Comprehensive Sexuality Education for Gender-Based Violence Prevention

Mariana Buenestado-Fernández
University of Cantabria, Spain

Azahara Jiménez-Millán
University of Córdoba, Spain

Francisco Javier Palacios-Hidalgo
University of Córdoba, Spain

A volume in the Advances in Educational Technologies and Instructional Design (AETID) Book Series

Published in the United States of America by
IGI Global
Information Science Reference (an imprint of IGI Global)
701 E. Chocolate Avenue
Hershey PA, USA 17033
Tel: 717-533-8845
Fax: 717-533-8661
E-mail: cust@igi-global.com
Web site: http://www.igi-global.com

Copyright © 2024 by IGI Global. All rights reserved. No part of this publication may be reproduced, stored or distributed in any form or by any means, electronic or mechanical, including photocopying, without written permission from the publisher. Product or company names used in this set are for identification purposes only. Inclusion of the names of the products or companies does not indicate a claim of ownership by IGI Global of the trademark or registered trademark.

Library of Congress Cataloging-in-Publication Data

Names: Buenestado-Fernández, Mariana, 1988- editor. | Jiménez-Millán, Azahara, 1982- editor. | Palacios-Hidalgo, Francisco Javier, 1993- editor.

Title: Comprehensive sexuality education for gender-based violence prevention / edited by Mariana Buenestado-Fernández, Azahara Jiménez-Millán, Francisco Javier Palacios-Hidalgo.

Description: Hershey, PA : Information Science Reference, [2024] | Includes bibliographical references and index. | Summary: "The book's chapters delve into multiple critical areas: the integration of inclusive curricula in schools, the crucial role of families in young people's sexuality education, and the collaboration between activists, schools and education stakeholders to strengthen the prevention of gender-based violence"-- Provided by publisher.

Identifiers: LCCN 2024011705 (print) | LCCN 2024011706 (ebook) | ISBN 9798369320532 (hardcover) | ISBN 9798369345412 (paperback) | ISBN 9798369320549 (ebook)

Subjects: LCSH: Gender-based violence--Prevention. | Sex instruction for children. | Sex instruction for teenagers.

Classification: LCC HV6250.4.W65 C654 2024 (print) | LCC HV6250.4.W65 (ebook) | DDC 362.88082--dc23/eng/20240429

LC record available at https://lccn.loc.gov/2024011705

LC ebook record available at https://lccn.loc.gov/2024011706

This book is published in the IGI Global book series Advances in Educational Technologies and Instructional Design (AETID) (ISSN: 2326-8905; eISSN: 2326-8913)

British Cataloguing in Publication Data
A Cataloguing in Publication record for this book is available from the British Library.

All work contributed to this book is new, previously-unpublished material. The views expressed in this book are those of the authors, but not necessarily of the publisher.

For electronic access to this publication, please contact: eresources@igi-global.com.

Advances in Educational Technologies and Instructional Design (AETID) Book Series

Lawrence A. Tomei
Robert Morris University, USA

ISSN:2326-8905
EISSN:2326-8913

Mission

Education has undergone, and continues to undergo, immense changes in the way it is enacted and distributed to both child and adult learners. In modern education, the traditional classroom learning experience has evolved to include technological resources and to provide online classroom opportunities to students of all ages regardless of their geographical locations. From distance education, Massive-Open-Online-Courses (MOOCs), and electronic tablets in the classroom, technology is now an integral part of learning and is also affecting the way educators communicate information to students.

The **Advances in Educational Technologies & Instructional Design (AETID) Book Series** explores new research and theories for facilitating learning and improving educational performance utilizing technological processes and resources. The series examines technologies that can be integrated into K-12 classrooms to improve skills and learning abilities in all subjects including STEM education and language learning. Additionally, it studies the emergence of fully online classrooms for young and adult learners alike, and the communication and accountability challenges that can arise. Trending topics that are covered include adaptive learning, game-based learning, virtual school environments, and social media effects. School administrators, educators, academicians, researchers, and students will find this series to be an excellent resource for the effective design and implementation of learning technologies in their classes.

Coverage

- Online Media in Classrooms
- Web 2.0 and Education
- Instructional Design
- Adaptive Learning
- Instructional Design Models
- K-12 Educational Technologies
- Collaboration Tools
- E-Learning
- Educational Telecommunications
- Hybrid Learning

> IGI Global is currently accepting manuscripts for publication within this series. To submit a proposal for a volume in this series, please contact our Acquisition Editors at Acquisitions@igi-global.com or visit: http://www.igi-global.com/publish/.

The Advances in Educational Technologies and Instructional Design (AETID) Book Series (ISSN 2326-8905) is published by IGI Global, 701 E. Chocolate Avenue, Hershey, PA 17033-1240, USA, www.igi-global.com. This series is composed of titles available for purchase individually; each title is edited to be contextually exclusive from any other title within the series. For pricing and ordering information please visit http://www.igi-global.com/book-series/advances-educational-technologies-instructional-design/73678. Postmaster: Send all address changes to above address. Copyright © 2024 IGI Global. All rights, including translation in other languages reserved by the publisher. No part of this series may be reproduced or used in any form or by any means – graphics, electronic, or mechanical, including photocopying, recording, taping, or information and retrieval systems – without written permission from the publisher, except for non commercial, educational use, including classroom teaching purposes. The views expressed in this series are those of the authors, but not necessarily of IGI Global.

Titles in this Series

For a list of additional titles in this series, please visit: http://www.igi-global.com/book-series/advances-educational-technologies-instructional-design/73678

Encouraging Transnational Learning Through Virtual Exchange in Global Teacher Education
Alina Slapac (University of Missouri-St. Louis, USA) and Cristina A. Huertas-Abril (University of Córdoba, Spain)
Information Science Reference • copyright 2024 • 424pp • H/C (ISBN: 9781668478134) • US $215.00 (our price)

Utilizing Visuals and Information Technology in Mathematics Classrooms
Hiroto Namihira (Otsuma Women's University, Japan)
Information Science Reference • copyright 2024 • 264pp • H/C (ISBN: 9781668499870) • US $220.00 (our price)

Reshaping Learning with Next Generation Educational Technologies
James Braman (Community College of Baltimore County, USA) Alexis Brown (Community College of Baltimore County, USA) and Mary Jo Richards (Community College of Baltimore County, USA)
Information Science Reference • copyright 2024 • 242pp • H/C (ISBN: 9798369313107) • US $235.00 (our price)

Utilizing AI for Assessment, Grading, and Feedback in Higher Education
Nasser Hamed Al Harrasi (University of Technology and Applied Science, Oman) and Mohamed Salah El Din (Majan University College, Oman)
Information Science Reference • copyright 2024 • 376pp • H/C (ISBN: 9798369321454) • US $255.00 (our price)

Applied Linguistics and Language Education Research Methods Fundamentals and Innovations
Hung Phu Bui (University of Economics Ho Chi Minh City, Vietnam)
Information Science Reference • copyright 2024 • 281pp • H/C (ISBN: 9798369326039) • US $245.00 (our price)

Utilizing AI Tools in Academic Research Writing
Anugamini Priya Srivastava (Symbiosis Institute of Business Management Pune, Symbiosis International University, Pune, India) and Sucheta Agarwal (Institute of Business Management, GLA University, Mathura, India)
Information Science Reference • copyright 2024 • 296pp • H/C (ISBN: 9798369317983) • US $230.00 (our price)

Strategies and Digital Advances for Outcome-Based Adult Learning
Janice E. Jones (Carroll University, USA) and Mette L. Baran (Cardinal Stritch University, USA)
Information Science Reference • copyright 2024 • 239pp • H/C (ISBN: 9781799847489) • US $215.00 (our price)

AI Approaches to Literacy in Higher Education
Oscar Oliver Eybers (University of Pretoria, South Africa) and Alan Muller (University of Pretoria, South Africa)
Information Science Reference • copyright 2024 • 285pp • H/C (ISBN: 9798369310540) • US $235.00 (our price)

701 East Chocolate Avenue, Hershey, PA 17033, USA
Tel: 717-533-8845 x100 • Fax: 717-533-8661
E-Mail: cust@igi-global.com • www.igi-global.com

Table of Contents

Foreword xiv

Preface xvi

Chapter 1
Sex Education and Gender-Based Violence Against Indigenous Women in Mexico 1
    Adriana Medina-Vidal, Independent Researcher, Mexico
    Adrian Palma-Patricio, UACM Cuautepec, Mexico

Chapter 2
Navigating the Tension of Holistic Sexual Reproductive Health Curriculum in Three States of
SADC Using Rogers Diffusion of Innovation Theory 22
    William Chakabwata, University of South Africa, South Africa
    Ronika Mumbire, Independent Researcher, Zimbabwe

Chapter 3
Texts, Critical Literacy, and Their Effect on Students' Insight of Gender Equality: A Qualitative
Study in a Spanish HE Context 44
    Tú Anh Hà, Universitat Rovira i Virgili, Spain
    Cristina A. Huertas-Abril, University of Córdoba, Spain

Chapter 4
Spanish Contemporary Women's Writing as a Tool to Teach CSE: A Case Study on Crónica del
Desamor and Amor, Curiosidad, Prozac y Dudas 63
    Mazal Oaknín, University College London, UK

Chapter 5
Dialogic Talks and Photographic Narration: Strategies for University Teaching With a Gender
Perspective 81
    Azahara Jiménez-Millán, University of Cordoba, Spain
    Elisa Pérez Gracia, University of Cordoba, Spain

Chapter 6
Empowering Education Against Gender Violence: Practical Tools and Insights for Teaching Comprehensive Sex Education in Mexico 102
    Rosa Elena Durán González, Universidad Autónoma del Estado de Hidalgo, Mexico
    Berenice Alfaro-Ponce, Tecnologico de Monterrey, Mexico

Chapter 7
Girl-Child Formal Education: A Strategy in Mitigating Male-Based Supremacy Syndrome in the Traditional IGBO Society 116
    Bruno Onyinye Umunakwe, University of Nigeria, Nsukka, Nigeria

Chapter 8
Classical Violence: Teaching Mythology Against Gender-Based Violence 135
    Francisco Sánchez Torres, Universidad de Córdoba, Spain

Chapter 9
Theoretical Approach to the Concept of Modern Homonegativity: Strategies for Prevention and Intervention in the Educational Field 152
    Adrián Salvador Lara Garrido, Universidad de Almería, Spain
    José Ramón Márquez Díaz, Universidad de Huelva, Spain

Chapter 10
Comprehensive Sexual Education: Analysis of Psychoeducational Materials 171
    Karen Elin Acosta Buralli, CONICET, Universidad de Buenos Aires, Argentina
    María Luisa Silva, CONICET, Argentina
    Jazmín Cevasco, CONICET, Universidad de Buenos Aires, Argentina

Chapter 11
AIALL and Queer Language Education to Prevent Gender-Based Violence: Using Artificial Intelligence for Lesson Planning 189
    Francisco Javier Palacios-Hidalgo, University of Córdoba, Spain
    Cristina A. Huertas-Abril, University of Córdoba, Spain

Chapter 12
Comprehensive Sexuality Education as a Preventive Strategy Against Gender-Based Violence in the Digital Sphere: A Training Proposal 211
    Mariana Buenestado-Fernández, Universidad de Cantabria, Spain

Chapter 13
Cyberbullying: Gender-Based Violence in Reverted Muslim Women 229
    Sabina Civila, Universidad de Huelva, Spain

Chapter 14
Online Protection Measures to Prevent Sexting Among Minors 246
    José-María Romero-Rodríguez, Universidad de Granada, Spain
    Blanca Berral-Ortiz, Universidad de Granada, Spain
    José-Antonio Martínez-Domingo, Universidad de Granada, Spain
    Juan-José Victoria-Maldonado, Universidad de Granada, Spain

Chapter 15
Sexual (Mis)information: Pornography and Adolescence in the Digital Space 265
    Elizabeth-Guadalupe Rojas-Estrada, National Council of Humanities, Science, and
        Technology, Mexico
    Arantxa Vizcaíno-Verdú, Universidad Internacional de la Rioja, Spain
    Mónica Bonilla-del-Río, European University of the Atlantic, Spain

Compilation of References 285

About the Contributors 333

Index 339

Detailed Table of Contents

Foreword xiv

Preface xvi

Chapter 1
Sex Education and Gender-Based Violence Against Indigenous Women in Mexico 1
Adriana Medina-Vidal, Independent Researcher, Mexico
Adrian Palma-Patricio, UACM Cuautepec, Mexico

In this chapter, the authors analyze the relevant socio-demographic aspects of the indigenous population in Mexico and examine young women's access to sexual and reproductive health information and education in rural areas, as well as the context of discrimination and violence they face throughout their lives for being young, female, indigenous and from a low socio-economic class. The authors discuss the case of the binnizá women of Juchitán, Oaxaca, to show how they experience multiple forms of violence within their communities and resist the violence of the hegemonic medical system, which undermines indigenous knowledge and weakens the traditional medical systems that are part of the cultural and social survival of the communities.

Chapter 2
Navigating the Tension of Holistic Sexual Reproductive Health Curriculum in Three States of SADC Using Rogers Diffusion of Innovation Theory 22
William Chakabwata, University of South Africa, South Africa
Ronika Mumbire, Independent Researcher, Zimbabwe

The chapter explores the provision of comprehensive sex education (CSE) and the antecedent challenges. A case of three states, namely Namibia, South Africa, and Zimbabwe, is undertaken, in order to illuminate the obstacles related to the implementation of this curriculum. The aims of comprehensive sexuality education are also explored in order to demonstrate the indispensable nature of this curriculum. CSE has faced resistance in many countries, due to the way it was implemented. The chapter argues for implementation of CSE curriculum, using Rogers's theory of diffusion of innovation (DIO), to overcome challenges related to the implementation of this indispensable curriculum for young people. The chapter is undergirded by the poststructural feminism, social cognitive and diffusion of innovation theories.

Chapter 3
Texts, Critical Literacy, and Their Effect on Students' Insight of Gender Equality: A Qualitative Study in a Spanish HE Context 44
    Tú Anh Hà, Universitat Rovira i Virgili, Spain
    Cristina A. Huertas-Abril, University of Córdoba, Spain

This study investigates the effect of critical literacy on university students' insight of gender equality. It aims to propose a guideline to teach critical reading, and assesses the influence of texts and critical reading on students' perception of gender equality. Students (n = 40) were guided to identify the author's purpose behind the text by delving into the text itself and connecting it with the background surrounding the text. Then students' perceptions of gender equality and their opinions about the influence of critical reading on their understanding of gender equality were collected through a survey. Qualitative content analysis was employed to analyze the data collected from students. The findings showed that critical reading not only offered students more perspectives and new ideas to see an issue, but also helped them reflect on the topic of gender equality itself and what they had already understood of gender equality. This benefits students' metacognition and showcases an effective way of gender equality education.

Chapter 4
Spanish Contemporary Women's Writing as a Tool to Teach CSE: A Case Study on Crónica del Desamor and Amor, Curiosidad, Prozac y Dudas 63
    Mazal Oaknín, University College London, UK

This chapter presents a pedagogical proposal for a contemporary Spanish literature lesson in which students work on key social-emotional skills while carrying out textual analysis. Taking selected excerpts from Montero's Crónica del desamor and Etxebarria's Amor, curiosidad, prozac, y dudas, the chapter will capitalize on women's writing's potential to educate students on gender-based violence and raise awareness of the importance of sexuality education as a preventative measure. The proposed text-based discussions raise key issues of comprehensive sexuality education and give students the ability to reflect on what constitutes a healthy relationship and how to identify signs of an unhealthy relationship.

Chapter 5
Dialogic Talks and Photographic Narration: Strategies for University Teaching With a Gender Perspective 81
    Azahara Jiménez-Millán, University of Cordoba, Spain
    Elisa Pérez Gracia, University of Cordoba, Spain

Currently, the levels of gender violence are unsustainable in a society that upholds the principles of respect, coexistence and justice. Likewise, it is important to emphasize that the features of contemporary society, characterized by immersion in new technologies, social networks and artificial intelligence, have led to the appearance of events related to gender violence in new digital contexts. In this context, education plays a key role, and it is seen as essential to adopt a cross-curricular and intersectional approach, which in the case of Spain still represents a pending challenge. This chapter presents a teaching-learning process framed in feminist pedagogy, applied in the university environment of the Education Degrees of a Spanish public university. In this process, sessions have been carried out based on dialogic discussion and photographic narration from a gender perspective. The main objective was to provide students with pedagogical tools that to raise awareness and encourage critical thinking.

Chapter 6
Empowering Education Against Gender Violence: Practical Tools and Insights for Teaching
Comprehensive Sex Education in Mexico 102
    Rosa Elena Durán González, Universidad Autónoma del Estado de Hidalgo, Mexico
    Berenice Alfaro-Ponce, Tecnologico de Monterrey, Mexico

This chapter critically examines the shortcomings of sex education in Mexican schools, tracing its historical evolution in the context of governmental and global health policies. Initially, sex education in Mexico was predominantly biological; however, it has since expanded in response to societal changes. The chapter underscores the importance of a comprehensive educational approach that not only provides minors with knowledge, but also equips them with self-esteem, respect for others, and tools for self-protection. It explores the debate over who should bear the responsibility for educating children on these matters—parents, teachers, or both through a collaborative approach. Furthermore, the chapter offers practical guidelines and activities for educators, aiming to prepare children for a safer, more informed future. It advocates for an educational methodology that is contemporary, engaging, and free from dogmas and social prejudices.

Chapter 7
Girl-Child Formal Education: A Strategy in Mitigating Male-Based Supremacy Syndrome in the
Traditional IGBO Society 116
    Bruno Onyinye Umunakwe, University of Nigeria, Nsukka, Nigeria

In this chapter, the study presents the socio-cultural backdrop of traditional Igbo society, aiming to investigate the status of the girl-child and the crucial role of formal education in dismantling deeply entrenched societal structures that perpetuated male dominance. Employing a historical analysis, the study draws information from a variety of sources, including journals, books, articles, periodicals, and the internet. The major emphasis in this chapter was the enrolment of girl-child in formal schooling system which actively involves writing and reading. Education becomes a fundamental right that has restored an equitable society by curbing gender marginalization and discrimination. The study recommends that the government and relevant stakeholders should ensure accessible education through the elimination of environmental barriers to quality education.

Chapter 8
Classical Violence: Teaching Mythology Against Gender-Based Violence 135
    Francisco Sánchez Torres, Universidad de Córdoba, Spain

This chapter offers an examination of Greek and Roman myths in the context of university-level teaching with a focus on Gender-Based Violence (GBV) prevention. The aims can be summarized as follows: providing a sufficient methodological framework through which open the analysis of myths to critical approaches and proposing techniques and ways of interlacing these critical approaches in the classroom. Consequently, mythology as a group of discourses will be examined to identify the qualities of myth as a powerful means of reification for cultural practices from a semiotic approach. Furthermore, a series of in-class experiences will be provided, preceded by an analysis of the concept of GBV and its application in the context of Greek and Roman mythology, its tradition and its reception through the ages.

Chapter 9
Theoretical Approach to the Concept of Modern Homonegativity: Strategies for Prevention and Intervention in the Educational Field 152
    Adrián Salvador Lara Garrido, Universidad de Almería, Spain
    José Ramón Márquez Díaz, Universidad de Huelva, Spain

The aim of this chapter is twofold. On the one hand, to analyze the concept of homonegativity, and its main manifestations, as well as its relationship with other factors such as sexist attitudes. On the other hand, it aims to collect pedagogical strategies that can be used by teachers to promote educational spaces free of discrimination and respectful of affective-sexual diversity. A theoretical model is presented that analyses homonegativity and manifestations which, following a parallel path to other phenomena such as sexist attitudes, include more subtle and modern aspects that characterize modern homonegativity. There are also certain socio-demographic and ideological variables that influence the display of these behaviors by teachers. A number of strategies for the promotion of positive attitudes in the educational environment in relation to affective-sexual diversity are selected. The conclusions point to the need to offer specific training to teachers in order to provide them with resources and skills to promote inclusive educational spaces.

Chapter 10
Comprehensive Sexual Education: Analysis of Psychoeducational Materials 171
    Karen Elin Acosta Buralli, CONICET, Universidad de Buenos Aires, Argentina
    María Luisa Silva, CONICET, Argentina
    Jazmín Cevasco, CONICET, Universidad de Buenos Aires, Argentina

Gender violence is a problem of central relevance since its consequences are fatal and affect the world's population. Comprehensive sexual education (CSE) is considered a key tool to apply gender violence prevention (PGV) strategies. However, the adequate implementation of CSE depends largely on teacher training. Therefore, the objective of this chapter is to improve the understanding of psychoeducational materials on CSE and PGV intended for teachers. The role of causal connectivity of a material on general CSE and one specifically on PGV from a manual for secondary school teachers designed by the Ministry of Education of Argentina (2022) was analyzed. The results demonstrated the predominance of a low level of causal connectivity in both materials. Considering the role of causal connectivity, as a textual characteristic that facilitates comprehension, could optimize the development of CSE and PGV materials for teachers and, consequently, contribute to the training and implementation of CSE and PGV.

Chapter 11
AIALL and Queer Language Education to Prevent Gender-Based Violence: Using Artificial Intelligence for Lesson Planning 189
    Francisco Javier Palacios-Hidalgo, University of Córdoba, Spain
    Cristina A. Huertas-Abril, University of Córdoba, Spain

The rise in gender-based violence demands urgent attention and action. As violence rates against women and trans and gender non-conforming people have increased alarmingly, there is an imperative need to review how today's societies fail to protect minoritized groups. Moreover, artificial intelligence has undoubtedly acquired relevance on the public scene, both seen as a threat and an ally to boost and fight against this type of violence. Following the socially and culturally responsive language teaching and English for social purposes and cooperation approaches, this chapter presents a teaching proposal to address gender-based violence in the language classroom. The tasks are designed following a non-biased gender and queer lens and taking advantage of different Artificial Intelligence tools. It aims to offer language teachers a practical guide for lesson planning and promote artificial intelligence assisted language learning. Ultimately, the chapter attempts to show the potential of queer language education to fight gender-based violence.

Chapter 12
Comprehensive Sexuality Education as a Preventive Strategy Against Gender-Based Violence in the Digital Sphere: A Training Proposal.. 211
    Mariana Buenestado-Fernández, Universidad de Cantabria, Spain

Comprehensive sexuality education is presented as a fundamental preventive strategy against gender violence in the digital sphere. In this context, a training program is proposed that specifically addresses this problem. The proposal seeks to equip individuals with solid knowledge about sexuality, consent, and healthy relationships online, with the aim of counteracting gender violence that manifests itself in cyberspace. By integrating a gender perspective into sexuality education, the authors aim to empower people to recognize and combat forms of digital violence, thus promoting safer and more respectful online environments. This holistic approach seeks to prevent the perpetuation of harmful stereotypes and behaviors, promoting a digital culture that supports gender equality and mutual respect.

Chapter 13
Cyberbullying: Gender-Based Violence in Reverted Muslim Women 229
    Sabina Civila, Universidad de Huelva, Spain

Gender-based violence in the digital environment affects women from various communities, and Muslim reverted women are no exception. According to the National Observatory of Technology and Society, 54% of women have experienced assault on honor and privacy in the digital environment. However, for Muslim revert women, the situation is further complicated due to the intersection of gender violence and Islamophobic attitudes amplified by social media. Online hate speech directed at Muslim revert women takes various forms from offensive comments to threats, intensifying gender Islamophobia. Therefore, this chapter delves into how gender Islamophobia expands through social media and affects reverted women and the different stigmas they face due to changes in religion. In conclusion, despite Islamophobia being the current subject of study, there is limited research specifically addressing the discrimination faced by Muslim revert women. Future research directions were proposed to contribute to this area of study.

Chapter 14
Online Protection Measures to Prevent Sexting Among Minors 246
    José-María Romero-Rodríguez, Universidad de Granada, Spain
    Blanca Berral-Ortiz, Universidad de Granada, Spain
    José-Antonio Martínez-Domingo, Universidad de Granada, Spain
    Juan-José Victoria-Maldonado, Universidad de Granada, Spain

This chapter explores sexting among minors in the digital era, focusing on Spain. It delves into sociocultural, technological, and psychological factors contributing to sexting, highlighting evolving norms, device access, and peer pressures. The impact of a lack of awareness and education on sexting is emphasized. The discussion stresses collaborative online protection, including parental controls, government policies, and educational programs. The chapter underscores the critical role of online protection, proposing holistic prevention approaches. It emphasizes early-age awareness and education for safe online behaviors, recommending programs in schools and families. European frameworks like the DigComp enhance digital competencies, and Spain's legal stance protects minors. Commitment at national and European levels is evident, with training and awareness crucial. Collaboration between teachers and families is emphasized for prevention, creating a supportive environment for responsible technology use.

Chapter 15
Sexual (Mis)information: Pornography and Adolescence in the Digital Space 265
 Elizabeth-Guadalupe Rojas-Estrada, National Council of Humanities, Science, and
  Technology, Mexico
 Arantxa Vizcaíno-Verdú, Universidad Internacional de la Rioja, Spain
 Mónica Bonilla-del-Río, European University of the Atlantic, Spain

The escalating prevalence of pornography consumption among the youth has raised significant concern within the scientific community. This study aims to systematically examine scholarly literature on adolescence and engagement with pornography. Employing a conceptual framework, a qualitative literature review was conducted. Data analysis involved compiling abstracts and employing the AI coding system of Atlas.ti 23. These narrative approaches include (1) adolescent online health and pornographic education, (2) youth sexual identity shaped by online pornographic content, (3) and government policies promoting (in)formed sex education. The study's conclusions underscore the detrimental effects of unregulated access to online pornographic content on adolescents, manifesting in distorted self-image, diminished self-esteem, and altered body perceptions. This phenomenon highlights the imperative of promoting comprehensive sex education. Media literacy is identified as a pivotal initiative to foster understanding of stereotypical representations and their societal and personal impacts.

Compilation of References 285

About the Contributors 333

Index 339

Foreword

Addressing a dramatic reality such as Gender-Based Violence involves recognizing its complexity and the need to work from a global and coordinated approach. In the field of law, legislation is an essential tool in the fight against Gender-Based Violence, as evidenced by the Spanish Organic Law on Comprehensive Protection Measures against Gender-Based Violence of 2004, the Organic Law for the Effective Equality of Women and Men of 2007, and the Organic Law on Comprehensive Guarantees of Sexual Freedom of 2022. Likewise, political institutions, security forces, associations and entities are essential actors, as shown by the active role they have been playing in recent decades. However, the commitment and awareness of society as a whole is necessary to achieve the end of Gender-Based Violence, and education is a decisive factor in this objective, as illustrated in the present book, *Comprehensive Sexuality Education for Gender-Based Violence Prevention*.

The people responsible for editing this book, whom I thank for their invitation to write this foreword, as well as the authors of the different chapters, belong to various higher education institutions, both national and international. Universities, through teaching, research, transfer of knowledge and innovation, must play a fundamental role in preventing, detecting, and proposing solutions to end Gender-Based Violence, as well as demonstrating zero tolerance for any violent behavior. However, universities must also be safe spaces where human rights are respected and where all people can exist in freedom. In this regard, it is worth recalling the *MeToo* University movement, which calls for the visibility of cases of sexual and gender-based harassment in the field of higher education.

Gender-Based Violence is a public health issue and in no context can it be shielded behind the label of cultural tradition. To this end, as illustrated in some of the chapters of this book, an intersectional perspective allows us to deepen our understanding of this problem, highlighting how the different categories of discrimination come together and give rise to complex realities.

Another of the contributions of this edited book is the look it casts on digital scenarios, an omnipresent area in our daily reality that especially affects the young population. Reports such as *EU Kids Online* 2020 or studies like *La situación de la violencia contra las mujeres en la adolescencia en España*, by the Spanish Ministry of Equality, or those developed by the Queen Sofia Centre on youth and digital media, warn about the perception of Gender-Based Violence among young people and the increase in sexism. In addition, various studies indicate that this sector of the population, as prosumers, have a good level in the use of technology and digital networks, but do not have a critical attitude towards the media, something that can and should be worked on in the classroom, as reflected in some of the proposals in this volume.

As for affective and sexuality education, there is indeed scientific evidence of its benefits in the construction of a more egalitarian society and, despite this, it is still not present in the formal educational context. The doubts, concerns, and expectations that young people develop during this stage regarding

Foreword

sexuality lead to the acceptance of the normative, and to risky behaviors and challenges to fit into the social model of the group, without forgetting that sexuality is essential in the process of confirming hegemonic and normative gender roles. In the face of this, work must be done to generate healthy and democratic relationships with young peoples, without over-responsibilizing or blaming them.

Finally, it is necessary to thank the co-editors of this book, as well as the authors, for their commitment and dedication to this task. The analyses carried out, the perspectives offered, and the alternatives proposed undoubtedly contribute to the firm commitment to fight against Gender-Based Violence through education.

Silvia Medina Quintana
University of Córdoba, Spain

Preface

In the pursuit of advancing human rights and fostering healthy relationships, Comprehensive Sexuality Education (CSE) stands as a cornerstone for combating gender-based violence (GBV). Our world is in dire need of proactive measures to address the alarming statistics that reveal the pervasive nature of GBV. As editors of this comprehensive reference book, it is with great conviction that we present this collective effort to bridge the gap between education and prevention.

Drawing from the invaluable insights of scientific literature and the expertise of international bodies, we embrace a holistic approach to sexuality education. Recognizing that sexuality is not solely confined to the biological realm, but intricately woven into the fabric of our emotional, social, and cultural dynamics, we affirm the need for a multifaceted understanding. This book is not just a compilation of facts and figures; it is a call to action rooted in evidence-informed approaches.

The urgency of our mission cannot be overstated. The staggering prevalence of GBV demands nothing short of a concerted effort across sectors and borders. With SDG 5.2 as our guiding beacon, we aspire to equip young people with the knowledge and skills necessary to dismantle harmful stereotypes, foster empathy, and cultivate healthy relationships. It is through education that we empower individuals to challenge the status quo and forge a path towards a more equitable future.

In the pages that follow, readers will find a diverse array of perspectives and insights, each contributing to a richer understanding of the intersection between CSE and GBV prevention. From the integration of inclusive curricula in schools to the pivotal role of families in shaping attitudes towards sexuality, each chapter offers practical strategies and resources for implementation.

In Section 1 of the book, "Sexuality Education and in Diverse Social and Cultural Contexts", the focus is on sexuality education within diverse social and cultural landscapes. Chapter 1, "Sex Education and Gender-based Violence Against Indigenous Women in Mexico", authored by Adriana Medina-Vidal and Adrian Palma-Patricio, delves into the intersection of sex education and gender-based violence against indigenous women in Mexico. In Chapter 2, "Navigating the Tension of Holistic Sexual Reproductive Health Curriculum in Three States of SADC Using Rogers Diffusion of Innovation Theory", William Chakabwata and Ronika Mumbire examine the complexities of implementing a holistic sexual reproductive health curriculum in three states of the Southern African Development Community, using Rogers Diffusion of Innovation Theory. Chapter 3, "Texts, Critical Literacy and their Effect on Students' Insight of Gender Equality: A Qualitative Study in a Spanish HE Context", presents a qualitative study conducted in a Spanish higher education context investigates the impact of texts and critical literacy on students' understanding of gender equality developed by Tú Anh Hà and Cristina A. Huertas-Abril. Lastly, in Chapter 4, "Spanish Contemporary Women's Writing as a Tool to Teach CSE: A Case Study on *Crónica del Desamor* and *Amor,*

Preface

Curiosidad, Prozac y Dudas", Mazal Oaknín explores how contemporary Spanish women's writing can serve as a valuable tool in CSE through a case study of two novels, *Crónica del Desamor* and *Amor, Curiosidad, Prozac y Dudas*.

The second section of the book is entitled "Interventions and Proposals to Empower Young People in Gender Violence Prevention and Sexual Education" and includes six chapters on how to bring both existing and evidence-based approaches to gender-based violence prevention through comprehensive sexuality education into the classroom. The first chapter of the section corresponds to Chapter 5, "Dialogic Talks and Photographic Narration: Strategies for University Teaching with a Gender Perspective", in which Azahara Jiménez-Millán and Elisa Pérez Gracia develop an innovative pedagogical intervention based on dialogical learning and the use of photography to learn about young people's conceptualization of gender violence and their proposals. In Chapter 6, "Empowering Education Against Gender Violence: Practical Tools and Insights for Teaching Comprehensive Sex Education in Mexico", Rosa Elena Durán González and Berenice Alfaro-Ponce present a pragmatic plan consisting of a series of interesting proposals for educators to integrate essential components of sexuality education into their pedagogical practices. Bruno Onyinye Umunakwe presents in Chapter 7, "Girl-Child Formal Education: A Strategy in Mitigating Male-Based Supremacy Syndrome in the Traditional IGBO Society", a qualitative study using the historical method to assess the need for girls' schooling and its impact on the repositioning of the male supremacy syndrome affecting traditional Igbo society. In Chapter 8, "Classical Violence: Teaching Mythology Against Gender-Based Violence", Francisco Sánchez Torres outlines some guidelines to help orient the study and teaching of Greco-Roman mythology at university level, providing an approach that makes a crucial contribution to raising awareness of gender-based violence. Adrián Salvador Lara and José Ramón Márquez Díaz in Chapter 9, "Theoretical Approach to the Concept of Modern Homonegativity: Strategies for Prevention and Intervention in the Educational Field", present a theoretical paper that analyzes, on the one hand, the concept of homonegativity and its perpetuation among teachers and, on the other hand, discusses the main pedagogical strategies for its prevention and intervention. Finally, in Chapter 10, "Comprehensive Sexual Education: Analysis of Psychoeducational Materials", Karen Elin Acosta Burallis, María Luisa Silva and Jazmín Cevasco delve into the conceptualization of Psychoeducation in such a way that reflect on the importance of developing CSE materials that properly promote learning on gender violence prevention.

The third section of the book is entitled "Digital Space and Online Behavior", and it includes five chapters that deal with how GBV can be perpetuated but, at the same time, fought in the digital era. The first chapter of the section is Chapter 12, "AIALL and Queer Language Education to Prevent Gender-Based Violence: Using Artificial Intelligence for Lesson Planning", in which Francisco Javier Palacios-Hidalgo and Cristina A. Huertas-Abril provide an interesting teaching proposal to address GBV in the language classroom by combining the Socially and Culturally Responsive Language Teaching and English for Social Purposes and Cooperation approaches and the use of Artificial Intelligence. In Chapter 13, "Comprehensive Sexuality Education as a Preventive Strategy against Gender-Based Violence in the Digital Sphere: A Training Proposal", Mariana Buenestado-Fernández proposes a training program to equip learners with solid knowledge about sexuality, consent and healthy relationships online to make them better citizens of the digital era. Sabina Civila reflects in Chapter 14, "Cyberbullying: Gender-based Violence in Reverted Muslim Women" on how gender Islamophobia is growing because of social media and how this affects the perpetuation of stigma on reverted women. In Chapter 15, "Online Protection Measures to Prevent Sexting Among Minors",

José-María Romero-Rodríguez, Blanca Berral-Ortiz, José-Antonio Martínez-Domingo and Juan-José Victoria-Maldonado examine sexting practices among Spanish minors, focusing on the different factors that contribute to it. Finally, Elizabeth-Guadalupe Rojas-Estrada, Arantxa Vizcaíno-Verdú and Mónica Bonilla-del-Río examine in Chapter 16, "Sexual (Mis)information: Pornography and Adolescence in the Digital Space", the prevalence of pornography consumption among young people, showing the urgent need to promote CSE to fight stereotypes associated to sexual practices as well as to prevent manifestations of distorted self-image, diminished self-esteem, and altered body perceptions among younger generations.

We extend our deepest gratitude to the contributors who have generously shared their expertise and experiences. It is our hope that this book will serve as a valuable resource for researchers, educators, health professionals, social workers, and policymakers alike. Together, let us embark on this journey towards a world free from GBV, where every individual is empowered to live authentically and without fear.

Mariana Buenestado-Fernández
University of Cantabria, Spain

Azahara Jiménez-Millán
University of Córdoba, Spain

Francisco Javier Palacios-Hidalgo
University of Córdoba, Spain

Chapter 1
Sex Education and Gender-Based Violence Against Indigenous Women in Mexico

Adriana Medina-Vidal
https://orcid.org/0000-0002-3414-4307
Independent Researcher, Mexico

Adrian Palma-Patricio
UACM Cuautepec, Mexico

ABSTRACT

In this chapter, the authors analyze the relevant socio-demographic aspects of the indigenous population in Mexico and examine young women's access to sexual and reproductive health information and education in rural areas, as well as the context of discrimination and violence they face throughout their lives for being young, female, indigenous and from a low socio-economic class. The authors discuss the case of the binnizá women of Juchitán, Oaxaca, to show how they experience multiple forms of violence within their communities and resist the violence of the hegemonic medical system, which undermines indigenous knowledge and weakens the traditional medical systems that are part of the cultural and social survival of the communities.

INTRODUCTION

In this chapter, we analyze the complex situation of violence experienced by indigenous women in relation to sexual and reproductive education in rural community contexts in Mexico, using an intersectional and decolonial qualitative approach, and focusing on the case study of the *binnizá* women in Juchitán de Zaragoza, Oaxaca.

In addition to the situation of marginalization and poverty suffered by indigenous women, there is also psychological, physical, economic, and sexual violence both in their homes and in their communities. As far as the attention of the biomedical system is concerned, in Juchitán obstetric violence has been

DOI: 10.4018/979-8-3693-2053-2.ch001

documented, reflected in forced sterilization and the imposition of contraceptive devices; or the lack of intercultural perspectives in the medical and educational spheres, which constitutes a flagrant violation of their sexual and reproductive rights. Consequently, there is an urgent need to implement evidence-based public policies from an intercultural, intersectional and decolonial perspective that allows for the design and implementation of culturally appropriate health promotion and sexual education programs, considering the experiences and subjectivities of indigenous women. Especially, we are conceiving the educational area in terms of popular education instead institutional one, because the gender-based violence against indigenous linked to their sexuality occurs in institutional areas like the health system and schools, but mainly in the everyday life.

BACKGROUND

In order to explore the situation of multiple and intertwined violences of indigenous women through the case of the *binnizá* women in Juchitán, we first approached the theoretical and methodological foundations of both the intersectional and decolonial perspectives, which allow for an understanding of the different inequalities and structural violences of indigenous women in a way that is intertwined with gender, class, sexuality, and the processes of racialization as manifestations of power and oppression, focused from the Global South.

We use an intersectional and decolonial qualitative methodology to understand the sexual education of the indigenous population in Mexico, and especially of indigenous women in Oaxaca, as a problem that requires an understanding of the situation of the historical complexity of the indigenous population in Mexico, but also of some socio-demographic data.

In this order of ideas, the article is based on the intersectional and decolonial analysis of the health system that is linked to the case study: *binnizá* women in Juchitán. We privilege some secondary sources, but also some interviews, to demonstrate the urgent need for the design and implementation of public policies, educational programs based on popular education more than institutional ones, and community health promotion work, with documented evidence, to enable indigenous women to reorient their sexual and reproductive health in terms of intersectional and decolonial qualitative methodology.

Intersectionality

The intersectionality approach emerged when black feminists expressed dissatisfaction with the patriarchal attitudes of black male activists and the ethnocentrism of white feminists, and argued that to address their experiences, it was necessary to look at how gender, race and ethnic identities were interrelated (Wade, 2000; hooks, 2004). It became clear that these social categories had been used in a homogeneous way, without recognizing that situations such as sexual violence or women's dependence on a man's wage were different for each sector of the female population. Moreover, abstract social categories are combined in specific historical contexts, resulting in matrices of domination (Hill Collins, 1998). In Latin America and the Caribbean, feminists have also made their marginalized status visible and initiated a process of decolonization. For example, de la Cadena (1992) noted that indigenous women in the Cuzco region are the last link in the chain of subordination and have traditionally not had access to sources of power; over time, women have been allowed to inherit land and position themselves in the communal space, but in a limited way.

Gender is a theoretical variable that cannot be separated from the other oppression axes. Categories such as race, gender and class are interrelated (Cumes, 2009). Oppressions intersect (hooks, 2004), so it is necessary to analyze the mutual constitution of gender, ethnicity, and class without compartmentalizing or hierarchizing oppressions to account for how they are interconnected and articulated (Brah, 1991). Moving away from a single axis (gender, ethnicity/race, or social class) means analyzing reality in a more complex way and maintaining an intersectional perspective. The reality of white and mestizo women is different from that of indigenous and Afro-descendant women: the former have been privileged in the context of colonization and slavery, while the latter have worked for centuries as slaves, on the streets as vendors, and at home as domestic servants or prostitutes.

The following are some of the most important advances in the use of intersectional analysis in Latin America. Quijano (2002) introduced the concept of the coloniality of power and set out a way of understanding the intersection of race and gender. Placing the Americas at the center of the narrative of modernity, he argues that the capitalist pattern of power classifies people along three axes (labor, gender, and race) and proposes that it is the category of race that has a transversal and permanent place in the configuration of the modern/colonial capitalist pattern of power. Lugones (2008) points out that gender is as fictitious and important a category as race and suggests that they should be merged to make intersections visible to adequately interpret women of color. Mendoza (2010) warns that colonizers and colonized men made a gendered social pact to exclude white and non-white women from access to citizenship and politics, and to lose control over their bodies. Segato (2015) argues that patriarchy is not a colonial invention, but humanity's most archaic and enduring political structure. For her, the first colony is women's bodies (Sieder, 2017).

In short, intersectionality explores the complex interrelationships between different manifestations of power and oppression that work together to normalize different forms of violence and create hierarchies according to class, race, gender, and sexuality. Furthermore, this approach highlights how these interactions shape the lives of men and women and influence their social relations, experiences, and perspectives according to their position in these complex categories (Sieder, 2017; Al-Faham et al., 2019). This approach has also been reflected upon from the Global South by other theoretical approaches, such as decolonial ones.

Decoloniality

The decolonial approach focuses on challenging and dismantling colonial power relations and decolonizing mentalities, institutions, and practices. Postcolonial and decolonial approaches critique multiculturalism, which crystallizes and fixes racial identities. Postcolonial studies began with the decolonization of India in 1947 and judged the notion of race in an overlapping way with other categories such as 'subalternity'. On the other hand, decolonial studies analyze the origin of race as a category that emerges in a particular historical and social moment to classify populations in the Americas and to shape relations of domination on a global scale.

Spivak (2011) wrote a seminal postcolonial feminist work whose central argument is that the subaltern subject - representing oppressed groups, the proletariat, women, indigenous groups, and the peasantry - remains silent in the capitalist historical narrative. In the text, the author deconstructs the subaltern, exposing the monolithic category on which its identity is based; and calls on intellectuals to avoid speaking for the subaltern by reproducing neo-colonial schemes of political, economic, and cultural domination.

According to Mohanty's (2008) postcolonial gaze, engaging with 'Third World feminisms' involves two simultaneous processes: deconstructing and dismantling Western hegemonic feminisms and creating a contextualized autonomous feminism. The author analyses the "Third World Woman" from Western feminist texts to examine their analytical principles and political implications in the context of the hegemony of Western academia. In these texts, the average Third World woman is portrayed as sexually constrained, ignorant, poor, uneducated, tradition-bound, domestic, confined to the family, and victim. However, these women are not a homogeneous and pre-constituted group placed within the various "underdeveloped" social structures but are constituted through social relations. On the other hand, although Western women present themselves as educated, modern, in control of their bodies and sexuality, and with the freedom to make their own choices, this is not necessarily the reality.

One of the most important decolonial feminists in Latin America is Rivera Cusicanqui. She dedicated herself to criticizing patriarchy, machismo, and violence against Indian women and workers. She avoids pigeonholing into a single theoretical perspective, challenging the dominant and engaging in dialogue with writers from different theoretical currents to create a configuration of concepts that allows her to understand the sociological processes of her region. She has repeatedly stated that a decolonial discourse goes hand in hand with a decolonizing theory and practice, openly criticizing some academics recognized by universities in the United States who subscribe to a theoretical, racialized, and exoticized multiculturalism. The author argues that while men inherit and map the land, women inherit and map relations outwards, thus articulating a 'dynamic cultural fabric that unfolds and reproduces itself to encompass the border and mixed sectors - the *Ch'ixi* sectors - that contribute their vision of personal responsibility, privacy and individual rights associated with citizenship' (Rivera Cusicanqui, 2010).

Postcolonial and decolonial feminism converge and diverge; broadly speaking, postcolonial feminism is a deconstructive project, while decolonial feminism is a constructive project. However, Spivak, Mohanty and Rivera Cusicanqui are feminists committed to an ongoing critique of Eurocentrism, imperialism, and capitalism. In this sense, it is important to break down the boundaries between feminists in the South to engage in dialogue with each other to critically reflect on their goals and methods, to engage in anti-colonial struggles, and thus to confront the hegemonic projects of the North (Asher, 2017).

Intersectional and Decolonial Qualitative Methodology

It is a methodological challenge to analyze the complex situation of indigenous women in rural areas because it requires an understanding of the forms of violence they face, which include physical or interpersonal, domestic, psychological, symbolic, political, and structural violence based on their race, space, ethnicity, class, and gender (Bourgois, 2001). This violence comes from the state, their families, their communities, their partners, white or mixed-race women, among others. It is women who have higher rates of illiteracy and poor health than men in their communities. It is essential to examine forms of violence from the perspective of intersectionality, which means understanding the concrete circumstances of people's lives and avoiding: assuming a priori that one form of violence is more important than another for all indigenous women; observing only the direct manifestations of physical violence; imposing definitions of gender-based violence without considering their contexts; denying the multiple and complex causality of violence; and ignoring women's perceptions and experiences (Sieder, 2017).

In general, the most appropriate methodology should consider how women perceive, experience, and understand different forms of gender-based violence in specific contexts of socio-economic, political, and racial violence; what actions these women take to confront forms of oppression; and what effects these actions have (Hernández, 2009, 2010; Sieder, 2017). It is desirable that such research recognizes the heterogeneity of women's experiences, includes a historical perspective on local gender-based violence, collects information on gender-based violence in rural and indigenous areas, uses ethnically disaggregated statistics, includes an analysis of the links between forms of violence, includes an emic analysis of how women contextually understand the forms of violence that affect their lives, and integrates the relational (family, partner, community, boss, etc.) and situational (political, economic, social, cultural, etc.) dimensions. It integrates the relational (family, partner, community, bosses, etc.) and situational (political, economic, social, and cultural) dimensions of the analysis of gender inequalities and violence (Millán, 2014; Figueroa and Sierra, 2020).

The substrate of this intersectional and decolonial qualitative methodology is the ethnographic method, specifically linked to the anthropological tradition in the social sciences (Creswell, 1998). This method "involves a strategy of approaching reality that allows us to rethink the way knowledge is constructed in social practice, while at the same time requiring, in an essential way, a fundamental commitment on the part of the researcher in his or her fieldwork and in his or her relationship with social actors" (Ameigeiras, 2006:109). The ethnographer offers a narrative about the lives of particular people, emphasizing individuals and their ever-changing relationships, rather than focusing on the presumed homogeneity, coherence, and timeless structure of the supposed 'group' (Angrosino, 2015). It is preferable for the researcher to engage with the members of the group under study and establish a dialogical relationship with them (Bourgois, 2006). Their text should locate both the researcher and the researched, and highlight women's voices, opinions, and agency (Lamas, 2018).

The intersectional and decolonial qualitative methodology employed in this article it is also an epistemology and conceptual framework to understand the of sex education and gender-based violence against indigenous women in Mexico. In order to explain this complex issue, we analyze, at first glance, the challenge of the sex education within the education system in Mexico, and the difficulties of not only a intercultural education, but decolonial one.

MAIN FOCUS OF THE CHAPTER

Sexuality Education for the Indigenous Population in Mexico

According to the World Health Organization (WHO), sexual health is "...a state of physical, mental and social well-being related to sexuality, which is not the absence of disease, dysfunction or disability. Sexual health requires a positive and respectful approach to sexuality and sexual relationships, and the ability to have pleasurable and safe sexual experiences, free from coercion, discrimination, and violence" (WHO, 2006). Sexuality is a central aspect of human beings, including aspects such as gender, gender identities and roles, sexual orientation, eroticism, pleasure, intimacy, and reproduction (UNFPA, 2014). The Pan American Health Organization (OPS, 2008) considers sexual health to be a continuum of physical, psychological, and socio-cultural well-being related to sexuality, so that people can freely and responsibly express their sexual capacities, leading to personal and social well-being.

In this regard, we understand the sexual education within the framework of a wide notion of education. We are not conceptualizing necessarily the educational area related to the formal or institutional education but linked to the cultural learning in the everyday life of indigenous people, particularly indigenous women. And this includes all the gender learning and practices who enables their health or those who limits and conducts them to be violated and vulnerated in their sexual and reproductive rights.

People with sexual and reproductive health are able to enjoy a satisfying and safe sexual life, have the right to decide whether or not to have children, choose safe and accessible family planning methods, decide on the number and spacing of these children, receive adequate medical care during pregnancy and childbirth, avoid violence that may affect their integrity and health, and have access to sufficient information to make free and informed choices. All people have the right to comprehensive sexuality education (CSE) to make free, responsible, and informed choices to prevent unplanned pregnancies and sexually transmitted diseases (UNFPA, 2020), regardless of gender, age, ethnicity, class, sexual orientation, and marital status.

Adolescents and young people between the ages of 12 and 29 need knowledge and skills to enjoy sexual health, have respectful relationships and protect their rights throughout their lives. However, the teaching of sexuality remains a gap in the Mexican education system (Fonllem, n.d.). Including it in the curriculum at all levels of education could prevent many of the problems that society faces daily, such as sexual violence, forced marriages, teenage pregnancies, maternal deaths and hate crimes against women and people of sexual diversity, among others.

We must recognize that the sex education in México have been a battlefield within the Mexican state and the cultural imaginary. Since the earlies 1930's the mexican religious and civil conservative groups have tried to influence in the educational policy arguing that sexuality concerns to a private sphere and have refused the possibility to include the sex education in the public education. It was not until the 1970's decade that the Mexican state includes officially sex education into the curricula.

Since then, the official sexual educational programs have transited to the biological and anatomical view to the most recently contents in terms of sexual and reproductive health and rights to the prevention of Sexually Transmitted Diseases (STD's), and Human Immunodeficiency Virus (HIV), and unintended pregnancy.

Despite these notable efforts of public educational policy, it is necessary to incorporate a decolonial and intersectional perspective aimed to the indigenous people and clearly to the indigenous women, not only in the formal and basic system education but un the everyday life through the popular education, with epistemologies and methodologies employed by the health promotion in the different projects of community health interventions. To work against gender-based violence that indigenous women in Mexico suffer is to seek their sexual and reproductive, through the lens of popular education, and let them construct by themselves the social conditions to empower and change their own gender and sexual reality with their own projects and cultural visions.

Indigenous women in México are objects of multiple structural inequalities and violence, like the absence of the access to the formal or institutional education with intercultural and decolonial perspectives. The modern and postrevolutionary project of Mexico always was a mestizo nation project, the indigenous people was forgotten, but inequalities inside indigenous people are deeper between indigenous women, because the hegemonic gender order, privileges the access to education to the indigenous men, relegating indigenous women the unpaid domestic labor, unpaid care work and gender roles linked to sexual lives.

This article focuses on a case study of binnizá (zapotec) women in Juchitán de Zaragoza, Oaxaca, and analyze some dimensions that influences in their gender practices learnings linked to their sexual and reproductive life. We assert how the lack of sexual educational with intersectional and decolonial perspective affects their fertility rate, how the structural poverty and marginality of young rural indigenous women are interrelated with the constrains in the access to the health system and why it is absolutely necessary incorporate tge intersectional and decolonial perspective only in the health system but in the educational one; and at the time in the health sexual and reproductive promotion at the community health through the lens of popular educational in the everyday life.

Mexico's Indigenous Population and Fertility Rate

Mexico is a multi-ethnic, pluricultural and multilingual country due to the presence and diversity of indigenous and Afro-Mexican peoples*. According to the 2020 Population and Housing Census, 19.4% of Mexico's population (23,229,089 people) self-identify as indigenous at the municipal level. Regarding the estimate of the indigenous population in households, 9.5% (11,979,483 persons) declared themselves to be speakers of an indigenous language. The four ethnic groups with the largest populations are Nahuatl, Maya, Zapotec and Mixtec. Although the presence of indigenous peoples has been recorded in all the states of the country, they are concentrated in 8 states: Chiapas, Oaxaca, Veracruz, Puebla, Yucatan, Guerrero, Mexico, and Hidalgo. Although self-identification is a criterion for indigenous populations, the use of language and traditions are elements to be considered in the ethnic universe.

The precariousness of the living conditions of the country's indigenous population is systematically greater than that of the non-indigenous population; the existing gaps between the well-being of the indigenous and non-indigenous populations in 2018 are not different from those identified in 2008 (CONEVAL, 2019). In 2018, 69.5% of the population living in poverty was indigenous, did not have enough income to consume a food basket and had three or more social deprivations. The most common deprivations among the indigenous population are access to social security, access to basic services in the home and educational backwardness. Fifty per cent of the indigenous population live in rural areas, with most indigenous communities concentrated in the south-southeast of the country.

These structural problems affect the exercise of sexual and reproductive rights by indigenous adolescents. Some patterns have been observed among indigenous and non-indigenous adolescents in Latin America: the percentage of indigenous adolescents who had their first sexual intercourse before the age of 15 is higher than among non-indigenous adolescents, due to cultural pressures and lack of sexual education; the onset of sexual life among indigenous adolescents occurs in the context of couple relationships; and early motherhood is more common among indigenous women (Naciones Unidas, 2011). This situation suggests that, on the one hand, traditional models of sexuality and reproduction persist among indigenous youth, leading to higher fertility rates among young women. On the other hand, there is a greater educational gap among young indigenous women, which limits their access to sexual and reproductive health information and education.

During the three-year period from 2011 to 2013, the total fertility rate for Mexican women living in rural areas was 2.81 children per woman, for women living in urban areas it was 2.04 children, and for women who speak an indigenous language it was 2.98 children. Women who speak an indigenous language show a higher propensity to become pregnant during adolescence, with 54.0 per cent of them becoming mothers at this stage, compared to 45.9 per cent of those who do not speak an indigenous language. Regarding the use of contraceptive methods among sexually active adolescents, 63.0 per cent of those who speak an indigenous language do not use them, in contrast to 60.0 per cent of those who do not speak an indigenous language and use them (INEGI, 2018).

Some changes in adolescent fertility rates were reported between 2014 and 2018. Adolescent girls living in indigenous households increased their fertility rate by 2.8 per cent, from 84.7 per cent births in 2014 to 87.1 per cent in 2018. In comparison, non-indigenous adolescents decreased their fertility rate by 9.5 per cent, from 76.2 per cent births in 2014 to 69 per cent births in 2018 (CONAPO, 2021a). This disparity is due to a combination of factors, including poor information in rural indigenous areas, low access to contraceptive methods and social and cultural restrictions on their use, cultural constructions and values of motherhood and womanhood linked to gender identity and ethnicity, access to comprehensive sexuality education, protection from violence, and access to relative citizenship status in the family and community.

Inequality and Exclusion of Young Rural Indigenous Women

The community exerts strong control over indigenous girls, and often the strategy to gain minimal control over their choices is to marry and have a child (Bonfil, 2014). The transition from childhood to adulthood occurs through marriage and parenthood, as adolescence is an emerging phenomenon in indigenous societies. The truth is that parents often encourage their daughters to begin their sexual life so that they will soon find a partner who will take them in and provide for them, not realizing that they are leading them to a fate of no schooling, no preparation for work and no life project.

In indigenous cultures, the concept of complementary duality, which justifies the hierarchical distinction between women and men, their different spheres of activity and their subordination to each other, confines women to the domestic sphere and to caring for the family. Indigenous girls are married at a young age to older men; they do not decide for themselves the number and spacing of their children; their families control their actions, movements, and ideas; men decide for them; and they receive less schooling. From adolescence onwards, women accumulate greater disadvantage and exclusion; and under these conditions they are more exposed to gender-based violence, which exacerbates the conditions of subordination, victimization, and harassment.

Gap Between the Health System and Indigenous Women

There is a gap between the perspective of health workers and that of indigenous users; most health workers are unaware of their patients' health practices and are therefore less able to communicate with them and treat them with dignity and respect. Several studies have documented the issue of sterilization and the imposition of contraceptive devices, which directly violates their right to choose and has been identified as the most obvious manifestation of obstetric violence (Belli, 2013). Research has shown that 50 per cent of indigenous beneficiaries of the Oportunidades program received skilled care at birth, compared to 79 per cent of non-indigenous women. Indigenous women also have less access to laboratory tests and vaccinations, limited access to prenatal care services and a delay in the start of reproductive life (Freyermuth-Enciso, 2014).

Women living in indigenous areas have higher mortality rates than non-indigenous women. Some of the factors involved in this situation are the geographical accessibility of health services and infrastructure, the availability of financial resources to transport a woman with an obstetric emergency, basic knowledge of health risks (Juárez-Moreno et al., 2021) and the perception that women are more likely to have a higher mortality rate than those who do not (Juárez-Moreno et al., 2021) and the perception that they are more likely to have a higher mortality rate (Freyermuth-Enciso, 2014).

In the indigenous region of Los Altos de Chiapas, the doctor-patient relationship is problematic, doctors are reviled, and the indigenous population distrusts them for various reasons (Freyermuth-Enciso, 2014). Health workers do not speak the local language and discriminate against the knowledge and practices of women themselves and/or traditional midwives, which means that users do not receive sufficient, clear, timely and truthful information; and as a result, women are unable to make free choices about the care they receive. In the south of Yucatan, it has been reported that medical personnel do not speak Mayan, do not understand the indigenous concept of the body and illness, and even disregard the wisdom of traditional medicine. Mayan women avoid going to the health center because their prenatal and postnatal practices are not respected; institutional biomedical practices are applied without considering women's opinions; it is lost that pregnant and parturient women feel uncomfortable and ashamed when attended by male doctors; and women are attended exclusively by monolingual medical residents without intercultural training (Mendoza, 2018).

Intersectional and Decolonial Analysis of the Health System

Biomedicine is the hegemonic medical system that imposes its ideas, undermines indigenous knowledge, and weakens traditional medical systems that are part of the cultural and social survival of communities (Gamlin and Berrio, 2020). The indigenous traditional medical system has a concept of well-being that is holistic and collective, encompassing spirituality and social and environmental dynamics; this contrasts with the hegemonic view, which is both individualistic and biological and relates to behavior (Menéndez, 1992; Valeggia and Snodgrass, 2015). From an indigenous perspective, illness focuses not only on biological processes but also on the broader social and historical context in which illness occurs (Zárate Hernández, 2009).

Biomedicine has contributed to improving the health of indigenous people, but its discriminatory and imposing colonialist perspective, together with the inadequacy of the health system in Mexico, has led the population to refrain from seeking care. Contrary to the approach that portrays indigenous women as passive victims of structural violence, Gamlin and Berrio (2020), drawing on the role of agency in post-critical anthropology, note that indigenous women actively participate in reshaping the health care process in a variety of ways: going to traditional doctors because they provide them with greater cultural and social security, resisting certain forms of medical treatment, refusing care, and seeking courts to defend their rights.

Tének and Nahua women in San Luis Potosí have developed strategies to resist the practices of the hegemonic medical model and incorporate indigenous knowledge and community resources, articulating the benefits of both perspectives. Some of these strategies include: accessing public health care while continuing to use local midwives; prioritizing maternity advice from their mothers, mothers-in-law, midwives and partners over advice from doctors; going to the midwife because they have a better chance of not having a caesarean section; choosing the mobile brigade over the hospital because it is geographically and culturally closer; delaying their approach to health institutions and not being rigorous in their prenatal consultations; among others (Flores et al., 2022).

Case Study: Binnizá Women in Juchitán de Zaragoza, Oaxaca

Oaxaca is home to the largest number of indigenous groups (16) in the country, and its population is spread across eight regions. Fifty-one per cent of the Oaxacan population lives in rural areas (less than

2,500 inhabitants), 23 per cent in transitional areas (2,500 to 14,999 inhabitants) and 26 per cent in urban areas (more than 15,000 inhabitants). The most widely spoken indigenous languages are Zapotec, Mixtec, Mazatec and Mixe. The average level of education of the indigenous population aged 15 and over is 5.4 years, i.e. they have not completed primary education. The illiteracy rate among the indigenous population aged 15 and over is 25.1% (Erken, 2021).

The Zapotec people call themselves *binnizá,* which means 'people who come from the clouds'. The Zapotecs have lived in the state of Oaxaca for at least 3,500 years, in the regions of the Sierra Norte, the Valles Centrales, the Sierra Sur, Tuxtepec, the Isthmus of Tehuantepec and the coast of Oaxaca, in a total of 220 communities (INPI, 2017). There are phonetic and cultural differences among the Zapotecs (clothing, food, and housing). The traditional political system of the Zapotec indigenous community is the *mayordomías*[1] of the patron saint, whose tools are the community organization: kinship ties and alliances between groups (Ruíz, 2011). The Zapotecs of the Isthmus of Tehuantepec are mainly concentrated in the municipalities of Santo Domingo Tehuantepec and Juchitán de Zaragoza.

While the average fertility rate in Mexico is 68.5 births per 1,000 adolescents (CONAPO, 2021b), in Oaxaca it reaches 94 births (Ramírez, 2022). In addition, statistics in this state register a high maternal mortality rate, which is attributed to the sum of marginalized conditions (Freyermuth 2019). The municipality of Juchitán de Zaragoza ranks second in pregnancies among girls under the age of 15 and third among adolescents aged 15-19 and is one of the 40 municipalities in Oaxaca with a gender alert declaration (DIGEPO, 2019).

Throughout the state, cultural stereotypes, both indigenous and colonial, associated with patriarchy and domination over women persist, creating conditions conducive to systemic violence against Oaxacan women (Fernández-Tapia, 2021). Social values, traditions and practices have led men to perceive themselves as having the power to control and dominate the bodies and sexuality of women, young women, and girls. Oaxaca is one of the states with the highest incidence of sexual violence in Mexico, but only 5% of cases are known because they are not reported. The main places where sexual violence occurs are homes and schools. In 2013, the Oaxacan Civil Code was amended to prohibit marriage before the age of 18 and to reduce the fertility rate, but despite these and other efforts, the fertility rate remains high (Reyes Alavez & Ramírez Vargas, 2022).

Some authors have argued that there is a 'third gender' in the Juchitán region: the *muxes*, who are biologically male and do not fully identify with either male or female roles. Far from reinforcing the myth that *muxes* are the sexual initiators of men, it is more appropriate to argue that some men seek out *muxes* for sex because they are more sexually open, since cultural and social norms in the region make it difficult to have sex with women before marriage (Borruso, 2002; Dávalos, 2017; Gutiérrez, 2021). Until a few years ago, the practice of bride kidnapping was widespread among underage couples, which consisted of grooms stealing their brides, taking them home and, with the consent of the boy's relatives, testing the girl's virginity (the groom inserts his fingers into the vagina, breaks the hymen and stains a handkerchief with blood) (Barabás & Bartolomé, 1999). The blood on the handkerchief is a necessary test to obtain the family's consent to have sex at that moment in a room prepared for the occasion, after having announced it to the whole community with fireworks, and the next day the date of the wedding is agreed with the bride's family (Dalton, 2010). This is a form of control and sexual violence against women.

The rite of kidnapping is still practiced in Juchitán, but only in the southern part of the city (not in the north, where families of a higher socio-economic status live), and although some young women are no longer virgins, tricks are performed to imitate the blood of the hymen breaking. This is the only way to fulfil the ideal of a woman's role in the community and to have the opportunity to be a wife and mother. Some of the traditional beliefs about gender roles that persist are: a woman who has lost her virginity and has access to pleasure also loses her feminine characteristics; the community rejects women who have not become virgins at marriage, have no children, are unmarried or divorced; men can have access to premarital sex to enrich their masculinity; the man decides the number and spacing of children; women agree not to use contraception so that the man will not accuse them of infidelity; and men have the right to be unfaithful. Overall, men control women's bodies and sexuality, dominant masculinities, and gender-based violence remain deeply entrenched.

In indigenous communities, remaining a virgin until marriage is associated with a woman's value and the perceived respect of others (Karver et al., 2016). The community stigmatizes girls who have sex before marriage, it is seen as dishonoring the parents if virginity is lost, and they become the subject of gossip by others. Alongside this situation, motherhood is seen as defining women and their womanhood. Women's value is centered on their ability to have children, and not having children means being less of a woman in the eyes of community members. Gender-based violence in the form of communal violence has the greatest impact on indigenous women in Oaxaca. This category does not exclude other forms of gender-based violence but encompasses them in an environment of close coexistence that cannot be attributed solely to community dynamics (Briseño-Maas and Bautista-Martínez, 2016). Women are embedded in a complex system of oppression that operates through multiple and simultaneous structures, in which discrimination based on gender, race/ethnicity, age, sexual orientation and other factors, including poverty, interact, resulting in a continuum that encompasses a wide range of manifestations and degrees of violence.

Violence against women begins in the micro-spaces where structural deficiencies such as inequality and marginalization are expressed. Women suffer psychological, physical, economic, and sexual violence in their homes and communities. Increasing alcoholism among men has contributed to the rise in violence against women. To understand the historical and social context of gender violence in Juchitán, we interviewed a public servant who has been the director of culture in the municipality of Juchitán for several years. He explained that the construction of the Pan-American Highway in the 1950s made it easier for the Carta Blanca brewery to enter Juchitán. But since the only alcoholic drinks consumed by the population were mezcal and taberna (a drink like pulque but made from the coyol palm), it was not easy to encourage the consumption of beer.

Carta Blanca found that one of the most important social practices in the community was the construction of the *enramada*[2], which was used as a venue for traditional festivities. The construction of the *enramada* was a social gathering place where 20 to 30 men would come together to cut the reeds and then weave them into three-meter-long canvases, which were then unrolled and tied to the crossbeams of the *enramada*. The women participated by preparing breakfast for the men and the mezcal producers. The brewery then offered the men iron structures and tarpaulin roofs, chairs, ice and even tables, on the condition that they would buy beer at a special price. As they gradually accepted, the social fabric was eroded by the loss of the *enramada* structure and alcohol consumption increased exponentially, becoming a regional public health problem. Nowadays, beer is consumed in most *velas* celebration, and everyone at the party knows that he or she cannot arrive without carrying at least one carton or contributing financially to the purchase of the drink. According to the public servant, the alcoholism induced by the brewery is a major factor in the high rate of domestic violence in Juchitán and in the increase in aggression against women, which has become entrenched.

The population is very identified with the customs of their ancestors and tries to keep them alive with great solemnity and, interestingly, this phenomenon recurs in different areas. One event that illustrates this phenomenon is the revival of the traditional dress for the *velas*. In the 1960s, a dress was required (white guayabera and dark trousers for men, and regional costume for women), but in the 1980s it became so flexible that young people could wear any dress. In the early 1990s, the members of one of the sails felt that this was degrading and decided to reintroduce the requirement to wear traditional dress. Soon after, the rest of the *velas* "understood the importance of recovering something important for the Zapotec identity, not just a costume, but a solemnity that represents the most important of the festivities," according to the public servant. Now, the dress code is very strict for all the *velas*.

This new wave of recovery of traditions and celebrations also includes the revival of the indigenous language. Although Juchitán has a high percentage of Zapotec speakers (52%, or around 65,000 inhabitants) compared to other nearby municipalities such as Tehuantepec (6%, or around 3,500 inhabitants, most of whom are over 60 years old), over the last 20 years workshops have been held in schools to strengthen the language, and it has been possible to increase the statistics by 1% (from 60,000 in 2000 to 65,000 speakers today). According to the public servant, efforts are also being made to revive the tradition of the *enramadas* because of their importance to the social fabric.

Although there is no direct link between the strict use of traditional dress to attend the *velas*, the revival of the Zapotec language and the construction of the *enramadas* and violence against women, it is possible to observe that the population's strong identification with the customs of their ancestors and their intention to keep them alive has led to an interest in recovering traditional practices that devalue women and make them inferior to men. Some of these practices are the rite of bride kidnapping and early pregnancy, which could be reflected in the increase in teenage pregnancy statistics in the community in 2019 compared to 2017. These practices have disadvantaged women for generations and are now taking place in a context of increased violence, according to the public servant.

Social inequalities are linked to gender inequalities, which in turn lead to further gender-based violence. Indigenous women who decide to go to judicial institutions to file a complaint are confronted with the naturalization and acceptance of male violence, the lack of awareness and training of the personnel in charge, and the lack of translators with a gender perspective, which makes it practically impossible for them to file a formal complaint and follow it up (Briseño-Maas and Bautista-Martínez, 2016). Unfortunately, they have also experienced the lack of intercultural vision and gender perspective in public health institutions.

Only 17.5% of health centers in Oaxaca have staff who speak the local indigenous language, although 57.1% serve the indigenous population (Sachse, et al., 2012). There is a general lack of interpreters and translators to provide health services to users in indigenous languages, and there are no sexual and reproductive health dissemination materials in indigenous languages (ILSB, 2021). The ILSB (n.d.) conducted a study on the intercultural approach to service provision in rural and urban health units in two municipalities in Oaxaca and found that patients are not asked about their affiliation and mother tongue when they register; there is a lack of staff to provide intercultural health services and no link with traditional midwives; sexual and reproductive health materials do not mention male co-responsibility; and adolescent girls seeking information are discriminated against if they are not accompanied by an adult.

There have been several cases of obstetric violence in Oaxaca because of negligence and discrimination in the authoritarian medical system. The violence has been greater among indigenous women, who have suffered humiliation, ridicule, rejection, discrimination, and exclusion through situations such as the placement of intrauterine devices without authorization, being subjected to poorly performed caesarean sections and denial of care, forcing women to give birth on the lawn, in bathrooms or on hospital pavements (Gutiérrez, 2017). For its part, CIDH (2014) documented the following cases of obstetric violence in Oaxaca from 2015 to 2020: obstetric violence and inadequate medical care in the Hospital Rural Solidaridad no. 34 of the Mexican Social Security Institute in Tlaxiaco; obstetric violence and inadequate medical care at the Hospital Rural Oportunidades no. 35 of the Mexican Social Security Institute in Santiago Jamiltepec; obstetric violence and violation of health protection in the hospitals of the Ministry of Health; obstetric violence, inadequate medical care and loss of life in the Hospital Rural Oportunidades no. 66 of the IMSS in Santiago Juxtlahuaca; and obstetric violence, violations of reproductive freedom and autonomy, of the right to choose the number and spacing of children and of health protection in the General Hospital of Juchitán de Zaragoza "Macedonio Benítez Fuentes" of the Ministry of Health. Therefore, the CNDH (National Commission for Human Rights) proposes to train obstetricians and gynecologists to avoid discrimination against women, to implement a model of intercultural care with a humanized approach, to link the health system with traditional midwifery and to organize a human rights awareness workshop in universities.

SOLUTIONS AND RECOMMENDATIONS

The power dynamics in the relationship between health professionals and indigenous women have a direct impact on the quality of therapeutic communication. The solution could begin by questioning and rethinking the way in which medical personnel interact with the indigenous population they serve, recognizing that acting as intercultural mediators would facilitate a dialogue between different worldviews, rather than perpetuating attempts to colonize indigenous thought, which translates into another form of violence experienced by indigenous women. The institutional health system and the traditional health system can be linked through an intercultural, human rights and gender perspective.

The health system should ensure the availability of contraceptive methods in indigenous communities, provide them unconditionally and respect the sexual rights and privacy of adolescents and young people. An intercultural perspective, complemented by biomedicine, can unleash processes of violence against women. Medical personnel should be trained to dialogue with people of different cultures, including speaking an indigenous language and knowing and understanding indigenous myths, rituals, values, and customs, to prevent early pregnancy and maternal mortality. Midwives should be integrated into the institutional health system (through certification) by claiming, valuing, and respecting the practice of midwifery, as they have multiple knowledge of the human being, the functioning of body parts and organs, and a conception of the person-body balance anchored in the universe and nature.

It is necessary to implement public policies with an intercultural and gender perspective, culturally appropriate health promotion and sexual education programs that consider the meanings, values, perceptions, and practices of different indigenous groups regarding their bodies, couple life, sexuality, illness and both traditional and current ways of caring for their health. It is recommended that such programs be designed with indigenous women so that they themselves can affirm their own knowledge and adopt the strategies they consider appropriate in accordance with their world view.

FUTURE RESEARCH DIRECTIONS

It is necessary to deepen the research on indigenous peoples in general with a gender perspective, and to define it in terms of women's sexual and reproductive health, since it is in this area that inequality manifests itself in an intersectional way. Particularly with regard to the state of Oaxaca, it is recommended that the multiple dimensions of sexual and reproductive health be studied, such as courtship, initiation of sexual practices, cultural construction of desire, mutual consent, sexual abuse and coercion, conjugality, exercise of sexuality, reproduction, interruption of pregnancy, motherhood, breastfeeding, among others, in order to establish participatory action research projects that allow the construction of public policies based on documented evidence, as well as the transformation of their cultural environments through critical pedagogies.

It will be necessary to use pedagogical approaches to comprehensive sexuality education in dialogue, critical and collaborative indigenous women's contexts between the different sectors involved, such as formal education, primary health care and communities. Popular education or other pedagogies that are collectively and communally constructed as epistemologies and methodologies can contribute to the complex articulation of formal and informal education.

CONCLUSION

In this chapter we analyze the sexual and reproductive education of indigenous women in Mexico through an intersectional and decolonial approach; we address the context of marginalization and the problems that have become more acute in indigenous communities in recent years, and their relationship with the exercise of sexual and reproductive rights by young indigenous women; We have compiled some of the divergences between biomedical practices and the traditional indigenous perspective to show the gap between the health system and indigenous women; and we have deepened the case of *binnizá* women in Juchitán de Zaragoza, Oaxaca, using the intersectional and decolonial qualitative methodology.

The formulation of the case study allowed us to articulate demographic statistics, ethnographic studies, analyses of violence against women, legislative changes, increased alcoholism among men and aggression against women, community and intra-family violence, the tendency to reinstate traditions in various fields, the lack of awareness among staff of judicial institutions, and the various ways in which medical personnel have discriminated against and violated indigenous women; to make visible the inclusion of these women in a complex system of oppression that discriminates against them on the basis of gender, race/ethnicity, class and age. One of the limitations of our study is the inclusion of testimonies from *binnizá* women about their vision of the forms of violence that affect their lives, their disagreements with the health system, and their strategies for resisting the practices of the hegemonic medical model and incorporating the knowledge and resources of their community. This study is a starting point for future analysis.

REFERENCES

Al-Faham, H., Davis, A. M., & Ernst, R. (2019). Intersectionality: From Theory to Practice. *Annual Review of Law and Social Science*, *15*(1), 247–265. doi:10.1146/annurev-lawsocsci-101518-042942

Ameigeiras, A. R. (2006). El abordaje etnográfico en la investigación social [The ethnographic approach in social research]. In I. Vasilachis de Gialdino (coord.), Estrategias de investigación cualitativa [Qualitative research strategies] (pp. 107-151). Gedisa.

Angrosino, M. V. (2015). Recontextualización de la observación. [Recontextualisation of the observation] In *N.K. Denzin & Y.S. Lincoln (coords.) Manual de investigación cualitativa. Volumen IV Métodos de recolección y análisis de datos [Handbook of qualitative research. Volume IV Methods of data collection and analysis]*. (pp. 203–234). Gedisa.

Asher, K. (2017). Spivak and Rivera Cusicanqui on the Dilemmas of Representation in Postcolonial and Decolonial Feminisms. *Feminist Studies*, *43*(3), 512–524. doi:10.1353/fem.2017.0041

Barabás, A. & Bartolomé, M. (1999). Configuraciones Étnicas en Oaxaca. [Ethnic Configurations in Oaxaca]. Ethnographic Perspectives for Autonomies [Perspectivas Etnográficas para las Autonomías]. INAH, INI.

Belli, L. (2013). La violencia obstétrica: otra forma de violación a los derechos humanos [Obstetric violence: another form of human rights violation]. *Revista Redbioética [Redbioethics Journal]*, *1*(7), 25-34. https://redbioetica.com.ar/wp-content/uploads/2018/11/Art2-BelliR7.pdf

Bonfil, P. (2014). Introducción [Introduction]. En P.Bonfil (coord.), Derechos y salud sexual y reproductiva entre jóvenes indígenas: hacia la construcción de una agenda necesaria [Sexual and reproductive health and rights among indigenous young people: towards the construction of a necessary agenda] (pp. 13-42). GIMTRAP.

Borruso, M. M. (2002). *Hombre, mujer y muxe'en el Istmo de Tehuantepec*. Plaza y Valdés.

Bourgois, P. (2001). The Power of Violence in War and Peace. Post-Cold War Lessons from El Salvador. *Ethnography*, *2*(1), 5–34. https://escholarship.org/uc/item/8w69708b. doi:10.1177/14661380122230803

Brah, A. (1991). Difference, diversity, differentiation. *International Review of Sociology*, *2*(2), 53–71. doi:10.1080/03906701.1991.9971087

Briseño-Maas. M. L.; & Bautista-Martínez, E. (2016). La violencia hacia las mujeres en Oaxaca. En los caminos de la desigualdad y la pobreza [Violence against women in Oaxaca. On the roads of inequality and poverty]. *Revista LiminaR. Estudios Sociales y Humanísticos [Journal LiminaR. Social and Humanistic Studies]*, *XIV* (2), 15-27.

Carosio, A. (2023). Embarazo adolescente, desigualdad y violencia en América Latina y el Caribe. [Teenage pregnancy, inequality and violence in Latin America and the Caribbean] In K. Batthyány (Ed.), *Desigualdades y violencias de género en América Latina y el Caribe [Inequalities and gender-based violence in Latin America and the Caribbean]*. (pp. 117–212). CLACSO.

Comisión Interamericana de Derechos Humanos (CIDH). (2014). *150 Período de Sesiones: Salud materna y denuncias de violencia obstétrica en México.* https://tinyurl.com/wjyfkwn

CONAPO. (2021a). Segunda fase de la Estrategia Nacional para la Prevención del Embarazo Adolescente 2021-2024 [*Second phase of the National Strategy for the Prevention of Adolescent Pregnancy 2021-2024*].CONAPO.https://www.gob.mx/cms/uploads/attachment/file/703251/Segunda_fase_de_la_ENAPEA_2021-2024_ajuste_forros_030222_small.pdf

CONAPO. (2021b). La situación Demográfica de México [*Mexico's Demographic Situation*]. CONAPO. https://www.gob.mx/conapo/documentos/la-situacion-demografica-de-mexico-2021

CONEVAL. (2019). La pobreza en la población indígena de México, 2008-2018 [*Poverty among Mexico's indigenous population, 2008-2018*]. CONEVAL. https://www.coneval.org.mx/Medicion/MP/Documents/Pobreza_Poblacion_indigena_2008-2018.pdf

Creswell, J. W. (1998). *Qualitative inquiry and research design: Choosing among five traditions.* Sage Publications, Inc.

Cumes, A. (2009). Multiculturalismo, género y feminismos: mujeres diversas, luchas complejas. *Participación y políticas de mujeres indígenas en contextos latinoamericanos recientes*, 29-52.

Dalton, M. (2010). *Mujeres: Género e Identidad en el Istmo de Tehuantepec, Oaxaca* [*Women: Gender and Identity in the Isthmus of Tehuantepec, Oaxaca*]. CIESAS.

Dávalos Vázquez, N. Q. (2017). Alguien ya robó mujer: virginidad y rito de paso en un barrio binnizá de Juchitán, Oaxaca [Someone has already stolen a woman: virginity and rite of passage in a Binnizá neighborhood in Juchitán, Oaxaca]. Master's thesis in Social Anthropology, El Colegio de San Luis.

de la Cadena, M. (1991). Las mujeres son más indias": Etnicidad y género en una comunidad del Cusco. [Women are more Indian: Ethnicity and gender in a Cuzco community]. Isis International Journal [Isis International Journal], 16.

DIGEPO. (2019). *Síntesis del embarazo adolescente en el municipio de Juchitán de Zaragoza* [*Synthesis of adolescent pregnancy in the municipality of Juchitán de Zaragoza*]. DIGEPO.

Erken, A. (2021). United Nations Population Fund-The UNFPA strategic plan, 2022-2025 Annex 1. https://www.unfpa.org/unfpa-strategic-plan-2022-2025-dpfpa20218

Fernández-Tapia, J. (2021). Abuso sexual a niñas en Oaxaca:¿ problema legal o cultural? *Revista Innova Educación*, *3*(3), 7–32. doi:10.35622/j.rie.2021.03.001

Figueroa Romero, D., & Sierra Camacho, M. T. (2020). Alertas de género y mujeres indígenas: interpelando las políticas públicas desde los contextos comunitarios en Guerrero, México. *Canadian Journal of Latin American and Caribbean Studies/Revue canadienne des études latino-américaines et caraïbes*, *45*(1), 26-44.

Flores, Y. Y. R., Pérez, O. L., & Moreno, M. J. (2022). Resistencias y sincretismo indígena de mujeres ténck y nahuas de San Luis Potosí, México, en la experiencia del autocuidado durante el embarazo y parto. *Revista de el Colegio de San Luis*, *12*(23), 1–31. doi:10.21696/rcsl122320221409

FMI, ECMIA, y CHIRAPAQ. (2020). *Mujeres indígenas de las Américas a 25 años de Beijing. Avances, brechas y desafíos* [*Indigenous women of the Americas 25 years after Beijing. Progress, gaps and challenges*]. FMI, ECMIA, CHIRAPAQ.

Fondo de Población de las Naciones Unidas. UNFPA (2020). *Orientaciones técnicas y programáticas internacionales sobre educación integral en sexualidad fuera de la escuela.* https://www.unfpa.org/es/publications/orientaciones-tecnicas-y-programaticas-internacionales-sobre-educacion-integral-en

Fonllem, M. E. T. Género y sexualidad. Políticas públicas sobre los derechos sexuales y reproductivos en méxico (2000-2015). *Salud reproductiva, medio ambiente y género*, 19.

Freyermuth-Enciso, M. G. (2014). La mortalidad materna y los nudos en la prestación de los servicios de salud en Chiapas: Un análisis desde la interculturalidad. *LiminaR*, *12*(2), 30–45. doi:10.29043/liminar.v12i2.340

Gamlin, J., & Berrio, L. (2020). Critical anthropologies of maternal health: Theorising from the field with Mexican indigenous communities. *Critical medical anthropology: Perspectives in and from Latin America*, 42-68.

Guerrero, D. G. (2017). Capítulo 10. Prevención del embarazo adolescente en el estado de Oaxaca mediante armonización de marco legal. *Índice*, 135.

Gutiérrez, N. (2017). Violencias en Oaxaca: pueblos indígenas, conflictos post electorales y violencia obstétrica. *Violencia y paz. Diagnósticos y propuestas para México*, 315-349.

Gutiérrez España, J. A. (2021). *El intrépido vuelo de las mariposas istmeñas a la Ciudad de México. Muxeidad, identidad de género y corporalidad en contexto migratorio* [*The intrepid flight of the Isthmian butterflies to Mexico City. Muxeidad, gender identity and corporeality in a migratory context*].

Hernandez, R. A. (Ed.). (2008). *Etnografías e historias de resistencia: mujeres indígenas, procesos organizativos y nuevas identidades políticas* (pp. 15–40). Centro de Investigaciones y Estudios Superiores en Antropología Social.

Hernández Castillo, R. A. (2010). Violencia de Estado y violencia de género: Las paradojas en torno a los derechos humanos de las Mujeres en México [State violence and gender-based violence: the paradoxes surrounding women's human rights in Mexico]. *Trace (México, DF)*, *57*, 86–98.

Hill Collins, P. (1998). La política del pensamiento feminista negro. *Qué son los estudios de mujeres*, 253-312.

Hooks, B. (2004). Mujeres negras. Dar forma a la teoría feminista. *Otras inapropiables. Feminismos desde las fronteras*, 33-50. ILSB (n/d). *Juventudes evalúan servicios de salud sexual y reproductiva a través de mecanismos de transparencia y rendición de cuentas en Oaxaca* [*Youth evaluate sexual and reproductive health services through transparency and accountability mechanisms in Oaxaca*]. ILSB. https://ilsb.org.mx/embarazoenadolescentes/assets/files/Oaxaca.pdf

ILSB. (2021). *Recomendaciones para prevenir el embarazo en adolescentes por medio de los servicios de salud sexual y reproductiva en Oaxaca* [Recommendations for preventing adolescent pregnancy through sexual and reproductive health services in Oaxaca]. ILSB. https://ilsb.org.mx/wp-content/uploads/2021/12/LPN_Incidencia_Oaxaca-H-web_VF.pdf

INEGI. (2018). *Encuesta Nacional de la Dinámica Demográfica (ENADID) 2018* [National Survey of Demographic Dynamics (ENADID) 2018]. INEGI.

INEGI. (2020). *Censo de Población y Vivienda, 2020* [Census of Population and Housing, 2020]. INEGI.

INPI. (2017). *Etnografía del pueblo zapoteco del Istmo de Tehuantepec (Binnizá)* [Ethnography of the Zapotec People of the Isthmus of Tehuantepec (Binnizá)]. INPI. https://www.gob.mx/inpi/articulos/etnografia-del-pueblo-zapoteco-del-istmo-de-tehuantepec-binniza

Juárez-Moreno, M., López-Pérez, O., Josefa Raesfelda, L., & Durán-González, R. E. (2021). Sexualidad, género y percepción del riesgo a la infección por VIH en mujeres indígenas de México [Sexuality, gender and HIV risk perception among indigenous women in Mexico]. *Saúde Soc. São Paulo, 30*(2), 1-12. https://doi.org/ doi:10.1590/S0104-12902021200399

Karver, T. S., Sorhaindo, A., Wilson, K. S., & Contreras, X. (2016). Exploring intergenerational changes in perceptions of gender roles and sexuality among Indigenous women in Oaxaca. *Culture, Health & Sexuality, 18*(8), 845–859. doi:10.1080/13691058.2016.1144790 PMID:26928352

Lamas, M. (2018). ¿Activismo académico? El caso de algunas etnógrafas feministas. *Cuicuilco. Revista de ciencias antropológicas, 25*(72), 9-30.

Lugones, M. (2008). Colonialidad y género. *Tabula rasa*, (9), 73-102.

Mendoza, A. (2018). X-ilah k'oha'an (parteras) y personal médico alópata en la atención del embarazo y el parto de mujeres mayas de Yucatán y Quintana Roo. *Salud reproductiva, medio ambiente y género, 55*.

Mendoza, B. (2010). La epistemología del sur, la colonialidad del género y el feminismo latinoamericano. *Aproximaciones críticas a las prácticas teórico-políticas del feminismo latinoamericano, 1*, 19-36.

Menéndez, E. (1992). Modelo hegemónico, modelo alternativo subordinado, modelo de autoatención. Caracteres estructurales. *La antropología médica en México, 1*, 97-111.

Millán, M. (2014). Alcances político-ontológicos de los feminismos indígenas. *Más allá del feminismo: caminos para andar*, 119-144.

Mohanty, C. (2008). Bajo los ojos de occidente. Academia Feminista y discurso colonial. *Descolonizando el feminismo: teorías y prácticas desde los márgenes, 1*, 1-23.

Naciones Unidas. (2011). *Salud de la población joven indígena en América Latina. Un panorama general* [Health of the young indigenous population in Latin America. An overview]. Naciones Unidas.

OPS. (2008). *La Salud Sexual y Reproductiva de los Adolescentes y los Jóvenes: Oportunidades, Enfoques y Opiniones* [Adolescent and Youth Sexual and Reproductive Health: Opportunities, Approaches and Views]. OPS.

Quijano, A. (2002). Colonialidad del poder, globalización y democracia [Coloniality of power, globalisation and democracy]. Revista de Ciencias Sociales [Social Science Journal], 4 (7-8), 1-23.

Ramírez Izúcar, C. (2022). Retos para la Prevención del Embarazo en Adolescentes en Oaxaca [Challenges for the Prevention of Adolescent Pregnancy in Oaxaca]. *Oaxaca Población siglo XXI [Oaxaca Population 21st century]*, 47, 31-40. https://productosdigepo.oaxaca.gob.mx/recursos/revistas/revista47.pdf

Reyes Alavez, DRamírez Vargas, R. (2022). Preventing Adolescent Pregnancy in Oaxaca [Prevención del Embarazo en Adolescentes en Adolescentes en Oaxaca [Preventing Adolescent Pregnancy in Oaxaca]. Oaxaca Población siglo XXI [Oaxaca Population 21st century], 47, 41-45.

Rivera Cusicanqui, S. (2010). Ch'ixinakax utxiwa: una reflexión sobre prácticas y discursos descolonizadores [Ch'ixinakax utxiwa: a reflection on decolonising practices and discourses]. Tinta Limón.

Ruíz Medrano, E. (2011). Un breve recorrido bibliográfico por la historia de los pueblos zapotecos de Oaxaca [A brief bibliographic tour through the history of the Zapotec peoples of Oaxaca] [*Anthropological Dimension*]. *Dimensión Antropológica*, *18*(52), 57–80.

Sachse, M., Azalia Pintado, P. S., & Lastra, Z. (2012). Calidad de la atención obstétrica, desde la perspectiva de derechos, equidad e interculturalidad en centros de salud en Oaxaca [Quality of obstetric care from the perspective of rights, equity and interculturality in health centres in Oaxaca] [*CONAMED Journal*]. *Revista CONAMED*, *17*(1), s4–s15.

Segato, R. L. (2015). The Critique of Coloniality in Eight Essays. And an anthropology on demand [The Critique of Coloniality in Eight Essays. And an anthropology on demand]. Prometheus.

Sieder, R. (2017). Introduction. Indigenous women and legal pluralities in Latin America: rethinking justice and security [Introduction. Indigenous women and legal pluralities in Latin America: rethinking justice and security]. In Rachel Sieder (Ed.), Exigiendo justicia y seguridad: Mujeres indígenas y pluralidades legales en América Latina [Demanding Justice and Security: Indigenous Women and Legal Pluralities in Latin America] (pp.13-50). CIESAS.

Spivak, G. C. (2011) *Can the Subaltern Speak?* Editorial El cuenco de plata. [1988]

UNFPA. (2014). UNFPA Operational Guidelines for Comprehensive Sexuality Education: A Human Rights and Gender-Based Approach [UNFPA Operational Guidelines for Comprehensive Sexuality Education: A Human Rights and Gender-Based Approach]. UNFPA.

Valeggia, C. R., & Snodgrass, J. J. (2015). Health of Indigenous Peoples. *Annual Review of Anthropology*, *44*(1), 117–135. doi:10.1146/annurev-anthro-102214-013831

Vázquez, N. Q. D. (2017). *Alguien ya robó mujer: virginidad y rito de paso en un barrio Binnizá de Juchitán.*

Wade, P. (2000). Raza y etnicidad en Latinoamérica [Race and ethnicity in Latin America]. Abya-Yala. doi:10.26530/OAPEN_625258

WHO. (2006). *Defining sexual health: Report of a technical consultation on sexual health*. World Health Organization.

ADDITIONAL READING

Altamirano-Jiménez, I. (2010). Neoliberalism, Racialised Gender and Indigeneity. In B. Hokowhitu, (Eds.), *Indigenous Identity and Resistance. Researching the Diversity of Knowledge* (pp. 193–206). Otago Press University.

Carsten, J. (2004). *After kinship* (Vol. 2). Cambridge University Press.

Lozano, C. P. M. (2005). El esquema cultural de género y sexualidad en la vida cotidiana. Una reflexión teórica. *Culturales*, *1*(2), 30–62.

Martin M. K. y Voorhies, B. (1978). *The Woman: An Anthropological Approach.*

Ortner, S. (1979). ¿Es la mujer con respecto al hombre lo que la naturaleza con respecto a la cultura? *Antropología y feminismo*, 109-131.

Pérez, J. B. (2013). *Espacios de lucha contra el racismo y sexismo Mujeres y vida cotidiana.*

Rubin, G. (2015). El tráfico de mujeres: notas sobre la economía política del sexo. *Género: la construcción cultural de la diferencia sexual. -(Pública-Género; 1)*, 35-91.

Stone, L., & King, D. E. (2018). *Kinship and gender: An introduction*. Routledge.

KEY TERMS AND DEFINITIONS

Binnizá: It is the name the Zapotecs use for themselves. It means people who come from the clouds.

Decoloniality: It is a perspective that analyses the origin of race as a category that emerges at a particular historical and social moment to classify the population in the Americas and to configure relations of domination on a global scale.

Hegemonic Medical Model: It is a system with a scientific, bureaucratic, undemocratic, and uniform perspective that contrasts health with illness and focuses on identifying symptoms and possible treatments. It is an ethnocentric model, claiming that only Western medical knowledge is valid; it is also androcentric and lacks a gender perspective.

Intercultural Approach: Recognizes the coexistence of different cultures and facilitates communication, exchange, and connection, respecting identities and defending their interrelationship.

Intersectionality: This is an approach that explains the phenomenon whereby two or more social categories interact, multiplying disadvantage and discrimination.

Muxes: People who were born biologically male and do not fully identify with masculine or feminine roles.

Velas: Community festival of the Zapotecs of the Isthmus. They are nighttime celebrations that are carried out by the mayordomías during the month of May and in Juchitán they are dedicated to the patron saint of San Vicente.

Zapotec: They are the indigenous people who settled in the state of Oaxaca before the Spanish conquest and colonization.

ENDNOTES

*   Two per cent of the population (2,576,213 people) self-identify as Afro-Mexican or Afro-descendant (INEGI, 2020).
1   It is a position in the Catholic religion given to those in charge of organizing celebrations in honor of patron saints or community festivals. The *mayordomía* expresses the solidarity and cohesion of the group.
2   It is a temporary structure made from the branches of a local tree or shrub that is used to shelter people from the sun.

Chapter 2
Navigating the Tension of Holistic Sexual Reproductive Health Curriculum in Three States of SADC Using Rogers Diffusion of Innovation Theory

William Chakabwata
https://orcid.org/0000-0002-4224-5239
University of South Africa, South Africa

Ronika Mumbire
Independent Researcher, Zimbabwe

ABSTRACT

The chapter explores the provision of comprehensive sex education (CSE) and the antecedent challenges. A case of three states, namely Namibia, South Africa, and Zimbabwe, is undertaken, in order to illuminate the obstacles related to the implementation of this curriculum. The aims of comprehensive sexuality education are also explored in order to demonstrate the indispensable nature of this curriculum. CSE has faced resistance in many countries, due to the way it was implemented. The chapter argues for implementation of CSE curriculum, using Rogers's theory of diffusion of innovation (DIO), to overcome challenges related to the implementation of this indispensable curriculum for young people. The chapter is undergirded by the poststructural feminism, social cognitive and diffusion of innovation theories.

INTRODUCTION

The chapter will submit an overview of the tension that is characterized by the introducing of comprehensive sexual education (CSE), in the SADC states and ways in which this may be tackled by employing Roger's Diffusion of Innovation theory (DOI). The chapter commences by submitting the rationale for holistic CSE globally, by using statistics of prevalence of cases of gender based violence (GBV) and avers that the proliferation of cases of GBV in the three countries reflects a lack of knowledge, skills and attitude in the area of CSE. The three countries that will be surveyed in this study are Namibia, South Africa and Zimbabwe are all located in southern Africa and are a part of the Southern African Development Community (SADC). South Africa has been selected to be a part of this chapter, due to its highly acclaimed progressive legislation on reproductive health. South Africa has also ratified a number of international declarations on reproductive health. In Zimbabwe the predominant form of contraceptive is the oral pill, which is widely propagated by international organisations such as United Nations Populations Fund (UNFPA. It is the gendered nature of perception towards reproductive health that drives gender-based violence (GBV). Comprehensive sexuality education (CSE), has potential to reduce GBV, by the way it equips learners with competencies that are based on empirical data on human development, communication skills, empathy and gender identity and reciprocal respect. CSE has the potential to inculcate in learners the skills to develop appropriate skills in relationships. Namibia was also selected to be a part of this chapter, due to the constrictions that teenagers face in accessing health and reproductive services as a consequence of paucity of information, negative attitudes from nurses and lack of parental support tends to hinder access to the much needed services. Rogers's diffusion of innovation model will be employed to explain how the three countries may introduce innovation. The chapter presents a background to the study of case studies of Namibia, South Africa and Zimbabwe, attitude towards CSE are interrogated, and aims of CSE, theoretical underpinnings of the chapter follow with the recommendations and conclusions being presented.

BACKGROUND TO THE STUDY

Comprehensive Sexuality Education (CSE) evolved over time from initially being subject that was taught by medical doctors at schools level supported by biology educators who utilised rarefied terms that young adolescents could not relate to (IPPF European Network, 2012).In the 1980s sexuality education due to the advent of HIV/AIDS, became more expressive in order to demonstrate risks associated with unsafe sex. The didactic approach became more learner- centred and active learning methods were used (IPPF European Network, 2012). The priority of instruction was to ensure that learners do not engage in risky sexual behaviour that could lead to unplanned pregnancies and also to eschew sexually transmitted infections (STIs). The weakness of this approach was that it was premised on the assumption that focalised sex as the priority for young people, and this was replaced with a more holistic curriculum that sought to develop self -esteem, better decision making in relationships, knowledge of sexuality and sexual identities,defining boundaries in life and gender based violence.

Pourkazemi et al (2020) avers that one critical element of CSE is the human reproductive health and it is very essential especially for girls and women and for preserving the health of the society. Comprehensive Sexual Education (CSE) helps to fortify children with knowledge that they need to protect themselves from sexual abuse. CSE encapsulates provision of information on sexually transmitted infections (STIs) which include AIDS and hepatitis, counselling, inculcating a sense of responsibility in both males and females regarding cultural norms and values, family planning and other services available druing pregnancy and care of the child after birth. The curriculum for CSE focalises more on the youth. This realisation led to the development of a curriculum termed CSE, which subsumed all that was taught under life skills and additional skills and knowledge.

Making the CSE prioritise the youth is prudent because they are more likely to engage in risky behaviour such as substance abuse, smoking and partaking in unprotected sexual activities. Risky sexual behaviours exposes adolescents to challenges such as HIV, hepatitis and STIs, in addition to pregnancies, engaging in unsafe abortion and neonatal challenges and issues to related to being a mother.The significance of CSE is also foregrounded in the Sustainable Development Goals (SDGs) which explicate the provision of reproductive health services and institutionalising it into policies and practices of countries (Pourkazemi et al,2020). It is acknowledged that one of the key ways of realising Sustainable Development Goal Target 3.7 by 2030 has to be general access to sexual and comprehensive reproductive health care services, which encompass family planning, provision of information and education. Reproductive health education is also intended to be designed into strategic plans of nations.

The legal basis of CSE may be encapsulated as Universal Declaration of Human Rights (UDHR, 1948), Convention on the Elimination of Discrimination against Women and Children (CEDAW, 1979) and Maputo Declaration (2003) among many others. For Southern African nations the most far reaching agreement was the Maputo Protocol on Women's Rights of 2003, which averred that men and women must be granted an equal opportunity to enjoy human rights. The Maputo protocol had significant ramifications for human rights for women in the way it foregrounded reproductive rights for women agreed to abolish numerous harmful practices for women (United Nations, 2024).

Fang et al.,(2020) noted that the implementation of Sexual Reproductive Health (SRH) is impacted by a diversity of cultural beliefs and practices in different countries In spite of its noble intentions, CSE still confronts major implementation obstacles for young people, particularly in developing countries, due to variables such as religious convictions that adolescent must not be exposed to sexual content, constrictions from cultural taboos, paucity of financial resources,unwillingnes by many teachers to engage on diversity of sexualities and a dearth of policy frameworks to uphold reproductive rights. Other impediments that function at individual level to inhibit the implementation of CSE innovation are stigma associated with accessing services for adolescents, fear, constricted knowledge, misceonceptions of such programmes, lack of financial autonomy among a host of other inhibitory variables. Other impediments that are prevalent in developing countries are a lack of accurate data on pre—marital sex, unsafe abortion, and sexual coercion.

The international Conference on Population and Development (ICPD) Programme of Action proposed a definition of reproductive health as

... people are able to have a satisfying and safe sex life and that they have a capability to reproduce and the freedom to decide if, when and how often to do so. Implicit in this last condition are the right of men and women to be informed and to have access to safe, effective and affordable, and acceptable methods of family planning of their choice, as well as other methods of their choice for regulating of fertility which are not against the law... (Sadana, 2002, p. 407)

Reproductive health is incoporated in SDGs under target 3.7 which envisages that by 2030 access to reproductive and health services and family planning will become universal. Venketsamy (2020) highlights the importance of holistic sexually reproductive health education in combating child sexual abuse. It is also foregrounded that holistic reproductive health education curriculum has potential to address high levels of gender –based violence (GBV) in our societies. In many countries which include South Africa, Namibia and Zimbabwe, CSE is taught as a component of lifeskills curriculum. CSE has potential of addressing violence and intolerance towards people who include lesbians, gay,bisexual,transgender,intersex, queer, asexual (LGBTIQA), since sexuality is fundamental to citizenship and identity.

CSE curriculum is being implemented globally in order to address the diverse needs of young people in different contexts. UNFPA (2020) explicated Asia has more than 1,8billion young people in the age category of 10-24 in Asia and Pacific Regions in countries designated as low and middle income. Although the socio and economic context is not homogenous, young people in that region have constricted access to comprehensive sexual reproductive health information and services. Of the 13million girls who lack access to contraceptives globally, about half are located in the Asia-Pacific Region culminating in an approximate 3,7 million adolescents giving birth in the region per annum. The same report assert that 82,000 young people are infected by HIV annually in that region.

Ronconi et al., (2023) noted that among the countries in Latin America which include Argentina, Bolivia, Brazil, Chile, Colombia, Costa Rica, Cuba, Ecuador, Honduras, Mexico, Nicaragua,Paraguay, Peru and Dominican Republic, there is an incipient regulatory architecture for the implementation of CSE. However, when it comes to a holistic implementation of this curriculum there are still challenges in schools. It is also conceded that the degree of family resistance, when it comes to teaching CSE. In the case of Honduras, Bolivia, Colombia, and Peru, the legal framework in these states grants family a huge role to decide what to incoporate in CSE.

The United States diplays a gamut of views on CSE. The controversy in the United States has evolved around issues of content for CSE, responsibility for teaching the curriculum, and the issue of age appropriateness of the information. Consequently different states have adopted different policies in relation to CSE. Guanci & Blackburn (2022) postulated that:

- 38 states in the US has made the teaching CSE mandatory and HIV education;
- 28 states insisted that abstinence be foregrounded in CSE;
- 19 indicated that sexual activity must be probed only in the context of marriage;
- 6 states made it legal to undermine sexual orientations different from binary of male and female;
- 7 states asserts that sex education must be evidence based, relevant to the age of the child, appropriate to culture and not value laden;
- 2 states do not support CSE to use religion for its legitimacy.

Mbizvo, et al., (2023) averred that early pregnancies at school level has the consequences of exacerbating gender disparities by exposing young adolescent and young women to poverty and hindering them from accessing resources. School attrition due to early and unintended pregnancy (EUP), particularly for girls is an outcome of constricted sexual and reproductive health (SRH) knowledge which also exposes them to other risks such as HIV, sexually communicated infections and sexual and gender-based violence (SGBV).The intersection of all these forces has the capacity of holding women in a vicious place of deprivation limiting them from realising their economic potential and from making meaningful contribution to their societies. Empirical research that focalises on unequal power relationships and human rights displayed a positive effect on predominant health variables such as pregnancy, STIs, and childbirth and by implication suggesting that CSE has potential to be more impactful (Mbizvo, et al., 2023; Haberland, 2015; Denno, et al, 2015).

The Southern African Development Community (SADC), is an economic development platform that is constituted of Angola, Botswana, Comoros,Democratic Republic of Congo, Eswatini, Lesotho, Madagascar, Malawi, Mauritius, Mozambique, Namibia, Seychelles, South Africa, United Republic of Tanzania, Zambia and Zimbabwe. In Sub-Sahara Africa, the challenges that have necessitated the introduction of CSE is the dominance of a young adolescent population constituting 23%, high rates of sexually transmitted infections (STIs), limited academic attainment, prevalence of child marriages, unplanned pregnancies and high attrition in schools (Chawhanda, et al.,2021).

In the SADC states, it is acknowledged that CSE, education is offered in all states with differences that are attributed to cultural contexts presenting opportunities and challenges. Chawhanda, et al.,(2021) study which included Kingdom of Eswatini, Lesotho, Malawi, Mozambique, South Africa, and Zambia, noted that teachers tended to avoid topics such as abortion, sexual diversity, sexual diversity use of condoms were neglected, while topics such as substance abuse, HIV,STIs, gender equality were taught. The reasons offered by teachers and learners for shunning the topics were the teachers' cultural and religious beliefs and perceptions that teaching about condoms and abortion encouraged learners to engage in sex. Children in the study were reticent to engage parents on sexual education at home as it was seen to violate the protocol of parental respect. Research showed that in Zambia, Mozambique and Malawi, intiation into adulthood gives the child consent that they can marry and engage in unprotected sex, propelling child to marry due to socio-economic factors and also the harsh reality that the marriage may bring financial relief to the family (Kok, et al., 2021).

THE AIMS OF COMPREHENSION SEXUALITY EDUCATION

United Nations Scientific and Cultural Organisation (UNESCO,2024) postulates that CSE is a school based approach to instruction that helps to develop cognitive,emotional,physical and social components of sexuality.The pronounced goals of comprehensive sexuality education is constitutive of a lifelong process of securing information, constructing attitudes beliefs and norms that are linked to relationships, intimacy and identity (Lukolo & van Dhyke, 2015). Sexuality education also subsumes "sexuality development,reproductive health,interpersonal relationship,affection,intimacy, body image and gender roles (Lukolo & van Dhyke, 2015, p. 35). In addition reproductive health includes counselling, educating, providing information on sex and instituting responsibility in both sexes on norms and values regarding sex, and counselling on HIV/AIDS, use of contraceptives and abortion,and provision of prenatal care services and among many other options. Reproductive health is one of the chief components of human health. The target audience for reproductive health education are adolescence who are prioritised by virtue of their proclivity to engage in risky behaviours such as smoking, drinking, and indulging in unsafe sex practices.

United Nations Fund for Population Activity (2015,p 4) added that the comprehensive sexuality education is

" a right-based and gender-focussed approach to sexuality education whether in school or out of school. CSE is curriculum based education that aims to equip children and young people with the knowledge, skills, attitudes and values that will enable them to develop a positive view of their sexuality, in the context of their social and emotional development by embracing a holistic view of sexuality and sexual behaviour which goes beyond a focus on prevention of pregnancy and transmission of sexual infections.

A study that was conducted in South Africa by Lukolo & van Dhyke (2015) expounds on the escalation of child sexual abuse in South Africa and how schools are introducing life skills education as a counterpoise to gender based violence (GBV). Adolescents are vulnerable to GBV due to multiple factors which include " alcohol consumption, drug abuse, high risk sexual behaviour, sexually transmitted diseases, sexual assault, escape from home, unrestrained sex in the family, history of robbery, imprisonment, and living in a drug hangout" (Lukolo & van Dhyke, 2015, p. 6). CSE empowers learners to develop self esteem, valuing human rights and gender equality and also to be tolerate of people diverse sexuality, ethnicity and race.It is for this reason that the teaching of CSE is premised on the presupposition it can be an effective tool for eliminating gender- based violence which has become pervasive globally. Venketsamy & Kinear, (2020) added that the proliferation of cases of child abuse and sexual violence has made CSE an imperative as strategy to eliminate this aberration.

It is in response to the escalating incidents of child sexual abuse and gender based violence that the South African Department of Basic Education (DBE), working in conjunction with the Department of Health (DoH), intiated the a comprehensive strategy on HIV/AIDS, sexually transmitted infections and Tuberculosis (TB) 2012-2016 (DBE), 2017). The primary trajectory of CSE in South Africa is to multiply the knowledge and skills in the area of HIV, STIs and TB among learners,teachers and administrators . The programme also seeks to diminish sexual hazardous behaviour among learners and also to reduce learner drop -out rate from school particularly from among vulnerable groups. In South Africa the sexual reproductive rights rights that CSE seeks to uphold in young people are enshrined in the constitution which foregrounds that every child has a right to be fortified from harm and preserved from abuse, and every child must have access to quality education in order for them to become assertive when it comes to protecting their rights.

The Constitution of Namibia also echoes the same sentiments on children rights in Article 15 (2) which avers that children are protected from deleteriousness effects to their mental health, physical, spiritual, moral or social development. GBV and sexual abuse is deleterious to children's health. The same sentiments are captured in the constitution of Zimbabwe Article 15 (2), which declare that children must be secured from hazardous to their emotional, physical, mental, or spiritual, social and moral development.

Panchaud, et al., (2019) observed that CSE that focalises on gender equality,human rights and empowerment displayed capacity to emhance attitudes of learners, build their self esteem,emhance communication skills and decision making and also develop positive attitudes towards gender. Studies have also demonstrated the importance of a sound policy architecture in facilitating CSE in schools. The following sections delves into the case of Namibia, South Africa and Zimbabwe.

NAMIBIA

UNAIDS (2013) survey in Namibia noted that one women in the country, will experience GBV in their life cycle. Keulder & Amakoh (2022) observed that Namibia rating on the Global Gender Gap Index from a group of 156 countries was 6th position.Namibia also occupies a third position among African states assuming a position after Rwanda and South Africa in terms of women representation in parliament. Namibia National Gender Policy (2010-2020,p29) postulate a clear stance on GBV by explicating GBV as applying to "all forms of violence that apply to women,girls and men and boys because of the unequal power relations between them". In the National Gender Policy GBV is attributed to power disparity between men and women and low literacy levels, cultural norms and values that subordinate positions of women and people of sexual diversity.

The impact of GBV has ramifications on families, communities and families. GBV occurs across socio-economic classes, religious affiliation, age and geographical location (Venketsamy & Kinear, 2020). Namibia Statistical Agency (2021) averred that Namibia developed a national gender policy that embeds monitoring and evaluation. Data obtained in 2013, which was the only current data availabe alluded that 14% of the girls and women in the age category 16-49 had suffered from incidences of gender based violence in 2012. The same survey showed that women in the same age group of 15-49 had experienced domestic violence after the age of 15. The survey indicated that some of the girls who had experienced domestic violence did not seek professional assistance.

UNESCO (2024) explained that in Namibia CSE has a an extensive pedegree which can be traced to independence in 1990, when CSE was integrated in School Health and Life Skills Education. The rationale for the introduction CSE were high incidents of new HIV among adolescents, predominantly high levels of teen pregnancies, and multiple incidents of STIs. Given that Namibia has a predominantly young population constituting 66% of people situated below the age of 30. The rate of HIV infection among the adolescents in the category of 15-24 is 43%. It was these statistics that motivated a rapid curriculum intervention through CSE in schools. The government introduced a new curriculum innovation called My Life is My Choice which where integrated in biology, life skills and life sciences, which was intended to develop in learners the competence to make effective decisions in areas such as HIV and STIs in the 1990s (UNESCO, 2024).The government also introduced in primary schools a new curriculum intervention termed the Window of Hope, which was intended to develop competency among learners to make effective decisions in the areas of HIV and also to build self- esteem. In 2012/13 the government embarked on a massive efforts tp revise the curriculum with the intention of ensuring that CSE is introduced in schools.

UNESCO (2024) noted that efforts to scale up CSE by the government were resisted by faith based organisations, which saw the CSE in pejorative terms encouraging promiscuity among learners and lobbied the government to backtrack on its commitment to the scaling up of CSE curriculum. Teachers lacked confidence in engaging learners on CSE curriculum content and parents were reluctant to intiate conversation on CSE with their children. The government of Namibia has resolved to engage faith based organisations on CSE curriculum prior to its full scale implementation.

Dyasi (2024) indicated that some religious leaders made a commitment to allow for the teaching of CSE at the International Conference on AIDS and STIs (ICASA) in 2021.The religious leaders demonstrated a commitment to ensuring that learners are exposed to CSE. In Namibia CSE, is embedded in Life Skills/Life Orientation subject. The religious leaders acknowledged the central role played parents, gurdians and teachers in implementing CSE. At the same conference the religious leaders reiterated the significance of CSE in promoting self respect and human rights among learners.

SOUTH AFRICA

Venketsamy (2020) avers that child sexual molestation has been escalating in South Africa with 54 cases of sexual assault against primary school children being reported in 2017, at a school in Gauteng. In Soweto a security guard was charged for sexual assault of rape and sexual assault of 87 school girls at a primary school in Soweto (PiJoos, 2017).In order to address this scourge, many schools in South Africa have instituted CSE, in Life Skills Curriculum, in order to help learners to acquire competencies of tackling GBV.

Centre for the Study of Violence and Reconciliation (2016) conducted a survey on GBV in South Africa for the purpose of informing its programme on gender prevention. The same report implicated the state for its ineptitude in implementing a clear policy framework to address GBV. In spite of the progress that has been made in enhancing the position of women in society, GBV still remains high in South Africa. Forces that drive GBV are identified as religious, cultural and political variables. Although men also experience GBV, statistics show women tend to experience a disproportionate amount of GBV. Centre for the Study of Violence and Reconciliation (2016,p) avers that GBV subsumes "physical, sexual, psychological violence occurring in families and in the community, battery, sexual harassment, forced prostitution, and trafficking in women".

Thusi & Mlambo (2023) asserted that the legislation, Criminal Amendment Act 32 of 2007, in South Africa acknowledges the potential for both sexes to engage in GBV. In many cases GBV can encapsulate physical, emotional, social well being and also includes lacerations, bruises, and assaults that causes genital pain during urination and sexual disorders (Thusi & Mlambo,2023,p73). Domestic violence tends to be prevalent than other forms of violence such as physical violence, emotional violence, economic violence and femicide. Physical violence takes the form "hitting, slapping, and pushing" while emotional violence connotes acts involves "verbal abuse, name calling, and belittling" and sexual violence which also very common assumes the form "rape, sexual harassment, sexual exploitation and exploitation for sexual purposes" (Centre for the Study of Violence and Reconciliation, 2016, p7).

Comprehensive Sexuality Education was a component of the education system in South Africa since 2000 (Department of Basic Education, 2004). CSE was situated within Life Skills and Life orientation in order to ascertain that learners acquire skills on sexuality, gender and relationships. The declared intention of CSE was to ensure that learners were able to transition to adulthood in a health way and with competencies to make decisions that are prudent in relationships. Koch & Wemeyer (2021) averred that although there was a decline in new rates of HIV infections in South Africa, young people in the category of 15-24 years constituting 34% of new infections in 2017. HIV infections is also gendered, with women constituting 15,6%, which translate to three quarters of people in the category of 20-24 year old young people living with HIV. There is a preponderant high rate of unintended pregnancies in South Africa among tenagers with the child bearing rate at 7% between 2009 and 2018. It is in the light this stark reality that the Department of Basic Education sought to strengthen the teaching of CSE in South Africa.

Koch & Wemeyer (2021) demonstrated that CSE is experiencing a host of challenges which include teacher factors, community and parental resistance. Some teachers habour sentiments that sexuality issues are too discreet to be tackled in an open forum such as a classroom. There is also an asymmetrical relationship between what the teachers ought to teach in the official CSE curriculum and what the communities conceives to be acceptable. An abstinence only approach focus tends to be a predominant and safer approach for many teachers and heteronomativity is upheld at the expense of other forms of sexuality.Parents and other stakeholders such as faith based groups have resisted governments efforts to buttress the teaching of CSE in schools by creating a hashtag #LeaveOurKidsAlone' in 2020 in which more than 100 000 people vocalised resentment against CSE curriculum. The next case study explores the experience of implementing CSE in Zimbabwe.

ZIMBABWE

A brief background of the three countries is presented in this part of the chapter. Magezi & Manzanga (2019) averred that women are exposed to various forms of abuses globally.In Zimbabwe, gender based violence incidents are still astronomical.A survey conducted by the Zimbabwe Demographic Health Survey (2015) indicated that one in three woman have been exposed to gender-based violence (GBV) from the age of 15. The same survey showed that the number of women who reported being exposed to GBV escalated from 29,9% in 2010 to 34,8% in 2015. The majority of the incidents of GBV are perpetrated by a male partner who may be a current boy friend, ex- boy friend or husband. The survey showed sexual rape as a major form of violence perpetrated against women. The same survey demonstrated an array of excuses for GBV as arguing with a male partner, going out without seeking permission from a male partner, burning food, refusing to engage in sex, neglecting children and infidelity.The rise in cases of GBV makes CSE indispensable in Zimbabwe due to the way it has potential to help transform practices that uphold GBV and also equip learners with skills for effective decision-making, help build their self-esteem and transform attitudes towards gender norms.

Mazhambe & Mushunje (2023) opines that Zimbabwe Demographic Health Survey indicated that 1 in 3 women between the age of 15-49 has encountered physical violence and one in four women was exposed to sexual violations since the age of 15. Most of these incidents are perpetrated by close family members and child marriages are also prevalent in Zimbabwe with 1 in 3 girls being given in marriage before the age of 18. The most preponderant form of violence is from close partners. Zimbabwe has a legal framework that is intended to safeguard women and children from GBV, such as the constitution that forbids discrimination on any basis which includes gender, race and ethnicity.

Siziba (2020) in a study on institutional response to gender-based violence observed that women continue to be experience all forms of emotional phyiscal and sexual violence. The same study averred that the mere enactment of laws does not automatically translate to implementation of protection of women from violence. The drivers of gender –based violence in Zimbabwe were identified as "alcohol abuse, low level of education for the survivor, cultural standards and practices, use of mobile devices and marital status" (Siziba,2020,piii). The same study attribute gender- based violence to unequal power dynamics between men and women and social and cultural values that do not condemn violence. It is in this context that CSE becomes an indispensable innovation in the fight to expunge gender- based violence.

Mahoso et al. (2023) expounds that prevailing economic hardship in Zimbabwe impel young children to engage in sexual activity early in life. Other legislation includes the Domestic Violence Act of 2006, the Criminal Law Codification and Reform Act, the children Act and National Gender Policy. Mazhambe & Mushunje (2023) expounds that Zimbabwe economy was already in a state of recession prior to the advent of COVID 19, and thereafter the economy continued to contract due to multiple factors which include the fiscal policy pursued by the government. The government has also been battling a intractable budget deficit for many years including 2019 and 2020.

UNFPA Zimbabwe (2024) declare that CSE is grounded in guidance and counselling curriculum. As in other countries the curriculum endevours to develop in learners the holistic aspects which include physical, emotional,cognitive and social. The curriculum also seeks to empower learners to deal effectively with issues of Gender Based Violence (GBV). The school curriculum has been reviewed in order to buttress life skills, and comprehensive sexuality education,HIV/AIDS and GBV education which has to be taught from infant to secondary school level in the revised curriculum framework of Curriculum Framework of 2015-2022. Guidance and Counselling was promoted in the country from 2000 in order to address topical issues such as HIV/AIDS and endemic teen marriages. Obstacles that were being encountered included lack of skills among teachers to teach the curriculum, teachers inability and unwillingness to converse on sex related issues in class, and resistance from parents and gurdians who are sceptical regarding the aims of the subject.

ATTITUDES TOWARDS COMPREHENSION SEXUALITY EDUCATION

Lukolo & van Dhyke (2015) explicated the aversion which is rooted in cultural beliefs of parents, towards engaging their children on sexuality education. Parents holds sentiments of inadequcy in terms of knowledge competence needed to engage children on sexuality education. Both teachers and parents have explicated concerns over children learning graphic sexual content at school (Venketsamy, 2020). At the same time it is also averred that parents and teachers have a predominant influence on the decision of children to engage sex (Venketsamy & Kinear, 2020).

Mahoso et al. (2023) noted that in Zimbabwe, teachers are uncomfortable with communication on CSE and they also feel constricted with the language to use in class and are reluctant to teach the subject leading to repercussions from parents. The attitudes of teachers were also noted to impede the implementation of CSE. The prevailing perception in Zimbabwen society is that sexual education is congruous to people approaching marriage and adolescence. There is also a perception in Zimbabwe that if children are taught CSE, it will provoke them to start engaging in sexual activities (Mahoso et al. 2023).

Venketsamy & Kinear (2020) observed that social cultural and religious norms of the society can have an effect on the receptivity of communities to comprehensive sexuality education. Schools are impacted by the cultural context where the schools are situated and some parents and community members hold sentiments which express that CSE can make learners to engage in premature sexual activities. In order to be relevant CSE must respond to the views and needs of the people in the society. This capacity to adapt CSE to the needs of the communities and the messages that they communicate on sex, gender and sexuality, in which schools are embedded is considered effective programming of curriculum innovation. The attitudes of communities will influence the extent to which educators will delve into CSE sexuality content. It is also postulated that the parents have a role to engage their children on sexuality education and relationships. Studies have shown that parents are reluctant to engage children on risky sexual behaviour and also on subjects that are perceived to be taboo (Ascraft & Murray, 2017; Berglas et al., 2014).

Rudoe & Ponford (2023) expounded that relationship and sex education was mooted in Britain in 2020,with the subject being made mandatory in all primary schools that were funded by the government. Data that emerged from the study by Rudoe & Ponford (2023), Mullis et al.,(2021) and Department of Education (2019) showed that at a global level numerous studies display that multiple parents were interested in engaging children on CSE, however they tend to lack knowledge and confidence on the topic. Politicians have also contested the position of CSE in schools. This implies that the attitudes of politicians towards CSE is just as complex as those of other stakeholders like parents, caregivers and religious leaders. It has also been contested in England regarding the responsibility for administering sexual education, if it lay with the state or the parent. The Universal Declaration of Human Rights places the locus of administering CSE, in the hands of the parents and caregivers. The teaching of sexual education in England took a new trajectory with the rise of sexually transmitted infections, which made it mandatory for the state to come up with an intervention at school level. In the course of time, around 1970s, the mandate for the teaching of sex education became more centred on the government, as the rights of the child began to supersede the rights of the parents (Rudoe & Ponford, 2023).

Studies that were done in London and Ireland indicated that for many males and females, schools were perceived to be an idle vehicle for sex education (Rudoe & Ponford, 2023). Studies by Mullis et al.(2021), Astle et al.,(2022), Morawska et al., (2015) in Ireland, England, Australia and United States .explicate a sense of embarrassment, fear of the consequences of children engaging in sex, and dearth of knowledge as reasons for the parents' reluctance to engage with their children on sex education. Other impediments which were identified were termed as cultural barriers which include social factors inherent in the community and cultural obstacles such as assumptions that children have secured knowledge on sex elsewhere, perceptions that sex was taboo, rooted in culture and religious proclivity, age of parents, generational disparity, gender and perceptions that males can not engage on sex with their daughters. It was also noted that female parents who were more open- minded tended to be more willing to engage on sexual topics with their children.

Mbizvo, et al., (2023) noted that in studies that were conducted in Zambia, there was no evidence of decline in in-school pregnancies when learners were taught sexuality education without supporting SRH services. It was also noted that implementing CSE was impeded by parental resistance, perceived incompatibility of the curriculum with the prevailing social norms, limited training and paucity of resources for teachers, discomfort of the teachers in using the materials and lack of integration of the curriculum with the provision of required sexual reproductive health services.

Wekesah et al. (2019) conceded that in Sub-Sahara Africa major impediments to the introduction of CSE are social cultural norms that are strengthened by statutory instruments which are premised on the assumption that stereotype the demonstration and condom use as being unalawful. In some of the states teachers are not allowed to delve into issues communities consider as taboo such as mastubation, homosexuality and abortion. Absinence seems to be the major embraced prescription in some of these societies. In cases where teachers find a conflict between their values and those of the society, they adopt a neutral stance that is proselytise moral values upheld in the community. Teachers values and sentiments of the community becomes in many societies more poignant than that of the CSE curriculum.

A study that was conducted in Lesotho reflected that parents were not opposed tonCSE curriculum per se but the content and didactics employed (Wekesah et al. 2019). Most of the instruction on sex at home in many societies were predominantly admonishing the children based on the parent's experience of what the child ought to do (Nambambi & Mufune, 2011; Nyarko, 2014). Parents had a proclivity to uphold values in the CSE curriculum that converged with their beliefs and discarded content that was contrary. Parents would also censor teachers who taught content that was not aligned to their beliefs and this had an effect of undermining the curriculum. Parents in Ghana also contested the age at which CSE can be taught to chidren, arguing that introduction at a very early age may be injurious to children. In Ethiopia, parents contended that the structure of the CSE must be redesigned so that at primary school level the curriculum must accentuate abstinence, while at secondary school level abstinence, condoms and contraceptices are focalised.

Some of the teachers faced constraints which included paltry training in didactics, a tendency to fall back into unhelpful habits of teaching after professional development due to hostile school environment,lack of motivation, dearth of teaching and learning resources, and syllabuses that are overcrowded (Berglas, Constantine, & Ozwe, 2014) Sidze, et al., 2017). In some schools CSE is incorporated into other subjects subjects such as Home Economics as is the case in Zambia, and management in Ghana rendering it inaccessible to learners who are not registered in those subjects. Finally,most countries in sub-Sahara Africa lack culturally appropriate content to unpack sensitive topics such as abortion,masturbation and homosexuality.

THEORETICAL UNDERPINNINGS

The chapter also draws from post structural feminist theory in order to unravel the global prevalence of GBV practices. Finally Rogers's diffusion theory is illuminated in order to advocate the successful way of implementing CSE. The diffusion theory is taken as appropriate because the introduction of CSE in many countries is a huge innovation. The Albert Bandura Social Learning theory is also probed in order to shed light on how children acquire anti-social behavior

POSTSTRUCTURAL FEMINIST THEORY

There are multiple and diverse strands of poststructural theory which are bound together by tenets which include probing objectivity, metanarratives and reason. Postsructuralism engages in theorising on facts,ontology and epistemology by scrutinising discourse knowledge and power (Willet & Etowa, 2023). Poststructural theory Feminist research helps to illuminate the gender inequities and inequalities in society and also challenges hegemonic narratives (van Wijlen & Aston, 2019). Brown & Ishmail, (2019) declare that poststructuralism feminism has its genesis in the intellectual movements termed poststructuralism that came to the fore in the 1960s onwards. The eminent proponents of post-structural theory are Derrida, Chris Weedon and Foucault who have probed the essentialist views of gender associated with modernity. Poststructuralism questions the premises of traditional knowledge construction and perceive reality as constructed from language. In this ontology it is also acknowledged that language is value laden but a tool for political articulation that displays the interests abd biases of the dominant group in the society.

Post structural feminism holds that gender is constructed in discourse and the groupings of male/female as being historically located and positioned in a social context as opposed to being a fixed entity. van Wijlen & Aston (2019) averred that post-structural feminism deconstructs unequal power dynamics which are inherent in our gendered society. Post –structural feminism offers insights on the relationship between power and privilege in society. Poststructural feminism probes which discourses are exerting influence on individual consciousness at different levels, that is conscious and unconscious to influence individual subjectivities and how individual lives are impacted by systemic and individual influences. In the context of this chapter Michael Foucault view on power and how it is deployed are used to illustrate the way gender based violence manifest in societies. The Foucaldian perspective helps to overcome the pigeonhole approach that is associated with other feminist views and displays the exercise of power as taking a multidimensional perspective as opposed to being unidirectional.

Cannon et al.(2015) averred that in poststructural feminism deconstruct binaries in order to show how they function. The binaries which include men/women,heterosexual/ and homosexual are by nature unstable leading to treatment of the second category such as women as inferior. Identities are constituted within and by discourse people respond by enacting resistance to them. Other feminist theory perceive power as being exercised in a undirectional way by males, Foucault argues that even women can exercise power and take enact gender based violence in relationships. Evidence abounds of males being subjected to GBV, although females tend to bear the brunt of GBV in a disproportionate way (Kalimaposo et aal. 2022; Kalimaposo et aal. 2022;). Postsructural feminism rejects the notion that man monopolise power in a static form and that women are always victims who only have to react in self defence. A binary approach obfuscate the way people deploy power in terms of who has power and how they use it. This chapter adopts the poststructural feminist argument that women can not be homogenised and discussed outside the framework of their history and other particularities.

Poststructural feminism also acknowledges that women are different in many ways that include race, age, class, nationality, education among many other variables. Ronconi et al., (2023) explicated the formation of the modern state was rooted in a binary mindset, from which sex at birth was related to inequalities in which women are disadvantaged at brith in relation to males. This is th worldview that has generated gender based violence that women and children face and other groups such as LGBT+. The next section takes parse of the Roger's Theory of Diffusion of Innovation (DOI).

ROGER'S THEORY OF DIFFUSION (DOI)

Nepal & Nepal (2023) averred that the Innovation Diffusion Theory was developed by Roger (1962) and it posits a model on how new ideas spread and technology across diverse cultures. This model of Diffusion of Innovation is relevant to the teaching of holistic reproductive health education, and ways in which these ideas may be approached in culures that are not a part of the Global North. Diffusion of Innovation (DOI) refers to the manner in which innovation is transmitted to members of a social system over time. The central tenet of the theory is the premise that new concepts are emerging daily and the key issue is communication is central to disseminating the concepts to communities.

The major assumption is that the attitude that people are likely to develop towards the innovation depends on how the information is spread (Makovhololo,2017; Rogers, 1962). DOI endevours to explain the diffusion of innovation in diverse areas that include agriculture, public health and family planning. An innovation avails to people a new way of probing an issue in order to address it. Individuals tend to struggle with numerous questions as they seek to comprehend the essence of the innovation and if it gives them a better alternative (Rogers, 1962). In order to deal with uncertainty that is presented by an innovation individuals would begin to search for information particularly from their peers. The exchange of information about the innovation occurs within the context of interpersonal networks. The way in which an innovation is spreadly is predominantly a social process in which people perceptions are transmitted from one person to the next.

Roger (1962) explicate that ensuring that people embrace a new idea is a complex process, in spite of the merits that the innovation offers. It is for that reason that many people who intend to introduce any innovation struggle with the rate at which an innovation spreads. This observation is also pertinent to the spread of CSE. An appreciation of the local context and culture of a people is a key to the diffusion of any innovation. Rogers, (1962, p30) explained that diffusion involves:

(1) "a process by an innovation
(2) is communicated through certain channels
(3) over time
(4) among members of a social system."

The adopters who embrace an innovation early are termed early adopters and those who get onboard latter are termed late adopters. The rate of adoption is determined by the perceived merits of the idea which include relative advantage,compartibility,complexity,trialability and observability.

Relative advantage alludes to the extent to which an innovation is seen as being superior to the one it supersedes in either social or economic basis. If perceptions are high that the merits are benefial, then the rate of adoption may escalate. Compartibility connotes the extent to which an innovation is aligned to the current values or previous experiences of potential adopters. In the case of CSE, there was resistance from the people because of the way it upended existing cultural beliefs and taboos on sexuality of young people, gender and relationships. Compatibility implies that the value system or worldviews of a community may have to change if they are to embrace the innovation. Complexity refers to the extent to which technical terms and concepts are made accessible to the people. Triability means the extent to which ideas can be tested empirically on a limited scale. Trialability helps to reduce uncertainty that people have regarding the innovation. Observability refers to the level at which an idea's success may be seen by others. The results that are visible are likely to stimulate discussion regarding the innovation.

The success of comprehensive sexuality education has capacity of of equipping learners with skills to combat Gender Based Violence and also with knowledge of the reproductive system, has to take into account the cultural sensitivities of societies that are situated in the global South and where sensitivities and taboos to discussions on sex are still dominant.The nature of illustrations used in learning resources, the language and the depth of content on sexuality, has to take into account what diverse communities consider appropriate, possibly sharing some information gradually and as communities embrace the ideas the content and graphics may be increased. Most countries in the global North are in the post modern stage where Sigmund Freud theories has influenced discussion on sex and also the production of movies that has less sexual sanctions.In comparison to the global south there is a lot of sensitivities regarding discussion on sex and these have to be taken into account when it comes to issues of content that is shared, how it is shared and age of the learners and also breadth and depth of data.

The key to the diffusion of this innovation of CSE is to identify the key stakeholders in the implementation of the curriculum. A study that was conducted by Rudoe & Ponford (2023) in England displayed that parents and caregivers are the key to the design and implementation of CSE. The implication of this observation is that the efforts have to be exerted by the government and other stakeholders in this sector to ensure that the chief stakeholders embrace the merits of this innovation in helping to build learners self esteem, reduce gender inequality and to make better life choices in the area of relationships.

THE SOCIAL LEARNING THEORY

GBV is a multifaceted phenomenon that transpires at various levels such as individual, in relationships and community dimensions. Research on GBV foreground the behaviour as a learned phenomenon, which implies that when an individual is exposed to instruction such as CSE curriculum, they have the potential to unlearn the disposition. Bandura et al., (1963) posited that children acquire expectations and behaviours from what they observe in their environment. In a series of experiments Bandura was able to demonstrate that children who were exposed to adults acting in any aggressive way tended to immitate that aggressive behaviour with dolls.

Siziba (2020) explicate the Development approach illustrate that children when they are placed in a situation where violence is displayed particularly boys, tend to simulate the same disposition in their relationships,instituting a cycle of GBV. Consequently, when children are exposed to violence they learn that it is acceptable way of dealing with issues and they mimic the behaviour. The SIT avers that disposition to GBV is an acquired behaviour, which is internalised through observation and use of rewards and punishment (Akers, 2017). When children are exposed to violence they tend to legitimise the use of violence in their lives latter in life. Research has shown that the transmission of violence from one generation to the next, may transpire in the life of the people perpertrating violence or those who survive it.

Children who are exposed to abuse by parents or other caretakers are likely either to perpetrate violence or to be exposed to it. Women who survived sexual abuse are likely to experience recurring sexual abuse as adults (Powers et al.,2017). Girls who are exposed to sexual abuse are at risk of engaging in premature sex, engage in multiple sexual relations and also to take part in drug abuse. Having multiple sexual relations also places women at risk of GBV, as men compete to engage them . Childhood exposure to sexual relations has an effect on the structure of the brain and to impact a person personality development. Abuse of children tends to create the corollary of GBV in children through a number of process that range from modelling and also changes in the brains structure and the consequent effect on the development of the brain. Children who originate from communities that are destitute are likely to be experience polytrauma which include withholding of food, name calling, violence which makes the child more prone to perpetrating GBV latter in life (Cosme,2021). Research also demonstrate that perpetrating GBV is not confined to children who were exposed to sexual abuse only,although exposure to violence increases the likelihood of violence. It is therefore critical to protect children from potential abuse by teaching them CSE, so that they are empowered to report cases of sexual abuse, and also grow up with a different mindset towards gender norms, sexuality and GBV.

DISCUSSION OF IMPEDIMENTS TO INTRODUCING CSE

The introduction of CSE is an innovation in many countries that requires careful navigation. It is for that reason that Rogers's model of diffusion of innovation becomes indispensable. The spread of innovation depends on an appreciation of local cultural context and the central role networks plays in the process. By implication the spread of an innovation is perceived as more dependent on social network than being a mere technical process. Activating effective social networks in the spread of innovations such as CSE, requires the identification and utilization of opinion people and social models in the communities (Rogers, 1962). Opinion leaders in the context of African countries which include chiefs, religious leaders, politicians, journalists and educators have capacity to influence the rate at which an innovation is adopted.

Innovations such as CSE have to be perceived as ideas emerging from the local context not as an imposition from outsiders. This means building the capacity of influential people in communities to embrace innovations so that they can activate the local social networks to accept the innovation. Stakeholders such as the government, donor community and Non-Governmental Organisations

(NGOs), have to concentrate resources on ensuring that the influential people comprehend the rationale for a CSE curriculum and that they also take part in the design of the curriculum prior to its implementation in schools. This can transform the process of curriculum implementation from being a linear process to a dialectical process, which displays reflexivity. The studies that were conducted in Zambia displayed a number of challenges in implementing CSE, which included parental resistance to the curriculum materials, discomfort that teachers felt with the learning materials, lack of integration between the school teaching and the associated reproductive health services and also negative attitudes towards the curriculum.

Ronconi et al., (2023) postulated that standards may be employed in CSE which include legality, comprehensiveness, transversality, teacher training and role of family. Transversality means that the CSE must not be taught in isolation in the school context but must be linked to all the other subjects. These standards are postulated to guide policy in terms of implementation of CSE. States have to pronounce a commitment to eliminate discrimination that women and other groups such as LGBT+ face constituted on the basis of sexual disparities. Ronconi et al., (2023) opined that CSE must assume a holistic approach that acknowledges the sexual rights of all people including LGBT+.. This is rooted on the premise that gender is not a binary and on international proclamation that acknowledges the rights of LGBT+. It is important that children be engaged on CSE in a way that is appropriate to their age.

Teachers are chief agents for the successful implementation of CSE. It is for that reason that they are prepared to assume a transformative role in the teaching of CSE in schools, during the preparation period and also through on-going staff development and training.

RECOMMENDATIONS

Based on the foregoing discussion, it is noted that it is critical that parents and care givers of adolescents are involved in the design and implementation of the CSE curriculum. These are the key stakeholders who have the capacity to make the innovation succeed through the diffusion of the innovation social networks. Workshops and training events need to be conducted by influential people in the communities in order to accelerate the rate of technological innovation of CSE. It is paramount to ensure that the implementation is not taken as a mere technical process, but communication that enables communities to converge or diverge Son issues.

Roger's characteristics of innovations that are perceived by individuals also need to be taken into account when implementing a CSE curriculum. It is important to ensure that communities perceive the CSE curriculum as beneficial to them so that there is rapid adoption. This can be realized by ensuring that influential people take part in spreading the benefits of the curriculum in their communities. Compatibility means that during implementation, it is vital that a discussion be initiated by stakeholders regarding the values of the curriculum and prevailing cultural norms in order to realize change in norms of the community. The curriculum resources that are used to diffuse the CSE curriculum must be easy to comprehend and use so that it does not frustrate the people who may want to adopt the new innovation by its complexity. Trial of the CSE curriculum may also be done at a few local schools and the results shared with all stakeholders. It is significant that people in the communities are able to see the benefit of the CSE by publishing in media the results from the curriculum and also engaging communities on different forum's on the outcome. Finally, the school curriculum must be aligned to the provision of community reproductive health services so that learners are able to implement their knowledge from school.

CONCLUSION

The chapter has highlighted the importance of CSE curriculum in building learners self-esteem, reducing gender disparities, reducing incidences of GBV, eliminating unplanned pregnancies among many other benefits. Although CSE is vital for many communities it faces resistance in many communities from parents, caregivers, politicians and other influential stakeholders. It is for that reason that we can draw lessons from Roger's diffusion of innovation in order to realize accelerated adoption of the CSE curriculum in many countries.

REFERENCES

Akers, R. (2017). *Social Learning and Social Structure: A general theory of crime and deviance*. Tranaction Publishers. doi:10.4324/9781315129587

Ascraft, A., & Murray, P. (2017). Talking to parents about adolescent sexuality. *National Centre for Biotechnology Information, 64*(2), 305–320. PMID:28292447

Astle, S., Toews, G. L., Topham, L., & Vennum, A. (2022). To talk or not to talk: An analysis of parents' intentions to talk with children about different sexual topics using the theory of planned behaviour. *Sexuality Research & Social Policy, 19*(2), 705–721. doi:10.1007/s13178-021-00587-6

Berglas, N., Constantine, N., & Ozwe, E. (2014). A rights-based Approach to Sexuality Education: Conceptualization, Clarification and Challenges. *Perspectives on Sexual and Reproductive Health, 46*(2), 63–72. doi:10.1363/46e1114 PMID:24785652

Brown, A., & Ishmail, K. J. (2019). Feminist theorizing of men and masculinity: Applying Feminist Perspective to Advance College Men Maculinity Praxis. *Threshold, 42*(1), 17–35.

Cannon, C., Lauve-Moon, K., & Buttell, F. (2015). Intimate partner Violence through Poststructural feminism, Queer Theory and the Sociology of Gender. *Social Sciences (Basel, Switzerland), 4*(3), 668–687. doi:10.3390/socsci4030668

Cannon, C., Lauve-Moon, K., & Buttell, F. (2015). Re-Theorizing Intimate Partner Violence through Post-Structural Feminism, Queer Theory, and the Sociology of Gender. *Journal of Social Sciences, 4*, 668–687.

Centre for the Study of Violence and Reconciliation. (2016). *Gender Based Violence in South Africa: A brief Review*. Centre for the Study of Violence and Reconciliation.

Cosme, G. (2021). A Social Learning Understanding of Violence. *Academia Letters, Articles 1019*. doi:10.20935/AL1019

DBE. (2017). *DBE national policy on HIV, STIs and for learners educators, school support and officials.* Pretoria: Government Printers.

Denno, D., Hoopes, A., & Chandra-Mouli, V. (2015). Effective strategies to provide adolescent sexual and reproductive health services and to increase demand and community support. *Journal of Adolescence, 56*(1), 1–14. PMID:25528977

Department of Education . (2019). *Relationships Education, Relationships and Sex Education (RSE) and Health and Education: Statutory Guidance for Governing Bodies, Proprietors,Head Teachers, Principals, Senior Teachers Teams.* London: Dff.

Dyasi, M. (2024, 1 20). *UNFPA Namibia.* Retrieved from Comprehensive Sexuality Education https://namibia.unfpa.org/en/news/importance-comprehensive-sexuality-education-africas-young-people-0

Fang, J., Tang, S., Tan, X., & Tolhurst, R. (2020). Achieving SDG related sexual and reproductive health targets in China: What are appropriate indicators and how we interpret them? *Reproductive Health, 17*(84), 1–11. doi:10.1186/s12978-020-00924-9 PMID:32487257

Haberland, N. (2015). The case for addressing gender and power in sexuality and HIV education: A comprehensive review of evaluation studies. *International Perspectives on Sexual and Reproductive Health, 41*(1), 31–42. doi:10.1363/4103115 PMID:25856235

IPPF European Network. (2012). *Sexuality Education in Europe and Central Asia.* IPPF European Network.

Kalimaposo, K., Mukando, M., Milupi, I., Mubita, K., & Hambulo, F. (2022). Men's Expeience ofgender based violence in selected Compunds of Lusaka Urban. *International Journal of Social Science and Education Research Studies*, 717-733.

Keulder, C., & Amakoh, K. (2022). Amid progress on Women's Rights Namibians see gender based violence as a priority issue to adress. *Afrobarometer Dispatch*, (513), 1–19.

Lukolo, L., & van Dhyke, A. (2015). Parents' Participation in the Sexuality Education of Their Children in Rural Namibia: A Situational Analysis. *Global Journal of Health Science, 7*(1), 35–45. PMID:25560329

Magezi, V., & Manzanga, P. (2019). Gender-based violence and efforts to address the phenomenon: Towards a church public pastoral care intervention proposition for community care intervention proposition for community development in Zimbabwe. *Hervormde Teologiese Studies*, •••, 1–9. doi:10.4102/hts.v75i4.5532

Mahoso, T., Venketsamy, R., & Finestone, M. (2023). Cultural Factors Affecting the Teaching of Comprehensive Sexuality Education in Early Grades in Zimbabwe. *Global Journal of Human Social -Social Science: C Sociology and Culture, 23*(5), 1-13.

Makovhololo, P. (2017). Diffusion of Innovation theory for Infomation technology decision making in organisational strategy. *Journal of innovation theory for Information technology decision making in organisational strategy*, 461-481.

Mazhambe, R., & Mushunje, M. (2023). Evidence generation for sustained impact in the response to from the SRHR Africa Trust Zimbabwe. *Frontiers in Global Women's Health*, 1–7. doi:10.3389/fgwh.2023.1135393 PMID:37746322

Mbizvo, M., Kasonda, K., Muntalima, N.-C., Joseph, G., Inambwe, S., Namukonda, E., & Kangale, C. (2023). Comprehensive Sexuality Education Linked to sexual reproductive health services reduces early and unitended pregnancies among in-school adolescent girls in Zambia. *BMC Public Health*, *23*(348), 1–13. PMID:36797703

Ministry of Gender and Child Welfare. (2010). *National Gender Policy (2010-2020)*. Ministry of Gender and Child Welfare.

Morawska, A., Grabski, M., & Fletcher, R. (2015). Parental confidence and preferences for communication with their child about sexuality. *Sex Education*, *15*(3), 235–248. doi:10.1080/14681811.2014.996213

Mullis, M., Kastrinos, E., Taylor, W. G., & Bylund, C. (2021). International Barriers to Parents-Child Communication about Sexual and Reproductive Health Topics: A Qualitative Systematic Review 21 (4). *Sex Education*, *21*(4), 387–403. doi:10.1080/14681811.2020.1807316

Nambambi, N., & Mufune, P. (2011). What is talked about when parents discuss Sex with Children: Family Based Education in Windhoek, Namibia. *African Journal of Reproductive Health*, *15*(4), 120–129. PMID:22571114

Namibia Statistical Agency. (2021). *Namibia National Gender Statistics Assessment*. Namibia Statistical Agency.

Nepal, S., & Nepal, B. (2023). Adoption of digital banking: Insights from UTAUT Model. *Journal of Business and Social Sciences*, *VIII*(1), 17–34.

Nyarko, K. (2014). Parental Attitude towards Sex Education at Lower Primary in Ghana. *International Journal of Elementary Education*, *3*(2), 21–29. doi:10.11648/j.ijeedu.20140302.11

Panchaud, C., Keogh, S., Stillman, M., Awusabo-Asare, K., Motta, A., Sidze, E., & Monzon, A. (2019). Towards Comprehensive Sexuality Education: A comparative Analysis of the Policy environment surrounding school-based sexuality education in Ghana, Peru, Kenya, and Guatemala. *Sex Education*, *19*(3), 277–296. doi:10.1080/14681811.2018.1533460

PiJoos. I. (2017). *Sexual assault claims at primary school: Lesufi slams principal*. News24. https://www.news24.com/news24/sexual-assault-claims-at-primary-school-lesufi-slams-principal-20171123

Pourkazemi, R., Janighorban, M., Boroumandfar, Z., & Mostafavi, F. (2020). A comprehensive reproductive health program for vulnerable adolescent girls. Pourkazemi et al. *Reproductive Health 17* (3), 1-6. PMID:31915022

Powers, R., Cochran, J., Maskaly, J., & Sellers, C. (2017). Social Learning Theory, Gender and Intimate Partner Violencnt Victimisation: A strucrural Equation Approach. *Journal of Interpersonal Violence*, 1–27. PMID:29294768

Rogers, E. (1962). *Diffusion of Innovations*. Free Press.

Rudoe, N., & Ponford, R. (2023). Parental attitudes to school- and home-based, sex and health education:Evidence from a crosssectional study in England and Wales, Sex Education. *Sex Education.* doi:10.1080/14681811.2023.2257602

Sadana, R. (2002). Definition and measurement of reproductive health. *Bull Wold Health Organ*, 407-9.

Sidze, E., Keogh, M., Mulupi, S., Egesa, C., Mutua, M., Muga, W., & Chimaraoke, I. (2017). *From Paper to Practice: Sexuality Education Polcies and their implication in Kenya.* Guttmacher Institute and African Population and Health Research Centre.

Siziba, E. (2020). (Submitted in). Gemder-Based Violence in Zimbabwe: Acritical analysis of Institutional Response. *Partial Fulfilment of the Requirement of the Doctorof Philosophy in Sociology: University of Pretoria.*

South Africa Country. (2018). *Prevention of Violence against women and girls Stakeholder Network Analysis.* South Africa: South Africa Country Report.

Thusi, X., & Mlambo, V. (2023). South Africa Gender Based Violence: An Exploration of a single sided Account. *EUREKA Social and Humanities*, (2), 73–80. doi:10.21303/2504-5571.2023.002734

Thusi, X., & Mlambo, V. (2023). South Africa's Gender Based Violence: An exploration of a single sided account. *Social and Humanities*, (2), 73–80. doi:10.21303/2504-5571.2023.002734

UNAIDS. (2013). *Gender-Based Violence (GBV) in Namibia: An exploratory assessment and Mapping of GBV Response services in Namibia.* UNAIDS.

UNESCO. (2021). *The journey towards comprehensive sexuality education:Global Status Report.* UNESCO.

UNESCO. (2024, 01 20). *UNESCO Namibia.* Namibia Comprehensive Sexuality Education. https://education-profiles.org/sub-saharan-africa/namibia/~comprehensive-sexuality-education

United Nations Fund for Population Activity . (2015). *Incorporating comprehensive sexuality education within Basic and Higher education of Learning in KwaZulu- Natal .* KwaZulu Natal: UNFPA.

van Wijlen, J., & Aston, M. (2019). Applying post -structuralism as framework for exploring infant feeding interactions in the neonatal intensive care unit. *The CanadiAN Journal of Critical NursinDiscourse*, *1*, 59–72.

Venketsamy, R. (2020). A comprehensive reproductive health program for vulnerable adolescent girls. *Reproductive Health*, *13*(13), 1–6.

Venketsamy, T., & Kinear, J. (2020). Strengthening comprehensive sexuality education in the curriculum for the early grades. *South African Journal of Childhood Education*, *10*(1), 1–9. doi:10.4102/sajce.v10i1.820

Wekesah, F. M., Nyakangi, V., Onguss, M., Njagi, J., & Bangha, M. (2019). *Comprehensive Sexuality Education in Sub-Sahara Africa.* Forum for African Women Educationalist.

Willet, A., & Etowa, J. (2023). A Critical Examination of epistemologival congruence between intersectionality and feminist post structuralism: Towards an intergrated frameworkfor health related research. *Nursing Inquiry, 30*, 1–12.

ADDITIONAL READING

Chawhanda, C., Ogunlela, T., Mapuroma, R., Ojifinni, O., Bwambale, M., Levin, J., & Ibisomi, L. (2021). Comprehensive sexuality education in six Southern African countries: Perspectives from learners and teachers. *African Journal of Reproductive Health, 25*(3), 60–71. PMID:37585842

Council of Europe. (2024). *Comprehensive Sexuality Education Protects Children and heps build a safer, inclusive society.* Council of Europe. https://www.coe.int/ca/web/commissioner/blog/-/tag/discrimination

Deveaux, M. (1994). Feminism and Empowerment: A critica Reading of Foucalt. *Feminist Studies, 20*(2), 223–247. doi:10.2307/3178151

Marquardt, J. (2022). School-based sexuality Education in Europe and Central Asia. *European Journal of Public Health, 32.* doi:10.1093/eurpub/ckac129.740

Mquirmi, N. (2024). *How post-structural feminism and its focus on the concept of gender provide an innovative challenge to the status quo within Security Studies.* Policy Centre for the New South. https://www.policycenter.ma/publications/how-post-structural-feminism-and-its-focus-concept-gender-provide-innovative-challenge

Parker, R., Kaye, W., & Lazarus, J. V. (2009). Sexuality Education in Europe: An overview of Current. *Sex Education, 9*(3), 227–242. doi:10.1080/14681810903059060

Pierre, N. (2000). Poststructural Feminism: An overview. *International Journal of Qualitative Studies in Education : QSE, 13*(5), 477–515. doi:10.1080/09518390050156422

UNESCO. (2024, 01 20). *Health and Education Resource Centre.* Standards for Sexuality Education in Europe: Guidance for Implementation. https://healtheducationresources.unesco.org/library/documents/standards-sexuality-education-europe-guidance-implementation

Vanwesenbeeck, I. (2024). *Comprehensive Sexuality Education.* Oxford. https://oxfordre.com/publichealth/display/10.1093/acrefore/9780190632366.001.0001/acrefore-9780190632366-e-205;jsessionid=B32FD487C7B5ABFB920819A80BF5D858

Yilmaz, E. (2023). Attitudes towards sexual education among midwifery students. *European Journal of Midwifery, 7*(November), 1–2. doi:10.18332/ejm/172511 PMID:38023947

KEY TERMS AND DEFINITIONS

Curriculum: A course of instruction or subject.
Diffusion: The way ideas spread through a social system.

Discourse: A narrative or view on any issue.
Feminism: A movement that is committed to the uplifting of women and equality between sexes.
Innovation: A new idea or concept.
Metanarrative: A world view that is taken for granted as being universal.
Poststructural: perspectives that hold that truth is uncertain and that language and context determines what we hold to be true.
Reflexivity: checking one's beliefs, biases and practices in the course of work.

Chapter 3
Texts, Critical Literacy, and Their Effect on Students' Insight of Gender Equality:
A Qualitative Study in a Spanish HE Context

Tú Anh Hà
https://orcid.org/0000-0002-6450-3390
Universitat Rovira i Virgili, Spain

Cristina A. Huertas-Abril
https://orcid.org/0000-0002-9057-5224
University of Córdoba, Spain

ABSTRACT

This study investigates the effect of critical literacy on university students' insight of gender equality. It aims to propose a guideline to teach critical reading, and assesses the influence of texts and critical reading on students' perception of gender equality. Students (n = 40) were guided to identify the author's purpose behind the text by delving into the text itself and connecting it with the background surrounding the text. Then students' perceptions of gender equality and their opinions about the influence of critical reading on their understanding of gender equality were collected through a survey. Qualitative content analysis was employed to analyze the data collected from students. The findings showed that critical reading not only offered students more perspectives and new ideas to see an issue, but also helped them reflect on the topic of gender equality itself and what they had already understood of gender equality. This benefits students' metacognition and showcases an effective way of gender equality education.

DOI: 10.4018/979-8-3693-2053-2.ch003

INTRODUCTION

Based on the work of Michielsen and Ivanova (2022), gender equality is a fundamental content of comprehensive sexuality education that are derived from both the Standards for Sexuality Education in Europe (2010) and the International Technical Guidance on Sexuality Education (ITGSE) in 2018. However, the European Commission (2023) pointed out that gender equality is challenged in and through education in the European context through textbooks and learning materials. In fact, the European Commission (2023) pointed out the unbalanced representation of males and females in textbooks and they are often portraited with stereotypes, which are not always easy to be recognized. Moreover, there is an increasing number of online learning materials that are not evaluated in terms of opportunities and threats that they can bring to learners' perception about gender and gender equality. This raises an issue of using texts and more importantly, understanding texts and the message they convey as well as critically thinking and questioning the message transferred through texts. Schools and teachers can select and remove texts in a curriculum to avoid students absorbing gender biases and stereotypes, but they cannot avoid what students are exposed to outside schools. Therefore, it is pivotal to equip learners with critical literacy to identify the purpose behind each text, question the message of the text, and see an issue from different perspectives in order to have independent judgement and take independent actions instead of sinking in and being led by different sources of information and opinions. This can be one of the solutions for the challenge related to gender equality that textbooks and learning materials pose.

Texts play a significant role in various academic subjects as a means of communication and transmission of knowledge to students. Alexopoulos et al. (2022) consider texts as written or spoken compositions that convey messages and a substantial amount of knowledge. This means texts have the ability to transfer concepts related to gender, gender biases, and stereotypes. As texts continue to be disseminated through diverse channels (i.e., articles, social media posts, videos, and advertisements), it has become crucial for individuals to possess the skills to understand and interpret the information presented. This entails going beyond the surface-level meaning of the text and being able to recognize the underlying messages, subtext, and potential biases. In addition, the lack of critical reading skills among students is a prevalent issue nowadays, not only among Asian students but also among their Western counterparts, as pinpointed by studies like Le et al. (2021), Mohd Zin et al. (2014), Felipe (2014), and Vidal-Moscoso & Manríquez-López (2016), among others.

In this study, by focusing on texts in our study, the authors aim to address the need for improved critical literacy and promote a deeper understanding of gender equality issues. This chapter is going to present the concept of gender equality as a part of comprehensive sexuality education, texts and education for gender equality which emphasize the role of critical literacy. Based on the aforementioned concepts, this current chapter intends to propose and assess an intervention integrating texts and critical literacy to help students develop critical thinking of gender equality.

BACKGROUND

Comprehensive Sexuality Education

According to Michielsen and Ivanova (2022), Europe has a rich history of incorporating sexuality education into school curricula. This practice originated in Sweden in 1955 and gradually spread to many other European countries in the following decades. According to the European Expert Group on Sexuality Education, the emphasis of sexuality education has evolved over time to align with public health priorities. Initially, the focus was on preventing unintended pregnancies during the 1960s and 1970s. As the HIV epidemic emerged in the 1980s, education about preventing the transmission of the virus became an important component. In the 1990s, raising awareness about sexual abuse was incorporated into sexuality education. In the 2000s, the curriculum expanded to address issues such as combating sexism, homophobia, and online bullying, while nowadays, discussions surrounding gender norms and gender inequality have gained prominence within sexuality education. This demonstrates how the subject has adapted and expanded to encompass a broader range of topics over the years.

In the European context, and according to Michielsen and Ivanova (2022), there are two significant guidance documents that provide definitions and descriptions of sexuality education. The first is the 2010 Standards for Sexuality Education in Europe, which was published by the World Health Organization (WHO) European Office and the German Federal Centre for Health Promotion. This document outlines the recommended standards for sexuality education in Europe. The second important guidance document is the 2018 International Technical Guidance on Sexuality Education (ITGSE), which was jointly developed by the United Nations Educational, Scientific and Cultural Organization (UNESCO) and other United Nations (UN) agencies (UNESCO, UNAIDS, UNFPA, UNICEF, UN Women & WHO, 2018). This guidance builds upon the initial version released in 2008 and provides updated recommendations for sexuality education globally. According to Michielsen and Ivanova (2022), there are key characteristics of comprehensive sexuality education, based on both the Standards for Sexuality Education in Europe (2010) and the ITGSE (2018), as it should be:

- based on scientifically accurate information
- started at birth and be incremental
- age- and developmentally appropriate
- curriculum-based
- comprehensive and based on a holistic concept of well-being, which includes health
- based on a human-rights approach and on gender equality
- culturally relevant and context appropriate
- transformative; and
- able to develop life skills needed to support health choices.

It can be seen that the key characteristics of comprehensive sexuality education emphasizes gender equality as its foundational content (Michielsen & Ivanova, 2022). Other attributes are related to an approach for comprehensive sexuality education, such as based on a human-rights approach, curriculum based, culturally relevant and context appropriate, age and developmentally suitable. With gender equality as the content for comprehensive sexuality education, the next question that needs to be clarified is "what is the concept of gender equality?".

Gender Equality

Gender equality, according to the European Institute for Gender Equality (EIGE), implies that:

the interests, needs and priorities of both women and men are taken into consideration, thereby recognising the diversity of different groups of women and men. Gender equality is an issue that should concern and fully engage both men and women equally. Equality between women and men is seen both as a human rights issue and as a precondition for, and indicator of, sustainable people-centered development (European Commission, 2023, p. 8).

The Council of Europe (2015) defines gender equality as: "equal visibility, empowerment, responsibility and participation for both women and men in all spheres of public and private life. It also means an equal access to and distribution of resources between women and men" (p. 5). It can be seen that in the European context, gender equality is related to equal opportunities to be involved, take responsibility and have an equal allocation and access to resources in all areas of life. The EIGE also points out gender bias as: "prejudiced actions or thoughts based on the gender-based perception that women are not equal to men in rights and dignity" (European Commission, 2023, p. 8).

Nevertheless, there is a problem with the word "equal" that the Council of Europe (2015) and the EIGE proposed, as it seems to give the same things for different people and forgets the diversity of human society. Men and women are naturally different for their biological features which can lead to their differences in various domains, including their capacity and needs. The WHO recognizes the problem of the word "equal" and puts forward the concept of "gender equity" besides "gender equality". In addition, the concept of "gender equality", according to the WHO, is not defined as to provide equal things for men and women, instead it is defined as "the absence of discrimination on the basis of a person's sex in opportunities, the allocation of resources and benefits, or access to services" (European Commission, 2023, p. 9). By erasing the discrimination of a person's sex in opportunities, the distribution of resources and access to services, it ensures that gender inequality is prohibited in society without mentioning conferring the same things for both men and women. And gender equity is understood as "the fairness and justice in the distribution of benefits and responsibilities between women and men. The latter concept recognizes that women and men have different needs and power, and that these differences should be identified and addressed in a manner that rectifies the imbalance between the sexes" (European Commission, 2023, p. 9).

In Spain, the context of this study, the Constitution of 1978, in its article 14, establishes: "Spaniards are equal before the law and may not in any way be discriminated against on account of birth, race, sex, religion, opinion or any other personal or social condition or circumstance" (Spanish Constitution, 1978, p. 11). This is the moment in which the legal basis for equality is laid, reversing the Spanish legislation of the Francoist period, and has as an important milestone the approval of the law of divorce, in June 1981 (Subirats, n. d.). It was also in the 1980s that governmental bodies responsible for equality policies began to be created in Spain, such as the Instituto de la Mujer (Women's Institute), created in 1983. This is an autonomous body within the Ministry of Social Affairs, whose purpose is precisely to design and promote equality policies in Spain. Moreover, Article 9.2 of the Spanish Constitution sets forth the obligation of the public authorities to promote the conditions for the equality of the individual and of the groups in which they are integrated to be real and effective. Despite this, it is not until the 2000s when the Organic Law 1/2004, of December 28, on Integral Protection Measures against Gender Violence, and the Organic Law 3/2007, of March 22, for the effective equality of women and men were passed.

In the last years, however, numerous advances have occurred. The Royal Decree 2/2020, of January 12, which restructures the ministerial departments, created in its article 1 the Ministry of Equality, and in its Article 20 determines that it is responsible for the proposal and execution of the Government's policy on equality and of the policies aimed at making equality between women and men real and effective and the eradication of all forms of discrimination. Likewise, the Royal Decree 455/2020, of March 10, which develops the basic organic structure of the Ministry of Equality, specifies that the Ministry of Equality is also responsible for the prevention and eradication of the different forms of violence against women, as well as the elimination of all forms of discrimination based on sex, racial or ethnic origin, religion or ideology, sexual orientation, gender identity, age, disability or any other personal or social condition or circumstance (Ministerio de Igualdad, 2024). Currently, as can be seen from the above, there are specific regulations in Spain on equality between women and men, the fight against gender violence, LGTBI rights and non-discrimination on the grounds of ethnic or racial origin, as well as various regulatory projects promoted by the Ministry of Equality in the areas of its competence.

Finally, it must be noted that in this study, the concept of gender equality is perceived by integrating the two concepts of "gender equality" and "gender equity" that WHO proposed, so gender equality is to avoid discrimination based on one's sex in opportunities, the distribution of resources and benefits, or access to services, and to create social justice and fairness in the allocation of benefits and responsibilities based on the recognition of different needs and power of men and women.

Texts as the Means to Transfer the Concept of Gender

Texts are often mentioned in language learning, however, all other subjects at school use texts as the means of communication and transferring knowledge to students. Although texts are popular in learning in general, the definition of texts is often found in the context of language learning. According to Ur (2012), a text is "a piece of writing or speech which we use for language learning. It can be studied as a complete and autonomous unit: the reader or listener can therefore understand it without necessarily knowing the context, even if it was originally an extract from a book, a conversation, etc." (p. 28). According to Alexopoulos et al. (2022), texts serve as a medium of conveying a substantial amount of knowledge and message including the concept of gender, gender biases and stereotypes. In this study, a text is understood as a piece of writing or speech that transfers a message. Nowadays, we are living in the world of information, each day, each individual interacts with different types of texts for everyday conversation such as emails or through media including advertisements, news articles and social media. Therefore, the ability to understand the message conveyed through texts is essential for each person so as not to sink in the pool of information and be led by others without recognizing their purposes. For gender education, it is necessary to help learners build the ability of understanding the message that each text is trying to transfer and for which purpose or from what motivation that the message is generated. With that ability, learners can recognize different assumptions and notions of gender, gender stereotypes and gender biases, especially the purpose of conveying that message in order not to be led by others' ideas of gender, to find out their gender identity, be themselves and live their life instead of basing on others' concept and lose their own selves.

Texts and Education for Gender Equality

With the appearance of texts on different channels, especially through media, and the necessity of providing individuals with the capacity of understanding the message transferred through texts, media literacy education emerged as the result with the aim of integrating popular culture media in educational settings and provide students with the skills to critically analyze and identify the message of such media (Puchner et al., 2015). Related to media literacy education is the concept of critical media literacy. Critical media literacy is a framework that aims to analyze and understand the hidden power messages conveyed through media and develop the ability to resist and challenge these messages (Puchner et al., 2015; Share, 2009). The aim of critical media literacy is to focus on social justice issues. From that point, critical media literacy can be exploited for education of gender equality, as gender equality is a matter of social justice. While there are widespread calls for incorporating critical media literacy into education and recommendations on how to teach it, there is relatively limited empirical research examining its effectiveness in educating students about social justice issues (Puchner et al., 2015).

The central notion of critical media literacy is critical literacy for some reasons. In the 21st century, the concept of literacy is not limited only in the ability to read and write, instead it has gone beyond to embrace different modes of communication. According to Coyle and Meyer (2021), textual fluency covers the competence to exchange a message via different means such as visuals, audios, texts, etc. These different means of communication are actually related to media that can transfer a message through different channels, such as movies, advertisements (visuals) or podcasts (audios). Furthermore, different researchers (i.e., Flynn, 1989; Norris et al., 2012; Shor, 1999; Wilson, 2016) argue that critical literacy requires critical thinking that involves questioning, challenging the concept transferred through different modes, which is the main notion of critical media literacy. For example, Norris et al. (2012) contend that "critical literacy encourages readers to question, explore, or challenge the power relationships that exist between authors and readers. It examines issues of power and promotes reflection, transformative change, and action" (p. 59). Moreover, when mentioning critical literacy, several authors (Norris et al., 2012; Shor, 1999; Wilson, 2016) refer to the act of reading which can be perceived as the act of interpreting a message with the agency of authors and readers, therefore, in critical literacy, texts still play at the central rather than other modes of communication.

According to the European Commission (2023), some challenges regarding gender equality in and through education in the European context include textbooks and learning materials, including:

(i) There is progress in recent years to address textbook biases, however it is still limited.
(ii) The collaboration between two sectors: (i) textbook and learning publishers and (ii) responsible national authorities to take actions regarding gender equality in textbook and learning materials has not been effective.
(iii) With the increasing use of online materials, it is still vague about the opportunities and threats that this brings about and how policy makers can best address this issue.
(iv) Women and men are not only represented unbalancedly in textbooks, but also pictured with stereotypes. In addition, a number of stereotypes are subtle instead of being flagrant, and the initiative to tackle the issue is to remove (classic) texts but this measure is questioned for its appropriateness and if there are alternatives to replace it.
(v) The matter of terminology and inclusive language.

It can be seen from the challenges of gender equality in and through education in Europe that there are many problems raised surrounding textbooks and learning materials. Among them, the use of online resources with its opportunities and threats, and the question about the effect and appropriateness of omitting (classic) texts implying subtle gender stereotypes, call for the necessity of constructing critical literacy for learners. With critical literacy, learners can understand, question and challenge the message including gender stereotypes or biases conveyed through (classic) texts, not only those in textbooks but also other texts that they can face in reality. This helps them to form their independent thinking and be on the way to find their own values and personal identity in which gender is an essential component. We cannot avoid learners interacting with a great amount of information each day (containing online resources), but we can help them to form a safeguard which is critical literacy to ward off threats from various sources of information.

With critical literacy education as the means for gender equality, the main focus of this chapter encompasses the following points: critical literacy education for gender equality, the position of texts in critical literacy education, and the study's intervention.

MAIN FOCUS OF THE CHAPTER

Critical Literacy for Gender Equality

Shor (1999) perceives literacy as social action that evolves individuals as agents within a larger culture through language use. According to this author, critical literacy is a process of being conscious of one's experience as historically built within specific power relations. Critical literacy relates to questioning the social construction of self and understanding how language shapes and impacts individuals' perceptions and experiences. This notion of critical literacy put forward is related to the formation of self-identity which is influenced by relationships surrounding one and the whole society, and critical literacy requires individuals' consciousness of the social construct of oneself that is affected by language including texts. What Shor (1999) proposes can explain the formation of gender identity which not only depends on biological factors but also the social concept of gender having existed in society no matter of individuals' recognition and conveyed to them through texts. And critical literacy for gender equality requires each person to understand the social concept of gender that contributes to the construction of their self and how texts influence their thinking and perception of gender.

Traditionally, literacy only concerns reading and writing, therefore, critical literacy is often conceptualized surrounding reading and writing in a critical way. According to some researchers (Norris et al., 2012; Priyatni & Martutik, 2020), critical literacy involves identifying, questioning, challenging the concept transferred through texts as a means of communication. Norris et al. (2012) argue that "critical literacy encourages readers to question, explore, or challenge the power relationships that exist between authors and readers. It examines issues of power and promotes reflection, transformative change, and action" (p. 59). Priyatni and Martutik (2020) contend that critical reading requires a set of skills and knowledge, such as analyzing, synthesizing, logical reasoning, understanding of history, society, rhetoric and different perspectives. Among them, two typical cognitive features are reasoning and reflecting in which its two typical cognitive attributes are reasoning and reflecting. Reasoning is to evaluate what is being read with reasons and evidence while reflecting is to question and assess the validity of the information and message conveyed in the text.

In the 21st century, literacy has evolved beyond traditional reading and writing skills to encompass a broader range of communication modes. This expanded view of literacy recognizes the importance of understanding and effectively utilizing various modes of communication, including visuals, audios and other non-textual modes. Textual fluency, as proposed by Coyle and Meyer (2021), emphasizes the ability to communicate and comprehend information across multiple modes of communication. It involves not only understanding written texts but also effectively interpreting and creating meaning from visual representations and other non-textual forms of communication. This expanded perspective acknowledges the increasing prevalence of multimedia and multimodal information in our digital age. Within the framework of critical literacy, this expanded definition of literacy recognizes the need for individuals to critically engage with and analyze information presented through different modes. Critical literacy involves actively seeking credible sources of information, questioning and evaluating inputs received in various forms (visuals, audios, texts, etc.), and considering multiple perspectives on an issue.

By incorporating critical literacy skills across different modes of communication, individuals can develop a more comprehensive understanding of the complexities of the media landscape, engage in informed decision-making, and actively participate in shaping their own interpretations and responses to messages conveyed through different media forms. From that view, critical literacy is closely related to the concept of critical media literacy. According to Puchner et al. (2015), critical media literacy emerged as a subset of the broader media literacy education (MLE) movement that gained momentum in the 1990s. The common pedagogical goals of critical media literacy include the following:

i. Social construction of media messages: media messages are not objective but are constructed and influenced by social, cultural, and political factors.
ii. Examination of media construction tools and methods: critical media literacy seeks to explore the techniques, strategies, and processes employed in creating media content that are not shown to the audience, including aspects such as editing, framing, and representation.
iii. Understanding audience reception: critical media literacy acknowledges that different audience groups may interpret and understand media messages in various ways, influenced by their backgrounds, experiences, and perspectives.
iv. Unveiling values and ideologies: critical media literacy aims to uncover the underlying values, beliefs, and ideologies embedded within media texts, drawing attention to how these influence audience perceptions and shape societal norms and expectations.
v. Recognition of intentional messaging: critical media literacy recognizes that media producers purposefully craft messages to achieve specific goals, such as promoting products, shaping public opinion, or perpetuating certain narratives.

It can be seen that both critical literacy and critical media literacy focus on identifying the message conveyed via a mode of communication and the purpose of creating the message through analyzing different techniques that are used to generate the message, as well as being aware of the social factors that participate in the construction of the message. This means not only to understand the text itself (textual comprehension), but also critically think of the message created through the text and social factors that are involved in the formation of the message. Different modes of communication have different techniques to generate a message. In this study, we opt to focus on texts instead of other materials such as videos or audios for education for gender equality for some reasons. First, the popularity of texts across curriculum requires learners to be equipped with critical literacy to find out the meaning and main ideas of the texts, evaluate them with reasons, evidence and give their own opinions. Second, the lack of critical reading in students is a popular phenomenon, not only among Asian students (Le et al., 2021; Mohd Zin et al., 2014) but also among their Western peers (Felipe, 2014; Vidal-Moscoso & Manríquez-López, 2016). With the bloom of social networks such as Facebook, Instagram, TikTok, it can be easier and faster to upload and watch photos and videos on social media rather than write and read a note. Therefore, there can be an argument that with the digital world when information is transferred faster with visuals, audios rather than texts, it is more necessary to provide learners with critical media literacy than only critical literacy focusing on texts. However, we believe that with the ability to identify and question a message expressed in a text, individuals can have critical thinking to question what they see and what they hear in other modes of communication.

In this study, critical literacy is perceived as the ability to identify the message conveyed through texts, understand the techniques constructing the message, especially the social factors such as social norms, politics that influence the construction of the texts which in turn can impact the readers. Then question the message transferred and acknowledge that self-identity including gender identity is affected by different social factors via texts as one means of communication. Therefore, critical literacy requires both textual understanding and critical thinking. Hence, critical literacy for gender equality helps learners to identify the message of gender transferred through text, evaluate that message and give their own opinions. In addition, learners are aware of the social factors that contribute to the formation of the message about gender that is conveyed in texts. The texts play as the input to develop both critical literacy as the competence and the concept of gender, gender equality, gender biases and stereotypes as the knowledge. Based on the texts and the concept of critical literacy, the study proposed a critical reading model to help students with their critical literacy to approach gender issues. The intervention of the study is presented in the next section.

Figure 1. Texts and critical literacy for gender equality
Source: Authors' own elaboration

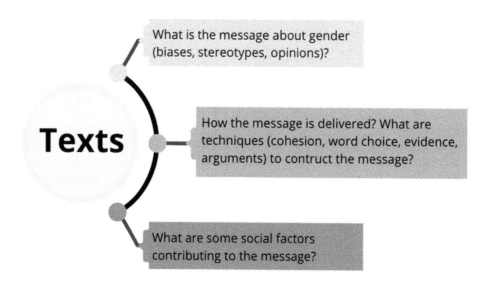

The Intervention

Design of the Intervention

The proposed model aims to assist students in comprehending texts and developing critical thinking skills. In order to understand the text, students are encouraged to not only grasp the meaning of sentences and identify the main idea but also discern the author's message and purpose. The model consists of two stages: (i) identifying the author's purpose and (ii) responding to the author.

In the first stage, students are required to determine the author's purpose by considering both the content within the text and the external context. Outside the text, students should consider the context in which the text is written, including the author, the time period, the situation, the genre, and the topic. They need to ask questions such as: Who is the author? What is the context? What is the topic? How is the topic perceived during that time, especially in a specific context? This process helps students gain a deeper understanding of the background in which the text is situated. They can explore different types of sources, such as visuals and audios, to gather further information about the text's underlying context.

Regarding the content within the text, students engage in reading activities to extract the author's message. They first need to answer the question, "What does the author say?" This involves identifying the topic, main ideas, arguments, and supporting evidence used by the author. By doing so, students can form an initial overview of the text. They can then make predictions about the upcoming content and subsequently confirm or revise their predictions as they continue reading, following the suggestion of Correia (2006).

Next, students delve into the question, "How does the author say?" They focus on the author's choice of words, rhetorical devices, types of coherence (such as cause and effect, chronology, compare and contrast, spatial-temporal coherence, problems and solutions), and cohesive devices to uncover the meaning and message conveyed by the text. Students evaluate how the evidence is organized and whether it logically supports the author's argument. They also examine the connections between different pieces of evidence and their relevance to the overall argument. By analyzing the author's attitude expressed through their arguments, word choice, and use of coherence types, students can deduce the purpose of the text. Inferences can be drawn by connecting textual findings (main ideas, arguments) with the contextual information.

In the second stage, after determining the author's purpose, students are encouraged to respond to the text by expressing their own opinions and explanations. They can indicate whether they agree with the author's opinion or present alternative arguments. Engaging in discussions with their peers allows them to exchange perspectives and consider different viewpoints. This aspect of the model is designed to foster critical thinking as it provides an opportunity to share diverse opinions and challenge one's own assumptions through interaction with others (Brookfield, 2012). The inclusion of discussions enables students to explore various aspects of an issue that may not be fully addressed in individual tasks, allowing for a more comprehensive understanding.

The Text

The text chosen to conduct the intervention is about gender equality, especially women and their role in building a sustainable world titled 'Gender equality 'fundamental prerequisite' for peaceful, sustainable world' published by the UN in March, 2022. There are some reasons to choose this text. The text focuses on the equality between women and men, especially in terms of leadership and points out the domination of men in global decision-making structures which lead to wars and human crisis in different places of the world. Later in 2023, the European Commission (EC) also identified the lack of women's representation in educational management in European contexts. According to the EC (2023), some challenges of gender equality in and through education include the fact that while women are inclined to pursue careers in education more often than men, they continue to be underrepresented in positions of managers at higher levels and broader decision-making structures at the level of school leadership (European Commission, 2023, p. 20). This again proves the argument that the UN published before in 2022. Among different issues related to gender equality, we believe that the imbalance in power between females and males in making decisions at top-down level which can affect the lives of a number of people should be recognized and discussed as this not only influences a specific individual but a large number of persons regardless of their gender.

Piloting the Intervention

Participants

The piloting phase of the two-stage critical reading model was carried out in the Spring semester of the academic year 2021-22. The proposal was tested in the context of "English as a Foreign Language for Primary Education Teachers", a compulsory course of the 3rd Year of the Degree in Primary Education and the Double Degree in Primary Education and English Studies of the University of Córdoba, Spain.

There were 40 students voluntarily participating in the study, using the convenience sampling method. In the session, students were required to read the text, then identify the message that the text transferred and give their opinions about the message. The lesson was delivered by the researchers of the current study, following the two-stage critical reading of the intervention. The whole lesson lasted for 120 minutes. After that, students had 15 minutes to write down their feedback for the intervention, specifically focusing on their insight of gender. This aims to evaluate the effect of the intervention on students' perception of gender equality.

Study participants had the following distribution regarding gender: 31 women (79.49%) and 8 men (20.51%). Moreover, 36 participants (92.31%) were Spanish and had Spanish as their first language, while 3 (7.69%) participants were international students (origins: India, Italy and Turkey). The overall English proficiency of the students was intermediate-advanced (B2-C1 level according to the CEFR).

Instrument

The instrument used to carry out the pilot and obtain feedback from students includes the text titled 'Gender equality 'fundamental prerequisite' for peaceful, sustainable world' published by the UN in March, 2022 (https://news.un.org/en/story/2022/03/1114072) and the following questions: "In your opinion, do you think that the reading and the activities of the intervention that you experienced in class support you to have critical thinking about women's rights and gender equality? To what extent, how does it help / does not help?" The list of questions was distributed after the teaching experience via Google Forms in English. The participants were informed about the objective of this research, and they all gave their explicit informed consent, and all the responses were anonymized prior to the content analysis.

Data Collection and Data Analysis

The data was collected right after the students finished their lesson by using Google forms with the questions presented in the Instrument. Following the recommendations by Arbeláez and Onrubia (2014), the study has followed three phases to analyze data: i) theoretical phase – a preliminary analysis useful to know possible approaches to the phenomenon; ii) descriptive-analytical phase, in which data are analyzed; and iii) interpretation phase, in which meaningful explanations are given to the findings obtained. The data were then analyzed and visualized, using Excel and Atlas.ti (v. 23 for Windows).

In the theoretical phase, the researchers agreed to apply qualitative content analysis to analyze the data. With qualitative content analysis, the data collected from surveys is examined and organized into various codes and categories. These codes represent specific ideas or themes found in the data. Data is analyzed and categorized based on the two types of relationship among ideas: similarity and contiguity relations (Maxwell & Chmiel, 2014). This approach aims to identify connections among different codes and groups, allowing to construct themes, categories and subcategories. The two researchers agreed that the requirements of qualitative content analysis (Schreier, 2014, p. 175) should be utilized for the coding frame. These requirements include: (i) uni-dimensionality (main categories represent a distinct and specific dimension, theme, or concept of the material), (ii) mutual exclusiveness (there should be no overlap or ambiguity in assigning members to subcategories within one main category), (iii) exhaustiveness (all significant themes, concepts, or dimensions of the material must be represented by the categories). The requirement of mutual exclusiveness does not imply that each unit can only be coded once. Instead, each unit can be coded multiple times, but each unit should be assigned to only one subcategory within a specific main category. With the first phase, the frame formed to analyze the data identified by the researcher includes the two main categories: (i) feedback about the content of the text, (ii) feedback about critical literacy skills (Figure 2).

Feedback for the Intervention

The Text

A majority of students argued that the text has the following positive attributes: (i) provide new ideas and different views to see gender equality (21 participants, 52%), (ii) provoke reflection on the topic of gender equality and their already thoughts about the topic (12 participants, 30%). Three students (7.5%)

Figure 2. Frame to analyze the data collected after the intervention
Source: Authors' own elaboration

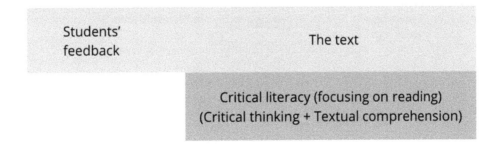

believed that the text motivates them to act for gender equality. Only a few students did not find the text to provide a new argument (1 participant). For example, some participants said:

I strongly think it has been a good opportunity to support my critical thinking about women's rights and gender equality since there are some aspects in the text that I have not thought about before and are pretty related with this problem (Participant 29).

I think it has been an interesting class. The text makes me think about things I have never thought about before. It helps me to understand some things that happen in the world (Participant 21).

Critical Literacy

Regarding critical literacy, students pointed out different ways that the intervention helped them with their critical literacy, including (i) being aware of the different issues related to gender equality and their unconscious thinking about the issues (7 participants, 17.5%), (ii) reflection on the topic and individuals' unconscious thinking of the topic (12 participants, 30%), (iii) critically thinking of the topic (9 participants, 22.5%), (iv) analyzing the text (3 participants, 7.5%), (v) understanding better ideas and their purpose (3 participants, 7.5%), (vi) finding out the relationship among ideas and connecting different parts or ideas of the text (3 participants, 7.5%), (vii) connecting the text itself to the context outside the text (2 participants, 5%). Different codes can be divided into two main categories: critical thinking and textual comprehension (Figure 3).

Regarding students' feedback about the impact of the intervention on their critical thinking, it can be interpreted that by helping students with their awareness of different issues in gender equality such as the influence of the pandemic on females and males, as well as the role of women in global leadership,

Figure 3. Students' feedback on the effect of the intervention on their critical literacy
Source: Authors' own elaboration

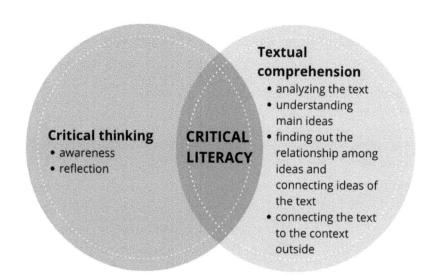

students could then start reflecting on the topic of gender equality itself and their own assumptions of gender equality, which facilitated their critical thinking of the topic. For example, some students shared how the intervention helped them to be aware of different issues of gender equality and their unconscious thinking of the topic:

I have never really thought about how the world crisis affects women in different ways than men, so it was very interesting to bring this topic up and to be able to talk about it in class (Participant 37).

I think that the text and the activity that we have done help us to be aware of gender equality and make us think about our unconscious thinking of it (Participant 31).

With awareness of different issues of gender equality, students could then reflect on the topic and their own thinking:

There are many interrelated aspects that we are not aware of if we do not carry out this type of activities and deeper reflections (Participant 39).

I strongly think that this experience in class supports people to have critical thinking about women's rights and gender equality. Some people do not want to face this problematic yet, thinking that this is something invented by women for having more rights than men. But this is far from reality. Women have so much to fight for, and this kind of activities spreads awareness about this social issue (Participant 15).

About students' textual comprehension, from students' answers, it can be seen that the intervention supported them in analyzing the texts so they could understand the main ideas better and recognize the relationship among the ideas in order to find out the message of text.

I think that the reading and the activities done in class will help me to think more critically about women's rights and gender equality as I can read texts and understand better the ideas and their purpose in the text as well as the relationship between them (Participant 11).

Yes, I do because thanks to everything we have done today, I have learned new ways of analyzing a text before going through it. Moreover, I have learned new things or I have considered new things that I didn't take into account before regarding gender equality and I'm sure it will help me to be more aware of the situation and take action to promote gender equality (Participant 40).

Finally, as critical literacy requires not only to understand the text but also to be aware of the social factors that contribute to form the message of the text, the intervention also aimed to help students link the text to the context that it raised. One student shared that by linking the text itself to the context, they could understand the text better and think of text critically.

I had never related gender equality or women's rights with the actual world situation and I think that was the reason why at first I did not really understand the text. So, after understanding the text I think that it has helped me to have critical thinking (Participant 24).

PRACTICAL IMPLICATIONS AND FUTURE RESEARCH DIRECTIONS

As stated in participants' responses, critical literacy and gender equality require further attention in the context of pre-service teacher training. In this light, the authors have identified a series of practical implications of developing critical literacy among future teachers at the same time the selection of texts help them increase their awareness on the importance of gender equality. By increasing pre-service teachers' critical literacy, they would be able to:

- be aware of unbalanced gender representation in the learning materials they use in their lessons and try to compensate for this unequal situation with supplementary resources.
- identify and avoid gender stereotypes in their lessons, especially when the stereotypes appear to be subtle and not blatant.
- have more insight into the impact of both manifest and subtle biases and stereotypes in learning materials as well as in students' attitudes and behaviors.
- evaluate and filter online materials. Although there is research on gender stereotypes in textbooks, more and more teachers and students use online materials. Teachers then need to evaluate and filter those materials to avoid gender bias, as well as increase their students' critical literacy to discriminate among texts.
- use appropriate terminology and inclusive language, avoiding terminology which may be outdated, biased and/or inappropriate.
- increase awareness against all types of gender-based violence and abuse among their students, including sexist jokes, discrimination, bullying and even physical violence.
- lead initiatives to mainstream gender equality and raise awareness against gender violence in the learning materials they use.
- address gender biases associated with teacher expectations, especially in teacher education programs.
- introduce gender equality across all subject areas to eradicate stereotypes about gender roles.

There is no doubt that pre-service teachers (as well as in-service teachers) and educators need training in how to recognize gender stereotyping in their lessons and how to discuss this topic with their students, for which critical literacy is essential. It is clear that our findings should be interpreted considering certain limitations. On the one hand, the results are only based on the self-reported opinions and experiences of the participants, which is necessarily subjective. For this reason, future research should consider using additional data-gathering techniques to obtain more reliable data. On the other hand, the sample of the study is limited due to the exploratory nature of the research, and only pre-service teachers from a single context were recruited. Future analyses should then consider expanding the sample size and the variety of participants in order to obtain conclusions that can be extrapolated to other contexts. Despite these limitations, the present study could be seen as a first step in the investigation of the connection of critical literacy and awareness of gender biases and against gender violence, especially among pre-service Primary Education teachers. Research in this area should aim to improve teacher training and teaching practice related to critical literacy and, ultimately, to prevent students from assuming gender-associated stereotypes and help them fight against gender violence.

CONCLUSION

This chapter addresses two key interrelated issues: on the one hand, the lack of critical reading skills among students (cf. Felipe, 2014; Le et al., 2021, Vidal-Moscoso & Manríquez-López 2016); and on the other hand, the necessary awareness of the importance of gender equality and the fight against gender violence. Despite its relevance, this is a field scarcely explored yet, especially among pre-service teachers.

In general, the findings presented here are positive as they reveal that pre-service teachers agree on the fact that critical literacy is a relevant tool to increase gender equality and fight against gender violence. Moreover, our findings highlight that pre-service teachers feel that they need to be specifically trained to develop their critical literacy to promote a non-biased and more equal learning environment and educate the democratic citizens of tomorrow's society. In this sense, the authors consider that pre-service teachers (as well as in-service teachers) and educators need training in how to recognize gender stereotyping in their lessons and how to discuss this topic with their students, for which critical literacy is essential. Our findings should encourage researchers, teachers and education stakeholders to continue reflecting on the necessity to develop critical literacy to support gender equality as part of the integral growth of individuals.

REFERENCES

Alexopoulos, C., Stamou, A. G., & Papadopoulou, P. (2022). Gender representations in the Greek primary school language textbooks: Synthesizing content with critical discourse analysis. [IJonSES]. *International Journal on Social and Education Sciences, 4*(2), 257–274. doi:10.46328/ijonses.317

Arbeláez, M., & Onrubia, J. (2014). Análisis bibliométrico y de contenido. Dos metodologías complementarias para el análisis de la revista colombiana [Bibliometric and content analyses. Two complementary methodologies for the analysis of the Colombian journal Educación y Cultura] *Revista de Investigaciones UCM, 14*(23), 14–31. doi:10.22383/ri.v14i1.5

Brookfield, S. D. (2012). Critical theory and transformative learning. In E. W. Taylor & P. Cranton (Eds.), *The handbook of transformative learning: Theory, research, and practice* (pp. 131–146). Jossey-Bass.

Correia, R. (2006) Encouraging critical reading in the EFL classroom. *English Teaching Forum, 1*, 16–27.

Council of Europe. (2015). *Gender Equality Strategy 2014 – 2017*. Council of Europe. https://rm.coe.int/1680590174

Coyle, D., & Meyer, O. (2021). *Beyond CLIL: Pluriliteracies teaching for deeper learning*. Cambridge University Press. doi:10.1017/9781108914505

European Commission. (2023). *Issue paper on gender equality in and through education* (edited by B. van Driel, V. Donlevy & M. M. Roseme). Working Group on Equality and Values in Education and Training. European Education Area Strategic Framework. https://bit.ly/3HzxQXT

Felipe, M. (2014). Reading habits of pre-service teachers / Trayectorias de lectura del profesorado en formación. *Culture and Education / Cultura y Educación, 26*(3), 448–475.

Flynn, L. L. (1989). Developing critical reading skills through cooperative problem solving. *The Reading Teacher*, *42*(9), 664–668.

Le, H. V., Chong, S. L., & Wan, R. (2022). Critical reading in higher education: A systematic review. *Thinking Skills and Creativity*, *44*, 101028. doi:10.1016/j.tsc.2022.101028

Maxwell, J., & Chmiel, M. (2014). Notes toward a theory of qualitative data analysis. In U. Flick (Ed.), *The SAGE handbook of qualitative data analysis* (pp. 21–34). SAGE Publications. doi:10.4135/9781446282243.n2

Michielsen, K., & Ivanova, O. (2022). *Comprehensive sexuality education: Why is it important? Study requested by the FEMM committee*. Policy Department for Citizens' Rights and Constitutional Affairs. European Parliament. https://bit.ly/48NaoSN

Mohd Zin, Z., Wong, B. E., & Rafik-Galea, S. (2014). Critical reading ability and its relation to L2 proficiency of Malaysian ESL learners. *3L. The Southeast Asian Journal of English Language Studies.*, *20*(2), 43–54. doi:10.17576/3L-2014-2002-04

Norris, K., Lucas, L., & Prudhoe, C. (2012). Examining critical literacy: Preparing preservice teachers to use critical literacy in the early childhood classroom. *Multicultural Education*, *19*(2), 59–62.

Priyatni, E. T., & Martutik. (2020). The development of a critical–creative reading assessment based on problem solving. *SAGE Open*, *10*(2), 2158244020923350. doi:10.1177/2158244020923350

Puchner, L., Markowitz, L., & Hedley, M. (2015). Critical media literacy and gender: Teaching middle school students about gender stereotypes and occupations. *The Journal of Media Literacy Education*, *7*(2), 23–34. doi:10.23860/jmle-7-2-3

Schreier, M. (2014). Ways of doing qualitative content analysis: Disentangling terms and terminologies. *Forum Qualitative Sozialforschung / Forum: Qualitative. Social Research*, *15*(1). doi:10.17169/fqs-15.1.2043

Share, J. (2009). *Media literacy is elementary: Teaching youth to critically read and create media*. Peter Lang. doi:10.3726/978-1-4539-1485-4

Shor, I. (1999). What is critical literacy? *The Journal of Pedagogy, Pluralism and Practice*, *1*(4), 2. https://bit.ly/4a0xl5j

Spanish Constitution. (1978). *The Spanish Constitution, passed by the Cortes Generales in Plenary Meetings of the Congress of Deputies and the Senate held on October 31, 1978. Ratified by the Spanish people in the referendum of December 6, 1978. Sanctioned by His Majesty the King before the Cortes on December 27, 1978*. https://bit.ly/437rpVT

Subirats, M. (n. d.). *La evolución de las políticas públicas de igualdad [The evolution of public policies on equality]*. https://bit.ly/3uXfj50

UNESCO. UNAIDS, UNFPA, UNICEF, UN Women, & WHO. (2018). *International technical guidance on sexuality education. An evidence-informed approach*. https://bit.ly/42gvHKn

Ur, P. (2012). *A course in English language teaching* (2nd ed.). Cambridge University Press. doi:10.1017/9781009024518

Vidal-Moscoso, D., & Manríquez-López, L. (2016). El docente como mediador de la comprensión lectora en universitarios [The teacher as a mediator of reading comprehension for university students]. *Revista de la Educación Superior* [Journal of Higher Education]. *XLV*, *177*(1), 95–118.

WHO, & BZgA (World Health Organization Regional Office for Europe, & German Federal Centre for Health Promotion). (2010). *Standards for Sexuality Education in Europe: A Framework for Policy Makers, Education and Health Authorities and Specialists*. WHO. https://bit.ly/3TnWxx2

Wilson, K. (2016). Critical reading, critical thinking: Delicate scaffolding in English for Academic Purposes (EAP). *Thinking Skills and Creativity*, *22*, 256–265. doi:10.1016/j.tsc.2016.10.002

ADDITIONAL READING

Banegas, D. L., & Gerlach, D. (2021). Critical language teacher education: A duoethnography of teacher educators' identities and agency. *System*, *98*, 102474. doi:10.1016/j.system.2021.102474

Canett Castro, K. M., Fierro López, L. E., & Martínez Lobatos, L. (2021). Towards a critical literacy with a gender approach in the teaching of literature. *Diálogos sobre educación. Temas actuales en investigación educative [Dialogues on education. Current issues in educational research]*, *12*(23), 00019. doi:10.32870/dse.v0i23.965

Gómez Castillo, Y. D., & Castañeda-Trujillo, J. E. (2023). English Language Learners Making Sense of Social Issues through A Critical Literacy Cycle. *Cuadernos de Lingüística Hispánica*, *41*(41), 1–19. doi:10.19053/0121053X.n41.2023.16093

Huertas-Abril, C. A., & Palacios-Hidalgo, F. J. (2022). La formación docente inicial en temáticas LGBTIQ+ y de género: Estudio cualitativo de las opiniones del profesorado [(Spanish) Initial teacher training in LGBTIQ+ and gender issues: A qualitative study of teachers' opinions]. In K. Álvarez y A. Cotán (Coords.) Construyendo identidades desde la educación [Building identities from education] (pp. 398–417). Dykinson.

Huertas-Abril, C. A., & Palacios-Hidalgo, F. J. (2023). LGBTIQ+ education for making teaching inclusive? Voices of teachers from all around the world. *Environment and Social Psychology*, *8*(1). https://bit.ly/49c2p1p

Khan, C. (2020). Fostering a critical consciousness in ELT: Incorporating a women, gender and sexuality course in a bilingual education university program in Bogota, Colombia. *Pedagogy, Culture & Society*, *28*(3), 403–420. doi:10.1080/14681366.2019.1649713

Palacios-Hidalgo, F. J. (2023). *Enseñanza de lenguas social y culturalmente responsable* [Socially and culturally responsible language teaching]. Editorial Comares.

Palacios-Hidalgo, F. J., Huertas-Abril, C. A., & Villegas-Troya, C. (2023). La traducción pedagógica en la enseñanza de inglés como lengua extranjera: superando los sesgos de género del profesorado de educación primaria en formación [Pedagogical translation in teaching English as a foreign language: overcoming gender biases of pre-service primary education teachers]. In J. Cabero-Almenara, C. Llorente-Cejudo, A. Palacios-Rodríguez & M. Serrano-Hidalgo (Coords.), Mejorando la enseñanza a través de la innovación educativa [Improving teaching through educational innovation] (pp. 645–655). Dykinson.

Teise, K. L., Mpisi, A., & Groenewald, E. (2020). Raising Consciousness of Gender Oppression through a Transformed Curriculum. *Africa Education Review*, *17*(6), 27–45. doi:10.1080/18146627.2021.1979894

KEY TERMS AND DEFINITIONS

Critical Literacy: Pragmatic curriculum approach that integrates engagement in social, political, and cultural dialogues along with the examination of textual and discursive mechanisms, their impacts, and the stakeholders involved.

Critical Thinking: Thinking processes that involve examining existing data, evidence, observations, and arguments to make informed judgments through the use of logical, critical, and impartial analyses and assessments.

Gender Bias: A prejudiced inclination toward a person or group based on their gender. This bias can be shown as a predisposition, partiality, prejudice, or predilection when selecting, representing or making decisions about a person or group. It is understood as an erroneous approach to equality between people that can generate unequal and discriminatory behavior in which there is a certain favoritism towards one gender, even unconsciously.

Gender Equality: State of equal ease of access to resources and opportunities regardless of gender, as well as the state of valuing behaviors, aspirations and needs equally, regardless of gender.

Pre-Service Teacher: A student enrolled in a teacher training program who needs to fulfill degree prerequisites, including coursework and practical training, to obtain a teaching license to be able to work as a teacher.

Text: A piece of writing or speech that transfers a message.

Textual Comprehension: Also called "reading comprehension", is the ability to process and interpret texts, understand their meaning and significance, and connect them with the reader's previous, existing knowledge.

Chapter 4
Spanish Contemporary Women's Writing as a Tool to Teach CSE:
A Case Study on Crónica del Desamor and Amor, Curiosidad, Prozac y Dudas

Mazal Oaknín
University College London, UK

ABSTRACT

This chapter presents a pedagogical proposal for a contemporary Spanish literature lesson in which students work on key social-emotional skills while carrying out textual analysis. Taking selected excerpts from Montero's Crónica del desamor and Etxebarria's Amor, curiosidad, prozac, y dudas, the chapter will capitalize on women's writing's potential to educate students on gender-based violence and raise awareness of the importance of sexuality education as a preventative measure. The proposed text-based discussions raise key issues of comprehensive sexuality education and give students the ability to reflect on what constitutes a healthy relationship and how to identify signs of an unhealthy relationship.

INTRODUCTION

This chapter presents a pedagogical proposal for a contemporary Spanish literature lesson in which students with an advanced level of Spanish are offered opportunities to work on key social-emotional skills such as empathy, integrity and openness while learning about how to construct healthy relationships and acting as allies and gender-equality advocators. This aim is in line of CSE (Comprehensive Sexuality Education), which consists of accurate, age-appropriate education that children and adolescents have the right to receive in order to learn about sexuality and their sexual and reproductive health, which is key for their health and survival. According to the World Health Organization, offering quality CSE and equipping students with the knowledge and values that help them to protect

DOI: 10.4018/979-8-3693-2053-2.ch004

their health, develop respectful, responsible social and sexual relationships and protect other people's rights results in long-term positive health outcomes and a lower risk of violence, exploitation and abuse. The proposal is based on the second-year module SPAN0082 Cultural Minorities in Spanish Contemporary Literature, taught as part of the BA Spanish and Latin American Studies in University College London (UCL). This module provides an introduction to the latest literary, political and social changes in contemporary Spain, introducing students to the question of the existence, or not, of a Spanish literature describable as women's writing. By analysing works by Rosa Montero, Dulce Chacón, Lucia Etxebarria and Najat El Hachmi, the module considers the role that writing by women plays in written accounts of collective identities, in providing alternatives to traditional fictional gender stereotypes, in promoting a feminist awareness and in portraying new definitions of Spanishness. Taking selected excerpts from Rosa Montero's *Crónica del desamor* (1979) and Lucía Etxebarria's *Amor, curiosidad, prozac y dudas* (1996), the chapter will capitalise on women's writing's potential to educate students on the very pressing topic of gender-based violence and raise awareness of the importance of sexuality education as a preventative measure.

Besides equipping our students with the means to carry out a critical analysis of the texts and to broaden their understanding of the cultural, social and political context of the Spanish Transition to democracy and the country's entry intro globalisation, the texts also have the potential to prompt classroom discussion on the feminist discourses, misogyny and gender-based violence described in the novel. This chapter ultimately aims to demonstrate how for Spanish literature students, contemporary women's writing can help raise awareness of the pervasiveness of gender-based violence across different decades and political contexts. On the one hand, in facilitating these discussions, tutors can play a pivotal role as agents of gender equality and societal change. On the other, the proposed text-based discussions raise key issues of comprehensive sexuality education and give students the ability to reflect on what constitutes a healthy relationship and how to identify signs of an unhealthy relationship.

BACKGROUND

Gender-based violence and sexism are predominant themes in both *Crónica del desamor* and *Amor, curiosidad, prozac y dudas*. These disproportionately affect women and girls and include violations against fundamental rights such as domestic and sexual violence, lack of access to education and reproductive freedom. Indeed, recent digital movements such as the #Me Too campaign continue to bring to the forefront and denounce the prevalence of gender-based domestic and sexual violence. According to global figures, 27% of women aged 15-49 have experienced physical and/or sexual violence from their partner. These figures also estimate that these violent patterns start early, with 24% of girls and young women aged 15-19 and 26% of women aged 19-24 having suffered violence at least once since the age of 15 (Sardinha et al., 2022). As universities discuss ways to take their commitment to EDI (equality, diversity and inclusion) further, the European Expert Group on Sexuality Education (2016) has recommended that gender-based violence be prevented through a quality sexuality education that also comprehends teaching about the emotional, social and cultural factors of healthy human relationships (UNESCO, 2018).

The texts singled for this pedagogical proposal have been chosen for their particular relevance to the "cultural moments" Colmeiro (2011) has described as the "three particular cultural moments in contemporary Spain that have shaped the construction of memory and collective identity: the post-civil war dictatorship, the democratic Transition, and the post-transition process of European integration and globalization" (p. 24). *Crónica del desamor* is a fictional account of the late Franco and early Transition period. The central character is a single-mother, and issues involving maternity take centre stage in this literary reflection of the sense of double disappointment liberal women faced in post-Franco's Spain. In spite of the greater freedom and rights introduced during the Transition, Montero's protagonists experience the political disillusionment that accompanied the end of the Franco regime, and this disillusionment has spread to their personal lives. Although their testimonies include the memories, voices, and stories of different women, the similarity of their personal and emotional circumstances would suggest that they form a multiple, collective protagonist (Nieva de la Paz, 1998, p. 651). Montero defines this as a novel closely linked to a generational reality (Montero, 2009), and above all, what these women have in common is their rejection of the Francoist ideal of woman, and their scepticism with regard to the uncertain changes that other more progressive solutions could offer. Alongside the political reinvention of Spain during the Transition, the protagonist Ana and her friends feel the need to re-invent themselves as liberated women, whilst the patriarchal, misogynistic attitudes of the Franco years remain very much in place.

In terms of the novel's content and style, the testimonial aspects of *Crónica del desamor* have been the subject of various studies. Myers (1988) notes its journalistic style. Davies (1994) and Knights (1999) focus on its metafictional status as a novel written by an author who is a journalist producing a narrator and Ana, who is a journalist writing a novel. Marcote (1988), Kerbavaz (2015), and Bezhanova (2017) have all considered Montero's first novel to be a statement of collective disillusionment depicting the contemporary mood of the Spanish liberal and left-wing population. Attention has been drawn to the narrator (Bellido Navarro, 1992), and to her function as the voice of the novel's ideological message (Martínez-Quiroga, 2015; Bárcenas Bautista, 2008). Other studies have highlighted the novel's groundbreaking feminist analysis of Spanish society (Nieva de la Paz 1988; Montero Rodríguez, 2006). Nieva de la Paz (1998) focus on the way the novel fictionalises Montero's personal experience, and other critics focus on its reflection of the difficult position of women, more generally, at this time (Nieva de la Paz, 2004; Manteiga, 1988). Nonetheless, despite the vivid portrayal of sexual abuse and unhealthy relationships in the novel, none of these accounts appear to acknowledge the opportunity for students to foster key social-emotional skills such as inclusivity, recognising their emotions, understanding one's thoughts and feelings, and managing conflictive situations whilst raising awareness about gender-based violence and preventing it through the learning of healthy relationships.

Amor, curiosidad, prozac y dudas' author Lucía Etxebarria believes that writing by women has a role to play in written accounts of collective identities, in providing alternatives to traditional fictional gender stereotypes, and in promoting a feminist awareness (Senís Fernández, 2001). With over 100,000 copies sold in less than a year, the novel was a literary success that turned Etxebarria into an overnight star, and whose immediate fame prompted its film adaptation in 2001. The novel was published in 1997, only five years after Barcelona's hosting of the Olympic Games and Seville's hosting of the EXPO 92. Francisca López believes that these events, among others, "aided in the recognition of Spain as a modern nation outside of its borders; at the same time, such recognition reinforced Spaniards' and their nation's own identification with the process of modernity at the local level" (López, 2008). This timing therefore seems key to the novel's success, and Henseler attributes this to the fact that it "connected with a twenty-to thirty-something generation that saw its concerns, its passions, and its needs mirrored in the destiny of 'las chicas Etxebarria'" (Henseler, 2004, p. 698). These "chicas Etxebarria" are the Gaena sisters, whose interrelated crises and struggles motivate the narrative. Although all three attended a nun's school and were brought up by a conservative and strict mother, each ended up following a totally different path in life, which is seen by Bosse (2007) as an attempt "to flesh out the multiplicity of the female subject" (p. 69). The eldest, Ana, got married at a young age to a good-hearted but passive man, and she now spends her days vegetating and crying in her beautiful home. Rosa, two years her junior, is an extremely successful, high-flying businesswoman who is dependent on Prozac and has no life outside her career. Finally, Cristina, the youngest sister and nominally a doctoral student, divides her existence between her work in Planeta X, a bar well-known as a drugs haven, medicating herself with recreational sex, drugs and alcohol, and missing her ex-boyfriend Iain. Cristina attributes her promiscuity to her unusually high levels of testosterone, and Exceso de testoterona was precisely the novel's initial title, "later changed due to the opposition on part of the publishing house" (Bosse, 2007, p. 67). As Gareth Wood (2013) sums it up, "*Amor* is the story of three sisters, women whose lives have taken divergent paths, but who are united in their dysfunctionality and ultimate unhappiness" (p. 277).

Etxebarria (2003) explains that all three characters are stereotypes and that this responded to her desire to make a testimonial and sociological novel about the Spanish women of her generation, about their struggles, problems, disappointments (p. 116). Indeed, Senís Fernández (2001) argues that the construction of female subjectivity in Etxebarria's novels is inseparable from her feminist commitment, and the theme of gender-based violence, which occupies a prominent place in mainstream feminist agendas, also is key in the plot of *Amor, curiosidad, prozac y dudas*.

Nonetheless, both critics that have praised the novel, including Henseler (2004), Bourland Ross (2006), Almeida (2003), and Carrillo Zeiter (2005), and those less impressed by it, such as Tsuchiya (2002) and López (2008), focus on the conflicts experienced by the three sisters, and appear to ignore the importance of the novel's message that despite their differences in terms of age, political opinions, education and sexuality, Cristina, Ana and their mother Eva suffer gender-based violence. Not only can the text teach our students that this problem affects the lives of all women, regardless of their origin, race, culture, religion, sexuality or social class, but it also highlights the message that not all survivors have the same access to support or recognition. Indeed, stereotypes can create obstacles to assistance, making some groups more likely to suffer from domestic violence (Simpson and Helfrich, 2014).

The following pedagogical proposal will present selected excerpt from the novels with a view to not only developing students' close reading skills and critical thinking, but also to raise awareness of the fact that despite the many political, cultural and social changes that Spanish society has undergone in recent decades, and despite the fact that the country currently boasts what is widely considered to be one of the European Union's most advanced set of laws on gender-based violence, about 100 women have been murdered annually in Spain in recent years, around half of them by current or former intimate partners (*New York Times*, 2023, 17 February).

By working on selected excerpts from *Crónica del desamor* and *Amor, curiosidad, prozac y dudas*, this pedagogical proposal will provide practical examples of the different ways in which sexuality education can be embedded in the literature classroom, equipping our students with an appropriate understanding of sexuality and gender and with the tools to identify healthy and unhealthy relationships, therefore fighting discrimination and violence. The two novels studied depict instances of gender-based violence in a variety of forms – sexual, verbal, socio-economic, emotional, physical – and in a variety of settings – at the workplace, in a marriage, in a friendship, in public transport, at university. Each of the two proposals presented here combine a selected excerpt with a set of questions to be firstly discussed by students in small groups. Secondly, lecturers are encouraged to prompt a classroom discussion aimed at promoting the key values of comprehensive sexuality education as stated in the UNESCO toolkit.[1]

OPPORTUNITIES FOR CSE IN *CRÓNICA DEL DESAMOR*

The shortcomings of the Transition and the resulting political malaise generated a sense of cultural disenchantment, particularly with the anti-Franco sectors of the population, marked by the disillusion with the pragmatic transactional aspect of the Transition and the general dissolution of collective hopes of the past and the former unity of the anti-Franco resistance. Indeed, the political context that set the framework for the way that the novels of the Transition came to be haunted both by the death of the dictator and an anticipated future that did not arrive. More than thirty years of nationalist rule in Spain, during the 1970s, Franco's health was visibly failing. In 1974 the Caudillo fell ill and Prince Juan Carlos took over as Head of State. After the dictator's death in 1975, the newly instated King Juan Carlos set in motion the changes necessary for the Transition to democracy (Spires, 1996, p. 12). Initial enthusiasm soon led to a sense of disillusionment, as the end of the regime did not automatically usher the utopian future many had hoped for (Neuschäfer, 2011). Hence, the uncertainty surrounding the Transition provoked apathy in a population unaccustomed to the liberties it had just gained. While the Pactos de Moncloa (Madrid, 1977) played a pivotal role in the peaceful transition to democracy, the pact of oblivion that accompanied them masked the oppression of 'los vencidos' by the Franco regime: an oppression that, until the fall of the regime, had counted on the legitimizing authority of the State to back them up. In spite of the agreements reached by Adolfo Suárez's government, ensuring the main political parties were represented in the Congreso de los Diputados, and that business associations and trade unions would provide important fundamental rights to Spanish citizens, the spirit of the Transition did not allow the Spanish people to talk about their past.

Pessimism, apathy, and disillusionment recur, thematically, in the most highly regarded Transition and post-Transition novels (Vater, 2020). In *Crónica del desamor*, this sense of disenchantment extends to themes hitherto repressed, such as abortion, gender-based violence, divorce, single motherhood and the role of sexual preference in the workplace, making this novel a pioneering addition to the work of Montero's male peers and an important tool for a feminist analysis of Spanish society. In its depiction of verbal, emotional and sexual violence against women, Montero's transgressive, anti-patriarchal narrative voice provides a ground-breaking account of repressed female memory that highlights the link between contemporary existential female angst and the indoctrination of women during the Regime.

In the novel the account of the on-going effects of sexual discrimination can seem overly intrusive. The section, below, for example, introduces the topic of Ministry jobs for sexual favours to a letter the protagonist Ana is attempting to write to her son, Curro's, father Juan:

"Juan: supongo que te sorprenderá recibir esta carta [...]"

Y Ana suspira, desolada: le es más fácil escribir hacia el pasado que aventurarse al futuro.

Su cara tenía una blandura feminoide y especial, blandura de muslo viejo, con la mejilla desplomada y temblorosa:

- Ahora está cerrada la admisión hasta el año que viene, pero... ¿cómo te llamas, guapa?

- Ana Antón.

[...]

- Te gustaría entrar en el ministerio, ¿verdad?

- Sonreía amable y blando esperando la respuesta, conociéndola de antemano, seguro de su poder. Y ella tenía que decir que sí, que le gustaría muchísimo [...]

- Sí, señor

- Pero no me llames señor, Anita, si ya somos buenos amigos, ¿no?

- Era como un mareo, y Ana era aún muy joven, y él era poderoso [...] y él sonreía, y ella se sentía incómoda y culpable [...] y Ana comprendió que sí, que era eso que estaba temiendo, que el tipo la esperaba, la acechaba.

- Y tendremos que ser más amigos todavía – aquí carraspeó, dudando, luego añadió con rapidez – porque te vendría bien repasar un poco tu francés [...] Como comprenderás, yo soy un hombre muy ocupado, pero estoy dispuesto a darle un empujoncito a tu francés. (Montero, 1979, pp. 93-96)

"Juan, I suppose you will be surprised to receive this letter [...]"

And Ana sighs, devastated – It is easier for her to write to the past than to venture into the future.

His face had a special, feminine softness, the softness of an old thigh, with a slumped and trembling cheek:

- Now admission is closed until next year, but... what's your name, love?

- Ana Anton.

- You would really like to work for this ministry, right?

- He smiled kindly and softly, waiting for the answer, knowing it in advance, sure of its power. And she had to say yes, she would like it very much [...]

- Yes, sir

- But don't call me sir, Anita, we're already good friends, aren't we?

- It was like a dizziness, and Ana was still very young, and he was powerful [...] and he smiled, and she felt uncomfortable and guilty [...] and Ana understood that yes, it was exactly what she was afraid of, that man was waiting for her, stalking her.

Spanish Contemporary Women's Writing as a Tool to Teach CSE

- And we will have to be even closer friends - here he cleared his throat, hesitating, then quickly added - because it would be good for you to brush up on your French [...] As I'm sure you understand, I am a very busy man, but I am willing to help you with your French. (My translation)

In order to analyse this excerpt, students are divided into small groups and asked to discuss the following questions:

- How is the topic of sexual harassment in the workplace introduced in the novel?
- How does the voice of the narrator express a double-interior-discourse?
- How are Ana's feelings conveyed? Do you feel the personal is political in this excerpt?
- Which linguistic expressions are pointing at the harassment that is taking place?
- Which techniques have been employed in order to enhance identification with readers?
- Why is 30-year-old Ana still haunted by what happened when she was 17 and which narrative devices have been employed to depict a connection with the readers' present moment?

On the one hand, in terms of textual analysis, the protagonists that make up the multiple narrative voices in *Crónica del desamor* are mediated through the character of Ana, a journalist and single mother of thirty, who functions as a kind of prototype for all her female friends. Their everyday stories are also mediated through an omniscient narrator, who has access to their memories and emotions. Alongside the political reinvention of Spain during the Transition, Ana and her friends feel the need to re-invent themselves as liberated women. *Crónica del desamor* uses a third-person, indirect mode that is interrupted by the free-indirect voices, thoughts, and dialogues of the protagonists. The uncanny resonances of these multiple, dissident female voices contribute to what Bakhtin refers to as the "double voice" effect: a blending of authorial and narrative voice(s) that draws the reader in, enhancing identification. On the other hand, lecturers are encouraged to direct students answers towards a general discussion that promotes the key values of comprehensive sexuality education:

- Human rights approach: the discussion will emphasise that Ana has a right to education, work and non-discrimination. Students become aware of the fact that their own rights must be acknowledged and respected.
- Gender equality: our students learn that gender norms under the Franco regime favoured unequal and inequitable relationships and learn the tools to create relationships based on empathy and respect.
- Culturally relevant and context appropriate: as our students prepare to join the professional world, they learn to analyse and challenge the ways in which cultural structures, norms, and behaviours affect their relationships within professional and other types of settings.
- Transformative: although the novel is set in the Transition to democracy, students recognise that harassment in the workplace still happens nowadays. Although Ana is a young, white, heterosexual, Spanish woman, students admit that this and other forms of gender-based violence happen across all socio-demographics and learn to treat others with respect and acceptance regardless of their differences.
- Developing self-efficacy: by analysing the signs of an imbalanced, abusive professional relationship in the excerpt, our students reflect on the information around them and gain the tools to make informed decisions, express themselves effectively and react assertively.

OPPORTUNITIES FOR CSE IN *AMOR, CURIOSIDAD, PROZAC Y DUDAS*

In *Amor, curiosidad, prozac y dudas*, the protagonist Cristina, while perhaps embodying a new generation of Spanish women that are the product of the far-reaching social shifts resulting from Spain's globalisation and closer integration with its European neighbours, is still haunted by its Francoist past. Indeed, Cristina appears doomed to repeat the fate of her mother, who was financially and physically abused by her husband. Cristina sees in her boyfriend Iain the person who will rescue her from her states of existential anguish. Having met him at a particularly vulnerable time, she just like her mother before her, quickly comes to idealise him. And, just as her mother turned a blind eye to her own partner's short-comings, Cristina turns a blind eye to the fact that her knowledge of Iain is superficial, to the fact that he still has feelings for his ex-partner, and to the warnings of her sisters and friends.

Although Cristina is not, as far as we are told, physically abused by Iain, their relationship is a tempestuous one, plagued by violent shouting, self-harming on Cristina's part, frequent attacks of jealousy, and a constant sense of insecurity and self-doubt that threated to destroy her mental stability:

Una vez bebió demasiado y cuando salimos del bar empezó a gritarme. Siguió gritando hasta que llegamos a casa. Le dije que yo no era suya, que no era de nadie y que hacía con mi cuerpo lo que me daba la gana. Que no soporto que me griten. Que ya he oído suficientes gritos a lo largo de mi vida […]. Pero el seguía gritando. Cuchillos en los oídos. Cogí mi propio cuchillo […]. Levanté la mano. Dirigí el cuchillo hacia mi brazo. Me hice un tajo profundo a lo largo del antebrazo. Vi la sangre correr. […] En la casa de socorro tuve que explicar que me había cortado preparando la ensalada […] De vuelta a casa él me besó el brazo y las puntas de los dedos, una por una. Aseguró que lo sentía […] Cada vez que acababa yo repetía que luego tendría que irse. Que no pensaba verle más. Que podía follarme todo lo que quisiera y que eso no cambiaría las cosas. Dijo que si le pedía que se marchara no volvería más. Le respondí que ya sabía dónde estaba la puerta. Le vi marcharse y no dije una palabra. Quería morirme. (Etxebarría, 1996, pp. 89-90)

Olvídate del sida y de las drogas, de las bombas nucleares, de los experimentos genéticos, de la manipulación de la información por parte del poder. La verdadera amenaza, la más presente, son los celos y el deseo, el éxtasis, el arrebato, el momento en que te tocará derribar las estructuras sobre las cuales asentaste tu equilibro mental. La pasión es la amenaza más presente, no importa lo racional que creas que eres. Nadie está a salvo. (p. 172)

One time he drank too much and when we left the bar he started yelling at me. He continued screaming until we got home. I told him that I wasn't his, that I didn't belong to anyone and that I did with my body whatever I wanted. That I can't stand being yelled at. That I have already heard enough screams throughout my life […]. But he kept screaming. Knives in my ears. I took my own knife […]. Raised my hand. I aimed the knife at my arm. I got a deep gash along my forearm. I saw the blood running. […] At the hospital I had to explain that I had cut myself while preparing the salad. On the way home he kissed my arm and the tips of my fingers, one by one. He said he was sorry […] Every time he finished, I repeated that he would have to leave later. That I didn't plan to see him again. That he could fuck me all he wanted and that wouldn't change things. He said that if I asked him to leave, he wouldn't come back. I replied that he already knew where the door was. I watched him leave and didn't say a word. I wanted to die. (My translation)

Forget about AIDS and drugs, about nuclear bombs, about genetic experiments, about the manipulation of information by those in power. The true threat, the most present, is jealousy and desire, ecstasy, rapture, the moment in which you will have to tear down the structures on which you established your mental balance. Passion is the most present threat, no matter how rational you think you are. No one is safe. (My translation)

With the purpose of examining this excerpt, students are divided into small groups and asked to discuss the following questions:

- After numerous excerpts in which Cristina expresses her infatuation with Iain, how is the topic of gender-based abused introduced in the novel?
- Which role does Cristina's sexuality play in this abusive relationship?
- How does Cristina's narrative voice differ from her sassy, humoristic tone in previous chapters of the novel? How is Etxebarria's feminist commitment represented in this excerpt?
- Which literary devices are used to depict psychological abuse? Why do you think Cristina links recent scientific developments to emotions such as jealousy and possessiveness?
- How does Cristina's bravado stand in contrast to her lack of assertiveness when it comes to Iain?

Senís Fernández (2001) argues that the construction of female subjectivity in Etxebarria's novels is inseparable from her feminist commitment. Focussing firstly on her essay, *La letra futura*, and the prologue to *Nosotras que no somos como las demás*, and secondly on a selection of her novels, *Amor, curiosidad, prozac y dudas*, *Beatriz y los cuerpos celestes*, and *Nosotras que no somos como las demás*, he explores the reiteration of Etxebarria's political and feminist ideas in her fiction. He correctly distinguishes three resources related to the use of a first-person narrator: the remembrance of the past, the alternation of speeches and direct opinions (2001).

Indeed, the three characters of *Amor, curiosidad, prozac y dudas* narrate their own life stories in the first person. Cristina, in charge of eighteen sections, is the main narrator, whilst the remaining ten sections are equally divided by Ana and Rosa. However, rather than focusing exclusively on the novel's feminist discourses, López (2008) has noted that in their narrations, the characters:

reveal the different discourses that the female subject must contend with in her search for self-understanding. Some of these discourses, such as the more traditional ones learned in Catholic school and in the home, are wholly predictable in a twentieth-century female novel about female development. Others, however, such as those characteristic of advanced capitalism and disseminated by global popular culture, are less predictable.

López's view is that although these discourses may be intended to be liberating and ironic, they often fail to demonstrate the full extent of their damaging consequences for female subject formation or to unmask the on-going contradictions placed on women by traditional discourses of femininity (2008). Similarly, lecturers are encouraged to direct students' answers towards the fact that, in spite of all the important advances achieved in terms of equality between the sexes, Cristina represents a grave issue affecting young Spanish adults from all classes and educational backgrounds. In Spain today, generally high levels of education mark a stark contrast to the fact that, as expert Fernando Fernández-Llebrez (2012) explains, there is an element of continuity between young women and women of other generations: the belief that it is not worth arguing when there is a relationship problem. The combination of this discussion and the textual analysis of the excerpt promotes the study of key values of comprehensive sexuality education:

- Human rights approach: the excerpt will highlight the idea that Cristina's right to health and safety must be acknowledged and respected. Based on previous passages of the novel, the discussion will remark upon the ways in which other characters advocate for Cristina's rights.
- Gender equality: our students learn that in spite of progressive laws, gender-based abuse is still a grave problem in Spanish society and that it is crucial to acquire the tools to create relationships based on empathy and respect.
- Culturally relevant and context appropriate: our students will recognise that despite Cristina's extroverted personality, feminist ideas and sexual liberation, the cultural structures, norms, and behaviours she has inherited continue to affect her relationship.
- Transformative: throughout the novel Cristina is constructed as a highly likeable character and the numerous references to Generation X culture and grunge music reinforces the notion that gender-based violence happen across all periods and socio-demographics.
- Developing self-efficacy: by analysing the signs of an imbalanced, abusive intimate relationship in the excerpt, our students reflect on what distinguishes toxic infatuation from a healthy relationship and acquire the tools to make informed decisions, express themselves effectively and react assertively.

RECOMMENDATIONS FOR FURTHER PEDAGOGICAL APPLICATIONS

A Health Humanities Perspective

The interdisciplinary field of Health Humanities seeks to investigate the cultural meaning and lived experiences of wellbeing and illness through humanities and creative or fine arts. Through a focus on questions of health, health care and well-being, the study of *Crónica del desamor* and *Amor, curiosidad, prozac y dudas* can include the discussion of a series of major medical themes that, according to international guidance (UNESCO et al., 2018; UNFPA, 2014;[2] WHO Regional Office for Europe and BZgA, 2010[3]) should be addressed as part of a comprehensive sexuality education programme.

Hence, further pedagogical proposals could highlight *Crónica del desamor*'s treatment of the topic of abortion. The main protagonist, Ana rememorates how her sister-in-law Teresa was forced to undergo an illegal abortion, whilst Ana's wealthier friend Candela had the choice to travel to London to have a termination. Students will learn that abortion was illegal under Franco, and this prohibition was enforced with very invasive government action. Given that the law was not passed until 1985, abortion was still illegal practice during the Transition, when *Crónica del desamor* was written. Although it was not uncommon for well-off Spanish women to travel overseas in order to obtain abortions, other not so wealthy women were forced to put up with clandestine, high-risk terminations in Spain. According to a U.S. Library of Congress Country Study on Spain, a 1974 government report estimated that there were about 350,000 such abortions each year, which gave Spain one of the highest ratios of abortions to live births among advanced industrial countries (Solsten&Meditz, 1990). Likewise, the narration of Candela's visit to the gynaecologist, where she is openly criticised for her choice of contraceptives, is a thinly disguised denouncement (on the part of the narrator) of the drawbacks of the sexual liberation that occurred after the Transition. Through the textual analysis and the thematic discussion of these excerpts, students are educated on important comprehensive sexuality education topics such as sexual and reproductive health, contraception and unintended pregnancy and sexual and reproductive rights.

With regards to *Amor, curiosidad, prozac y dudas*, the study of Ana and Cristina's mental health would also allow us to teach our students about suicidal thoughts, self-harm, depression and anxiety. The relationship between Iain and Cristina is a tempestuous one, plagued by violent shouting, self-harming on Cristina's part, frequent attacks of jealousy, and a constant sense of insecurity and self-doubt that threated to destroy her mental stability. On the other hand, the hazardous cocktail of stimulants and tranquillizers that Ana uses to self-medicate and to suppress her sense of powerlessness and depression lands her in hospital. What has provoked Ana's crisis is the realisation that she has not overcome her traumatic rape by Antonio, and that the traditional life as the housewife of a husband she doesn't love is nothing but a failed revenge now that Antonio is dead. The relevant textual excerpts provide ample opportunity for students to learn about saying no to sex, communicating within relationships, developing decision-making skills and obtaining support, which are basic themes in a comprehensive sexuality education programme.

The Fostering of Soft Skills

Not only does the study and discussion of the texts we have selected allow our students to work on their Spanish literacy skills (reading, writing, speaking and listening), but by reflecting on their depictions of gender-based abuse they can also embrace EDI values, appreciate difference and develop emotional skills. In recent years, universities have become increasingly aware of the fact that the influence that soft skills have on performance in the professional world is greater than hard skills, as concluded by studies such as Ibrahim et al. (2017). Moreover, studies conducted by the Stanford Research Institute and the Carnegie Mellon Foundation among Fortune 500 CEOs revealed that 75% of long-term job success results from soft skills mastery and only 25% from technical skills (Doyle, 2021). Hence, in view of this, universities are increasingly dedicated to the issue of ensuring that study programmes should also involve the development of professional and personal abilities in the form of all-encompassing soft skills such as leadership, innovation, creativity, critical analysis, autonomy, and cooperation with others.

Particularly, future pedagogical proposals in this line could complement close textual analyses of the literary excerpts selected for this chapter with role play activities with which students could develop socio-emotional skills such as empathy, respect, inclusion, and reciprocity. Students could be divided into small groups and based on an excerpt, each student could be assigned a character/role with a series of questions that allow them to develop a background story. These background stories and the ensuing dialogues would involve the fostering of a number of soft skills and life skills for health and well-being that are part of a comprehensive sexuality education programme. Table 1 shows a suggested activity for one group of students analysing one of the excerpts in *Amor, curiosidad, prozac y dudas*.

The Use of Intersectional Texts

As already examined, the novels *Crónica del desamor* and *Amor, curiosidad, prozac y dudas* illustrate that gender-based violence reaches women of all personalities, educational levels, and ages. However,

Table 1. List of proposed characters/roles, questions to construct the characters' background stories and soft skills and areas of comprehensive sexuality education developed for a class on Amor, curiosidad, prozac y dudas

Student character/role	Questions to construct the character's background story	Soft skills and areas of comprehensive sexuality education developed
Cristina	• Are you happy in your relationship? • Do you think Iain and you are equal partners? • Is your relationship affecting your mental health?	Decision-making, gender-equality, gender-based violence, cultural and social norms
Cristina's best friend	• Do you think Cristina is safe? • Is she confiding in you? • Do you think she is fully consenting?	Empathy, safety, emotional abuse
Iain	• How do you think Cristina feels in your relationship? • Do you think she is fully consenting?	Consent, bodily autonomy, emotional abuse
Cristina's sister	• How can you bridge your personal differences in order to help your sister? • How can you help Cristina? • Do you think she would feel judged by you?	Inclusion, respect, non-discrimination

the characters Ana Antón in *Crónica del desamor* and Cristina and Ana Gaena in *Amor, curiosidad Prozac y dudas* are all white, heterosexual, young, able-bodied, middle-class, educated Spanish women. In order to adequately raise awareness of the fact that gender-based violence also affects women of different cultural backgrounds, nationalities, races, ethnicities, disabilities, ages, sexualities, education levels and religions, it seems crucial for future pedagogical proposals to take into account the importance of intersectionality as a vehicle to grasp invisible power relations and the ways in which inequality can be shaped by them.

Professor Kimberly Crenshaw first coined the term intersectionality in 1989, and this theory is now key to numerous fields including anthropology, economics, gender studies, queer studies and political sciences. Intersectionality examines the ways in which numerous social forces, social identities, categories and ideological instruments are expressed and legitimized through power and disadvantage. As a response to the perceived limitations of the second wave of feminism, intersectionality was incorporated into the third feminist wave of the 1990s as it seeks to fill the gap caused by a rather narrow understanding of femininity that concerned itself mainly with the lives and experiences of white, upper middle-class women. In recent years, well-known activists and essayists such as Eddo-Lodge (2018), Saad (2020) and Gay (2014) have questioned mainstream feminism's principal preoccupation with disparities and oppressions of gender that centre in white women, sidelining the disparities and oppression of other intersections, such as race, religion, sexuality or body ability, that are just as important.

In view of the fact that new and innovative teaching practices flourish and given that universities are increasingly committed to developing an EDI agenda and to making the content of the research, materials and reading lists more inclusive, it seems ever-pressing to consider that our lessons should be intersectional. Indeed, the advantages of an intersectional approach to pedagogy have been highlighted by different studies such as Begum and Saini (2019), Shay (2016), Arday and Safia Mirza (2018), Bhambra, Gebrial&Nişancıoğlu (2018), Icaza&de Jong (2019) and Banks (2020). Taking into account that women's lives are intersectional, when choosing selected literary works that also serve the purpose to providing comprehensive sexuality education to our students and helping prevent gender-based violence, future pedagogical proposals should consider matters arising from race, ethnicity, class, religion, gender and nationality alongside gender. In this sense, the plots of novels such as Moroccan-Spanish writer Najat El Hachmi's *El último patriarca* (2008), Equatorian Guinean writer Trifonia Melibea Obono's *Herencia de bindendee* (2016) and *La bastarda* would allow us to explore the issue of gender-based violence from a variety of angles including post-colonialism, race, sexuality and class.

CONCLUSION

Based on selected excerpts from Rosa Montero's *Crónica del desamor* (1979) and Lucía Etxebarria's *Amor, curiosidad, prozac y dudas* (1996), this chapter has described a pedagogical proposal for a contemporary Spanish literature lesson highlighting the role played by women writing in written accounts of collective identities, in subverting traditional fictional gender stereotypes, in raising awareness of feminist concerns and in presenting a broader understanding of Spanishness. Both novels are representative of two key periods in Spanish contemporary history: namely, the Spanish Transition to democracy, and the Spanish entry into the European era of globalisation. This makes them especially valuable tools for the achievement of one of the module's aims – to provide an introduction to the latest literary, political and social changes in contemporary Spain. Indeed, both novels have been hailed for their respective feminist analyses of Spanish society at the time, and in both novels the themes of sexism, misogyny, and gender-based violence are dealt with in a graphic, raw manner. Hence, this chapter has capitalised on their potential to educate students on the very pressing topic of gender-based violence and raise awareness of the importance of sexuality education as a preventative measure.

The proposal presented was designed for the second-year module SPAN0082 Cultural Minorities in Spanish Contemporary Literature, a selective option of the BA Spanish and Latin American Studies in University College London (UCL) and was therefore aimed at advanced students of Spanish language. Nonetheless, it is also highly applicable to students who are native speakers of Spanish, just as the literary excerpts can also be incorporated into the Spanish language classroom in tune with educational views of language learning (Kramsch&Kramsch, 2000). The aim of the exercises presented here is two-fold. On the one hand, students are provided with the means to carry out a critical analysis of the texts and to deepen their knowledge of the cultural, social and political context of the periods studied. In this sense, the novels can help raise awareness of the pervasiveness of gender-based violence across different decades and political contexts. Different discussions have been suggested in order to prompt classroom discussion on the feminist discourses, misogyny and gender-based violence described in the novels. On the other hand, the proposed text-based discussions bring up important issues of comprehensive sexuality education and equip students with the ability to reflect on what constitutes a healthy relationship and how to identify signs of an unhealthy relationship.

The different sub-themes present in both novels also encompass chief medical themes that should be part of a well-rounded comprehensive sexuality education programme. In this sense, and in line with the field of Health Humanities, further suggestions for pedagogical proposals based on the texts studied have highlighted the theme of abortion in *Crónica del desamor* and the theme of mental health in *Amor, curiosidad, prozac y dudas*.

Moreover, by reflecting on the texts' treatment of these issues and on their depictions of gender-based abuse, students can also embrace EDI values, appreciate difference and develop emotional skills. To this end, this chapter has suggested a role-play activity in which students are divided in small groups and tasked with the creation of a background story for a given character based on a series of pointers aimed at fostering a number of key socio-emotional skills and areas of comprehensive sexuality education.

This chapter has also acknowledged the limitations of the texts selected, in as much as their characters are all white, middle-class, educated, young, body-abled, heterosexual Spanish women. With the aim of raising awareness of the fact that gender-based violence occurs across all socio-demographics, texts such as *El último patriarca*, *Herencia de bindendee* and *La bastarda* have been recommended for an intersectional approach.

By using well-chosen literary texts that deal with the issue of gender-based violence in a balanced, honest and educational manner, and by prompting safe discussions that teach key issues of comprehensive sexuality education, lecturers can play a pivotal role as agents of gender equality and societal change. By acting as allies and gender-equality advocators through the teaching of key social-emotional skills such as empathy, integrity and openness, they can equip the students with the tools to prevent and eradicate gender-based violence.

REFERENCES

Almeida, L. (2003). As Meninas Más na Literatura de Margaret Atwood e Lucía Etxebarría. *Espéculo: Revista de Estudios Literarios, 25*.

Arday, J., & Mirza, H. S. (2018). *Dismantling race in higher education: racism, whiteness and decolonising the academy*. Palgrave Macmillan. doi:10.1007/978-3-319-60261-5

Bárcenas Bautista, C. (2008). La mujer española y la deconstrucción del discurso misógino en Crónica del desamor, La función delta, y Te trataré como una reina de Rosa Montero. [Tesis Doctoral, University of Houston].

Begum, N., & Saini, R. (2019). Decolonising the Curriculum. *Political Studies Review, 17*(2), 196–201. doi:10.1177/1478929918808459

Bezhanova, O. (2017). Rosa Montero's La carne: Questioning the Culture of the Transition. *Cincinnati Romance Review, 43*, 134–149.

Bhambra, G. K., Gebrial, D., & Nisancioglu, K. (2018). *Decolonising the university*. Pluto Press. doi:10.2307/j.ctv4ncntg

Bosse, C. (2007). Becoming and Consumption: The Contemporary Spanish Novel. Lexington

Carrillo Zeiter, K. (2005). ...El amor y otras mentiras": Mujeres, sexo y amor en las novelas de Lucía Etxebarría. In A.-S. Buck & I. Gastón Sierra (Eds.), *El amor, esa palabra...": El amor en la novela española contemporánea de fin de milenio* (pp. 41–53). Iberoamericana Editorial Vervuert.

Colmeiro, J. (2011). Nation of Ghosts? Hunting, Historical Memory and Forgetting in Post-Franco Spain, *452F. Electronic journey of theory of literature and comparative literature, 4*, 17-31

Crenshaw, K. (1989). Demarginalizing the Intersection of Race and Sex: A Black Feminist Critique of Antidiscrimination Doctrine, Feminist Theory and Antiracist Politics. *University of Chicago Legal Forum*, *1989*, 1. https://chicagounbound.uchicago.edu/uclf/vol1989/iss1/8

Davies, C. (1994). *Contemporary Feminist Fiction in Spain. The Work of Montserrat Roig and Rosa Montero*. Berg.

Doyle, A. (2013, November 1). *Soft Skills List and Examples*. The Balance Careers; The Balance. https://www.thebalancecareers.com/list-of-soft-skills-2063770

Eddo-Lodge. (2018). *Why I'm No Longer Talking to White People About Race*. Bloomsbury.

Etxebarria, L. (1996). *Amor, curiosidad, prozac y dudas*. Debolsillo.

Etxebarría, L. (2000). *La letra futura*. Destino.

European Expert Group on Sexuality Education. (2016). Sexuality education – what is it? *Sex Education*, *16*(4), 427–431. doi:10.1080/14681811.2015.1100599

Fernández-Llebrez González, F. (2012). Malestares de género: identidad e inclusión democrática. *Foro interno: anuario de teoría política*, *12*, 29-59.

Gay, R. (2014). *Bad Feminist: Essays*. Harper Perennial.

Henseler, C. (2003). *En sus propias palabras: escritoras españolas ante el mercado literario*. Torremozas.

Henseler, C. (2004). Pop, Punk, and Rock & Roll Writers: José Ángel MañAs, Ray Loriga, and Lucía Etxebarria Redefine the Literary Canon. *Hispania*, *87*(4), 692–702. doi:10.2307/20140874

Ibrahim, R., Boerhannoeddin, A., & Bakare, K. K. (2017). The effect of soft skills and training methodology on employee performance. *European Journal of Training and Development*, *41*(4), 388–406. doi:10.1108/EJTD-08-2016-0066

Icaza, R., & De Jong, S. (2018). Introduction: decolonization and feminisms in global teaching and learning: a radical space of possibility. In Decolonization and Feminisms in Global Teaching and Learning (pp. xv-xxxiv). (Teaching with Gender book series). Routledge.

Kerbavaz, K. (2015). La lengua de Margarita: El silencio impuesto y la escritura activista en Crónica del desamor. *Revista de Filología y Lingüística de La Universidad de Costa Rica*, *41*(2), 55–65.

Knights, V. (1999). *The Search for Identity in the Narrative of Rosa Montero*. Edwin Mellen Press.

López, F. (2008). Female Subjects in Late Modernity: Lucía Etxebarría's *Amor, Curiosidad, Prozac y Dudas*. *Dissidences*, *2*(4)

Manteiga, R. (1988). The Dilemma of the Modern Woman: A Study of the Female Characters in Rosa Montero's Novels. In R. C. Manteiga, C. Garlerstein, & K. McNerney (Eds.), *Feminine Concerns in Contemporary Spanish Fiction by Women* (pp. 113–123). Scripta Humanistica.

Marcote, R. M. (1998). Voices of Protest in Rosa Montero's *Crónica del desamor*. *Neophilologus*, *82*(1), 63–70. doi:10.1023/A:1004237420813

Martínez-Quiroga, P. (2015). Humor, feminismo y crítica social en la novela española contemporánea. *Bulletin of Spanish Studies: Hispanic Studies and Researches on Spain, Portugal, and Latin America*, 92(6), 931–949. doi:10.1080/14753820.2014.947854

Ministerio de la Presidencia. (1977). *Los pactos de la Moncloa*. Secretaría General Técnica.

Montero, R. (2009). *Crónica del desamor*. Alfaguara.

Montero Rodríguez, S. (2006). La autoría femenina y la construcción de la identidad en Crónica del desamor de Rosa Montero. *Revista de Filología y Lingüística de La Universidad de Costa Rica*, 32(2), 41–54. doi:10.15517/rfl.v32i2.4289

Myers, E. D. (1988). The Feminist Message: Propaganda and/or Art? A Study of Two Novels by Rosa Montero. In R. C. Manteiga, C. Garlerstein, & K. McNerney (Eds.), *Feminine Concerns in Contemporary Spanish Fiction by Women* (pp. 99–12). Scripta Humanistica.

Neuschäfer, H.-J. (2011). Habíamos ganado la guerra: Sobre la obra de la autora catalana Esther Tusquets. In J. Reinstädler & D. Ingenschay (Eds.), *Escribir después de la dictadura. La producción literaria y cultural en las posdictaduras de Europa e Hispanoamérica* (pp. 137–142). Vervuert Verlag. doi:10.31819/9783954871094-007

Nieva de la Paz, P. (2004). *Narradoras españolas de la transición política: textos y contextos*. Fundamentos.

Ross, C. B. (2006). Sex, Drugs and Violence in Lucía Etxebarria's Amor, curiosidad, Prozac y dudas. In A.-P. Durand & N. Mandel (Eds.), *Novels of the Contemporary Extreme* (pp. 153–162). Continuum International Publishing Group.

Saad, L. (2020). *Me and White Supremacy. How to Recognise your Privilege, Combat Racism and Change the Word*. Quercus Books.

Sardinha, L., Maheu-Giroux, M., Stöckl, H., Meyer, S. R., & García-Moreno, C. (2022). Global, regional, and national prevalence estimates of physical or sexual, or both, intimate partner violence against women in 2018. *Lancet*, 399(10327), 803–813. doi:10.1016/S0140-6736(21)02664-7 PMID:35182472

Senís Fernández, J. (2001). Compromiso feminista en la obra de Lucía Etxebarría. *Espéculo. Revista de Estudios Literarios*, 18.

Shay, S. (2016, June 13). *Decolonising the curriculum: it's time for a strategy*. The Conversation. https://theconversation.com/decolonising-the-curriculum-its-time-for-a-strategy-60598

Simpson, E. K., & Helfrich, C. A. (2014). Oppression and Barriers to Service for Black, Lesbian Survivors of Intimate Partner Violence. *Journal of Gay & Lesbian Social Services*, 26(4), 441–465. doi:10.1080/10538720.2014.951816

Solsten, E., & Meditz, S. W. (1990). Spain, a Country study. Department of the Army.

Spires, R. C. (1996). *Post-Totalitarian Spanish Fiction*. University of Missouri Press.

Tsuchiya, A. (2002). The "New" Female Subject and the Commodification of Gender in the Works of Lucía Etxebarria. *Romance Studies*, 20(1), 77–87. doi:10.1179/ros.2002.20.1.77

UNESCO. (2018). *International technical guidance on sexuality education: An evidence-informed approach; overview*. UNESCO. https://bit.ly/44JqCcN

Vater, K. J. (2020). *Between Market and Myth: The Spanish Artist Novel in the Post-Transition, 1992-2014*. Bucknell University Press.

Wood, G. (2013). The Naturalist Inheritance in *Amor, curiosidad, prozac y dudas* by Lucía Etxebarria. *Hispanic Research Journal, 14*(3), 273–290. doi:10.1179/1468273713Z.00000000049

ADDITIONAL READING

Moi, T. (2002). Sexual/Textual Politics. Routledge. Labanyi, J. (2002). Castrating Identity in Contemporary Spain: Theoretical Debates and Cultural Practice. Oxford University Press.

Montero, R. (1982). *Cinco años de País*. Debate.

Montero, R. (2004). *La loca de la casa*. Punto de Lectura.

Moszczyńska, K. (2009). *La vida devorada (novela, mujer y sociedad en la España de los noventa)*. Instituto de Estudios Ibéricos e Iberoamericanos de la Universidad de Varsovia.

Oaknín, M. (2019). *Feminism, Writing and the Media in Spain*. Peter Lang. doi:10.3726/b11488

Widiyono, W. (2019). The Role of Soft Skills in Preventing Educated Unemployment: A Phenomenological Approach of University Graduates in Jakarta. *International Journal of Humanities and Social Science, 9*(5). Advance online publication. doi:10.30845/ijhss.v9n5p25

Yunus, K., & Li, S. (2005, October 1). Matching Job Skills with Needs. Bu*siness Times*.

KEY TERMS AND DEFINITIONS

CSE: Comprehensive Sexuality Education. It consists of accurate, age-appropriate education that children and adolescents have the right to receive in order to learn about sexuality and their sexual and reproductive health, which is key for their health and survival.

EDI: Equality, Diversity, and Inclusion. It ensures fair treatment and opportunity for all, with the objective of eliminating prejudice and discrimination due to an individual group's character traits.

Franco Regime: Spain was controlled by general and dictator Francisco Franco (1892–1975) from 1939 until his passing. He came to power during the terrible Spanish Civil War when his Nationalist forces toppled the democratically elected Second Republic with the assistance of Nazi Germany and Fascist Italy. Taking on the moniker "El Caudillo" (The Leader), Franco suppressed the language and culture of the Basque and Catalan areas of Spain, persecuted political opponents, condemned the media, and exercised total authority over the nation.

Gender Equality: A situation in which gender has no bearing on who is able to obtain certain opportunities or rights.

Gender-Based Violence: Any kind of violence committed against an individual or group of individuals due to their real or perceived gender, sex, sexual orientation, and/or gender identity.

Healthy Relationship: A relationship in which there isn't any power disparity. Couples share decision-making authority, respect one another's independence, and are free to act independently without fear of reprisal or vengeance.

Socio-Emotional Skills: Social and emotional intelligence is crucial in interpersonal relationships. Socio-emotional skills support us in feeling empathy, forming wholesome connections, and controlling our emotions.

Spanish Transition: As Franco grew older, some of the regimen's prohibitions progressively relaxed, and the nation moved towards democracy after his passing. The process commenced with the political elites left over from the Franco regime's attempt to reform the institutions of the dictatorship through existing legal means.

Textual Analysis: A method used to examine and interpret texts by analysing their content, style, structure, purpose, and underlying meanings.

ENDNOTES

[1] https://csetoolkit.unesco.org/toolkit/getting-started/what-comprehensive-sexuality-education.

[2] https://www.unfpa.org/sites/default/files/pub-pdf/EN-SWOP14-Report_FINAL-web.pdf

[3] https://www.icmec.org/wp-content/uploads/2016/06/WHOStandards-for-Sexuality-Ed-in-Europe.pdf

Chapter 5
Dialogic Talks and Photographic Narration:
Strategies for University Teaching With a Gender Perspective

Azahara Jiménez-Millán
University of Cordoba, Spain

Elisa Pérez Gracia
University of Cordoba, Spain

ABSTRACT

Currently, the levels of gender violence are unsustainable in a society that upholds the principles of respect, coexistence and justice. Likewise, it is important to emphasize that the features of contemporary society, characterized by immersion in new technologies, social networks and artificial intelligence, have led to the appearance of events related to gender violence in new digital contexts. In this context, education plays a key role, and it is seen as essential to adopt a cross-curricular and intersectional approach, which in the case of Spain still represents a pending challenge. This chapter presents a teaching-learning process framed in feminist pedagogy, applied in the university environment of the Education Degrees of a Spanish public university. In this process, sessions have been carried out based on dialogic discussion and photographic narration from a gender perspective. The main objective was to provide students with pedagogical tools that to raise awareness and encourage critical thinking.

INTRODUCTION

Currently, the levels of gender violence are unsustainable in a society that upholds the principles of respect, coexistence and justice. Despite the progress in the fight for women's rights and gender equality and the promulgation of laws such as the recent Organic Law 10/2022, of September 6 about comprehensive guarantee of sexual freedom in Spain, the gender violence continues to prevail. This problem

DOI: 10.4018/979-8-3693-2053-2.ch005

persists due to the influence of various interconnected factors, such as the persistence of gender norms and stereotypes rooted in society, social and economic inequality, among others.

In this context, it is essential to highlight the meaningful contributions of Judith Butler to the field of gender studies. Her approach to the problem of gender violence is based on her theory of gender performativity and her criticism of binary and heteronormative gender norms. Butler maintains that gender violence arises as a direct consequence of the imposition of these restrictive norms, and she advocates challenging them and working towards a more inclusive society free of gender violence (Cano, 2021). From the perspective of gender studies, gender violence is conceived as a manifestation of structural and systematic violence that perpetuates and reinforces the aforementioned gender norms (Butler, 2017).

Likewise, it is important to emphasize that the features of contemporary society, characterized by immersion in new technologies, social networks and artificial intelligence, have led to the appearance of events related to gender violence in new digital contexts. In this sense, prominent researchers have highlighted the close relationship between technology and gender violence, pointing out how these digital tools can facilitate and perpetuate gender violence and harassment (for example, Baym, 2006; Criado-Pérez, 2020; Franks, 2022).

Therefore, the problem of gender violence requires a comprehensive approach that involves all spheres of society for its treatment and prevention. In this context, education plays a key role, and it is seen as essential to adopt a cross-curricular and intersectional approach, which in the case of Spain still represents a pending challenge (Barriuso-Ortega et al., 2022; Garzón Fernández, 2016). In this sense, the implementation of comprehensive sexuality education emerges as a crucial educational approach. This is not limited only to providing information on biological and reproductive aspects, but also addresses psychosocial issues, sexual diversity, and the promotion of gender equality. These elements are necessary to integrate into the educational curriculum and offer a comprehensive vision that contributes to combating gender violence from its roots.

At the same time, the inclusion of the gender perspective in university teaching is positioned as a crucial element, since it promotes critical reflection about power relations and gender inequalities (Salazar, 2021). From this perspective, university students can acquire an understanding of the roots and dynamics of gender violence, while developing skills to analyze and address this problem both in their immediate environment and in their future careers as teachers. Previous research focused on feminist teaching (García-Cano et al., 2022; García-Cano et al., 2023) has explored the influence of equality policies on teaching innovation, offering revealing conclusions that range from opportunity and opportunism.

Diverse studies have focused on the analysis of methodologies and their contribution to feminist pedagogy. For example, María García-Cano and Eva F. Hinojosa-Pareja (2016) carried out a systematization of the contributions of Service-Learning, identifying four fundamental elements: interdependence, communication, responsibility and care. Mireia Foradada and Sara López (2023), for their part, explored the use of the autobiographical story as a feminist teaching method, with the purpose of denaturalizing hegemonic knowledge and allowing the deconstruction of mechanisms of inequality. A previous project that combined photography with Service-Learning allowed us to delve deeper into aspects linked to feminist pedagogy, such as the valorization of personal experiences and the subjective dimension in the process of knowledge construction, as well as transcending the individual to the collective and, ultimately, to the political.

In this sense, pedagogical talking is presented as an effective tool to address these issues in the educational environment. This space for dialogue and reflection allows both students and teachers to express their interpretations of the text, listen to different perspectives and build knowledge collectively

(Alexander, 2020). Through dialogic discussion, it is possible to explore and analyze issues related to gender, equality and gender violence, encouraging critical reflection. By providing a safe environment that promotes active listening, you contribute to the understanding and recognition of the experiences of others, which can lead to changes in attitudes and behaviors.

Furthermore, it is important to clarify that although the terms "abuse," "assault," "harassment," and "mistreatment" share some similarities in that they all involve harmful behaviour toward other people, there are subtle differences in their definitions and connotations (Kiekens et al., 2022). Abuse involves the improper or unfair use of power or resources, in this case, in the context of personal relationships, especially in the sexual area. It may include behaviors that cause physical, emotional, or psychological harm. Aggression involves an act of violence or hostile behavior directed toward another person. In the sexual context, sexual assault includes any non-consensual act of a sexual nature that causes harm or discomfort to the victim. Harassment or bullying involves unwanted, repetitive behaviors that create a hostile or intimidating environment for the victim. In the sexual sphere, sexual harassment refers to unwanted conduct of a sexual nature that violates the boundaries of consent and may occur in work, educational or social settings. Finally, abuse involves unfair, cruel or abusive treatment of another person. It can manifest itself in various ways, whether physically, emotionally, verbally or psychologically (Hequembourg, Livingston & Wang, 2020).

In this sense, our positioning in this chapter coincides with the contemporary feminist theory of Judith Butler, which is far from the current binary system male/female and the need to rethink the proposals linked to the ethics of responsibility towards non-violent coexistence (Cano, 2021). We believe that Butler's perspective (Butler, 2020) and queer pedagogies (Sánches-Sáinz, 2019) are the required stance from the field of education to keep on progressing in equality. Actually, she points out that the violence we see is correlated with the reactions to the processes in which we are usually immersed. Thus, we should recognize that it is a continued fight in which principles are on our side.

Thus, in line with the approach and context presented, this chapter aims to know university students' perceptions about gender violence, the importance they give to this issue as well as the strategies they believe could be helpful for its prevention from the educational perspective.

GENDER BASED VIOLENCE

Gender-based violence (GBV) is a pervasive social issue that transcends geographical, cultural, and socioeconomic boundaries (Muluneh et al., 2020). Due to its complexity, it is important to provide a comprehensive understanding of the multifaceted nature of gender-based violence, exploring its origins, manifestations, and impact on individuals and societies.

Understanding the origins of gender violence requires a comprehensive examination of various contributing elements (Jewkes & Morrell, 2019; Hankivsky, 2020):

- Socialization and Gender Norms: From an early age, individuals are socialized into gender roles and expectations. Stereotypes and rigid norms associated with masculinity and femininity can contribute to power imbalances and the normalization of violent behaviors.
- Patriarchal Structures: Societal structures often reflect patriarchal norms, where power is concentrated in the hands of men. This power dynamic can perpetuate attitudes and behaviors that

subordinate women and other gender minorities, fostering an environment conducive to gender violence.
- Historical and Cultural Factors: Historical practices and cultural norms play a significant role in shaping attitudes towards gender. Some cultures may have traditions or beliefs that perpetuate gender inequalities, contributing to the acceptance or normalization of violence against certain genders.
- Economic Inequality: Economic disparities can exacerbate gender-based violence. In societies where women and marginalized genders have limited access to resources, education, and economic opportunities, they may be more vulnerable to violence and exploitation.
- Power Imbalances: Gender-based violence often stems from power imbalances, where one gender is granted more social, economic, or political power than another. These imbalances create conditions in which violence can be used as a tool to maintain control and dominance.
- Intersectionality: The intersectionality of various social identities (race, class, sexuality, etc.) contributes to unique experiences of gender-based violence. Intersectional factors can compound vulnerabilities and increase the risk of violence for individuals who belong to multiple marginalized groups.
- Cultural Relativism and Legal Systems: Some societies may justify or tolerate gender violence due to cultural relativism, where practices are viewed through the lens of cultural norms. Additionally, gaps or inadequacies in legal systems may contribute to impunity for perpetrators of gender-based violence.
- Media Influence: Media can shape and reinforce cultural attitudes towards gender. Stereotypical portrayals of gender roles and normalization of violence in media content can contribute to the perpetuation of harmful behaviors.
- Psychological and Individual Factors: Individual factors, including psychological issues, can contribute to gender-based violence. These may include issues related to anger management, control, or a history of trauma.
- Lack of Education and Awareness: Insufficient education about gender equality and human rights can contribute to the perpetuation of harmful stereotypes and attitudes. Communities with limited access to education may struggle to challenge traditional norms that normalize gender violence.

Therefore, addressing the origins of GBV requires an intersectional approach. Efforts should focus on challenging societal norms, promoting gender equality, implementing effective legal frameworks, and providing education and support to communities to break the cycle of violence and create a culture of respect and equality. This last tool, education should be considered as a primary strategy to approach GBV at all levels (Schneider & Hirsch, 2020).

EDUCATION STRATEGIES TO PREVENT GENDER VIOLENCE

Education plays a pivotal role in preventing GBV by fostering a culture of respect, equality, and understanding. One of the key aspects of education is the promotion of awareness and sensitivity towards gender issues. By integrating gender equality into educational curricula, students are exposed to diverse perspectives and learn to challenge stereotypes and biases. This helps break down traditional gender norms and expectations, reducing the likelihood of perpetuating harmful attitudes that contribute to violence

(Rosa, Drew & Canavan, 2020). Moreover, education empowers individuals with the knowledge and skills to recognize and address GBV. Students equipped with a comprehensive understanding of consent, healthy relationships, and the impact of power dynamics are better positioned to navigate situations that may lead to violence. Education also plays a crucial role in dismantling ingrained cultural and societal norms that perpetuate GBV, fostering a more inclusive and equitable society (Le & Nguyen, 2020).

Beyond individual empowerment, education can catalyze systemic change. When educational institutions actively promote gender equality, they contribute to the creation of a society that rejects violence against any gender. Teachers, as influencers and role models, play a crucial role in shaping attitudes and behaviors. By promoting respectful communication and empathy in the classroom, educators can inspire the next generation to value equality and reject violence.

In the case of Higher Education, preventing GBV requires a multi-faceted approach that addresses both individual and systemic factors. One strategy is the implementation of comprehensive educational programs that focus on consent, healthy relationships, and bystander intervention (Bondestam & Lundqvist, 2020). These programs can empower students with the knowledge and skills to recognize and prevent instances of gender-based violence, fostering a campus culture that prioritizes respect and consent.

Another crucial strategy is the establishment of clear and enforceable policies against GBV within academic institutions. This includes implementing effective reporting mechanisms, conducting thorough investigations, and ensuring that survivors are supported throughout the process. Creating a safe and confidential reporting environment encourages survivors to come forward, while holding perpetrators accountable contributes to a safer campus environment. Institutional commitment to gender equality is paramount. Higher education institutions can actively work towards creating inclusive and equitable spaces by promoting diversity in leadership, faculty, and curriculum (Laursen & Austin, 2020). By addressing gender disparities and biases, institutions can contribute to changing the broader societal attitudes that perpetuate gender-based violence.

Engaging in community partnerships and collaborations is also essential. Higher education institutions can collaborate with local organizations, advocacy groups, and law enforcement to create a network of support and resources for survivors. This collaborative approach strengthens the response to gender-based violence and provides a more comprehensive support system for those affected. An example could be

Furthermore, fostering a culture of awareness and accountability through ongoing training for faculty, staff, and students is crucial. This could include seminars or dialogic talks involving the whole education community. Actually, dialogic talks are characterized by open and participatory communication, so they serve as a powerful tool in promoting women's empowerment in universities (Merrill, 2005). These interactive discussions create a platform for individuals to express their thoughts, share experiences, and engage in meaningful conversations about gender equality and women's empowerment. In addition, dialogic talks can effectively foster inclusive spaces where diverse voices and perspectives are valued and by encouraging open dialogue, universities can ensure that the experiences and concerns of women, including those from marginalized backgrounds, are heard and acknowledged. This inclusivity helps in addressing the intersectionality of gender with other identities. Dialogic talks offer higher education institutions a dynamic and inclusive approach to promoting women's empowerment by cultivating an environment where women feel supported, valued, and empowered to excel in their academic and professional pursuits.

Lastly, photographic narration, a strategy that combines visual storytelling and narrative, can be a compelling means to promote gender equity and raise awareness about gender issues in contemporary society. In recent years, scholars and activists have increasingly recognized the power of visual narratives in shaping perceptions. Utilizing photography and narration in tandem allows for a nuanced exploration of gender dynamics, shedding light on the multifaceted aspects of gender equity (Simmonds, Roux & Avest, 2015). Moreover, the impact of visual communication in challenging gender stereotypes seems to have a deep effect (Liebenberg, 2018), so photovoice can be seen as a dynamic tool to deconstruct ingrained gender norms by visually presenting diverse narratives that showcase the richness of gender identities and roles.

METHODOLOGY

Study Design

Case study research is the design used for this investigation. The case study in education research is extremely useful in order to understand context, communities and individuals since its main distinctive feature is its interest in a particular case (Hamilton & Corbett-Whittier, 2012). Therefore, we believe it the most appropriate method so as to know in depth students' perceptions about gender violence, its relevance and the strategies they consider to be suitable for its prevention.

This research has been developed throughout four well differentiated phases explained in the following table (Table 1).

Context and Participants

This study has been developed at the University of Córdoba (Spain), in the Faculty of Education Sciences and Psychology. In particular, participants belong to the subject of Diversity, Coexistence and Inclusive Education within the Early Childhood Education Degree. 63 students took part of this study (4%men and 66% women).

Table 1. Phases of the research

PHASE	ACTIVITIES
1. Preparatory phase	- Scientific literature review - Research problem definition (objectives and research questions)
2. Study design	- Design the instruments - Participants selection
3. Field work	- Data gathering
4. Data analysis	- Project creation (ATLAS.ti v. 23) - Data analysis
5. Study report	- Writing the chapter

Dialogic Talks and Photographic Narration

This subject includes in its syllabus the curricular contents organized into three blocks: 1) Coexistence in a world of transformation; 2) Citizenship Education, human rights and ethics of care; 3) Diversity and equal opportunities. Each block is made up of two topics:

1. Conditioning factors of coexistence in a global world.
2. Inclusive model as educational positioning.
3. Citizenship, participation and democracy.
4. The ethics of care as an exercise of citizenship.
5. Multiculturalism and interculturality in school.
6. Coeducation and equality at school.

This research was carried out at the end of topic 4. One of the strategies we use in the subject is the dialogic talks for the reason that they allow students to dialogue, redefine and give meaning to the text, relating it to their personal experiences and the context where they live. It is based on the idea that each individual reflection and production of meaning is enriched and expanded through interaction with others. Thus, after finishing the dialogic talk about the ethics of care (Camps, 2021), the questionnaire was given to the students.

Instruments

One questionnaire was used in order to gather the information for answering the research objectives. It was design *ad-hoc* based on previous studies on the same topic (e.g. Taylor et al., 2021). The questions were organized in two different blocks. On the one hand, it deals with questions related to students' perceptions about gender violence, its importance and the strategies to prevent it from higher education. These questions were: What do you understand about gender violence?; How important is this social problem for you?; What do you think could be done to prevent it?; How could higher education work in order to prevent it?; What strategies do you think could be used in higher education to prevent it?

On the other hand, students were asked to take a picture and use it as a metaphor connecting it with the text used in the dialogic talk and gender violence. Moreover, they algo have to argue about it.

Therefore, using different types of questions has allowed us to triangulate (figure 1) the data and provide greater rigor to the study.

Analysis Procedure

The analysis procedure was organized in three different stages. Firstly, primary documents and data were prepared and organized for analysis. Secondly, the coding process (Strauss & Corbin, 2016) was carried out with the use of the software. Two types of coding strategies were used: a) Open coding: the analytical process by which codes are identified as concepts and their properties and dimensions are discovered in the data (590 codes were identified); b) Axial coding: process of relating categories to their subcategories, called "axial" because coding occurs around the axis of a category, and links the categories in terms of their properties and dimensions.

Figure 1. Data triangulation

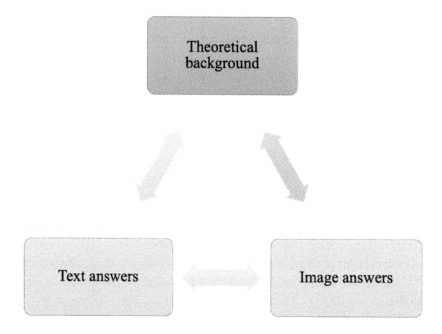

RESULTS

The results are presented according to the objectives of the study. On the one hand, we deal into the students' perceptions about the concept of gender violence and its importance. On the other hand, we focus on the strategies they believe could help to prevent this violence from the educational field.

1. Concept

University students who take part in the study refer to the concept of gender violence from varied perspectives and positionings.

Gender violence is important because it can affect your life, your freedom, your dignity, your physical, psychological or sexual integrity, your safety, etc. Gender violence is a structural problem that predominantly affects women and girls. It is a serious violation of human rights. It is important to address the issue openly and measure its importance to understand it and propose actions that lead to healthy and constructive coexistence among all people in society. (Case 30)

When university students of the Early Childhood Education Degree are asked about the concept of gender, their answers are always linked to sex (man/woman) or sexual orientation. And in a minimal number of cases, sexual identity is referred to, such as the following quote: "Gender violence is understood when a person suffers discrimination, aggression or intimidation for some reason due to their sexual condition, sexual identity or sexual orientation." (Case 21).

There is a majority link that relates gender violence towards women, both adults and adolescents and girls, "To remedy this, the first thing is to educate the new generations to have adequate relationships so that at no time do situations of aggression or rape towards women, educating them in respect" (case 13) "Physical or verbal aggression that is generally done to women by their partners or ex-partners, it also occurs when some type of discrimination, harassment or degradation occurs due to their gender, simply for being a woman." (Case 56). The LGTBI community is also referred to, but a lower frequency of appointments also refers to the male sex:

I understand gender violence as the physical or verbal aggression of the male gender against a woman or a person from the LGTBI community. This aggression would be different if it were an aggression towards the male gender since it would not receive this name. (Case 44)

It is true that the victims are usually women, although this does not mean anything that men are not affected. (Case 61)

Violence exerted by a woman towards a man, or a man towards a woman, is considered gender violence. (Case 18)

Therefore, there are contrary positions in relation to its conceptualization, and although there is a majority that considers the female sex as the object of violence, exercised by men, there is a lower incidence of responses that are defined in the opposite direction. Then, this is relevant when planning educational actions to address it.

Furthermore, a central idea is the previous relationship or connection in some way between victim and aggressor. As one student indicates:

Gender violence is defined as some type of discrimination or aggression based on gender identity or sexual orientation. It normally occurs towards women regardless of their age or living condition by people normally linked to them by an emotional relationship. (Case 8)

This is relevant because in GBV prevention strategies this element can be crucial in establishing "healthy" relationships, fleeing from other types of harmful relationships or what are called "toxic relationships."

What is mostly consistent is a conception linked to a "position of inequality" in which the dignity of the person is affected:

It is the psychological, physical and sexual damage affecting the female sex and that threatens her dignity, integrity and freedom. It deals with an inequality in which the male sex is above the female sex. (case 42)

A situation of inequality that is always linked to the female sex:

Gender-based violence is violent acts that target a person based on their gender or that disproportionately affect people of a specific gender. This violence can be physical, sexual, psychological or economic. Although gender violence can affect anyone, regardless of their sex, women and girls are the main victims due to unequal power structures and traditional gender norms. (Case 39)

In these cases, the idea of a structural inequality seems to coincide with the positioning although it is not manifested in a generalized way but rather the fact of being a structural problem is not frequently referred to:

Gender violence is important because it can affect your life, your freedom, your dignity, your physical, psychological or sexual integrity, your safety, etc. Gender violence is a structural problem that predominantly affects women and girls. It is a serious violation of human rights. It is important to address the issue openly and measure its importance to understand it and propose actions that lead to healthy and constructive coexistence among all people in society. (Case 21)

Gender violence is understood as any violent act or aggression, based on a situation of inequality in a system of relations of domination of men over women that has or may result in physical, sexual or psychological harm, including threats." and coercion or deprivation of liberty, whether they occur in the public sphere or in family or personal life. It has its origin in gender inequality, the abuse of power and the existence of harmful norms. (Case 30)

Even, in some cases, critical positions and very defined positions are evident; these cases are the use of the concept of patriarchy and machismo in today's society, explained as the origin of inequality that gives rise to the situation of power and gender violence.:

Gender violence is a reality that women experience every day, existing because of patriarchy and great machismo. It is a reality that this is physical, verbal and psychological violence directed towards a woman by a man. There are many people who in the 21st century still do not understand that this exists and that it causes suffering and can end the lives of many women. Only those of us who have suffered this know what it truly is; Only we know that it accompanies you every day. We must make the new generations understand the importance of communication and respect so that this ends and patriarchy disappears so that women can live freely and without feeling objectified for the simple fact of being a woman. (Case 52)

Gender violence has been and continues to be one of the clearest manifestations of inequality, subordination and the power relations of men over women. This type of violence is based on and is carried out by the subjective difference between the sexes. In short, women suffer violence for the mere fact of being women, and the victims are women of any social stratum, educational, cultural or economic level. Gender violence is that which is exercised against women by those who are or have been linked to them through emotional relationships (partners or ex-partners). The aggressor's objective is to cause harm and gain control over the woman, which is why it occurs continuously over time and systematically in form, as part of the same strategy. (Case 12)

On the other hand, it is identified with aggression in its diversity of typologies: verbal, physical, psychological or sexual:

I understand gender violence when some type of discrimination or aggression occurs, whether due to your gender identity, your gender expression and even your sexual orientation. I also understand violence when it is physical and a person attacks another, whether by pushing, breaking, mutilating, etc. It also exists psychologically or emotionally through actions that offend or humiliate a person and attack that person's self-esteem. (Case 29).

In addition, the duration of the violence is referred to, considering that it usually occurs continuously over time:

Gender violence is that which is exerted on women by those who are or have been linked to them by relationships of affectivity (couples or ex-partners). The objective of the aggressor is to cause harm and gain control over the woman, which is why it occurs continuously over time and systematically in the form, as part of the same strategy. (Case 57)

Gender violence is a type of physical, psychological, sexual and institutional violence, exercised against any person or group of people on the basis of their sexual orientation, gender identity, sex or gender. That is to say, it is a harm that is done to women either by exes or partners. It occurs when they suffer some type of discrimination, sexual or physical assault. Gender violence has different manifestations, such as acts that cause suffering or harm, threats, coercion or other deprivation of freedoms. (Case 28)

On other occasions, the terms used to define gender violence by university students, the vast majority of whom are adolescents, are the terms "abuse" and "harassment."

In the first case, the concept of abuse refers to ideas such as the one expressed by one of the students:

I understand by gender violence, any abuse that is exerted (psychological or physical) on the other gender, which causes insecurity, fear, even a trauma for the person for life. Physical violence would be just the iceberg of all the acts that inhibit the other person, leaving them without trust and under your control. (Case 1)

On the other hand, it is linked to different areas of action: both the public sphere and the more private waiting area:

Gender violence is understood as any violent act or aggression, based on a situation of inequality in a system of relations of domination of men over women that has or may result in physical, sexual or psychological harm, including threats." and coercion or deprivation of liberty, whether they occur in the public sphere or in family or personal life. (Case 30)

These acts are manifested in all areas of social and political life, including the family itself, the State, education, the media, religions, the world of work, sexuality, social organizations., coexistence in public spaces or culture. (Case 43)

All in all, students describe the concept of GBV connected with diverse types of violence (figure 2), even as a synonym of maltreatment. Moreover, although to a lesser extent, students refer to domestic violence or violence towards men.

Figure 2. Concept of gender violence

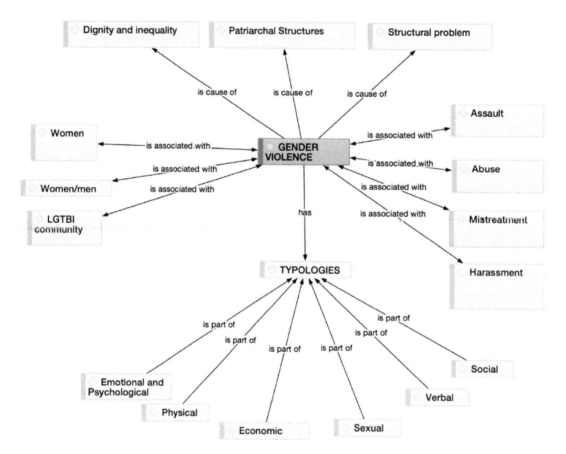

2. Strategies

Students have a wide range of ideas about the strategies (figure 2) that may be used in higher education so as to prevent GBV.

As indicated in the previous section, the approach must be holistic, transversal and from multiple perspectives: legislative changes, training of practicing teachers in the different educational stages; sensitization and awareness with the aim of creating a culture that allows living in gender.

To do this, as premises the consideration is contemplated to be an issue linked to Rights and, specifically, Women's Rights and its approach must be from childhood.

These strategies could be classified as follows:

- Legislative: creation of policies and protocols to support victims. For example, measures linked to the prevention and early detection of signs of gender violence and help to victims:

In order to prevent gender violence, it would be necessary to monitor the people who carry it out, since many times the victims report it and in the end nothing happens against the person who reported it, because there is no tests or something, so a follow-up should be done to be able to verify that that person is committing gender violence and not wait for the victim to end in the worst possible way. (Case 24).

First, victims must be listened to, and offered a safe space in which they can speak with confidence and feel heard, free of prejudice and blame. Another way to prevent violence would be education, that is, questioning the traditional characteristics assigned to men and women, pointing out the stereotypes they constantly face and letting boys and girls know that there is nothing wrong with being different. You should also recognize the signs of violence, identify them and help the victim get out of that situation, without hoping that the person who perpetrates the violence will "change. (Case 58)

The idea of the need to strengthen legislation is also stressed. In this sense, a student quotes: "implement and enforce effective laws that protect victims and punish aggressors." (Case 39). Another student explains it in the same direction as harsher penalties:

In my opinion, gender violence is an issue of great importance since it is ending the lives of women every day, and no matter how many talks are given on this topic, activities in schools, institutes... in order to avoid it, It is a reality to comment on how it continues to happen and how normalized we have it. I think that greater penalties should be imposed for those guilty of these undesirable acts and thus be able to ensure that this devastating situation that torments us almost daily ends once and for all. (Case 36)

- Educational: education is a large-scale issue that involves all areas of society and not only school and formal training. Therefore, the need to address this problem holistically from home as well is indicated. Here it links with an ethic of care and co-responsibility:

Some time ago, at school, mothers must be the main example for boys and girls; They should be the main models that demonstrate what is right and what is not in reference to this very important issue. To do this, boys and girls must be involved in household chores, without distinguishing between men and women to carry out a certain action. We should never excuse or ignore sexist comments, jokes, sarcasm, anecdotes or jokes, since this is the main avenue for future abuse and violence, both verbal and physical. It is very important to get involved with families through the AMPA of the schools in order to claim the importance of gender violence. (Case 19)

Thus, teacher training and implementation of programs for students, and in parents' associations and families. From early childhood and in all educational stages and not only the approach from a specific subject but also in a transversal way:

Violence in education is a fundamental issue that must be developed within the classrooms, from childhood I would say. In education, it is not enough to just talk about violence, but to implement that detention or avoidance. It can be carried out by holding workshops, and above all by getting in touch with people who have suffered this problem on themselves or close family members, to be able to know well the causes, the consequences, what it causes in themselves... all this and work In a cooperative manner, violence greatly favors avoidance or detention. (Case 38)

To prevent this problem, awareness can be raised from a young age, with stories or activities that are attractive to them and through which they learn. Also carrying out campaigns and programs, with real cases that tell their experiences and thus raise awareness and empathize with the situations they have experienced. (Case 13)

Some students also refer to the importance of considering early childhood as a tool for the detection and prevention of gender violence:

Teach respect for people from a very young age. Teach them what people's rights are, educate them with values and that this overprotection can be harmful in some cases. Education is a key tool to eradicate gender violence. We can use resources to work on these situations, for example in books for teenagers about gender violence, we see how different forms of violence against women are reported: physical, psychological, social, family abuse... This is how they bring them closer to this reality. as spectators and provide tools so that they know how to detect and combat it and live relationships based on equality and respect. (Case 28)

Then, students also refer to different strategies that could be applied within Higher Education contexts. Not only do they allude to general aspects such as create safe spaces of dialogue, promote respect and empathy, design and implement research projects and eliminate sexist stereotypes "A series of programs could be applied to reduce sexism, reduce bullying among peers and improve relationships". But they also make mention of specific strategies:

- Mentoring programs. Some students devote quite importance to this strategy. For instance: "Tutoring programs aimed at strengthening relationships between the school, parents and adolescents and children, to prevent risk behaviors and teach how to resolve conflicts." (Case 49)
- Photo-narration. In the context of GBV, photo-narration can make visible and give voice to the experiences of the affected people, raise awareness about the problem and generate empathy in those who view it. Images can powerfully convey the consequences of violence and show the importance of building relationships based on respect and equality. Furthermore, through photo-storytelling, values of equality and diversity can be promoted, gender stereotypes challenged, and critical reflection on the social and cultural norms that perpetuate violence. Photo-narration has the potential to generate empathy in those who observe it, by visually and emotionally showing the consequences and suffering caused by gender violence. Through these shocking images, people can be sensitized and made aware of the importance of preventing and eradicating this problem. Furthermore, photo-storytelling can help break the silence and stigma surrounding gender violence, giving a voice to victims and generating a space for reflection and debate in university classrooms.

This tool can be very effective in addressing sensitive topics such as gender violence in university classrooms. It could be used through awareness and education sessions, photography and storytelling in which students can take photographs that represent situations related to gender violence. In addition, I could hold reflection and awareness sessions in which students could give their different points of view on gender violence and reflect them through photography. (Case 17)

With this tool, in universities, it can be used so that male and female students know differences and discriminate in which photos of violent or sexist acts appear, no matter how minimal they may be. This can be used in different cases, such as: - Workshops and photography projects. - Research projects. - Exhibitions. - Classroom discussions. - Creation of awareness campaigns. - Creation of educational resources. - Interdisciplinary work. (Case 30)

It is important that, when using photo-storytelling, university students must know how to foster a safe and respectful environment to discuss sensitive topics such as gender violence; Ethics and privacy regulations must be respected when working with images and testimonies of affected people.

They believe, photo-narration also promote non-verbal communication that is extremely useful in vulnerable situations:

Dialogic Talks and Photographic Narration

Photovoice can be a useful tool for gender violence, information can be extracted from each of the images, what it transmits to the person and to the rest. You can study and analyze the images, in order to think about what you want to transmit and communicate to others. Images are a type of non-verbal communication, which often say more than words, which is why it is a very useful tool for preventing different types of violence. Using images you can transmit and experience many emotions that these attacked people have suffered. (Case 43)

And to awaken critical consciousness:

Photo-narration can be used in university classrooms as a tool to address gender violence. Students can create visual stories using photographs, reflecting on gender stereotypes, power relations, and the consequences of violence. This encourages critical awareness and dialogue on the topic. (Case 37)

Moreover, it may be effective to reinforce emotional knowledge, know the group, promote group cohesion and increase awareness:

The potential that I consider that photo-narration has in the prevention of gender violence is to see how people feel and to know more or less the "backpack" that each person carries, since we always see, so to speak. the "facade" that is, a minimal part of what that person is. With this activity that we have practiced in class I have minimally understood what fulfills my classmates, what brings them happiness, what absences hurt them; So to speak, I have known that each person is much more than what we can simply observe. (Case 61)

Photovoice can prevent gender violence because if X people are given a narrative of photos in which they are victims of gender violence and in which the changes that can occur can be observed to have, we can raise awareness among different people so that they can understand how it is not a good thing and they should fight to end this type of violence. In addition, it can also have an impact if someone has a victim of gender violence in their environment and can see photos from before they suffered it, so they will understand much better. (Case 24)

In short, for the prevention of gender violence, the creation of a culture free of stereotypes that coexists in real equality between genders is a priority. To this end, work in higher education around the creation of critical awareness is essential to move towards social change.

Higher education plays a crucial role in the prevention of gender violence, influencing the training of future leaders, professionals and citizens. Since those of us who are training in higher education are going to be the future of society, it is in our power to change it and eradicate the problems found in it. Higher education has an important role in training future generations and can contribute greatly to the prevention of gender violence by promoting a culture of gender equality, respect and non-violence in its academic community. (Case 31)

- **Sensitization and awareness.** Both from and to family environments, educational and socio-educational institutions, and society in general. A social conscience is advocated where all people are aware of the situation and its relevance and, to this end, the role of non-profit associations and NGOs that contribute to this task is emphasized:

Meetings, workshops and conferences could be held to inform us more about the problem and raise awareness among people who do not know the real importance of this type of violence. In addition, donations could be made to associations related to victims of gender violence to offer our help. (Case 17)

Moreover, they highlight that gender violence prevention strategies are important from early childhood:

Talk about consent, physical autonomy and accountability to girls and boys from a young age and also listen to what they have to say about their experience in the world, so in this way we can prevent multiple problems from a young age. (Case 28)

Similarly, there is also evidence of certain fatigue with the current situation of gender violence, which leads to two positions being expressed: on the one hand, one more optimistic towards its eradication and on the other hand, we find positions related to a feeling of not achieving real equality and a drastic reduction of gender violence in the short term:

"Gender violence continues to be a reality that we have to face daily. Although there are many social norms in our society, together we can promote and carry out activities that little by little help us achieve gender equality and eradicate gender violence." (Case 58)

I think that there is no 100% effective prevention against violence, although we should raise more awareness in society, from different points of view. On the one hand, we should carry out more dynamic campaigns, so that they attract people to raise awareness about gender violence and link both men and women to these dynamics. On the other hand, I consider that the consequences with which the perpetrators of violent acts are punished are not harsh enough, therefore, they do not take their actions seriously, without giving them importance. (Case 50)

The need for a holistic multiple approach with continuity over time is highlighted too:

To address this issue, it is important that educational institutions take active steps to create a safe and respectful environment for all students; it requires a holistic approach and continued commitment from the entire educational community. (Case 31)

CONCLUSION

To conclude, it is important to point out that students do have their positioning regarding the concept of GBV and their own perceptions about which strategies could be useful so as to prevent it from the educational field, specifically, from higher education institutions. Overall, the study highlights the complexity of the perception of gender violence among university students and emphasizes the need for a holistic approach that combines education, awareness and creating effective supportive environments.

The study reveals that there is a significant level of awareness among university students about the existence of GBV. Most recognize the seriousness of the problem and its impact on society. Despite this general awareness, there is a gap in perception of the magnitude and severity of GBV. Some students may minimize certain behaviours or fail to recognize some cases, highlighting the need for deeper understanding and lifelong education.

As indicated, a holistic and interdisciplinary approach is key. Introducing diverse strategies both general and specific ones could help its prevention. We consider the approach in class to pedagogical and theoretical texts about and from the perspective of city ethics and, in addition, working with didactic strategies around dialogue, of interest for raising awareness. In this sense, the approaches expressed by the education students have been aligned with an institutional approach, from all the institutions of society, from education in all its educational and non-formal and informal stages and from social associations.

In summary, gender violence refers to the non-consensual mistreatment of a person with the sole purpose of causing harm. It can manifest itself in many forms, including physical, economic, psychological and sexual violence. It is a serious social problem that interrupts the development of a country and has a negative impact on the health and well-being of the affected people. To prevent this violence,

Figure 3. GBV prevention strategies

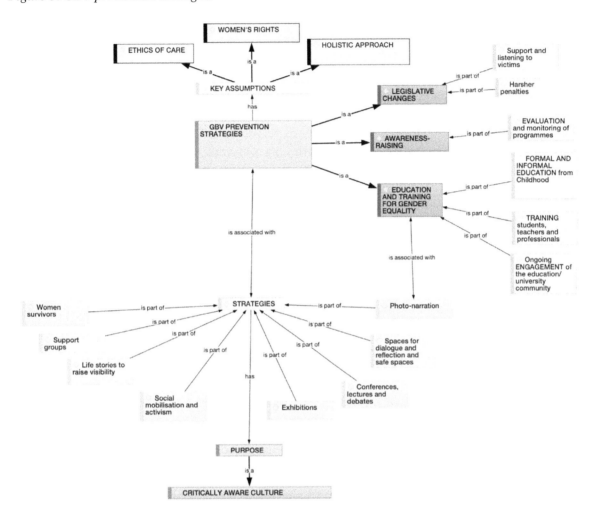

it is important to educate ourselves, reflect on gender equality, eliminate prejudices and stereotypes, promote respect and non-discrimination, organize educational campaigns and information conferences, provide support to victims and report cases of abuse.

In the field of higher education, talks and educational campaigns can be held to raise awareness about gender violence and promote gender equality in university classrooms. Furthermore, photo-narration can be an effective tool to work on gender violence, since it allows us to tell stories and visualize other people's experiences through images and descriptions. It can also be useful to learn about cases of gender violence and promote empathy and consciousness in the university community. In addition, dialogic talks and photo-narration have proven to be powerful tools in higher education for preventing gender-based violence. Engaging students in open and constructive dialogues allows them to explore diverse perspectives and challenge preconceived notions about gender roles and relationships. These discussions foster a deeper understanding of the complexities surrounding gender-based violence, encouraging empathy and critical thinking.

Future lines of research on strategies to prevent gender-based violence in university settings may focus on a multi-dimensional approach that integrates prevention, intervention, and support systems. Moreover, investigations could delve into the effectiveness of diverse educational programs and teaching strategies that promote awareness, consent, and bystander intervention, targeting both students and faculty. Additionally, understanding the intersectionality of gender-based violence with factors like race, sexual orientation, and socio-economic status is essential for crafting inclusive and effective strategies that address the diverse needs of the university community.

In summary, education serves as a powerful tool in the prevention of GBV. It not only equips individuals with the knowledge to challenge harmful norms but also cultivates a societal mindset that fosters respect, empathy, and equality, ultimately contributing to the eradication of GBV.

REFERENCES

Alexander, R. (2020). *A dialogic teaching companion*. Routledge. doi:10.4324/9781351040143

Barriuso-Ortega, S., Heras-Sevilla, D., & Fernández-Hawrylak, M. (2022). Análisis de programas de educación sexual para adolescentes en España y otros países / Analysis of sex-education programs for teenagers in Spain and other countries. *Educare (San José), 26*(2), 329–349. doi:10.15359/ree.26-2.18

Baym, N. K. (2006). The Emergence of On-line Community. In S. Jones (Ed.), *Cybersociety: communication and community* (pp. 35–68). Sage.

Bondestam, F., & Lundqvist, M. (2020). Sexual harassment in higher education–a systematic review. *European Journal of Higher Education, 10*(4), 397–419. doi:10.1080/21568235.2020.1729833

Butler, J. (2017). *Cuerpos aliados y lucha política: hacia una teoría performativa de la asamblea / Allied bodies and political struggle: towards a performative theory of the assembly*. Paidós.

Butler, J. (2020). *Sin miedo. Formas de resistencia a la violencia de hoy / Without fear. Forms of resistance towards today's violence*. Taurus.

Camps, V. (2021). *Tiempo de cuidados: otra forma de estar en el mundo / Care time: another way of being in the world*. Arpa.

Cano Abadía, M. (2021). *Judith Butler. Performatividad y vulnerabilidad / Judith Butler. Performativity and vulnerability*. Shackleton.

Criado Pérez, C. (2020). *La mujer invisible. Descubre cómo los datos configuran un mundo hecho por y para los hombres / The invisible woman. Discover how data shapes a world made by and for men*. Editorial Seix Barral.

Foradada, M., & López, S. (2023). El relato autobiográfico como método docente feminista / The autobiographical story as a feminist teaching method. *Educar, 59*(1), 83–97. doi:10.5565/rev/educar.1581

Franks, M. A. (2022). Speaking of Women: Feminism and Free Speech. *Feminist Frictins: Key Concepts and Controversies*. Signs. http://signsjournal.org/franks/

García-Cano, M., Buenestado-Fernández, M., Hinojosa-Pareja, E. F., & Jiménez-Millán, A. (2022). Innovación docente para la igualdad y para la diversidad en las políticas universitarias de España / Teaching innovation for equality and diversity in university policies in Spain. *Aula Abierta, 51*(1), 75–84. doi:10.17811/rifie.51.1.2022.75-84

García-Cano, M., & Hinojosa-Pareja, E. F. (2016). Coeducación en la formación inicial del profesorado: de la transversalidad a la vivencia a través de la ética del cuidado / Coeducation in initial teacher training: from transversality to experience through the ethics of care. Multiárea. *Revista de didáctica, 8,* 61-86. doi:10.18239/mard.v0i8.1122

García-Cano, M., Hinojosa-Pareja, E. F., Buenestado-Fernández, M., & Jiménez-Millán, A. (2023). A statutory requirement: Teaching innovation for gender equality at university. *Women's Studies International Forum, 96,* 102673. doi:10.1016/j.wsif.2022.102673

Garzón Fernández, A. (2016). La educación sexual, una asignatura pendiente en España / Sexual education, a pending subject in Spain. *Biografía, 9*(16), 195–203. doi:10.17227/20271034.vol.9num.16biografia195.203

Hamilton, L., & Corbett-Whittier, C. (2012). Using case study in education research. *Sage (Atlanta, Ga.).*

Hankivsky, O. (2020). Women's Health, Men's Health, and Gender and Health: Implications of Intersectionality. *Social Science & Medicine, 258,* 113136. PMID:22361090

Hequembourg, A. L., Livingston, J. A., & Wang, W. (2020). Prospective associations among relationship abuse, sexual harassment and bullying in a community sample of sexual minority and exclusively heterosexual youth. *Journal of Adolescence, 83*(1), 52–61. doi:10.1016/j.adolescence.2020.06.010 PMID:32736276

Kiekens, W. J., Baams, L., Fish, J. N., & Watson, R. J. (2022). Associations of relationship experiences, dating violence, sexual harassment, and assault with alcohol use among sexual and gender minority adolescents. *Journal of Interpersonal Violence, 37*(17-18), NP15176–NP15204. doi:10.1177/08862605211001469 PMID:33719695

Laursen, S., & Austin, A. E. (2020). *Building gender equity in the academy: Institutional strategies for change.* Johns Hopkins University Press. doi:10.1353/book.78724

Le, K., & Nguyen, M. (2020). How education empowers women in developing countries. *The B.E. Journal of Economic Analysis & Policy, 21*(2), 511–536. doi:10.1515/bejeap-2020-0046

Liebenberg, L. (2018). Thinking critically about photovoice: Achieving empowerment and social change. *International Journal of Qualitative Methods, 17*(1), 1609406918757631. doi:10.1177/1609406918757631

Merrill, B. (2005). Dialogical feminism: Other women and the challenge of adult education. *International Journal of Lifelong Education, 24*(1), 41–52. doi:10.1080/026037042000317338

Muluneh, M. D., Stulz, V., Francis, L., & Agho, K. (2020). Gender based violence against women in sub-Saharan Africa: A systematic review and meta-analysis of cross-sectional studies. *International Journal of Environmental Research and Public Health, 17*(3), 903. doi:10.3390/ijerph17030903 PMID:32024080

Rosa, R., Drew, E., & Canavan, S. (2020). An overview of gender inequality in EU universities. *The Gender-Sensitive University*, 1-15.

Sánchez Sáinz, M. (2019). *Pedagogías Queer. ¿Nos arriesgamos a hacer otra educación? / Queer Pedagogies. Do we risk doing other education?* Catarata.

Schneider, M., & Hirsch, J. S. (2020). Comprehensive sexuality education as a primary prevention strategy for sexual violence perpetration. *Trauma, Violence & Abuse, 21*(3), 439–455. doi:10.1177/1524838018772855 PMID:29720047

Simmonds, S., Roux, C., & Avest, I. T. (2015). Blurring the boundaries between photovoice and narrative inquiry: A narrative-photovoice methodology for gender-based research. *International Journal of Qualitative Methods, 14*(3), 33–49. doi:10.1177/160940691501400303

Strauss, A., & Corbin, J. (2016). *Bases de la investigación cualitativa: técnicas y procedimientos para desarrollar la teoría fundamentada / Bases of qualitative research: techniques and procedures to develop grounded theory*. Universidad de Antioquia.

Taylor, S., Calkins, C. A., Xia, Y., & Dalla, R. L. (2021). Adolescent perceptions of dating violence: A qualitative study. *Journal of Interpersonal Violence, 36*(1-2), 448–468. doi:10.1177/0886260517726969 PMID:29294897

ADDITIONAL READING

Alp Yilmaz, F., & Şener Taplak, A. (2021). Relationship between self-esteem, perception of gender and attitudes towards dating violence among university students. *Perspectives in Psychiatric Care, 57*(2), 911–919. doi:10.1111/ppc.12634 PMID:33047315

Graham, L. M., Embry, V., Young, B. R., Macy, R. J., Moracco, K. E., Reyes, H. L. M., & Martin, S. L. (2021). Evaluations of prevention programs for sexual, dating, and intimate partner violence for boys and men: A systematic review. *Trauma, Violence & Abuse, 22*(3), 439–465. doi:10.1177/1524838019851158 PMID:31262233

Moletsane, R. (2023). Using photovoice to enhance young women's participation in addressing gender-based violence in higher education. *Comparative Education, 59*(2), 239–258. doi:10.1080/03050068.2022.2146394

Prados Garacía, C. (Coord.) (2023). Adolescencia, redes sociales y violencia de género digital / Adolescence, social networks and digital gender violence. *Tirant humanidades*.

Ranea Triviño, B. (2021). *Desarmar la masculinidad / Disarming masculinity*. Catarata.

Ruiz-Eugenio, L., Puigvert, L., Ríos, O., & Cisneros, R. M. (2020). Communicative daily life stories: Raising awareness about the link between desire and violence. *Qualitative Inquiry, 26*(8-9), 1003–1009. doi:10.1177/1077800420938880

Schneider, M., & Hirsch, J. S. (2020). Comprehensive sexuality education as a primary prevention strategy for sexual violence perpetration. *Trauma, Violence & Abuse, 21*(3), 439–455. doi:10.1177/1524838018772855 PMID:29720047

Sosa, V., & Imhoff, D. (2023). Socialización política de género en la infancia. *Psicología Política, 23*(56), 98–114.

Zwiers, J., & Crawford, M. (2023). *Academic conversations: Classroom talk that fosters critical thinking and content understandings*. Routledge. doi:10.4324/9781032680514

KEY TERMS AND DEFINITIONS

Abuse: It involves the improper or unfair use of power or resources, in this case, in the context of personal relationships, especially in the sexual area. It may include behaviors that cause physical, emotional, or psychological harm.

Assault: It has to do with an act of violence or hostile behavior directed toward another person. In the sexual context, sexual assault includes any non-consensual act of a sexual nature that causes harm or discomfort to the victim.

Dialogic Talk: Is a form of communication or conversation characterized by open and interactive exchanges between participants. In dialogic talk, individuals engage in a mutual and dynamic exchange of ideas, opinions, and information.

Gender Based Violence: It refers to any harmful act that is perpetrated against an individual's will and is based on socially ascribed gender differences between males and females.

Harassment: It means unwanted, repetitive behaviors that create a hostile or intimidating environment for the victim. In the sexual sphere, sexual harassment refers to unwanted conduct of a sexual nature that violates the boundaries of consent and may occur in work, educational or social settings.

New Masculinities: It refers to men who are committed to relationships between equals, rejecting inequalities and being aware of the privileges that being a man implies in the society in which we live. They want to break with the culture of inequality and be allies against all forms of violence against women.

Photovoice: Is a participatory research methodology that combines photography and community engagement to empower individuals to express their perspectives on a particular issue or topic.

Chapter 6
Empowering Education Against Gender Violence:
Practical Tools and Insights for Teaching Comprehensive Sex Education in Mexico

Rosa Elena Durán González
Universidad Autónoma del Estado de Hidalgo, Mexico

Berenice Alfaro-Ponce
Tecnologico de Monterrey, Mexico

ABSTRACT

This chapter critically examines the shortcomings of sex education in Mexican schools, tracing its historical evolution in the context of governmental and global health policies. Initially, sex education in Mexico was predominantly biological; however, it has since expanded in response to societal changes. The chapter underscores the importance of a comprehensive educational approach that not only provides minors with knowledge, but also equips them with self-esteem, respect for others, and tools for self-protection. It explores the debate over who should bear the responsibility for educating children on these matters—parents, teachers, or both through a collaborative approach. Furthermore, the chapter offers practical guidelines and activities for educators, aiming to prepare children for a safer, more informed future. It advocates for an educational methodology that is contemporary, engaging, and free from dogmas and social prejudices.

INTRODUCTION

In this chapter, we will delve into the key aspects on incorporating sex education to preschool and elementary school education programs, explaining each topic in a clear and structured manner. We will begin by discussing who should take responsibility for this crucial education: is it the parents, the teachers, or should it be a collaborative effort? Then, we will explore challenges present in the modern era and how different groups may sort and navigate them, albeit with a focus on a classroom environment. At last,

DOI: 10.4018/979-8-3693-2053-2.ch006

we will also provide some fundamental concepts necessary for teachers. Our goal with this chapter is to provide a practical and straightforward analysis that will empower educators in addressing these critical challenges, thereby preparing children for a safer, healthier, and better-informed future.

BACKGROUND

Sex education programs in schools across Mexico have fallen short of effectively addressing the social problems associated with sexuality. This shortfall can be attributed to the relatively recent introduction of these initiatives. According to Chandra-Mouli et al. (2018), sex education in Mexico has undergone significant evolution, adapting in response to societal changes within the country. However, despite these efforts, there remains a need for further improvement to comprehensively address the complex issues surrounding sexuality in educational settings.

The first consideration for including such content in school curricula was made by the Ministry of Public Education in 1932. However, due to societal resistance, it was not until 1974 that topics related to sexuality were incorporated into the Natural Sciences curriculum for 6th grade in primary schools and into Biology for all three grades of secondary school. These topics covered adolescent development, physical and mood changes, anatomical differences between boys and girls, primary and secondary sexual characteristics, the reproductive systems of women and men, the menstrual cycle, fertilization, and embryonic development (Heredia Espinosa & Rodríguez Barraza, 2021). The content was taught primarily from a biological perspective.

Secondly, the intention behind incorporating sexual content in schools was influenced by two main factors. One was the government's population policy aimed at reducing birth rates. The other was the global context of the 1960s, a period marked by significant developments in human sexuality research and changing social attitudes. This era witnessed groundbreaking studies like those of Kinsey in 1948 and (Masters & Johnson, 2012) in the 1960s, which played a pivotal role in the sexual revolution. Influences such as the contraceptive pill were notable outcomes of this research. Although the Mexican government seemed to admire and accept the sexual openness of 'first world' countries, particularly the United States, domestically, it maintained a conservative approach.

For decades, this conservative stance, supported by government policies, societal norms, and religious authorities, limited the scope of sexual education in Mexico, keeping the population largely uninformed about these issues. In the case of Mexico, there is a separation of church and state guaranteed by the constitution. However, the institution with the most influence in the public schooling system is the catholic church, which in 2020 increased its following up to 78% of the population, according to INEGI data (INEGI, 2020).

Today, limiting access to information is challenging due to its easy availability on the Internet. While this has its advantages, the disadvantages often overshadow them. The pervasive use of computers and smartphones means minors are exposed around the clock to an overwhelming amount of online information. Much of this information presents sexuality and the human body in distorted ways, as numerous sites have pornographic objectives, are driven by profit motives, or engage in extortion and mental manipulation. Both minors and unsuspecting adults who visit these sites can become victims of individuals or criminal groups (Stoilova et al., 2021).

MAIN FOCUS OF THE CHAPTER

Issues, Controversies, Problems

Such prohibitions and taboos have their origin in Catholicism teachings, which have been reinforced by groups influential in education. The stance of the catholic church on this topic has been summarized in the document "Familiaris consortio", emitted in 1981 by Ioannis Pauli PP. II; in which it says sexual education is a fundamental right and responsibility for the parents, therefore it can only be carried out on their direction, be it at home or at school, thus they are unable to impose a sex education program which the parents may oppose and have no control over. At home, the parents should watch their language to respect the "natural modesty" of their children to prevent their words from inciting them to sin, on the contrary, children should appreciate human sexuality and chastity as gifts to be cared for and developed. Besides taking away authority from public schools, it does not provide parents with the necessary elements to educate their children in the topic, limiting the sexuality practice to marriage (Castañeda, 1996).

On the other hand, several non-profit organizations and Parent-Teacher Associations are linked to catholic hierarchy, political parties, state or nation-wide authorities to censor and stop sexual education programs, instead encouraging conservative texts. Citing an example, the Unión Nacional de Padres de Familia (Nation-wide Parents Association) supported the text 'The cult of sexuality' (Kramsky, 1993) in which on top of declaring itself against contraceptive methods, claims masturbation can cause severe physical and psychological harm to the point of madness (Szasz, 1998).

Some education authorities are also united against an integral sexual education. In August 2008, the government of Distrito Federal published the book 'Your future in freedom: On responsible sexual and reproductive health' which according to Marcelo Ebrard, governor at the time, had updated information with medical and scientific backup, in an open and direct way, free of taboos and fanatism, as well as free of lies and half-truths (Garduño, 2018).

Masters and Johnson (1983), highlighted in the 1960s that "children have been taught by adults to view the human body as indecent and that being naked is something to be avoided at all costs" (p. 298). It's important to understand that various sexual practices, including intercourse and its variants, are not inherently bad as long as they involve consenting adults and are aimed at mutual pleasure. This does not mean that young people cannot engage in such practices, but they should do so voluntarily and with full awareness. However, the types of images circulating on the web are often not of this nature. There are numerous websites whose purpose is the commercial exploitation of sex, protected under the guise of 'freedom of expression' and a lack of international regulation in this field. These sites often disregard the potential harm they may cause.

Distorted images of sexuality are ubiquitous, not just on the internet, but also in television programs during family viewing times, movies, magazines, video games, and more. These representations are part of multimillion-dollar industries and are unlikely to disappear, even if we choose to ignore them (Zachari et al., 2018). This prevalence underscores the necessity of education in schools. It's crucial to provide minors with scientific knowledge that is free from dogmas and social prejudices, current, engaging, age-appropriate, and tailored to their knowledge needs. Equally important is equipping them with tools for self-esteem, self-respect, respect for others, and self-protection. This approach is key to leading a healthy and fulfilling life in all its aspects, including the prevention of sexual violence (Schneider & Hirsch, 2020).

SOLUTIONS AND RECOMMENDATIONS

Who Is Responsible for the Sexual Education of the New Generations?

This issue became a point of contention during the Cárdenas government's proposal to integrate sex education into school curricula. Numerous parents' organizations resisted, deeming it inappropriate for schools to address such topics. Their success meant that these subjects remained confined to the home until the 1970s, when the government took the initiative to include them in education. However, this debate resurfaces with each proposed educational reform concerning sex education.

Education by Parents

In many families, discussions about sexuality have become a sensitive issue. Some parents feel it's their responsibility to address it, while others, out of ignorance or fear, prefer schools to handle it. Some delegate this task to religious institutions. However, a common approach is avoidance: many parents sidestep the issue, believing that 'life is the best school' and leaving their children to figure things out on their own. This often leads to crucial topics being overlooked at home, with parents failing to openly address their children's questions about (Pick de Weiss et al., 1993). This lack of dialogue often stems from adults' own ignorance; they, too, were once left to navigate life independently. These tensions are reflected in communication statistics, where between 40% and 97% of teenagers wish their parents would share more information about sexuality, while 58% to 64% of parents express a desire to discuss sexuality before their children finish elementary education (Ramírez et al., 2006).

Rarely do parents take the time to explain to their children about the sexual functions of their bodies, menstruation, intercourse, pregnancy, abortion, masturbation, among others. For Orcasita et al. (2018) family communication has proven insufficient when relative to sexuality topics, more than 50% of the younger population considered limited the information available as well as the needed trust to talk about sexuality topics. The consequences of this are evident: the number of pregnant adolescents in Mexico, which has the highest rate of such cases (UNAM, 2021). These young women often face harsh consequences, such as being disowned by their parents for 'failing them,' becoming single mothers at a young age, or, in worse cases, being forced into marriage. Others become part of the statistics on deaths from clandestine abortions, either due to fear of talking to their parents or because of their unwillingness to take responsibility for a child. As for young men, a lack of proper information about taking care of their bodies can lead to issues like premature ejaculation, erectile dysfunction, and other sexual dysfunctions. Both men and women, without adequate information to protect themselves, are at risk of contracting venereal diseases, AIDS, suffering from neurosis, or even contemplating suicide.

The results of a sexuality study ran with parents or adults in charge of public middle school students from downtown Monterrey, Nuevo León, revealed that only a minority (14%) considered they should be the ones in charge of teaching sex education to their children, which already means a certain openness for third-party institutions to become involved with the sexual education of their children. Although most of the interviewed (96.2%) consider sexual education crucial for their children, half or less of them have spoken with them on topics such as sexual content on television (50.2%), sexual content on internet (32.6%), sexually transmitted diseases (46.8%), AIDS (54.7%), and condom usage (37%). More than 75% of the parents thought that talking about condom usage with their kids would influence them to hold sexual relationships. The reasons they had for not talking about these matters were the following:

lack of awareness or efficiency (33.3%) shame or embarrassment (28.9%), inappropriate age (10.4%), or their child was of the opposite sex (5.9%) (Ramírez et al., 2006).

Education by Teachers

In the 80's, with the appearance of AIDS in the world, the health education program was incorporated in all grades from a physiological and anatomical perspective (Reis & Seidl, 1989); sexuality was approached from a medical perspective, since the objective was to warn about diseases and negative consequences of the exercise of sexuality (such as AIDS or unwanted pregnancies). The following decade, the Ministry of Public Education initiated a process of reforms that are still ongoing; encouraging a focus on values, people's wellbeing, or as at present, emphasizing the culture of prevention, respect for human rights and inclusion (Pick et al., 2003). From a theoretical and pedagogical point of view, the contents to be taught by teachers may be fine, however, this is hardly put into practice because most of them, despite their good will, teachers lack sufficient information to develop the topics in order to provide students with the tools to develop their autonomy and to take care of their bodies and exercise their sexuality in a respectful and responsible way. Other times, their moral stance or religious restrictions prevent them from addressing these issues, mentioning them lightly or overlooking them.

A qualitative study with three Elementary school teachers from Mexico City revealed they lacked proper training in sexual education, teaching students a reproductive approach without an integral perspective. These deficiencies tracked back to the lack of an integral sexual education during their professional training, while only one of them had taken sexuality classes by their own volition, (Álvarez, 2019).

The best evidence that school programs have not yielded the expected results are the statistics. In the State of Hidalgo "seven out of every 10 pregnancies of young women of school age occurred among women between 15 and 29 years old, but one out of every six was between 15 and 19 years old. Between 2011 and 2013, the population between 12 and 19 years old was interviewed about sexual practices; 20% of women have already started an active sexual life; 33% of them do not use protection methods against pregnancy and 51.9% have become pregnant; 10.7% were pregnant during the interview. In the case of men, 25.5% between 12 and 19 years old, have already had sexual intercourse; 14.7 did not use any contraceptive method" (Escamilla & Guzmán, 2017). In addition to pregnancies, clandestine abortions, unwanted children with interruption of life plans, etc., this generates an increase in sexually transmitted infections (STIs), which is of concern and should occupy social policies.

Preventing these issues is best achieved through comprehensive sex education. When young people decide to be sexually active, they will do so with or without parental consent. The goal of sex education is not to encourage or discourage sexual activity but to provide adequate, effective, and scientific information. This enables young people to be aware, informed, and protected, helping them avoid life-altering consequences (Goldfarb & Lieberman, 2021). The earlier they start learning about these topics, the more aware they will become, leading to better decisions in their youth and as adults.

Therefore, educating students is a collective responsibility that involves parents, teachers, and society. Teachers, well-informed and supported by the community, are often the primary point of contact for schoolchildren. Their pedagogical training allows them to blend scientific knowledge with didactic methodologies, presenting the information in a formal yet engaging manner appropriate for each age group. Teachers are known for their innovation, dynamic approaches, and ability to seek support from peers or specialists. Their daily interaction with students also fosters trust, making them role models.

For sex education to be effective and relevant, teachers need to consider several preliminary aspects, as highlighted in recent research. Iyer and Aggleton (2013) note the impact of teachers' beliefs and attitudes on young people's sexual and reproductive health. Ollis (2016) emphasizes the importance of adequate teacher preparation for handling sexuality issues in the classroom. Kehily (2002) explores how educators' personal sexual history and professional experience influence their teaching approach. Breuner et. al. (2016) stress the need for evidence-based, developmentally appropriate sex education, with guidance from pediatricians, schools, and experts to help young people make safe and informed decisions. Maia and Vilaça (2017) examine teachers' perceptions of students' sexuality, advocating for continuous training. Goldman and Collier-Harris (2017) provide valuable resources for designing effective educational programs.

Consequently, it is advisable for teachers to hold preliminary meetings to unify criteria and avoid confusion when discussing topics with parents and students. These meetings can determine how topics should be adapted according to educational level, region, and customs. While the core content remains the same, methodology and pedagogical considerations will vary by age group. It is also beneficial for teachers to integrate sexuality topics across different subjects like mathematics, Spanish, history, or geography. This approach allows for discussions on figures, problems, historical facts, or cultural aspects of sexuality locally and globally, following active school methodologies.

FUTURE RESEARCH DIRECTIONS

Preliminary Considerations for Teachers Who Will Be Teaching Sex Education

To achieve comprehensive sexual education, UNESCO (2018) suggests involving community settings in non-formal educational programs to raise awareness among parents, caregivers, and community leaders. In formal educational settings like schools, (Pérez, 2021) advocate for social pedagogy as foundational, considering social, cultural, political, civic, and religious contexts. This holistic approach to sexual education considers methodological and theoretical factors across preventive, corrective, and optimizing levels. It includes a social-educational diagnosis of individuals and an examination of environmental realities to inform methodological decisions through dialogue. Due to its strong social components, the following themes are to be considered:

- Initial Assessment: Before beginning the program, evaluate the age group, socioeconomic background, religion, customs, and traditions of the participants.
- Diagnosis: Pose a series of questions to determine the students' existing knowledge and their areas of greatest interest. Assess what topics are suitable to teach based on their age.
- Preparation of the Topic: Allocate appropriate time for each session, considering the school grade. Use of audiovisual materials, case studies, and occasionally inviting a health professional (who could be a parent) may be beneficial.
- Development of the Topic: Avoid lengthy, monotonous lectures to maintain student engagement. If a teacher is asked a question they do not know the answer to, they should admit their ongoing learning process in the field of sexuality and commit to researching the answer. Pretending to know or inventing an answer is not advisable.

- Language: Use appropriate and inclusive language when teaching. Harmonize the terminology used to describe various topics, as body parts might be named differently across cultures. Even young children should be encouraged to use correct terminology, such as penis, vagina, testicles, breasts, and buttocks.
- Encourage Collective Work: Engage parents, administrative staff, and school directors by informing them about the topics being covered, so they can reinforce these lessons at home and in subsequent grades. The sex education program is a multi-year process, not a one-time lecture; thus, any pending topics will eventually be addressed as students progress through school.
- Engaging Community Leaders: In cases where there is resistance among the community, sensitizing community leaders to the benefits of comprehensive sex education for schoolchildren can help. Here, the teacher or workshop leader also serves as a mediator, prepared to address conflicts that may arise.

Critical social-educative actions are above all participation oriented, reflective and dialogical, hence its joint proposition with students, parents and directors. It is contextualized to the attention of historical, cultural, economic, and political situations in actions that promote awareness, inclusion, and a humanized, inclusive, democratic and ethical approach (Pérez, 2021).

Sexuality: Basic Concepts

In the field of sexology have emerged several concepts hard to understand and retain in memory, new scientific discoveries and a sexual movement carried out by socially repressed or excluded groups, have given voice, presence, essence and human value to people who every day take on their new gender identities and fight for legal recognition and against discrimination and intolerance; being a delicate topic, the challenge in transmitting it to our students, children and adolescents will be related to trying to remain neutral and provide only educational information, especially in the spheres of traditionalist families; it is likely some students will feel identified (recent national and international studies (Australia) report interesting findings regarding the age at which children are aware of their gender identity from early childhood, between 3 and 7 years old), (INEGI, 2021), (Marino et al., 2023), or will simply feel inquisitive and befitting to know more, as knowledge advances, discrimination towards diversity will gradually become understanding and social inclusion, it is from education where changes and social shifting are generated.

Before being teachers, we are human beings ourselves, and we may or may not agree with current concepts. However, I believe it is necessary to convey scientifically demonstrable information from all perspectives and to remain neutral when explaining to students the reasons behind the different positions on current sexual diversity and gender ideology. This is to provide the reasons and approaches from various viewpoints, giving students the opportunity to broaden their research and develop their own criteria. It is essential for them to learn to listen, be tolerant, and respect all human beings as equals, while also expecting respect for themselves.

These topics could be handled more deeply from 5th grade or in middle school, but if asked before such grades, they are not to be evaded and should explained in the simplest way possible, until the students' concerns are satisfied, especially in the aspect of respect and tolerance for diversity. Also in the United States a similar management method is used, according to the National Sex Education Standard, which provides guidelines, tools and suggestions to gradually educate children in comprehensive sexual education, according to age and level of education (Future of Sex Education Initiative, 2020). We will start with definitions of the most common vocabulary, although they are still pending and yet to appear. I will also use some of Concepción Garriga's definitions and the National Sex Education standards itself (Future of Sex Education Initiative, 2020).

Gender: A role, identity and self-expression culturally related to the sex assigned at a person's birth, coded as male or female, based on the sexual and reproductive anatomy of their body. Gender is a social construct; therefore, it is possible to reject or modify the socially assigned one and develop it until a person can feel true to themselves (Future of Sex Education Initiative, 2020).

Gender Ideology: A social movement born from feminism, which fights for recognition of equal rights and opportunities for women in the face of traditional anthropocentrism, against gender violence, as well as the legal right to abortion when women request it. Later the HLGBITTTQ+ movement would join due to similar ideals. The differentiation between sex and gender would allow people to live recognizing themselves with the gender they identify with regardless of the sex with which they were born or were coded at birth, (UNESCO, 2018).

Gender ideology first emerged as an expression in the Catholic Church; In 1997, the Belgian Monsignor Schooyans wrote the book L'Évangile face au désordre mundo (The gospel in the face of world disorder), which may probably be the first known time where it is mentioned in a complaint against gender ideology (Mena-López & Ramírez Aristizábal, 2018).

Currently, gender is considered a social and not a natural construct; attitudes learned under the cultural parameters of a society at a given time; yet within feminism, there are sectors which only accept women born with a uterus and/or vagina in their movement and reject other genders.

The conservative point of view alleges the origin of gender ideology to be of conceptually leftist political intentions to break into public policies, with roots in radical feminism and gender diversity, claims it an attempt to change the concept of the biologically sexed human nature in two genders, man and woman, according to genetic codes. For gender ideology, each person should choose the gender to which they want to belong, as well reject the acknowledgement of their assigned gender at birth, favoring the one they identify themselves with, but according to the chromosomes, a man is a man and a woman is a woman (Laje Arrigoni, 2019), hate oriented violence both verbally and physically has also been increasing.

On the other hand, those who defend gender ideology reject all discrimination and violence against people's sexual diversity, seeking equal rights regardless of their sexual orientation or identity, citing the scientific evidence in the field of Social Psychology, Sociology or Neurobiology which continues to reaffirm that trans women are women not because they want to, but because that is how they identify and feel (Bambú, 2019). They are supported by neurosciences and they argue social norms and laws have been made for the conservation of an anthropocentric state which is afraid of losing the power preserve it has always maintained. Currently they are supported and recognized by International Organizations, making progress in the recognition of their rights.

It is not a matter easy to tackle, needing more study and dialogue. Violence against ciswomen, transwomen, homosexuals and others by men has always been evident, a global movement came to remove the foundations of our society and will have a determining and profound impact in our concepts and future relationships.

Woman: In several countries, considered to be "all people who feel like women and present and represent themselves as such, whatever they biologically are. They can be 46 XY (Chromosomally Male) with androgen insensitivity, or H to M trans people in any phase of transition. The term biowoman or ciswoman refers to a sex-gender coincidence", meaning, women born biologically, women who feel like women (Garriga i Setó, 2015).

Man: all people who feel like men and present and represent themselves as such, whatever they are biologically. Bioman or cisman is also a sex-gender coincidence, (he is a man who was born biologically a man and feels like a man) (Garriga i Setó, 2015).

Transgender: Biowoman who wishes to live as a man without changing her sex, or a bioman who wishes to live as a woman without surgical interventions" (Garriga i Setó, 2015). Person whose gender identity and/or expression does not correspond to their sex assigned at birth. This term is generally used to encompass various identities related to gender non-conformity (Future of Sex Education Initiative, 2020). They self-identify as men or women, but this gender does not correspond to the one assigned to them at birth based on the physical characteristics of their sexual organs (UNAM, 2019).

Transsexual: They seek to change or have changed medically-through hormonal therapies or surgery- their sexual characteristics to become feminized or masculinized, (UNAM, 2019).

Transvestite (Crossdresser): Behavioral expression of sexuality conceptualized as a preference for using clothing, mannerisms, accessories, or language attributed to the opposite gender (Álvarez, 2011). In other words, a person who wears clothing and adopts attitudes of the opposite sex for various reasons, regardless of their sexual and gender identity.

Biological or chromosomal sex: Biological characteristics that define humans as male or female. Although these sets of biological characteristics are not mutually exclusive, as there are individuals who possess characteristics of both sets, they tend to differentiate humans as male or female (UNESCO, 2018), XY chromosomes define physically male individuals, and XX chromosomes define physically female individuals.

Gender identity: "Gender identity" is the way each person considers themselves as a man, woman, or another gender based on their way of being, thinking, feeling, and acting, which may or may not correspond with their birth sex (INEGI, 2021).

Sexual orientation: The capacity of a person to feel attracted, romantically or sexually, to women, men, individuals of both sexes, or others, or to not feel attracted (INEGI, 2021).

Gender expression: The way people manifest their gender externally, such as through clothing, appearance, or mannerisms in their behavior (Future of Sex Education Initiative, 2020)

CONCLUSION

Sex education is an essential tool equipping children to navigate the complexities of the modern world, and Mexico being rooted in historical complexities and cultural nuances, demands a multifaceted approach for meaningful progress. The ongoing debate over the primary purveyor of sex education – whether it be parents, teachers, or a collaborative effort between the two – underscores the gravity of the subject matter. However, beyond this discourse lies a shared responsibility that transcends individual roles, calling for a unified effort involving families, educators, and broader societal structures.

The proposed strategies offer a pragmatic blueprint for educators to integrate essential sexual education components into their pedagogical practices. By recognizing and accommodating diverse family backgrounds and community contexts, these strategies aim to mitigate the pervasive effects of historical shame and misinformation surrounding sexuality. Moreover, they emphasize the critical role of educators as facilitators of knowledge, guiding children through age-appropriate discussions and activities that foster informed decision-making and bodily autonomy.

Looking ahead, the imperative lies in refining didactic approaches to early sex education, ensuring that concepts are conveyed with sensitivity, accuracy, and cultural relevance. Such an approach not only empowers children to navigate the complexities of their burgeoning identities but also cultivates a culture of respect, consent, and inclusivity within educational settings and beyond.

Ultimately, the provision of comprehensive sex education is not merely a matter of individual rights but a collective endeavor aimed at safeguarding the well-being and dignity of future generations. By embracing this shared responsibility and fostering an environment of open dialogue and mutual support, we can pave the way for a safer, healthier, and more informed society.

REFERENCES

Álvarez, E. (2019). *¿Qué saben los maestros de primaria sobre educación sexual? Procesos de formación docente en torno a la educación sexual y la sexualidad: Estudio de casos.* Área Temática 08. Procesos de Formación, COMIE. 1–10. https://www.comie.org.mx/congreso/memoriaelectronica/v15/doc/0661.pdf

Álvarez, J. L., & Jurgenson, G. (2011). Travestismo, transexualidad y transgénero. *Revista De Estudios De Antropología Sexual, 1*(3), 55–67. https://revistas.inah.gob.mx/index.php/antropologiasexual/article/view/573

Bambú, T. (2019, March 27). El feminismo radical, un gran incomprendido. *Pikara Magazine.* https://www.pikaramagazine.com/2019/03/feminismo-radical-incomprendido/

Breuner, C. C., Mattson, G., Breuner, C. C., Adelman, W. P., Alderman, E. M., Garofalo, R., Marcell, A. V., Powers, M. E., Mph, M., Upadhya, K. K., Yogman, M. W., Bauer, N. S., Gambon, T. B., Lavin, A., Lemmon, K. M., Mattson, G., Rafferty, J. R., & Wissow, L. S. (2016). Sexuality Education for Children and Adolescents. *Pediatrics, 138*(2), e20161348. doi:10.1542/peds.2016-1348 PMID:27432844

Castañeda, A. J. (n.d.). La enseñanza de la iglesia católica sobre la educación sexual según familiaris consortio, 37. *Aciprensa* https://www.aciprensa.com/Familia/edusex1.htm

Chandra-Mouli, V., Gómez, L., Plesons, M., Lang, I., & Corona, E. (2018). Evolution and Resistance to Sexuality Education in Mexico. *Global Health, Science and Practice, 6*(1), 137–149. doi:10.9745/GHSP-D-17-00284 PMID:29602869

Collier-Harris, C. A., & Goldman, J. D. G. (2017). What educational contexts should teachers consider for their puberty education programmes? *Educational Review, 69*(1), 118–133. doi:10.1080/00131911.2016.1183592

Escamilla Gutiérrez, M., & Guzmán Saldaña, R. (2017). Educación Sexual en México ¿Misión de la casa o de la escuela? *Educación y Salud Boletín Científico de Ciencias de La Salud Universidad Autónoma Del Estado De Hidalgo, 5*(10). Advance online publication. doi:10.29057/icsa.v5i10.2478

Future of Sex Education. (2020). *National Sex Education Standars, Core content and skills, K-12*. The Future of Sex Education.

Garduño, G. V. (2018). Educación Sexual: una polémica persistente. *Instituto Nacional para la Evaluación de la Educación, 11*. https://www.inee.edu.mx/educacion-sexual-una-polemica-persistente/

Garriga i Setó, C. (2015). Una revisión crítica de los conocimientos actuales sobre la sexualidad y el género (II). *Aperturas Psicoanalíticas: Revista Internacional de psicoanálisis, 51*. https://aperturas.org/articulo.php?articulo=0000918&a=Una-revision-critica-de-los-conocimientos-actuales-sobre-la-sexualidad-y-el-genero-II

Goldfarb, E. S., & Lieberman, L. D. (2021). Three Decades of Research: The Case for Comprehensive Sex Education. *The Journal of Adolescent Health: official publication of the Society for adolescent. Medicine, 68*(1), 13–27. doi:10.1016/j.jadohealth.2020.07.036 PMID:33468103

Heredia Espinosa, A. L., & Rodríguez Barraza, A. (2021). Antecedentes de la educación sexual en México a un siglo de su creación: eugenesia y moral. *Elementos 121*, 45–51. https://elementos.buap.mx/directus/storage/uploads/00000005801.pdf

INEGI. (2021). *INEGI- Censos de población y vivienda 2010-2020*. INEGI. https://cuentame.inegi.org.mx/monografias/informacion/mex/poblacion/diversidad.aspx?tema=me&e=15#:~:text=78%20%25%20de%20la%20poblaci%C3%B3n%20es%20cat%C3%B3lica

INEGI. (2021). *Encuesta Nacional sobre Diversidad Sexual y de Género*. INEGI.

Ioannis, PP. II. (1981). *Familiaris Consortio*. Libreria Editrice Vaticana.

Iyer, P., & Aggleton, P. (2012). *Sex education should be taught, fine...but we make sure they control themselves': teachers' beliefs and attitudes towards young people's sexual and reproductive health in a Ugandan secondary school*. University of Sussex. https://hdl.handle.net/10779/uos.23419181.v1

Kehily, M. J. (2002). Sexing the Subject: Teachers, pedagogies and sex education. *Sex Education, 2*(3), 215–231. doi:10.1080/1468181022000025785

Laje, A. (2019, december 2). *¿De dónde viene la ideología de género?* [Video]. Youtube. https://www.youtube.com/watch?v=dAaUhVTYfo0

Maia, A. C. B., & Vilaça, T. (2017). Concepções de professores sobre a sexualidade de alunos e a sua formação em educação inclusiva. *Revista Educação Especial, 30*(59), 669. doi:10.5902/1984686X28087

Marino, J. L., Lin, A., Davies, C., Kang, M., Bista, S., & Skinner, S. R. (2023). Childhood and Adolescence Gender Role Nonconformity and Gender and Sexuality Diversity in Young Adulthood. *JAMA Pediatrics, 177*(11), 1176. doi:10.1001/jamapediatrics.2023.3873 PMID:37747725

Masters, W. H., & Johnson, V. E. (2012). *El vínculo del placer*. Colección Relaciones Humanas Y Sexología, 1. GRIJALBO.

Masters, W. H., Levin, R. J., & Johnson, V. E. (1983). *El vínculo del placer: un nuevo enfoque del compromiso sexual*. Grijalbo.

Mena-López, M., & Ramírez Aristizábal, F. M. (2018). Las falacias discursivas en torno a la ideología de género. *Ex Aequo - Revista Da Associação Portuguesa de Estudos Sobre as Mulheres*, 37. doi:10.22355/exaequo.2018.37.02

Ollis, D. (2016). 'I felt like I was watching porn': The reality of preparing pre-service teachers to teach about sexual pleasure. *Sex Education*, *16*(3), 308–323. doi:10.1080/14681811.2015.1075382

Orcasita, L. T., Cuenca, J., Montenegro, J. L., Garrido, D., & Haderlein, A. (2018). Diálogos y Saberes sobre Sexualidad de Padres con Hijos e Hijas Adolescentes Escolarizados. *Revista Colombiana de Psicología*, *27*(1), 41–53. doi:10.15446/rcp.v27n1.62148

Pérez, V. M.-O. (2021). Pedagogía social y educación social. *Revista Educação Em Questão*, *59*(59). Advance online publication. doi:10.21680/1981-1802.2021v59n59ID24018

Pick, S., Givaudan, M., & Poortinga, Y. H. (2003). Sexuality and life skills education: A multistrategy intervention in Mexico. *The American Psychologist*, *58*(3), 230–234. doi:10.1037/0003-066X.58.3.230 PMID:12772430

Pick De Weiss, S., Diaz R., Andrade Palos, P., & Gribble, J.N. (1993). Teenage sexual and contraceptive behavior: the case of Mexico. *Advances in Population: psychosocial perspectives*, 1:229-49.

Ramírez Aranda, J. M. González. González. J. M., Cavazos. Ríos. J. J., & Ríos. Garza. T. (2006). Actitudes de los padres sobre sexualidad en sus hijos, valores y medidas preventivas de SIDA. *RESPYN, Revista Salud Pública y Nutrición*, *7*(1). https://respyn.uanl.mx/index.php/respyn/article/view/159

Reis, J., & Seidl, A. (1989). School Administrators, Parents, and Sex Education: A Resolvable Paradox?. *Adolescence*, *24*(95)-639–645.

Schneider, M., & Hirsch, J. S. (2020). Comprehensive Sexuality Education as a Primary Prevention Strategy for Sexual Violence Perpetration. *Trauma, Violence & Abuse*, *21*(3), 439–455. doi:10.1177/1524838018772855 PMID:29720047

Stoilova, M., Livingstone, S., & Khazbak, R. (2021, february). *Investigating Risks and Opportunities for Children in a Digital World: A rapid review of the evidence on children's internet use and outcomes.* UNICEF, 1–82.

Szasz, I., & Lerner, S. (1998). *Sexualidades en México: algunas aproximaciones desde la perspectiva de las ciencias sociales*. El Colegio de México. doi:10.2307/j.ctvhn0bgv

UNAM. (2019, July 26). *La UNAM te explica: Transexualidad.* Fundación UNAM. https://www.fundacionunam.org.mx/unam-al-dia/la-unam-te-explica-transexualidad/

UNAM. (2021, September 3). Mexico, first place in teenage pregnancies among OECD countries. *Boletín UNAM*. UNAM. https://www.dgcs. unam.mx/boletin/bdboletin/2021_729.html

UNESCO. (2018). *Orientaciones técnicas internacionales sobre educación en sexualidad Un enfoque basado en la evidencia*. UNESCO. https://unesdoc.unesco.org/ark:/48223/pf0000265335

UNESCO. (2018). *El rol del sector de educación en la EIS*. UNESCO. https://csetoolkit.unesco.org/es/toolkit/el-caso/el-rol-del-sector-de-educacion-en-la-eis

Zachari, A., Sabri Nawar, Y., & Javaherizadeh, E. (2018). The impact of sexuality in advertisements on consumers purchase behaviour: A social media perspective. *The Business and Management Review*, *9*(4), 1–18.

ADDITIONAL READING

Arevalo, E. A. M. (2023). The challenge of educating men: How to change attitudes and behaviors to prevent gender-based violence. *Sinergias Educativas*, *8*(4). doi:10.37954/se.v8i4.426

Elboj-Saso, C., Iñiguez-Berrozpe, T., & Valero-Errazu, D. (2022). Relations with the educational community and transformative beliefs against gender-based violence as preventive factors of sexual violence in secondary education. *Journal of Interpersonal Violence*, *37*(1-2), 578–601. doi:10.1177/0886260520913642 PMID:32253970

Parkes, J. (2015). *Gender-based violence in education*. UNESCO.

Roza, V., & Martín, C. (2021). *Sexual and Gender-based Violence: Road Map for Prevention and Response in Latin America and the Caribbean*. Inter-American Development Bank. doi:10.18235/0003819

Tsapalas, D., Parker, M., Ferrer, L., & Bernales, M. (2021). Gender-based violence, perspectives in Latin America and the Caribbean. *Hispanic Health Care International; the Official Journal of the National Association of Hispanic Nurses*, *19*(1), 23–37. doi:10.1177/1540415320924768 PMID:32515230

Vanner, C. (2021). Education about gender-based violence: Opportunities and obstacles in the Ontario secondary school curriculum. *Gender and Education*, *34*(2), 134–150. doi:10.1080/09540253.2021.1884193

Villardón-Gallego, L., García-Cid, A., Estévez, A., & García-Carrión, R. (2023). Early Educational Interventions to Prevent Gender-Based Violence: A Systematic Review. *Health Care*, *11*(1), 142. doi:10.3390/healthcare11010142 PMID:36611602

KEY TERMS AND DEFINITIONS

Asexual: People who feel no desire or attraction to anyone.

Bisexual: People who are attracted to both males and females for intimate and sexual relationships.

Comprehensive Sex Education: An educational approach that covers all aspects of sexuality for informed decision-making. It is an effective means of preventing sexual and gender-based violence, unintended pregnancy at all ages, especially among adolescents, and sexual health to prevent sexually transmitted diseases.

Gender Perspective: Includes analysis of the social environment in terms of gender differences and how these differences affect the experiences of individuals and groups. In the context of sex education, it addresses how gender influences sexuality.

Homosexual: People born male who are attracted to other men for sexual relations.

Intersex: A condition in which an individual exhibits varying degrees of sexual characteristics of both sexes.

Lesbian: People born female who are attracted to other women for sexual relations.

Nonbinary: People who, regardless of their biological sex at birth (male or female), do not identify with either gender; they embody both masculine and feminine simultaneously. They ask to be addressed with inclusive language, for example, instead of "compañero" or "compañera," they prefer "compañere".

Pansexual: A person who can have sexual relations with anyone, regardless of biological sex, gender, or sexual orientation.

Queer: Includes all sexual diversity, LGBTTTIAQ and non-binary. One can belong to any group, but being queer is elective; there are those who do not define themselves as queer. Cisgender people do not fall under this classification.

Chapter 7
Girl–Child Formal Education:
A Strategy in Mitigating Male-Based Supremacy Syndrome in the Traditional IGBO Society

Bruno Onyinye Umunakwe
https://orcid.org/0000-0002-7187-8238
University of Nigeria, Nsukka, Nigeria

ABSTRACT

In this chapter, the study presents the socio-cultural backdrop of traditional Igbo society, aiming to investigate the status of the girl-child and the crucial role of formal education in dismantling deeply entrenched societal structures that perpetuated male dominance. Employing a historical analysis, the study draws information from a variety of sources, including journals, books, articles, periodicals, and the internet. The major emphasis in this chapter was the enrolment of girl-child in formal schooling system which actively involves writing and reading. Education becomes a fundamental right that has restored an equitable society by curbing gender marginalization and discrimination. The study recommends that the government and relevant stakeholders should ensure accessible education through the elimination of environmental barriers to quality education.

INTRODUCTION

Formal education/schooling remains a verified instrument in mitigating socio-cultural prejudices. Karram (2023) sustains that formal education simultaneously address problem of gender inequality on multiple levels - economic, social, political, health and cultural. Further, Lakhotiya (2023) sustains that, formal education plays crucial roles in advancing gender equality by empowering individuals, challenging stereotypes, fostering inclusive environments, and advocating for equal opportunities. By this, formal education creates avenue where everybody (including the girl-child) has equal legal access to basic necessities of life. Though scholars established that all educational systems including formal education are significant for societal transformations, but to determine each of their related

DOI: 10.4018/979-8-3693-2053-2.ch007

proportions remain uncertain because driving home a comprehensive definition of education will always leave the researcher to contrasting views. One of the recognized techniques to address this conceptual issue was given by Chazan (2022). It suggests that the meaning of education could be approached considering three perspectives: first descriptive, which involves explaining the nature and meaning of the term using various words to clarify either the essence of the phenomenon or how the term should be interpreted. Second programmatic, that advocates or prescribes a specific belief about what education ought to be or achieve. This dimension considers less the intrinsic nature or language of education but more focused on promoting a particular educational practice deemed desirable. Third. stipulative definitions which serve a utilitarian purpose, functioning as linguistic agreements or pacts that facilitate smooth discussions without requiring constant reiteration of the definition. Though Chazan (2022)'s suggestion is relevant, it is limited in giving feasible techniques that can facilitate the regular articulation of this concept.

Based on the search for the meaning of education, scientists and researchers have deployed a widely accepted method. This engages linguistic derivation search through a well-known approach called 'etymology'. While this method is considered relevant in grasping educational concepts, the frequency tends to be misleading due to the potential ambiguity arising from its application, as it may not always yield a clear and specific definition. Education, from the linguistic origin could be traced back to its Latin roots, encompassing various terms such as 'educare', signifying the process of nurturing and upbringing; 'educere,' indicating the act of drawing out or revealing; 'educo,' suggesting leading out of; and 'educatum,' representing the act of teaching or instruction. The mixt interpretations offered through these linguistic roots highlight the challenge of establishing a cohesive definition of education. As a point of departure, the linguistic trace 'educare' – 'to lead out' assumed to have captured the perspectives of experts, form the base in comprehending the meaning of education in this study. This seems paramount since the goal is to guide searching minds through the misery of curiosity (Arslan, 2018). In addition, the dependency on derivative root is to offer original interpretation rather than relying on a mere scholastic definition.

Being 'to lead out', formal schooling fit well in this dimension because it sustains a well-structured and organized processes in acquiring knowledge, skills, attitudes, and values during the instructional process. This brings to limelight the school setting when discussing formal education (Öz & Kayalar (2021). This includes the development of the child's latent faculties through structured curriculum by the processes of reading and writing under schooling system. Though the central focus of this chapter is on the impacts of girl-child education in eliminating male base supremacy in the Igbo traditional society, the study has furnished students with the creative skills, ideas, beliefs and expressions that every gender is an agent of social development. This begins with brief descriptions of study purpose, research questions, methodology, literature review, theoretical framework and discussions. This description is not intended to be a complete course in historical development on gender inequality but will raise awareness of the issues involved in male-based syndrome and the impacts of formal education which is also inclusive.

STATEMENT OF THE PROBLEM

The idea of 'girl-child' as appears throughout this study pertains specifically to the baby-girl, the young daughter of the family, the wife, the mother and the many roles that the woman assumes in the course of her life. Universal Declaration of Human Rights (UDHR), established on December 10, 1948, at Palais de Chaillot in Paris, France, by the UN General Assembly in reaction to the heinous acts that deeply disturbed humanity during the Second World War, serves as a cornerstone for freedom, justice, and equality. Evaluating human rights on the basis for these principles has been instrumental in advancing the cause of gender equality, marking a significant accomplishment of the declaration. The preamble and Article 26 of the Universal Declaration recognize and grant individuals the right to education, emphasizing the importance of education in reinforcing respect for human rights and fundamental freedoms. Hence, human right to education establishes an inclusive environment that promotes development. According to USAID (2008), education is widely recognized as a valuable asset that enhances personal well-being and contributes to the progress of a nation. Providing education to both genders results in comparable improvements in their future earnings and broadens prospects for boys and girls alike. Nevertheless, educating girls yields numerous extra socio-economic advantages that positively impact entire communities. These advantages encompass heightened economic output, elevated household incomes, postponed marriages, diminished fertility rates, and enhanced health and survival rates for infants and children. Beyond these aforementioned goals, formal education has closed the global gender gap in employment and assures equal access for women and men to quality work and leadership positions. This therefore establishes significant ground in promoting education for all in Igbo society, denoting that all children, not just the male-child, must be given the chance to complete their education in a safe environment.

RESEARCH OBJECTIVE AND QUESTIONS

The objective of this research is to investigate how girl-child formal education addresses the sociocultural issue of male-child supremacy in the traditional Igbo society. Moreover, it also aims at answering the following research questions:

1. Which factors contributed to women marginalization?
2. How does girl-child formal education addresses women marginalization?
3. To what extent does girl-child education impact socioeconomic development?
4. What are the psychological impacts of girl-child education?

LITERATURE REVIEW

Features of Formal Education

Formal education which involves an intentional and organized teaching process built upon a specified curriculum, conducted within the school environment. According to Johnson and Majewska (2022), formal education aligns effectively with restricted curriculum models, emphasizing organized learning. This educational system is well-known by structured learning with linear objectives, facilitated through direct teaching behaviors, and is both intended and acknowledged by both educators and learners. Johnson and Majewska (2022) further sustain that within formal education, acquiring knowledge typically places a focus on cognitive aspects and can be acknowledged or assessed through the attainment of qualifications. Hence, education occurs within academic establishments and often centers on propositional knowledge. By propositional knowledge, it depicts theoretical understanding (such as 'knowledge-that') and differs from practical knowledge, encompassing abilities, techniques, and skills (for instance, knowledge-how') (Rata, 2019). There seems to be flaws in this idea because formal education also inculcates practical/technical knowledge as seen among learners that graduated through polytechnics and colleges of agriculture, science and technologies. However, formal education includes preschool, primary schools, secondary schools, and higher education institutions such as colleges, trade or technical schools, and universities. It typically occurs in a classroom setting, led by qualified educators who provide structured instruction (Aguzie & Umunakwe, 2019). In Nigeria as instance, formal education begins with pre-primary and continuing through primary and secondary school and through training at the tertiary institution and at the professional level. This educational approach involves specialized personnel, physical facilities, specific tools, a defined curriculum, and set objectives. This shows that educational institutions and instructors within formal learning are tasked with creating schedules and utilizing instructional methods, including explicit actions aimed at imparting knowledge and managing classrooms. These actions may involve demonstrating, explaining, providing feedback, making corrections, and setting learning goals. Moreover, formal education is characterized with specific age brackets, regular tuition fee, chronological grading system, a syllabus and subject-oriented which has to be covered within a specific time period. It is deemed essential for everyone, and the process involves awarding diplomas to those who successfully complete it, emphasizing the mandatory nature of attendance. These features characterized formal education (Öz & Kayalar, 2021). Formal education moreover specifies minimum requirements for learner participation, such as the duration of attendance or guided learning hours (Moldovan & Bocoş-Binţinţan, 2015, Jung & Choi, 2016). Summing up, formal education involves the schooling or analogous educational experiences individuals undergo prior to embarking on their careers or life journeys.

Formal education establishes that the teaching and learning processes must be effectively managed to ensure both cognitive advancement and social growth by clearly setting of guidelines and a curriculum that outlines a structured and progressively sequenced educational framework, starting from pre-school and extending through university. This does not depict that learning cannot occur on the fringes of, or outside of formal curriculum arrangements rather, formal education targets academic studies, specialized programs, and institutions that provide comprehensive technical and professional training on a full-time basis. Alnajjar (2021) informs that under formal education, various courses with different scopes are offered within this system, and the existence of a formal course implies the necessity of a well-defined and planned curriculum. By this, while all educational systems follow formal pattern of transferring knowledge, formal education has a well-organized curriculum which is contingent upon having a structured curriculum in place. This enhances undergoing a training with the aim of obtaining a certificate or diploma, which empties in the prospects for higher education so as to improve professional careers and guarantee good job opportunities.

Curriculum

Existing literature confirm abundant individual idea when defining the concept of 'curriculum'. Etymologically, the term originates from the Latin word 'curere', meaning 'to run a course.' In essence, it signifies a subject with specific objectives designed to yield educational outcomes for learners. According to Uwak (2018), the term curriculum denotes specifically a carefully organized series of instructional plans aimed at guiding students' educational activities and encounters in alignment with the instructional goals and objectives set by schools. Mizan (2022) agrees that the term curriculum pertains to the educational content and teachings provided within a school, educational institution, or a particular course or program. Similarly, it is a systematically structured framework for facilitating educational activities. However, curriculum is metaphorically likened to a race; consequently, it functions as an active agent driving educational activities forward.

Curriculum comprises standards-based experiences through which students engage in and proficiently acquire information and skills. Karakuş (2021) argues that curriculum goes beyond simply selecting content and employing specific methods; it encompasses both planned and spontaneous activities that engage students. A well-thought-out, tested, and adjusted curriculum fosters student-teacher interaction within an educational setting. By aligning with the physical facilities and resources of the school, curriculum aims to attain targeted goals and make a meaningful contribution to societal development. By this, curriculum serves as a comprehensive framework, encompassing a model and a document that incorporates the structuring of the educational setting, choices made by educators concerning the learning journey, and the perspectives of society, families, and external authorities. Iyekekpolor and Uveruveh (2023) suggests four elements of curriculum to include: (i) goals and objectives; (ii) content or subject and subject matter; (iii) learning experiences; and (iv) evaluation since there is not universally accepted or precise definition of the concept. In his '12 musts', Uwak (2018, p.31) notes that before a program should qualify as a curriculum, it must possess these characteristics:

1. Must be a written document
2. Must address or contain academic activities
3. Must be sequentially (systematically) drawn
4. Must be set up by experts (in the field)
5. Must tackle the current needful issues
6. Must be directed and guided by instructors
7. Must be learners-centered
8. Must focuses on the specific subject matter
9. Must focuses on specific areas of the subject matter
10. Must involve teaching and learning processes
11. Must clearly state the aim, the goal and the objective
12. Must at its implementation achieve the needed aims, goals and objectives

Bhardwaj and Hooda (2022) further sustain on the features of a good curriculum:

1. It should be creative.
2. It should be flexible.
3. It should be related to real life learning.
4. It should be psychologically sound.
5. It must provide the better scope to cultivate the skills and attitude for development.
6. It should be innovative and practical so that the student automatically generates their interest top learn the new concept.
7. It should be professional and updated according to requirement of market (present and future).
8. Increase awareness in students.

Based on the detailed explanations, the primary aim of the curriculum is to efficiently foster learning and enrich the knowledge of students, with the intention of influencing their attitudes, shaping their characters, and instilling positive moral values. Curriculum functions as a fundamental reference for educators, outlining essential elements for successful teaching and learning. The impact is to guarantee that each student can partake in challenging academic endeavors. Hence, the design, arrangement, and considerations of a curriculum are crafted to enhance students' learning in a more effective and streamlined manner. By this, to adequately facilitate teaching and learning, the curriculum should encompass necessary objectives, methodologies, resources, and assessments. (Mizan, 2022). Curriculum as a framework includes various components like aims and objectives, subject matter, instructional approaches, methods, and the structuring of educational encounters. The effectiveness of teaching mostly hinges on integrating curriculum components that exhibit strong interconnections. For example, failing to apply the appropriate teaching method or technique in the classroom renders it impossible to achieve the goals and objectives of a course. However, the way curriculum is organized, viewed, arranged and conceptualized is of fundamental importance in the achievement of educational objectives. Esu (2011) divides curriculum into the following:

1. Subject-centered curriculum emphasizes on school subjects and their internal subdivisions. Advocates of this curriculum organization approach endorse systematic planning, advocating for a curriculum structured around knowledge or discipline. This include: what should be taught – the subject and how to make the subject interesting in order to convey the knowledge successfully. Hence, the starting point of what is to be learnt is knowledge (subject).
2. Child-centered or experience curriculum places a strong emphasis on catering to the learner's needs and interests. The organization of this curriculum prioritizes the learner's experience. Advocates of this approach assert that the learner should be the focal point of the learning process, with the child's problems, interests, and needs serving as the central considerations. Additionally, the learner's interests are seen as instrumental in promoting the understanding of the subject matter, influencing the content and structure of the teachings.
3. Core curriculum concentrates on fundamental aspects of daily life activities or social functions and issues within a social system. It is a curriculum geared towards problem-solving, incorporating specific subjects deemed suitable for all members of society. Additionally, this curriculum is rooted in the needs, interests, problems, and aspirations of society, with the learner's needs and interests being encompassed within the societal context. This approach allows learners to directly engage with and study the societal problems. It does not specifically address the immediate needs of the child and does not extensively focus on the values associated with social function.
4. Broadfield or integrated curriculum Focus on different interconnected topics characterizes this curriculum, which emerged as a departure from the traditional subject-centered approach to education. It bears resemblance to a core curriculum but distinguishes itself by consolidating diverse fields of study into a cohesive unit. This educational approach involves combining two or three subjects or disciplines. However, a challenge associated with broadfield curriculum lies in determining a universal understanding of what everyone should learn.
5. Hidden curriculum is associated with instruction at the classroom level. It encompasses the unintentional learning experiences that children gain from the inherent structure and organization of public schools, as well as from the actions and attitudes of teachers and administrators who are prepared to facilitate learning. Examples of the hidden curriculum include the implicit messages

and lessons derived from the overall structure of schools. These lessons are acquired without deliberate intent, originating from the social environment and involving the transmission of values, norms, and beliefs.

The diverse educational resources, including books, maps, teacher's guides, toys, and additional materials, empower both teachers and learners to assess the achievement of course objectives upon the completion of the educational program.

Strengths of Formal Education

Strengths of formal education lies within the pattern, and this makes it unique from other systems of education. Typically defined and structured, formal education is managed by educational stakeholders such as state or regional agencies, to standardize learning practices across various locations within a system (Mpofu, 2013). This facilitates the refinement, regulation, and control of education for the sake of efficiency, productivity and equal socioeconomic opportunities. By this, formal curricula elevate the importance of specific skills and knowledge deemed valuable to society. For instance, the curriculum can be utilized to ensure the inclusion of certain teachings in schools, including social and personal values. Veronica (2022) and Souto-Otero (2022) sustain that structured education which occurs in a regulated environment aim to educate students. Formal education occurs within a school environment, where multiple students gather in a classroom under the guidance of a qualified and certified subject instructor. Plato (2022) highlights the followings as strengths of formal education:

1. A well-organized educational framework and up-to-date course materials are provided.
2. Qualified and experienced instructors convey knowledge to students through a systematic and structured learning process.
3. The approach ensures that students' progress to both intermediate and final examinations.
4. The institutions are logically and effectively managed, culminating in the official recognition of certificates. Successful completion opens up job opportunities for the students.

The specified nature of formal learning also supports the accumulation of shared knowledge beyond specific contexts, contributing to enhanced social mobility. The recorded, propositional knowledge nurtured through disciplinary communities possesses generalizable qualities, making it applicable in diverse situations (Herțanu et al. 2023). Access to this esteemed knowledge, based on ability rather than social connections or status, holds the potential to empower learners from disadvantaged or marginalized groups (gender inequality). At a national level when a formal curriculum is mandated, this will expose most learners to common ideas and knowledge, mitigating any inequality of access among different groups in the national population. Compared to other forms of learning, formal learning supports well-established evaluation and assessment methodologies. The testing and assessment practices within formal education and training draw upon a long history of practical application, research, and theoretical foundations.

Weaknesses of Formal Education

The weaknesses of formal education revolve within its inability to fully capture the dynamic nature of educational processes. This falls short in conveying the entirety of teachers' actions, teachings, and contributions within classrooms, as well as the diverse experiences of learners in those educational settings. In the light of Bamkin (2020, p. 236), "whilst [the written curriculum] ... considers the teachers' perspectives and planning for core areas of moral education, it overlooks the minutiae of everyday teaching practices and efforts made outside the curriculum 'hot-spots'." Using this information, formal written curricula can be evaluated since it does not capture the individual interpretations and delivery styles of each teacher, nor do they reflect the perspectives and experiences of learners as they engage with the curriculum. Matambo (2018) agrees that formal education frequently met with lukewarm dedication in communities that seek to uphold their cultural integrity. As a result, formal education in these societies has not managed to significantly alter people's perspectives. In instances where it has had an impact, the transformation appears superficial. Equally, Yuvi (2020) expresses that students with varying levels of ability, both high and low achievers, as well as those with special talents or facing challenges, are typically placed in the same classroom under the instruction of the same teachers. This system hinders the swift advancement of gifted students, as some may be eager to cover more syllabuses within limited time but face obstacles. Moreover, the diverse mix of learners create mental strain among the students and structured education represents a somewhat unnatural approach to teaching and learning, as it involves the creation of artificial situations during the instructional process.

Given the diversity among schools and teachers, the official curriculum may not provide a comprehensive understanding of how it is implemented in classrooms. Some learners do not respond favorably to formal education, leading to notable dropout rates in certain global formal teaching programs (Busse et al., 2019). Ng (2020) argues that informal settings may be more conducive for some learners, as formal curricula are occasionally perceived as inflexible and one-sided, and some students may resist teacher-directed instruction. Interacting with theoretical knowledge that is detached from personal experience might discourage certain learners. For instance, when educators introduce disconnected and unfamiliar mathematical formula, it can result in some individuals losing interest in attending mathematics classes. Formal educational is challenging to replace intuitive concepts, as instructors must challenge what learners have previously acquired. Consequently, it seems necessary to supplement the abstract nature of certain formal learning with hands-on experiences, such as visits to museums and planetariums. The results for indigenous and non-indigenous learners may differ when following formal curricula. When a curriculum is crafted to favor one group over others, it may harbor biases that disadvantage or alienate other groups. Other weaknesses of formal education as contained in Educational News (2019) include:

1. Sometimes, brilliant students are bored due to the long wait for the expiry of the academic session to promote to the next stage.
2. Chance of bad habits' adoption may be alarming due to the presence of both good and bad students in the classroom.
3. Wastage of time as some lazy students may fail to learn properly in spite of motivation by the professional trainers.
4. Costly and rigid education as compared to other forms of learning.

5. Some unprofessional and non-standard education system may cause the wastage of time and money of the students which leads to the disappointment from formal education and argue them to go for non-formal education.

While formal education plays a crucial role in challenging learners' mistaken intuitive concepts, particularly regarding gender issues, studies establish that relying solely on formal learning approaches may not be enough to dispel misconceptions among younger learners or to overcome their naive scientific ideas. Additionally, there is a suggestion that depending solely on formal learning methods may limit teachers' pedagogic freedom, potentially influencing the overall learning experience.

Despite its weaknesses, the existence of curriculum that promotes improving of knowledge through reading and writing distinguishes formal education from other educational systems particularly traditional or indigenous education as found in the traditional Igbo society.

Traditional Igbo Society

Igbo society is among core ethnic groups of Nigeria presently inhabiting the southeastern region of the country. It covers five states of Abia, Anambra, Ebonyi, Enugu, and Imo. Like other traditional ethnic groups of Nigeria, the Igbo society has unique culture or norms that identify them wherever being discussed despite civilization. In a preface on 'Things Fall Apart' written by Chinua Achiebe (1999) inform that one notable characteristic of Igbo society was the absence of centralized political systems. Instead, the Igbo people resided in self-governing villages and towns, overseen by their elders. Generally, they structured themselves into patrilineages—groups organized based on descent from fathers to sons—with only a few deviations from this pattern. In an agreement, Nwabude (2022) states that, a predominant feature of traditional Igbo society is that it is organized in a hierarchical patriarchal order which is much embedded in the belief that a male-child is superior to a female-child. The idea of a patriarchal society is the feelings that male children are unique, stronger and fit for the public space while female-children are feeble, weak, and breeders of children (Umunakwe, 2023). Embedded in gender roles where each gender has different tasks in the society, patriarchal culture confines women's roles to domestic responsibilities often reference that the appropriate place for women is in the kitchen (Ofozoba, 2020). This affects the way (even of recent) a girl-child is subjugated, undervalued and discriminated leading to gender disparities in the traditional Igbo society. While some believe the veracity of this theory to be reinforced either by natural, structural or sociocultural factors, the girl-child inherently accepts her roles to be submissive and suitable only for domestic purposes.

However, in the traditional Igbo society, significant gender imbalances persist, where women and girls face disadvantages across various domains and lack the same opportunities as men. These disparities are evident in nearly all public sectors, including unequal access to essential social services, property rights disparities, and enduring gender gaps in both the labor market and the public sphere (Ukaegbu & Oguejiofor, 2022). Ojukwu and Ibekwe (2020) agreeing with the interpretation state that women experience different forms of discrimination, including physical and emotional abuse, throughout their entire lives, from childhood to death. Various discriminatory practices are imposed on women, and the subordination they face exposes them to harmful cultural and traditional norms.

The prevalence of a patriarchal system influences gender-biased laws and customs, leading to a lack of gender equity and freedom. Women are often sidelined to contribute to issues that affect them, they were only allowed to talk through their men. There are cases of cultural discriminatory practices such as widowhood and female genital mutilation practices. In summary, the prevalent bias against women is primarily rooted in patriarchal norms, shaping societal expectations and roles to relegate women to a subordinate status.

Traditional Igbo Educational System

Traditional Igbo society conveyed and received knowledge through oral literature, encompassing folktales, myths, proverbs, and songs which primarily took place within the family and village levels (Okoro, 2018). Emeagwali (2006) holds that people in different regions across the African continent including the Igbo, employed a diverse array of symbols and motifs to communicate their ideas. Elders who served as educators and unquestionable authorities taught the youths either in groups or on individual basis on the history, cultural legacy, traditions, and laws pertinent to the society. They were also trained in essential skills like hunting, construction of huts, local fabrications, textile manufacturing, crafting metallic tools, wine tapping, traditional and herbal medicine production, food processing, wood carving, among various other practices. Iwunna et al. (2021) express that education in Igbo land predates the arrival of white missionaries. It did not involve writing, structured classrooms, or formal written instruction. Instead, teaching was conducted orally, and any knowledgeable elder could act as a teacher without the need for certificates or formal classrooms. In this traditional educational setup, there was no prerequisite for a certificate or physical classroom; rather, the oral curriculum was integrated into the cultural norms and traditional values of the Igbo people. Iwunna et al. (2021) present further that the educational system that existed in Igbo land at that time aimed to equip the Igbo people with the skills necessary for self-sufficiency. This indigenous education imparted valuable lessons to girls, teaching them the virtues of being supportive wives who respected their husbands and raised their children with moral values. Young men, on the other hand, were instructed on the importance of strength, hard work, adherence to the law, respect for elders, and preservation of cultural values. This native form of education played a crucial role in shaping individuals who later became traditional healers, house builders, blacksmiths, woodworkers, food processors, midwives, and various other skilled professionals. The indigenous form of education played a crucial role in facilitating the transmission of cultural values, beliefs, norms, history, and language among the Igbo people across generations.

The Igbo traditional educational system not only promoted active involvement of Igbo individuals in community development but also instilled in the youth a commitment to the cultivation of virtuous character. Throughout Igbo history, there has been a longstanding tradition of fostering an appreciation for high moral standards, exemplifying the core principles of the indigenous education of the Igbo community. Using folk stories as a medium, the Igbos endeavored to impart lessons and contribute to the establishment of a morally upright and crime-free Igboland (Duruoma & Derefaka, 2019). In the light of Onuora et al. (2019), Igbo traditional education is commonly identified and categorized as informal learning which takes place within the family household or compound, where adults, parents, and elders in the community naturally serve as the educators for the children who act as pupils or students. In Igbo communities, the elders are responsible to pass down traditional knowledge to the younger generation. They are entrusted with the task of guiding the youth towards responsibility, mental balance, skills development, and self-sufficiency. Primarily, the elders ensure that the younger individuals grow up with strong moral values and a resilient character. Igbo traditional education employs both conscious and unconscious methods and is passed down from one generation to the next, extending even to those yet to be born. This educational process begins in early childhood and continues through adolescence until adulthood, where the individual is expected to have acquired the necessary skills to be independent and self-reliant.

THEORETICAL FRAMEWORK

The theoretical framework guiding this study anchored on critical pedagogy theory, propounded by Paulo Freire (1921-1997). Freire states that, it is possible to free people from silence culture and the trap of ignorance only through education and awareness. According to Nyirenda (2018) and Chalaune (2021)'s Freire's idea of critical pedagogy was influenced by his early life experiences which could be trace back to residing among underprivileged children and later, as he matured, working alongside impoverished laborers. These encounters inspired his belief that ignorance, illiteracy, and a culture of silence stem from prevailing economic, social, and political conditions in society. For Freire, the educational system serves as a key tool in perpetuating this culture of silence (Mahmoudi et al., 2014). Relying on innovative perspective on the learning concept, Freire establishes that individuals raised in a culture of silence who may believe that social, political, and economic systems are unchanging and insurmountable, find it difficult to draw upon their own abilities to transcend these structures. Freire argues that individuals should not perceive the structures around them as an unchangeable reality without any hope of escape. Instead, they should recognize the potential for change in their circumstances. He advocates for establishing a dialogue-based relationship among individuals to cultivate a critical and active environment, promoting education as a dynamic and progressive process (Shih, 2018). Hence, the fundamental goal of education is to attain a heightened critical awareness that empowers individuals to lay the foundation for their advancement. In this pursuit of progress, considerations like gender, age, race, and societal and political constraints are disregarded (Rugut & Osman, 2013).

Freire, however, endeavors to empower marginalized individuals, shifting them from being passive recipients of education to active participants in their self-governance and liberation. In pursuit of this objective, learners are encouraged to engage in actions that facilitate the transformation of their communities, primarily achieved through emancipatory education. By employing a method that involves questioning and addressing problematic issues in the learners' lives, critical thinking is cultivated, leading to the development of a heightened awareness. This critical awareness empowers individuals to enhance their lives and assume responsibility, essential steps in constructing a more just and equitable society. Consequently, critical pedagogy is often described as a force that challenges various forms of dominance, oppression, and subordination, ultimately aiming to free those who are oppressed.

RESEARCH METHODOLOGY

This is a qualitative study which adopted historical method in evaluating the need in enrolling a girl-child in school and the impacts towards repositioning male-based supremacy syndrome affecting the traditional Igbo society. That et al. (2021) express that historical research entails methodically and impartially reconstructing past events by gathering, assessing, validating, and combining evidence to establish factual information and arrive at well-supported conclusions, frequently in connection to specific hypotheses. Based on the belief that history only happens once, this method aims to establish that progress in qualitative research involves incorporating historical research findings into the ever-expanding body of scientific knowledge. In the realm of education, each study goes beyond mere empirical observation. This integration of historical research is crucial for fostering innovation, development, and improvement in both theory and practice. The overarching aim is to retrieve and understand ideas and meanings from the past, which can significantly influence and shape the present and future. However, delving into the history of pedagogical thinking is more than just reconstructing the past; it presents an opportunity to uncover the meaningful dimensions of a tradition that can serve as inspiration and motivation for current and future endeavors. Additionally, it entails leveraging past experiences and research to enhance the understanding of valuable notions and concepts accumulated over time (Albulescu, 2018).

ADVENT OF FORMAL SCHOOLING IN TRADITIONAL IGBO SOCIETY

Existing literature on the evolution of formal education in Igbo society anchored on the activities of European missionaries and colonialists. According to Okoro (2018), since the introduction of schooling system also known as western system of education in Nigeria in which Igboland became a part by the Christian missionary, the arrival of Catholics marked the initial presence in Nigeria. Guided by Portuguese traders, who founded a seminary on Sao-Tome Island, near the Nigerian coast, in 1571. The purpose was to educate Africans as clergy and educators. Progressing from Sao-Tome, they extended their efforts to Warri, establishing schools and spreading the Gospel. In the light of Frankema (2021), the penetration of formal education commenced through the influence of European missionaries, who frequently imparted not only religious teachings but also non-religious subjects. Following the Berlin Conference of 1884/85, formal alterations were made to the education systems, aligning them more closely with European standards. The various colonial authorities employed slightly varied approaches, yet they uniformly hindered African access to education. They employed strategies such as imposing European languages as the medium of instruction and restricting the curriculum to exclude any content related to Africa. In Igboland however, the British heavily relied on missionaries and churches to impart Euro-centric perspectives. Systematically, this triggered the building of learning centers known as schools with planned and systematic curriculum basically to create awareness that everyone irrespective of the gender shares equal opportunities. In the account of Ezeudu et al. (2013), the first primary school in Onitsha commenced on Monday, November 15, 1858, accommodating 14 girls aged 10 to 16, who were initially without clothing. Taylor, the founder, provided them with garments, although the boys displayed no inclination to participate. Subsequently, in 1864, Taylor established both day and night schools for young slaves, marking the initiation of educational endeavors. The day school enrolled 50 pupils, while the night school had 70 on its roster. Funding for the boarding house was sustained through contributions from charitable organizations abroad. Notably, this emerged system of education promoted inclusiveness which increased enrolment rate that brought sociocultural transformations among which is, gender parity.

CONTRIBUTIONS OF FORMAL SCHOOLING TOWARDS GENDER PARITY IN TRADITIONAL IGBO SOCIETY

The enrolment of girl-child in formal schooling contributed enormously to creating room for gender parity. By engaging in curricula and non-curricula activities with the male counterpart, the girl-child developed a deep sense of belonging by connecting with diverse groups of people who are likely to share similar interests, ideas or goals. The formation of feminist movements in Nigeria such as Women in Nigeria (WIN), National Women's Union, Federation of Ogoni Women Association, Non-governmental Women's Human Rights Organization, Federation of Nigeria Women's Society, Aba Market Women Organization, Abeokuka Women's Union, Widows Association of Nigeria, amongst others (Aguzie et al., 2019) were as results of collaboration during schooling. These movements attended to different women's rights issues within the private sphere of the family and in the public arena such as sexual and reproductive health; poverty; economic empowerment; violence against women; property ownership; peace and security; leadership development and political participation, among others. Learning in the same environment with their male counterparts created the spirit of discernment that every gender has equal rights. This triggers various feminist movements and formulations of various laws to eliminate subjugation of women in every ramification (Levtov, 2013). Obviously, a child who experiences a sense of connection within a circle of friends is more likely to aspire to positive transformation, personal development, and societal advancement. A supportive community of like-minded friends can significantly contribute to fostering change and nurturing children who have the potential to become future leaders in their communities. Again, regular engagement with classmates from diverse socioeconomic backgrounds exposes the female child to varying perspectives, cultivating empathy and enhancing their ability to connect with individuals holding different views. Consequently, social interaction plays a crucial role in the cognitive development of a child, underscoring its significance in the realm of child education.

In the light of Cotton (2022), for decades now, promoting girls' education has been recognized as a key strategy to counteract the persistent challenges of poverty and disease afflicting substantial areas of cultural societies. By this, girl-child access to education does not only enhances the attainability of MDGs 2 and 3 but also contributes positively to the remaining six Goals. Research shows that girls who are educated are more likely to have wider knowledge of primary healthcare than girls who are not educated. However, girl-child access to education does not only transforms their destinies but also impacts the well-being of their future children. Moreover, it enables them to actively contribute to the socioeconomic decisions in the society which is strengthened through the prioritizing of equal and inclusive education as a fundamental right, provision of gender-sensitive and inclusive curricula, creating rooms for equal and accessible educational opportunities in traditionally male-dominated fields like science, technology, engineering, and mathematics (STEM). By this, women engage in esteemed professions such as medicine, engineering, agriculture, legislations, banking, amongst others. Example of notable women in the southeast of Nigeria include: Nneka Onyeali-Ikpe, Ukonwa Ojo, Adaobi Nwakuche, Chinyere Okorocha, Nkemdilim Uwaje Begho, Ngozi Okonjo Iwuala, Oby Ezekwesiri.

However, providing education to girls produces even more significant outcomes. When girls receive an education, they typically postpone marriage, have fewer yet healthier offspring, and play a more substantial role in both family earnings and national productivity. In essence, investing in the education of girls may potentially generate a higher return on investment than any other available investment in the developing world (USAID, 2008). To Haralambos and Holborn (2004), schools function as meritocratic establishments where uniform standards are employed for all students, regardless of inherent characteristics like social class, gender, or family background. The enrolment of the girl-child in formal schooling have paved way for their independence, reducing the burden of depending on their male counterparts in every matter.

CONCLUSION

Over time, the emphasis in education has primarily been on ensuring equal access for both genders, aiming to narrow the enrollment disparity between girls and boys. It is deduced that formal education has deeply encouraged and improved the integration of girl-child in the socioeconomic, political, administrative and technological affairs thereby rejecting the traditional way of seeing the girl-child as mentally inferior. Though there has been a lack of adequate emphasis on issues like retention, academic achievement, and the overall quality and applicability of education. Offering a high-quality and pertinent education will not only contributes to enhanced enrollment and retention rates but also ensures that both boys and girls can fully reap the advantages of their educational experiences. As a matter of recommendation, stakeholders should ensure that every barrier to girl-child education is destroyed, and girls should enroll and complete at least 9 years of quality education in a safe and supportive community environment and also acquire the skills they need to lead healthy and productive lives.

REFERENCES

Achiebe, C. (1999). *Things fall apart*. AWS.

Aguzie, D. O., & Umunakwe, B. O. (2019). The contributions of philosophy in sustaining education in Nigeria. *Multidisciplinary Journal of Social Science Education*, 114–124. (Maiden edition).

Aguzie, D. O., Umunakwe, O. B., & Akaire, C. B. (2019). Aristotle's philosophy of gender inequality: Its implications for transformative leadership practices in the Nigerian politics. *Interdisciplinary Journal of Gender and Women Development Studies*, *3*(1), 138–153.

Albulescu, I. (2018). The historical method in educational research. [AJHSSR]. *American Journal of Humanities and Social Sciences Research*, *2*(8), 185–190.

Alnajjar, E. A. M. (2021). The impact of a proposed science informal curriculum on students' achievement and attitudes during the Covid-19. *International Journal of Early Childhood Special Education (INT-JECSE)*, *13*(2), 882–896. doi:10.9756/INT-JECSE/V13I2.211131

Arslan, H. (Ed.). (2018). *An introduction to education*. Cambridge Scholars Publishing.

Bamkin, S. (2020). The taught curriculum of moral education at Japanese elementary school: The role of classtime in the broad curriculum. *Contemporary Japan*, *32*(2), 218–239. doi:10.1080/18692729.2020.1747780

Bhardwaj, S., & Hooda, K. (2022). Impact of innovative process in teaching –learning. [AJCS]. *Amity Journal of Computational Sciences*, *3*(2), 19–23.

BusseR.LischewskiJ.SeeberS. (2019). Do non-formal and informal adult education affect citizens' political participation during adulthood? *JSSE - Journal of Social Science Education, 18*(4), 5–24. doi:10.4119/jsse-1443

Chalaune, B. S. (2021). Paulo Freire's critical pedagogy in educational transformation. *International Journal of Research-GRANTHAALAYAH*, *9*(4), 185–194. doi:10.29121/granthaalayah.v9.i4.2021.3813

Chazan, B. (2022). *What is 'education'? Principles and pedagogies in Jewish education.* Palgrave Macmillan., doi:10.1007/978-3-030-83925-3

Cotton, A. (2021). *The importance of educating girls and women – the fight against poverty in African rural communities.* United Nations. https://n9.cl/ebm89

Duruoma, N. B., & Derefaka, A. A. (2019). Indigenous training and learning among the Agbaelu people of central Igboland, Nigeria. *Port Harcourt Journal of History & Diplomatic Studies*, *6*(3), 1–16.

Educational News. (2019). *Types of education: Formal, informal & non-formal.* Educational News. https://n9.cl/m6kdi

Emeagwali, G. T. (2006). Africa and the textbooks. In G. T. Emeagwali (Ed.), *Africa and the academy* (pp. 1–30). Africa World Press, Inc.

Esu, A. E. O. (2011). The concept of curriculum. In A. F. Uduigwomen & K. Ogbinaka (Eds.), *Philosophy of education: An analytical approach* (pp. 122–134). Joja Educational Research and Publishers Limited.

Ezeudu, F. O., Nkokelonye, C. U., & Ezeudu, S. A. (2013). Science education and the challenges facing its integration into the 21st century school system in a globalized world: A case of Igbo nation. *US-China Education Review B*, *3*(3), 172–182.

Frankema, H. P. E. (2021). The origins of formal education in sub-Saharan Africa: Was British rule more benign? *European Review of Economic History*, *16*(4), 335–355. doi:10.1093/ereh/hes009

Haralambos, M., & Holborn, M. (2004). *Sociology themes and prospective.* Harper Collins Publishers.

Herțanu, M., Soponaru, C., & Păduraru, E. A. (2023). Formal education vs. informal education in the Roma community - A silent confrontation where nobody wins. *Frontiers in Education*, *8*, 1–8. doi:10.3389/feduc.2023.1225113

Iwunna, P., Ndukwu, E. C., Dioka, B. O., Alaribe, O. C., & Alison, O. J. (2021). History of Igbo people and education: A psychological implication. *Historical Research Letter*, *53*, 51–61.

Iyekekpolor, S. A. O., & Uveruveh, F. (2023). Curriculum development and evaluation: New dimensions to enriching Mathematics Education in Nigeria. *African Journal of Mathematics and Computer Science Research*, *16*(1), 8–13. doi:10.5897/AJMCSR2022.0913

Johnson, M., & Majewska, D. (2022). Formal, non-formal, and informal learning: What are they, what are they, and how can we research them? Research report. Cambridge University Press & Assessment.

Jung, H., & Choi, E. (2016). The importance of indirect teaching behaviour and its educational effects in physical education. *Physical Education and Sport Pedagogy*, *21*(2), 121–136. doi:10.1080/17408989.2014.923990

Karakuş, G. (2021). A literary review on curriculum implementation problems. *Shanlax International Journal of Education*, *9*(3), 201–220. doi:10.34293/education.v9i3.3983

Karram, A. (2023). *Education as the pathway towards gender equality*. N9. https://n9.cl/miwacx

Lakhotiya, A. (2023). *The role of education in promoting gender equality*. N9. https://n9.cl/7r3lqq

Levtov, G. R. (2013). *Promoting gender equity through schools: Three papers on schooling, gender attitudes, and interventions to promote gender equity in Egypt and India* [PhD thesis, University of Michigan]. https://n9.cl/pcatr

Mahmoudi, A., Khoshnood, A., & Babaei, A. (2014). Paulo Freire critical pedagogy and its implications in curriculum planning. *Journal of Education and Practice*, *5*(14), 86–92.

Matambo, E. (2018). Formal against indigenous and informal education in sub-Saharan Africa: The battle without winners. *Indilinga*, *17*(1), 1–13.

Mizan, R. M. (2022). What is curriculum? Definition and importance of curriculum. N9 https://n9.cl/7tnwn

Moldovan, O., & Bocoş-Binţinţan, V. (2015). The necessity of reconsidering the concept of non-formal education. *Procedia: Social and Behavioral Sciences*, *209*, 337–343. doi:10.1016/j.sbspro.2015.11.245

Mpofu, J. (2013). Relevance of formal education to third world countries national development. *Journal of Research & Method in Education (IOSR-JRME)*, *1*(5), 64–70.

Ng, H. H. (2020). Towards a synthesis of formal, non-formal and informal pedagogies in popular music learning. *Research Studies in Music Education*, *42*(1), 56–76. doi:10.1177/1321103X18774345

Nwabude, A. A. R. (2022). Traditional African (the Igbo) marriage customs & the influence of the western culture: Marxist approach. *Open Journal of Social Sciences*, *10*, 224–239. doi:10.4236/jss.2022.102016

Nyirenda, J. E. (2018). The relevance of Paulo Freire's contributions to education and development in present day Africa. https://n9.cl/b1pv4

Ofozoba, C. A. (2020). A philosophical reflection on gender inequality and the status of women in the 21st century Nigeria social environment. *The International Journal of Humanities & Social Studies*, *8*(10), 123–129. doi:10.24940/theijhss/2020/v8/i10/HS2010-036

Ojukwu, E. V., & Ibekwe, U. E. (2020). Cultural suppression of female gender in Nigeria: Implications of Igbo females' songs. *Journal of Music and Dance*, *10*(1), 1–13.

Okoro, S. I. (2018). The Igbo and educational development in Nigeria, 1846-2015. [IJHCS]. *International Journal of History and Cultural Studies, 4*(1), 65–80. doi:10.20431/2454-7654.0401005

Onuora, N. T., Obiakor, E. E., Obayi, J. I., & Chinagorom, L. C. (2019). Igbo traditional education: A panacea to the nation's unemployment debacle. *International Network Organization for Scientific Research (INOSR). Arts and Management, 5*(1), 42–55.

Öz, R., & Kayalar, T. M. (2021). A comparative analysis on the effects of formal and distance education students' course attendance upon exam success. *Journal of Education and Learning, 10*(3), 122–131. doi:10.5539/jel.v10n3p122

Plato, N. (2022). Advantages and disadvantages of education and its implementation. *Global Science Research Journals, 3*(3), 1–2. doi:10.15651/2437-1882.22.3.038

Rata, E. (2019). Knowledge-rich teaching: A model of curriculum design coherence. *British Educational Research Journal, 45*(4), 681–697. doi:10.1002/berj.3520

Rugut, E. J., & Osman, A. A. (2013). Reflection on Paulo Freire and classroom relevance. *American International Journal of Social Science, 2*(2), 23–28.

Shih, Y. H. (2018). Some critical thinking on Paulo Freire's critical pedagogy and its educational implications. *International Education Studies, 11*(9), 64–70. doi:10.5539/ies.v11n9p64

Souto-Otero, M. (2022). Validation of non-formal and informal learning in formal education: Covert and overt. *European Journal of Education Research, Development and Policy*, 365–379. doi:10.1111/ejed.12464

That, V. V., Vinh, P. P., & Dung, Q. M. (2021). Methods of historical data analysis and criticism in historical research. *Baltic Journal of Law & Politics, 14*(2), 244–256. doi:10.2478/bjlp-2021-00019

Ukaegbu, P., & Oguejiofor, J. O. (2022). Marginalization of women in Igbo tradition: Myth or reality? *Nnamdi Azikiwe Journal of Philosophy, 13*(2), 271–283.

Umunakwe, B. O. (2023). Philosophical mediation between patriarchal theory and feminism: A reflection on Igbo society. In D. Okocha, M. Yousaf, & M. Onobe (Eds.), *Handbook of research on deconstructing culture and communication in the global south* (pp. 283–295). IGI Global. doi:10.4018/978-1-6684-8093-9.ch018

United States Agency International Development. (USAID). (2008). *Education from a gender equality perspective*. USAID. https://n9.cl/4fu4h

Uwak, S. O. (2018). Curriculum definition: A misleading philosophy. *International Journal of Advancement in Development Studies, 13*(2), 27–34.

Veronica, L. (2022). Formal education: Understanding its meaning and importance. *International Journal of Education Research and Review, 10*(2), 1–2.

Yuvi. (2020). *Disadvantages of formal, informal and non-formal education*. Yogiraj Notes. https://n9.cl/gk3is

ADDITIONAL READING

Alek, & Nguyen, V. T. (2023). Verbal phatic expressions in EFL student teachers' classroom interactions. *The Journal of Language Learning and Assessment, 1*(1), 44–56.

Bouchama, N., Ferrant, G., Fuiret, L., Meneses, A., & Thim, A. (2018). *Gender inequality in West African social institutions. West African Papers, No. 13*. OECD Publishing., doi:10.1787/fe5ea0ca-

Ejumudo, O. B. K. (2013). Gender equality and women empowerment in Nigeria: The desirability and inevitability of a pragmatic approach. *Developing Country Studies, 3*(4), 59–66.

Emordi, O. A. T., Sengupta, P., & Ikednma, A. H. (2021). Women, marginalisation and politics in Africa and Asia. *Integrity Journal of Arts and Humanities, 2*(2), 27–35. doi:10.31248/IJAH2021.019

Ferber, S., Fourie, J., & Selhausen, M. F. (2023). The rise of education in Africa. *The History of African Development*. Retrieved from: https://n9.cl/g9s3u

Hallum, C., & Obeng, W. K. (2019). *The West Africa inequality crisis*. OXFAM. https://n9.cl/lq9px

Ibrahim, J. (2019). *The first lady syndrome and the marginalisation of women from power: Opportunities or compromises for gender equality?* N9. https://n9.cl/fykak

Medina, S. Y. (2022). The history and development of education in Afrika. N9. https://n9.cl/hgx94q

Oyenuga, O. F., & Idowu, O. (2022). The school and contemporary education in Nigeria: Lessons from John Dewey. *Journal of Philosophy and Culture, 10*(2), 24–28. doi:10.5897/JPC2021.0099

UNICEF. (2020). *Adolescent girls in West and Central Africa: Data brief*. UNICEF. https://n9.cl/4r3te

Wuryaningrum, R. (2023). Phatic communication and its implications for online learning motivation. *AIP Conference Proceedings, 2679*(January), 060008. doi:10.1063/5.0111632

KEY TERMS AND DEFINITIONS

Discrimination: This an unjust or prejudicial treatment of different categories of people, particularly on the ground of sex.

Education: It involves more than just going to school and the ability to read and write although basically, it involves all experiences that an individual acquires inside or outside the school. Education is the totality of human activities which aims at sustaining the individual physically, mentally, morally and socially for the benefit of the society.

Formal Education: This presupposes that teaching-learning must be properly harnessed so as to ensure the mental growth and social development. It involves a consciously planned instructional process based on prescribed syllabus and carried on in the school. Formal education encompasses elementary schools, secondary schools, and post-secondary schools (colleges, trades or technical schools, and universities).

Girl-Child: The idea of 'girl-child' as appears throughout this study pertains specifically to the baby-girl, the young daughter of the family, the wife, the mother and the many roles that the woman assumes in the course of her life.

Inclusiveness: This depicts that none of the groups or parties involved in a practice is excluded.

Paternalism: A systematic organization of male supremacy and female subordination.

Traditional Igbo Society: This constitutes people inhabiting the southeastern Nigeria before colonization.

Chapter 8
Classical Violence:
Teaching Mythology Against Gender-Based Violence

Francisco Sánchez Torres
Universidad de Córdoba, Spain

ABSTRACT

This chapter offers an examination of Greek and Roman myths in the context of university-level teaching with a focus on Gender-Based Violence (GBV) prevention. The aims can be summarized as follows: providing a sufficient methodological framework through which open the analysis of myths to critical approaches and proposing techniques and ways of interlacing these critical approaches in the classroom. Consequently, mythology as a group of discourses will be examined to identify the qualities of myth as a powerful means of reification for cultural practices from a semiotic approach. Furthermore, a series of in-class experiences will be provided, preceded by an analysis of the concept of GBV and its application in the context of Greek and Roman mythology, its tradition and its reception through the ages.

INTRODUCTION

The study of the Ancient World, namely Greek and Roman mythology, stands as a bridge connecting the past with the present, offering profound insights into the intricate tapestry of the Classical traditions and receptions in our cultures. Beyond being tales of gods and heroes that served for the purpose of identifying the ancient communities and their shared cultural values, these myths serve as conduits of discourse, not only encapsulating the ethos, values, and societal constructs of the remote past, but also reinforcing contemporary values and social structures. This chapter embarks on a comprehensive journey within ancient mythology to delve into the intersections with contemporary issues, particularly the pervasive presence of Gender-Based Violence (GBV) in the classical stories of Rome and Greece that nowadays form a cultural canon in any Humanities class.

Ancient Greek and Roman mythology, with its narratives cherished throughout History, serves as a captivating lens through which students can explore the multifaceted aspects of human existence. As

DOI: 10.4018/979-8-3693-2053-2.ch008

we traverse the corridors of the Classical Tradition, the focus extends beyond the surface-level tales, prompting a critical examination of myths as intricate forms of discourse. These narratives are not isolated entities but rather complex expressions that mirror the collective consciousness, moral quandaries, and societal norms of their respective cultures. Furthermore, they transcended the boundaries of the ancient societies, as they became cultural contents to be imitated or used as arguments for or against particular values and structures.

Deconstructing the layers of discourse embedded within these myths is a crucial academic endeavour. By viewing myths as dynamic communicative tools, students can discern the nuanced dialogues that shaped the ancient worldview and also became tools for shaping the following eras. The analysis of mythological discourse unveils the moral and ethical underpinnings that guided ancient societies, providing a foundation for understanding cultural identity, historical perspectives and the progression of culture.

Moreover, the Classical Tradition extends, as said, beyond the boundaries of Antiquity to embrace the contemporary classroom. Reinterpreting mythology considering present-day issues transforms these ancient narratives into living dialogues that resonate with the challenges and complexities of the contemporary world. This interdisciplinary approach not only enriches the field of Classical Studies but also fosters critical thinking skills, encouraging students to draw connections between the past and the present.

Transitioning seamlessly into the contemporary landscape, the discourse expands to encompass GBV, a pervasive issue within the classical world. In the background of Spanish university-level education, our exploration acknowledges the challenges faced by the discipline while underscoring the relevance of introducing transversal contents into the teaching process. The intersection of mythology and GBV provides students with a perspective that will help them navigate the complexities of power dynamics, and the historical roots of GBV culturally speaking.

Guiding students through these conversations requires a pedagogical approach that considers the sensitivity of the topic. Our experiences in university-level teaching reveal the importance of creating a safe space for open dialogue, allowing students to engage critically with the material. With academic rigor sufficient to approach the topic, educators can facilitate a nuanced exploration of GBV and mythology, helping students decipher the implications of cultural symbols for contemporary society.

As the researchers proceed on the topics of this paper, the study of ancient mythology as discourse and its contemporary relevance provides readers and scholars with unvaluable material towards a deeper understanding of how our culture was shaped by its controlling powers. Students will not only enrich their understanding of the Classical Tradition but also equip themselves with the tools to dissect and contribute to discussions on pressing societal issues with a perspective ranging longer that the scope of a few decades. A journey through time and discourse that bridges Antiquity with the present turns out to be of extraordinary value for the pursuit of knowledge and awareness about the consequences of violence (GBV in this case) being legitimised by culture.

In the ensuing sections, the researchers shall delve deeper into the intricacies of ancient mythological discourse and its relevance in the contemporary classroom, followed by an exploration of the application of GBV awareness techniques to teaching. Through these analyses, the researchers aim to provide a comprehensive understanding of how the past continues to shape our present, ensuring that the echoes of ancient voices resonate as contextualised in the critical dialogue our society must engage with for the interpretation of its sources.

It is the researchers' belief that there is a great need for studies akin to the one presented in this book. Furthermore, the lack of university-level studies about mythology and its impact on GBV awareness

Classical Violence

implies that the methodologies used in this chapter are still in development. However, it may serve as a propeller for further, deeper studies.

THE STUDY OF MYTHOLOGY AND ITS REINTERPRETATIONS

To start a comprehensive study of ancient mythology and its use in class, it is imperative to first consider mythology as a dynamic discourse. It can be regarded as a complex language through which societies communicate their values and perceptions. Mythological narratives are not static tales but living expressions that engage with the human experience across time. This conceptualization serves as the bedrock for our exploration, as we introduce our students into the entangled threads of mythological discourse and its evolution through History.

The reinterpretation of mythology has been a testament to its enduring relevance. In the Renaissance, classical myths were revisited as artists and thinkers sought inspiration in the ideals of ancient Greece and Rome, shaping a cultural revival which was defined by their interpretation of the Ancient World on the crossroads of their own era. The Enlightenment witnessed a critical reassessment aligned with the shifting concepts of reason and morality during the European political and economic transformation. The 19th and 20th centuries brought forth a wide range of perspectives – from positivist thought to feminist and queer studies – that revitalised the study of the Greco-Roman culture.

This historical panorama underscores the need for an adequate methodology when approaching the study of myths. An interdisciplinary approach, weaving together discourse analysis, historical and cultural examination, becomes essential. By tracing the evolution of mythological interpretations, scholars can discern patterns, shifts, and cultural influences, providing a nuanced understanding. With this methodology, the application of myths in the classroom gains depth, ensuring a proper understanding of the relationship between their cultural values and their relevance towards particular discourses within society.

Myths as Discourse

Qu'est-ce qu'un mythe, aujourd'hui? [...] le mythe est une parole. (Barthes, 1957, p. 211)

Roland Barthes and his work *Mythologies* will be the starting point for our study of mythology as a discourse. The semiotic system Barthes proposed began with the simple proposition that the researchers have quoted after the title of this section. Myth is a word. Although it may seem an obvious derivation from the etymology of the Greek word *mythos* 'word, story, tale', this statement hides a much more intricate and nuanced explanation. Before moving onto Barthes semiotic system for myths, the researchers see it fit to provide the readers with a couple of notes about the word *mythos* and its usage in Antiquity.

According to the LSJ dictionary[1], the meaning of *mythos* can be divided into two blocks, being the first one 'word, speech, conversation'. Then, *mythos* can be understood as anything uttered with a certain meaning. The second meaning is 'story, tale, fable', and, as the dictionary notes, it was not primarily opposed to *logos* as a dichotomy of truth and falsehood. However, the stories referred to as *mythoi* had the characteristics of being told. The word *mythos* is, therefore, entangled in the thread of those etymologies related to utterance and verbal expression, further removed from the comprehension derived from reading or deciphering symbols.

Barthes (1957, pp. 211-226) kept in mind the flexibility of this concept in his development of the myth as a semiotic system. Closely following Ferdinand de Saussure's steps, Barthes considered the myth as part of the semiotic system of discourse, namely a secondary system. Taking the structuralist scheme of *signifiant/signifié | signe*, Barthes introduced a subsystem through which myth works. Barthes represents it as the same system but taking the *signe* from the first structure and turning it into the *signifiant* of this second structure. Thus, the scheme would be:

([signifiant/signifié | signe] signifiant) / signifié | signe

Being the second *signe* the association of the second *signifiant* and the *signifié*, having come the second *signifiant* from the previous association of the first structure into a full *signe*. Furthermore, Barthes' exposition on his analysis of myth as a discourse presents two characteristics that become crucial for our methodology to be operative. Firstly, the three-fold decipherment of the myth, which presupposes three ways of receiving and decoding a myth in a sort of dialectical interpretation of the processes through which the receiver understands the message contained in both systems[2]. Barthes' third reading of the myth provides us with an unvaluable tool towards the application of this methodology to the classroom, as it helps students understand the intricate cognitive processes underlying the reception of a given myth in any format.

The second element of the analysis comes intimately interlaced to this first one, that is, Barthes' conceptualisation of myth as a *parole dépolitisée*. Myth acts as a naturalising and reifying agent[3], making the natural out of the constructed[4] (Barthes, 1957, pp. 252-256). Myth as a discourse is a powerful tool in the history of cultural constructs if understood according to Barthes' proposal, as it becomes the normalising agent. The implications derived from the acceptance of this as an operative approach will be explained later.

Another relevant proposal comes from Johan Degenaar's work. In his examination of myth as a discourse, he framed mythical discourse analysis within three temporalities. This framework begins with the premodern discourse (Degenaar, 2007, pp. 2-3), which represents the stage in which the myth is understood as being real and part of the individual that receives it, not being there any critical distance. The following stage is categorised as modern discourse, in which there is a "critical attitude towards the assumptions of premodern discourse" (2007, p. 4). At this point, the Degenaar introduces the special case of the Ancient Greek culture, in which there is a critical and rationalised interpretation of myths. However, the discussion demonstrates how both stages coexisted, as well as it must be accepted that the rationalised Greek worldview was crucial to the development of the interpretation of myths. The modern discourse, therefore, emphasises the rational, the explanation of the myth as linked to the factual, although there is a need for the myth as naturalising agent "which legitimises social behaviour and political action" (Degenaar, 2007, p. 6). The last of the discourses is the postmodern one, in which there is an ironic relationship to the previous ones. The irony resides in the fact that the postmodern starts from the premise that experience cannot be univocally understood. Therefore, the irrational – or primitive – and the rational – or modern – are subsequently possibilities towards the understanding of the myth. The postmodern discourse focuses on the "diversity of contexts in which it plays a role" (2007, p. 7), being the analysis of its usage and context the real value of the myth. Myth consequently becomes subsidiary, relative and wholly dependent on the circumstances surrounding its appearance and reproduction.

Degenaar's proposal seems to us an update of Barthes' three-fold process of understanding a myth, in a methodology that puts chronological epistemology at the centre of the interpretation. The postmodern

Classical Violence

discourse links the interpretation of myth back to the *parole dépolitisée*, as the analysis of myth in context reveals its function as a normalising agent for dominant ideas in any given situation. Robert Segal examines in his essay on Bruce Lincoln's *Theorizing Mythology* the view that links myth to ideology (2021, p. 156), and criticises the thought that the modern and postmodern turn in myth theory entails the consideration of it as ideology, at least in exclusive terms (2021, p. 167). Moreover, in an essay about myth and politics, Segal emphasised how myth theorists – divided in rationalists or romantics – tied the political to religion. Myths, therefore, could be part of a religion or could transcend its religious function, without being it a necessity, however, the loss of its political power. Segal, when summarising Mircea Eliade's and Malinowski's view on myth and the political, states that "myth traces back the origin of present-day social phenomena and in that sense bolsters them. Myth thus brings the sacred forward to the present. But surely myth also takes one out of the present and back to the past" (2021, pp. 175-176).

An interpretation of myth as such unravels then a plethora of analytical tools to understand the process of reception and reproduction of mythology according to any given social and political context. Before turning to the classroom and how it can be used, it is necessary to introduce another key element for our methodology: the application of this framework for analysing the mythological phenomena.

Reinterpreting Mythology

An analysis of a rather cliché myth – Medusa's figure – will be enough. In order to begin our study of mythology, an approach to the ancient sources is needed. Mainly, two ancient authors deal with the figure of Medusa: Apollodorus in his *Bibliotheca* and Ovid in the *Metamorphoses*. The former offers the following information (Apollod. 2.4):

ἦσαν δὲ αὗται Σθενὼ Εὐρυάλη Μέδουσα. μόνη δὲ ἦν θνητὴ Μέδουσα· διὰ τοῦτο ἐπὶ τὴν ταύτης κεφαλὴν Περσεὺς ἐπέμφθη. εἶχον δὲ αἱ Γοργόνες κεφαλὰς μὲν περιεσπειραμένας φολίσι δρακόντων, ὀδόντας δὲ μεγάλους ὡς συῶν, καὶ χεῖρας χαλκᾶς, καὶ πτέρυγας χρυσᾶς, δι' ὧν ἐπέτοντο. τοὺς δὲ ἰδόντας λίθους ἐποίουν.

Their names were Stheno, Euryale, and Medusa. Only Medusa was mortal, and for that reason it was her head that Perseus was sent to fetch. The Gorgons had heads with scaly serpents coiled around them, and large tusks like those of swine, and hands of bronze, and wings of gold which gave them the power of flight; and they turned all who beheld them to stone. (Hard [trans.], 1997, p. 66)

This monstrous description will be commented, but first it may be compared to the account the latter gives about the same figure (Ov. *Met.* 4.772-801):

Narrat Agenorides gelido sub Atlante iacentem
esse locum solidae tutum munimine molis;
cuius in introitu geminas habitasse sorores
Phorcidas, unius partitas luminis usum.
Id se sollerti furtim, dum traditur, astu
supposita cepisse manu perque abdita longe
deviaque et silvis horrentia saxa fragosis
Gorgoneas tetigisse domos, passimque per agros

perque vias vidisse hominum simulacra ferarumque
in silicem ex ipsis visa conversa Medusa.
Se tamen horrendae clipei, quem laeva gerebat,
aere repercusso formam adspexisse Medusae,
dumque gravis somnus colubrasque ipsamque tenebat,
eripuisse caput collo; pennisque fugacem
Pegason et fratrem matris de sanguine natos
addidit et longi non falsa pericula cursus,
quae freta, quas terras sub se vidisset ab alto
et quae iactatis tetigisset sidera pennis.
Ante exspectatum tacuit tamen. Excipit unus
ex numero procerum quaerens, cur sola sororum
gesserit alternis inmixtos crinibus angues.
Hospes ait: "Quoniam scitaris digna relatu,
accipe quaesiti causam. Clarissima forma
multorumque fuit spes invidiosa procorum
illa: neque in tota conspectior ulla capillis
pars fuit. Inveni, qui se vidisse referret.
Hanc pelagi rector templo vitiasse Minervae
dicitur. Aversa est et castos aegide vultus
nata Iovis texit; neve hoc inpune fuisset,
Gorgoneum crinem turpes mutavit in hydros.

Their guest then mentioned a freezing glen at the foot of Mount Atlas,
tightly enclosed by a fortification of massive rocks.
Two sisters had lived by the valley's entrance, the daughters of Phorcys,
who shared the use of a single eye, which Perseus had craftily
stolen as one was passing it on to the others, by slipping
his hand underneath, thus forcing the Graiae to give him directions.
He travelled through rocky regions remote and secluded, littered
with broken trees, and finally came to the home of the Gorgons.
Across the fields and along the tracks he had seen the statues
of men and of beasts transformed to stone at the sight of Medusa.
He, however, had only looked on those terrible features
as they were reflected in bronze, on the shield which he held in his left hand;
and while Medusa as well as her adders lay buried in sleep,
he had lopped her head from its neck. In consequence, swift-winged Pégasus
sprang from his mother's blood, along with his brother Chrysáor.
Perseus also narrated the dangers he'd faced on his long voyage,
naming the seas and the lands he had viewed from his flight through the air,
and all the stars which he'd lightly brushed with his beating wings,
but his audience wanted more. He was asked by one of the court
why Medusa, alone of her sisters, had snakes entwined in her hair.
'That is an excellent question,' responded the guest; 'let me give you

Classical Violence

the answer. Medusa was one an exceedingly beautiful maiden,
whose hand in marriage was jealously sought by an army of suitors.
According to someone who told me he'd seen it, her marvellous hair
was her crowning glory. The story goes that Neptune the sea god
raped this glorious creature inside the shrine of Minerva.
Jove's daughter screened her virginal eyes with her aegis in horror,
and punished the sin, by transforming the Gorgon's beautiful hair
into horrible snakes.' (Raeburn [trans.], 2004, pp. 169-171)

A brief commentary on both sources will suffice, as the application of it on the classroom for teaching mythology and generating consciousness on gender-based violence will give further details on how mythological discourse works. Apollodorus' text – later chronologically than Ovid's but generally considered to be based on older sources – gives a description of the Gorgons and Medusa inserted in a more fantastical approach. Ovid's account, however, includes more details about the origin of Medusa, although the unrealistic portrait of the snake-haired female is kept in the artificial but coherent sense with which Conradie (1977, pp. 52-54) characterises Greek myth in his explanation on Kirk's remarks about the lack of imaginative thought in classical mythology. In this explanatory tale about how Medusa was punished for being so beautiful – for beauty is a gendered concept – that Neptune raped her, Ovid placed the most influential characterisation of this mythological figure.

Consequently, the classical tradition mixed the creature with the appealing young woman, and devised the hybrid monster that pervades the arts. Painting and sculpture have produced works of art that reimagine the figure, according to the circumstances of the moment. Rubens, Benvenuto Cellini, Michelangelo Merisi da Caravaggio – maybe in the most famous depiction –, Antonio Canova or Arnold Böcklin have reenacted from the 16th century onwards Medusa slain by Perseus, presenting her as a young woman in an expression of horror after being decapitated. In cinema, the apparition of Medusa has been featured in films ranging from the second decade of the 20th century to the next. The 1925 silent film *The Gorgon's Head*, belonging to the MET collection, depicts the mythological tale of Perseus; when Medusa is killed in minute 10:30, she is depicted as a fantastical creature, female-like but covered in scales, with reptilian physical traits.

Another famous depiction of Medusa in cinema appears in *Clash of the Titans* (1981), where the creature is depicted as fully non-human – the same representation was featured in the film's remake in 2010 –. An updated version of Medusa was portrayed by the actress Uma Thurman in the adaptation of the book series *Percy Jackson*. In this version, a completely human Medusa who conceals her petrifying gaze under sunglasses rejects the trend in cinema that had represented her as a monster. However, the depiction of Medusa as a monster that needs to be killed was challenged by the 2008 sculpture by Luciano Garbati *Medusa with the Head of Perseus*, which went viral ten years later, coinciding with the *#MeToo* movement. In this depiction, it is Medusa that holds Perseus' head separated from his body. The surrounding polemic does not conceal the fact that it was an answer to Benvenuto Cellini's sculpture of Perseus holding the head of Medusa and that it used the frequent devise of recreation to invert a narrative[5].

This brief survey shows how a myth – deeply intertwined with GBV – becomes a discourse. It can be unlimitedly told, retold, reinterpreted, reimagined, and recycled throughout History. Medusa's case demonstrates how the myth turns out to be a sort of tissue – in Barthes' notion of text – which can be used to ornate and reify social structures and cultural practices such as violence against women in an apology of sexual abuse, as well as a powerful instrument for contesting the very same dynamics that had been previously legitimised. In the following section we will examine the concept of GBV and how it can intersect with this methodology for the study of myths in the classroom of Classics.

GENDER-BASED VIOLENCE AND THE CLASSICAL WORLD FOR THE CLASSROOM

GBV stands as a pervasive issue with profound societal ramifications, recognized and addressed by institutions such as the European Commission. In its official communications, the European Commission delineates GBV as encompassing various forms of violence, including physical, sexual, psychological, and economic abuse, perpetrated against individuals based on their gender or gender identity. This conceptualization serves as a cornerstone for understanding the complexities of GBV and the importance of addressing it comprehensively within academic discourse and societal frameworks.

In the previous section, it has become apparent that mythological narratives represent a field through which to explore and dissect the dynamics of gender-based violence. Drawing upon the insights provided by the European Commission's definition, we propose an examination of the temporal and cultural boundaries, delving into the mythological realm to elucidate its relevance on GBV.

Within the classroom, the application of GBV concepts to the study of mythology manifests in various forms, shaping and enriching the educational experience. Through in-class discussions, students engage with mythological narratives, critically examining the depictions of power dynamics, gender roles, and interpersonal relationships inherent within these stories. By contextualizing mythological themes within the framework of GBV, students gain a deeper understanding of the societal structures and cultural norms that both inform and reflect instances of violence based on gender.

Moreover, experiential learning activities provide students with opportunities to explore GBV concepts within mythological contexts through a series of teaching techniques that will be examined. Also, these pedagogical approaches need not only to foster a deeper engagement with the material but also encourage empathy, critical thinking, and dialogue surrounding issues of gender-based violence. In doing so, the classroom becomes a dynamic space for exploration and reflection, where theoretical concepts intersect with life, yielding insights that reach beyond the confines of the academic world. Through the exemplification of these in-class experiences, this section aims to illustrate the transformative potential of this intersection.

Gender-Based Violence and Greco-Roman Mythology

Our interpretation of the concept of Gender-Based Violence (GBV) will derive from the official documents issued by the European Commission, the Council of Europe and also the European Union Agency for Fundamental Rights (FRA), although this interpretation will not be exempt from a review of some critical aspects. The FRA, in a survey published in 2014 compares the definitions given by various official political institutions about GBV. The United Nations (UN) proposed for the first time a working definition in the Declaration on the Elimination of Violence Against Women (FRA, 2014, p. 9), which stated that GBV was "any act of gender-based violence that results in, or is likely to result in, physical, sexual or psychological harm or suffering to women […] whether occurring in public or in private life".

Another worldwide recognition act came from the Fourth World Conference on Women in Beijing in 1995, which included detailed references to cultural practices such as female genital mutilation or marital rape. In 2011 the Council of Europe adopted the so-called Istanbul Convention, which addressed the term of GBV for the first time in a European context.

The European Commission offers a webpage with a somewhat brief but handy summary of the concept's definition and practical application. According to the European Commission, GBV stands as the "violence directed against a person because of that person's gender or violence that affects persons of a particular gender disproportionately". In practice, the following information is focused on violence against women and lists a series of forms and examples of GBV. The Council of Europe, on its part, ended last year their *Gender Equality Strategy 2018-2023*, which was a continuation of the *Gender Equality Strategy 2014-2017*. In the text of the strategy, it includes a particular mention to disadvantaged groups within the main victims of GBV, which were largely ignored in previous official documents; these are racialised women, disabled women[6], or migrant and refugee women (2018, p. 11).

Taking these documents into account, a working definition of GBV can be any violence, whether physical, sexual, psychological, or social – including economical –, directed towards individuals because of their non-compliance to gender structures within a given social context. Women and girls have been the historical focus when talking about gender, but according to research from various decades, it can be understood that there is an increasingly growing number of individuals that have suffered many forms of GBV, without it contributing to the invisibility of the structural violence against women (Graaff, 2021). Feminised men[7], non-binary people, intersex individuals, or trans people in general must not be forgotten in all their intersections – for they are racialised, belong within an economic setting or present varying degrees of ability and disability – in our understanding of GBV. As feminist and queer theory research has demonstrated, the coercive violence all feminised genders suffer is precisely based on gender division and structures, and it would be methodologically both insufficient and unwise to establish criteria to determine whether gender-based violences can be classified and, ultimately, prioritised according to a hierarchy.

What is the role of mythology in this methodological framework? It is not difficult to find examples of these violences in our classical myths, whether in the classical sources or the later reinterpretations. The researchers believe that a series of powerful examples can be given to emphasise this intersection.

Sexual and physical violence against feminised genders makes the greater part of mythology which includes GBV. In the previous section Medusa was introduced, but many other examples can be brought up. The *Iliad* revolves around Achilles' wrath, which was caused by Agamemnon's taking Briseis – a young priestess held captive as war-trophy – from him after giving back Chryseis, another female slave, to her father Chryses. From a beginning marked by the impossibility for women to decide on their bodily autonomy – a cultural practice that was pretty much extended throughout the history of Ancient Greece and differed in several aspects in Rome –, the rest of the story continues until the death of Achilles' mate Patroclus takes place. Ovid's *Metamorphoses* – widely considered one of the most influential works from Antiquity – uses poetry to tell stories such as Daphne's, whom Apollo tried to rape but escaped transformed into a laurel bush (*Met.* 1.473-567); or Ganymede's, a young man who was given to Zeus by his family to be his cupbearer (*Met.* 10.152-161); or Caenis, a woman who asks to become a man after being raped by Poseidon and is granted both her wish and invulnerable skin, and later joins Jason's expedition to retrieve the Golden Fleece (*Met.* 12.189-209).

Sexual violence against women and other feminised individuals is, therefore, deeply entangled within myths that have shaped the cultural taste of Europe and, by means of the colonisation, many other non-European cultures.

Psychological violence also plays an important role in the construction of some of the most influential characters from mythology. Medea, for example, fulfilled the stereotype of the "mad woman", but her characterisation turns out to include several traits that became very popular y later reinterpretations and retellings of the myth. Medea, coming from Colchis, was alien to Greece, and so the character cannot be estranged from the idea of embodying Otherness. Also, her links to magic and sorcery depict her as a wise woman and underscores the need for the society to punish her exceeding the limits of female decorum. As Robert Cowan writes, she is a "foreigner, barbarian, witch, infanticide, demi-goddess" that "stands on the other side of any boundary drawn around what is normative" (Cowan, 2010, p. 40). Both in Euripides' and Seneca's account of the myth, the psychological violence that the character faces drives the character's acts, as her being abandoned by Jason, mocked by his new bride, and shunned by the Greek society causes her final revenge against the system.

These are but a portion of the examples that could be brought up in class. Greco-Roman mythology's rich range of tales allows for an examination not only of the original, documentary sources, but their progression, as it has been already said. Any of the mentioned myths, as well as many others – the rape of the Sabine Women (Ov. *Ars am.* 1.101-136), Hylas being abducted by the nymphs (Theoc. 13) –, depict gender-based violences and have been pervasively retold across formats and media. This represents an excellent opportunity for reflection in class; for if myths have the function, according to Barthes, of reification, its artistic and literary constant recreation has the power to turn them into a beauty standard or an aspirational attitude. A critical approach is required to prevent the automatization of this cultural content, which we will exemplify in the following subsection.

In-Class Experiences and Proposals: Talking about GBV and Mythology in University-Level Teaching

In the next paragraphs, a description of the experiences including GBV in the study of classical mythology in university-level teaching will be provided, but beforehand a brief overview of the pedagogical environment needs to be given. The situation of the study of Classics and the ancient Greco-Roman world in Spain will also not be approached, as there are no recent and academically availed studies published yet[8].

The setting for the experiences here described and the proposals suggested is as follows. The University of Córdoba does not offer Undergraduate courses on Classics yet, but it does include units on Latin and Greek languages, literature, and cultures in the programmes of other Human Sciences courses, such as Spanish, English, History, Film and Culture or Cultural Management. The presence of these units is not balanced, as the literary and philological courses receive most of the credit points. In the case of the study of mythology and culture, the main units are "Mitología clásica" (Classical Mythology), "Cultura clásica" (Classical Culture), belonging to the course on Cultural Management, and also "Cultura clásica en el cine" (Classical Culture in Film), and "Mito en la cultura digital" (Myth in Digital Culture), inserted in the programme of the course on Film and Culture. These units deal with various aspects of the ancient Greco-Roman world, underscoring the importance of using the original sources properly, as well as approaching the study of temporally distant cultures critically.

Currently, our teaching experience has been in the unit *Myth in Digital Culture*, which explores the reception of the ancient myths in contemporary culture, with a focus on the arts and media that feature digital tools or environments. Such is the case of film, videogames, digital sculpture, animation, or music. This unit is offered to students in their last course year as part of the optative branch of units. Despite not being technically involved in the expected contents in a Film and Culture course – at least in terms of being a unit on film techniques or filmic analysis –, it is one of the most popular optative units in the programme, with a regular number of more than 15 or 20 students per year, equating approximately half the enrolled students globally. Its enrolment rate responds mainly to the satisfaction of the students after passing the unit *Classical Culture in Film*. Consequently, the profile of the students in this unit is very diverse, with interests in mythology ranging from a creative drive to mere curiosity to understand cultural productions from a deeper and more appealing perspective.

This environment should only be considered ideal for the introduction of critical approaches to classical mythology, due to the lack of interest for traditional, philological perspective on behalf of the students. As such, the content of the unit includes an examination of contemporary theories and how they can be applied to the study of myths. As an example, not far from GBV but not focused on it, the researchers cite a session on Cyborg Theory and myths involving living statues or automata (such as Pygmalion's myth as told by Ovid). Students read the classical piece by Donna Haraway (1994), and then research on ancient testimonies about the interest towards artificial intelligence and beings. Ovid's text is discussed in a roundtable and students try to draw parallels coming from the contemporary arts.

This inquiry made in class on the body, its limits and its conceptualisation soon leads to the matter of GBV. At this point of the teaching program, a series of activities are devised to encourage critical thinking and raise awareness about the implications of the mythological discourse for the sublimation of content favouring or challenging GBV. The next subsections will refer teaching situations and experiences. The researchers believe it necessary to underline that all these experiences include a content-warning for the students, as they deal with violence and other sorts of disturbing content.

Mythological Violence Through Nina Bunjevac's Bezimena (2018)

This teaching experience, which occurred in 2022, proposed students the examination of Nina Bunjevac's powerful graphic novel *Bezimena* (2018) and the pervasive presence of mythological elements surrounding the narrative. The students were asked to read the book before the session, and to take notes about the characteristics of the narration, the drawing style and any other details that may have caught their attention. In the classroom, the instructor and the students read together about the Artemis/Diana in Greco-Roman mythology[9], the tale of Actaeon (Ov. *Met*. 3.138-252) and its reception in the arts through paintings and other works of art. Then, they are given the following worksheet as a home assignment:

Write an essay (800-1000 words) in which you analyse Nina Bunjevac's *Bezimena*. The essay must answer the following questions:

1. What elements from the novel have an explicit connection with Greek mythology?
2. What mythological episodes present in the novel are linked to the goddess Artemis?
3. Identify the aesthetical processes involved in the author's remediation of the classical content.
4. Reflect on the importance of the mythological parallelism for expressing contemporary sexual violence.

Students are strongly encouraged to research on contemporary topics and create a bridge between past and present. Their analysis of the myth requires them to understand the layers of meaning culturally embedded in the discourse, and how the author responds to it and challenges the tradition through her work.

Sacrificing the Other in Myth: Medea in Pasolini and Correa

Belonging to the teaching unit celebrated in 2023, this experience required students to work in groups – as part of a cooperative learning process – to look for different characteristics in the configuration of Medea in Pier Paolo Pasolini's film (1969) and Alessandro Correa's short film *Medea* (2017), in comparison to Seneca's homonymous play. They were also given secondary literature on both Medea and postcolonial theory, regarding migration and the construction of the cultural other – primarily a selection of passages from Homi Bhabha (1994) and the classical text by Gayatri Spivak (1988).

In the next session, students were asked to distribute the information in a sheet of paper, using colours and graphical elements to create a visually appealing poster about the mythological figure of Medea. After that, they were asked to recreate a monologue (300-500 words) by Medea inspired by the primary sources and the secondary literature. These monologues were read in class and discussed critically. The reception of this activity was particularly popular.

A Proposal for Experiential Learning: Living Mythological Statues

Experiential Learning, as proposed by David A. Kolb, was developed theoretically by J. Dewey, K. Lewin, J. Piaget, or L. Vygotsky to underscore the idea that every human being really begins their acquisition of knowledge when it is applied to their life. According to Kolb (2015, pp. 37-49), experiential learning has a series of characteristics, such as that the learning process needs to be understood as a process, not as a result; that it is based on continuous experience, born through the resolution of conflicts; also that learning requires the learner to holistically adapt to the world in an exchange of experiences that derives in the learning process, which is none other than the generation of new knowledge.

The proposal the researchers make in this subsection comes from another teaching experience with the same group during the year 2023. It was called *Heroic Sculptures*, and required students to work cooperatively to recreate famous myths by means of props, their bodies and the physical space of the classroom. The results were immediate, as students started researching on myths, their sources, and envisioning how they could be put to practice in a performance or bodily representation.

Inevitably some myths appeared that involved a degree of GBV, because a group of students represented the myth of Europa (Ov. *Met.* 2.833-875), particularly the moment in which Europa gets on the bull, which is Zeus in disguise, and then the bull takes her into the sea. Although the myth does not portray explicit violence – and therefore the students did not reflect on the potentialities of what they were really portraying –, it implies a later sexual violence that is only known to those that are already acquainted with the mythical tale.

As a result, it can be a powerful idea to suggest something of the sort, such as a retelling of the myths involving GBV from a critical perspective and following the experiential learning technique. Instead of portraying violence, the living sculptures can be used to challenge the classical myth through the body. Of course, this proposal must be carefully examined by the instructors, who must know very well their students, as any experiential learning process involving the body may have important psychophysical significance and consequences.

CONCLUSION

Throughout these pages we have outlined some directions to help orient the study and teaching of Greco-Roman mythology while introducing contents related to GBV at a university level. These notes emphasised the importance of an understanding of mythology as a source of a plethora of discourse that have shaped the artistic and cultural tastes of not only European elites, but also the mainstream perceptions about beauty and practices that can be socially acceptable. This approach crucially contributes to the application of content to generate awareness about GBV, as it fosters a critical view of mythology and the contextual nuances that determine how it has to be understood, always in dependence of the historical moment, the social trends and the culturally institutionalised practices. It is, nevertheless, a rather unexplored approach for study, as the researchers have noted at the beginning of the chapter[10].

The researchers have also included some examples coming from in-class experiences, that put Greco-Roman mythology in a scope of analysis which facilitates both its acquisition and its consideration as an epistemological instrument for challenging discourses that have historically favoured GBV. These experiences range from traditional activities, such as essay-writing, roundtable discussions or secondary literature reading, to other proposals that break the expected monotony by using unusual elements for intellectual learning, such as the body and performance.

As a conclusion, the researchers believe that two questions could be briefly addressed. The first question is the adaptability of this proposal to other settings or contexts. The researchers of this chapter devote their study and research to Classics, but of course other mythologies and culture will offer fruitful experiences. This is not restricted to the Greco-Roman culture, but it can be applied easily to mythological environments as influential as the classical.

The second question is the situated nature of the teaching process regarding this matter. There is always a degree of situational awareness required for every learning and teaching process, but in this case, as the cited studies by the Agency for the Fundamental Rights (2014) and the Council of Europe (2018) point out, GBV is deeply tied to the cultural practices of a society. In this case, the researchers believe that GBV can vary from even microscopical spheres of society in the sort of continuum Yadav & Horn (2021) describe, and therefore the instructors need to develop a particular sense of anticipation towards what could easily derive into the generation of more undesired GBV. Considering, as again these official documents express, the backlash regarding Human Rights, the use of a powerful cultural content such as mythology in order to produce consciousness about GBV must be carefully devised not to become, as myths often do, a dog whistle for more violence.

The classical world keeps being the cultural referent for European societies, as it is deeply entangled in our institutions, as well as in many cultural practices and products that are both a source of inspiration and debate. The need for a debate about our mythological tales, that still shape mainstream content, is evident. Moreover, reflecting about GBV and establishing critical approaches to the ancient world and its ever-influential culture has become urgent in the educational environment.

REFERENCES

Barthes, R. (1957). *Mythologies*. Editions du Seuil.

Bhabha, H. K. (1994). *The location of culture*. Routledge.

Bunjevac, N. (2018). *Bezimena*. Fantagraphics.

Casey, E., Carlson, J., Two Bulls, S., & Yager, A. (2018). Gender Transformative approaches to engaging men in gender-based violence prevention: A review and conceptual model. *Trauma, Violence & Abuse*, *19*(2), 231–246. doi:10.1177/1524838016650191 PMID:27197533

Cicogna, M., & Rossellini, F. (Producers), & Pasolini, P. P. (Director). (1969). *Medea* [Film]. Euro International Film.

Conradie, P. J. (1977). The literary nature of Greek myths: A critical discussion of G. S. Kirk's views. *Acta Classica*, *20*, 49–58.

Correa, A. (Director). (2017). *Medea* [Film]. YouTube. https://goo.su/fKsUgy

Council of Europe. (2018). *Gender equality strategy 2018-2023*. Documents and Publications Production Department, Council of Europe. https://goo.su/JyW5E

Cowan, R. (2010). A stranger in a strange land: Medea in Roman republican tragedy. In H. Bartel (Ed.), *Unbinding Medea: Interdisciplinary approaches to a classical myth from antiquity to the 21st century* (pp. 39–52). Legenda.

de la Noy, K., Fay, W., Harris, L., Iwanyk, B., Jashni, J., McMillan, K., & Tull, T. (Producers), & Leterrier, L. (Director). (2010). *Clash of the titans* [Film]. Warner Bros. Pictures.

Degenaar, J. (2007). Discourses on myth. *Myth and Symbol*, *4*(1), 1–14. doi:10.1080/10223820701673973

del Río Ferres, E., Megías, J. L., & Expósito, F. (2013). Gender-based violence against women with visual and physical disabilities. *Psicothema*, *25*(1), 67–72. PMID:23336546

Deping, L. (2009). A semiotic perspective of mythical discourse. *Chinese Semiotic Studies*, *2*(1), 1–19. doi:10.1515/css-2009-0103

Doniger, W. (2016). Invisibility and sexual violence in Indo-European mythology. *Social Research*, *83*(4), 847–877. doi:10.1353/sor.2016.0058

European Commission. (n. d.). *Gender-based violence (GBV) by definition* [Webpage]. https://goo.su/ukD8cb

European Union Agency for Fundamental Rights. (2014). *Violence against women: An EU-wide survey*. Publications Office of the European Union. https://goo.su/BqG3Yi

Evans, B. (2020). Myths of violence. *Journal of Humanitarian Affairs*, *2*(1), 62–68. doi:10.7227/JHA.035

Graaff, K. (2021). The implications of a narrow understanding of gender-based violence. *Feminist Encounters: A Journal of Critical Studies in Culture and Politics*, *5*(1), 12. https://doi.org/ doi:10.20897/femenc/9749

Graves, R. (2011). *The Greek myths: The complete and definitive edition*. Penguin.

Grimal, P. (1992). *Dictionary of classical mythology*. Penguin.

Haraway, D. (1994). A manifesto for cyborgs: Science, technology, and socialist feminism in the 1980s. In S. Seidman (Ed.), *The Postmodern Turn New Perspectives on Social Theory* (pp. 82–116). Cambridge University Press. doi:10.1017/CBO9780511570940.007

Hard, R. (1997). *Apollodorus. The library of Greek mythology*. Oxford University Press. [trans.]

Harryhausen, R., & Schneer, C. H. (Producers), & Davis, D. (Director). (1981). *Clash of the titans* [Film]. Metro-Goldwyn-Mayer.

Kolb, D. (2015). *Experiential learning: Experience as the source of learning and development*. Pearson.

Moog-Grünewald, M. (Ed.). (2008). *Mythenrezeption. Die antike mythologie in literatur, musik und kunst von den anfängen bis zur gegenwart*. J. B. Metzler.

Praeg, L., & Baillie, M. (2011). Sexual violence: Mythology, infant rape and the limits of the political. *Politikon: South African Journal of Political Studies, 38*(2), 257–274. doi:10.1080/02589346.2011.580126

Raeburn, D. (2004). *Ovid. Metamorphoses. A new verse translation*. Penguin Books. [trans.]

Rajan, V. G. J. (2011). *Myth and violence in the contemporary female text*. Routledge.

Rosenfelt, K., Columbus, C., Barnathan, M., & Radcliffe, M. (Producers), & Columbus, C. (Director). (2010). *Percy Jackson & the Olympians: The lightning thief* [Film]. 20th Century Fox.

Segal, R. (2021). *Myth analyzed*. Routledge.

Spivak, G. C. (1988). Can the subaltern speak? In C. Nelson & L. Grossberg (Eds.), Marxism and the interpretation of culture (pp. 271–313). Macmillan.

The Met (uploader). (2020-present). *The Gorgon's head, 1925. From the vaults* [Film]. YouTube. https://goo.su/RRWwrT

Yadav, P., & Horn, D. M. (2021). Continuums of violence: Feminist peace research and gender-based violence. In T. Väyrynen, S. Parashar, É. Féron, & C. C. Confortini (Eds.), *Routledge handbook of feminist peace research* (pp. 105–114). Routledge. doi:10.4324/9780429024160-12

ADDITIONAL READING

Bornstein, K. (1994). *Gender outlaw: On men, women, and the rest of us*. Routledge.

Butler, J. (1993). *Bodies that matter: On the discursive limits of sex*. Routledge.

Butler, S. (Ed.). (2016). *Deep classics: Rethinking classical reception*. Bloomsbury Academic.

Kearney, R. (2003). *Strangers, gods and monsters: Interpreting otherness*. Routledge.

Martindale, C., & Thomas, R. F. (Eds.). (2006). *Classics and the use of reception*. Blackwell. doi:10.1002/9780470774007

Russo, N. F., & Pirlott, A. (2006). Gender-based violence: Concepts, methods and findings. *Annals of the New York Academy of Sciences*, *1087*(1), 178–205. doi:10.1196/annals.1385.024 PMID:17189506

Sandoval, C. (1995). Cyborg feminism and the methodology of the oppressed. In C. Hables Gray (Ed.), *The cyborg handbook* (pp. 407–422). Routledge.

Segal, R. (2023). *Myth theorized*. Equinox Publishing. doi:10.1558/isbn.9781781798652

KEY TERMS AND DEFINITIONS

Classical Reception: It is the counterpart of the Classical Tradition, encompassing the studies that reflect on how the Greco-Roman culture is reinterpreted, reimagined, and retold.

Classical Tradition: It refers to the processes through which the Greco-Roman material and immaterial culture has been transmitted throughout History (conservation, edition, etc.).

Cooperative Learning: A pedagogical approach that puts the focus of the teaching and learning process in developing a notion of cooperation in the students. Cooperative techniques emphasise teamwork and collaboration in order to achieve general goals, rather than individual benefits.

Critical Approaches to Classics: Any critical approach to Classics proposes methodological procedures that challenge colonising and hierarchical structures based on the presumption that the Greco-Roman culture is inherently superior to any other culture.

Experiential Learning: It refers to a pedagogical approach based on the use of direct experience in learning. Experiential learning techniques rely on making learners confront real or nearly real situations.

Feminised Genders: From the perspective of queer studies, gender and sex are both social constructs that respond to a social division originated in the distribution of labour and the economy of production in two main genders: masculine and feminine. As such, the masculine gender corresponds to the highest hierarchy, whereas anything else can be subject to feminisation and assume a passive stance. This concept allows a methodological analysis that includes cis and trans women, non-binary people, and de-masculinised cis and trans men.

Mythical Discourse: It refers to the methodological framework that considers myths as a text, and therefore susceptible to changes according to the producer of the discourse, as complying to circumstantial characteristics, such as the cultural context.

ENDNOTES

[1] The entry for μῦθος (*mythos*) can be consulted in the following URL: https://goo.su/U2Qh

[2] The thesis of this dialectical interpretation would be the first reception according to Barthes (1957, p. 234), which requires going for a literal meaning of the myth. Its antithesis would be the second interpretation, through which the deformation between the signifier and the signified is understood and the myth deconstructed (1957, p. 235). Barthes proposes a synthesis as the third interpreta-

3. Partly due to the quality of making ungrammatical and unreasonable elements operative when inserted within the mythological discourse, as Lu Deping demonstrates (2009, pp. 7-8).
4. Barthes' words depict the concept with such eloquence that it would be a mistake not to include them: "[l]e mythe ne nie pas les choses, sa fonction est au contraire d'en parler; simplement, il les purifie, les inocente, les fonde en nature et en éternité, il leur donne une clarté du constat" (1957, p. 253)
5. This is not an uncommon phenomenon, especially when regarding mythological figures. Margaret Atwood's *The Penelopiad* (2005) claims an alternative reception of Penelope waiting for Odysseus; Kamila Shamsie's *Home Fire* (2017) offers a retelling of a contemporary, Muslim Antigone facing racism and insecurity in Europe; Madeline Miller's *Circe* (2018) proposes another version for the ancient sorceress. In cinema, Maria Callas' depiction of Medea in Pasolini's homonymous film (1969) gave psychological depth to the stereotype of the deranged woman which had been the common representation of the sorceress from Colchis. Away from the mythological world, contemporary literature has challenged the representation of female characters in modern works; such is the case of Jean Rhys' *Wide Sargasso Sea* (1966), which focused on Bertha Mason, the 'madwoman in the attic' from Charlotte Brontë's *Jane Eyre* (1847).
6. Del Río Ferres et al. (2013) inform about the difficulties and limitations there are when studying the case of disabled women. Most of the times, their being excluded from higher education, or the professional domain determines a very high level of violence in their lives that has surpassed official expectations (p. 71).
7. About the importance of raising awareness among men – feminised or nor –, Casey et al. (2016) underscore "that as a critical and holistic domain, social action is inclusive of all genders' and communities' efforts and is therefore the point at which men's engagement ceases to be a separate consideration or goal" (p. 242). It needs not to be a focus, but surely one of the tools to achieve a proper level of consciousness about GBV.
8. Some organisations, such as the Sociedad Española de Estudios Clásicos (SEEC), or newspapers have published surveys and other texts on the matter. There is, however, no reliable data to really estimate the impact of the latest reforms on education and the conditions of instructors.
9. Useful works for the study of mythology, such as the mythography written by Grimal (1992), Graves (2011) or Moog-Grünewald (2008), are also included. These works are crucial, for they help students locate myths within the ancient sources and provide a brief description, in which the authors hardly ever omit violence-related ones.
10. There are examples of secondary literature about sexual violence in mythology (Praeg & Baillie, 2011; Rajan, 2011; Doniger, 2016), as well as how the concept of myth functions as a naturalizing agent for violence (Evans, 2020). There are, nevertheless, no proper, university level studies that emphasize the role of using mythology as a means towards creating awareness about GBV.

Chapter 9
Theoretical Approach to the Concept of Modern Homonegativity:
Strategies for Prevention and Intervention in the Educational Field

Adrián Salvador Lara Garrido
https://orcid.org/0000-0002-0529-1594
Universidad de Almería, Spain

José Ramón Márquez Díaz
https://orcid.org/0000-0001-9255-629X
Universidad de Huelva, Spain

ABSTRACT

The aim of this chapter is twofold. On the one hand, to analyze the concept of homonegativity, and its main manifestations, as well as its relationship with other factors such as sexist attitudes. On the other hand, it aims to collect pedagogical strategies that can be used by teachers to promote educational spaces free of discrimination and respectful of affective-sexual diversity. A theoretical model is presented that analyses homonegativity and manifestations which, following a parallel path to other phenomena such as sexist attitudes, include more subtle and modern aspects that characterize modern homonegativity. There are also certain socio-demographic and ideological variables that influence the display of these behaviors by teachers. A number of strategies for the promotion of positive attitudes in the educational environment in relation to affective-sexual diversity are selected. The conclusions point to the need to offer specific training to teachers in order to provide them with resources and skills to promote inclusive educational spaces.

DOI: 10.4018/979-8-3693-2053-2.ch009

INTRODUCTION

International scientific literature shows differences in the treatment and acceptance of lesbian, gay and bisexual (hereinafter, LGB) people. Specifically, in the European context, homosexuality is still conceived as a source of discrimination and social rejection (ILGA-Europe, 2023). This is reflected in the educational sphere, as schools are seen as hostile spaces for LGB students. Comprehensive Sexuality Education (hereinafter, CSE) is considered a useful tool for including sexual orientation, gender identity and expression (hereinafter, SOGIE) diversity in the educational curriculum, as it contributes to addressing stigmatisation, discrimination and violence towards those sexual orientations that do not respond to normative canons (Granero-Andújar et al., 2023). The work of professionals in the field of education is a key element for the promotion of quality CSE, which allows for educational spaces free of discrimination and respectful of homosexuality (Fernández-Hawrylak et al., 2022; Pichardo and de Stéfano, 2020). Therefore, it is suggested that initial and continuous teacher training in sexuality education should be guaranteed, as well as the need for specific preparation in the area of sexual orientation, gender identity and expression (Barozzi and Ruiz-Cecilia, 2020; Coulter et al., 2021). However, it is concluded that teachers have little training in these issues (Barozzi and Ruiz-Cecilia, 2020; Fernández Hawrylak et al., 2022; Martínez et al., 2013). This fact can lead to the emergence of prejudices and negative attitudes that have an impact on professional work (Lara-Garrido et al., 2023).

In the specific case of attitudes, negative behaviours towards LGB students continue to be perpetuated, which reinforces a climate that reproduces both binary (male-male and female-female) and heterosexual logic and has repercussions on the attention paid to students who deviate from these norms (Bartholomaeus et al., 2017; Coulter et al., 2021). Those studies focused on analysing these attitudes coincide in pointing out the existence of a series of components that give rise to one of the most current explanatory models, such as homonegativity (Quezada, 2016). It is therefore necessary to explore this term in greater depth, as well as to explain the relationship that exists with other factors, such as sexist attitudes. In this way, we can contribute to the adoption of the necessary strategies to address homonegativity in teachers and enable them to include content on SOGIE as part of a quality CSE.

Based on the above, this work pursues a twofold objective. On the one hand, it is interested in analysing the concept of homonegativity and its main manifestations in order to focus on modern homonegativity, as well as its perpetuation in teachers. On the other hand, it tries to address those pedagogical strategies that result in its prevention and intervention. To this end, the main contributions to the scientific literature on the study of attitudes, in general, and towards homosexuality, in particular, in teachers and their relationship with other factors, such as sexist behaviour, will be reviewed. Likewise, the evolution of these attitudes towards more subtle and modern manifestations will be shown, housing the proposal of a theoretical model that frames the manifestation of these attitudes. Finally, the main strategies for addressing homonegativity in teachers will be reviewed to enable them to offer CSE and advocate both respect and peaceful coexistence in schools.

THEORETICAL APPROACH TO THE CONCEPT OF ATTITUDE

Hall and Rodgers (2019) argue that attitudes are one of the main elements in the dynamics of prejudice and discrimination. Attitudes refer to those evaluative positions that an individual holds towards an object or focus of evaluative judgement, which refers to anything that can be evaluated from a favourable or unfavourable dimension (Hall & Rodgers, 2019; Maio et al., 2019). They can also present different degrees of value (e.g. negative, positive or neutral) and intensity (e.g. strongly or slightly negative) (Maio et al., 2019).

Research that has attempted to analyse the structure of attitudes has presented different explanatory models, one of the most influential and current being the multicompetent model of attitude (Maio et al., 2019). This model states that attitudes are composed of cognitive, affective and behavioural components (see Figure 1) (Arnau-Sabatés & Montané-Capdevilla, 2010; Maio et al., 2019). First, those thoughts and beliefs related to the object of the attitude allude to the cognitive component (Hall & Rodgers, 2019). Second, feelings and emotions that are linked to the attitude object are part of the affective component (Arnau-Sabatés & Montané-Capdevilla, 2010). Finally, past, present and future behavioural experiences towards the attitude object are included in the behavioural component (Maio et al., 2019).

The prediction and implementation of attitudes would be determined by the influence of these three elements (Ajzen & Fishbein, 2005; Arnau-Sabatés & Montané-Capdevilla, 2010). In this sense, they independently affect attitude response, although they are interrelated (Maio et al., 2019). Similarly, attitudes can generate responses in each of these dimensions (Ajzen & Fishbein, 2005; Hall & Rodgers, 2019). It should be noted that prejudice is seen as a specific type of negative attitude, directed towards people who belong to a certain social group (Navas-Luque & Cuadrado-Guirado, 2020).

THEORETICAL ASPECTS OF ATTITUDES TOWARDS SEXUAL ORIENTATION, GENDER IDENTITY AND EXPRESSION

Those studies aimed at analysing attitudes towards SOGIE coincide in pointing to the existence of different theoretical aspects that contribute to explaining prejudice towards this diversity.

Queer Theory

Research that focuses its efforts on analysing the approaches of Queer theory attempts to break with the essentialist view of sex, gender and sexual orientation, in order to adopt a constructionist perspective that determines the variability of meanings of what is considered to be male and female (Barozzi and Ruiz-Cecilia, 2020; Riggs and Treharne, 2017).

Figure 1. The Multicompetent model of attitude
Source: Maio et al. (2019)

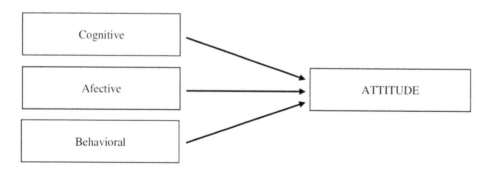

Sex and gender are underpinned by a binary system that responds to a socio-political end, which is human reproduction (Riggs and Treharne, 2017). Therefore, the heteronormative matrix refers to those social discourses in relation to sexual identity that promote the existence of two congruent sexes with two hierarchical and mutually complementary genders, which are expressed on the basis of heterosexuality (Carrera-Fernández et al., 2019). Based on a feminist approach, there are different contributions that seek to question heteronormativity and gender binarism, as well as the derived behaviours that discriminate and exclude. De Beauvoir (1949) denaturalised gender, considering it to be a cultural construction of sex that determines the way a woman or man is. Subsequently, one of the main fundamental theorists of Queer theory, Judith Butler (1999), deconstructed the sex-gender binarism, as she considered that gender is not related to sex nor does it respond to this classification. Therefore, she pointed out that people could not be classified only as male/male and female/female which, according to Carrera-Fernández et al. (2014, p. 654) "demonstrates that the sex of a body is a matter of degrees and not a classification into one of two complementary, closed and mutually exclusive categories".

Attitudes Towards Sexual Orientation, Gender Identity, and Expression

SOGIE refers to different affective-sexual orientations and the ways in which a person identifies and/or expresses their gender in an inclusive way and is understood as a source of collective wealth (Sánchez-Sáinz et al., 2016). The inclusion of this diversity through content in the school curriculum aims, on the one hand, to question normative thinking and the systems on which gender and sexuality are based (Meyer et al., 2015; Staley and Leonardi, 2019). On the other hand, incorporating educational practices that promote equality and non-discrimination of LGBT students (Meyer et al., 2015; Staley and Leonardi, 2016). However, there are some barriers that have an impact on the implementation of this issue, pointing to the attitudes of the educational community towards SOGIE (Bartholomaeus et al., 2017; Staley and Leonardi, 2019). These attitudes are based on sexual stigma which refers to stereotypes, prejudice and discrimination towards people motivated by their sexual orientation (Barrientos-Delgado et al., 2019; Morrison et al., 2016).

Evolution of Attitudes Towards Sexual Orientation, Gender Identity, and Expression

Since Weinberg defined homophobia as the fear or personal discomfort that heterosexual people may experience when interacting with homosexual people (Herek, 2004), this term has experienced a number of limitations that have affected its conceptualisation. One of them alludes to the view of the sex-gender binomial, so that homophobia is related to the expression of practices or behaviours that are associated with the opposite gender (Carrera-Fernández et al., 2019; D'Amore et al., 2022). Furthermore, it reflects the predominance of heterosexuality over other sexual orientations. Therefore, the definition of homophobia has undergone an evolution that includes those violent behaviours that have been the basis for conceptualising negative attitudes motivated by sexuality and gender.

On the one hand, both homophobia and biphobia share traits because attraction to people whose gender identity is similar is considered a transgression of the heterosexual norm (López-Sáez et al., 2020). In addition, Baiocco et al. (2020) add that bisexual people do not respond to the monosexuality associated with homosexual relationships. Morrison et al. (2019) point out that biphobia is the product of a double dichotomy delimited between heterosexual-homosexual and male-female. They also mention that this term has evolved into binegativity, which refers to prejudiced attitudes towards bisexual people.

On the other hand, breaking the sex-gender binarism is still punished and pathologised (Carrera-Fernández et al., 2014). Those who defy this binary gender division are considered homosexual. In this sense, Norton and Herek (2012) consider that transphobia and homophobia share similar constructs, as the structure of prejudice towards trans* people is similar to prejudice towards homosexual people. Transphobia refers to the fear or hatred of people who do not conform to socially established gender expectations such as masculine women, feminine men, and transvestites, transsexuals or transgender people (Hill, 2003; Hill and Willoughby, 2005).

Multicompetent Model of Attitudes Towards Affective-Sexual Diversity

The multi-competent model proposed by Maio et al. (2019) has been applied to the analysis of attitudes towards homosexual people. Callender (2015) argues that prejudice towards homosexual people includes an individual level, which refers to the perpetuation of this prejudice through self-reinforcing relationships between stereotypes (cognitive component), sexual prejudice (affective component) and discrimination (behavioural component).

Discrimination and hostility towards homosexual people have experienced an evolution parallel to other phenomena such as sexist attitudes and racism/xenophobia (Carrera-Fernández et al., 2018; Morrison and Morrison, 2011). From a feminist approach, discrimination that is rooted in gender, cultural, sexual orientation or gender identity prejudices is due to the construction of a hegemonic identity that privileges a few people and shows an imbalance of power (Gentlewarrior et al., 2008; Hicks and Jeyasingham, 2016). Heras-Sevilla and Ortega-Sánchez (2020) point out that due to the process of socialisation and gender pressure, these attitudes are learned and developed throughout life, which influences the willingness to perform certain behaviours, to a greater or lesser extent, inclusive or egalitarian. In this sense, they point to sexist behaviours, which imply a predisposition towards the differential treatment of men and women. These attitudes define what is proper to men and women, and therefore have repercussions on the way people relate to each other and interact with each other.

Manifestations of sexism have evolved from more traditional and explicit expressions to more modern and subtle ones (Morrison & Morrison, 2002; Pon, 2009). Similarly, negative attitudes towards homosexuality have followed a parallel path. There are different theoretical models that attempt to analyse hostility and rejection towards lesbian and gay people, one of the most widespread being that of Herek (2004). This model refers to overt and behavioural expressions of prejudice towards homosexual people such as verbal or psychological violence (e.g. teasing, insults and rumours) and physical aggression (Morell-Mengual et al., 2020; Saleiro et al., 2022). However, factors such as the normative pressure exerted by society to encourage respect for affective-sexual diversity and the promotion of equality have contributed to the emergence of more subtle or implicit expressions (Morrison & Morrison, 2002; Morrison et al., 2009). These expressions imply respect but not full acceptance of homosexual people, leading to rejection or exclusion that makes it difficult for them to express their sexual orientation (Molero et al., 2017; Rodríguez-Castro et al., 2013).

Currently, one of the most relevant approaches in the international context is the study of homonegativity (Quezada, 2016). According to Morrison and Morrison (2011, p. 2573), it refers to "that negative affective, cognitive and behavioural element towards those who are perceived, correctly or incorrectly, as gay men or lesbian women". Modern homonegativity harbours those more subtle and indirect attitudes of rejection and discrimination (Frías-Navarro et al., 2015; Rye & Meany, 2010) and reflects the following beliefs (Morrison & Morrison, 2002, p. 18): "(a) homosexual people are making unnecessary demands to change their status quo; (b) discrimination towards homosexual people is a thing of the past; and (c) homosexual people exaggerate their sexual preference, which prevents them from assimilating into mainstream culture".

Discriminatory attitudes towards affective-sexual diversity owe their success to stereotypical, biased and incorrect information about the construction of sexual orientation (Rodríguez-Castro et al., 2013). Following the multicompetent model of attitudes (Maio et al., 2019), this aspect derives in the existence of certain beliefs that refer to one's own knowledge about homosexuality that are included as the cognitive component of attitudes (Morrison & Morrison, 2002). These beliefs refer to false myths or misconceptions that are culturally accepted and lead to a negative attitude towards homosexuality. The affective component includes feelings towards homosexual people that are associated with positive or negative evaluations and that determine the predisposition to react in favour of or against this group. Finally, the intention, the desire to do something or the acceptance of certain behaviours allude to the behavioural component.

Stereotypes, prejudices and discrimination towards affective-sexual diversity can be carried out at different levels of processing, with the explicit (i.e. conscious) and implicit (i.e. unconscious) process being the most important. In this regard, Callender's (2015, p. 4) proposed cognitive-affective-behavioural model describes the main components of prejudice towards homosexual people, their associations and the factors mediating between them (see Figure 2). This model reflects descriptive and predictive properties, which can be interpreted from different levels of complexity. In relation to the first level, the links between stereotypes, prejudice and discrimination are described. Regarding the second level, two subcomponents are established within each category that reflect implicit processes (stereotypes that characterise gay men and lesbian women as people who break with the norms of how the genders should act, aversive prejudice and subtle discrimination) and explicit processes (stereotypes supported by positive beliefs of gender non-conformity, as well as implicit in the identification of homosexual people, explicit prejudice and overt discrimination). Finally, the third level describes those factors that mediate how the subcomponents interact with each other.

Modern Homonegativity in Teachers: Sociodemographic and Ideological Variables

The study of modern homonegativity in teachers has been linked to both socio-demographic and personal (e.g. gender identity) and ideological (e.g. political inclination) variables. On the one hand, the perpetuation of a hegemonic model of masculinity and the normalisation of both heterosexual practices may determine that gender identity and sexual orientation influence the display of negative attitudes towards homosexuality. Furthermore, contact with LGB people decreases prejudice and stereotypes towards LGB people. In short, teachers who identify as male, heterosexual and without friendships and/ or positive contact with LGB people show greater modern homonegativity (Bartholomaeus et al., 2017; Foy & Hodge, 2016; Heras-Sevilla & Ortega-Sánchez, 2020; Scandurra et al., 2017).

On the other hand, this larger sample of modern homonegativity is also related to teachers whose religious beliefs and political ideologies promote heteronormativity and traditional gender roles (Baiocco et al., 2020; Lara-Garrido et al., 2023; Westwood, 2022). Likewise, beliefs about the conceptualisation of homosexuality are identified as another relevant factor in justifying attitudes towards homosexual

Figure 2. Cognitive-affective-behavioural model of prejudice towards homosexual people
Note: *Bold boxes show the linking of explicit thoughts, feelings or behaviours, while faint boxes reflect implicit ones. Dotted boxes show a mixture of explicit and implicit thoughts. The arrows reflect the psychological linkages connecting the different sub-components, while those in bold and faint allude to explicit and implicit sub-components. The dashed arrow reflects the indirect linkage by which discrimination influences stereotypes. Source: Callender (2015, p. 4).*

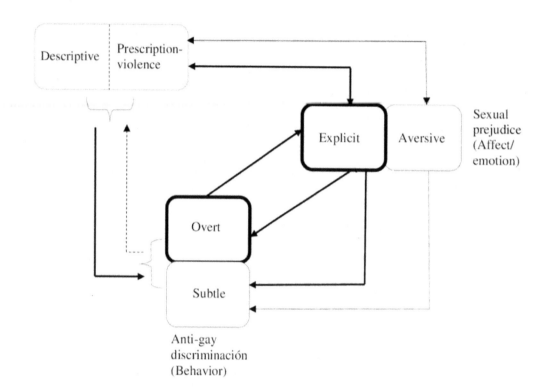

people. Teachers who associate homosexuality with environmental factors and/or an individual's choice reflect greater modern homonegativity than those who link it to genetic factors. This may be due to the belief that homosexuality may be a social influence and/or is a lifestyle choice of the individual, which is linked to worse attitudes towards homosexual people (Costa et al., 2018; Frías-Navarro et al., 2015). However, associating homosexuality with genetic factors refers to it being an inherent and uncontrollable characteristic, which is related to better attitudes (Lara-Garrido et al., 2023).

MODERN HOMONEGATIVITY AND CSE

CSE refers to a process of quality teaching and learning about the emotional, cognitive, physical and sexual aspects of sexuality and reproductive health, where values and beliefs related to these issues are explored (Fernández-Hawrylak et al., 2022; Sperling, 2021). For this reason, it implies addressing the DAS since, according to Granero-Andújar (2023, p. 97), "it is necessary to offer the necessary skills, knowledge and values for its normalisation, valorisation and respect". It is also contemplated in legislation[1] which stipulates that such education will include the specific needs of LGTBI people, avoiding any kind of stigmatisation or discrimination.

While the visibility of non-hegemonic forms of sexuality is claimed through CSE, there are still many difficulties in addressing SAD in a full and comprehensive manner. On the one hand, there is an unequal treatment of the contents in favour of the treatment of aspects such as the risks related to sexually transmitted infections, as well as unwanted pregnancies and their prevention. It also leads to the reproduction of discriminatory messages that perpetuate the different forms of violence suffered by those who do not conform to sexual norms (Granero-Andújar, 2023). On the other hand, the work of the body of education professionals to achieve a diverse and egalitarian affective-sexual education is highlighted (Fernández-Hawrylak et al., 2022; Granero-Andújar, 2023). However, it is suspected that the perpetuation of homonegativity among teachers may be a barrier to the provision of CSE. Taking into account the multicompetent model of attitude, the possession of erroneous knowledge about SSA may have an impact on certain stereotypes, myths, false beliefs and prejudices that influence the greater or lesser possession of negative attitudes towards this issue (Lara-Garrido et al., 2023). In addition to the above, the absence of specific training to improve knowledge and, consequently, attitudes towards SOGIE among teachers may influence the attention to CSE that integrates content related to this issue (Fernández-Hawrylak et al., 2022).

Modern Homonegativity in Teachers: Strategies for Prevention and Intervention

As has been indicated so far, modern homonegativity is present in various contexts of society; however, it is more accentuated in some contexts than in others, for example, in the educational sphere, where people are increasingly diverse and, at the same time, more homogeneous. Faced with this fact, teachers and future teachers must be trained in the subject of SOGIE, as they form an active and elementary part of the work of preventing, detecting, intervening and eradicating violence, in its different manifestations, from educational institutions (Barragán and Pérez-Jorge, 2020).

In general terms, teachers trained in affectivity and sexuality will be able to adapt the objectives and contents, among other curricular elements, of their programmes to respond to the interests and needs of students in this regard. In addition, they will take advantage of any everyday situation, such as a conversation that arises, a conflict, a television programme or any starting point to address the subject so that students feel free to express their doubts and concerns in this regard.

As Sánchez-Torrejón (2021) indicates, naturalness, a sense of humour and one's own experiences as a starting point for working on this type of subject are usually the recommendations among teachers.

However, the main fear, among others, of teachers when dealing with the subject of SOGIE is determined by families (López, 2005). Even so, teacher training and updating should facilitate this aspect by also considering collaboration with families and giving importance to the relationship with them. In this respect, parents' ideas must be accepted and taken into account. Otherwise, we will have a source of conflict from which the students will always suffer the most.

In short, we find ourselves in a society in movement, which changes and adapts to realities, and where education must try to keep pace as far as possible. For this reason, as well as in the classroom, we will also find diversity in the cloisters. This, far from being a problem, should motivate us to move towards respect and knowledge. Thus, teachers make up a focal group on which to work on this issue, due to the need to work with their students and also with their colleagues (Díez-Gutiérrez and Muñiz-Cortijo, 2022).

Based on everything we have discussed so far, Moreno (2015) argues that it is up to teachers to select the strategies for SOGIE training, as well as to establish the pedagogical goals it pursues. In this regard, González-Falcón (2019) proposes taking into account the following characteristics, attending, in turn, to three major educational criteria:

- Individuality. This refers to the possibility of offering multiple options for action and appropriation, as well as variety through the offer of resources and materials under different choices, which allow multiple interests and pedagogical needs to be met.
- Active listening, confidence and autonomy. Non-sexist and non-segregationist, free of any exclusion on the basis of gender and/or culture, based primarily on the social and educational interests of the teachers themselves. In the same way, a physical organisation that represents the own and unique identity of the teaching group under a meaningful environment of meeting, communication and multiple social relationships is taken into account.
- Meaningful learning. Critical teaching competence is prioritised, thus favouring research and exploration skills based on the different ways of presentation, appropriation and pedagogical use.

Based on the premises outlined so far, some strategies to promote positive teacher attitudes towards SOGIE are as follows (Barragán and Pérez-Jorge, 2020; Pichardo and Puche, 2019; Resa Ocio, 2021; Russell, 2011; Russell et al., 2021; Warwick et al., 2004):

- Teacher opinion. It is useful to know what teachers think about SOGIE and what vision they have of how the subject is addressed in the educational institution. To this end, inclusive debates can be carried out, in which the hegemony of heteropatriarchy in the different spheres of society and, more specifically, in the educational sphere, can be questioned. On the other hand, it is also possible to reflect on subordinated gender and sexual identities in an uncritical way.
  - Create anti-discrimination and anti-bullying strategies to promote positive attitudes among teachers towards SOGIE. All members of the educational community should work collaboratively to create caring educational institutions. To this end, it is essential that educational institutions include inclusive policies, anti-discrimination regulations, content related to CSE sexuality education and bullying prevention measures. In line with the pedagogy used, Sears (1999, p. 5) describes queer pedagogy as "creating elementary classrooms that challenge categorical thinking, promote interpersonal intelligence, and foster critical consciousness". Also, we find transformative pedagogy and "aims to create critical consciousness and to promote an analysis of the processes of mindset construction. Its methodology addresses inequity and discrimination by deconstructing stereotypes and prejudices" (Bedford, 2002, p. 138).
  - Raise awareness among all the people in the different educational institutions so that they know how to act in situations of SOGIE discrimination. In this case, ongoing teacher training in SOGIE is essential to achieve an inclusive education system, a system that caters for the diversity of students. In this sense, not only LGB associations or groups are the institutions or people who should offer courses and/or workshops, but such training should also be offered by the Administration, the Ministry of Education or the Departments of Education of each autonomous community. In short, apart from courses and conferences, other strategies

- should also be offered to work on SOGIE, such as: teaching groups, congresses, working groups, appropriate literature, debates, etc.
- Introduce information about SOGIE in curricula. SOGIE-related content should always be present in all curricula at all educational stages. According to Díaz de Greñu and Parejo (2013), SOGIE should be reflected in the School Education Project, Curriculum Project, Classroom Programming and Diversity Attention Plan. With regard to the organisation of educational institutions' regulations, it is important that all members work together, with the fundamental aim of reducing discriminatory behaviour related to SOGIE; that is, to create opportunities for people to increase their knowledge and critically reflect on the consequences that can arise from prejudice and social exclusion. Inclusive language should also be used (to promote diversity, respect, equality and non-acceptance of sexual discrimination), learning materials (such materials should be made available to all who request them), inclusive educational practices, cooperative learning, peer support, discussions, taking into account learners' preconceptions, etc. In addition to this, work must be done on information linked to gender and, more broadly, SOGIE, which must be reoriented, as there are erroneous conceptions about it.
- Availability of all sources of information related to SOGIE. Each educational institution should provide the usual information channels to make known all sources of information related to SOGIE.

For their part, Donoso and Velasco (2013) argue that universities should include and promote teaching and research on equality in a cross-cutting manner at all levels of academic training, thus preventing the emergence of discriminatory attitudes towards minority groups.

Likewise, de Stéfano et al. (2015) stated the importance of creating qualitative techniques to foster positive attitudes in students towards the phenomenon of SOGIE. Initially, the technique of participant observation should be used to get to know and analyse the particularities of individuals. Subsequently, a set of workshops on bodily, SOGIE and family diversity is implemented. Behaviours, discourses and attitudes should be recorded in the workshops, in order to continue generating new strategies, which will make it possible to continue working on the phenomenon of SOGIE from different approaches.

Cava and Musitu (2002), similarly, highlighted that, in order to develop an inclusive educational community, it is essential to develop values such as coexistence, acceptance of student diversity, empathy, and other personal and social resources of the teacher body. Along the same lines, Domínguez and Vázquez (2015) stated that, in order to develop the values mentioned in this same paragraph, it is necessary to work cooperatively and in heterogeneous groups.

In turn, intervention programmes are also resources that can be created and worked on in educational institutions to improve relations between all people, prevent discriminatory behaviour towards certain groups of individuals and favour the social inclusion of all students (Garaigordobil & Oñederra, 2010). Taking these intervention programmes into consideration, we agree with Garrido and Morales (2014) that a greater number of resources should be included to address discriminatory behaviour and to promote attention to SOGIE. It is urgent to work on the issue of SOGIE in the initial and ongoing training of teachers, with the aim of creatin quality educational centers for all, centers that act under the democratic principles of the right to equal opportunities and to choose one sexual orientation or another without receiving discriminatory treatment.

CONCLUSION

This paper aims to analyse the concept of homonegativity, its main manifestations and its relationship with other factors such as sexist attitudes, as well as its perpetuation in teachers according to sociodemographic, personal and ideological variables. In addition, pedagogical strategies are shown aimed at its approach by teachers and that contribute to offering quality ESI in their teaching work.

Attitudes towards sogie are articulated in different theoretical aspects that explain prejudice towards LGB people. Specifically, these attitudes are related to other behaviours such as sexist behaviours, as they are based on similar constructs that have resulted in a parallel evolution in their manifestation towards more modern or subtle forms. The concept of modern homonegativity encompasses the different components and their relationships and is therefore considered appropriate for the analysis of negative attitudes towards homosexuality (Morrison & Morrison, 2002).

Furthermore, there are different socio-demographic and personal variables, as well as ideological variables that determine the sample of modern homonegativity in teachers. As stated and substantiated above, teacher training in CSE and SOGIE is a priority (Fernández-Hawrylak et al., 2022). The analysis of teachers' attitudes and the factors that determine their expression can be oriented towards the improvement of training (Coulter et al., 2021).

Following the previous line, all this can be carried out through education, which advocates the implementation of a socialization process that, as far as possible, transcends the boundaries of school institutions. Indeed, there are everyday learning experiences outside their formal framework. Even so, based on Cifuentes-Zunino et al. (2020), the school is a privileged space for preventing, detecting and intervening, in our case, modern homonegativity: it plays an important role in the legitimisation of stereotyped models.

As Moreno-Sánchez (2021, p. 1) points out, hierarchisation and belonging to a social class, to an ethnic group, the fact of presenting certain physical characteristics or gender, among many other aspects, "are some of the issues that determine the socialisation process and, more broadly, the educational process, highlighting the complexity of educational organisations".

For this, we must be trained, a training that can be supported by the different regulations in which respect for SOGIE is defended and promoted (Granero-Andújar & Márquez-Díaz, 2022). A clear example of this is Organic Law 3/2020, of 29 December, which modifies Organic Law 2/2006, of 3 May, on Education (LOMLOE, 2020), which adopts a gender equity perspective through co-education and promotes equal opportunities between women and men at all educational stages, the prevention of gender-based violence, as well as tolerance towards SOGIE.

Precisely, if we focus on the university education stage, future teachers, as well as active teachers, must have adequate training in this subject, among other aspects, to design, implement and evaluate training proposals, through which, as far as possible, the problem of modern homonegativity can be eradicated, a problem increasingly linked to more subtle and difficult to detect behaviour, such as looks, gestures, etc. (Fernández-Hawrylak et al, 2022; Hernáinz & Márquez, 2011; Penna, 2015). In this way, following Moreno-Sánchez (2013), we will manage to create an inclusive school; that is, a school free of any type of discrimination and/or violence in its multiple manifestations.

REFERENCES

Ajzen, I., & Fishbein, M. (2005). The Influence of Attitudes on Behavior. In D. Albarracín, B. T. Johnson, & M. P. Zanna (Eds.), *The Handbook of Attitudes* (pp. 173–222). Lawrence Erlbaum Associates, Inc.

Arnau-Sabatés, L., & Montané-Capdevilla, J. (2010). Aportaciones sobre la relación conceptual entre actitud y competencia, desde la teoría del cambio de actitudes. *Electronic Journal of Research in Educational Psychology*, 8(3), 1283–1302. doi:10.25115/ejrep.v8i22.1416

Baiocco, R., Pistella, J., & Morelli, M. (2020). Coming Out to Parents in Lesbian and Bisexual Women: The Role of Internalized Sexual Stigma and Positive LB Identity. *Frontiers in Psychology*, 11, 1–11. doi:10.3389/fpsyg.2020.609885 PMID:33363501

Barozzi, S., & Ruiz-Cecilia, R. (2020). Training in gender and sexual identities in EFL teaching. Participants' contributions. *Onomázein. Revista de Lingüística. Filología y Educación*, 6(6), 84–103. doi:10.7764/onomazein.ne6.05

Barragán, F., & Pérez-Jorge, D. (2020). Combating homophobia, lesbophobia, biphobia and transphobia: A liberating and subversive educational alternative for desires. *Heliyon*, 6(10), 1–14. doi:10.1016/j.heliyon.2020.e05225

Barrientos-Delgado, P., Montenegro, C., & Andrade, D. (2022). Perspectiva de Género en Prácticas Educativas del Profesorado en Formación: Una Aproximación Etnográfica. *Revista Internacional de Educación para la Justicia Social*, 11(1). doi:10.15366/riejs2022.11.1.013

Bartholomaeus, C., Riggs, D. W., & Andrew, Y. (2017). The capacity of South Australian primary school teachers and pre-service teachers to work with trans and gender diverse students. *Teaching and Teacher Education*, 65, 127–135. doi:10.1016/j.tate.2017.03.006

Butler, J. (1990). *Gender trouble: Feminism and the subversion of identity*. Routledge.

Callender, K. A. (2015). Understanding antigay bias from a cognitive-affective-behavioral perspective. *Journal of Homosexuality*, 62(6), 782–803. doi:10.1080/00918369.2014.998965 PMID:25530128

Carrera-Fernández, M. V., Almeida, A., Cid-Fernández, X. M., Vallejo-Medina, P., & Rodríguez-Castro, Y. (2019). Patrolling the boundaries of gender: Beliefs, attitudes and behaviors toward trans and gender diverse people in Portuguese adolescents. *International Journal of Sexual Health*, 32(1), 40–56. doi:10.1080/19317611.2019.1701170

Carrera-Fernández, M. V., Cid-Fernández, X. M., Almeida, A., González-Fernández, A., & Lameiras-Fernández, M. (2018). Attitudes Toward Cultural Diversity in Spanish and Portuguese Adolescents of Secondary Education: The Influence of Heteronormativity and Moral Disengagement in School Bullying. *Revista de Psicodidáctica*, 23(1), 17–25. doi:10.1016/j.psicod.2017.07.004

Carrera-Fernández, M. V., Lameiras-Fernández, M., Rodríguez-Castro, Y., & Vallejo-Medina, P. (2014). Spanish adolescents' attitudes toward trans people: Proposal and validation of a short form of the Genderism and Transphobia Scale. *Journal of Sex Research*, 51(6), 654–666. doi:10.1080/00224499.2013.773577 PMID:23767992

Cava, J., & Musitu, G. (2002). *La convivencia en la escuela*. Paidós.

Cifuentes-Zunino, F., Pascual, J., & Carrer-Russell, C. (2020). Acoso escolar por orientación sexual, identidad y expresión de género en institutos de educación secundaria catalanes. *Revista de Educación Inclusiva, 13*(2), 153-174. https://revistaeducacioninclusiva.es/index.php/REI/article/download/604/584

Costa, P. A., Carneiro, F. A., Esposito, F., D'Amore, S., & Green, R. J. (2018). Sexual Prejudice in Portugal: Results from the First Wave European Study on Heterosexual's Attitudes Toward Same-Gender Marriage and Parenting. *Sexuality Research & Social Policy, 15*(1), 99–110. doi:10.1007/s13178-017-0292-y

Coulter, R. W. S., Colvin, S., Onufer, L. R., Arnold, G., Akiva, T., D'Ambrogi, E., & Davis, V. (2021). Training pre-service teachers to better serve LGBTQ high school students. *Journal of Education for Teaching, 47*(2), 234–254. doi:10.1080/02607476.2020.1851137 PMID:33986557

D'Amore, S., Wollast, R., Green, R. J., Bouchat, P., Costa, P. A., Katuzny, K., Scali, T., Balocco, R., Vecho, O., Mijas, M. E., Aparicio, M. E., Geroulanou, K., & Klein, O. (2022). Heterosexual University Students' Attitudes Toward Same-Sex Couples and Parents Across Seven European Countries. *Sexuality Research & Social Policy, 19*(2), 791–804. doi:10.1007/s13178-020-00511-4

De Beauvoir, S. (1949). *El segundo sexo*. Éditions Gallimard.

De Stéfano, M., Puche, L., & Pichardo, J. I. (2015). El compromiso de la investigación social en la construcción de otra escuela posible. *Revista Interuniversitaria de Formación del Profesorado, 82*(29), 50-54. https://www.redalyc.org/pdf/274/27439665004.pdf

Díaz de Greñu, S., & Parejo, J. (2013). La promoción de la igualdad y el respeto de la diversidad afectivo sexual: Bases de un programa de orientación y tutoría para educación secundaria. *Revista Española de Orientación y Psicopedagogía, 24*(3), 63–79. doi:10.5944/reop.vol.24.num.3.2013.11245

Domínguez, J., & Vázquez, E. (2015). Medidas de atención a la diversidad: Perspectiva del equipo de orientación específico. *Revista de Estudios e Investigación en Psicología y Educación, 11*, 1–4. doi:10.17979/reipe.2015.0.11.87

Donoso, T., & Velasco, A. (2013). ¿Por qué una propuesta de formación en perspectiva de género en el ámbito universitario? *Profesorado, Revista de Currículum y Formación del Profesorado, 17*(1), 71-88. https://www.ugr.es/~recfpro/rev171ART5.pdf

Fernandez-Hawrylak, M., Alonso-Martínez, L., Sevilla-Ortega, E., & Ruiz-Ruiz, M. E. (2022). Inclusión de la Diversidad Sexual en los Centros Educativos desde la Perspectiva del Profesorado: Un Estudio Cualitativo. *Revista Internacional de Educación para la Justicia Social, 11*(2), 81–97. doi:10.15366/riejs2022.11.2.005

Foy, J. K., & Hodge, S. (2016). Preparing Educators for a Diverse World: Understanding Sexual Prejudice among Pre-Service Teachers. *Prairie Journal of Educational Research, 1*(1). doi:10.4148/2373-0994.1005

Frías-Navarro, D., Monterde-i-Bort, H., Pascual-Soler, M., & Badenes-Ribera, L. (2015). Etiology of Homosexuality and Attitudes Toward Same-Sex Parenting: A Randomized Study. *Journal of Sex Research, 52*(2), 151–161. doi:10.1080/00224499.2013.802757 PMID:24024528

Garaigordobil, M., & Oñederra, J. (2010). *La violencia entre iguales*. Pirámide.

Garrido, M. R., & Morales, Z. (2014). Una aproximación a la homofobia desde la psicología. Propuestas de intervención. *Psicología, Conocimiento y Sociedad*, *4*(1), 100–109. https://www.redalyc.org/pdf/4758/475847268005.pdf

Gentlewarrior, S., Martin-Jearld, A., Skok, A., & Sweetser, K. (2008). Culturally Competent Feminist Social Work. *Affilia*, *24*(3), 210–222. doi:10.1177/0886109908319117

González-Falcón, I. (2019). *Variables didácticas y organizativas para la innovación y el liderazgo educativo. Guía docente*. Servicio de Publicaciones de la Universidad de Huelva.

Granero-Andújar, A. (2023). *Educación afectivo-sexual y colectivo LGTBIQ. Una relación de encuentros y desencuentros*. Octaedro. doi:10.36006/09142-1

Granero-Andújar, A., & Márquez-Díaz, J. R. (2022). Análisis de la normativa estatal española y autonómica andaluza en lo referido al colectivo LGTBI en el marco educativo. *Educare (San José)*, *26*(3), 1–24. doi:10.15359/ree.26-3.29

Hall, W. J., & Rodgers, G. K. (2019). Teachers' attitudes toward homosexuality and the lesbian, gay, bisexual, and queer community in the United States. *Social Psychology of Education*, *22*(1), 23–41. doi:10.1007/s11218-018-9463-9

Heras-Sevilla, D., & Ortega-Sánchez, D. (2020). Evaluation of sexist and prejudiced attitudes toward homosexuality in Spanish future teachers: Analysis of related variables. *Frontiers in Psychology*, *11*, 572553. doi:10.3389/fpsyg.2020.572553 PMID:33013607

Herek, G. M. (2004). Beyond "Homophobia": Thinking About Sexual Prejudice and Stigma in the Twenty-First Century. *Sexuality Research & Social Policy*, *1*(2), 6–24. doi:10.1525/srsp.2004.1.2.6

Hernáinz, E., & Márquez, D. (2011). *Manual Educativo para la Diversidad*. Fundación Reflejos de Venezuela, Unión Afirmativa de Venezuela y Amnistía Internacional Venezuela.

Hicks, S., & Jeyasingham, D. (2016). Social Work, Queer Theory and After: A Genealogy of Sexuality Theory in Neo-Liberal Times. *British Journal of Social Work*, *46*(8), 2357–2373. doi:10.1093/bjsw/bcw103

Hill, D. B. (2003). Genderism, transphobia, and gender bashing: A framework for interpreting anti-transgender violence. In B. Wallace & R. Carter (Eds.), *Understanding and dealing with violence: A multicultural approach* (pp. 113–136). SAGE., doi:10.4135/9781452231723.n4

Hill, D. B., & Willoughby, L. B. (2005). The Development and Validation of the Genderism and Transphobia Scale. *Sex Roles*, *53*(7-8), 531–544. doi:10.1007/s11199-005-7140-x

ILGA-Europe. (2023). *Annual Review of the Human Rights Situation of Lesbian, Gay, Bisexual, Trans and Intersex people in Europe and central Asia*. ILGA. https://www.ilga-europe.org/report/annual-review-2023/

Jaffe, K. D., Dessel, A. B., & Woodford, M. R. (2016). The nature of incoming graduate social work students' attitudes toward sexual minorities. *Journal of Gay & Lesbian Social Services*, *28*(4), 255–276. doi:10.1080/10538720.2016.1224210

Lara-Garrido, A. S., Álvarez-Bernardo, G., & García-Berbén, A. B. (2023). Conocimientos hacia la Homosexualidad y Homonegatividad Moderna en Estudiantes de Educación Universitarios. *Revista Internacional de Educación para la Justicia Social, 12*(2), 213–229. doi:10.15366/riejs2023.12.2.012

López-Diosdado, M. (2016). Aprender a vivir juntos: una asignatura pendiente en la formación docente. *Revista Nacional e Internacional de Educación Inclusiva, 9*(2), 215-224. https://revistaeducacioninclusiva.es/index.php/REI/article/download/61/56

López-Sáez, M. Á., García-Dauder, D., & Montero, I. (2020). Correlate Attitudes Toward LGBT and Sexism in Spanish Psychology Students. *Frontiers in Psychology, 11*, e2063. doi:10.3389/fpsyg.2020.02063 PMID:32973622

Maio, G. R., Haddock, G., & Verplanken, B. (2019). *The psychology of attitudes and attitudes change* (3rd ed.). SAGE.

Martínez, J. L., González, E., Vicario-Molina, I., Fernández-Fuertes, A. A., Carcedo, R. J., Fuertes, A., & Orgaz, B. (2013). Formación del profesorado en educación sexual: Pasado, presente y futuro. *Magister, 25*(1), 35–42. doi:10.1016/S0212-6796(13)70005-7

Meyer, E. J., Taylor, C., & Peter, T. (2015). Perspectives on gender and sexual diversity (GSD)-inclusive education: Comparisons between gay/lesbian/bisexual and straight educators. *Sex Education, 15*(3), 221–234. doi:10.1080/14681811.2014.979341

Molero, F., Silván-Ferrero, P., Fuster-Ruiz de Apodaca, M. J., Nouvilas-Pallejá, E., & Pérez-Garín, D. (2017). Subtle and blatant perceived discrimination and wellbeing in lesbians and gay men in Spain: The role of social support. *Psicothema, 29*(4), 475–481. doi:10.7334/psicothema2016.296 PMID:29048306

Morell-Mengual, V., Gil-Llario, M. D., & Gil-Juliá, B. (2020). Prevalencia e influencia de la violencia homofóbica sobre la sintomatología depresiva y el nivel de autoestima. *Informació Psicològica, 120*, 80–92. doi:10.14635/IPSIC.2020.120.6

Moreno, F. (2015). Función pedagógica de los recursos materiales en Educación Infantil. *Revista de Comunicación Vivat Academia, 133*, 12–25. doi:10.15178/va.2015.133.12-25

Moreno-Sánchez, E. (Coord.). (2013). *La urdimbre sexista: violencia de género en la escuela primaria.* Aljibe.

Moreno-Sánchez, E. (2021). Violencia de género en la escuela: hay una oportunidad para la prevención. The Conversation.

Morrison, M. A., Kiss, M. J., Parker, K., Hamp, T., & Morrison, T. G. (2019). A systematic review of the psychometric properties of binegativity scales. *Journal of Bisexuality, 19*(1), 23–50. doi:10.1080/15299716.2019.1576153

Morrison, M. A., & Morrison, T. G. (2002). Development and validation of a scale measuring modern prejudice toward gay men and lesbian women. *Journal of Homosexuality, 43*(2), 15–37. doi:10.1300/J082v43n02_02 PMID:12739696

Morrison, M. A., & Morrison, T. G. (2011). Sexual Orientation Bias Toward Gay Men and Lesbian Women: Modern Homonegative Attitudes and Their Association With Discriminatory Behavioral Intentions. *Journal of Applied Social Psychology*, *41*(11), 2573–2599. doi:10.1111/j.1559-1816.2011.00838.x

Morrison, M. A., Morrison, T. G., & Franklin, R. (2009). Modern and Old-fashioned Homonegativity Among Samples of Canadian and American University Students. *Journal of Cross-Cultural Psychology*, *40*(4), 523–542. doi:10.1177/0022022109335053

Morrison, T. G., Bishop, C. J., Morrison, M. A., & Parker-Taneo, K. (2016). A Psychometric Review of Measures Assessing Discrimination Against Sexual Minorities. *Journal of Homosexuality*, *63*(8), 1086–1126. doi:10.1080/00918369.2015.1117903 PMID:26566991

Navas-Luque, M. y Cuadrado-Guirado, I. (Coords.). (2020). *El estudio del prejuicio en Psicología Social*. Editorial Sanz y Torres.

Norton, A. T., & Herek, G. M. (2012). Heterosexuals' attitudes toward transgender people: Findings from a national probability sample of US adults. *Sex Roles*, *68*(11-12), 738–753. doi:10.1007/s11199-011-0110-6

Penna, M. (2015). Homofobia en las aulas universitarias: Un meta-análisis. *Revista de Docencia Universitaria*, *13*(1), 197–200. doi:10.4995/redu.2015.6445

Pichardo, J. I., & de Stefano, M. (2020). *Somos Diversidad. Actividades para la formación de profesionales de la educación formal y no formal en diversidad sexual, familiar, corporal y de expresión e identidad de género*. Ministerio de Derechos Sociales y Agenda 2030, y Ministerio de Igualdad. https://www.igualdad.gob.es/ministerio/dglgtbi/Documents/SomosDiversidad_DIGITAL_0707.pdf

Pichardo, J. I., & Puche, L. (2019). Universidad y diversidad sexo-genérica: Barreras, innovaciones y retos de futuro. *Methaodos. Revista de Ciencias Sociales*, *7*(1), 10–26. doi:10.17502/m.rcs.v7i1.287

Pon, P. (2009). Cultural Competency as New Racism: An Ontology of Forgetting. *Journal of Progressive Human Services*, *20*(1), 59–71. doi:10.1080/10428230902871173

Quezada, F. (2016). Una medida de la homonegatividad breve, unidimensional e independiente de los efectos positivos y negativos: Evidencia de validez de la escala de Wrench en Chile. *Salud y Sociedad*, *7*(1), 10–28. doi:10.22199/S07187475.2016.0001.00001

Riggs, D. W., & Treharne, G. J. (2017). Queer Theory. In B. Gough (Ed.), *The Palgrave Handbook of Critical Social Psychology* (pp. 101–121). Springer Link. doi:10.1057/978-1-137-51018-1_6

Rodríguez-Castro, Y., Lameiras-Fernández, M., Carrera-Fernández, V., & Vallejo-Medina, P. (2013). Validación de la Escala de Homofobia Moderna en una muestra de adolescentes. *Anales de Psicología*, *29*(2), 523–533. doi:10.6018/analesps.29.2.137931

Russell, S. T. (2011). Challenging homophobia in schools: Policies and programs for safe school climates. *Educar em Revista*, *39*(39), 123–138. doi:10.1590/S0104-40602011000100009

Russell, S. T., Bishop, M. D., Saba, V. C., James, I., & Ioverno, S. (2021). Promoting School Safety for LGBTQ and All Students. *Policy Insights from the Behavioral and Brain Sciences*, *8*(2), 160–166. doi:10.1177/23727322211031938 PMID:34557581

Saleiro, S. P., Ramalho, N., de Menezes, M. S. y Gato, J. (2022). *Estudo Nacional sobre as necessidades das pessoas LGBTI e sobre a discriminação em razão da orientação sexual, identidade e expressão de género e características sexuais*. Comissão para a Cidadania e Igualdade de Género.

Sánchez-Sainz, M., Penna-Tosso, M., & Rosa-Rodríguez, B. (2016). *Somos como somos: Deconstruyendo y transformando la escuela*. Los Libros de la Catarata.

Scandurra, C., Picariello, S., Valerio, P., & Amodeo, A. L. (2017). Sexism, homophobia and transphobia in a sample of Italian pre-service teachers: The role of socio-demographic features. *Journal of Education for Teaching*, 43(2), 245–261. doi:10.1080/02607476.2017.1286794

Sperling, J. (2021). Comprehensive sexual health education and intersex (in)visibility: An ethnographic exploration inside a California high school classroom. *Sex Education*, 21(5), 584–599. doi:10.1080/14681811.2021.1931834

Staley, S., & Leonardi, B. (2016). Leaning In to Discomfort: Preparing Literacy Teachers for Gender and Sexual Diversity. *Research in the Teaching of English*, 51(2), 209–229. doi:10.58680/rte201628875

Staley, S., & Leonardi, B. (2019). Complicating What We Know: Focusing on Educators' Processes of Becoming Gender and Sexual Diversity Inclusive. *Theory into Practice*, 58(1), 29–38. doi:10.1080/00405841.2018.1536916

Warwick, I., Chase, E., Aggleton, P. y Sanders, S. (2004). *Homophobia, sexual orientation and schools: A review and implications for action*. DfES.

ADDITIONAL READING

Bejarano, M. T., Martínez, I., & Blanco, M. (2019). Coeducar hoy: Reflexiones desde las pedagogías feministas para la despatriarcalización del currículum. *Tendencias Pedagógicas*, 34, 37–50. doi:10.15366/tp2019.34.004

Butler, J. (1990). *Gender trouble: Feminism and the subversion of identity*. Routledge.

De Beauvoir, S. (1949). *El segundo sexo*. Éditions Gallimard.

Diversity and Childhood. (2021). *Diversidad e infancia: Cambiando las actitudes sociales hacia la diversidad de género en los niños de toda Europa*. Unión Europea.

Gavilán, J. (2016). *Infancia y transexualidad*. Los Libros de la Catarata.

Granero Andújar, A. (2023). *Educación afectivo-sexual y colectivo LGTBIQ: Una relación de encuentros y desencuentros*. Octaedro. doi:10.36006/09142

Granero-Andújar, A. (2023). *Educación afectivo-sexual y colectivo LGTBIQ. Una relación de encuentros y desencuentros*. Octaedro. doi:10.36006/09142-1

Guash, O. (2006). *Héroes, Científicos, Heterosexuales y Gays. Los varones en la perspectiva de género*. Bellaterra.

Marine, S. (2017). Changing the frame: Queering access to higher education for trans* students. *International Journal of Qualitative Studies in Education : QSE, 30*(3), 217–233. doi:10.1080/09518398.2016.1268279

McBride, R. S. (2021). A literature review of the secondary school experiences of trans youth. *Journal of LGBT Youth, 18*(2), 103–134. doi:10.1080/19361653.2020.1727815

McBride, R. S., & Neary, A. (2021). Trans and gender diverse youth resisting cisnormativity in school. *Gender and Education, 33*(8), 1090–1107. doi:10.1080/09540253.2021.1884201

Navas-Luque, M. y Cuadrado-Guirado, I. (Coords.) (2020). *El estudio del prejuicio en Psicología Social*. Editorial Sanz y Torres.

Pichardo Galán, J. I., de Stéfano Barbero, M., Faure, J., Sáenz, M., & Williams Ramos, J. (2015). *Abrazar la diversidad: propuestas para una educación libre de acoso homofóbico y transfóbico*. Instituto de la Mujer y para la Igualdad de Oportunidades.

Sánchez-Sáinz, M. (2019). *Pedagogías Queer: ¿Nos arriesgamos a hacer otra educación?* Los Libros de la Catarata.

WE PROJECT. (2020-2022). *Promoting work-based equality for LGBT+Q+ YOUNG*. Unión Europea.

KEY TERMS AND DEFINITIONS

Active Listening: Communication skill in which you pay full attention to what the other person is saying, understand their point of view, show interest and respond appropriately.

Heteronormativity: Hierarchical system from which derives a sex-gender binarism that identifies two opposite and differentiated genders (male/male vs. female/female), from which a series of roles and behaviours arise that are considered specific to one or the other gender. It also normalises heterosexual sexual relations and practices (Carrera-Fernández et al., 2019).

Homophobia: Phobia or pathological fear of being with a homosexual person in an enclosed space (Herek, 2004).

Inclusive Language: A form of communication that seeks to avoid discrimination and exclusion of people on the basis of their individual characteristics. It consists of using language that makes diversity visible and promotes equal rights and opportunities for all people.

Intervention Strategy: A detailed plan designed to address and resolve issues related to teaching and learning processes. This strategy is designed to identify and address the barriers that prevent students from reaching their full potential, thereby providing them with the support they need to succeed in the educational environment.

Meaningful Learning: The process by which learners relate new information to their prior knowledge, experiences and values, creating strong and lasting connections in their memory.

Modern Homonegativity: Set of affective, cognitive and behavioural components that determine negative attitudes towards homosexual persons. It moves away from traditional prejudice based on moral objections and includes more subtle and modern attitudes of rejection and discrimination (Morrison & Morrison, 2011).

Multicompetent Model of Attitude: A model that determines that attitudes are evaluations of an object that include cognitive, affective and behavioural components. The direct and independent influence of these three factors explains attitude prediction and performance (Ajzen & Fishbein, 2005; Maio et al., 2019).

Prevention Strategy: Planned and coordinated action whose main objective is to prevent the occurrence of risk situations or problems in the school environment. This strategy can cover different areas such as bullying prevention, promotion of positive coexistence, addiction prevention, sex education, among others.

Transphobia: Fear or hatred of people who do not conform to socially established gender expectations such as masculine women, feminine men and transvestites, transsexuals or transgender people (Hill, 2003).

ENDNOTE

[1] *Ley 4/2023, de 28 de febrero, para la igualdad real y efectiva de las personas trans y para la garantía de los derechos de las personas LGTBI*, in Spain, and *Lei nº 61/2018, de 21 de Maio. Aprova a Estratégia Nacional para a Igualdade e a Não Discriminação 2018-2030*, in Portugal, among others.

Chapter 10
Comprehensive Sexual Education:
Analysis of Psychoeducational Materials

Karen Elin Acosta Buralli
CONICET, Universidad de Buenos Aires, Argentina

María Luisa Silva
CONICET, Argentina

Jazmín Cevasco
CONICET, Universidad de Buenos Aires, Argentina

ABSTRACT

Gender violence is a problem of central relevance since its consequences are fatal and affect the world's population. Comprehensive sexual education (CSE) is considered a key tool to apply gender violence prevention (PGV) strategies. However, the adequate implementation of CSE depends largely on teacher training. Therefore, the objective of this chapter is to improve the understanding of psychoeducational materials on CSE and PGV intended for teachers. The role of causal connectivity of a material on general CSE and one specifically on PGV from a manual for secondary school teachers designed by the Ministry of Education of Argentina (2022) was analyzed. The results demonstrated the predominance of a low level of causal connectivity in both materials. Considering the role of causal connectivity, as a textual characteristic that facilitates comprehension, could optimize the development of CSE and PGV materials for teachers and, consequently, contribute to the training and implementation of CSE and PGV.

INTRODUCTION

In the last decade, Comprehensive Sexual Education (CSE) has become an important part of education. In fact, many countries have advocated for legislation to promote CSE, and o international organizations

DOI: 10.4018/979-8-3693-2053-2.ch010

have highlighted its importance for student health. One of their recommendations involves improving the resources promoting educational practices of comprehensive sexual education (CSE) and prevention of gender violence (PGV). In relation to this, it has been observed that to facilitate the instruction of CSE, it is important to promote the comprehension of CSE and PGV materials, especially when they are part of teacher training courses. This chapter focuses on analyzing the causal connectivity of statements, as a textual feature that facilitates comprehension, in two psychoeducational teaching materials on CSE and PGV. These materials are part of teaching training materials that are included in teacher training courses by the Department of Education of Argentina.

Psychoeducational materials on CSE are crucial for the prevention of complex social problems. There is extensive literature that highlights how psychoeducational interventions on CSE, and systematic training can help solve and prevent social problems such as gender violence, teenage pregnancy, dating violence, absences and limitations of parental co-responsibilities in upbringing and care, etc. (Badrlah et al., 2023; Fonner et al., 2014). These problems have been observed to have a high prevalence, especially in societies and communities in which relationships exhibit asymmetry, and in which gender minorities face exclusion and social disadvantages.This social injustices are transmitted from generation to generation. These patterns in which unequal relationships are formed with gender norms that perpetuate violence are usually characterized as "patriarchal schemes of domination" (Gregorio et al., 2023; Makleff et al., 2020).

Evidence about the positive impact of promoting learning about CSE has generated that in different countries, especially in Latin America, CSE content has been included in the school curriculum. As was suggested, the importance of CSE has been highlighted by international organizations. It should also be noted that legislation must be accompanied by resources that allow its implementation (UNESCO, 2021). Considering this, it is crucial that teachers have appropriate training. Materials that are part of teacher training courses tend to include booklets or handbooks with focus on expository content and include self-assessment and reflection activities (Carman et al., 2011). However, teacher training courses do not tend to include instruction on how to teach CSE (Ahmed et al., 2006).

This gap points to the need to promote CSE training in Teacher training institutions and, and to develop teaching training materials that facilitate learning (Vanwesenbeeck et al., 2016). Considering prior studies, we can propose that if these materials are revised, learning can be facilitated. In consequence, the aim of this work is to contribute to the promotion of the development of psychoeducational materials focused on CSE. With this aim, we will examine the establishment of causal connections among statements in sample texts that were developed in Argentina. We focus on these connections, given that previous studies have recognized that establishing causal connections facilitate comprehension (Cevasco & Acosta Buralli, 2023). The aim of this chapter is to analyze the role of causal connectivity in two psychoeducational materials: one based on general CSE content and another on PGV. Both materials are included in a handbook for highschool teachers designed by the Ministry of Education of Argentina (2022).

The chapter shows the following organization: the first section presents the conceptual framework of Psychoeducation and some pedagogical guidelines relevant to the development of teaching materials. The second section reviews prior studies on these issues. The following sections present the analysis of Psychoeducation materials, identify some possible gaps, and provide recommendations for future studies. Finally, we reflect on the importance of developing CSE materials that properly promote learning on the PGV.

THE ROLE OF CAUSAL STRUCTURE IN PSYCHOEDUCATIONAL MATERIALS

Psychoeducation in the XXI Century: Sexual Education and Prevention of Gender Violence

Psychoeducation emerged around the 1950s. It was originally applied to the reeducation of children by Catholic educators and voluntary scout movements (Gendreaud, 1983), the discipline became a legitimate and recognized practice in Europe (Le Blanc, 2004). Pioneers Psychoeducation precursors were Canadian, such as Jeannine Guindon, Gilles Gendreau and Euchariste Paulhus. The first practitioners worked with youth at risk applying re-education programs, based on the promotion of self-awareness and empowerment inspired by the epigenetic theories of Piaget and Erickson (Guindon, 1995). This allowed them to articulate educational and psychological theories. Since then, Psychoeducation was established as a subdiscipline that articulates psychology and education (Bégin et al., 2012; Dionne, 2008; Potvin, 2003).

Psychoeducation considers the emerging complexities of the educational realities of the XXI century (Coll et al., 1992). Psychoeducation covers both situations that involve learning and teaching in formal environments, as well as the management of coexistence and ties in the most varied contexts and face diverse questions. In formal education settings, Psychoeducation takes all educational community members as the recipients of its interventions, that is, its application is not restricted to student problems (Maldonado, 2017). In this sense, it provides a framework for intervention techniques taking into account the social relationships in terms of social practices (Ramírez Botero, 2017). It is essential in the discipline to continuously review the approach to praxis, from the problem definition to the consideration of each process in which participants are involved.

Considering this, it would be desirable for every psychoeducational approach both its design, implementation and elaboration to be interdisciplinary scientific work based. We believe that psychoeducational practice would allow us to modify social practices and reflect about it. We named this process *"feedback"* (Maldonado, 2017). In sum, this discipline not only builds explanatory theory around the psychoeducational problem, but also develops intervention programs based on action and resources included in educational processes. This dynamic generates a new approach to solve the difficulty, which, in turn, optimizes its theoretical dimension. Therefore, the above represents a practical theoretical feedback cycle that starts and arrives from the real needs of educational communities (Banz Liendo & Valenzuela Schmidt, 2004). Indeed, various studies highlight the relevance of Psychoeducation and demonstrate its favorable results both in the elaboration of psychoeducational resources (Camero Callao, 2023) and in the interventions carried out (Aizcorbe & Gallo, 2023; Sáez Delgado et al., 2023).

CSE is considered to include psychoeducational content, given that it involves socio psychological issues learnings, such as sexual orientation and identity, sexual attraction, communication, relationship skills, parenting, contraception, safe sex, gender norms, consent, decision making and PGV (Goldfarb & Constantine, 2011). Through prevention programs, CSE addresses behavioral risk factors, in order to reduce social risk factors (Schneider & Hirsch, 2020). A related crucial social problem is gender violence (Pispira et al., 2022). Gender violence has been considered a violation of human rights, including the sexual and reproductive rights of girls and women around the world (WHO, 2021). Present materials that promote the construction of healthy relationships based on human rights to students, and providing tools that allow the development of skills with a gender perspective, CSE provides comprehensive strategies to prevent GBV and promote gender equality (Acosta Buralli et al. al., 2023; Makleff et al., 2020).

Causal Networks in Psychoeducational Resources

During discourse comprehension, causal connections are established among statements. This allows readers or listeners to construct a coherent mental representation (Manrique, 2020).

The establishment of causal connections has been examined by the *Causal Network Model* (Trabasso & Sperry, 1985). This Model proposes that the causal structure of a narrative is organized as a network, in which each node represents events that can hold multiple causes or consequences (Girón Alconchel, 2023). The Model provides some criteria to determine the existence of a connection between two statements: temporal priority (the cause must be prior to the consequence), operativity (the cause must be operative when the consequence occurs) and necessity in the circumstances (we should be able to propose that, if the cause is not had occurred, neither would have the consequence).

For example, if we read (London, 1903), "1. Every hour was full of shock and surprise, 2. He had been thrown into the heart of essential things.", we can establish that statement 2 causes statement 1, given that it presents an event that is temporally prior (2. "It had been thrown", 1. "it was"), is active or operative when statement 1 occurs, and is necessary for statement 1 to occur (Mackie, 1980).

Prior studies indicate that those statements that have a higher number of causal connections tend to be judged as more important (McMaster et al., 2012; Trabasso & Sperry, 1985), identified as main ideas (Cevasco et al., 2020), and recalled more quickly than those with low causal connectivity (Karlsson et al., 2019).

Few studies have examined the role of causal connectivity in psychoeducational materials. Among them, Acosta Buralli and Cevasco (2022a) examined the role of causal connectivity in the comprehension of CSE material presented to preservice teachers. Statements with high causal connectivity were more included in answers to comprehension questions than those that had a low level of causal connectivity. The authors concluded that causal connectivity has a significant effect on the comprehension of these materials. In a similar study, Pispira et al. (2022) examined college students' comprehension of gender violence prevention materials. They observed that establishing causal connections also facilitated students' learning. However, the materials used in both studies were oral interviews, and not handbooks. That is, they were not expository texts.

Considering the importance of developing psychoeducational materials that facilitate learning about CSE and effective PGV, this chapter will examine the role of causal connectivity in specific psychoeducational materials prepared by the Department of Education of Argentina.

CSE IN ARGENTINA: ITS EDUCATIONAL IMPLEMENTATION

Challenges to the Implementation of CSE

Law 26,150 (2006) establishes that CSE is a mandatory subject in all schools in Argentina (Alessi et al., 2023). Its incorporation into the curriculum has been recommended by international organizations (UNESCO, 2019; UNFPA, 2014; WHO, 2015).

Comprehensive perspective of sexuality considers not only the biological aspects but also the psychological, emotional, social and ethical aspects. The recipients are preschool, elementary and highschool students who attend public and private schools in Argentina. Law 26,150 determines that the contents of CSE are not only key for physical and psychological health but are considered part of human rights

(Faur & Gogna, 2016). One of the effects of the regulations has been the promotion of academic and social demand for the implementation of CSE (Vargas et al., 2012), which encouraged the increase in teacher training. Mandatory reading materials have been designed since 2009 annually regarding the Ministry of Education of Argentina.

The materials are open access and include information on the foundations and strategies for addressing CSE at all levels and educational areas (Boccardi, 2023).

It can also be proposed that this demand impacts the publishing field, which means that the publication of titles that address different aspects of this area increases. For example, if we review briefly the catalog of an Argentine publishing house dedicated to the teachers (Noveduc, 2024), we can see that a specific area on CSE has been included in the digital library. This shows the important role of CSE among educational materials: 22% of the materials were offered from 2011 to 2017, while the remaining 78% corresponds to the lapses of 2018 and 2023. This suggests that, despite the CSE law having been passed in 2006, materials on CSE have increased in recent years.

The Ministry of Education also promotes teacher training. It can be observed that the National Comprehensive Sexual Education Program, of the observatory of Education for Human Rights, Gender and CSE, offers face-to-face and virtual training for teachers, educational management teams, supervision and community organizations. These involve a workload of 210 hours of virtual coursework over three months. As well as national courses that address specific topics, and instructional strategies with a workload of 40 virtual hours and a duration of 2 months. Finally, the National Program offers training sections focused on problems of educational practice. In these training sections, teachers can participate in weekly sessions of 1.30 hours for a month, synchronously or asynchronously.

However, despite the availability of materials and specific training, its implementation in educational institutions has been considered inadequate or limited (Safitri, 2021). Likewise, the implementation of CSE has faced obstacles from both school institutions and the families, teachers, authorities and students (Romero, 2021; Valdés et al., 2021). It should be noted that children and adolescents have the right to access CSE training, therefore, it is expected that this right would not be neglected or undermined due to the limitations of teacher training (Carman et al., 2011).

One of the causes of this failure can be attributed to the inadequate training of teachers on the subject (Klein, 2021). In this regard, previous studies found that although teachers recognize the relevance of teaching CSE content, they are aware that they were not adequately trained (Acosta Buralli & Cevasco, 2022b). We have to point out that unlike training that involves other content (for example, physical science content), in the case of CSE contents, teachers must assume an active role, seeking transformations in social representations about the gender norms that perpetuate violence, and the promotion of critical thinking to mitigate its reproduction (Ronconi et al., 2023). It has been proposed that the emotional bonds of trust and pedagogical authority that teachers display when teaching CSE are what make their interventions effective and generate positive changes in their students (Romero, 2023). It is possible that the quality of the emotional links that teachers promote with the CSE content may represent a key factor in promoting students to take ownership of the content, and make healthy decisions that contribute to gender equality (Fajardo, 2022). Teaching CSE represents a challenge for teachers on a personal level, not only with respect to reviewing the social representations that they hold, but also their own experiences related to identity and sexuality. Therefore, learning and teaching CSE involve reflection that must be accompanied by comprehensive training (Alessi, 2023; Gamba, 2018). This means that CSE teaching contents require a constant strengthening through training processes (Faur, 2019)

In summary, despite the mandatory implementation of the CSE since 2006, its implementation has not been satisfactory, some situations can be reversed (for example deficits in specific teacher training), others, however, are more difficult to approach. To solve this problem, it has been proposed that the application of CSE should start from an educational intention based on the development of systematic teaching strategies scientific evidence- based along with a contextualized analysis of childhood realities (Sacán & Villafuerte, 2023). We believe that this kind of approach will facilitate the implementation of psychoeducational perspectives.

Design of CSE Psychoeducational Resources Evidence Based

As mentioned above, Psychoeducation has demonstrated its effectiveness in solving critical social problems (Aizcorbe & Gallo, 2023). We consider that, given that PGV is a complex problem included within the contents of the CSE (Bucheli & Rossi, 2019), it is necessary to design and elaborate CSE psychoeducational resources with an evidence-based perspective.

Reviewing the research carried out on CSE materials, we can recognize that they have focused on the different types of content and not in the form of transmitting them. Yang et al. (1999) analyzed 274 CSE materials from the Korean educational system: videos, books, CDs, and slides. Half of these materials only had general and non-specific information about CSE.

Ferguson et al. (2008) also analyzed CSE materials in the Netherlands. The research was carried out over a period of 10 months, in which they selected materials on CSE produced in the Netherlands during 2003 and 2008 aimed at high school students. The results demonstrated that these materials are characterized by consistent messages oriented to sexuality, safe sex and contraception and are associated with a high rate of safe sex practices in their recipients. Considering that sexual health behaviors are influenced by factors such as politics, religion, access to affordable and accessible health services, sociocultural norms and attitudes, researchers relate the social acceptance of adolescent sexuality at the national level with the elaboration of adequate CSE resources. These factors vary both within and between nations. For example, the link between religion and politics in the United States is quite different from that in the Netherlands, and this impacts the policies, funding, and sexual health programs. The Netherlands normalizes and accepts adolescent sexuality (Schalet, 2000) by the belief that adolescents can be ready for sexual activity when in the context of a relationship and the use of appropriate contraception (Schalet, 2000). Although at the time the research was carried out in 2008 the topics were still presented from a perspective of reducing risky sexual behaviors, the researchers emphasize that the topics were presented in a positive way, normalizing sexuality, not inducing fear and shame in young people.

In Argentina, few studies have analyzed CSE materials. Boccardi (2023) analyzed CSE resources for teacher training developed between 2009 and 2012, and during 2022 by the Ministry of Education. He observed that in the materials produced between 2009 and 2012, hetero-cis-sexual regulations prevail, leaving out other identities, erotic-sexual relationships, and family configurations, while the material produced in 2022 allows sexual diversity to be installed as a critical perspective that crosses the approach to CSE.

Despite the relevance and increase of Psychoeducation materials regarding CSE, it should be noted that we have not found studies that address the need to build knowledge, so that the design of psychoeducational materials on CSE responds to characteristics assumed by the comprehension of discourse and learning (Acosta Buralli et al., 2023). Considering this, the chapter presents an analysis of two texts included in training material intended for secondary level teachers in Argentina. Given that the purpose of our work is to build guidelines and methodological tools that, based on scientific evidence, allow the design of psychoeducational materials, we consider the role of causal connectivity in their comprehension (Cevasco & Acosta Buralli, 2023). We expected that main textual ideas would have high causal connectivity (Cevasco & Acosta Buralli, 2023). We also expected that both materials would show a high number of causal connections, because both belong to the same publisher, and their topics are related, since PGV is one of the main contents of the CSE. This analysis allows us to examine if CSE contents are presented in a complementary manner to the PGV contents or if they are conceived separately.

THE ROLE OF CAUSAL CONNECTIONS IN PSYCHOEDUCATION MATERIALS: DISCOURSE ANALYSIS

Corpus

The selection of text to be analyzed should accomplish some criteria: it might display current content and approaches on CSE (Appendix 1) and PGV (Appendix 2), it should have institutional support from educational authorities, and it should take into account the specific characteristics of the Argentine educational system. We picked up for the analysis the latest update (2022) of "CSE school references" part 1 presented by the Directorate of Education for Human Rights, Gender and CSE, endorsed by the Ministry of Education of Argentina. The document has proposals to promote the implementation of CSE in schools. The material supports an CSE perspective based on respect for Human Rights to address the priority learning cores that make the contents mandatory at the secondary level. It is intended for all teachers in general, but specifically for those who are part of the CSE reference team. This team was formed after the Federal Congress of Education approved Resolution N° 340/18 that promotes that all schools in the country have a teaching team that acts as CSE references with an interdisciplinary approach and functions as a link with the jurisdictional teams and with the institutional project of each establishment. The design and elaboration of the material is, in part, a product of the "Spotlight" Initiative, a global alliance between the European Union and the United Nations to eradicate violence against women and girls worldwide (Ministry of Education of the Argentine Nation, 2022).

The selected corpus considers texts addressed to teachers and educational management staff at the secondary level.

The criteria by which we select the texts were:

1. The texts should have a similar length, that they are in the range of 440 and 540 words, as a limit none of the texts will exceed 540 words.
2. The texts should have the characteristics of thematic advancement and organization in accordance with what has been characterized as an expository text, with a prevalence of explanatory sequences (Calsamiglia & Tusón, 1997).
3. The texts, in addition to explanatory sequences, include argumentative sequences that substantiate the pedagogical relevance of including content on CSE and gender violence prevention.

Two texts were selected: one on CSE in general, called "Assessing affectivity" (page 15), and another on PGV called "General fundamentals" (page 69). The first we will call Text 1 (T1) and the second Text 2 (T2).

Regarding the structure and purpose, T1 presents introductory content, and its purpose is to provide argumentative/theoretical support to the contents of the following chapters. T2, for its part, develops informative questions about behaviors that are characterized as gender violence, in turn developing the approach that allows for the construction of prevention strategies based on the contents of the CSE.

Analysis Procedure

The instruments were segmented into clauses.

In order to determine the number of causal connections, we proceeded according to the guidelines proposed by Trabasso and Sperry (1985). They establish that the existence of a causal connection between two statements is determined by considering the relationship between the causally related events. The causal connection involves temporal priority necessity and operativity. Thus, the event described in the statement under analysis, considered as a cause, must be temporally prior to the one considered a consequence, and be operative or active when the event considered a consequence is mentioned. Furthermore, the event must be necessary for the consequence event to occur. From these criteria, two independent judges derived a causal network for each text, and then compared their scores. It was observed that there was an agreement in 82% of the cases. In cases where there was disagreement, the judges reached an agreement through discussion.

Subsequently, an analysis was carried out to identify the causal connectivity in each text. To do this, the number of connections of each clause was counted; those that belonged to a range between 1 and 5 number of connected statements were considered to have low causal connectivity, while those that had a range between 5 and 10 connected statements were considered to have low causal connectivity. A medium level of causal connectivity and, finally, clauses that had between 10 and 15 connected clauses were identified as clauses with high causal connectivity. On the other hand, within the number of connections identified, what percentage of them corresponded to connections between the texts was selected.

Results

Table 2, Figure 1a nd Figure 2 show the causal connections:

As can be seen, the texts present causal connections, which demonstrates that both have cohesive thematic linking relationships, which suggests that they are conducive texts to promote learning (Cevasco & van den Broek, 2019). However, when we analyze the causal connectivity, we observe that low causal connectivity predominates. That is, there are fewer clauses connected to each other. Regarding the comparison between the texts, it is evident that in the PGV material low causal connectivity predominates to a greater extent, while in the CSE material, there is a higher percentage of medium and higher than in PGV.

Table 1. Detail the number of words and clauses in T1 and T2

Instrument	T1	T2	total
Number of words	498	534	1.032
Number of clauses	51	74	125

Source: Own elaboration

Table 2. The number of causal connections when and, therefore, the number of clauses with low, medium and high causal connectivity that each text presents

Level of causal connectivity	T1	T2
Low	67%	86%
Mid	19%	8%
High	14%	6%

Source: Own elaboration

Figure 1. Level of causal connectivity of text 1 on CSE
Source: Own elaboration

Instrument	T1	T2	total
Number of words	498	534	1.032
Number of clauses	51	74	125

Figure 2. Level of causal connectivity of text 2 on PVG
Source: Own elaboration

Level of causal connectivity	T1	T2
Low	67%	86%
Mid	19%	8%
High	14%	6%

Regarding the analysis to demonstrate the percentage of causal connectivity existing between the texts, the results showed 13% of clauses connected between the texts, while the remaining 83% belonged to connected clauses within the same text.

The following is an example of a T1 clause that is causally connected to a T2 clause:

34. rejection of all forms of violence (T1)

122. to ensure that these and future generations do not suffer violations of rights (T2).

As can be seen, the phrase [rejection of a form of violence] is a material and necessary cause that allows us to understand that the ultimate goal of this action is [to prevent successive generations] from suffering violations of rights. As we can see, the causal link between both texts, although it exists, is low and also appeals to general notions, not linked to specific issues, even of a practical nature. Thus, for example, we did not find connections that explain how CSE training prevents the violation of rights, an issue that, for example, could have been included by mentioning awareness-raising activities for the modification of patriarchal structures and silence of violations. For example, mentioning the need to create and strengthen support networks among women, which allow the monitoring and prevention of situations of gender violence.

These observations lead us to conclude that the thematic advancement structure that allows the integration of the contents of both texts is presented with a low index of causal connectivity, many of which are of a general or abstract type. This observation leads us to assume that both explanatory texts, despite being focused on promoting that comprehenders learn about CSE and PGV, conceive it as a relationship between knowledge of an expository nature, as if they were content from other disciplinary areas and not knowledge of a nature. procedural. This conception may help us understand why their impact on teacher training is low space and in the visibility of the teaching community.

SUGGESTIONS FOR CSE RESOURCES ELABORATION

In this chapter, we have reviewed the emergence and relevance of Psychoeducation as a framework to produce effective interventions in order to reduce social critical problems. One of the core issues is the elaboration of materials aiming to cope with preventive care and self-care behaviors, specifically on CSE and PGV. In this sense, studies revised, mainly working with discourse analysis, have proved that design and elaborate Psychoeducation materials would be focused in promoting a better comprehension and learning. In this sense a large number of future teachers recognize their own limitations when teaching CSE content. As we have seen, these limitations are not solved solely with content-type training, since the comprehensiveness and complexity of the representations and practices that are questioned from the CSE approach must be addressed. This task is crucial, considering the high rates of gender-based violence crimes, attacks and abuses. Consequently, it is necessary for different disciplines to work together trying to provide people with knowledge to build a future where healthy relationships with others and with one's own body prevail.

With regard to the need for multidisciplinary work in the development of psychoeducational materials, cognitive psychology could make greater evidence-based contributions. Previous research has highlighted that promoting the establishment of causal discursive connections is essential to encourage deep processing of the content of the material; Therefore, it is a key cognitive skill to promote learning (Cevasco & van den Broek, 2019). Furthermore, other studies have examined the role of this skill applied to tasks that promote the reader's strategic processes and, in turn, enhance the development of this skill. Among them, answering causal or elaboration questions (tasks that require the comprehender to generate an explanation about a specific event described in the text (Ammaturo & Cevasco, 2023; Pispira et al., 2022) and note taking (Acosta Buralli & Cevasco, 2022a). These studies have observed that encouraging comprehenders to focus on those parts of the text with greater causal connectivity facilitates recall and greater reflection on the main ideas of the text, even for students with learning disabilities (McMaster et al., 2012).

Although it should be noted that research on the role of causal connectivity in learning from expository texts on Psychoeducation is still developing, we consider that the results of our analysis may allow us to make recommendations. Taking into account that clauses with a high number of causal connections influence the construction of a coherent mental representation of the topic, and therefore, promote comprehension and facilitate learning. The results showed that most of both materials have a low level of causal connectivity, and the text on CSE has a higher level of high and medium causal connectivity compared to that of PGV. Based on what has been developed, it could be recommended that causal connectivity be considered a variable to take into account to promote the learning of future psychoeducational productions. On the other hand, it could be considered that in future materials there is a higher percentage of causal connections between the texts, taking into account that there is a thematic relationship between the materials, because the PGV (T2) is one of the contents of the CSE (T1), and which belong to the same didactic manual, it would be relevant to consider this variable in future studies. In turn, based on the evidence of previous studies, it could also be suggested to include interventions that promote or enhance greater attention to those events with greater causal connectivity, such as the generation of causal questions or elaboration questions (Ammaturo & Cevasco, 2023; McMaster et al., 2012; Pispira et al., 2022), or note taking (Acosta Buralli & Cevasco, 2022a).

EVIDENCE-BASED CONTRIBUTIONS TO IMPROVE CSE AND PVG TEACHING

We have seen previously that to promote the implementation of CSE and PGV, it is necessary that the teachers are adequately trained. Therefore, it is necessary that teacher training materials are adequately prepared in order to promote comprehension. Applying learning strategies that have been shown to be effective in other types of materials could be an option to promote the comprehension of psychoeducational texts on CSE and PGV in teacher training. In this chapter, causal connectivity has been selected as a tool that has proven to have an impact on the comprehension of discourse and was applied to create a Causal Network that allows the analysis of the contents. The results demonstrated a predominance of the low level of causal connectivity in both materials and a slightly higher percentage of medium and high causal connectivity in the CSE material over the PGV material. It is expected that future research can contribute to the analysis of the causal connectivity of psychoeducational materials, considering the analysis by topic and not by clause, in order to identify what type of topic has greater causal connectivity in the text. On the other hand, it could also be taken into account for future guidelines to ask trained judges for their contribution to identify the main ideas of the material and show whether causal connectivity plays a role in the selected ideas. Although these studies have been carried out with the selection of main ideas by participants, they have not been carried out from the perspective of judges trained in linguistics.

Finally, a percentage of 13% of causal connectivity was observed between the texts. However, previous research has not tended to examine the degree of causal connectivity that two texts belonging to the same topic and the same teaching manual should have to optimize learning. It is expected that future research will establish what is the optimal percentage of causal connectivity between texts. It would also be important for future studies to examine the interaction between establishing causal connections and performing other tasks such as note-taking (Acosta Buralli & Cevasco, 2022a) or elaboration questions (Pispira et al., 2022), since has proposed that these tasks promote processes.

CONCLUSION

Children and teenagers have a right to CSE. Therefore, it is important that it will not be neglected, due to gaps in teacher training (Carman et al., 2011). In consequence, it is key that the researchers contribute to the development of psychoeducational teaching materials on CSE and PGV that focus on teacher training (Faur, 2019). The analyses that we presented in this chapter indicate that promoting the establishment of causal connections can make a contribution to this, and promote the implementation of high quality CSE.

ACKNOWLEDGMENT

We thank Joselyn Pispira for her contribution to this work.

REFERENCES

Acosta Buralli, K., & Cevasco, J. (2022a,19-21 July). *The role of causal connectivity and note-taking condition in the comprehension of spoken and written discourse about the importance of comprehensive Sex Education by Argentine college students.* [Conference]. 32nd Annual Meeting of the Society for Text and Discourse. Society for text and discourse.

Acosta Buralli, K., & Cevasco, J. (2022b). Educación sexual integral en la formación de docentes de educación física en Argentina y México [Comprehensive Sexual Education in the training of Physical Education teachers in Argentina and Mexico]. *Lecturas Educación Física y Deportes*, 27(288), 2–15. doi:10.46642/efd.v27i288.3386

Acosta Buralli, K., Pispira, J., Cevasco, J., & Silva, M. L. (2023). Development of psychoeducational materials on integral sexual education and prevention of gender violence based on evidence. *Salud, Ciencia y Tecnología - Serie de Conferencias, 2,* 124. https://doi.org/ doi:10.56294/sctconf2023124

Ahmed, N., Flisher, A., Mathews, C., Jansen, S., Mukoma, W., & Schaalma, H. P. (2006). Process evaluation of the teacher training for an AIDS prevention programme. *Health Education Research*, 21(5), 621–632. doi:10.1093/her/cyl031 PMID:16740671

Aizcorbe, G. M., & Gallo, M. N. (2023). La psicoeducación como una tecnología educativa [Psychoeducation as an educational technology]. *Innova Educa*, 3(3), 79–92.

Alessi, D., Barrena, M. A., & Ronconi, M. F. (2023). Desafíos políticos y pedagógicos en torno a la ESI [Political and pedagogical challenges around CSE]. In A. Peláez, M. Incháurregui, & M. Severino (Eds.), Escribir la ESI: saberes, debates y desafíos desde experiencias docentes [Writing the ESI: knowledge, debates and challenges from teaching experiences]. Editorial de la Universidad Nacional de La Plata (EDULP).

Ammaturo, A., & Cevasco, J. (2023). The Role of the Establishment of Causal Connections and Elaboration Question Answering Tasks in the Comprehension of Spontaneous Narrative Discourse by Argentine College Students. *Reading Psychology*, 45(2), 1–22. doi:10.1080/02702711.2023.2276453

Badriah, S., Tambuala, F., Herlinah, L., Mariani, D., Nurcahyani, L., & Setiawan, H. (2023). The effect of comprehensive sexual education on improving knowledge, attitudes, and skills in preventing premarital sexual behavior in adolescents. *KONTAKT-Journal of Nursing & Social Sciences related to Health & Illness*, 25(1), 50-56. doi:10.32725/kont.2023.004

Banz Liendo, C., & Valenzuela Schmidt, M. (2004). *La intervención psicoeducativa en la escuela y el rol del psicólogo educacional* [Psychoeducational intervention in school and the role of the educational psychologist]. Ediciones Universidad Diego Portales.

Bégin, J. Y., Bluteau, J., Arseneault, C., & Pronovost, J. (2012). Psychoeducation in Quebec: Past to Present. *Ricerche Di Pedagogia E Didattica. Journal of Theories and Research in Education, 7*(1). doi:10.6092/issn.1970-2221/2681

Boccardi, F. (2023). La diversidad sexual en el discurso estatal de la Educación Sexual Integral en Argentina. Un análisis sociosemiótico de los materiales didácticos oficiales. [Sexual diversity in the state discourse of Comprehensive Sexual Education in Argentina. A socio-semiotic analysis of official teaching materials]. *Espacios en Blanco. Serie Indagaciones, 33*(2), 31–31. doi:10.37177/UNICEN/EB33-375

Bucheli, M., & Rossi, M. (2019). Attitudes toward intimate partner violence against women in Latin America and the Caribbean. *SAGE Open, 9*(3). doi:10.1177/2158244019871061

Calsamiglia, H., & Tusón, A. (1997). *Las cosas del decir. Manual de análisis del discurso* [The things of saying. Discourse analysis manual]. Editorial Ariel.

Camero Callo, P. A. (2023). *Diseño de material psicoeducativo para contribuir en el bienestar psicológico afectado por la infodemia por Covid-19 en jóvenes cusqueños. [Design of psychoeducational material to contribute to the psychological well-being affected by the Covid-19 infodemic in young people from Cusco]* [Undergraduate Thesis, Universidad San Ignacio Loyola]. USIL Repositorio Institucional. https://hdl.handle.net/20.500.14005/13045

Carman, M., Mitchell, A., Schlichthorst, M., & Smith, A. (2011). Teacher training in sexuality education in Australia: How well are teachers prepared for the job? *Sexual Health, 8*(3), 269–271. doi:10.1071/SH10126 PMID:21851765

Cevasco, J., & Acosta, K. (2023). Construction of coherence in the comprehension of narratives: Studies on the importance of the establishment of causal connections, gaps in current research and future directions. *Papeles del Psicólogo, 44*(1), 45–54. doi:10.23923/pap.psicol.3010

Cevasco, J., Muller, F., & Bermejo, F. (2020). The role of discourse marker presence, causal connectivity and prior knowledge in the comprehension of topic shifts. *Current Psychology (New Brunswick, N.J.), 39*, 1072–1085. doi:10.1007/s12144-018-9828-4

Cevasco, J., & van den Broek, P. (2017). The importance of causality processing in the comprehension of spontaneous spoken discourse. *Ciencia Cognitiva, 11*(2), 43–45.

Cevasco, J., & van den Broek, P. (2019). Contributions of causality processing models to the study of discourse comprehension and the facilitation of student learning. *Psicologia Educativa, 25*(2), 159–167. doi:10.5093/psed2019a8

Coll, C., Palacios, J., & Marchesi, A. (1992). *Desarrollo Psicológico y Educación II*. Psicología de la educación escolar [Psychological Development and Education II: Scholar education psychology]. Alianza.

Dionne, J. (2008). Los orígenes de la psicoeducación [The origins of psychoeducation]. In M. B. Vizcarra, & J. Dionne (Eds.), El desafío de la intervención psicosocial en Chile: aportes desde la psicoeducación [The challenge of psychosocial intervention in Chile: contributions from psychoeducation] (pp. 25-34). RIL editores.

Fajardo, D. P. C. (2022). Educación sexual integral en la escuela [Comprehensive sexual education at school]. *Revista Unimar*, *40*(1), 136–151. doi:10.31948/Rev.unimar/unimar40-1-art7

Faur, E. (2019). La Catedral, el Palacio, las aulas, la calle. Disputas en torno a la Educación Sexual Integral [The Cathedral, the Palace, the classrooms, the street. Disputes around Comprehensive Sexual Education]. *Mora (Buenos Aires)*, *25*(1), 227–234.

Faur, E., & Gogna, M. (2016). La Educación Sexual Integral en la Argentina. Una apuesta por la ampliación de derechos. [Comprehensive Sexual Education in Argentina. A commitment to the expansion of rights] In I. E. Ramírez Hernández (Ed.), *Voces de la inclusión interpelaciones y críticas a la idea de "Inclusión" escolar* [*Voices of inclusion, questions, and criticisms of the idea of School "inclusion"*]. (pp. 195–227). Praxis Editorial.

Ferguson, R. M., Vanwesenbeeck, I., & Knijn, T. (2008). A matter of facts... and more: An exploratory analysis of the content of sexuality education in The Netherlands. *Sex Education*, *8*(1), 93–106. doi:10.1080/14681810701811878

Fonner, V. A., Armstrong, K. S., Kennedy, C. E., O'Reilly, K. R., & Sweat, M. D. (2014). School based sex education and HIV prevention in low- and middle-income countries: A systematic review and meta-analysis. *PLoS One*, *9*(3), e89692. doi:10.1371/journal.pone.0089692 PMID:24594648

Gamba, C. (2018). *La reflexión sobre nosotros/as mismos/as: los procesos de subjetivación docente y la educación sexual integral como tecnología de gobierno* [*Reflection on ourselves: the processes of teacher subjectivation and comprehensive sexual education as a technology of government*] [Master's thesis, FLACSO]. Repository FLACSO Andes.

Gendreau, G. (1983). L'intervention, la formation et la recherche en psycho-éducation: Un bref retour sur le passé [Intervention, training and research in psycho-education: A brief look back at the past]. *Revue Canadienne de Psycho-Éducation*, *12*(2), 75–82.

Girón Alconchel, J. L. (2023). Construcciones causales, consecutivas e ilativas. [Causal, consecutive and illative constructions] In G. Rojo, V. Vázquez Rozas, & R. Torres Cacoullos (Eds.), *Sintaxis del español* [*Spanish Syntax*]. (pp. 229–244). Routledge.

Goldfarb, E. S., & Constantine, N. A. (2011). Sexuality education. In B. Brown & M. J. Prinstein (Eds.), *Encyclopedia of Adolescence* (pp. 322–331). Elsevier Academic Press. doi:10.1016/B978-0-12-373951-3.00086-7

Gregorio, X. E., Silva, M. L., Pispira, J., & Rubbo, Y. (2023). The ideological discursive framework in femicide journalistic chronicles: María Soledad Morales' crime as a leading case. *Comunicación y Sociedad (Guadalajara)*, *8607*(0), 1–28. doi:10.32870/cys.v2023.8607

Guindon, J. (1995). Les étapes de rééducation des jeunes délinquants...et des autres [*The stages of rehabilitation of young delinquents... and others*]. Sciences et Culture.

Karlsson, J., Jolles, D., Koornneef, A., van den Broek, P., & Van Leijenhorst, L. (2019). Individual differences in children's comprehension of temporal relations: Dissociable contributions of working memory capacity and working memory updating. *Journal of Experimental Child Psychology*, *185*, 1–18. doi:10.1016/j.jecp.2019.04.007 PMID:31077975

Le Blanc, M. (2004). Qu'est-ce que la psychoéducation? Que devrait-elle devenir? Réflexion à la lumière de l'expérience montréalaise [What is Psychoeducation? What should it become? Reflection in light of the Montreal experience]. *Revue de psychoédcuation, 33*(2), 289-304.

Mackie, J. L. (1980). *The Cement of the Universe*. Clarendon Press., doi:10.1093/0198246420.001.0001

Makleff, S., Garduño, J., Zavala, R. I., Barindelli, F., Valades, J., Billowitz, M., Silva Márquez, V. I., & Marston, C. (2020). Preventing intimate partner violence among young people—A qualitative study examining the role of comprehensive sexuality education. *Sexuality Research & Social Policy*, *17*(2), 314–325. doi:10.1007/s13178-019-00389-x

Maldonado, H. (2017). *La psicoeducación: Neo ideas para abordar problemáticas psicoeducativas* [*Psychoeducation: Neo ideas to address psychoeducational problems*]. Editorial Brujas.

Manrique, M. S. (2020). Tipología de procesos cognitivos. Uma ferramenta para análise educacional [Typology of cognitive processes. A tool for educational analysis]. *Educación (Lima)*, *29*(57), 163–185. doi:10.18800/educacion.202002.008

McMaster, K. L., van den Broek, P., Espin, C. A., White, M. J., Rapp, D. N., Kendeou, P., Bohn-Gettler, C., & Carlson, S. (2012). Making the right connections: Differential effects of reading intervention for subgroups of comprehenders. *Learning and Individual Differences*, *22*(1), 100–111. doi:10.1016/j.lindif.2011.11.017

Ministerio de Educación de la Nación Argentina. (2022). *Referentes Escolares de ESI. Educación Secundaria: parte 1* [*CSE School References. Secondary Education: Part 1*]. Ministerio de Educación de la Nación. Dirección de Educación para los Derechos Humanos, Género y ESI. http://www.bnm.me.gov.ar/giga1/documentos/EL007797.pdf

Noveduc. (2024). *Comprehensive sexual education catalog*. Noveduc. https://www.noveduc.com/catalogo/educacion-sexual-integral/?mpage=2

Pispira, J., Cevasco, J., & Silva, M. L. (2022). Gender-based violence in Latin America (Ecuador and Argentina): Current state and challenges in the development of psychoeducational materials. *Discover Psychology*, *2*(1), 48. doi:10.1007/s44202-022-00060-4

Potvin, P. (2003). Pour une alliance réussie entre la pratique et la recherche en psychoéducation [For a successful alliance between practice and research in psychoeducation]. *Revue de Psycho-Éducation*, *32*(2), 211–224.

Ramírez Botero, A. (2017). La intervención psicoeducativa y la psicología educativa: Una diferencia necesaria. [Psychoeducational intervention and educational psychology: A necessary difference] In M. Riaño Garzón, S. Carrillo Sierra, J. Torrado Rodriguez, & J. Espinosa Castro (Eds.), *Contexto educativo: convergencias y retos desde la perspectiva psicológica* [*Educational context: convergences and challenges from the psychological perspective*]. (pp. 35–57). Ediciones Universidad Simón Bolivar., doi:10.17081/bonga/1158.c3

Romero, G. (2021). Sentidos en disputa en torno a la "transversalización" de la educación sexual integral en Argentina [Disputed meanings around the 'mainstreaming' of comprehensive sexual education in Argentina]. *Revista Mexicana de Investigación Educativa, 26*(88), 47–68.

Romero, G. (2023). Los regímenes de género escolares como geopolíticas educativas estratégicas. Aportes para pensar la transversalidad de la Educación Sexual Integral [School gender regimes as strategic educational geopolitics. Contributions to think about the transversality of Comprehensive Sexual Education]. *La ventana. Revista de estudios de género, 7*(57), 41-74.

Ronconi, L., Espiñeira, B., & Guzmán, S. (2023). Educación sexual integral en América Latina y el caribe: Dónde estamos y hacia dónde deberíamos ir [Comprehensive sexual education in Latin America and the Caribbean: Where we are and where we should go]. *Latin american legal studies, 11*(1), 246-296. doi:10.15691/0719-9112Vol11n1a7

Sacán, J. G., & Villafuerte, F. U. (2023). Resultados de conocimientos, actitudes y prácticas (CAPS) de la primera cohorte del curso Reconoce, Oportunidades Curriculares en ESI [Knowledge, attitudes and practices (KAP) results of the first cohort of the Recoce, Curricular Opportunities in CSE course]. In M. Samudio Granados, & C. Terán Fierro (Eds.), Educación integral de la sexualidad: reflexiones críticas desde distintas miradas [Comprehensive sexuality education: critical reflections from different perspectives] (pp. 169-190). Universidad Nacional de educación del Ecuador.

Sáez Delgado, F., López Angulo, Y., Mella Norambuena, J., Sáez, Y., & Lozano Peña, G. (2023). Programa psicoeducativo aplicado en el profesorado como mecanismo de retribución a las escuelas participantes de una investigación [Psychoeducational program applied to teachers as a remuneration mechanism for schools participating in research]. *LATAM Revista Latinoamericana de Ciencias Sociales y Humanidades, 4*(1), 3728–3741. doi:10.56712/latam.v4i1.522

Safitri, P. (2021). Peer Education sebagai Upaya pencegahan HIV/AIDS. [JAK]. *Jurnal Abdimas Kesehatan, 3*(1), 87–92. doi:10.36565/jak.v3i1.161

Schalet, A. (2000). Raging hormones, regulated love: Adolescent sexuality and the constitution of the modern individual in the United States and The Netherlands. *Body & Society, 6*(1), 75–105. doi:10.1177/1357034X00006001006

Schneider, M., & Hirsch, J. S. (2020). Comprehensive Sexuality Education as a Primary Prevention Strategy for Sexual Violence Perpetration. *Trauma, Violence & Abuse, 21*(3), 439–455. doi:10.1177/1524838018772855 PMID:29720047

Trabasso, T., & Sperry, L. L. (1985). Causal relatedness and importance of story events. *Journal of Memory and Language, 24*(5), 595–611. doi:10.1016/0749-596X(85)90048-8

UNESCO. (2019). *From ideas to action: addressing barriers to comprehensive sexuality in the classroom.* UNESCO. https://unesdoc.unesco.org/ark:/48223/pf0000371091

UNESCO (2021). *The journey towards comprehensive sexuality education: global status report.* UNESCO. doi:10.54675/NFEK1277

UNFPA. (2014). *Operational guidance for comprehensive sexuality education. A Focus on Human Rights and Gender.* UNESCO. https://www.unfpa.org/sites/default/files/pub-pdf/UNFPA_OperationalGuidance_WEB3_0.pdf

Valdés, S., Ulm Yarad, D., & Moreno, C. (2021). ¿Qué obstáculos perciben los docentes respecto a la implementación de la educación sexual integral en las escuelas secundarias? [What obstacles do teachers perceive regarding the implementation of comprehensive sexuality education in secondary schools?]. *Revista de Educación en Biología, 3*(Número Especial), 249-251. https://congresos.adbia.org.ar/index.php/congresos/article/view/704

Vanwesenbeeck, I., Westeneng, J., De Boer, T., Reinders, J., & Van Zorge, R. (2016). Lessons learned from a decade implementing Comprehensive Sexuality Education in resource poor settings: The World Starts With Me. *Sex Education, 16*(5), 471–486. doi:10.1080/14681811.2015.1111203

Vargas, M. A. F., Aguilar, C. A., & Jiménez, A. G. (2012). Educación sexual: Orientadores y orientadoras desde el modelo biográfico y profesional [Sexual education: Counselors from the biographical and professional model]. *Educare (San José), 16*, 53–71. doi:10.15359/ree.16-Esp.7

World Health Organization. (2015). *Sexual health, human rights and the law.* World Health Organization. https://apps.who.int/iris/bitstream/handle/10665/175556/9789241564984_eng.pdf

World Health Organization. (2021). *Violence against women.* World Health Organization. https://www.who.int/es/news-room/fact-sheets/detail/violence-against-women

Yang, S. O., Baik, S. H., & Jeong, G. H. (1999). Analysis of materials for sexual education in Korea. *Journal of Korean Academy of Community Health Nursing, 10*(2), 508–524.

ADDITIONAL READING

Acosta Buralli, K. (2022). Educación Sexual Integral en institutos de formación docente en Argentina [Comprehensive Sexual Education in teacher training institutes in Argentina]. *Maskana, 13*(1), 30–35. doi:10.18537/mskn.13.01.04

Ben-Anath, D. (2005). The role of connectives in text comprehension. *Studies in Applied Linguistics and TESOL, 5*(2), 1–27. doi:10.7916/salt.v5i2.1569

Castro, I. E., & Sujak, M. C. (2014). "Why can't we learn about this?" Sexual minority students navigate the official and hidden curricular spaces of high school. *Education and Urban Society, 46*(4), 450–473. doi:10.1177/0013124512458117

Ninsiima, A. B., Coene, G., Michielsen, K., Najjuka, S., Kemigisha, E., Ruzaaza, G. N., Nykato, V. N., & Leye, E. (2020). Institutional and contextual obstacles to the sexuality education policy implementation in Uganda. *Sex Education, 20*(1), 17–32. doi:10.1080/14681811.2019.1609437

O'Brien, H., Hendriks, J., & Burns, S. (2021). Teacher training organisations and their preparation of the pre-service teacher to deliver comprehensive sexuality education in the school setting: A systematic literature review. *Sex Education, 21*(3), 284–303. doi:10.1080/14681811.2020.1792874

Rollston, R., Wilkinson, E., Abouelazm, R., Mladenov, P., Horanieh, N., & Jabbarpour, Y. (2020). Comprehensive sexuality education to address gender-based violence. *Lancet, 396*(10245), 148–150. doi:10.1016/S0140-6736(20)31477-X PMID:32615078

Schneider, M., & Hirsch, J. S. (2020). Comprehensive sexuality education as a primary prevention strategy for sexual violence perpetration. *Trauma, Violence & Abuse, 21*(3), 439–455. doi:10.1177/1524838018772855 PMID:29720047

Trabasso, T., & Langston, M. (1998). Modeling causal integration and availability of information during comprehension of narrative texts. In H. Herre van Oostendorp & S. Goldman (Eds.), *The construction of mental representations during reading* (pp. 25–60). Lawrence Erlbaum Associates, Publishers.

KEY TERMS AND DEFINITIONS

Causal Connection: Relationships between clauses, mainly considering the events. One, the starting point, is the cause and the other, the result, is the consequence.

Causal Network Model: Theoretical model proposed by Trabasso & Sperry (1985) that studies the text causal relationships between events in a non-linear network format.

Clause: A string of words with a verb (or eventive form) that instantiates a predicate relationship from a subject.

Comprehensive Sexual Education: Theoretical perspective of teaching that proposes sexual education as a whole which includes sexuality from a physical, psychological and social perspective.

Gender Violence: Exercise of oppression, harm and control based on gender.

Psychoeducation: Articulation between the areas of education and psychology in order to cope socio- psychosocial problems.

Teacher Training: Education and learning process intended for teachers who have received or are in training.

Chapter 11
AIALL and Queer Language Education to Prevent Gender-Based Violence:
Using Artificial Intelligence for Lesson Planning

Francisco Javier Palacios-Hidalgo
https://orcid.org/0000-0002-4326-209X
University of Córdoba, Spain

Cristina A. Huertas-Abril
https://orcid.org/0000-0002-9057-5224
University of Córdoba, Spain

ABSTRACT

The rise in gender-based violence demands urgent attention and action. As violence rates against women and trans and gender non-conforming people have increased alarmingly, there is an imperative need to review how today's societies fail to protect minoritized groups. Moreover, artificial intelligence has undoubtedly acquired relevance on the public scene, both seen as a threat and an ally to boost and fight against this type of violence. Following the socially and culturally responsive language teaching and English for social purposes and cooperation approaches, this chapter presents a teaching proposal to address gender-based violence in the language classroom. The tasks are designed following a non-biased gender and queer lens and taking advantage of different Artificial Intelligence tools. It aims to offer language teachers a practical guide for lesson planning and promote artificial intelligence assisted language learning. Ultimately, the chapter attempts to show the potential of queer language education to fight gender-based violence.

DOI: 10.4018/979-8-3693-2053-2.ch011

INTRODUCTION

The concerning rise in gender-based violence (hereafter GBV[1]) demands urgent attention and action. In recent years, violence rates against women as well as against trans and gender non-conforming (TGNC) people have increased alarmingly (Human Rights Foundation, 2021; UN Women, 2023), stressing the imperative need to review how today's societies fail to protect minoritized groups. There are indeed several causes for this recent increase, such as the rise in online harassment due to the ease of access to the internet (Lismini et al., 2023), anti-LGBTIQ+ legislation in many countries (Bayrakdar & King, 2021), or racial, ethnic and social disparities around the world (Lynch & Logan, 2023), just to mention but a few. Moreover, Artificial Intelligence (AI) has undoubtedly acquired relevance in the public scene, both seen as a threat and an ally to boost but also fight against this type of violence (cf. Mahtani, 2023; United Nations Development Programme, 2023). Nevertheless, AI, if used ethically and appropriately, can be an effective tool to reduce GBV if certain measures are taken, for instance by ensuring that AI developers are trained in ethics, strengthening the protection of data privacy to prevent the misuse of personal information, and promoting quality sexuality education on how to recognize and combat the use of online tools for GBV, among other initiatives.

According to different scholars, international bodies and expert groups (i.e., European Expert Group on Sexuality Education, 2016; Schneider & Hirsch, 2020; UNESCO, 2018), it is precisely sexuality education that is vital for promoting informed, responsible, and equitable attitudes among individuals. Certainly, comprehensive sexuality education can help encourage healthy relationships based on respect, consent, communication, and empathy, as well as fight against discrimination and stigma related to sexual orientation and gender identity diversity (Goldfarb & Lieberman, 2021), and ultimately prevent GBV (Carrera-Fernández et al., 2021).

Comprehensive sexuality education can be integrated into various school disciplines, fostering a multidisciplinary approach to learning (Palacios-Hidalgo & Huertas-Abril, 2023a). Indeed, concepts related to sexual and reproductive health, sexual orientation, gender equality, identity and diversity, relationships and consent can be incorporated into subjects such as biology, psychology, ethics, and even languages. In the case of the latter, addressing issues related to sexuality (by teaching relevant vocabulary, using reading materials or simply fostering group discussions) may offer students opportunities to enhance their communication skills and, in turn, promote dialogue about essential topics that may eventually train them to stand against any form of GBV. In fact, specific approaches to language teaching can support the integration of topics related to sexuality education. Such is the case of English for Social Purposes and Cooperation (ESoPC; Huertas-Abril, 2018a) and, more generally, Socially and Culturally Responsive Language Teaching (SCR; Palacios-Hidalgo, 2023), both of which promote the teaching of languages through relevant social and cultural issues and encourage teachers to queer their lessons to promote inclusion, empathy and respect, challenge stereotypes and stigma, meet students' needs, and prepare informed and better citizens.

Bearing in mind all the aforementioned, this chapter presents a teaching proposal to address the integration of measures to prevent GBV in the language classroom. The tasks are designed following a non-biased gender and queer lens and taking advantage of different AI tools. The proposal aims to offer language teachers a practical guide for lesson planning and promote Artificial Intelligence Assisted Language Learning (AIALL). Ultimately, the chapter attempts to show the potential of queer language education and sexuality education to fight GBV.

BACKGROUND

Key Facts and Figures About GBV

According to the European Commission (n. d.), GBV refers to "violence directed against a person because of that person's gender or violence that affects persons of a particular gender disproportionately" (para. 1). In this light, the problematic increase in GBV has long been an unfortunate societal trend that requires urgent attention and action. Over recent years, rates of violence against women, TGNC people have surged (Human Rights Foundation, 2021; UN Women, 2023), emphasizing the imperative need for comprehensive reforms in our societies to fight GBV, prevent discrimination based on gender identity, and enhance the lives of victims.

There are indeed several factors that have intensified GBV, such as the democratization of access to technology, climate change, and the effects of the COVID-19 pandemic (UN Women, 2023), together with cultural and social norms and deeply rooted gender inequality that still exist in many parts of the world. Regarding cultural and social norms (which normally revolve around masculinity), there is no doubt that certain cultural and social standards that favor this type of violence and discrimination, particularly those related to masculinity and power dynamics (Piedalue et al., 2020), which eventually perpetuate a culture of violence. Likewise, gender inequality is also perpetuated by persistent traditional societal structures (Latzman et al., 2018) that not only contribute to increasing GBV but also maintain power relations of men over women and other minoritized gender identities. Nevertheless, there are other factors that contribute to the increase in GBV, including economic disparities that conduce to power imbalances in relationships, making it difficult for victims to leave abusive situations (Kiss et al., 2012), limited access (for any reason) to education that reinforce traditional gender roles and perpetuate poverty (John et al., 2020), and media representations and messages that eternalize gender stereotypes and objectify individuals (ElSherief et al., 2017), among others.

The European Institute for Gender Equality (2023), following the Istanbul Convention (also known as the Council of Europe Convention on Preventing and Combating Violence against Women and Domestic Violence, 2014), highlights four main types of GBV: physical, sexual, psychological and economic.

- Physical violence is defined as any action that inflicts physical harm because of illegal physical force, including restriction of freedom, severe and minor assault, and manslaughter.
- Sexual violence refers to any performed sexual act without consent, either in the form of sexual assault or rape.
- Psychological violence includes acts of psychological harm to a person, such as verbal insult, harassment and coercion.
- Economic violence includes all those acts that cause economic harm to an individual, like restriction of financial resources, education or professional opportunities, property damage, or failure to adhere to financial obligations towards other people.

In terms of figures, several reports have been developed with the aim of showing that GBV is very much present in every nook and cranny. For instance, UN Women (2023), the United Nations entity that is committed to gender equality and the empowerment of women, has highlighted different facts, especially with regard to GBV facilitated by technology: 10% of women in the European Union had experienced cyber-harassment from the age of 15 onward according to data from 2014; 49% of women in Uganda reported in 2021 that they had been affected by online harassment at some point in their lives; 85% of women in South Korea had faced hate speech online, findings resulting from a survey developed in 2016. In the majority of cases, this type of harassment includes facing inappropriate advances on social networks and receiving unsolicited or offensive sexually explicit messages. In any case, approximately 736 million women, representing 30 percent of women aged 15 and older, are estimated to have experienced physical and/or sexual intimate partner violence, non-partner sexual violence, or both at least once in their lifetime (UN Women, 2023).

In the case of Spain, a country that has fought a long struggle to achieve gender equality in recent years, the gender gap seems to be slowly closing, with data revealing great progress in the Gender Gap Index[2]. However, while the progress may seem encouraging, the reality is that Spain still struggles with pervasive violent sexism. In this sense, many women continue to endure aggressive abuse from their male partners or ex-partners, sometimes leading to death, and although the number of women killed because of GBV has fluctuated, it has generally decreased in the last decades (Statista Research Department, 2023a). Indeed, the most prominent peak was in 2008 with 76 deaths, whereas its lowest point was in 2021 with 48. However, figures regarding victims of GBV under protection measures seem to be different, with approximately 32,600 individuals living with special schemes to ensure their safety from aggressors in 2022 (Statista Research Department, 2023b).

Historically, discussions around GBV have often overlooked or marginalized the experiences of TGNC people (Wirtz et al., 2020). Certainly, TGNC individuals not only face internalized stigma but also negative societal messages and behavior, transphobia, and microaggressions that contribute to their emotional distress (Rood et al., 2017) and can also lead to the use of negative coping strategies such as drug abuse (Truszczynski et al., 2020). Indeed, TGNC people encounter a range of challenges in society, as highlighted by the (Human Rights Foundation, 2021[3]):

- Hostile political climate (Chan, 2023), as in many countries there is still no legal protection with regard to medical care or legal identification and recognition.
- Cultural marginalization and invisibility (Álvarez-Suárez, 2020), as TGNC people continue to be ignored and excluded from social participation in many areas of their lives, including education.
- Setbacks in education (Dueñas et al., 2022), as educational settings continue to be unwelcoming to TGNC students as a result of unresponsive education policies and/or discrimination from fellow students, teachers and other school staff.
- Employment discrimination (Di Marco et al., 2021), as TGNC individuals still encounter difficulties, intolerance and harassment in the workplace, barriers that are even higher for TGNC ethnic minorities.
- Exclusion from healthcare and social services (Scheim et al., 2022), as TGNC people are particularly vulnerable in terms of access to social services and healthcare, including finding health professionals who respect and affirm their identities.
- Barriers for immigrants, refugees and asylum seekers (Nematy et al., 2023), as not only TGNC but LGBTIQ+ people in general face high levels of discrimination and violence in several parts of the world, which forces them to flee from persecution based on sexual orientation and/or gender identity and look for asylum in other countries where they eventually encounter legal, societal and cultural obstacles.

- Physical and mental health disparities (Turban & Ehrensaft, 2018), as TGNC people can be more susceptible to mental health problems, such as depression, anxiety and even suicide, and bad physical health conditions.
- Intimate partner violence and sexual assault (Cogan et al., 2021), as TGNC people face high possibilities of discriminatory treatment when it comes to receiving care and justice after partner violence and sexual assault.
- Engagement in survival sex work (Kattari & Begun, 2017), as many TGNC individuals eventually engage in sex work in order to survive as a result of financial necessity derived from discrimination and economic barriers.

Given this array of challenges, it seems urgent to develop more inclusive and holistic dialogues and interventions concerning GBV and the experiences of TGNC people.

AI and AIALL, New Teaching Practices

Just like language learning has acquired great relevance in today's world, technological advances have also permeated all spheres of human life, including education and, more specifically, language teaching and learning (Huertas-Abril, 2021). Among the different existing technologies that are and have been applied to language education, AI has acquired relevance due to its multiple educational benefits, as indicated by Pratama et al. (2023):

[AI] has emerged as a transformational force in an ever-evolving digital age that has the ability to transform the educational landscape. The use of artificial intelligence to transform curricula is essential to building relevant and adaptive education of the future. [...] With this technology, the school curriculum can be transformed into a dynamic curriculum that is tailored to individual needs and focuses on developing skills that are relevant to the times. AI can be used to analyze large data sets and identify patterns that can inform instructional design and improve learning outcomes. (p. 351)

Similarly, AI has also become popular in language education:

[...] due to its efficiency and convenience. People can easily find different ways to learn a language now that smart devices and the Internet are more common. AI tools for learning a language can help students save time by doing specific tasks for them and giving them a more personalized learning experience based on their needs and progress. (Rebolledo & González-Araya, 2023, p. 7569)

In the same line, Huertas-Abril and Palacios-Hidalgo (2023) highlight the potential of AIALL, including its possibilities for timely and effective feedback and for students' practice of the target language at any time and place. The authors also pinpoint the positive effects of using AIALL for reducing learners' anxiety and, in turn, increasing their motivation and engagement. Moreover, other research also reveals several opportunities for AIALL, such as the fact that AIALL can facilitate personalized learning and help predict students' profiles, identify those at risk, and eventually reduce dropout rates (Huang et al., 2023), as well as expose learners to authentic uses and contexts to practice the target language and foster collaborative learning and social interaction (Kannan & Munday, 2018). Nevertheless, it seems urgent to train language teachers to integrate AIALL into their teaching (Huertas-Abril & Palacios-Hidalgo, 2023; Rebolledo & González-Araya, 2023).

AI has also been discussed as a tool to boost but also fight against GBV. On the one hand, AI has the potential to exacerbate GBV by the perpetuation of discrimination through biased algorithms, the collection of personal data that may compromise the safety of victims, and the misuse of technologies for the creation of fake content (Mahtani, 2023). On the other hand, AI not only can identify and address the risks of GBV more effectively but also offer immediate support (United Nations Development Programme, 2023). In any case, ethical considerations and collaboration among stakeholders are vital for ensuring that AI positively contributes to fighting GBV.

Socially and Culturally Responsive Language Teaching and English for Social Purposes and Cooperation

There is no doubt that learning languages other than one's mother tongue (or tongues) has become an essential requirement for 21st-century citizens to effectively function in the labor market, education, and almost every area of society (European Union, 2019; Eurydice, 2017; Mazzacani, 2019). As a result, several different types of approaches and methodologies have been developed in the last decades to guarantee that the teaching of languages is contextualized and that students are engaged and motivated to develop their communicative skills. In this sense, it is worth mentioning SCR (Socially and Culturally Responsive Language Teaching) and ESoPC (English for Social Purposes and Cooperation), two approaches to language teaching that foster the learning of languages among students through the integration of topics of social and cultural relevance in the classroom. On the one hand, SCR

is based on the use of diverse cultural references accessible to learners as well as socially relevant issues in order to enhance the learning of the target language. For this approach, it is essential to provide a teaching process that is concerned with the reality and the social and cultural problems of the present. In this light, a socially and culturally responsive language learning process entails that linguistic contents (i.e., grammar, vocabulary, and culture) and communicative skills need to be addressed through the direct and conscious inclusion of socially and culturally relevant issues (such as climate change, Sustainable Development Goals, animal abuse, immigration crisis, or health emergencies) that are close to the learners and that allow them to learn the target language in a contextualized and meaningful way. (Palacios-Hidalgo, 2023, p. 952)

SCR seeks to promote inclusion and respect for different social and cultural issues that are relevant in today's societies, while encouraging teachers to challenge misconceptions and stereotypes associated with them, raise awareness among learners, and train them as informed citizens of the world (Palacios-Hidalgo, 2023). All this is done by following the five fundamental principles of SCR, namely: (1) establishing language learning environments that revolve around learners' interests, experiences, and needs; (2) incorporating diverse culturally relevant references accessible to learners in order to enrich the language learning experience; (3) integrating the study and awareness of current and socially relevant issues to form the basis for developing learners' communicative competence and soft skills, including cooperative work, autonomy, critical and creative thinking; (4) acknowledging and appreciating diversity in all its forms as a fundamental component for comprehensive, inclusive, and universal learning; and (5) encouraging the inclusion and active engagement of learners through the cultivation of critical thinking and the fostering of both autonomous and cooperative learning (Palacios-Hidalgo, 2023).

Among other educational approaches, SCR is based on ESoPC, which is especially focused on the teaching of English[4]. The main objective of this approach is to foster the teaching and learning of English as a foreign language to help learners acquire and/or reinforce their communicative skills and also their social awareness, cooperation abilities, and civic values (Huertas-Abril, 2018a). According to Palacios-Hidalgo and Huertas-Abril (2023b),

ESoPC is interested in issues such as gender equality, animal abuse, environmental problems, fairtrade, food production policies, health emergencies, and immigration and refugees, among many others, which can all certainly be addressed in any educational stage (from pre-primary to higher education). By addressing these issues, ESoPC seeks the development of students' communicative competence in English while promoting cross-curricular learning and social awareness among learners. In this sense, for ESoPC it is key to work effectively on what has been defined as 'soft skills' that are essential in any context both inside and outside the classroom. These skills include personal attributes of a social and emotional nature that allow individuals to perform well in their environment, work well with others, and achieve their goals. (p. 39)

SCR and ESoPC are also technology-friendly language approaches, as both advocate for the use of technological and digital tools to enhance language teaching and learning (Palacios-Hidalgo, 2024, in press; Palacios-Hidalgo & Huertas-Abril, 2023b). In this light, the combination of SCR and ESoPC together with AIALL could not only bring interesting opportunities for personalizing the learning experiences of students and simulating real-life-like conversational scenarios (Huertas-Abril & Palacios-Hidalgo, 2023) but also provide possibilities to address socially relevant topics like GBV through communicative tasks.

Considering that SCR and ESoPC are concerned with integrating topics of social and cultural relevance in language education, both seem to be ideal approaches to incorporating comprehensive sexuality education in language education and making learners aware of and effectively trained to fight GBV. In the case of the former, research has already proved that ESoPC (and SCR by extension, as it is based on ESoPC) can be an optimal option to teach students about sexual and gender identity and diversity and, ultimately, promote inclusion and respect in the language classroom (Palacios-Hidalgo et al., 2023; Palacios-Hidalgo & Huertas-Abril, 2024, in press). Similarly, due to their interest in socially relevant themes ESoPC and SCR seem to be perfect for raising learners' awareness of the causes and consequences of GBV and training them to combat it. Therefore, the combination of both approaches with AIALL may be a powerful asset to bring comprehensive sexuality education to language education and, in turn, fight GBV.

AIALL TO PREVENT GBV: A TEACHING PROPOSAL

This section presents a proposal with different activities based on SCR and ESoPC that will allow teachers to address language content related to gender equality and GBV prevention. While the primary aim of this section is to provide teachers with suggestions for creating and implementing their own activities within their language lessons, these activities can also be directly applied in accordance with the instructions provided.

The first activity, "Bias Hunters" (Table 1), addresses the existence of gender stereotypes, especially those related to jobs. This activity is aimed at young learners and students with low levels of language proficiency, starting from A2 according to the CEFR[5] (Council of Europe, 2001, 2020) and for students aged 8 years and older. Nevertheless, the activity can be easily adapted to the characteristics and needs of the students. With this activity, both teachers and students will realize how biased AIALL tools can be.

The activity aims to show the numerous biases of AIALL tools regarding the relationship between jobs and gender. For example, when using "The teacher has a book in the hands" as a model prompt, the image presents a white (presumably cisgender) man with glasses and wearing a suit and tie (Figure 1),

Table 1. Activity "bias hunters"

Title	Bias Hunters
Recommended CEFR level	A2+
Recommended age	8+
Objectives	Gender equality and prevention of GBV: -To become aware of stereotypes associated with gender. -To reflect on gender stereotypes. -To be aware of the inequality between men and women. -To raise awareness about the biases that AI tools may have. Target language: -To practice descriptions and vocabulary related to jobs. -To express opinions in simple terms (agreement and disagreement). -To share own experiences in simple terms.
Grouping	Groups of 3-4 students and whole group.
Materials and preparation	No prior material or preparation is required.
AIALL tools	AI Image Gen in Canva.
Development	1. The teacher asks students to name different jobs, and then they ask them to reflect whether they associate this with men or women. 2. Students are asked to write one-sentence long descriptions of people doing their jobs, without any marks of gender (e.g., no gender pronouns like he or she, no possessive determiners). Example of sentence: "The teacher has a book on the hands". 3. The teacher checks that the sentences meet the non-gender requirement and asks the students to use these sentences as prompts in the AI Image Gen tool of Canva, which will generate an image based on the prompt. 4. Students share their images and reflect on how the AIALL tool presents the sentence they have created, especially paying attention to traditional gender-related roles. 5. Students draw in their groups the most accurate version of the sentence. If possible, the comparison of drawings can decorate the classroom.
Evaluation	The teacher can evaluate the construction of sentences in the target language. Moreover, informal assessment (e.g., through direct observation or checklists) can also be used to check that all students participate in group work, especially in the brainstorming phase and in the final reflection.
Alternatives and variations	A variation for this activity can be carried out using, for example, descriptions of families (e.g., a family with four members, two of them are adults and two of them are kids). Moreover, other AI image generation tools can be used, including DALL-E-3 or Midjourney. Finally, another alternative (especially with older students) can be implemented with automatic translation tools (e.g., DeepL, Google Translate) to see what gender marks AI uses when translating into the target language.

Source: Own elaboration

AIALL and Queer Language Education to Prevent Gender-Based Violence

even though women tend to choose careers in education more often than men (European Commission, 2023). The prompt is presented in the box on the top left of the application Canva.

Something similar happens when we use prompts related to other jobs traditionally associated with a specific gender (Figures 2 and 3).

It must be also taken into account when introducing the prompt given as a variation, "a family with four members, two of them are adults and two of them are kids,", that apart from a traditional family with a mother and a father, the tool is not precise and provides an image with five members (although the prompt indicated clearly that the family has only four), as shown in Figure 4.

The second activity is "Change the Story," which aims at re-reading and re-writing traditional fairytales where female characters (e.g., princesses) are rescued by male characters (e.g., warriors, princes) using AIALL tools.

This activity can generate numerous versions of traditional fairytales that can be real food for thought. For example, when using the prompt "Rewrite the story of Snow White with no gender biases" in ChatGPT (Figure 5), it automatically changes the pronouns and explicit references to male and female characters, as shown below:

The unmodified whole story re-written by ChatGPT reads as follows (bolds included by the chapter's authors):

Figure 1. AI generated image created in Canva for the prompt "English teacher with a book in the hands"
Source: Own elaboration

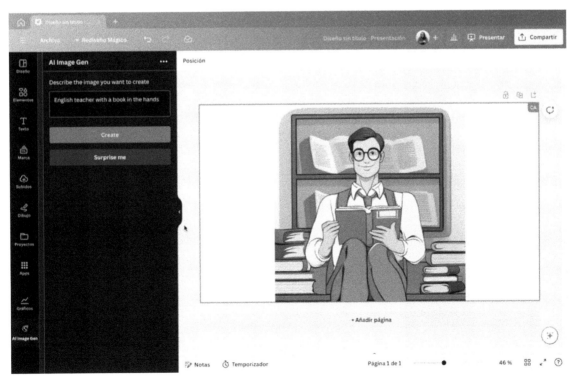

197

Figure 2. AI generated image created in Canva for the prompt "The secretary picked up the phone"
Source: Own elaboration

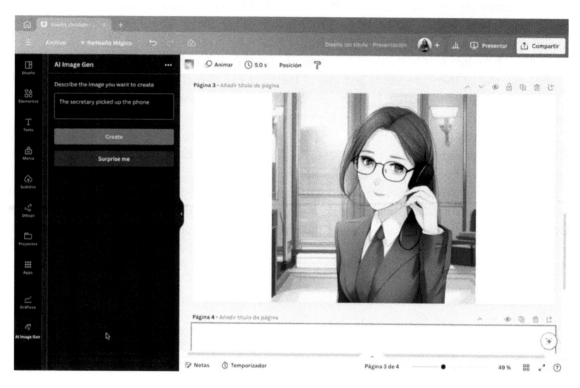

Figure 3. AI generated image created in Canva for the prompt "The nurse is healing the patient"
Source: Own elaboration

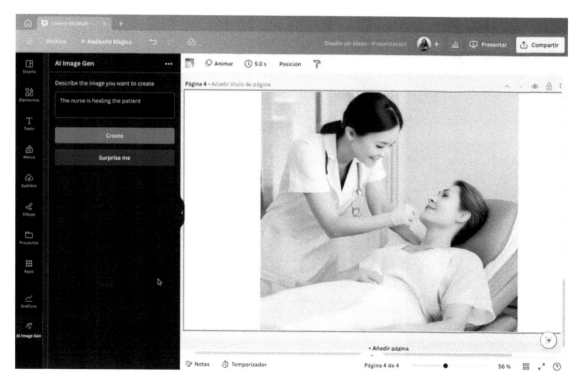

Figure 4. AI generated image created in Canva for the prompt "A family with four members, two of them are adults and two of them are kids"
Source: Own elaboration

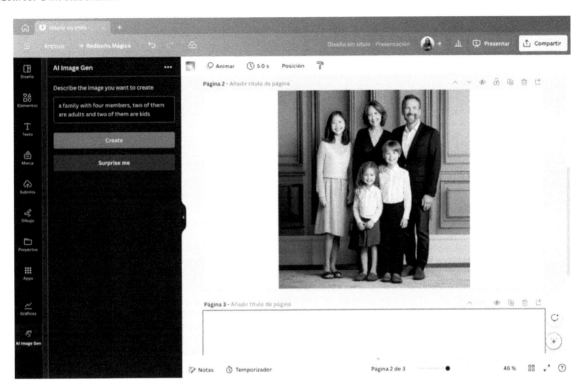

Once upon a time, in a land far away, there lived **a ruler** *who longed for a child. After much anticipation,* **their** *wish was granted, and* **they** *welcomed a baby into* **their** *castle.* **This child**, *named Snow White for* **their** *fair and radiant complexion, brought immense joy to the kingdom.*

As Snow White grew, **their** *kindness and compassion shone brightly, touching the hearts of all who knew* **them. Their** *gentle nature endeared* **them** *to both humans and animals alike. However,* **their** *happiness was short-lived as* **their** *beloved* **parent**, *the* **ruler**, *passed away, leaving Snow White in the care of* **their step-parent**, *who was initially kind but soon grew envious of Snow White's beauty and purity.*

The **step-parent**, *consumed by jealousy, ordered Snow White to be taken into the forest and disposed of. Yet, the hearts of those tasked with this cruel deed were softened by Snow White's innocence, and they could not bring themselves to harm them. Instead, they left Snow White in the depths of the forest, hoping* **they** *would find safety.*

Lost and alone, Snow White stumbled upon a quaint cottage deep in the woods, which belonged to seven miners. Taking pity on the weary traveler, the miners welcomed Snow White into their home. Grateful for their kindness, Snow White offered to help with the chores, and in return, the miners provided **them** *with shelter and protection.*

Table 2. Activity "change the story"

Title	Change the Story
Recommended CEFR level	B1+
Recommended age	12+
Objectives	Gender equality and prevention of GBV: -To become aware of stereotypes associated with gender. -To reflect on the gender stereotypes traditionally included in fairytales. -To be aware of the inequality between men and women. Target language: -To practice narrative writing in the target language. -To paraphrase and rewrite narrative texts.
Grouping	Individual task, groups of 3-4 students and whole group.
Materials and preparation	No prior material or preparation is required.
AIALL tools	ChatGPT.

Development	1. Students are given traditional fairytales with clear gender stereotypes, such as:
	  a) *Snow White*. Plot: Having lost her parents, Snow White is a princess who lives with her wicked stepmother. The stepmother poisons Snow White, who is placed by the dwarfs in a glass coffin in the forest. A prince finds her and kisses her while she is supposedly dead and breaks the spell. Controversial issues: the evil character of the stepmother; the necessity that a prince rescues the princess; the prince kisses the princess without consent (as she was supposedly dead).
	  b) *Sleeping Beauty*. Plot: The king and the queen have a daughter, the princess, but are told by a wicked (female) fairy that the princess will die when she pricks her finger on a spindle. The parents try to protect the princess by hiding her in the forest, but finally, she pricks her finger and instead of dying falls into a deep sleep. A prince finds her and kisses her, and breaks the spell. Controversial issues: the evil character of the female fairy; the overprotection of the parents; the necessity that a prince rescues the princess; the prince kisses the princess without consent.
	  c) *Peter Pan*. Plot: Wendy, John, and Michael Darling are going to bed when they are surprised by the arrival of Peter Pan and the fairy Tinker Bell, who have come to retrieve Peter's shadow. Peter reveals that he lives in the Never Land as captain of the Lost Boys, and the Darlings decide to go with them. After several adventures, the Darling children decide to go back home, but they are captured by the pirates. The boys are made to walk the plank and Wendy is tied to the mast, but Peter Pan rescues them, and the boys kill all the pirates. Finally, the children return to London, leaving Peter Pan to his perpetual boyhood. Controversial issues: Wendy, who is still a child, needs to act as a mother for her brothers and for the Lost Boys; Wendy, Tinker Bell and Tiger Lily (one of the "redskin braves") are jealous for Peter's affection; Peter needs to be the hero and rescue them all; Peter and the Lost Boys can be boys forever, while Wendy decides to go back to reality and grow old.
	  d) *Little Red Riding Hood*. Plot: A girl walks through the woods to bring food to her sickly grandmother. When the girl arrives at her grandmother's house, she notices the strange appearance of her "grandmother,", who is actually a wolf disguised as the grandmother. The wolf eats Little Red Riding Hood, and finally a male hunter kills the wolf and rescues the girl. Controversial issues: the girlish appearance of Little Red Riding Hood; the fact that the wolf eats the girl (sexual connotations); the necessity that a hunter rescues the girl.
	In groups, students discuss the roles of the different characters to identify gender stereotypes.
	2. Students need to rewrite individually the stories to avoid these gender stereotypes. For this purpose, they can use ChatGPT with specific prompts.
	3. Students share their newly, personal stories to fight against the traditional canon. They can also create their own illustrated eBooks including AI-generated images.

Evaluation	Written expression in the final products (tales) can be evaluated using rubrics to assess written production (e.g., rubrics proposed by Huertas-Abril, 2018c).
Alternatives and variations	As an alternative, instead of taking a fairytale and rewriting it, students can create a prompt so that ChatGPT creates a new story. This story should be analyzed in terms of gender biases, and students can try to identify (and modify) those biases.

Source: Own elaboration

Meanwhile, the **step-parent**, *believing Snow White to be no more, continued with* **their** *life, unaware of Snow White's resilience and the love* **they** *had found in the forest. But fate had other plans, for the*

Figure 5. AI generated text created in Chat GPT for the prompt "Rewrite the story of Snow White with no gender biases"
Source: Own elaboration

step-parent, *through chance encounters, learned of Snow White's continued existence and grew fearful of* **their** *potential return.*

Driven by fear and insecurity, the **step-parent** *devised a wicked plan to rid* **themselves** *of Snow White once and for all. Disguising* **themselves***, they sought out Snow White, offering a poisoned apple as a gesture of reconciliation. Unaware of the danger that lurked within, Snow White innocently took a bite, succumbing to the poison's deadly effects.*

Heartbroken, the miners mourned the loss of their dear friend, laying Snow White to rest in a glass coffin as a testament to **their** *enduring beauty and purity. News of Snow White's fate spread throughout the kingdom, touching the hearts of all who heard the tale.*

Yet, even in death, Snow White's spirit remained unbroken. Through the power of true love and compassion, **they were** *awakened from* **their** *slumber, the poison's grip vanquished forever. Reunited with their friends and loved ones, Snow White's story became a beacon of hope and resilience for generations to come, reminding all that goodness and kindness prevail, regardless of gender or station in life.*

The third activity (Table 3) presented here is entitled "Ending Violence against Women," and it is based on an infographic distributed by the Council of the European Union (2023). A section of these infographics is presented in Figure 6. The infographic will be used as an ice breaker to facilitate speaking among students, as well as to set a starting point for the core part of the activity.

Figure 6. Section of the infographic "Violence against women"
Source: Council of the European Union (2023)

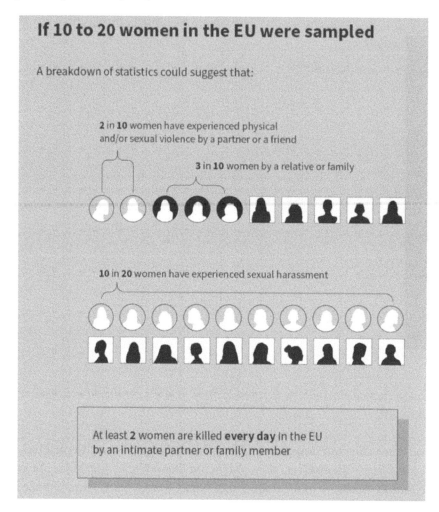

Considering both the topic and the range of vocabulary of the infographic, this activity is aimed at B1 level or more, and for students aged 14 or more.

PRACTICAL TEACHING IMPLICATIONS

Considering the current relevance of AIALL as well as the necessity of GBV prevention, it seems necessary to wrap up this chapter including five key practical teaching implications, namely:

- Regardless of the type of lesson, including language education, teachers should increase awareness against all types of GBV and abuse among students.
- Teachers should get updated training on AIALL tools prior to their use in the lessons in order to avoid all types of risks, including stereotypes or biases.

Table 3. Activity "ending violence against women"

Title	Ending Violence against Women
Recommended CEFR level	B1+
Recommended age	14+
Objectives	Gender equality and prevention of GBV: -To know facts and figures of GBV in the European Union. -To discuss about gender issues such as sexual violence, domestic violence and other relevant gender topics. -To share experiences observed in students' immediate environment related to gender inequality issues. -To raise awareness about GBV, both in the language lesson and beyond the walls of the classroom. Target language: -To express opinions both in written and in oral texts. -To share experiences and describe events that happened in the past. -To create a final product (video or presentation) that includes written and oral texts. -To foster autonomous learning and self-assessment of written texts in the target language.
Grouping	Groups of 3-4 students and whole group.
Materials and preparation	Digital or printed version of the infographic "Violence against women" (Council of the European Union, 2023).
AIALL tools	AI Text to Video Generators (e.g., Fliki, InVideo, Synthesia, Veed) and/or AI Text to Presentation Generators (e.g., Canva, Pitch, PopAI, SlidesAI).
Development	1. The teacher presents the infographic "Violence against women" distributed by the Council of the European Union (2023), which has six sections, namely: (i) The EU's proposal to end violence against women; (ii) What is gender-based violence?; (iii) If 10 to 20 women in the EU were sampled; (iv) A European woman's experience; (v) Societal cost of gender-based violence; and (vi) How do EU citizens view gender violence? 2. Students are then asked to write a text in the target language about GBV, using the infographic as a starting point. The texts can be argumentative or persuasive with the general aim of increasing awareness of the scourge of GBV. They can check the grammar and/or style by using AI tools such as Grammarly or Trinka (especially for English as a Foreign Language). 3. When students have the final version of the written text, they have to prepare a video or presentation. For this, students will use AI Text to Video Generators (e.g., Fliki, InVideo, Synthesia, Veed) and/or AI Text to Presentation Generators (e.g., Canva, Pitch, PopAI, SlidesAI). The final products should not be longer than three minutes and should be attractive to the general public. 4. All the 3- or 4-member groups will display their audiovisual products to the rest of the students so that they all can share their different perspectives on how to raise awareness against GBV. If students agree, the final products (videos or presentations) can be publicly uploaded onto social networks (e.g., Instagram, TikTok) to reach a wider audience. 5. Finally, the last task of this activity aims at getting feedback from the students. For this purpose, the teacher will ask questions to facilitate the discussion, including whether they enjoyed the discussion about GBV in the language class, whether they think that discussing gender issues can encourage their critical thinking, how they feel when sharing gender-related issues with others or how these topics can raise awareness of the problematic of GBV.
Evaluation	Written and oral expression in the final products (videos or presentations) can be evaluated using rubrics to assess oral and written production (e.g., rubrics proposed by Huertas-Abril, 2018b, 2018c).
Alternatives and variations	A variation of this activity could focus only on the written expression of the students. Students can create a 1- or 2-page essay about GBV and use an AI Text to Speech software (e.g., NaturalReader, ElevenLabs, PlayHT) to create an audio file. This way, students can create minipodcasts to raise awareness of GBV.

Source: Own elaboration

- Teachers need to be aware of the potential biases of AIALL tools so that they can also teach students how to identify and avoid gender-biased AI products.
- When using AIALL tools, both teachers and students should use appropriate, precise terminology and inclusive language, trying to avoid terminology that may be outdated, biased and/or inappropriate.

- Teachers must gain a deeper understanding of how both obvious and nuanced biases and stereotypes can affect AI-based language learning materials and also influence students' attitudes, behaviors and actions.

CONCLUSION

This chapter has attempted to reflect on the potential of AIALL for the integration of measures to prevent GBV in the language classroom. Furthermore, it has also shown how AI tools, despite offering great educational possibilities, are also biased, especially with regard to gender stereotypes, which may eventually contribute to intensifying GBV.

Bearing this in mind, certain ideas can be concluded from the teaching proposal presented here. First, it is necessary to address GBV and abuse in the classroom, as beyond language education, teachers play a crucial role in fostering a safe and inclusive learning environment for students. Therefore, it is essential for educators to incorporate discussions on GBV in their lessons with the aim of creating awareness and promoting a culture of respect and empathy among learners. Second, continuous training on AIALL tools is of paramount importance, considering the relevance of AI today. In this sense, ongoing training on AIALL can ensure that teachers are well-informed and prepared in the functionalities and potential risks associated with these tools, including the identification and avoidance of stereotypes or biases that may lead to situations of GBV. Third, and in connection with the previous idea, teachers must know the potential biases inherent in AIALL tools, as this awareness may empower them to guide their students in recognizing and avoiding gender biases present in AI. Moreover, sharing this knowledge can contribute to building critical thinking skills among learners when using AI.

Ultimately, this chapter underscores the critical importance of adopting a non-biased gender and queer lens in language education. By doing so, teachers can equip young students with the necessary tools to not only comprehend but actively combat GBV. This approach not only promotes a more inclusive and respectful learning environment but also contributes to shaping future generations that are adept at challenging societal norms and fostering a culture of equality and understanding that will be essential to making the world a better place.

REFERENCES

Álvarez-Suárez, L. (2020). Patologización e invisibilización de la identidad de género en España: ¿Qué debemos aprender de la legislación argentina? [Pathologization and invisibilization of gender identity in Spain: What should we learn from the Argentinean legislation?]. *Opinión Jurídica [Legal Opinion]*, *19*(39), 85–109. https://bit.ly/3tGDKTG

Bayrakdar, S., & King, A. (2021). LGBT discrimination, harassment and violence in Germany, Portugal and the UK: A quantitative comparative approach. *Current Sociology*, 1–21. doi:10.1177/00113921211039271

Carrera-Fernández, M. V., Lameiras-Fernández, M., Blanco-Pardo, N., & Rodríguez-Castro, Y. (2021). Preventing violence toward sexual and cultural diversity: The role of a queering sex education. *International Journal of Environmental Research and Public Health*, *18*(4), 1–15. doi:10.3390/ijerph18042199 PMID:33672323

Chan, A. S. W. (2023). Letter to the editor: Advocating worldwide social inclusion and anti-discrimination among LGBT community. Journal of Homosexuality, 70(5), 779–781. https://doi.org/ doi:10.1080/00918369.2021.2004869

Cogan, C. M., Scholl, J. A., Lee, J. Y., Cole, H. E., & Davis, J. L. (2021). Sexual violence and suicide risk in the transgender population: The mediating role of proximal stressors. *Psychology & Sexuality, 12*(1-2), 129–140. doi:10.1080/19419899.2020.1729847

Council of Europe. (2001). *Common European Framework of Reference for Languages: Learning, teaching, assessment.* Council of Europe. https://rm.coe.int/1680459f97

Council of Europe. (2014). *The Council of Europe Convention on preventing and combating violence against women and domestic violence.* Council of Europe. https://bit.ly/4246DpQ

Council of Europe. (2020). *Common European Framework of Reference for Languages: Learning, teaching, assessment. Companion volume.* Council of Europe. https://bit.ly/3PSYsaa

Council of the European Union. (2023). *Violence against women* (infographic). https://bit.ly/3SypFkJ

Di Marco, D., Hoel, H., & Lewis, D. (2021). Discrimination and exclusion on grounds of sexual and gender identity: Are LGBT people's voices heard at the workplace? *The Spanish Journal of Psychology, 24*(e18), 1–6. doi:10.1017/SJP.2021.16 PMID:33745498

Dueñas, J. M., Morales-Vives, F., Castarlenas, E., & Ferre-Rey, G. (2022). Trans students. Difficulties, needs and educational actions in Spain. *Gender and Education, 34*(5), 529–544. doi:10.1080/09540253.2021.1971160

ElSherief, M., Belding, E., & Nguyen, D. (2017). #NotOkay: Understanding gender-based violence in social media. *Proceedings of the International AAAI Conference on Web and Social Media, 11*(1), 52–61. 10.1609/icwsm.v11i1.14877

European Commission. (2023). *Issue paper on gender equality in and through education* (edited by B. van Driel, V. Donlevy & M. M. Roseme). Working Group on Equality and Values in Education and Training. European Education Area Strategic Framework. Publications Office of the European Union. https://bit.ly/3HzxQXT

European Commission. (n. d.). *Gender-based violence (GBV) by definition.* European Commission. https://bit.ly/3U2jUNr

European Expert Group on Sexuality Education. (2016). Sexuality education – what is it? *Sex Education, 16*(4), 427–431. doi:10.1080/14681811.2015.1100599

European Institute for Gender Equality. (2023). *Forms of gender-based violence.* European Institute for Gender Equality. https://bit.ly/47Tr4Hh

European Union. (2019). *Key competences for lifelong learning.* Publications Office of the European Union. https://bit.ly/3SkQWHx

Eurydice. (2017). *Eurydice brief: Key data on teaching languages at school in Europe.* Eurydice European Unit. doi:10.2797/828497

Goldfarb, E. S., & Lieberman, L. D. (2021). Three decades of research: The case for comprehensive sex education. *The Journal of Adolescent Health*, *68*(1), 13–27. doi:10.1016/j.jadohealth.2020.07.036 PMID:33059958

Huang, X., Zou, D., Cheng, G., Chen, X., & Xie, H. (2023). Trends, research issues and applications of artificial intelligence in language education. *Journal of Educational Technology & Society*, *26*(1), 112–131. doi:10.30191/ETS.202301_26(1).0009

Huertas-Abril, C. A. (2018a). Inglés para fines sociales y de cooperación (IFSyC): Contextualización y justificación. [English for Social Purposes and Cooperation (ESoPC): Contextualisation and rationale]. In C. A. Huertas-Abril & M. E. Gómez-Parra (Eds.), *Inglés para fines sociales y de cooperación. Guía para la elaboración de materiales* [English for Social Purposes and Cooperation: Guidance for materials design]. (pp. 9–24). Graó.

Huertas-AbrilC. A. (2018b). Oral presentation rubric (EFL teaching and learning). doi:10.13140/RG.2.2.17163.36649

Huertas-AbrilC. A. (2018c). Rubric for written assignments. doi:10.13140/RG.2.2.30585.13920

Huertas-Abril, C. A. (2021). *Tecnologías para la educación bilingüe* [Technologies for bilingual education]. Peter Lang., doi:10.3726/b17576

Huertas-Abril, C. A., & Palacios-Hidalgo, F. J. (2023). New possibilities of Artificial Intelligence-Assisted Language Learning (AIALL): Comparing visions from the East and the West. *Education Sciences*, *13*(12), 1234. doi:10.3390/educsci13121234

Human Rights Foundation. (2021). *Dismantling a culture of violence. Understanding violence against transgender and non-binary people and ending the crisis*. Human Rights Foundation. https://bit.ly/3Q1WZQ4

Ibrohimova, M., & Ziyaboyeva, S. (2022). English as a global language in XXI century. *The American Journal of Social Science and Education Innovations*, *04*(1), 5–8. doi:10.37547/tajssei/Volume04Issue01-02

John, N., Casey, S. E., Carino, G., & McGovern, T. (2020). Lessons never learned: Crisis and gender-based violence. *Developing World Bioethics*, *20*(2), 65–68. doi:10.1111/dewb.12261 PMID:32267607

Kannan, J., & Munday, P. (2018). New trends in second language learning and teaching through the lens of ICT, networked learning, and artificial intelligence. *Círculo de Lingüística Aplicada a la Comunicación*, *76*, 13–30. doi:10.5209/CLAC.62495

Kattari, S. K., & Begun, S. (2017). On the margins of marginalized: Transgender homelessness and survival sex. *Affilia*, *32*(1), 92–103. doi:10.1177/0886109916651904

Kiss, L., Schraiber, L. B., Heise, L., Zimmerman, C., Gouveia, N., & Watts, C. (2012). Gender-based violence and socioeconomic inequalities: Does living in more deprived neighbourhoods increase women's risk of intimate partner violence? *Social Science & Medicine*, *74*(8), 1172–1179. doi:10.1016/j.socscimed.2011.11.033 PMID:22361088

Latzman, N. E., D'Inverno, A. S., Niolon, P. H., & Reidy, D. E. (2018). Gender inequality and gender-based violence: Extensions to adolescent dating violence. In D. A. Wolfe & J. R. Temple (Eds.), *Adolescent Dating Violence. Theory, research, and prevention* (pp. 283–314). Academic Press. doi:10.1016/B978-0-12-811797-2.00012-8

Lismini, R., Narti, S., & Octaviani, V. (2023). Netnographic study of online gender-based violence (KBGO) on Twitter. *Journal of Science*, *12*(2), 1645–1661. doi:10.58471/scientia.v12i02.1430

Lynch, K. R., & Logan, T. K. (2023). Rural and urban/suburban victim professionals' perceptions of gender-based violence, victim challenges, and safety advice during the COVID-19 pandemic. *Violence Against Women*, *29*(5), 1060–1084. doi:10.1177/10778012221099987 PMID:35938486

Mahtani, N. (2023, May 21). *La violencia digital en tiempos de la IA, ¿otra amenaza más para las mujeres?* [*Digital violence in times of AI, another threat for women?*] El País. https://bit.ly/48EhvNW

Mazzacani, D. (2019). Foreign languages for the labor market: An analysis of the role of compulsory education in Europe. *Revista Internacional de Organizaciones*, *23*(23), 39–58. doi:10.17345/rio23.39-58

Nematy, A., Namer, Y., & Razum, O. (2023). LGBTQI+ refugees' and asylum seekers' mental health: A qualitative systematic review. *Sexuality Research & Social Policy*, *20*(2), 636–663. doi:10.1007/s13178-022-00705-y

Palacios-Hidalgo, F. J. (2023). Introducing the Socially and Culturally Responsive Language Teaching approach. In B. Pizà-Mir, J. G. Fernández-Fernández, M. M. Cortès-Ferrer, O. García-Taibo, & S. Baena-Morales (Eds.), *Currículum, didáctica y los Objetivos de Desarrollo Sostenible (ODS): Reflexiones, experiencias y miradas* [*Curriculum, didactics and the Sustainable Development Goals (SDGs): Reflections, experiences and perspectives*]. (pp. 950–966). Dykinson., https://bit.ly/3NqnddF

Palacios-Hidalgo, F. J. (2024 in press). The role of technology in Socially and Culturally Responsive Language Teaching: Exploring its potential in the language classroom. In *IA aplicada a la enseñanza y el aprendizaje* [*AI applied to teaching and learning*]. Dykinson.

Palacios-Hidalgo, F. J., Cosin-Belda, C., & Huertas-Abril, C. A. (2023). Queering EFL teaching through English for Social Purposes and Cooperation: A teaching proposal for Primary Education. In F. J. Palacios-Hidalgo & C. A. Huertas-Abril (Eds.), *Promoting inclusive education through the integration of LGBTIQ+ issues in the classroom* (pp. 139–160). IGI Global., doi:10.4018/978-1-6684-8243-8.ch008

Palacios-Hidalgo, F. J., & Huertas-Abril, C. A. (Eds.). (2023a). *Promoting inclusive education through the integration of LGBTIQ+ issues in the classroom*. IGI Global., doi:10.4018/978-1-6684-8243-8

Palacios-Hidalgo, F. J., & Huertas-Abril, C. A. (2023b). The potential of English for Social Purposes and Cooperation for the development of digital literacy. In P. Escudeiro, N. Escudeiro, & O. Bernardes (Eds.), *Handbook of research on implementing inclusive educational models and technologies for equity and diversity* (pp. 37–68). IGI Global., doi:10.4018/979-8-3693-0453-2.ch003

Palacios-Hidalgo, F. J., & Huertas-Abril, C. A. (2024, in press). Socially and Culturally Responsive Language Teaching: Queering the EFL classroom. In E. F. López-Medina, G. Beacon, M. Quinterno & X. Sotelo (Eds.), Queer studies in ELT. Brill.

Piedalue, A., Gilbertson, A., Alexeyeff, K., & Klein, E. (2020). Is gender-based violence a social norm? Rethinking power in a popular development intervention. *Feminist Review*, *126*(1), 89–105. doi:10.1177/0141778920944463

Pratama, M. P., Sampelolo, R., & Lura, H. (2023). Revolutionizing education: Harnessing the power of artificial intelligence for personalized learning. *Klasikal: Journal of Education. Language Teaching and Science*, *5*(1), 350–357. doi:10.52208/klasikal.v5i2.877

Rebolledo, R., & González-Araya, F. (2023). Exploring the benefits and challenges of AI-language learning tools. *International Journal of Social Sciences and Humanities Invention*, *10*(01), 7569–7576. doi:10.18535/ijsshi/v10i01.02

Rood, B. A., Reisner, S. L., Puckett, J. A., Surace, F. I., Berman, A. K., & Pantalone, D. W. (2017). Internalized transphobia: Exploring perceptions of social messages in transgender and gender-nonconforming adults. *International Journal of Transgenderism*, *18*(4), 411–426. doi:10.1080/15532739.2017.1329048

Scheim, A. I., Baker, K. E., Restar, A. J., & Sell, R. L. (2022). Health and health care among transgender adults in the United States. *Annual Review of Public Health*, *43*(1), 503–523. doi:10.1146/annurev-publhealth-052620-100313 PMID:34882432

Schneider, M., & Hirsch, J. S. (2020). Comprehensive sexuality education as a primary prevention strategy for sexual violence perpetration. *Trauma, Violence & Abuse*, *21*(3), 439–455. doi:10.1177/1524838018772855 PMID:29720047

Statista Research Department. (2023a, November 3). *Number of women that were killed in gender violence assaults in Spain from 2003 to 2022*. Statista Research Department. https://bit.ly/3RxlXpX

Truszczynski, N., Singh, A. A., & Hansen, N. (2022). The discrimination experiences and coping responses of non-binary and trans people. *Journal of Homosexuality*, *69*(4), 741–755. https://dooi.org/10.1080/00918369.2020.1855028. doi:10.1080/00918369.2020.1855028 PMID:33331799

Turban, J. L., & Ehrensaft, D. (2018). Gender identity in youth: Treatment paradigms and controversies. *Journal of Child Psychology and Psychiatry, and Allied Disciplines*, *59*(12), 1228–1243. doi:10.1111/jcpp.12833 PMID:29071722

UNESCO. (2018). *International technical guidance on sexuality education. An evidence-informed approach*. UNESCO. https://bit.ly/2NX4KG4

United Nations Development Programme. (2023, May 30). *Sara: La nueva herramienta de inteligencia artificial para combatir la violencia de género en Centroamérica [Sara: The new artificial inteligence tool to fight gender-based violence in Center America]*. United Nations Development Programme. https://bit.ly/3MbWZL9

Wirtz, A. L., Poteat, T. C., Malik, M., & Glass, N. (2020). Gender-based violence against transgender people in the United States: A call for research and programming. *Trauma, Violence & Abuse*, *21*(2), 227–241. doi:10.1177/1524838018757749 PMID:29439615

Women, U. N. (2023, September 21). *Facts and figures: Ending violence against women*. UN Women. https://bit.ly/3PDc49g

World Economic Forum. (2023). *Global gender gap report 2023*. World Economic Forum. https://bit.ly/499gQ6B

ADDITIONAL READING

Bin-Hady, W. R. A., Al-Kadi, A., Hazaea, A., & Ali, J. K. M. (2023). Exploring the dimensions of ChatGPT in English language learning: A global perspective. *Library Hi Tech*. Advance online publication. doi:10.1108/LHT-05-2023-0200

Ceballos Cano, M. V., & Huertas-Abril, C. A. (2024 in press). Artificial intelligence for teaching and learning English as a Foreign Language: A proposal for primary education. In *Tejiendo palabras: Explorando la lengua, la lingüística y el proceso de traducción en la era de la inteligencia artificial y la innovación docente [Weaving words: Exploring language, linguistics and the translation process in the age of artificial intelligence and teaching innovation]*. Dykinson.

Dewi, P., Yuliatin, R. R., & Sari, D. E. (2024). Tertiary EFL female and male students' perception in speaking class: Gender-based violence issue. *SALEE: Study of Applied Linguistics and English Education*, *5*(1), 97–109. doi:10.35961/salee.v5i1.1089

García-Molina, M., Huertas-Abril, C. A., & Palacios-Hidalgo, F. J. (2024 in press). The potential of AIALL: Exploring pre-service teacher attitudes. In *El factor relacional en la era de la IA [The relational factor in the age of AI]*. Dykinson.

Huertas-Abril, C. A., & Palacios-Hidalgo, F. J. (2023). New possibilities of Artificial Intelligence-Assisted Language Learning (AIALL): Comparing visions from the East and the West. *Education Sciences*, *13*(12), 1234. doi:10.3390/educsci13121234

Palacios-Hidalgo, F. J. (2023a). *Enseñanza de Lenguas Social y Culturalmente Responsable. Un enfoque para la enseñanza de idiomas en el siglo XXI [Socially and Culturally Relevant Teaching. An approch to teaching languages in the 21st century]*. Editorial Comares.

Palacios-Hidalgo, F. J. (2023b). Socially and culturally responsive language teaching materials: Guidelines for design. In E. Castro-León (Ed.), *Interrelaciones entre la imagen, el texto y las tecnologías digitales. Nuevas perspectivas en la enseñanza de las ciencias sociales [Interrelationships between image, text and digital technologies. New perspectives in the teaching of social sciences]* (pp. 764–780). Dykinson. https://bit.ly/3THg4co

Palacios-Hidalgo, F. J., Huertas-Abril, C. A., & Villegas-Troya, C. (2023). La traducción pedagógica en la enseñanza de inglés como lengua extranjera: superando los sesgos de género del profesorado de educación primaria en formación [Pedagogical translation in teaching English as a foreign language: overcoming gender biases of pre-service primary education teachers]. In J. Cabero-Almenara, C. Llorente-Cejudo, A. Palacios-Rodríguez & M. Serrano-Hidalgo (Coords.), Mejorando la enseñanza a través de la innovación educativa [Improving teaching through educational innovation] (pp. 645-655). Dykinson.

KEY TERMS AND DEFINITIONS

AIALL: Artificial Intelligence-Assisted Language Learning.
Artificial Intelligence: It refers to the development of computer systems capable of executing tasks that would typically require human intelligence (such as learning, problem-solving, and understanding natural language).
English for Social Purposes and Cooperation: An approach to teaching and learning English that focuses on the development of students' communicative and soft skills, social responsibility and cultural awareness through the use of socially and culturally relevant themes.
Gender-Based Violence: It refers not only to violence toward cisgender women but also to violence and discrimination caused to trans women, TGNC people.
Socially and Culturally Responsive Language Teaching: An approach to teaching and learning languages that focuses on the development of students' communicative and soft skills, social responsibility and cultural awareness through the use of socially and culturally relevant themes. It is based on Culturally Responsive Teaching, English for Social Purposes and Cooperation, and Universal Design for Learning.
TGNC: Trans and gender non-conforming.
Trans and Gender Non-Conforming People: An umbrella term encompassing anyone who does not conform to the gender assigned to them at birth.

ENDNOTES

[1] In this chapter, GBV not only includes violence toward cisgender women but also the violence and discrimination caused to trans women, TGNC people.

[2] A global indicator that sets a reference point concerning the state and evolution of gender parity, considering four aspects: economic participation and opportunity, educational attainment, health and survival, and political empowerment (World Economic Forum, 2023).

[3] Although these challenges refer to the United States, they are also applicable to many (if not all) parts of the world.

[4] Considering its role as the 'global language' or the modern 'lingua franca' (Ibrohimova & Ziyaboyeva, 2022).

[5] The Common European Framework of Reference for Languages, a standardized framework used to assess and describe language proficiency in a consistent and comprehensive way (Council of Europe, 2001, 2020).

Chapter 12
Comprehensive Sexuality Education as a Preventive Strategy Against Gender-Based Violence in the Digital Sphere:
A Training Proposal

Mariana Buenestado-Fernández
Universidad de Cantabria, Spain

ABSTRACT

Comprehensive sexuality education is presented as a fundamental preventive strategy against gender violence in the digital sphere. In this context, a training program is proposed that specifically addresses this problem. The proposal seeks to equip individuals with solid knowledge about sexuality, consent, and healthy relationships online, with the aim of counteracting gender violence that manifests itself in cyberspace. By integrating a gender perspective into sexuality education, the authors aim to empower people to recognize and combat forms of digital violence, thus promoting safer and more respectful online environments. This holistic approach seeks to prevent the perpetuation of harmful stereotypes and behaviors, promoting a digital culture that supports gender equality and mutual respect.

INTRODUCTION

The intersection between comprehensive sexuality education and the prevention of gender-based violence in the digital sphere is an essential field in the contemporary panorama. The omnipresence of information and communication technologies has brought innumerable benefits, but it has also triggered an alarming increase in situations of cyber gender-based violence, which disproportionately affects women and people of different genders (Yañez et al., 2023). In the face of this challenge, comprehensive sexuality education is revealed as a fundamental preventive strategy, capable of providing people with critical tools and knowledge necessary to function safely and respectfully in the digital

DOI: 10.4018/979-8-3693-2053-2.ch012

environment. Comprehensive sexuality education addresses not only the biological and reproductive aspects, but also the emotional, social, and ethical dimensions of human sexuality (Dey, 2020). Incorporating this perspective in the prevention of gender-based cyber violence involves recognizing the importance of autonomy, consent, effective communication, and mutual respect in the digital realm (Adams et al., 2021).

Comprehensive sexuality education thus becomes a key instrument for empowering individuals, providing them with the necessary skills to discern inappropriate behaviors, identify warning signs and respond proactively to risky situations. In the specific context of the digital sphere, comprehensive sexuality education can address issues such as online safety, respect for privacy, digital identity management, and critical awareness of gender representation in digital media (Henry & Powell, 2018). Encouraging reflection on these issues contributes to building responsible and ethical digital citizens capable of forging healthy online relationships and combating the spread of cyber gender-based violence (Gilliam et al., 2016). In addition, comprehensive sexuality education provides a space to challenge entrenched gender stereotypes, promoting equality and diversity in all aspects of life, including the digital realm (Azhar, 2023). By strengthening the foundations of comprehensive sexuality education, the groundwork is laid for a more equitable and just digital society, where cyber gender-based violence is proactively addressed and online communities are built based on respect, empathy, and inclusion (D'Ambrosi et al., 2018). Ultimately, integrating comprehensive sexuality education into the digital realm not only helps prevent online gender-based violence, but also helps cultivate a digital culture in which everyone can participate in a safe and enriching way (Faith, 2022).

Cyber gender-based violence is a complex issue that impacts individuals of all ages, genders and sexual orientations, representing a significant threat in the digital realm. International organizations have provided alarming data highlighting the magnitude and seriousness of this phenomenon. In 2020, a survey conducted by the World Wide Web Foundation revealed that 50% of young women had experienced gender-based cyberbullying. This type of online violence can manifest itself in various forms, including the dissemination of intimate images without consent, the spreading of offensive comments and virtual bullying. Similarly, the European Institute for Gender Equality, in its 2018 report, provides additional information, highlighting that 51% of young women express reluctance to participate in online discussions due to previous experiences of virtual harassment. This reluctance not only limits participation on digital platforms, but also has negative implications on the personal and professional development of the women affected. Also, a study conducted by Amnesty International in 2017 delves into the diversity of forms that cyber gender-based violence can take. According to this report, 23% of women have experienced some form of online abuse, ranging from sexist insults to threats of gender-based violence. This abuse not only affects the mental and emotional health of victims, but also creates a hostile digital environment that undermines gender equality and freedom of expression.

Legal frameworks play a crucial role in combating gender-based cyber violence by providing a regulatory framework to address this phenomenon. However, the complexity of online violence poses significant challenges to existing legislation. In many cases, existing laws have failed to keep up with technological advances and new forms of digital violence, leaving gaps in the protection of victims (Samara et al., 2017). Furthermore, gender-based cyber violence can transcend borders, posing additional challenges in terms of jurisdiction and international cooperation. Differences in attitudes towards gender-based cyber violence vary significantly by country or region. In Nordic countries such as Sweden, Norway and Finland, where a culture of gender equality prevails, strong laws and policies are often implemented to address gender-based violence, including cyber violence (Ortega et al., 2012). On the other hand, in some parts of the Middle East, cultural and religious norms may contribute to the tolerance or normalization of violence against women, influencing the perception and response to gender-based cyber violence. In the United States and Western Europe, although legal frameworks are generally strong, there may be disparities in perception and response due to cultural and political differences (Cáceres-Reche et al., 2019). In Southeast Asia, as in India, Malaysia or Indonesia, attitudes towards gender-based cyber violence are influenced by a mix of cultural traditions, religion and technological development (Maria Michael & Reyes, 2021). In sub-Saharan Africa, the response may be more limited due to infrastructure challenges and government priorities, and attitudes may vary considerably by country and socioeconomic circumstances (Varela et al., 2020). These examples illustrate how cultural, social and political contexts influence the perception and response to gender-based cyber violence around the world.

In 2017, the United Nations, in collaboration with the European Union, launched the Spotlight Initiative, a joint effort aimed at eradicating all forms of violence against women and girls. This initiative specifically addresses cyber gender-based violence, working both in the online and offline spheres. Likewise, the United Nations 2030 Agenda for Sustainable Development (2015), with its fifth goal focused on gender equality, drives programs and strategies to address cyber violence as an integral part of its overall approach. On the other hand, UNESCO (2019) has developed various tools, such as the "Gender and Media Guide", which examines gender portrayal in the media and its relationship to the normalization of gender-based cyber violence. The organization also advocates for the integration of digital citizenship education in education systems, addressing aspects such as online respect, digital safety and cyber gender-based violence awareness. In addition, UNESCO (2018) collaborates on research to better understand the scope of the problem and provides international technical guidance to develop effective strategies to combat digital gender-based and sexual cyber violence. These initiatives, often conducted in cooperation with governments and civil society organizations, seek a comprehensive approach to address this global challenge.

BACKGROUND

Cyber gender-based violence is a phenomenon that addresses the perpetration of violent acts through digital platforms, such as the internet, social networks, and electronic devices, with the specific objective of affecting a person or group based on their gender. This type of violence manifests itself in various ways, some of the most prominent being online harassment, non-consensual dissemination of intimate images, unwanted sexting, impersonation, sexual cyberbullying, as well as gender discriminatory comments and other forms of virtual aggression (Rodríguez-Castro et al., 2021). In the digital environment, cyber gender-based violence represents a multifaceted threat that requires comprehensive attention and the implementation of effective measures to eradicate it and protect the most vulnerable individuals (Donoso-Vázquez et al., 2017). Online harassment can take the form of intimidating messages, insults, threats, and defamation, creating a hostile environment that negatively affects the experience of those targeted by these actions (Wolford-Clevenger et al., 2016). Nonconsensual dissemination of intimate images involves sharing intimate material without the consent of the affected person, generating devastating consequences for their privacy and emotional well-being (Van Ouytsel et al., 2020). Unwanted sexting, which involves the unsolicited sending of sexual content, and impersonation to commit sexual cyberbullying are additional manifestations of gender-based cyberviolence that intensify the vulnerability of victims (Hasinoff, 2015). Moreover, gender discriminatory comments perpetuate harmful stereotypes and contribute to the normalization of sexist attitudes online (Yahner et al., 2015). Faced with this complex problem, it is important to implement educational, legal, and technological strategies to counteract gender-based cyber violence, thus ensuring a safe and equitable digital environment for all.

Cyber gender-based violence has existed since online interactions became a significant part of everyday life. As the internet and digital technologies evolved and became more accessible, forms of gender-based violence also moved into the digital realm. However, the term "cyber gender-based violence" and public awareness of this specific problem have been gaining prominence in recent decades as society recognizes the importance of addressing gender-based violence in all settings, including the digital (Peterson & Densley, 2017). There is no exact date for the inception of gender-based cyber violence, as it has evolved with the development of technology and the expansion of online presence. Over time, gender-based cyberviolence has become a crucial issue on the human rights and gender equity agenda, and organizations, governments, and activists are working to address this problem and protect those affected (Ramos et al., 2020).

Victims of cyberviolence can be individuals of any gender, although women tend to face a significant proportion of these cases (Rebollo-Catalan & Mayor-Buzon, 2020). Sexual cyberviolence affects individuals regardless of their age, sexual orientation, gender identity, or any other personal characteristics. However, various research and reports indicate that women and girls have experienced higher levels of sexual cyberviolence compared to other groups (Monteiro et al., 2023). Some factors contributing to women's vulnerability include gender stereotypes, sexual objectification, online harassment, nonconsensual dissemination of intimate images, and other forms of digital abuse (Cava et al., 2023). Importantly, men and people of other gender identities can also be victims of sexual cyberviolence, and attention to these experiences is equally crucial (Bajo-Perez, 2022). Intersecting identities, such as race, ethnicity, sexual orientation, disability, and socioeconomic status, are complexly intertwined with gender, helping to shape experiences of cyber violence (Warrier, 2022). For example, people who belong to minority groups may face increased vulnerability due to the intersection of multiple forms of online discrimination. Women from ethnic or racial minorities, as well as LGBTQ+ people with disabilities, may be exposed to specific forms of online harassment and abuse that reflect embedded prejudices in society. Additionally, socioeconomic status may influence people's ability to access resources and support to address cyberviolence.

Gender-based cyber-violence manifests itself through various interrelated reasons that reflect power dynamics and gender inequalities embedded in society. These causes include gender inequality, where cyberviolence acts as an amplifier of existing gender disparities, being fueled by stereotypes and cultural norms conducive to discriminatory online behaviors (Vizcaíno-Cuenca et al., 2024). Online anonymity adds another layer to the problem, as the ease of remaining anonymous may lead some people to feel more inclined to engage in abusive behaviors without facing direct consequences (Temple et al., 2016). Online impunity also contributes, as the lack of effective measures to track and punish perpetrators creates a sense of impunity, thus fostering more cases of abuse. Misinformation and lack of awareness about the impact of gender-based cyber violence, as well as a lack of education around gender respect and equality, are additional factors that fuel the perpetuation of this phenomenon (Reed et al., 2017). Cultural and social norms that tolerate or normalize gender discrimination influence online behaviors, reflecting entrenched sexist attitudes in society (Alsawalqa & Alrawashde, 2022). Cyberviolence is a complex phenomenon that is influenced by a series of social and cultural factors (Menabò et al., 2023). First, culture plays a crucial role in how online violence is perceived and handled. Cultural norms and social values can influence tolerance towards certain aggressive online behaviors, as well as people's willingness to report or intervene in cases of cyber violence. Additionally, social factors, such as gender, age, ethnicity, and sexual orientation, also play an important role. For example, people belonging to certain groups may be more vulnerable to cyber violence due to the discrimination and marginalization they face online. Likewise, power dynamics and social inequalities can exacerbate cyberviolence, as some individuals may use technology as a tool to exert control or dominance over others (Smith & Steffgen, 2013). The inappropriate use of technology, driven by rapid technological evolution that outpaces security and privacy measures, facilitates the perpetration of cyber-violence. Likewise, gender-based cyber violence can be a manifestation of the desire for control and power over people, especially in abusive relationship situations.

Gender-based cyberviolence can lead to serious and diverse consequences for those who experience it. These include significant emotional and psychological impact, resulting in stress, anxiety, depression, and other conditions that affect mental well-being (Pashang et al., 2019). In addition, victims may experience social isolation, feeling ashamed or fearful, making it difficult to seek support due to fear of stigma (Villora et al., 2019). Reputational harm is also a common consequence, as nonconsensual dissemination of intimate images or online defamation can have a considerable impact on the affected person's personal and professional reputation (Chiang et al., 2021). In some cases, cyber-violence can even threaten physical safety through leaking personal information or persistent harassment, generating dangerous situations (Melander & Hughes, 2018). Personal relationships, both friendships and family and couple relationships, are affected by gender-based cyberviolence, generating tensions and conflicts in these environments (Muñoz-Fernández et al., 2022). Likewise, victims may face limitations in their participation in online activities, as well as in accessing educational or employment opportunities, due to the fear of cyberviolence (Chan, 2023). The cycle of victimization is another reality, as people who have been victimized may be at risk of facing similar situations in the future, perpetuating the cycle if not adequately addressed. The experience of cyberviolence can also generate distrust in the use of online platforms, affecting participation and free expression in digital spaces (Stonard, 2020). In addition, the stress and anxiety associated with cyberviolence can have negative impacts on the physical health of the affected person (Butler et al., 2023). Online attacks and harassment can cause anxiety, depression, post-traumatic stress and other psychological disorders, negatively affecting people's self-esteem and self-confidence. Furthermore, repeated victimization in digital environments can generate a sense of helplessness and helplessness, further exacerbating the psychological impact (Bauman et al., 2013). The harmful effects of cyberviolence can also extend to offline life, affecting interpersonal relationships, academic and work performance, and even overall quality of life. It is essential to provide adequate support and resources to victims of cyber violence to help them recover and rebuild their emotional well-being, as well as promote awareness and prevention to mitigate these risks in today's digital society (Hinduja & Patchin, 2014). Supporting a victim of gender-based cyber violence involves providing comprehensive support that covers both the emotional and practical aspects. Firstly, it is essential to offer a safe and understanding space where the victim can express their emotions and concerns without fear of being judged. This may include providing emotional support, active listening, and validation of her feelings. Additionally, guidance should be provided on how to take steps to protect your online safety, such as blocking attackers, changing privacy settings on social media, and collecting evidence in case you decide to report the incident to the relevant authorities. It is also important to connect the victim with additional resources and support services, such as helplines, women's rights organizations and legal advice, so that she can receive the professional assistance necessary for her recovery and empowerment (Modecki, 2014).

Comprehensive sexuality education plays an essential role in preventing digital gender-based violence by providing knowledge, skills, and attitudes to address gender dynamics in the digital environment (Jiménez, 2019). Among the ways in which comprehensive sexuality education contributes to prevention are promoting respect and consent in all digital interactions, raising awareness about different types of digital gender-based violence, teaching digital literacy skills to protect oneself online demystifying gender stereotypes, fostering socioemotional skills to build healthy relationships, including cybersecurity issues to understand online risks, strengthening self-esteem and empowerment, and promoting responsible reporting to create safer and more responsible online environments (Del Prete & Pantoja, 2022; Ngidi & Kaye, 2022).

MAIN FOCUS

Sexual cyberbullying is positioned as an insidious variant of gender-based violence, revealing the omnipresence of these manifestations in the digital sphere. This specific form of violence involves the use of digital technologies to harass, threaten or humiliate people, with a particular focus on the gender variable. Sexual cyberbullying can range from the unsolicited sending of explicit images to the non-consensual dissemination of intimate material, perpetuating gender stereotypes and undermining the safety and dignity of victims. Recognizing sexual cyberbullying as an expression of gender-based violence is essential to address its deep roots and to work towards creating digital environments that promote equality, respect and the eradication of gender-based violence.

Promoting comprehensive sexuality education in digital environments proves to be an essential measure for the prevention of cyber violence and a significant contribution to eradicating online gender-based violence. By approaching sex education from a comprehensive perspective, individuals are empowered to understand the importance of respect, equality and consensually in their digital interactions. This approach not only provides information about cyber violence, but also develops critical skills to recognize and prevent risky situations. By raising awareness about the various forms of online gender-based violence, it promotes a cultural shift that challenges stereotypes and fosters a safe and respectful virtual environment. Comprehensive sexuality education in digital environments thus becomes a powerful tool to empower individuals and build online communities that reject gender-based violence.

Perspectives

The digital sphere, while bringing connectivity and access to information, also becomes a space and tool where cyber sexual violence can manifest itself, underscoring the urgent need for comprehensive education and preventive strategies to ensure a safe and respectful online environment.

On the one hand, the digital sphere has become a space conducive to cyber sexual violence, where the "manosphere" and "pornification" play a significant role. The manosphere refers to online communities

Figure 1. The digital sphere as a space and tool for cyber sexual violence

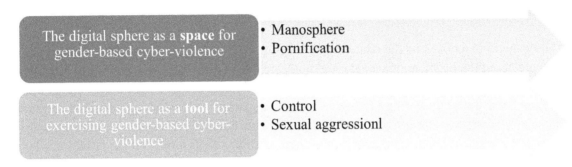

that promote misogynistic attitudes and harassing behaviors towards women, while pornification refers to the normalization and proliferation of explicit sexual content (Stahl et al., 2023). These phenomena contribute to the creation of a digital environment that facilitates sexual cyber violence, whether through virtual harassment, non-consensual distribution of intimate content, or objectification of individuals (Goldstein, 2020). In this context, it is important to address these problems through education, awareness and the implementation of preventive strategies, in order to transform the digital sphere into a space that promotes respect, equality and online safety.

On the other hand, the digital sphere has been transformed into a tool to exercise sexual cyber violence, manifesting itself through forms of control and sexual aggression online. This reality involves the use of technology to harass, intimidate or coerce individuals, either by sending unwanted messages, non-consensual dissemination of intimate images or emotional manipulation through digital platforms (Rebollo-Catalan & Mayor-Buzon, 2020). Control and sexual aggression in the digital realm reflect the ability of some individuals to take advantage of the vulnerabilities inherent in digital connectivity (Cripps & Stermac, 2018). Addressing these behaviors requires educational strategies that foster online respect, boundary awareness, and empowerment of individuals to protect against cyber sexual violence. This phenomenon highlights the urgent need to develop preventive measures and supportive resources to ensure a safe and respectful digital environment.

A TRAINING PROPOSAL

Developing a formative program on cyber sexual violence in youth is essential due to the increasing prevalence of online threats and their significant consequences. The digital age has integrated technology into the daily lives of young people, exposing them to risks such as cyber sexual harassment. A targeted educational program addresses the urgent need to raise awareness among young people about the various forms of sexual cyber violence, including non-consensual sexting, online harassment, and grooming. By understanding the risks, young people can develop skills to protect themselves and others by promoting ethical and respectful behavior online. In addition, a formative program facilitates access to supportive resources and creates an environment conducive to open dialogue, reducing the stigma associated with reporting experiences of cyber sexual violence. Ultimately, the development of these types of programs contributes to the creation of an informed and empowered youth capable of facing the challenges of cyberspace in a safe and aware manner. The following highlights the fundamental components that make up an educational program: objectives, content, methodology and evaluation.

- The general objectives of the educational program focus on raising awareness among young people about the problem of sexual cyberbullying, deepening their understanding of its emotional and psychological implications. In addition, it seeks to encourage ethical and respectful online behavior, highlighting the importance of empathy and consent in virtual interactions. Likewise, the program aims to equip students with effective strategies to prevent and respond to sexual cyberbullying, equipping them with practical tools and essential knowledge to navigate safely and responsibly in the digital environment. These objectives seek not only to inform, but also to empower young people to be active agents in creating safer and more respectful virtual environments.
- The formative contents of this educational program comprehensively address the phenomenon of sexual cyberbullying, highlighting its importance in the awareness and protection of young people. Initially, a clear understanding of sexual cyberbullying is provided, including definitions

Figure 2. General outline of the training program on sexual cyberbullying
Source: Own elaboration. Images creative common license.

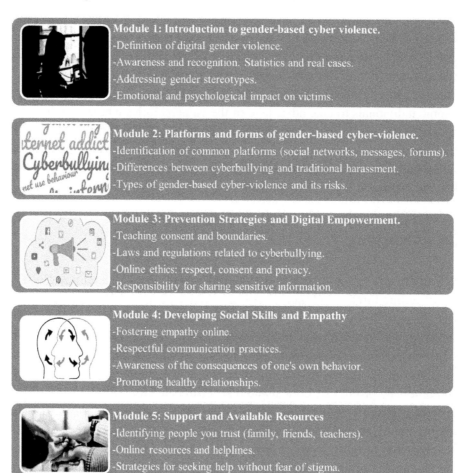

and current statistics to contextualize the problem. Subsequently, the various platforms and forms of cyberbullying are explored, allowing students to identify risks and potential situations. In addition, the legal and ethical framework of cyberbullying is addressed, informing about legal consequences, and promoting respectful and ethical online behavior. The central part of the program focuses on prevention strategies, including profile authentication, privacy settings and social skills for safe communication. Finally, resources and support are offered, both in terms of identifying trusted individuals and accessing specialized services. This comprehensive approach ensures that young people not only acquire theoretical knowledge, but also practical skills to address cyberbullying and build safer digital environments.

- The methodology of the educational program is based on participation and experiential learning. Through interactive classes, group discussions are encouraged, allowing young people to share experiences and perspectives. Practical activities include simulations of cyberbullying situations, giving students the opportunity to apply their knowledge in safe environments. In addition, multimedia resources, such as videos, testimonials, and infographics, are used to enrich understanding of the topic. To go even deeper, experts in cybersecurity and mental health can be invited to give specialized talks, providing valuable information and additional perspectives on cyberbullying and its consequences.

- Program evaluation can be carried out in a comprehensive manner, ensuring continuous monitoring of student progress. Participation in class and in various activities designed to strengthen understanding of the subject matter is valued. Knowledge is assessed through written tests that address key concepts and through group discussions that encourage the exchange of ideas. As a final project, students may have the opportunity to apply what they have learned through the creation of an online awareness campaign, promoting solidarity and the prevention of sexual cyberbullying in their virtual community. This evaluative approach seeks not only to measure content mastery, but also to cultivate practical skills and active engagement of participants in the fight against cyberbullying.

FUTURE RESEARCH DIRECTIONS

Sexual cyberbullying continues to be a phenomenon of growing concern in contemporary society, especially among youth, who are immersed in the digital age. In the quest to address and prevent this problem, future research in cyberbullying education can focus on several key directions.

- Assessing the psychological and social impact of cyberbullying emerges as a crucial component of a comprehensive understanding of this issue. A comprehensive investigation seeks to carefully analyze the emotional and psychological repercussions experienced by victims of cyberbullying, as well as to understand how these experiences affect the dynamics of online communities. It also examines the influence of sociocultural factors, such as age, gender, and cultural background, on the perception of and response to cyber sexual violence. This multidimensional approach provides deep insight, allowing not only to identify the dimensions of impact, but also to design more effective prevention and support strategies that address the psychosocial particularities of each individual and community.

- The development of technological prevention tools emerges as a crucial area of research in the fight against cyberbullying. Exploring the potential of technologies such as artificial intelligence and sentiment analysis aims at proactively identifying patterns of cyberbullying, enabling early intervention to prevent its spread. In parallel, critical evaluation of the effectiveness of security measures and privacy settings on online platforms becomes essential to strengthen user protection. This innovative approach not only addresses current challenges in the detection and mitigation of cyberbullying, but also contributes to the design of safer and more responsible digital environments through the implementation of efficient and ethical technological solutions.

- The integration of digital education into the school curriculum becomes essential research to address sexual cyberbullying from an educational perspective. It aims to examine how to effectively incorporate cyberbullying education into the curriculum, considering the specific needs of various age groups. This approach seeks not only to provide information about cyber sexual violence, but also to adapt the content appropriately for each stage of development. In addition, research is aimed at evaluating the effectiveness of specific educational programs, analyzing their long-term impact on students' attitudes and behaviors. By understanding how digital education can positively influence the awareness and behavior of young people, we seek to strengthen the capacity of educational institutions to proactively address sexual cyberbullying and promote responsible and ethical use of the digital environment.

- The analysis of trends and new forms of sexual cyberbullying is configured as an essential line of research to address the dynamic challenges presented by the digital environment. Staying alert to emerging trends, which may involve the use of new platforms and technologies, becomes crucial to anticipating and understanding changing forms of cyberbullying. This research seeks not only to identify current modalities, but also to anticipate potential future threats. Furthermore, it aims to investigate how rapid technological evolution may pose additional challenges in the fight against cyberbullying, analyzing the ability of existing security measures to adapt and protect users effectively. This proactive and future-oriented approach aims to provide essential information for the formulation of preventive strategies and continuous improvement of online security.

- The development of resilience strategies is presented as crucial research to provide young people with effective tools to confront cyberbullying and strengthen their emotional well-being. The exploration of these strategies seeks not only to mitigate the negative consequences of cyberbullying, but also to equip young people with skills that allow them to confront and overcome online adversities. The research focuses on understanding how education in socio-emotional skills an effective tool in this context can be, promoting empathy, self-esteem, and effective communication. By focusing on the development of resilience, this line of research seeks not only to prevent cyberbullying, but also to equip young people with the skills necessary to maintain their emotional well-being in the digital environment.

Figure 3. Future lines of research
Souce: Own preparation.

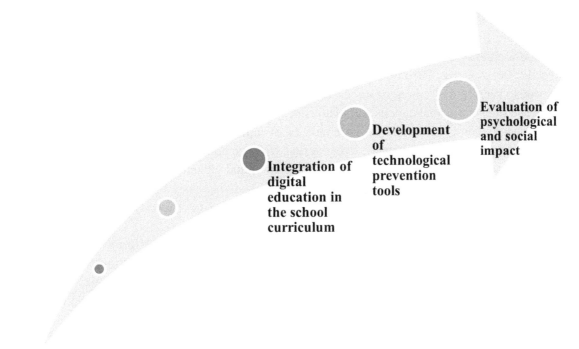

CONCLUSION

In the age of information and constant connectivity, education on cyber sexual violence emerges as an essential component to empower youth and cultivate safe and respectful digital environments. This specific form of violence, which ranges from cyberbullying to non-consensual sexting, has gained relevance as online interactions have become present in the lives of young people. Addressing this issue requires a comprehensive approach that not only informs, but also develops skills, fosters empathy and promotes a culture of digital respect. Awareness-raising stands as the fundamental starting point in education on cyber sexual violence. It involves providing young people, as well as educators and parents, with a clear understanding of the various forms that sexual violence can take in the digital environment. From anonymous cyberbullying to subtle grooming, awareness raising addresses the complexity of the problem and highlights the importance of recognizing early signs of violence to prevent its escalation. This first step is essential to create an open dialogue that demystifies cyber sexual violence and raises awareness about its impacts on an emotional, psychological and social level. Once the foundation of awareness is established, preventive strategies become a crucial component of cyber sexual violence education. Young people need to learn practical skills to protect themselves online, from appropriately setting privacy on their profiles to recognizing and avoiding risky situations. Promoting the development of social-emotional skills, such as empathy and self-esteem, also becomes essential. By strengthening these skills, young people are empowered to make ethical decisions and confront pressures online, building psychological resilience that allows them to confront cyber violence more effectively.

Intervention, both from a preventive and victim support perspective, is another critical aspect of cyber sexual violence education. Young people should understand how to recognize and report cyberbullying, as well as seek help when they need it. Developing a culture where victims feel supported and understood is essential to breaking the silence that often surrounds cyber sexual violence. Additionally, effective resources and support systems must be deployed to offer both emotional and legal help to those who have experienced cyber violence. The rapid evolution of technology poses additional challenges and underlines the need to keep up with emerging trends. Investigating and analyzing new forms of cyberbullying, such as the use of specific applications and platforms, is essential to adapt educational and preventive strategies. Education on cyber sexual violence must be dynamic and flexible, able to evolve alongside technology and social trends. Ultimately, cyber sexual violence education is not just about providing information, but about cultivating ethical and responsible digital citizens. It involves creating critical awareness about the impact of our actions online and understanding shared responsibility in building safe digital environments. Education on cyber sexual violence seeks to shape attitudes and behaviors, promoting empathy and respect in the digital age.

In conclusion, education on cyber sexual violence represents a collective effort to provide young people with the necessary tools to navigate cyberspace safely. From awareness to intervention and support, this holistic approach seeks not only to prevent cyber sexual violence, but also to build a generation of individuals who are informed, empathetic and capable of creating safer and more respectful digital communities.

REFERENCES

Adams, A., Lea, S. G., & D'Silva, E. M. (2021). Digital technologies and interventions against gender-based violence in rural areas. *International Criminal Justice Review*, *31*(4), 438–455. doi:10.1177/10575677211040413

Alsawalqa, R. O., & Alrawashdeh, M. N. (2022). The role of patriarchal structure and gender stereotypes in cyber dating abuse: A qualitative examination of male perpetrators experiences. *The British Journal of Sociology*, *73*(3), 587–606. doi:10.1111/1468-4446.12946 PMID:35644007

Amnesty International. (2017). *What is online violence and abuse against women?* Amnesty International. https://www.amnesty.org/en/latest/campaigns/2017/11/what-is-online-violence-and-abuse-against-women/

Azhar, S. (2023). "Too weak to fight, too scared to scream": Understanding experiences of sexual coercion of Black female adolescents through digital storytelling. *Sexualities*, *13634607231212841*, 13634607231212841. doi:10.1177/13634607231212841

Bajo-Pérez, I. (2022). Gender violence through Instagram: Descriptive study of women residing in Spain between 18 and 35 years old. *Sociología Y Tecnociencia*, *12*(2), 271–283. doi:10.24197/st.2.2022.271-283

Bauman, S., Toomey, R. B., & Walker, J. L. (2013). Associations among bullying, cyberbullying, and suicide in high school students. *Journal of Adolescence*, *36*(2), 341–350. doi:10.1016/j.adolescence.2012.12.001 PMID:23332116

Butler, L. C., Fissel, E. R., Gildea, B., & Fisher, B. S. (2023). Understanding intimate partner cyber abuse across partnership categories based on gender identity and sexual orientation. *Victims & Offenders*, *18*(1), 77–100. doi:10.1080/15564886.2022.2139032

Cáceres-Reche, M. P., Hinojo-Lucena, F. J., Navas-Parejo, M. R., & Romero-Rodríguez, J. M. (2019). The phenomenon of cyberbullying in the children and adolescents' population: a scientometric analysis. *Research in social sciences and technology, 4*(2), 115-128.

Cava, M. J., Castillo, I., Tomás, I., & Buelga, S. (2023). Romantic myths and cyber dating violence victimization in Spanish adolescents: A moderated mediation model. *Cyberpsychology (Brno)*, *17*(2). doi:10.5817/CP2023-2-4

Chan, E. (2023). Technology-facilitated gender-based violence, hate speech, and terrorism: A risk assessment on the rise of the incel rebellion in Canada. *Violence Against Women*, *29*(9), 1687–1718. doi:10.1177/10778012221125495 PMID:36226437

Chiang, J. T., Chang, F. C., & Lee, K. W. (2021). Transitions in aggression among children: Effects of gender and exposure to online violence. *Aggressive Behavior*, *47*(3), 310–319. doi:10.1002/ab.21944 PMID:33570759

Cripps, J., & Stermac, L. (2018). Cyber-sexual violence and negative emotional states among women in a Canadian university. *International Journal of Cyber Criminology*, *12*(1), 171–186.

D'Ambrosi, L., Papakristo, P., & Polci, V. (2018). Social media and gender violence: Communication strategies for a "new education". *Italian Journal of Sociology of Education*, *10*, 76–89. doi:10.14658/PUPJ-IJSE-2018-2-6

Del Prete, A., & Pantoja, S. R. (2022). The Invisibility of Gender-Based Violence in the Social Network. *Gender Studies*, *11*(2), 124–143. doi:10.17583/generos.9045

Dey, A. (2020). Sites of exception: Gender violence, digital activism, and Nirbhaya's zone of anomie in India. *Violence Against Women*, *26*(11), 1423–1444. doi:10.1177/1077801219862633 PMID:31379258

Donoso-Vázquez, T., Hurtado, M. J. R., & Baños, R. V. (2017). Las ciberagresiones en función del género. *Revista de Investigación Educacional*, *35*(1), 197–214. doi:10.6018/rie.35.1.249771

European Institute for Gender Equality. (2018). *Gender equality and youth: the opportunities and risks of digitalization*. EIGE. doi:10.2839/09510

Faith, B. (2022). Tackling online gender-based violence; understanding gender, development, and the power relations of digital spaces. *Gender, Technology and Development*, *26*(3), 325–340. doi:10.1080/09718524.2022.2124600

Gilliam, M., Jagoda, P., Jaworski, E., Hebert, L. E., Lyman, P., & Wilson, M. C. (2016). "Because if we don't talk about it, how are we going to prevent it?": Lucidity, a narrative-based digital game about sexual violence. *Sex Education*, *16*(4), 391–404. doi:10.1080/14681811.2015.1123147

Goldstein, A. (2020). Beyond porn literacy: Drawing on young people's pornography narratives to expand sex education pedagogies. *Sex Education*, *20*(1), 59–74. doi:10.1080/14681811.2019.1621826 PMID:35814266

Hasinoff, A. A. (2015). *Sexting panic: rethinking criminalization, privacy, and consent*. University of Illinois Press. doi:10.5406/illinois/9780252038983.001.0001

Henry, N., & Powell, A. (2018). Technology-facilitated sexual violence: A literature review of empirical research. *Trauma, Violence & Abuse, 19*(2), 195–208. doi:10.1177/1524838016650189 PMID:27311818

Hinduja, S., & Patchin, J. W. (2014). *Cyberbullying: identification. Prevention and Response*. Cyberbullying Research Center. https://cyberbullying.org/Cyberbullying-Identification-Prevention-Response.pdf

Jiménez, R. (2019). Multiple victimization (bullying and cyberbullying) in primary education in Spain from a gender perspective. *Multidisciplinary Journal of Educational Research, 9*(2), 169–193. doi:10.17583/remie.2019.4272

Maria Michael, J., & Reyes, M. E. (2021). Cyberbullying victimization as a predictor of depressive symptoms among selected adolescents amidst the COVID-19 pandemic. *Makara Human Behavior Studies in Asia, 25*(2), 145–152. doi:10.7454/hubs.asia.2161121

Menabò, L., Skrzypiec, G., Slee, P., & Guarini, A. (2023). What roles matter? An explorative study on bullying and cyberbullying by using the eye-tracker. *The British Journal of Educational Psychology*, e12604. doi:10.1111/bjep.12604 PMID:37186299

Modecki, K. L., Minchin, J., Harbaugh, A. G., Guerra, N. G., & Runions, K. C. (2014). Bullying prevalence across contexts: A meta-analysis measuring cyber and traditional bullying. *The Journal of Adolescent Health, 55*(5), 602–611. doi:10.1016/j.jadohealth.2014.06.007 PMID:25168105

Monteiro, A. P., Guedes, S., & Correia, E. (2023). Cyber Dating Abuse in Higher Education Students: Self-Esteem, Sex, Age and Recreational Time Online. *Social Sciences (Basel, Switzerland), 12*(3), 139. doi:10.3390/socsci12030139

Muñoz-Fernández, N., Sánchez-Jiménez, V., Rodríguez-deArriba, M. L., Nacimiento-Rodríguez, L., Elipe, P., & Del Rey, R. (2023). Traditional and cyber dating violence among adolescents: Profiles, prevalence, and short-term associations with peer violence. *Aggressive Behavior, 49*(3), 261–273. doi:10.1002/ab.22069 PMID:36585958

Ngidi, L. Z., & Kaye, S. B. (2022). Reducing school violence: A peace education project in KwaZulu-Natal, South Africa. *South African Journal of Education, 42*(2), 1989. doi:10.15700/saje.v42n2a1989

Ortega, R., Elipe, P., Mora-Merchán, J. A., Genta, M. L., Brighi, A., Guarini, A., Smith, P. K., Thompson, F., & Tippett, N. (2012). The emotional impact of bullying and cyberbullying on victims: A European cross-national study. *Aggressive Behavior, 38*(5), 342–356. doi:10.1002/ab.21440 PMID:22782434

Pashang, S., Khanlou, N., & Clarke, J. (2019). The mental health impact of cyber sexual violence on youth identity. *International Journal of Mental Health and Addiction, 17*(5), 1119–1131. doi:10.1007/s11469-018-0032-4

Peterson, J., & Densley, J. (2017). Cyber violence: What do we know and where do we go from here? *Aggression and Violent Behavior, 34*, 193–200. doi:10.1016/j.avb.2017.01.012

Ramos, A. M. G. (2020). Cyber-activism Against Sexual Violence: #BringBackOurGirls. *Debats: Revista de cultura, poder i societat*, (5), 233–244. doi:10.28939/iam.debats-en.2020-13

Rebollo-Catalan, A., & Mayor-Buzon, V. (2020). Adolescent bystanders witnessing cyber violence against women and girls: What they observe and how they respond. *Violence Against Women*, *26*(15-16), 2024–2040. doi:10.1177/1077801219888025 PMID:31779537

Reed, L. A., Tolman, R. M., & Ward, L. M. (2017). Gender matters: Experiences and consequences of digital dating abuse victimization in adolescent dating relationships. *Journal of Adolescence*, *59*(1), 79–89. doi:10.1016/j.adolescence.2017.05.015 PMID:28582653

Rodríguez-Castro, Y., Martínez-Román, R., Alonso-Ruido, P., Adá-Lameiras, A., & Carrera-Fernández, M. V. (2021). Intimate partner cyberstalking, sexism, pornography, and sexting in adolescents: New challenges for sex education. *International Journal of Environmental Research and Public Health*, *18*(4), 2181. doi:10.3390/ijerph18042181 PMID:33672240

Samara, M., Burbidge, V., El Asam, A., Foody, M., Smith, P. K., & Morsi, H. (2017). Bullying and cyberbullying: Their legal status and use in psychological assessment. *International Journal of Environmental Research and Public Health*, *14*(12), 1449. doi:10.3390/ijerph14121449 PMID:29186780

Smith, P. K., & Steffgen, G. (Eds.). (2013). *Cyberbullying through the new media: Findings from an international network*. Psychology Press. doi:10.4324/9780203799079

Stahl, G., Keddie, A., & Adams, B. (2023). The manosphere goes to school: Problematizing incel surveillance through affective boyhood. *Educational Philosophy and Theory*, *55*(3), 366–378. doi:10.1080/00131857.2022.2097068

UNESCO. (2018). *International technical guidance on sexuality education: an evidence-informed approach*. UNESCO. doi:10.54675/UQRM6395

UNESCO. (2019). *Gender, media & ICTs: new approaches for research, education & training*. UNESCO. https://unesdoc.unesco.org/ark:/48223/pf0000368963

United Nations. (2015). *Transforming our world: the 2030 Agenda for Sustainable Development*. UN. https://sdgs.un.org/2030agenda

United Nations & European Union. (2017). *Spotlight Initiative to end violence against women and girls*. UN. https://www.spotlightinitiative.org/

Van Ouytsel, J., Ponnet, K., & Walrave, M. (2020). Cyber dating abuse: Investigating digital monitoring behaviors among adolescents from a social learning perspective. *Journal of Interpersonal Violence*, *35*(23-24), 5157–5178. doi:10.1177/0886260517719538 PMID:29294845

Varela, J. J., Savahl, S., Adams, S., & Reyes, F. (2020). Examining the relationship among bullying, school climate and adolescent well-being in Chile and South Africa: A cross cultural comparison. *Child Indicators Research*, *13*(3), 819–838. doi:10.1007/s12187-019-09648-0

Villora, B., Yubero, S., & Navarro, R. (2019). Cyber dating abuse and masculine gender norms in a sample of male adults. *Future Internet*, *11*(4), 84. doi:10.3390/fi11040084

Vizcaíno-Cuenca, R., Romero-Sánchez, M., & Carretero-Dios, H. (2024). Making visible the myths about cyber-sexual violence against women: An analysis of social reactions toward victims on Twitter. *Journal of Interpersonal Violence*, *08862605231222876*, 08862605231222876. Advance online publication. doi:10.1177/08862605231222876 PMID:38243759

Warrier, S. (2021). Inclusion and Exclusion: Intersectionality and Gender-Based Violence. In R. Geffner, J.W. White, L. K. Hamberger, A. Rosenbaum, V. Vaughan-Eden, V.I. Vieth, Handbook of Interpersonal Violence and Abuse Across the Lifespan: A project of the National Partnership to End Interpersonal Violence Across the Lifespan (NPEIV) (pp. 2539-2552). Springer International Publishing.

Wolford-Clevenger, C., Zapor, H., Brasfield, H., Febres, J., Elmquist, J., Brem, M., Shorey, R. C., & Stuart, G. L. (2016). An examination of the Partner Cyber Abuse Questionnaire in a college student sample. *Psychology of Violence*, *6*(1), 156–162. doi:10.1037/a0039442 PMID:27014498

World Wide Web Foundation. (2020). *Survey - Young people's experience of online harassment*. Web Foundation. https://webfoundation.org/docs/2020/03/WF_WAGGGS-Survey-1-pager-1.pdf

Yahner, J., Dank, M., Zweig, J. M., & Lachman, P. (2015). The co-occurrence of physical and cyber dating violence and bullying among teens. *Journal of Interpersonal Violence*, *30*(7), 1079–1089. doi:10.1177/0886260514540324 PMID:25038223

Yañez, A. G. B., Alonso-Fernández, C., & Fernández-Manjón, B. (2023). Systematic literature review of digital resources to educate on gender equality. *Education and Information Technologies*, *28*(8), 1–26. doi:10.1007/s10639-022-11574-8 PMID:36747612

ADDITIONAL READING

Elshenraki, H. N. (Ed.). (2020). *Combating the Exploitation of Children in Cyberspace: Emerging Research and Opportunities*. IGI Global.

Flores, J. (2014). *Ciberviolencia de género y sexual en la adolescencia. Guía de apoyo para profesionales*. Pantallas Amigas.

Flynn, A., Powell, A., & Sugiura, L. (Eds.). (2021). *The Palgrave handbook of gendered violence and technology*. Springer.

Gjika, A. (2023). *When Rape Goes Viral: Youth and Sexual Assault in the Digital Age*. University of California Press.

Goldstein, A. (2020). Beyond porn literacy: Drawing on young people's pornography narratives to expand sex education pedagogies. *Sex Education*, *20*(1), 59–74. doi:10.1080/14681811.2019.1621826 PMID:35814266

Jiménez, R., & Triviño, L. (Coord.). (2023). *Pedagogía digital feminista en educación superior*. Dykinson.

Melander, L., & Hughes, V. (2018). College partner violence in the digital age: Explaining cyber aggression using routine activities theory. *Partner Abuse*, *9*(2), 158–180. doi:10.1891/1946-6560.9.2.158

Mishra, D., Le, A. N., & McDowell, Z. (2023). *Communication Technology and Gender Violence*. Springer.

Powell, A., & Henry, N. (2017). *Sexual violence in a digital age*. Springer. doi:10.1057/978-1-137-58047-4

Stonard, K. E. (2020). "Technology was designed for this": Adolescents' perceptions of the role and impact of the use of technology in cyber dating violence. *Computers in Human Behavior*, *105*, 106211. doi:10.1016/j.chb.2019.106211

Tavcer, D. S., & Dobkins, V. (2023). *Sexual Violence Policies and Sexual Consent Education at Canadian Post-Secondary Institutions*. Taylor & Francis. doi:10.4324/9781003332671

Temple, J. R., Choi, H. J., Brem, M., Wolford-Clevenger, C., Stuart, G. L., Peskin, M. F., & Elmquist, J. (2016). The temporal association between traditional and cyber dating abuse among adolescents. *Journal of Youth and Adolescence*, *45*(2), 340–349. doi:10.1007/s10964-015-0380-3 PMID:26525389

Vázquez, T. D., & Catalán, Á. R. (2018). *Violencias de género en entornos virtuales*. Ediciones Octaedro.

KEY TERMS AND DEFINITIONS

Image Cyberbullying: Refers to a form of online harassment in which intimate or personal images of a person are shared without their consent. This act may include the unauthorized distribution of photographs or videos of explicit sexual content, as well as the dissemination of compromising or private images with the intention of causing harm, humiliation, or embarrassment to the victim.

Non-Consensual Sexting: Refers to the practice of sharing messages, photographs, or videos of a sexually explicit nature of a person without their consent. In the context of sexting, which involves sending sexually suggestive content via text messages, messaging apps or social media, non-consensual sexting occurs when one party shares that intimate material without the agreement or knowledge of the other. person involved.

Online Grooming: An adult establishes a relationship with a minor online with the aim of gaining their trust and then exploiting them sexually.

Online Harassment: Refers to a pattern of hostile, threatening or intimidating behavior that takes place through digital platforms and social networks. This type of harassment involves the use of technology and online communication to harass, humiliate, defame, or cause emotional distress to a person. Online harassment can take many forms, including name-calling, threats, defamation, impersonation, unauthorized disclosure of personal information, and other malicious behavior.

Revenge Porn: Refers to the practice of sharing, disseminating, or distributing sexually explicit images or videos of a person, usually after a romantic or sexual relationship, without the consent of the person involved. In this context, the disclosure of such intimate material is intended to cause harm, embarrassment, or emotional suffering to the victim, and is often done as a form of revenge on the part of the person sharing the content.

Sextortion: A form of sexual exploitation that involves the coercive use of intimate material, such as sexually explicit images or videos, to extort money from the victim. In this context, the person threatens to reveal, or share said content in a non-consensual manner unless the victim complies with their demands. These demands may include sending more intimate material, performing certain actions, or even providing money. Sextortion typically occurs in online environments, where offenders can gain access to sensitive material and then manipulate the victim with the threat of public dissemination.

Sexual Cyberbullying: The practice of using digital platforms, such as social networks, instant messages, emails, or other online media, to carry out acts of harassment with sexual connotations towards a person. This behavior may include sending unsolicited messages, images, or videos of sexually explicit content, as well as the non-consensual dissemination of personal or intimate information. Sexual cyberbullying seeks to intimidate, embarrass, or cause emotional distress to the victim, and can manifest itself in a variety of ways, such as non-consensual sexting, online grooming, sextortion, image harassment and other forms of sexually motivated digital violence.

Sexual Identity Impersonation: The action of creating false online profiles for the purpose of deceiving other people about the user's sexual identity. In this context, sexual impersonation involves the creation of a fictitious digital presence that may include the use of photographs, personal information, and details about sexual preferences or experiences, all with the intention of deceiving or manipulating others.

Chapter 13
Cyberbullying:
Gender-Based Violence in Reverted Muslim Women

Sabina Civila
Universidad de Huelva, Spain

ABSTRACT

Gender-based violence in the digital environment affects women from various communities, and Muslim reverted women are no exception. According to the National Observatory of Technology and Society, 54% of women have experienced assault on honor and privacy in the digital environment. However, for Muslim revert women, the situation is further complicated due to the intersection of gender violence and Islamophobic attitudes amplified by social media. Online hate speech directed at Muslim revert women takes various forms from offensive comments to threats, intensifying gender Islamophobia. Therefore, this chapter delves into how gender Islamophobia expands through social media and affects reverted women and the different stigmas they face due to changes in religion. In conclusion, despite Islamophobia being the current subject of study, there is limited research specifically addressing the discrimination faced by Muslim revert women. Future research directions were proposed to contribute to this area of study.

INTRODUCTION

Gender-based violence in the digital environment has become a concerning phenomenon affecting women from various communities, and Muslim revert women are no exception. According to the National Observatory of Technology and Society (Observatorio Nacional de Tecnología y Sociedad, 2022), 54% of women have experienced assaults on their honor and privacy in the digital environment. However, for Muslim revert women, the situation is further complicated due to the intersection of gender violence and Islamophobic attitudes, a growing phenomenon exacerbated by the proliferation of social media (Fuentes-Lara & Arcila-Calderón, 2023).

DOI: 10.4018/979-8-3693-2053-2.ch013

Islamophobia manifests through the spread of stereotypes and prejudices contributing to a discriminatory discourse. In this context, the veil or hijab is used as a tool to justify and (re)victimize Muslim women. Jasmine Zine (2006), a pioneer in researching this type of discrimination, coined the term "gendered Islamophobia." She defines it as a specific form of ethno-religious and racialized discrimination targeting Muslim women, arising from historically ingrained negative stereotypes, and grounded in both individual and systemic forms of oppression. Additionally, the European Union Agency for Fundamental Rights, in its report on minorities and discrimination (2019), emphasizes the uniqueness of Islamophobia, especially concerning gender, highlighting the need to address this issue specifically and contextually.

As mentioned, social media has accelerated the spread of gender Islamophobia. These platforms contribute to the issue by disseminating misinformation and stereotypes, including false representations of Muslim women's attire, gender roles, and empowerment levels. Furthermore, social media is prone to the proliferation of hate speech, manifested through offensive comments and verbal attacks directed at Muslim women, thereby intensifying gender Islamophobia (Asociación Marroquí, 2022).

In this case, online hate speech received by Muslim revert women takes various forms, from offensive comments (traitor, mafia member...) to threats and stigmatization directed specifically at women (Soleimani, 2023). These expressions not only contribute to the creation of a hostile digital environment but also have severe consequences for the safety and well-being of women, especially those who have chosen to embrace the Islamic faith.

Gender-based hate speech not only perpetuates harmful stereotypes but also promotes discrimination, even inciting physical or psychological violence (Mateeva, 2022). In the digital context, this hate speech targeting Muslim revert women becomes an integral component of digital gender-based violence. Beyond widespread attacks, these women face derogatory labels such as "sexist" or "fucking *moro*", demonstrating a clear intersection between Islamophobia and sexism (Eckert et al., 2020).

What further exacerbates the situation is that these women not only endure the hatred from Islamophobic movements but also face rejection from their own community and questioning of their faith by the Muslim community (Civila & Jaramillo-Dent, 2022). This double stigma, originating from both outside and within their social circle, creates an additional burden for these women, who seek to share their experiences on social media as a form of expression and resistance. Reverted Muslim women find themselves at the intersection of two worlds. This internal struggle further underscores the urgent need for a comprehensive approach to address the unique challenges they face.

Despite Islamophobia being a current subject of study, there is a scarcity of research specifically addressing the discrimination faced by Muslim revert women or those in the process of conversion. Therefore, it becomes crucial to comprehensively address this issue to fully understand the challenges these women face on digital platforms and work towards creating a more inclusive and respectful online environment.

In this regard, to delve into this field of study, a theoretical exploration has been conducted through the most relevant international databases (Web of Science and Scopus), using the search criteria (Boolean) "gender violence" and "Muslim". Once the initial result was obtained (=968), the search was narrowed down to only social science journals, yielding a total of 378 documents across both databases, from 2014 to 2024. With these results, a literature review was carried out to correlate the current situation of the phenomenon with potential proposals for change.

SELECTION CRITERIA OF THE CORPUS

The present chapter is exploratory and descriptive, as it is primarily based on a literature review spanning the last 10 years (2014-2024) of the phenomenon of digital gender violence against women who have reverted to Islam. The development of the work has been mainly structured into two phases: i) the search and screening of documents, and ii) the analysis of the results obtained from the databases. The main objective is to understand and analyze the phenomenon of digital gender violence against women who have reverted to Islam and to identify proposals for change and future lines of research. Therefore, a search is conducted in both Web of Science and Scopus using the search criteria "Gender Violence" and "Muslim" from 2014 to 2024 in social science journals. The terms "revert", and "digital violence" are not included because no results are obtained with those search criteria. Figure 1 shows the results obtained from the different databases:

A total of 315 documents were analyzed in Scopus and 63 in Web of Science, refining only those related to the study object. During this process, the number of emerging citations of the articles was considered, with special emphasis on the most recent ones and those related to digital gender violence. Therefore, only the most cited documents related to digital violence were considered from all the emerging literature. This screening resulted in a total of 7 documents in Scopus and 1 in Web of Science.

BACKGROUND

Digital Gender-Based Violence: A Growing Phenomenon

The digital revolution, which began in the second half of the 20th century, transformed our lives in unimaginable ways. However, along with the benefits of global connectivity and instant information, a dark

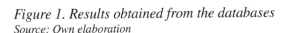

Figure 1. Results obtained from the databases
Source: Own elaboration

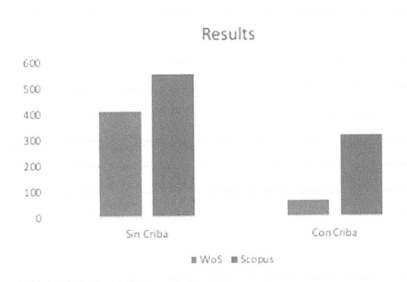

side has emerged, such as digital gender-based violence. Since the rise of technology and social media, social interaction has reached a new level of complexity. As we delve deeper into the digital world, the incidence of gender-based violence in this space also increases, especially since the COVID-19 pandemic has forced a global shift to online platforms (UN Women, 2023). Consequently, this is an issue of international concern, as reflected in Goal 5 of the 2030 agenda. This goal aims to achieve gender equality and requires urgent measures to eliminate the root causes of discrimination that continue to restrict women's rights in both the public and private spheres (United Nations, 2015).

Instead of serving as an equalizing force, technology has replicated and magnified existing gender inequalities, as indicated by gender and technology expert Dhrodia (2018). Toxic gender stereotypes and norms manifest themselves on existing social media platforms and websites, providing a refuge for misogyny and discrimination. In this session, the aim is to comprehend this phenomenon to later delve into gender-based violence in Reverted Muslim Women.

Digital gender-based violence encompasses a broad range of behaviors seeking to control, harm, or humiliate women through digital means. This can manifest in various forms, from harassment and defamation to the non-consensual sharing of intimate images, commonly known as "revenge porn" (Montero-Fernández et al., 2022). According to information provided by the World Health Organization (WHO) in 2021a, such aggression is emerging at increasingly younger ages, becoming a socially significant issue, as highlighted by Rodríguez-Castro and Alonso-Ruido (2015).

Moreover, the development of artificial intelligence (IA) has allowed for the perpetuation and dissemination of fake images of women, as observed in some cases (Dunn, 2020). This malicious act, often employed as a tactic of control and retaliation, underscores the urgency of legislating and addressing such behavior. The lack of clear and specific laws to tackle digital gender-based violence has left victims with few options for seeking justice. Furthermore, certain features of the digital environment, such as anonymity, virality, and disinhibition, encourage the amplification of these attitudes (Rodríguez-Darias & Aguilera-Ávila, 2018). However, anonymity decreases over time, and the identification of such crimes is proliferating.

Current legislation in many places has not evolved sufficiently to address the complexities of the digital era, leaving legal gaps and allowing perpetrators to evade accountability (Tovmasyan, 2022). According to a recent report by WHO (2021b), in 26 countries belonging to the Organization for Economic Cooperation and Development (OECD), domestic violence is not specifically included in their legislation. This highlights a significant gap in the protection of women's rights and the fight against this form of violence. However, it is important to note that currently, the Istanbul Convention stands out as the most comprehensive and exhaustive international treaty to address violence against women and domestic violence. Adopted in 2011 by the Council of Europe and open for signature in Istanbul, Turkey, this convention establishes a series of comprehensive measures to prevent, protect, and prosecute gender-based violence in all its forms.

On the other hand, the Budapest Convention on Cybercrime, adopted in 2001, represents the most significant international treaty in the fight against digital violence and cybercrimes. This convention provides a legal framework for international cooperation in the investigation and prosecution of cybercrimes, as well as measures to protect information systems and combat cybercrime. It is important to note that, while the Budapest Convention does not exclusively focus on digital violence against women, its general provisions on cybercrime and electronic evidence can be utilized to address this issue in the broader context of online criminality (Van Der Wilk, 2021).

One of the most challenging aspects of digital gender-based violence lies in the social perception of this issue. Often, this type of violence has been minimized or overlooked. Shame and stigma associated with being a victim of digital violence can lead to silence, allowing the problem to persist and grow (Civila et al., 2023). Nevertheless, awareness of digital gender-based violence is growing, along with the pressure to implement effective measures. The voices of activists and advocates are demanding changes, urging governments and technology companies to assume responsibilities and create a safe and equitable online environment.

Education and awareness are essential for changing the deeply rooted cultural attitudes that perpetuate gender-based violence. Therefore, educational and awareness programs should foster empathy, mutual respect, and adherence to ethical codes, to prevent violence. In addition, it is imperative for laws to evolve to specifically address this issue, providing a legal framework for prosecuting perpetrators. These initiatives aim to reduce the asymmetry between formal and informal institutions, question techniques justifying gender-based violence, and convey key messages about the social risks associated with such attitudes (Williams, 2023). These initiatives can actively promote the modification of cultural norms and elimination of stereotypes.

The previous reflection highlights the manifestation of gender-based discrimination, raising a crucial question: How does this issue amplify when a woman belongs to a minority? This complex dynamic is particularly evident in the experience of Muslim women residing in the West, who simultaneously face a double stigma as women and Muslims. Intersectionality, as an analytical framework, becomes relevant in this context, as it addresses the intricate and interconnected interactions between various forms of oppression and discrimination, such as gender and religion.

Gendered Islamophobia: Online Hate Speech

The intersection of religious and gender-based discrimination has fostered fertile ground in the digital world, where stereotypes and prejudices converge to impact the Muslim community, especially women. The gender-based violence Muslim women face in the West directly results from the gendered Islamophobia they experience because of their association with the Islamic religion (Moallem, 2021).

First and foremost, it is crucial to delve into the term Islamophobia, a concept that flourished in the West in the 1990s and has evolved to describe discrimination, prejudice, and hostility towards Islamic faith and its practitioners (Council of Europe, 2004). Gendered Islamophobia, specifically, manifests at the intersection of gender discrimination and Islamophobia, disproportionately affecting Muslim women in various aspects of their lives. According to Goikolea-Amiano (2012), gendered Islamophobia is an aversion to Islam, highlighted from a gender perspective, revealing that Muslim women are subjected to discrimination differently from Muslim men. This translates into their exclusion from the economic, social, and public life of a nation while simultaneously being victims of discrimination and persecution (Iner et al., 2022).

Gendered Islamophobia manifests subtly, but insidiously, in the digital realm, primarily through hate speech. According to Arcila-Calderón (2020), this phenomenon reveals that hatred is one of the most widely spread sentiments on social media. Hate speech targeting Muslim communities directly impacts women's social and political engagement. While such discourses do not encompass the entirety of social media, they manage to monopolize conversation; international studies indicate that at least 73% of comments on social platforms are negative towards Muslim women, thus fostering potential aggression (Martínez et al., 2022).

One of the most concerning aspects of this phenomenon is the objectification and stigmatization of Muslim women. Stereotypes rooted in ignorance and intolerance portray these women as oppressed, submissive, or even potential terrorists (Awan, 2016). These simplistic representations are not only inaccurate but also contribute to creating an environment where hatred and violence towards Muslim women are tolerated.

Algorithms designed to boost engagement often favor polarizing content, facilitating the spread of stereotypes and prejudice. Social media companies face the challenge of balancing freedom of expression with the responsibility to prevent the spread of hate on their platforms (Civila et al., 2023). However, it was observed that Islamophobic content circulating on social media not only spreads through the platforms' algorithms but also through the deliberate exploitation of the affordances these platforms offer to amplify the message. Many political parties have been observed disseminating inaccurate and polarized messages about the Muslim population. Furthermore, it is a fact that it is gaining more followers in the West (Daudi, 2022). This phenomenon significantly intertwines with the anti-Muslim ideology that has been promoted over centuries, as emphasized by Horsti (2017).

Many studies (Wachs et al., 2022; Brown, 2015; Nielsen, 2002) have revealed that facing online hate speech can exacerbate symptoms of depression and anxiety among affected individuals. Moreover, these discourses can have a detrimental impact on the personal development of the victim. According to research conducted by Ștefăniță and Buf (2021), two types of consequences are identified: short-term and long-term. Short-term consequences refer to immediate reactions such as fear, anger, or loneliness, while long-term consequences may include radicalization and support for extremist ideologies. In the case of racialized individuals or those perceived as such, encountering this type of discourse can also evoke feelings of inferiority and social exclusion. These communities are particularly affected by online discrimination, which can have serious repercussions on their emotional well-being and social integration.

Furthermore, in this case, the intimidation and threats experienced both online and offline can discourage women from expressing their opinions, participating in public debates, or exercising civil rights. This not only impacts their freedom of expression, but also perpetuates the exclusion of crucial voices in public discourse. Nevertheless, various studies have argued that Muslim women harness social media to generate counter-narratives and combat gendered Islamophobia. However, other scholars such as Civila and Jaramillo-Dent (2022) and Gómez et al. (2021) contend that the way the counter-narrative is created does not contribute to the creation of new discourses and perpetuates stereotypes.

Consequently, understanding the roots of this issues on social media is crucial to effectively address this issue. Ignorance and lack of knowledge of Islam and Muslim culture increase stereotypes. Education and the promotion of intercultural understanding are powerful tools for counteracting these misconceptions and fostering peaceful coexistence. Additionally, advocating for inclusive policies and combating systematic discrimination are fundamental steps towards eradicating gendered Islamophobia.

Moreover, in the case of gendered Islamophobia, a phenomenon of hostility towards women who, despite not coming from Muslim families, choose to embrace Islam and undergo conversion processes emerges on social media. The observation of this hostility towards non-Muslim women reverted to Islam raises fundamental questions about the notions of religious identity and sociocultural expectations. This phenomenon not only illustrates the intersection of gender and religion, but also highlights tensions in contemporary digital society regarding individual freedom of religious choice and traditional cultural expectations.

Muslims Reverted Stigma: External and Internal Struggles

Delving into our research focus, we explored the stigma faced by women who reverted to Islam. First, it is important to specify that we refer to as "reverts" those individuals who have chosen to renounce their faith and embrace a different one from their original or familial background (in this case, Islam). The reality faced by these individuals is intricately linked with the dynamics of colonialism and post-colonialism (Civila & Jaramillo-Dent, 2022). Consequently, this process not only involves spiritual exploration, but also carries an additional burden of social stigmatization.

The decision to embrace Islam is an intimate and personal journey influenced by a variety of factors ranging from spiritual reasons to individual life circumstances. However, for women who decide to revert to Islam, this process is often overshadowed by a triple stigma: the stigma associated with abandoning their original faith, stigma related to gender identity, and stigma linked to cultural expectations.

In this context, the decision to forsake traditional beliefs is perceived as a direct threat to patriarchal structures and Western tradition. According to Gilroy (2004), this act of change is seen as a betrayal of society, a rupture with established cultural norms, and is viewed as an act of rebellion against one's own culture. This challenge not only contradicts modern societies seeking to preserve a pure culture but also generates internal tensions for those making this decision. In addition, according to Tabassum (2003), women who choose to revert to Islam face rejection from friends and family members. Frequently, families present a choice between religion and relationships, associating the reversion to Islam with negative aspects, such as terrorism, devaluation of women, and polygamy.

In another aspect, reverted women face stigma linked to traditional gender expectations and roles. They often face accusations of conforming to established gender norms, including submissions, according to certain stereotypes. This is a consequence of Western societies' perception that Muslim women are often seen as submissive and subjected to sexist roles (Lems, 2024).

The second stigma associated with reversion also manifests in negative reactions from both the culture of origin and the new community into which they integrate. According to Al Areqi (2016), those undergoing reversion encounter significant acceptance challenges in both environments, creating a dichotomy of belonging. This difficulty extends beyond the social sphere, projecting onto digital platforms, where discrimination and rejection manifest through discriminatory content. Together, these stigmas and challenges present a complex scenario for women making decisions related to faith and identity, highlighting the tensions between tradition and change in an increasingly diverse world.

Additionally, as noted by Andujar (2024), some women opting for reversion to Islam may advocate for a westernized interpretation of religion. This phenomenon introduces an additional nuance, suggesting the possibility of masking racial identity and hiding under the umbrella of intersectional feminism. This perspective, advocating for the intersection of various forms of oppression, could be employed as a strategy to justify their religious choices, aligning with more widely accepted or progressive Western values. This, in turn, may foster non-acceptance within the Muslim community, creating a division between Muslims at two levels: level 1, those born into faith, and level 2, reverted Muslims.

This division not only reflects resistance towards reverted Muslims but also unveils intricate internal tensions that can emerge within the community. Non-acceptance of reverts may contribute to the formation of social and cultural barriers, hindering the development of a shared sense of belonging and cohesion within the Muslim community.

These stigmas are mirrored on social media, providing a perfect space for their amplification. Despite various studies (Obermaier et al., 2023; Naeem, 2022; Karjo et al., 2020) indicating that Muslim women face online hate speech, few delve into hate speech directed at reverted women. Civila and Jaramillo-Dent (2022) reveal that those in the reversion process become targets of attacks on social media. Outsiders perceive their choice as a threat to Western beliefs and values. On the other hand, individuals born into Islam question their identity and motivation for reversion. This phenomenon not only exposes the presence of individual ignorance and intolerance but also points to broader structures shaped by colonial and postcolonial narratives ingrained in contemporary society.

However, it is crucial to emphasize, as indicated by researchers such as Zulli and Zulli (2020), that there has also been active resistance to these harmful discourses. Resistance to hate speech on social media implies the existence of movements and voices that seek to counteract intolerance and promote intercultural dialogue.

MAIN FOCUS OF THE CHAPTER: Issues, controversies, problems

In addressing the issue of Cyberbullying: Gender-based Violence in Reverted Muslim Women, a series of issues, controversies, and challenges emerged, reflecting the complexity of this phenomenon. The controversy arises at the intersection of gender identity and religion, where women who have reverted to Islam face dual pressure: conforming to established gender norms and reconciling their identity within the context of a new faith. The tension between these forces can result in a conflicting experience in which women are caught between cultural and religious expectations, raising fundamental questions about individual autonomy and freedom of choice. In this chapter, I focus on exposing these dynamics from a critical standpoint, considering both historical narratives and contemporary actions that impact the experiences of these women.

On one hand, a fundamental problem lies in the persistence of patriarchal and traditional structures shaped by historical dynamics and the influence of colonialism. Female renunciation of their origins is perceived as a direct threat to these structures, which have been reinforced and perpetuated over time (Gylroy, 2004).

From this traditional perspective, women are assigned the responsibility of procreating and disseminating culture. Any deviation from established societal guidelines is seen as a threat to established social values (Nemoto, 2009). These views, steeped in persistent colonialism, rejected diversity as a valid lifestyle. Despite postcolonial rhetoric emphasizing the importance of diversity, in practice, these dynamics are tied to a set of social norms that hide new forms of colonialism. Therefore, the hate speech that this community receives falls under the umbrella of contemporary colonialism (Gray, 2013; Gylroy, 2004).

This contemporary discrepancy between the promotion of inclusion and diversity and postcolonial reality reinforces the stigmas and challenges faced by women who have embraced Islam. Consequently, this issue not only affects the social acceptance of Muslim women (reverts and non-reverts), but also restricts their autonomy and freedom of choice in a cultural context that, in many cases, still bears the scars of colonial history.

On the other hand, concerning contemporary actions that impact the experiences of these women, we encounter a virtual environment. On social media, Muslim women face, as mentioned earlier, a space in which postcolonial narratives spread and manifest in various ways. Despite the opportunity for social media to create new narratives, hatred proliferates. Cyberbullying reflects a lack of progress in combating colonial narratives that continue to influence public perception of these women.

However, the efforts and actions taken to address stigmatization still face numerous challenges. The lack of understanding of the complexity of identities after reversion and ingrained resistance to questioning cultural and religious norms limit the effectiveness of current efforts. Education and awareness are crucial; however, implementing educational programs that critically address these issues remains a challenge. A critical understanding of historical and contemporary dynamics, along with active engagement in changing cultural and religious norms that perpetuate stigma, is needed. Compared to current actions, there is a highlighted need for a broader approach and implementation of more effective measures to bring about significant changes in how these women are perceived and accepted in society.

After conducting the literature review, we have further observed that combating violence against women through legal frameworks poses a significant challenge. The two most prominent international treaties in this regard are outdated and do not adequately address contemporary technological issues such as artificial intelligence or social media platforms, which have proliferated since their inception. These treaties are thus considered obsolete, with the Budapest Convention (2001) particularly lagging behind. This presents a problem as women and girls remain inadequately protected against digital abuses in the face of rapidly evolving digital landscapes. Therefore, there is a critical need for updates and amendments to ensure that legal frameworks effectively address and combat digital gender-based violence.

SOLUTIONS AND RECOMMENDATIONS

Once the phenomenon is understood, it is especially relevant to explore solutions and offer recommendations to address the stigmas faced by women who have reverted to Islam and reduce hate speech on social media. In this way, the decolonization of the Internet and stereotypes rooted in this group will be promoted.

On the one hand, the implementation of awareness campaigns on social media that challenge stereotypes associated with the conversion to Islam is proposed. These campaigns should take advantage of social media and other digital platforms in order to reach a wide audience. The creation of educational content, personal testimonies, and open debates can contribute to understanding the complexities of this phenomenon, thereby fostering empathy and tolerance. Additionally, this will amplify the voices of women in this group, and their messages will reach further.

However, it is essential to work closely with social media platforms to implement more rigorous policies against the harassment of Muslim women, both converting and non-converting. This involves the creation of effective mechanisms to identify and eliminate hate speech. Moreover, it is crucial to promote the creation of support networks. Virtual communities can provide a safe space for sharing experiences, obtaining guidance, and showing mutual solidarity. Strategies such as those carried out by the Moroccan Association, in which a forum is used to share hate-inciting publications so that all participants can report them, can be promoted. It is also important to not share offensive content and not participate in discussions that promote hate speech.

The importance of reporting hate content on social media lies in the need to create safe digital spaces for all communities. Active reporting not only constitutes an act of defending individual rights but also a collective commitment to counteract hate speech. By reporting hate content, users contribute to the identification and removal of harmful messages, protecting victims and promoting digital safety. Furthermore, reporting raises public awareness about the severity of issues related to online hate, exerting pressure on platforms to strengthen their policies and implement more effective measures.

Additionally, developing media literacy strategies that promote counter-narratives and actively challenge the digital stigmas associated with Islam and its practitioners is crucial. Providing training on digital security and recognizing hate speech enables individuals to report it to platforms, allowing women to engage in online spaces critically and safely. Promoting positive narratives helps counteract hate speech by offering a constructive alternative to negative messages, as evidenced by previous research (Fuentes-Lara & Arcila-Calderón, 2023). This can involve creating content celebrating diversity and inclusion as well as highlighting the success stories of Muslim women.

Building upon the importance of media literacy in combating Islamophobia, it is essential to recognize the pivotal role it plays in reshaping perceptions and fostering a more inclusive digital environment. By providing people with the skills to understand the media, we empower them to differentiate between information and real stories, which helps break down stereotypes associated with Islam and its followers. This proactive approach not only improves security, but also acts as a powerful tool to stop the spread of discriminatory content. As individuals become better at recognizing and questioning portrayals, the Internet has become an inclusive space for women, allowing them to participate thoughtfully and confidently. Along with promoting perspectives and positive narratives, media literacy plays a role in driving change by creating a society that values diversity, challenges stereotypes, and actively opposes Islamophobic sentiments.

Another strategy involves collaborating with organizations dedicated to combating hate speech. These organizations can offer resources and tools to assist Muslim women and other communities in addressing these discourses. Additionally, they can provide emotional support and counseling to individuals who have experienced discrimination or online attacks. It is important to note that hate speech not only directly affects the targeted minority group but also has a negative impact on society.

FUTURE RESEARCH DIRECTIONS

Looking towards the future of research on violence against women, it is crucial to continue developing investigations in this area, as reports from various institutions indicate a persistent increase in violence against women. Furthermore, focusing on violence against Muslim revert women specifically brings the concept of digital identity to the forefront as a significant area of exploration.

In this context, digital identity refers to how Muslim women interact, are perceived, and experience digital life, considering the complex intersections with factors such as gender, religion, patriarchal structures, and postcolonial narratives. Digital identity has become a crucial framework connecting the contemporary experiences and challenges of Muslim women with the persistent influence of patriarchal structures and post-colonial narratives in the digital environment. This concept serves as a bridge between complex historical dynamics and contemporary actions, emphasizing its importance in comprehensively understanding and addressing current experiences in digital society.

Therefore, exploring how social media interactions influence the formation of religious and gender identities is essential to understanding the mechanisms that perpetuate or challenge stigma. Additionally, research must address intersectionality and examine how factors such as race, ethnicity, and socioeconomic status intertwine with religious and gender identities in the digital realm.

Another research avenue involves considering the psychological impact of narratives on these women on social media. Investigating the long-term consequences of cyberbullying and social exclusion is essential to designing effective interventions. Furthermore, exploring the opportunities offered by emerg-

Cyberbullying

ing technologies, such as artificial intelligence, in mitigating cyberbullying and hate speech represents a promising path.

The application of AI in mitigating hate speech remains unexplored. Despite advancements in machine-learning algorithms, there is a need to refine specific methods to address harmful online discourses. AI can play a fundamental role in analyzing linguistic patterns, cultural contexts, and emotions associated with messages, enabling a more precise and efficient detection of offensive content. Additionally, incorporating advanced natural language processing techniques could enhance contextual understanding, aiding in distinguishing between legitimate expressions and speech that incite hatred. Collaboration between ethics experts, programmers, and digital content specialists is crucial to developing AI solutions that are not only effective, but also ethical and respectful.

In the legal sphere, future research should consider legal and policy implications. Analyzing the effectiveness of existing legislation and proposing policy recommendations will contribute to creating a regulatory framework that protects the rights and dignity of Muslim women.

CONCLUSION

This chapter has delved into the issue of digital harassment and gender-based violence directed towards Western women who, for personal reasons, have chosen to revert to Islam. Throughout the text, we have emphasized the complex intersection of gender, religion, and discrimination, particularly in the context of social media. Consequently, as we examined the various dimensions of this phenomenon, several conclusions have been identified, and recommendations have been proposed to address these issues.

First, we examined the stigma associated with patriarchal structures. According to various consulted studies, historical and colonial dynamics significantly contribute to the stigma and hatred towards reverted women. Thus, it is evident that stereotypes ingrained in women are exacerbated in the case of this minority group and extend within the realm of social media, resulting in what is known as digital gender-based violence, closely linked to gender-based violence in general.

Additionally, it is important to note that digital gender-based violence not only affects women who have reverted to Islam but is also a problem that affects women of all religions and cultures. However, it is true that women who have reverted to Islam may be particularly vulnerable to digital gender-based violence due to the complex intersection of religion, gender, and their new identity. This underscores the need to continue working on preventing digital gender-based violence, as well as protecting and supporting victims. To achieve this, it is crucial to raise awareness in society about the severity of this phenomenon and promote education in values of equality and respect towards women. This aligns with the main objectives of the 2030 agenda and major institutions, such as UNHCR, UNESCO, and UNICEF.

According to the 2030 agenda, achieving gender equality by 2030 requires urgent measures to eliminate the root causes of discrimination that continue to restrict women's rights in both the public and private spheres. Among other things, it is necessary to amend discriminatory laws and actively adopt those that promote equality.

Second, the intersection between gender identity and religion creates significant tension for women who have reverted to Islam. This sets them apart from the hate speech directed at women in general and women born into Muslim families. These women find themselves caught between cultural and religious expectations, leading to rejection from both the society to which they belong and the community they join as new members.

This is framed within the concept of otherness, which refers to the construction of identity in relation to the perception and definition of the "other". In polarized societies, otherness can accentuate differences and contribute to the formation of opposing or contrasting identities. As observed throughout this chapter, in the context of women who have converted to Islam, otherness can manifest itself, influencing social perception, integration, and individual autonomy.

On the other hand, social media platforms have been found to play a crucial role in the spread of cyberbullying and gender-based violence. This is because, owing to the characteristics of these platforms, a culture of hate and gender discrimination flourishes. Hate comments, misogyny, and intolerance contribute to the creation of a hostile environment that discourages active and free participation by women. Throughout this chapter, three factors perpetuating hate speech towards this group are identified: (1) lack of effective policies to address hate speech, (2) lack of media education to develop the ability to create new narratives, and (3) characteristics of contemporary societies and postcolonialism for women who have reverted to Islam.

As a result, it is recommended to implement comprehensive educational programs that critically address these issues, promote acceptance of diversity, and challenge restrictive norms. Additionally, close collaboration with social media platforms is advised to enforce stricter policies against harassment, especially for Muslim women, and provide effective tools for identifying and eliminating hate speech. Regarding media education, there is a proposal to raise awareness of the importance of generating counter-narratives that foster understanding and tolerance.

The counternarrative emerges as an essential tool in the fight against hate speech, playing a crucial role in dismantling certain narratives. By challenging the stereotypes on which hate speech is based, the counternarrative seeks to counteract discrimination and promote understanding, highlighting alternative stories based on real experiences and human rights. Its value lies not only in challenging the foundations of hate speech, but also in constructing narratives that encourage understanding and alleviating tensions in societies. By highlighting shared humanity, the counter-narrative becomes a powerful tool for forging connections and promoting more compassionate dialogue among communities.

Finally, it is concluded that future research should focus on digital identity and explore how intersectional factors such as race, ethnicity, and socioeconomic status intersect with religious and gender identities in the digital realm. This could be achieved through deeper investigations into digital identity and its influence on discrimination, considering intersectional factors to better understand individual experiences.

ACKNOWLEDGMENT

This study was supported by the R+D+I Project (2019–2021), entitled Youtubers and Instagrammers: Media Competence in Emerging Prosumers, under code RTI2018–093303-B-I00, financed by the Spanish Ministry of Science, Innovation, and Universities, the European Regional Development Fund (ERDF), and the R+D+I project (2020–2022) entitled Instagramers and Youtubers for the Transmedia Empowerment of the Andalusian Citizenry. Media literacy of the Instatubers, with code P18-RT-756, was financed by the Government of Andalusia in the 2018 call for tenders (Andalusian Plan for Research, Development and Innovation, 2020) and the European Regional Development Fund (ERDF).

REFERENCES

Al Areqi, R. (2016). Hybridity/hybridization from postcolonial and Islamic perspectives. *Research Journal of English Language and Literature, 5*(1), 53–61. https://bit.ly/3BQdY10

Andujar, N. (January, 2024). *Los musulmanes conversos blancos como puente hacia el asimilacionismo* [White convert Muslims as a bridge to assimilation]. https://bit.ly/42LriPN

Arcila-Calderón, C., Blanco-Herrero, D., & Valdez-Apolo, M. B. (2020). Rechazo y discurso de odio en Twitter: Análisis de contenido de los tuits sobre migrantes y refugiados en español [Rejection and hate speech on Twitter: Content analysis of tweets about migrants and refugees in Spanish]. *Revista Española de Investigaciones Sociológicas, 172*(172), 21–40. doi:10.5477/cis/reis.172.21

Asociación Marroquí. (2022). *Mujeres tras el velo* [Women behind the veil]. Asociación Marroquí. https://bit.ly/48v4B3o

Awan, I. (2016). Islamophobia on social media: A qualitative analysis of Facebook's walls of hate. *International Journal of Cyber Criminology, 10*(1), 1–20. doi:10.5281/zenodo.58517

Brown, A. (2015). *Hate speech law: A philosophical examination.* Routledge. doi:10.4324/9781315714899

Budapest Convention. (2001). *Convention on CyberCrime.* Budapest Convention. https://bit.ly/3IaGaO2

Civila, S., De-Casas-Moreno, P., García-Rojas, A. D., & Hernando-Gómez, A. (2023). TikTok and the caricaturing of violence in adolescent romantic relationships. *Anàlisi: Quaderns de Comunicació i Cultura, 69,* 75–91. doi:10.5565/rev/analisi.3632

Civila, S., & Jaramillo-Dent, D. (2022). #Mixedcouples on TikTok: Performative hybridization and identity in the face of discrimination. *Social Media + Society, 8*(3). doi:10.1177/20563051221122464

Council of Europe. (2004). Introduction. Questions about the question. Chap. 1. In *Islamophobia and its consequences on young people.* European Youth Center. http://bit.ly/397kb6x

Daudi, I. (2022). *Islamophobia and the West: The making of a violent civilization.* Taylor and Francis., doi:10.4324/9781003323105

Dhrodia, A. (2018). Unsocial media: A toxic place for women. *IPPR Progressive Review, 24*(4), 380–387. doi:10.1111/newe.12078

Dunn, S. (2020). *Technology-facilitated gender-based violence: An overview.* Centre for International Governance Innovation. http://bit.ly/3HbrZb0

Eckert, S., O'Shay Wallace, S., Metzger-Riftkin, J., & Kolhoff, S. (2020). The best damn representation of Islam: Muslims, gender, social media and Islamophobia. *CyberOrient, 12*(1), 4–30. doi:10.1002/j.cyo2.20181201.0001

European Union Agency for Fundamental Rights. (2019). *Report on minorities and discrimination.* EU. https://bit.ly/3Tcd4UO

Fuentes-Lara, C., & Arcila-Calderón, C. (2023). El discurso de odio islamófobo en las redes sociales. Un análisis de las actitudes ante la islamofobia en Twitter [Islamophobic hate speech on social networks. An analysis of attitudes to Islamophobia on Twitter]. *Revista Mediterránea de Comunicación, 14*(1), 225–240. doi:10.14198/MEDCOM.23044

Gilroy, P. (2004). *Postcolonial melancholia*. Columbia University Press.

Goikolea-Amiano, I. (2012). *Feminismo y piedad: un análisis de género en torno a las conversas al Islam* [Feminism and Piety: A gender analysis around women converts to Islam]. Universidad del País Vasco.

Gómez-García, S., Paz-Rebollo, M., & Cabeza-San-Deogracias, J. (2021). Newsgames frente a los discursos del odio en la crisis de los refugiados [News games against hate speech in the refugee crisis]. *Comunicar, 29*(63), 123–133. doi:10.3916/C67-2021-10

Gray, H. (2013). Subject(ed) recognition. American Quarterly, 65(4), 771–798. https://doi.org/ doi:10.1353/aq.2013.0058

Horsti, K. (2017). Digital Islamophobia: The Swedish woman as a figure of pure and dangerous whiteness. *New Media & Society, 19*(9), 1440–1457. doi:10.1177/1461444816642169

Iner, D., Mason, G., & Asquith, N. L. (2022). Expected but not accepted: Victimisation, gender, and Islamophobia in Australia. *International Review of Victimology, 28*(3), 286–304. doi:10.1177/02697580221084115

Karjo, C. H., & Ng, A. (2020). Hate speech propaganda from and against Muslims in Facebook posts. *International Journal of Cyber Criminology, 14*(2), 400–416. doi:10.5281/zenodo.4766989

Lems, J. (2024). *Tomar la palabra. Islamofobia y participación política después del 15-M* [Taking the Floor: Islamophobia and Political Participation After the 15-M Movement]. Vernon Press.

Martínez, C., Van Prooijen, J. W., & Van Lange, P. (2022). A threat-based hate model: How symbolic and realistic threats underlie hate and aggression. *Journal of Experimental Social Psychology, 103*, 1044393. doi:10.1016/j.jesp.2022.104393

Mateeva, E. (2022). Hate speech in election campaigns. *Media and Language, 1*(11), 67–83. doi:10.58894/WTWA9930

Moallem, M. (2021). Race, Gender, and Religion: Islamophobia and Beyond. *Meridians (Middletown, Conn.), 20*(2), 271–290. https://www.muse.jhu.edu/article/856874. doi:10.1215/15366936-9547874

Montero-Fernández, D., García-Rojas, A. D., Hernando-Gómez, A., & Del-Río, F. J. (2022). Digital violence questionnaire. *Revista Electrónica de Investigación y Evaluación Educativa, 28*(2), 1–21.

Naeem, T. (2022). Muslims as terrorists: Hate speech against Muslims. *International Journal of Islamic Thought, 22*(1), 114–124. doi:10.24035/ijit.22.2022.245

Nemoto, K. (2009). *Racing romance*. Rutger University Press.

Nielsen, L. B. (2002). Subtle, pervasive, harmful: Racist and sexist remarks in public as hate speech. *The Journal of Social Issues, 58*(2), 265–280. doi:10.1111/1540-4560.00260

Obermaier, M., Schmuck, D., & Saleem, M. (2023). I'll be there for you? Effects of Islamophobic online hate speech and counter speech on Muslim in-group bystanders' intention to intervene. *New Media & Society*, *25*(9), 2339–2358. doi:10.1177/14614448211017527

Observatorio Nacional de Tecnología y Sociedad. (2022). *Violencia digital de género: Una realidad invisible [Digital gender-based violence: An invisible reality]*. Observatorio Nacional de Tecnología y Sociedad. https://bit.ly/46SMO5H

Rodríguez-Castro, Y., & Alonso-Ruido, P. (2015). Analysis of the speeches of the young people on violence in intimate relationships. *Revista de Estudios e Investigación en Psicología y Educación*, *2*, 015–018. doi:10.17979/reipe.2015.0.02.235

Rodríguez-Darias, A. J., & Aguilera-Ávila, L. (2018). Gender-based harassment in cyberspace. The case of Pikara magazine. *Women's Studies International Forum*, *66*, 63–69. doi:10.1016/j.wsif.2017.10.004

Soleimani, V. (2023). Sexist hate speech against women. In O. Pérez de la Fuente, A. Tsesis, & J. Skrzypczak (Eds.), *Minorities, free speech and the internet* (pp. 137–152). Routledge. doi:10.4324/9781003274476-11

Ștefăniță, O., & Buf, D. M. (2021). Hate speech in social media and its effects on the LGBT community: A review of the current research. *Romanian Journal of Communication and Public Relations*, *23*(1), 47–55. doi:10.21018/rjcpr.2021.1.322

Tabassum, F. R. (2003). Women who choose Islam. *International Journal of Mental Health*, *32*(3), 31–49. doi:10.1080/00207411.2003.11449590

Tovmasyan, G. (2022). The Nuanced Forms of Sexual Violence in the Online Environment. In S. Bedi (Ed.), *Cyber crime, regulations and security contemporary issues and challenges* (pp. 254–263). The Law Brigade Publisher., doi:10.55662/book.2022CCRS.015

United Nation Women. (2023). *How Technology-Facilitated Gender-Based Violence Impacts Women and Girls*. UN Women. https://bit.ly/42SFiqO

United Nations. (2015). *The sustainable development goals*. UN. https://sdgs.un.org/es/goals#history

Van der Wilk, A. (2021). *Protecting women and girls from violence in the digital age: the relevance of the Istanbul convention and the Budapest convention on cybercrime in addressing online and technology-facilitated violence against women*. Council of Europe.

Wachs, S., Gámez-Guadix, M., & Wright, M. (2022). Online hate speech victimization and depressive symptoms among adolescents: The protective role of resilience. *Cyberpsychology, Behavior, and Social Networking*, *25*(7), 416–423. doi:10.1089/cyber.2022.0009 PMID:35639126

Williams, C. (2023). Education and awareness raising to encourage formalisation. In C. Williams (Ed.), *A modern guide to the informal economy* (pp. 240–260). Elgar Publishing., doi:10.4337/9781788975612.00019

World Health Organization. (2021a). *Violence against women prevalence estimates*. World Health Organization. https://bit.ly/3IbPGQX

World Health Organization. (2021b). *Violence against women*. World Health Organization. https://bit.ly/40xAdBu

Zine, J. (2016). *Between orientalism and fundamentalism: Muslim women and feminist engagement.* In K. Hunt K. & Rygiel (Eds.), *Gendering the war on terror* (pp. 34-40). Routledge. https://bit.ly/47Eeb4C

Zulli, D., & Zulli, D. J. (2020). Extending the Internet meme: Conceptualizing technological mimesis and imitation publics on the TikTok platform. *New Media & Society*, *24*(8), 1872–1890. doi:10.1177/1461444820983603

ADDITIONAL READING

Civila, S., Romero-Rodríguez, L. M., & Civila, A. (2020). The demonization of Islam through social media: A case study of #Stopislam in Instagram. *Publications / MDPI*, *8*(4), 52. doi:10.3390/publications8040052

Gilroy, P. (2004). *Postcolonial melancholia.* Columbia University Press.

Gray, H. (2013). Subject(ed) recognition. American Quarterly, 65(4), 771–798. https://doi.org/doi:10.1353/aq.2013.0058

Hall, S. (1995). When was "The Post-Colonial"? Thinking at the limit. In I. Chambers & L. Curti (Eds.), *The post colonial questions* (pp. 237–256). Routledge., doi:10.4324/9780203138328

Hall, S. (1996). The west and the rest: Discourse and power. In S. Hall, D. Held, D. Hubert, & K. Thompson (Eds.), *Modernity: An introduction to modern societies* (pp. 185–227). Blackwell.

Meer, N. (2014). Islamophobia and postcolonialism: Continuity, orientalism and Muslim consciousness. *Patterns of Prejudice*, *48*(5), 500–515. doi:10.1080/0031322X.2014.966960

Snyder-Hall, R. C. (2010). Third-wave feminism and the defense of "Choice.". *Perspectives on Politics*, *8*(1), 255–261. https://www.jstor.org/stable/25698533. doi:10.1017/S1537592709992842

Wellman, B. (2001). Physical place and cyberplace: The rise of personalized networking. *International Journal of Urban and Regional Research*, *25*(2), 227–252. doi:10.1111/1468-2427.00309

Young, R. (2016). *Colonialism and the politics of postcolonial critique.* John Wiley & Sons. . ch1 doi:10.1002/9781119316817

KEY TERMS AND DEFINITIONS

Gender Islamophobia: It is a specific form of discrimination affecting Muslims based on their gender. It can manifest in attitudes or actions that discriminate or marginalize individuals or Muslim groups due to their gender identity, as well as gender stereotypes rooted in anti-Muslim prejudice.

Gender-Based Violence: Gender-based violence refers to any form of violence directed towards a person or group based on their gender. It can include physical, sexual, psychological, or economic aggression and is often rooted in power imbalances and unequal gender relations.

Hate Speech: It refers to any form of communication that spreads, promotes, or justifies hatred towards an individual or group based on characteristics such as race, religion, ethnic origin, gender, sexual orientation, disability, or other similar attributes. It can manifest in words, writings, gestures, or any other means of expression.

Islamophobia: It is the aversion, fear, prejudice, or discrimination against Islam and Muslim people, typically based on negative stereotypes, ignorance, or misunderstandings about the religion and its followers.

Post-Colonialism: It is a theoretical approach that analyzes the cultural, social, political, and economic consequences of colonialism once colonies have achieved political independence. It examines how colonial structures and dynamics continue to influence global relationships, national identities, and inequality after the colonial era.

Reverted: This term is often used to describe a person who has accepted and converted to Islam from another religion or belief.

Racism: Racism is discrimination, prejudice, or antagonism directed against people of certain races or ethnic groups, based on the belief that certain races are inherently superior or inferior to others. Racism can manifest in individual, institutional, or systemic actions that perpetuate racial inequality.

Chapter 14
Online Protection Measures to Prevent Sexting Among Minors

José-María Romero-Rodríguez
https://orcid.org/0000-0002-9284-8919
Universidad de Granada, Spain

Blanca Berral-Ortiz
Universidad de Granada, Spain

José-Antonio Martínez-Domingo
Universidad de Granada, Spain

Juan-José Victoria-Maldonado
Universidad de Granada, Spain

ABSTRACT

This chapter explores sexting among minors in the digital era, focusing on Spain. It delves into sociocultural, technological, and psychological factors contributing to sexting, highlighting evolving norms, device access, and peer pressures. The impact of a lack of awareness and education on sexting is emphasized. The discussion stresses collaborative online protection, including parental controls, government policies, and educational programs. The chapter underscores the critical role of online protection, proposing holistic prevention approaches. It emphasizes early-age awareness and education for safe online behaviors, recommending programs in schools and families. European frameworks like the DigComp enhance digital competencies, and Spain's legal stance protects minors. Commitment at national and European levels is evident, with training and awareness crucial. Collaboration between teachers and families is emphasized for prevention, creating a supportive environment for responsible technology use.

INTRODUCTION

In the digital contemporary era, the practice of sexting among minors has emerged as a phenomenon of intrinsic complexity, posing substantial challenges to the safety and well-being of the youth population.

DOI: 10.4018/979-8-3693-2053-2.ch014

In recent years, a significant increase in the popularity of social networking sites has been witnessed, attracting an extraordinary number of users, especially among the teenage demographic. Current data supports this trend. According to recent research from the EU Kids Online study, in Europe, approximately 85% of young people aged 13 to 16 are actively engaged on some social networking site (Smahel et al., 2020). Despite most of these sites setting a minimum age of 13 for creating a profile, it is noteworthy that a considerable percentage of younger children are also present on these platforms.

Although social media has attracted people of various ages in Spain, it is noteworthy that the younger generations were the most active in this realm. This fact is supported by statistics indicating that nearly 93% of the Spanish population between 16 and 24 years old were present on some social network. Similarly, the second age group with a high number of users was the 25 to 34 age range, with over 80%. Spaniards' interest in platforms like Instagram and Twitter diminishes as age increases. In this regard, around 45.1% of individuals aged 55 to 64 participated in social networks, while only around 30% of those aged 65 to 74 ventured to do so (Mena, 2022). Furthermore, research in social sciences suggests that smartphones with social media capabilities continue to be popular among young people, playing a central role in their relationships and shaping various aspects of their daily lives (Harari et al., 2020).

Ninety-five percent of Generation Z owns a smartphone, according to the Center for Generational Kinetics (GenHQ, 2018). In Spain, almost 90% of teenagers aged 14 to 16 have a smartphone, according to research on ICT and its impact on adolescent socialization. More than 50% of these young people use it for five hours or more daily. One in four even uses it for ten hours (Vannucci et al., 2019). Generation Z, also known as Gen Z, refers to individuals born roughly between the mid-1990s and the early 2010s. They are characterized by their digital nativity, having grown up in a world where technology, particularly smartphones and social media, is ubiquitous. Gen Z is known for being tech-savvy, adaptable to digital tools, and highly connected online. They are considered the first truly digital-native generation, shaping and being shaped by the digital landscape in profound ways.

The rapid evolution of information technologies has immersed minors in a digital environment where privacy and vulnerability coexist intrinsically (Vickery, 2017). The popularity of social media lies in the opportunity to receive, create, and share public messages at a low cost (Farsi, 2021). In this context, the implementation of online protection measures becomes imperative to counteract the inherent risks associated with the exchange of sexually explicit content. It is considered relevant to critically examine the effectiveness of such measures, unraveling their scope, limitations, and, fundamentally, their ability to address the psychosocial complexities linked to youth sexting (Raza et al., 2020).

This chapter aims to address youth sexting with the following objectives: comprehending and tackling the phenomenon of sexting among minors; identifying key risk factors leading to sexting; and determining national and international proposals to mitigate the negative effects of sexting.

CONTEXTUALISATION OF SEXTING AMONG MINORS

The phenomenon of sexting among minors, defined as the exchange of sexually explicit content through electronic devices, has emerged as a matter of growing concern in contemporary society. To contextualize this behavior, it is deemed necessary to explore the various factors contributing to its prevalence, integrating sociocultural, technological, and psychological aspects (Ojeda et al., 2020). The sociocultural environment plays a significant role in the prevalence of sexting among minors. The evolution of social norms regarding intimacy, sexuality, and communication has influenced the perception and acceptance of this practice (Molla-Esparza et al., 2020). Factors such as the liberalization of attitudes towards sexual expression and media exposure to sexual content contribute to its normalization among young people.

The widespread access to electronic devices, especially smartphones and social networks, has facilitated the practice of sexting among minors. Instant connectivity and the omnipresent availability of digital communication tools create a fertile ground for the proliferation of this behavior. The familiarity and proficiency of young people with digital technology also influence their involvement in sexting (Stoilova et al., 2021).

The context of interpersonal relationships, especially among peers, exerts significant pressure on minors' participation in sexting. The need to conform to social norms, the desire for acceptance, and peer influence can motivate young people to engage in this behavior, often driven by the search for validation and belonging (Dodaj et al., 2020). Lack of awareness of the risks associated with sexting and the absence of comprehensive education regarding digital responsibility and privacy contribute to its prevalence. Minors may sometimes not be fully aware of the legal, social, and emotional implications related to the online disclosure of intimate content (Ojeda and Del Rey, 2022).

In the contemporary scenario, where digital interaction among minors is an undeniable reality, the implementation of online protection measures is presented as an unavoidable need in response to the phenomenon of sexting (Setty, 2020). The practice of sexting, exposing minors to significant risks such as exploitation, cyberbullying, and non-consensual dissemination of intimate content, underscores the urgency of efficient online protection (Agnew, 2021). Given the inherent vulnerability of this demographic, the adoption of proactive safeguards becomes essential to counteract the harmful effects resulting from involvement in sexting.

Online protection is seen as a collaborative initiative, in which various stakeholders, from parents and educators to platform managers and policymakers, play fundamental roles (Yehya, 2021). This convergence of responsibilities rests on the recognition that the digital safety of minors cannot be addressed unilaterally but requires the concerted cooperation of all entities involved in the digital ecosystem. The critical importance of online protection lies in its ability to foster an educational and safe digital environment (Tran et al., 2020).

The implementation of parental control technologies, effective government policies, and specific educational programs serves as a bulwark against the risks associated with sexting. This proactive approach contributes to the creation of a digital culture that promotes responsibility and respect among young people (Tomczyk, 2020). Online protection, by preventing and mitigating risks associated with sexting, not only addresses immediate threats but also contributes to mitigating long-term consequences. By safeguarding the privacy and emotional well-being of minors, these measures assist in building a positive digital experience that reflects in their development over time (Stoilova et al., 2021).

RISKS OF SEXTING

The growing prevalence of sexting among minors, as highlighted in the comprehensive literature review, reflects a phenomenon that has garnered significant concern in the contemporary digital era. This behaviour, characterized by the exchange of sexually explicit content through electronic devices, has experienced an alarming increase among young people, raising substantial concerns about their well-being and online safety. Thus, the groundwork has been laid previously to address this emerging issue, emphasizing the urgent need for effective online protection measures.

In this context, the critical importance of understanding the risks associated with sexting among minors is underscored. Beyond mere prevalence, it is essential to comprehend the short and long-term implications of this practice on the mental health, reputation, and interpersonal relationships of young individuals. The review not only seeks to quantify the magnitude of the problem but also explores the underlying complexities surrounding this phenomenon, addressing psychosocial and cultural factors contributing to its proliferation (Mori et al., 2019).

Indeed, a recent systematic review found that the vast majority of longitudinal studies on risk factors for cyber deviant behavior have focused on cyberbullying, sexting, and cyber dating abuse, with little attention to cyber-dependent crimes such as hacking and the use/deployment of malware (Virgara & Whitten, 2023).

The dangers associated with sending sexually explicit content to online partners may be limited when teenagers share images anonymously with other peers (Van Ouytsel et al., 2021). However, the risk of coercion and sextortion related to sexting significantly increases when sending images to individuals they have never met outside the online environment (Wolak et al., 2018).

It should be added that the literature suggests that sexually explicit images are not secure within intimate relationships, and sexual messages can be redistributed as non-consensual pornography, often referred to as revenge porn. Revenge porn refers to situations in which a sexually explicit image or video of an individual is electronically distributed on a media platform without the depicted person's permission. Research indicates that 60% of individuals in a relationship have sent sexually explicit photos of their partners (Cole et al., 2020).

A specific study found that the relationships with other risk factors may depend on the context in which messages are shared. Young people who engage in sexting outside the context of a romantic relationship, possibly a riskier form of sexting, may also have a higher likelihood of involvement in other risky behaviours compared to those who practice sexting within an established romantic relationship (Van Ouytsel et al., 2018).

Additionally, it should be noted that young individuals participating in sexting are more likely to have experimented with substances such as alcohol, cigarettes, and marijuana. This correlation is possibly attributed to shared common risk factors (Temple et al., 2014; Maras et al. 2024).

So far, the literature suggests that sexting can involve both normal and risky sexual behaviors, or a combination of both. However, this assessment might depend on specific circumstances and the individual characteristics of the person engaging in sexting. Therefore, personality traits could provide a valuable contribution to our understanding of different types of sexting behaviors (Moreli et al., 2021).

On the other hand, the main types of sexting linked to its associated risks are determined (Dodaj et al., 2023):

1. Intimate partner pressure-induced sexting.
2. Retaliatory sexting.
3. Consensual sexting with an intimate partner.
4. Group-induced sexting pressure.
5. Sexting with the purpose of flirting with others.

The detailed exploration of various types of sexting constitutes an essential component of this section. It is acknowledged that sexting goes beyond the mere exchange of explicit images; it also encompasses the sending of messages with sexually suggestive connotations. This broad definition allows for capturing the diversity of behaviors associated with sexting and provides a comprehensive framework for understanding the complexity of this phenomenon in the context of minors (Dully et al., 2023).

Additionally, relevant statistics are incorporated to illustrate the alarming prevalence of sexting among adolescents. These statistics not only quantify the magnitude of the problem but also underscore the urgency of effective interventions. Numerical data provide an empirical basis for understanding the scale of the phenomenon, demonstrating that sexting is not an isolated or infrequent issue but rather a practice that affects a significant number of young individuals.

It's worth noting that the majority of sexting images are shared within the realm of romantic relationships, either as a flirtatious gesture or as an expression of trust and intimacy (Van Ouytsel et al., 2017). A comprehensive analysis of various sexting studies revealed that 14.8% of young people had shared and 27.8% had received sexually suggestive images (Madigan et al., 2018).

In the study conducted by Van Ouytsel et al. (2021), respondents were asked about the identity of the last person to whom they had sent a sexting image. Seventy percent of all respondents indicated that they had shared a text message in the context of a romantic relationship, either with a romantic partner or someone they were in love with. Analyzing by sexual orientation, it was observed that 73.2% of heterosexual teenagers and approximately half (47.1%) of LGB teenagers had shared sexting images with a potential romantic partner. These results suggest that focusing solely on abstinence in sexting education or highlighting the risks associated with sexting may be an ineffective strategy for most teenagers. Since most sexting images are shared in a context of trust, teenagers may not perceive these situations as risky when sending their images to a trusted romantic partner. Rather than focusing on risks, educational efforts might be more effective in highlighting the importance of mutual trust and responsibility when engaging in sexting within romantic relationships.

Another study investigated sexting behaviors, including sending text messages as well as nude or semi-nude images, among adolescents. Dolev-Cohen & Ricon (2020) collected data from 458 students (101 boys, 357 girls) to analyze the potential correlation between sexting and parenting styles, as well as manifestations of social control by parents. Around 30% of participants admitted to engaging in sexting, and approximately 32% claimed that mainly strangers had asked them to send nude or semi-nude photos. They also identified that sexting was more frequent among high school students compared to middle school students, and the solicitation of nude or semi-nude images was more common among boys than girls. Furthermore, the results indicated that lower social control by parents was associated with a higher likelihood of engagement in sexting, while the perception of a permissive parenting style was related to the solicitation of images from others. Additionally, teenagers rarely reported their sexting experiences to their parents or other significant adults, such as teachers.

Maheux et al. (2020) examined sexting in adolescents, a potentially risky behaviour, focusing on the relationship between teenagers' popularity and their perceptions of their peers' sexting. The research was conducted in a high school in the southeastern United States, where 626 teenagers completed surveys about sexual texting in the last year. Although 87.4% believed that popular teenagers in their class practiced sexting, only 62.5% of them had actually done so. There were no significant differences in sexting rates between popular and non-popular teenagers (54.8%). Those who thought that popular peers sexted were ten times more likely to do so themselves. Girls were more likely to sext when they believed their popular peers did not, but this difference disappeared if they believed they did. In summary, the study highlights the importance of peer status and perceptions of peer norms in teenage sexting.

Dodaj et al. (2020) conducted a year-long longitudinal study involving 216 girls and 143 boys, all aged between 15 and 17. In both study periods, participants completed the Sexting Behaviour Questionnaire and the Stress, Anxiety, and Depression Scale. The results revealed that approximately 30% of participants received sexually explicit text messages, while around 60% engaged in sexting. The prevalence rates of receiving and sending sexually explicit messages remained relatively stable over time, with significant variations by gender. Overall, participants reported that sexting primarily involved current or past romantic partners or friends, and the exchange of sexual messages did not exceed five people. It is noteworthy that they determined that anxiety and stress symptoms were more common among those who received sexting messages at the beginning of the study, while depression was more related to sending and receiving text messages in the follow-up. Stress was identified as a significant predictor of sexting in the initial study, and depression was associated with sending and receiving text messages in the follow-up. Therefore, this study confirms the prevalence of sexting among young people and suggests an association with negative consequences, especially in terms of anxiety, stress, and depression.

On the other hand, after identifying various recent research studies that provide relevant statistics on the addressed topic, the diversity of behaviors associated with sexting is highlighted. It is recognized that sexting goes beyond the exchange of explicit images, including messages with sexually suggestive connotations. The research underscores the importance of understanding the short and long-term risks on the mental health, reputation, and interpersonal relationships of young individuals.

Additionally, it is evidenced that the risk of coercion and sextortion increases when sending images to unfamiliar individuals outside the online environment. The variability in risks based on relationship contexts is emphasized. Furthermore, a correlation between sexting and substance use is noted, suggesting the presence of common risk factors.

The inclusion of specific statistics from reliable research in the analysis reinforces the urgency of addressing the issue of sexting among minors. These statistics not only quantify the magnitude of the phenomenon but also provide a solid empirical basis for comprehending its scale. By demonstrating that sexting is not an isolated or infrequent occurrence but rather affects a significant number of young individuals, the pressing need for effective intervention is highlighted.

Therefore, it is emphasized that the majority of sexting images are shared within the context of romantic relationships, either as flirtatious gestures or expressions of trust and intimacy. This finding suggests the importance of educational approaches that extend beyond simply highlighting the risks associated with sexting. Instead of exclusively focusing on abstinence or warning about dangers, educational initiatives may be more effective by emphasizing the significance of mutual trust and responsibility when engaging in sexting within established romantic relationships.

Delving into these aspects, it is acknowledged that young individuals may not perceive these situations as risky when sharing images with a romantic partner they trust. This underscores the complexity of sexting and the need for nuanced and contextualized educational approaches. Furthermore, it is suggested that sexting education should incorporate elements that promote healthy relationships, open communication, and awareness of the emotional and social implications of these practices, beyond simply cautioning about the risks.

The inclusion of specific statistics from reliable research and relevant studies adds credibility to the review. These data support the presented claims, providing a solid foundation for the urgency of addressing sexting among minors. By citing specific sources, the review establishes a direct link to existing academic research on the topic, reinforcing the rigor of the analysis and the need for immediate action (Karaian et al., 2015).

The urgency of effective interventions, highlighted in this section, underscores the critical need for preventive and corrective strategies (Bogner et al., 2023; Gavey et al., 2023). By revealing the prevalence of sexting among adolescents, the review positions this phenomenon as a public health issue that requires immediate attention. The section not only highlights the magnitude of the problem but also sets the stage for subsequent sections of the review, where existing measures will be analyzed, and recommendations will be proposed to address this challenge.

SOLUTIONS AND RECOMMENDATIONS

From the protection of minors and state regulation, government policies and regulations designed to control access to explicit content and protect minors from online exploitation are highlighted. Specifically in Spain, Organic Law 1/2015, of March 30, amending Organic Law 10/1995, of November 23, of the Penal Code regulates sexting as a criminal offense, and the use of sexually explicit images of minors is specifically addressed in Organic Law 11/1999, of April 30, amending Title VIII of Book II of the Penal Code, approved by Organic Law 10/1995, of November 23. However, this text focuses on examining technological tools that enable parental control, allowing parents to monitor and limit minors' online activity, establishing the school as a point for digital competence training. Online education is presented as an essential strategy to increase awareness among young people about the risks associated with sexting and to promote safe online behaviors. The collaboration between online platforms and organizations dedicated to child protection is also emphasized as a comprehensive approach to addressing this multifaceted challenge (Jang & Ko, 2023).

The imperative need to implement effective online protection measures is underscored as a fundamental and pressing component in ensuring the safety and well-being of individuals, particularly minors, within the digital landscape. This call to action extends beyond a mere acknowledgment, emphasizing the shared responsibility that spans across diverse stakeholders in the expansive digital ecosystem. From parents and educators to online platforms and policymakers, a collaborative effort is indispensable to foster a secure online environment for the younger generation.

Recognizing the evolving nature of online interactions, it is crucial to not only respond to current challenges such as sexting among minors but also to proactively anticipate and address potential future developments. The multifaceted approach requires the formulation and implementation of comprehensive strategies and policies that are not only reactive but also adaptive. This forward-looking perspective is imperative in ensuring that the protective measures put in place remain relevant and effective in addressing emerging trends and evolving patterns of online behavior among young people (Corcoran et al., 2022).

In this context, it is essential to address the notion of digital literacy, as it entails more than merely possessing technical skills; it refers to the ability to comprehend, evaluate, and critically utilize technology safely and effectively (Yustika & Iswati, 2020). It involves discerning online information, understanding the risks and benefits of engaging in digital platforms, and using technological tools to communicate, collaborate, and create content ethically and responsibly. In summary, digital literacy is crucial for empowering young people and turning them into competent and conscious digital citizens, capable of navigating the digital landscape safely and productively. Integrating digital literacy into educational policies and programs is essential for preparing future generations for the constantly evolving digital world (List et al., 2020).

As we navigate the dynamic digital landscape, it becomes evident that a one-size-fits-all solution is inadequate. Tailored strategies need to be developed, taking into account the nuanced nature of online interactions and the diverse needs of the youth. By fostering a culture of digital literacy, imparting knowledge to parents and educators, and actively involving online platforms in responsible content moderation, a holistic and collaborative approach can be established to mitigate the risks associated with minors engaging in inappropriate online behavior.

Within the European Union, there exists a comprehensive set of guidelines providing clear direction for teachers in the realm of digital training. These guidelines reflect a strategic focus on technology and its associated issues, establishing two crucial reference frameworks that serve as pillars for educational development. On one front, there is the DigCompEdu framework (Mora-Cantallops et al., 2020), designed specifically for educators. This framework delineates pedagogical dimensions, teacher competencies, and corresponding student competencies, forming a robust foundation for digital education.

The DigCompEdu framework's pedagogical dimensions are particularly noteworthy, encompassing various facets of digital education. Of significant importance are the areas of Student Empowerment and Development of Student Digital Competence. These dimensions emphasize the imperative to not only equip students with the necessary technical skills but also to cultivate their ability to harness digital tools effectively. Student Empowerment encourages the nurturing of students' own capacity to work with digital tools, instilling in them a sense of agency and confidence in navigating the digital landscape.

Moreover, the Development of Student Digital Competence within the DigCompEdu framework underscores the need for a comprehensive approach. This involves training students not only in the technical aspects of utilizing digital tools but also in fostering a deep understanding of security protocols and honing their problem-solving skills. In essence, it goes beyond mere technological proficiency to empower students with a holistic digital competence that encompasses responsible and secure use of digital resources.

On the other hand, DigComp (Kluzer et al., 2020) is proposed. This reference framework has the same objective as the previous one, to establish the level of digital competence of European citizens. It directly includes security along with competencies:

- Device protection
- Protection of personal and private information
- Protection of health and well-being
- Protection of the environment.

All these competencies focus on working on security as a means of protection against threats such as sexting. However, this framework not only establishes prevention methods but also proposes a series of competencies gathered in the problem-solving area. In addition to proposing the ability to solve technical problems, it is necessary to be aware of issues related to the increased use of technology, establishing competencies in:

- Technical problem-solving
- Identifying needs and technical responses
- Creative use of technology
- Identifying technological usage gaps

Amidst these initiatives, a noteworthy exemplar is the Do-It-Together HOL game-based learning project, an innovative venture presented by Kluzer and Pujol (2018). This project, conceived as a playful and dynamic educational endeavor, serves as a compelling tool to elucidate the intricacies of digital security. By immersing students in an interactive environment, it goes beyond the theoretical aspects of cybersecurity, delving into the practical implications and real-world risks associated with the misuse of technology.

The Do-It-Together HOL project, with its emphasis on interactivity, not only aligns seamlessly with the objectives of the DigCompEdu framework but also emerges as a progressive strategy to address the multifaceted challenges posed by the digital era. By explicating the psychological risks intertwined with digital security issues, this project becomes a pivotal instrument in shaping the digital acumen of students, fostering a generation that not only comprehends the technical facets of technology but also grasps its ethical and societal dimensions.

The prominent attention to digital security, privacy, and responsible digital citizenship in these frameworks offers a treasure trove of valuable information for educators and policymakers. In the educational context, where the integration of technology is increasingly ubiquitous, these frameworks provide key guidance to protect sensitive student information, promote ethical online behavior, and cultivate digital literacy. Educators can use these guidelines as practical tools to design pedagogical strategies that incorporate digital awareness and cybersecurity into the curriculum. Additionally, policymakers can leverage this information to develop robust regulations that address current and future challenges in the digital realm, ensuring a safe and conducive educational environment for learning. A detailed understanding of these frameworks enables education and policy professionals to make informed and proactive decisions in a constantly evolving digital world.

EDUCATIONAL STRATEGIES FOR SAFETY PROMOTION

As mentioned earlier, the stage in which there is a higher risk of experiencing sexting is during adolescence, and it is a problem particularly relevant to females as they are more likely to be victims (Ojeda et al., 2020). Therefore, it is essential to provide education before this age, gradually eliminating gender-related cultural elements and reflections and promoting responsible use of technology.

As a first course of action by teachers to promote sexting prevention, it is crucial to engage with families. The emergence of sexting during adolescence is not a random occurrence; rather, it coincides with the development of sexuality influenced by hormonal changes during this stage (Castelo-Rivas et al., 2023). Therefore, establishing a coordinated working plan with families is fundamental to facilitate the normal development of students' sexuality.

Expanding the nexus between education and healthcare, collaborative efforts between educators and health professionals emerge as a potent avenue for holistic student development. Beyond the conventional realms of academic instruction, this collaboration extends its reach into the critical domain of sexual and reproductive health. Integrating sexual and reproductive health programs into the educational environment becomes a pivotal strategy, especially when navigating the complexities of healthy sexual development during adolescence, as advocated by Denno et al. (2015).

It's also important to note that during this stage, social media has a significant impact and is often the medium through which sexting incidents occur (Fuentes & Nuñez, 2021). In response to this situation, parental control emerges as a preventive tool to avoid both misuse and excessive use of social media by minors (López-de-Ayala et al., 2020). While parental control may be perceived as excessive by adolescents, reality reveals that parental control over technological tools moderate's technology use, positively influencing the behavior and attitudes of adolescents (Martins et al., 2020).

Another aspect influencing the misuse of technology and, therefore, a higher risk of sexting, along with other issues associated with improper use of ICT, is the need for families to have greater knowledge in these areas. In-depth knowledge by families provides teachers with a privileged position for sexting prevention (Martins et al., 2020).

Regarding actions that teachers can take for prevention, it is important to note that institutions and teachers face challenges in directly preventing these issues. However, as a reference, it is interesting to consider the document: "ICT Security Training for Parents, Guardians, and Educators of Minors" (Ministry of Industry, Energy, and Tourism, n.d.), which provides a guide to learning situations focused on preventing these problems.

AWARENESS, PLATFORMS, AND PROGRAMMES

Within awareness, it is important to mention that there are multiple strategies, campaigns, and initiatives that have focused on preventing this issue, so some of them will be highlighted.

Firstly, the "Think Before You Post" program, an advertising campaign launched by the Ministry of Justice and the United States as a means of awareness. Although this campaign is old (2008), it has been one of the most influential awareness campaigns on the subject, especially due to the audio-visual production posted on YouTube: [Think Before You Post Video] (https://youtu.be/2qR8uSyTZH0).

Another initiative that has gained a lot of strength is the proposal of Safer Internet Day. This proposal is an idea designed by the European Union as a means of awareness, establishing February 6th as the international day for the fight for a safe internet. On this day, various entities, companies, and organizations offer specific free training on security. This initiative gains great impact through the creation and transmission of these ideas on the website they develop to share data and information about the event.

The Netsmartz initiative represents a forward-thinking approach to digital literacy, recognizing the need to start imparting essential knowledge about online safety and responsible internet usage at a young age. This web application goes beyond the conventional boundaries of traditional education, offering a multifaceted platform tailored specifically for students in their formative years. The initiative aligns with the understanding that cultivating a foundation of digital literacy from an early age is paramount in preparing the younger generation to navigate the complexities of the digital realm.

To conclude this section, special mention is made of one of the most elaborate and impactful school proposals at all levels. This initiative is known as "Cyber Civics." It provides guidance for all stakeholders who have an influence on students' educational stages. For schools as educational institutions, the "Social Media Kit for Schools" is highlighted. For educators, there are resources such as "Educator Resources," "FREE Educator Course," and "Educator Workshops." Tutors are provided with specific training through workshops and classes, along with resources they can use with the students they supervise. Additionally, there is a blog where they can contact the managers of the proposal and other tutors to address common questions and concerns, they may have.

SPECIFIC ACTIONS CARRIED OUT IN SPAIN

Focusing the characteristics of this chapter, it is necessary to emphasise the Spanish strategies for the prevention of the previously established problems. On the one hand, it can be seen that no country is generating a section of the curriculum that focuses on sexting or the prevention of sexual misconduct with different devices at any stage (López et al., 2023).

However, despite the fact that legislation is not generating a specific curriculum that focuses on resolving this problem, practices are being developed that focus on establishing protocols for intervention and action by centres. For example, the National Institute for Cybersecurity (INCIBE) has developed protocols and resources such as the one shown in Figure 1 or the one available at the following link: https://www.incibe.es/sites/default/files/contenidos/materiales/Campanas/sexting/is4k_actividad-didactica-sexting-basado-en-hechos-reales.pdf.

Another example in Spain that has stood out is the "Have you thought about sending that photo? which is promoted by the mobile phone company Orange Spain. This campaign is the representation in Spain of the US "Think Before You Post Video" campaign. Thus, INCIBE shows how the proposal with the greatest impact has had on this aspect in Spain.

Figure 1. Protocol for action in case of leaked student images
Source: Incibe (s/f) ¿Qué hacer si se filtran imágenes íntimas de un alumno/a?

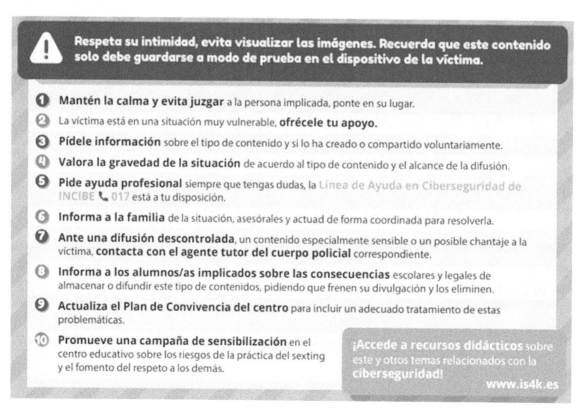

FUTURE RESEARCH DIRECTIONS

However, despite the implementation of these measures, the review also identifies challenges and limitations in their effectiveness. The section on ethical and privacy challenges explores the complexity of balancing the protection of minors with respect for their privacy and autonomy. Technological barriers and the need for constant updates to keep up with ever-changing technological developments are addressed, posing additional challenges. Cultural resistance and a lack of awareness in some environments hinder the acceptance and effectiveness of these online protection measures. The section concludes with a critical assessment of the current effectiveness of protection measures, emphasizing the need for a more holistic and adaptive approach (Dhirani et al., 2023).

Several scales have been developed to determine the factors influencing sexting behavior, as well as instruments gauging adolescents' perceptions of this issue and the likelihood of engaging in this risky behavior (Resett, 2019; Molla, 2021; Giménez-Gualdo et al., 2022). Therefore, as a future research direction, the idea of developing an intervention or a quasi-experimental design is proposed. The objective would be to delineate how cybersecurity training influences the possibilities or different areas that determine the likelihood of engaging in sexting.

CONCLUSION

The chapter comprehensively addresses the phenomenon of sexting among minors, contextualizing its emergence in the digital contemporary era. It highlights the growing prevalence of sexting, linking it to the increased use of social networks and electronic devices, especially among the younger population. A detailed overview of the situation in Spain is provided, emphasizing the active involvement of young people in digital platforms.

The text explores sociocultural, technological, and psychological factors contributing to the practice of sexting, considering the evolution of social norms, access to electronic devices, and the pressure from interpersonal relationships, especially among peers. The lack of awareness and comprehensive education is also emphasized as elements contributing to the prevalence of sexting among minors.

The relevance of online protection emerges as a central theme in the discussion, highlighting its collaborative nature involving various stakeholders, from parents and educators to platform managers and policymakers. Furthermore, the need for proactive measures, such as parental control technologies, government policies, and educational programs, is emphasized to counter the risks associated with sexting.

The work underscores the critical importance of online protection in today's digital age, not only to address immediate threats but also to mitigate long-term consequences. The fundamental role of these measures in building a digital culture that promotes responsibility and respect among young people is highlighted, contributing to a positive digital experience and long-term development. In general, the text provides a thorough and well-founded review of the issue of sexting among minors, addressing its multiple dimensions and proposing holistic approaches for prevention and continuous improvement.

In relation to the above, literature on online protection measures to prevent sexting among minors emphasizes the urgency of addressing this multifaceted issue significantly impacting the safety and well-being of young people in today's digital age. By synthesizing key findings, the need for a comprehensive response that combines preventive, educational, and regulatory measures to address the challenges posed by sexting among minors is highlighted.

It is essential to emphasize the importance of implementing preventive measures focusing on awareness and education. Promoting safe online behaviors from an early age through educational programs in both school and family settings is a fundamental strategy. These programs should not only inform about the risks associated with sexting but also foster a deeper understanding of the importance of privacy and respect in the digital world.

At the European level, through the European Union, key reference frameworks have been developed to enhance the digital competencies of the population. DigCompEdu focuses on the digital competencies of teachers, highlighting pedagogical dimensions and competencies for both teachers and students. On the other hand, DigComp establishes levels of digital competence for European citizens, including aspects of digital security, such as device protection, personal information, privacy, health and well-being, as well as the environment. While in Spain, the legal situation of sexting is clearly defined, specifically providing protection for minors.

These measures and approaches indicate a significant commitment both at the national and European levels to address the risks associated with sexting and the misuse of ICT. Training and awareness, for both teachers and students, are presented as fundamental pillars in these strategies, recognizing the importance of preparing society to interact safely and responsibly in the ever-evolving digital environment.

Finally, it is worth mentioning that collaboration between teachers and families is key in preventing sexting and promoting digital competencies. Family education, especially in the use of tools like parental control, contributes to a deeper understanding of online risks. These tools, though initially perceived as restrictive, play an important role in the safety of minors. Open communication between parents and teachers, along with the provision of informative resources, creates a supportive environment that strengthens awareness and responsible use of technology.

REFERENCES

Agnew, E. (2021). Sexting among young people: Towards a gender sensitive approach. *International Journal of Children's Rights*, *29*(1), 3–30. doi:10.1163/15718182-28040010

Bogner, J., Hadley, W., Franz, D., Barker, D. H., & Houck, C. D. (2023). Sexting as a Predictor of First-Time Sexual Behavior among At-Risk Early Adolescents. *The Journal of Early Adolescence*, *43*(4), 516–538. doi:10.1177/02724316221113351

Castelo-Rivas, W. P., Posligua-Castillo, M. J., Ruiz-Cordova, V. L., Apolo-Apolo, C. I., & Carpio-Chamba, J. L. (2023). Influencia de la Autoestima y el Apoyo Familiar en la Prevención del Sexting Adolescente. *Ciencia Latina Revista Científica Multidisciplinar*, *7*(4), 9995–10018. doi:10.37811/cl_rcm.v7i4.7684

Cole, T., Policastro, C., Crittenden, C., & McGuffee, K. (2020). Freedom to post or invasion of privacy? Analysis of US revenge porn state statutes. *Victims & Offenders*, *15*(4), 483–498. doi:10.1080/15564886.2020.1712567

Corcoran, E., Doty, J., Wisniewski, P., & Gabrielli, J. (2022). Youth sexting and associations with parental media mediation. *Computers in Human Behavior*, *132*, 107263. doi:10.1016/j.chb.2022.107263

Denno, D. M., Hoopes, A. J., & Chandra-Mouli, V. (2015). Effective strategies to provide adolescent sexual and reproductive health services and to increase demand and community support. *The Journal of Adolescent Health*, *56*(1), S22–S41. doi:10.1016/j.jadohealth.2014.09.012 PMID:25528977

Dhirani, L. L., Mukhtiar, N., Chowdhry, B. S., & Newe, T. (2023). Ethical dilemmas and privacy issues in emerging technologies: A review. *Sensors (Basel)*, *23*(3), 1151. doi:10.3390/s23031151 PMID:36772190

Dodaj, A., Sesar, K., & Jerinić, S. (2020). A prospective study of high-school adolescent sexting behavior and psychological distress. *The Journal of Psychology*, *154*(2), 111–128. doi:10.1080/00223980.2019.1666788 PMID:31566509

Dodaj, A., Sesar, K., Pérez, M. O., Del Rey, R., Howard, D., & Gerding Speno, A. (2023). Using vignettes in qualitative research to assess young adults' perspectives of sexting behaviours. *Human Technology*, *19*(1), 103–120. doi:10.14254/1795-6889.2023.19-1.7

Dolev-Cohen, M., & Ricon, T. (2020). Demystifying sexting: Adolescent sexting and its associations with parenting styles and sense of parental social control in Israel. *Cyberpsychology (Brno)*, *14*(1), 6. doi:10.5817/CP2020-1-6

Dully, J., Walsh, K., Doyle, C., & O'Reilly, G. (2023). Adolescent experiences of sexting: A systematic review of the qualitative literature, and recommendations for practice. *Journal of Adolescence*, *95*(6), 1077–1105. doi:10.1002/jad.12181 PMID:37157169

Farsi, D. (2021). Social media and health care, part I: Literature review of social media use by health care providers. *Journal of Medical Internet Research*, *23*(4), 1–21. doi:10.2196/23205 PMID:33664014

Gavey, N., Wech, A., Hindley, P., Thorburn, B., Single, G., Calder-Dawe, O., & Benton-Greig, P. (2023). Preventing image-based sexual coercion, harassment and abuse among teenagers: Girls deconstruct sexting-related harm prevention messages. *Sex Education*, 1–16. doi:10.1080/14681811.2023.2198205

Gen H. Q. (2018). *How Obsessed Is Gen Z with Mobile Technology?* GenHQ. https://genhq.com/how-obsessed-is-gen-z-with-mobile-technology/

Giménez-Gualdo, A. M., Sánchez-Romero, E. I., & Torregrosa, M. S. (2022). El lado oscuro de internet. ¿Predice el cyberbullying la participación en sexting? *Revista Latinoamericana de Psicología*, *54*, 112–119. doi:10.14349/rlp.2022.v54.13

Harari, G. M., Müller, S. R., Stachl, C., Wang, R., Wang, W., Bühner, M., Rentfrow, P. J., Campbell, A. T., & Gosling, S. D. (2020). Sensing sociability: Individual differences in young adults' conversation, calling, texting, and app use behaviors in daily life. *Journal of Personality and Social Psychology*, *119*(1), 204–228. doi:10.1037/pspp0000245 PMID:31107054

Jang, Y., & Ko, B. (2023). Online Safety for Children and Youth under the 4Cs Framework—A Focus on Digital Policies in Australia, Canada, and the UK. *Children (Basel, Switzerland)*, *10*(8), 1415. doi:10.3390/children10081415 PMID:37628414

Karaian, L., & Van Meyl, K. (2015). Reframing risqué/risky: Queer temporalities, teenage sexting, and freedom of expression. *Laws*, *4*(1), 18–36. doi:10.3390/laws4010018

Kluzer, S., Centeno, C., & O'Keeffe, W. (2020). *DigComp at work: the EU's digital competence framework in action on the labour market: a selection of case studies.* Publications Office. https://data.europa.eu/doi/10.2760/17763

Kluzer, S., & Pujol Priego, L. (2018). DigCompinto Action - Get inspired, make it happen. S. Carretero, Y. Punie, R. Vuorikari, M. Cabrera, & O'Keefe, W. (Eds.). JRC Science for Policy Report, EUR 29115 EN. Publications Office of the European Union. doi:10.2760/112945

Ley Orgánica 11/1999, de 30 de abril, de modificación del Título VIII del Libro II del Código Penal, aprobado por Ley Orgánica 10/1995, de 23 de noviembre. *Boletín Oficial del Estado 104*, de 1 de mayo de 1999, páginas 16099 a 16102. https://www.boe.es/eli/es/lo/1999/04/30/11

Ley Orgánica 1/2015, de 30 de marzo, por la que se modifica la Ley Orgánica 10/1995, de 23 de noviembre, del Código Penal. *Boletín oficial del Estado 77* de 31 de marzo de 2015, páginas 27061 a 27176. https://www.boe.es/eli/es/lo/2015/03/30/1

List, A., Brante, E. W., & Klee, H. L. (2020). A framework of pre-service teachers' conceptions about digital literacy: Comparing the United States and Sweden. *Computers & Education*, *148*, 103788. doi:10.1016/j.compedu.2019.103788

López, R., Hernández, D., & Martínez, K. P. (2023). Violencia Digital en las y los estudiantes de la Universidad Veracruzana. *Transdigital*, *4*(8), 1–17. doi:10.56162/transdigital221

Madigan, S., Ly, A., Rash, C. L., Van Ouytsel, J., & Temple, J. R. (2018). Prevalence of multiple forms of sexting behavior among youth: A systematic review and meta-analysis. *JAMA Pediatrics*, *172*(4), 327–335. doi:10.1001/jamapediatrics.2017.5314 PMID:29482215

Maheux, A. J., Evans, R., Widman, L., Nesi, J., Prinstein, M. J., & Choukas-Bradley, S. (2020). Popular peer norms and adolescent sexting behavior. *Journal of Adolescence*, *78*(1), 62–66. doi:10.1016/j.adolescence.2019.12.002 PMID:31841872

Maras, K., Sweiry, A., Villadsen, A., & Fitzsimons, E. (2024). Cyber offending predictors and pathways in middle adolescence: Evidence from the UK Millennium Cohort Study. *Computers in Human Behavior*, *151*, 108011. doi:10.1016/j.chb.2023.108011

Martins, M. V., Formiga, A., Santos, C., Sousa, D., Resende, C., Campos, R., Nogueira, N., Carvalho, P., & Ferreira, S. (2020). Adolescent internet addiction – role of parental control and adolescent behaviours. *International Journal of Pediatrics & Adolescent Medicine*, *7*(3), 116–120. doi:10.1016/j.ijpam.2019.12.003 PMID:33094139

Mena, M. (2022). *Uso de redes sociales. Los jóvenes de 16 a 24 años, los más activos en redes sociales en España [Use of social media. Young people aged 16 to 24, the most active on social media in Spain].* Statista. https://es.statista.com/grafico/28879/porcentaje-de-poblacion-que-ha-participado-en-redes-sociales-en-espana/#:~:text=Aunque%20las%20redes%20sociales%20han,alg%C3%BAn%20tipo%20de%20red%20social

Ministerio de industria, energía y turismo. (2018). *Capacitación en materia de seguridad TIC para padres, madres, tutores y educadores de menores de edad.* Ministerio de industria, energía y turismo. https://alumnosayudantes.files.wordpress.com/2018/03/unidades-didacticas-sexting_secundaria_red-es.pdf

Molla, C. (2021). *Sexting en adolescentes perfiles, prevalencias y desarrollo de la nueva escala de medida a-sexts* [Tesis doctoral, Universidad de Valencia].

Molla-Esparza, C., López-González, E., & Losilla, J. M. (2021). Sexting prevalence and socio-demographic correlates in Spanish secondary school students. *Sexuality Research & Social Policy, 18*(1), 97–111. doi:10.1007/s13178-020-00434-0

Mora-Cantallops, M., Inamorato-Dos Santos, A., Villalonga-Gómez, C., Lacalle-Remigio, J. R., Camarillo-Casado, J., & Sota-Eguizábal, J. M. (2022). *Competencias digitales del profesorado universitario en España: Un estudio basado en los marcos europeos DigCompEdu y OpenEdu* [The Digital Competence of Academics in Spain: A study based on the European frameworks DigCompEdu and OpenEdu]. Publications Office European Communities.

Morelli, M., Urbini, F., Bianchi, D., Baiocco, R., Cattelino, E., Laghi, F., Sorokowski, P., Misiak, M., Dziekan, M., Hudson, H., Marshall, A., Nguyen, T. T. T., Mark, L., Kopecky, K., Szotkowski, R., Toplu Demirtaş, E., Van Ouytsel, J., Ponnet, K., Walrave, M, & Chirumbolo, A. (2021). The Relationship between Dark Triad Personality Traits and Sexting Behaviors among Adolescents and Young Adults across 11 Countries. *International Journal of Environmental Research and Public Health, 18*(5), 5102. doi:10.3390/ijerph18052526 PMID:33806314

Mori, C., Temple, J. R., Browne, D., & Madigan, S. (2019). Association of sexting with sexual behaviors and mental health among adolescents: A systematic review and meta-analysis. *JAMA Pediatrics, 173*(8), 770–779. doi:10.1001/jamapediatrics.2019.1658 PMID:31206151

Ojeda, M., & Del Rey, R. (2022). Lines of action for sexting prevention and intervention: A systematic review. *Archives of Sexual Behavior, 51*(3), 1–29. doi:10.1007/s10508-021-02089-3 PMID:34791584

Ojeda, M., Del-Rey, R., Walrave, M., & Vandebosch, H. (2020). Sexting in adolescents: Prevalence and behaviours. *Comunicar, 28*(64), 9–19. doi:10.3916/C64-2020-01

Raza, S. A., Qazi, W., Umer, B., & Khan, K. A. (2020). Influence of social networking sites on life satisfaction among university students: A mediating role of social benefit and social overload. *Health Education, 120*(2), 141–164. doi:10.1108/HE-07-2019-0034

Resett, S. (2019). Sexting en adolescentes: Su predicción a partir de los problemas emocionales y la personalidad oscura. *Escritos de Psicología, 12*(2), 93–102. doi:10.24310/espsiescpsi.v12i2.10060

Setty, E. (2020). *Risk and harm in youth sexting: Young people's perspectives*. Routledge. doi:10.4324/9780429277344

SmahelD.MachackovaH.MascheroniG.DedkovaL.StaksrudE.ÓlafssonK.LivingstoneS.HasebrinkU. (2020). *EU Kids Online 2020: Survey results from 19 countries*. EU Kids Online. doi:10.21953/lse.47fdeqj01ofo

Stoilova, M., Livingstone, S., & Khazbak, R. (2021). *Investigating Risks and Opportunities for Children in a Digital World: A rapid review of the evidence on children's internet use and outcomes. Innocenti Discussion Paper 2020-03*. UNICEF Office of Research – Innocenti. https://lc.cx/oZifpZ

Temple, J. R., Le, V. D., van den Berg, P., Ling, Y., Paul, J. A., & Temple, B. W. (2014). Brief report: Teen sexting and psychosocial health. *Journal of Adolescence*, *37*(1), 33–36. doi:10.1016/j.adolescence.2013.10.008 PMID:24331302

Tomczyk, Ł. (2020). Skills in the area of digital safety as a key component of digital literacy among teachers. *Education and Information Technologies*, *25*(1), 471–486. doi:10.1007/s10639-019-09980-6

Tran, T., Ho, M. T., Pham, T. H., Nguyen, M. H., Nguyen, K. L. P., Vuong, T. T., Nguyen, T. H., Nguyen, T. D., Nguyen, T. L., Khuc, Q. L. V., & Vuong, Q. H. (2020). How digital natives learn and thrive in the digital age: Evidence from an emerging economy. *Sustainability (Basel)*, *12*(9), 1–21. doi:10.3390/su12093819

Van Ouytsel, J., Van Gool, E., Walrave, M., Ponnet, K., & Peeters, E. (2017). Sexting: Adolescents' perceptions of the applications used for, motives for, and consequences of sexting. *Journal of Youth Studies*, *20*(4), 446–470. doi:10.1080/13676261.2016.1241865

Van Ouytsel, J., Walrave, M., De Marez, L., Vanhaelewyn, B., & Ponnet, K. (2021). Sexting, pressured sexting and image-based sexual abuse among a weighted-sample of heterosexual and LGB-youth. *Computers in Human Behavior*, *117*, 106630. doi:10.1016/j.chb.2020.106630

Van Ouytsel, J., Walrave, M., Lu, Y., Temple, J. R., & Ponnet, K. (2018). The associations between substance use, sexual behavior, deviant behaviors and adolescents' engagement in sexting: Does relationship context matter? *Journal of Youth and Adolescence*, *47*(11), 2353–2370. doi:10.1007/s10964-018-0903-9 PMID:30073509

Vannucci, A., Ohannessian, C. M., & Gagnon, S. (2019). Use of multiple social media platforms in relation to psychological functioning in emerging adults. *Emerging Adulthood*, *7*(6), 501–506. doi:10.1177/2167696818782309

Vickery, J. R. (2017). *Worried about the wrong things: Youth, risk, and opportunity in the digital world.* MIT Press. doi:10.7551/mitpress/10653.001.0001

Virgara, J. L., & Whitten, T. (2023). A systematic literature review of the longitudinal risk factors associated with juvenile cyber-deviance. *Computers in Human Behavior*, *141*, 107613. doi:10.1016/j.chb.2022.107613

Wolak, J., Finkelhor, D., Walsh, W., & Treitman, L. (2018). Sextortion of minors: Characteristics and dynamics. *The Journal of Adolescent Health*, *62*(1), 72–79. doi:10.1016/j.jadohealth.2017.08.014 PMID:29055647

Yehya, F. M. (2021). Promising Digital Schools: An Essential Need for an Educational Revolution. *Pedagogical Research*, *6*(3), 1–10. doi:10.29333/pr/11061

Yustika, G. P., & Iswati, S. (2020). Digital literacy in formal online education: A short review. *Dinamika Pendidikan*, *15*(1), 66–76. doi:10.15294/dp.v15i1.23779

ADITIONAL READING

Agustina, J. R., & Gómez-Durán, E. L. (2016). Factores de riesgo asociados al sexting como umbral de diversas formas de victimización. Estudio de factores correlacionados con el sexting en una muestra universitaria. *IDP. Revista de Internet. Derecho y Política*, (22), 21–47. doi:10.7238/idp.v0i22.2970

Barrense-Dias, Y., Berchtold, A., Surís, J. C., & Akre, C. (2017). Sexting and the definition issue. *The Journal of Adolescent Health*, *61*(5), 544–554. doi:10.1016/j.jadohealth.2017.05.009 PMID:28734631

Del Rey, R., Ojeda, M., & Casas, J. A. (2021). Validation of the sexting behavior and motives questionnaire (SBM-Q). *Psicothema*, *33*(2), 287. PMID:33879302

Doyle, C., Douglas, E., & O'Reilly, G. (2021). The outcomes of sexting for children and adolescents: A systematic review of the literature. *Journal of Adolescence*, *92*(1), 86–113. doi:10.1016/j.adolescence.2021.08.009 PMID:34454257

Gassó, A. M., & Gómez-Durán, E. (2021). Psychopathological profile of sexting coercion perpetrators. *Spanish Journal of Legal Medicine*, *47*(4), 157–163. doi:10.1016/j.remle.2021.02.003

Gómez-García, G., Romero-Rodríguez, J. M., Rodríguez-Jimenez, C., & Ramos, M. (2020). Sexting among University Students: Links to Internet Addiction and Psychological Variables. *Journal of Drug and Alcohol Research*, *9*. doi:10.4303/jdar/236105

Mori, C., Cooke, J. E., Temple, J. R., Ly, A., Lu, Y., Anderson, N., Rash, C., & Madigan, S. (2020). The prevalence of sexting behaviors among emerging adults: A meta-analysis. *Archives of Sexual Behavior*, *49*(4), 1103–1119. doi:10.1007/s10508-020-01656-4 PMID:32072397

Sastre-Riba, S., & Romero, M. (2023). Alta capacidad: competencias sociales y cyberbullying. *Medicina*, *83*, 64-69. http://www.scielo.org.ar/scielo.php?script=sci_arttext&pid=S0025-76802023000300064&lng=es&tlng=es

KEY TERMS AND DEFINITIONS

Digital Behavior: Activities and actions carried out by individuals in online environments, including sexting, involving the exchange of sexually explicit content through electronic devices.

Interpersonal Relationships: Connections and emotional bonds between individuals, especially relevant when considering the implications of sexting on the quality of young people's interpersonal relationships.

Interventions: Planned and executed actions to address and resolve specific problems, in this case, measures to prevent or mitigate the risks associated with sexting among minors.

Online Education: Strategies and programs designed to inform and raise awareness among young people about safe and responsible practices when using digital platforms.

Online Protection Measures: Policies, tools, and strategies implemented to safeguard the safety and well-being of minors while navigating the digital world, including technological and regulatory measures.

Online Security: The set of measures and practices aimed at protecting the physical, emotional, and social integrity of young people while engaging in online activities, including the prevention of sexting.

Sexting: The act of sending, receiving, or sharing messages, images, or sexually explicit content through electronic devices, especially among minors, with implications for mental health, privacy, and online security.

Sextortion: The act of blackmail or coercion involving the use of explicit images, videos, or messages obtained from an individual, typically to extort money, additional explicit content, or other forms of cooperation, with the threat of public sharing if demands are not met.

Shared Responsibility: Recognition that various actors, such as parents, educators, online platforms, and policymakers, share the responsibility of addressing the issue of sexting among minors.

Chapter 15
Sexual (Mis)information:
Pornography and Adolescence in the Digital Space

Elizabeth-Guadalupe Rojas-Estrada
National Council of Humanities, Science, and Technology, Mexico

Arantxa Vizcaíno-Verdú
https://orcid.org/0000-0001-9399-2077
Universidad Internacional de la Rioja, Spain

Mónica Bonilla-del-Río
European University of the Atlantic, Spain

ABSTRACT

The escalating prevalence of pornography consumption among the youth has raised significant concern within the scientific community. This study aims to systematically examine scholarly literature on adolescence and engagement with pornography. Employing a conceptual framework, a qualitative literature review was conducted. Data analysis involved compiling abstracts and employing the AI coding system of Atlas.ti 23. These narrative approaches include (1) adolescent online health and pornographic education, (2) youth sexual identity shaped by online pornographic content, (3) and government policies promoting (in)formed sex education. The study's conclusions underscore the detrimental effects of unregulated access to online pornographic content on adolescents, manifesting in distorted self-image, diminished self-esteem, and altered body perceptions. This phenomenon highlights the imperative of promoting comprehensive sex education. Media literacy is identified as a pivotal initiative to foster understanding of stereotypical representations and their societal and personal impacts.

INTRODUCTION

The increasing prevalence of online pornography among younger demographics, exposing adolescents to explicit content, has reached considerable proportions due to rapid technological advancements and

DOI: 10.4018/979-8-3693-2053-2.ch015

development (Yunengsih & Setiawan, 2021). In this context, educators and families confront educational challenges in effectively addressing this issue. A primary risk associated with this phenomenon is the dissemination of sexual misinformation, evident in the assimilation of beauty standards, inaccurate sexual behaviors (Cerbara et al., 2023), or harmful stereotypes (Alexandraki et al., 2018).

In the exploration of their sexuality, adolescents often turn to the Internet or alternative media sources due to curiosity and a lack of opportunities or support from family or educators to gain knowledge about reproductive health, frequently accessing pornographic content (Meilani et al., 2020). However, such content may lead users, particularly adolescents, to misconceptions or unrealistic notions about the opposite sex, sexual behaviors, or sexual satisfaction (Revelo-Morejón, 2016).

The consumption of such audiovisual content can detrimentally influence the formation of sexual attitudes and behaviors (Yunengsih & Setiawan, 2021) and the comprehension of vital aspects such as identity, self-esteem, body satisfaction, or primary negative emotions (Cerbara et al., 2023). Thus, online pornography poses a challenge in today's hypermediatized society, given the ease of access and the array of available content across different devices.

During this critical developmental stage, adolescents might be particularly susceptible to the impacts of pornography (Meilani et al., 2023), potentially distorting their perceptions of sex, interpersonal relationships, violence, or consent (Alario-Gavilán, 2021), with potential consequences for both short-term and long-term sexual and emotional health (Román-García et al., 2021). Other worrisome aspects regarding adolescents' accessibility to online pornography are linked to addiction and excessive consumption (Pekal et al., 2018).

The immediate and ubiquitous availability of such pornographic content might lead to compulsive consumption, negatively affecting other facets of young people's lives, including their personal relationships within their close environment (family, friends, partners, etc.), as well as their psychological well-being or academic performance (Beyens et al., 2014). In this context, families and educators should assume a pivotal role in addressing digital sex education through strategies based on open communication to counteract media misinformation.

Furnishing accurate and comprehensive information can aid adolescents and young individuals in developing a nuanced understanding of human sexuality and adopting healthier attitudes and behaviors in the digital environment. Consequently, there is a pressing need to engage in discussions about the representations present in pornography to assist them in identifying and differentiating between fiction and reality.

The objective of this study is to investigate primary patterns in the generation of scholarly literature concerning adolescence and the engagement with pornography, with the purpose of delving into the themes, concerns, and associated risks inherent in this media activity that could impact the maturation of young individuals. Drawing insights from this scrutiny, a set of recommendations is proffered with the intention of alleviating potential adverse consequences stemming from the exposure to digital pornography.

METHOD

We adopted a conceptual approach in our research of adolescent digital pornography consumption by employing a qualitative literature review to explore emerging themes. We concentrated on contemporary research, leveraging prominent databases such as Web of Science (WoS) and Scopus, applying a search strategy involving the keywords "porn*" (in the title), "adolescent*" OR "teen*" (in the topic), AND "Internet*" (in the topic), combined with Boolean operators.

Our search criteria included a publication time frame (2020-2024), scientific article typology, language preferences (Spanish and English), and open access accessibility. As shown in Figure 1, the initial scan yielded 1,145 records (1,091 from WoS and 54 from Scopus). After exporting the results to Refworks for efficient reference management, we identified and removed 22 duplicate entries, resulting in a refined sample of 1,123 articles.

The subsequent manual filtering phase involved evaluating titles, abstracts, and keywords to adhere to our inclusion criteria. Papers lacking specificity in the object of the study (focusing on topics such as sexuality, sex education, or sexual health), addressing different age groups, or not exploring Internet-based pornographic consumption were excluded. Following this filtering process, the final sample consisted of 121 selected papers. Furthermore, supplementary material containing the selected studies and their respective references is available on Figshare at the following link: https://bitly.ws/3eToA.

Data Analysis

We conducted a comprehensive data analysis by compiling abstracts and employing the AI Coding system of the Atlas.ti 23 software. This step aimed to identify the prevailing themes across the studies. The analysis yielded ten main codes: age, government regulation, internationalization, technological media, pornography, psychopathologies, public health, methodology, sexual health, and youth behavior.

Figure 1. Selection process flow chart
Source: Own elaboration

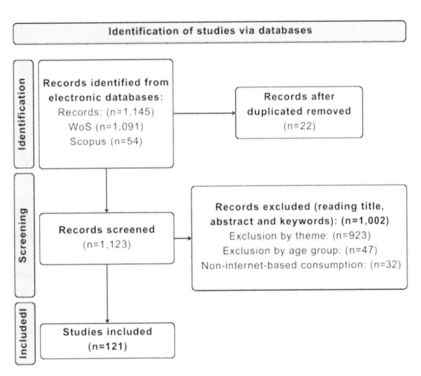

Additionally, over 1,000 subcodes were identified, forming the basis for three distinct memos or narrative approaches discussed in the subsequent sections: (a) adolescence online health and pornographic education, (b) young sexual identity constructed through pornographic content on the Internet, and (c) government policies to promote (in)formed sex education.

SEXUAL MISINFORMATION AND PORNOGRAPHY CONSUMPTION IN ADOLESCENCE: PREDOMINANT TOPICS

In the landscape of adolescent development, sexual misinformation and pornography consumption emerge as pivotal factors shaping attitudes, behaviors, and overall sexual health. This comprehensive exploration delves into the three interrelated approaches mentioned above.

Adolescent Online Health and Pornographic Education

The pervasive influence of the Internet has profoundly shaped the lives of adolescents, impacting various facets of their development, including health and sexual behavior. While acknowledging the ubiquity of online platforms, we delve into the potential consequences, both positive and negative, of adolescents' exposure to explicit content and elucidate the multifaceted dimensions of their online health in the digital age.

Educational Potential and Risks of Pornographic Exposure

As adolescents navigate the complexities of their burgeoning sexuality, exposure to pornography has become an integral part of their online experience. While some argue that it may serve as a source of sexual education (Pappas, 2021; Gesser-Edelsburg & Elhadi-Arabia, 2018; Goh et al., 2023), others have expressed concerns regarding its potential impact on mental health, relationships, and overall well-being (Raine et al., 2020; Svedin et al., 2023). Proponents of pornography argue that it may contribute to sexual education by providing adolescents with information about anatomy, consent, and various aspects of human sexuality (Rodríguez-Castro et al., 2021). Access to diverse perspectives and experiences through explicit content might help demystify certain aspects of sexuality that traditional education often fails to adequately address.

Acknowledging these potential educational benefits is crucial for fostering a nuanced understanding of adolescent online health. Conversely, concerns have been raised about the potential adverse effects of prolonged exposure to such uncontrolled explicit content. Research indicates correlations between excessive consumption of pornography and negative outcomes, such as distorted body image (Willis et al., 2022), unrealistic expectations (Wright & Herbenick, 2022), and diminished relationship satisfaction (Sommet & Berent, 2022). A comprehensive examination of these negative consequences is essential to inform interventions aimed at promoting educational and healthier online behaviors among adolescents (Charig et al., 2020). In this context, as delineated by Meilani et al. (2023), the active engagement of both families and communities alongside educational institutions is of paramount importance in guiding and supporting adolescents concerning the utilization of smartphones and social media platforms. This proactive involvement thwarts access to pornography and attenuates the perils associated with the development of precarious sexual behaviors. Furnishing comprehensive sexual education within both scholastic establishments and domestic settings serves as a potent mechanism for interrogating societal taboos and the uncritical embrace of beauty norms and sexual mores propagated through pornographic content (Cerbara et al., 2023). Specifically, the configuration of family dynamics has emerged as a pivotal determinant in mitigating excessive pornography consumption on online platforms (Li et al., 2023; Shek & Ma, 2012).

In agreement with this, Rivera et al.'s (2016) research underscores that a conducive intrafamilial milieu correlates positively with diminished pornography consumption, whereas adversarial intrafamilial dynamics and proclivities toward relational independence engender heightened consumption. Hence, these findings substantiate a discernible association between the inculcation of values and both online and offline risk-taking behaviors. Consequently, the efficacy of familial discourse in fostering candid conversations regarding pornography within an atmosphere of trust and comfort assumes critical significance in comprehending and managing adolescent consumption patterns (Jhe et al., 2023).

A primary legal consideration revolves around defining and regulating explicit pornographic content. Laws vary across jurisdictions, and what may be deemed explicit or harmful in one region may not be subject to the same restrictions elsewhere. Consequently, international consensus on the legal framework for explicit content, especially concerning minors, is essential. In the pursuit of protecting minors, lawmakers often grapple with the challenge of defining what constitutes explicit content (Principi et al., 2022). The rapidly evolving nature of online platforms and the diversity of available content pose challenges to creating a legal framework that is both comprehensive and adaptable. Striking balance involves considering cultural nuances, societal norms, and the evolving landscape of digital media (Byron et al., 2021).

Ethical and Collaborative Approaches to Address Explicit Content

Freedom of expression is also a right in democratic societies and any attempt to regulate explicit content must navigate this balance (Thurman & Obster, 2021). Censorship raises concerns about limiting individual freedoms, and critics argue that overly restrictive measures may infringe upon adults' right to access information freely (Sharma & Bleich, 2019). Furthermore, ethical considerations play a pivotal role in shaping the discourse on explicit content and adolescent online health. Ethical concerns extend beyond legality, delving into the questions of responsible content creation, dissemination, and consumption (Dudek et al., 2022). Content creators, platforms, and users all bear ethical responsibilities to ensure that explicit material is produced and consumed in a manner that respects human dignity and minimizes harm (Sanders et al., 2023).

In addition to legal and ethical considerations, collaboration among policymakers, technology companies, educators, and parents is fundamental. Technological solutions such as age verification tools and content filtering mechanisms can aid in enforcing legal restrictions. However, relying solely on technological solutions is insufficient, and a holistic approach that combines legal, ethical, and educational measures is essential (Fasih-Ramandi, 2019; McCormack & Wignall, 2024). Encouraging conversations about healthy sexuality, consent, and critical media literacy can empower adolescents to navigate the digital landscape responsibly.

Young Sexual Identity Construction through Pornography on the Internet

The Internet has undergone a transformative evolution in the pornography sector, encompassing traditional outlets such as television and print, as well as digital platforms. The diversity inherent in such explicit content is a significant contributor to the intricate dissemination of its current influence. Research by Idoiaga-Mondragon et al. (2024) or Bernstein et al. (2022) emphasizes the wide spectrum of sexually explicit material on the Internet, ranging from educational and consensual depictions to more potentially harmful portrayals. The heterogeneity of content exposes adolescents to different dilemmas of human sexuality (Vertongen et al., 2022), thereby complicating its potential impact on their evolving sexual identity.

According to a study conducted by Thurman and Obster (2021), 63% of young individuals access pornographic content through social media, whereas 47% do so through websites, with the latter exhibiting a higher prevalence of such content. In fact, youth perceive digital platforms as a source of anonymous secondary information, underscoring the vital importance of digital pornography literacy promoting authentic and practical information concerning sexuality and healthy relationships. This literacy initiative aids vulnerable youths in identifying and critically evaluating problematic messages encountered through pornography (Davis et al., 2020). Furthermore, some studies have demonstrated an association between frequency of pornography consumption and increased self-objectification and body comparison tendencies. Both genders are susceptible to body-related concerns linked to pornography, although not necessarily related to body shame (Maheux et al., 2021).

Building on this, the frequency of exposure emerges as a pivotal determinant of the degree of influence exerted by pornography. Prichard et al. (2013) emphasized that repeated exposure can contribute to the normalization of certain behaviors or attitudes. This normalization effect is essential in shaping adolescents' perceptions of what constitutes typical or acceptable behavior in sexual relationships (Löfgren-Mårtenson & Månsson, 2010). Moreover, individual differences among adolescents introduce another layer of complexity into the interplay between pornography and sexual attitudes. Martin-Hald and Malamuth (2008) and Frangos and Frangos (2011) highlighted the influence of pornography on cognitive development, personality traits, and preexisting beliefs about self-sexuality. This recognition of individual variability is instrumental in tailoring interventions to suit the diverse identity needs of adolescents.

Sexual Expectations and Unrealistic Experiences

Beyond these aspects, some authors have suggested that exposure to explicit material contributes to the formation of sexual fantasies, development of preferences (Attwood et al., 2018), and establishment of expectations within romantic relationships (de-Miguel-Álvarez, 2020). Another study added the role of explicit pornographic content in reinforcing and perpetuating gender stereotypes (Shor & Golriz, 2019). The portrayal of gender roles and dynamics in pornography has been identified as a contributing factor to the internalization of traditional societal expectations (Cerbara et al., 2023). Goldsmith et al. (2017) and Maheux et al. (2021) demonstrated the potential impact of explicit material on shaping body image ideals and beauty standards among adolescents. Pornographic depictions often present unrealistic and idealized representations of physical attributes, potentially contributing to body dissatisfaction and internalization of unattainable beauty norms (Byron et al., 2021).

The perpetuation of stereotypes in pornography extends beyond gender roles and body images. Cultural and racial stereotypes are also prevalent in explicit content (Vangeel et al., 2020). Adolescents exposed to such content may internalize and perpetuate harmful stereotypes related to ethnicity and cultural backgrounds (Fritz et al., 2021), impacting their understanding of diversity and contributing to prejudiced attitudes (Cowan & Campbell, 1994). In light of this, interventions should not only focus on the individual level, but also extend to broader societal and cultural contexts. Collaborative efforts involving educators, parents, and policymakers can foster media literacy that enables adolescents to critically analyze and deconstruct the stereotypes presented in pornography.

Government Policy to Minimize Risks and Promote (In)Formed Sex Education

The escalating political concern regarding online pornography consumption and sexual misinformation has led to a deeper understanding of the associated risks, public health impact, and vulnerability of specific population groups. These concerns are exacerbated by online environmental features such as anonymity and accessibility. Maddocks (2023) emphasizes that public opinion pressure and activism from various interest groups have focused on the necessity of addressing this phenomenon through legislative measures. Since the late nineties, most Western countries have enacted laws aimed at safeguarding children and adolescents from online abuse, primarily focusing on the production, possession, and dissemination of pornography via the Internet (Hyden, 2023; Martellozzo et al., 2020; Sharpe & Mead, 2021; Thurman et al., 2022).

Legislative Measures and Regulatory Challenges on Online Pornography

The traditional regulatory model, which is effective in the physical realm with precise territorial borders and focuses on the roles of producers and distributors, encounters new challenges in cyberspace (Yar, 2020). Various nations, including New Zealand, the United Kingdom, France, and Germany, have addressed the issue of minors' access to pornographic sites through an approach that, in its most basic form, requires users to confirm having surpassed a certain age (Keen et al., 2020). However, the evident deficiency of this method lies in the lack of independent controls to verify the accuracy of the age declared by the user, coupled with the widespread use of virtual private networks and browsers that can easily bypass these restrictions, undermining their effectiveness (Thurman & Obster, 2021).

Innovative Approaches to Combat Cybercrime and Protect Adolescents

To address the distribution of such materials and combat cybercrime more broadly, some governments have established specialized units dedicated to ensuring compliance with established regulations (Macilotti, 2020). An example is the National Office Against Illegal and Pornographic Publications in China under the Ministry of Public Security (Cui et al., 2021). On the other hand, relatively emerging forms of pornography, such as self-generated images and the non-consensual sharing of private images, commonly known as "revenge porn", have emerged as crucial topics of discussion and regulation in various jurisdictions (Gámez-Guadix et al., 2022). In the Mexican context, the "Ley Olimpia" stands out as a regional reference for addressing this issue, penalizing those who disseminate, share, or disclose intimate images without the consent of the involved person (Navas-Garcés & Nuñez-Ruiz, 2021).

Other strategies implemented outside the digital realm include awareness campaigns designed to educate society about the risks and consequences of digital violence (Herbitter et al., 2022), with a particular focus on non-consensual sharing of intimate material and the health and sociocultural risks of pornography consumption (Liang & Lu, 2012). A notable example is the campaign carried out by the Basque Institute for Women in Spain, under the slogan "Porn is a school of violence against women", to emphasize the notion that pornography can act as a mechanism that teaches and reinforces patterns of violence directed towards women (Emakunde, 2023).

Integrating Pornography Education Into Academic Curricula

However, despite the widespread condemnation of pornography and its consumption, Keen et al. (2020) point out that intermediaries in this industry often exert pressure to avoid specific legislation and reduce state intervention, censorship, regulatory costs, and their own responsibilities. Another crucial concern is that current measures tend to focus primarily on commercially oriented pornography, leaving social media platforms, video-sharing services, and streaming services beyond their scope (Sharpe & Mead, 2021). Evidence supports the claim that minors access explicit content through these platforms (Meilani et al., 2023; Pawlikowska et al., 2022).

These challenges underscore the need to address this phenomenon using more comprehensive approaches, including the incorporation of these issues into the educational realm to cultivate informed citizens about the importance of privacy, online respect, and the risks associated with the consumption and dissemination of pornographic material (Alexandraki et al., 2018). In this context, some countries have integrated topics related to pornography into their academic sexual education programs, such as Canada (Levin & Hammock, 2020), or have developed specific educational materials, as seen in the case of Ecuador's government (Ministerio de Educación, 2021), highlighting how pornography consumption can increase exposure to misinformation that reinforces harmful gender norms. Despite these advancements, initiatives often face resistance and controversy, especially from conservative groups, along with a lack of teacher training and adequate resources to effectively address the inclusion of this content in schools (López-Pacheco, 2021).

RECOMMENDATIONS AND CONCLUSION

In summary, unrestricted accessibility to online pornographic content has led to early exposure of adolescents to distorted representations that negatively impact their self-esteem and body perception, and foster the construction of unrealistic and violent expectations surrounding sex. This phenomenon not only raises concerns about the health and emotional well-being of young people, but also underscores the need to equip adolescents with critical tools to interpret and filter the content they consume.

It is crucial to acknowledge that sexual misinformation is intricately linked to the transmission and restriction of knowledge of sexuality over time (Canh et al., 2020). In addition, messages and violence associated with pornography have the potential to acquire an educational dimension that should not be underestimated (Alilunas et al., 2021). Therefore, strategies aimed at addressing this phenomenon require a comprehensive approach that goes beyond merely correcting informational errors or verifying a user's age. They should also promote an open, understandable, and healthy dialogue about sexuality.

While legislation on this matter has sought to evolve to address contemporary challenges in the digital era, it faces difficulties in keeping pace with the rapid expansion and diversification of online content (Yar, 2020). In light of this, there is an emphasis on the need for states to take concrete measures to promote greater awareness and education regarding pornography consumption. However, this action must go beyond mere awareness and encompass the establishment of regulatory frameworks that ensure access to comprehensive sexual education considering the diversity of experiences and realities faced by minors in the digital world.

In line with the insights of Argentine anthropologist Rita Segato (2003), it is imperative to ensure the dissemination of narratives, representations, and logics that enable a "reflective overcoming" of pornographic content; however, these efforts should be inversely proportional to the mechanisms perpetuating it. In this context, the following recommendations are proposed.

Media and Information Literacy (MIL) Is a Crucial Skill

Considering the potential of MIL as a strategy to address the phenomenon in question, its integration into the educational realm provides an opportunity to empower students to critically analyze the content they consume online. This initiative not only promotes understanding of stereotypical representations and their impact on social and personal perceptions, but also strengthens the ability to discern between fiction and reality, as well as between accurate information and misinformation (Testa et al., 2023a). Moreover, it stands out for its capacity to stimulate creativity and the critical production of content and messages, fostering healthy, respectful, and realistic narratives about sexuality and relationships (Vahedi et al., 2018).

According to Vahedi et al. (2018), critically comprehending the underlying interests, dynamics, and logic surrounding the production of such content enables the mitigation of social and cultural pressures that normalize or promote consumption as desirable. MIL also enables the teaching of self-regulation strategies, providing support to adolescents in managing their online time and handling emotions associated with explicit content, especially that involving violence. This empowers them to make conscious decisions about content consumption, including pornography (Scull et al., 2021). Ultimately, MIL has emerged as a tool for addressing online privacy and promoting ethical management of presence and identity in cyberspace (Voicu & Crăciun, 2023).

Educational Resources From the Perspective of MIL

A population with higher levels of media literacy, as highlighted by Calvo-González (2015), is better equipped to advocate policies and practices that regulate access to online pornography. Additionally, they are more adept at intervening and providing support to individuals who may experience issues related to consumption. In this context, Table 1 compiles curriculum materials and family guides addressing online pornography consumption, leveraging the principles of media literacy to understand and manage this phenomenon.

An integrative analysis of these materials revealed a concentration of efforts to demystify the distorted perceptions offered by pornographic content. They aim to foster healthier and more equitable online interactions, equip parents with tools to understand and openly engage with their children about the explicit content they consume, and provide general and basic information to confront sexual misinformation.

Collaboration Among Stakeholders

The establishment of a safe online environment and promotion of informed sexual education are shared responsibilities that require ongoing attention. Therefore, it is recommended to foster cooperation, both at the local and international levels, among the government, civil society, educational institutions,

Table 1. Educational resources from the perspective of MIL

Type of resource	Title	Author(s)	Description
Teaching unit	Digital identities	Calvo-González (2014)	This educational initiative, tailored for high school students, delves into the effects of social media and technology on young individuals' interactions and emotions. It offers a specific focus on analyzing these influences and actively challenging traditional stereotypes and myths, including those perpetuated by pornography.
Lesson	Media literacy and sexuality	SFUSD (2017)	This lesson is part of *Be Real. Be Ready* (2017) curriculum designed for high school students with the aim of exploring aspects related to sexuality and relationships.
Toolkit	Myth vs reality	Childnet International (2018)	This resource is tailored for high school students, with a primary focus on the authenticity of the online content. It utilizes videos as pedagogical tools to delve deeper into topics such as Internet pornography consumption.
Curriculum	The truth about pornography: A pornography literacy. Curriculum for high school students designed to reduce sexual and dating violence	Rothman et al. (2020)	This is a nine-session curriculum designed to critically analyze explicit content and raise awareness of the influence of media on the formation of social norms.
Activity	El porno: La industria que convierte a las mujeres en objetos [The porn industry: Turning women into objects]	Barbero-Reyes (2023)	This activity is part of the material created within the framework of the project *Ni zorras, ni héroes* (*Neither sluts nor heroes*), which aims to debunk the myths conveyed to minors through pornographic content.
Lesson	Pornografía y sexualidad [Pornography and sexuality]	García-Rojas & Salcines-Talledo (2023)	This lesson, designed for parents, is part of the guide *Educación afectiva y sexual en la familia* (*Emotional and sexual education in the family*) (2023).
Lessons	• I heard it 'round the Internet: Sexual health education and authenticating online information • Online relationships: Respect and consent • Sex in advertising	MediaSmarts (2024)	These lessons are part of the guide *Use, understand & engage: a digital media literacy framework for Canadian schools* (2024), which compiles nine key aspects of media literacy and provides educators with supportive lessons and interactive resources.
Lesson	Fantasy or reality? How sexually explicit media affects how we see relationships IRL	Advocates for Youth (2024)	This lesson is part of the *Rights, Respect, Responsibility: A K-12 curriculum* (2024), which not only addresses the fundamentals of sexual education but also focuses on developing specific skills to promote healthy behaviors in this area.

Source: Own elaboration

media industry, parents, and healthcare professionals. An exemplary demonstration of the significance of such collaborations is evident in the *#GeneraciónXXX* campaign [https://bitly.ws/3eIgc], led by the civil association Dale la Vuelta in partnership with the European Parliament. This initiative aims to shield children from the adverse effects of pornography in Spain. Furthermore, it advocates for the implementation of more efficacious measures regarding user verification, facilitated by the active engagement of diverse entities. Another noteworthy instance is the *Seguros en Internet portal* [https://bitly.ws/3eIgJ], developed by Telefónica in collaboration with the Peruvian Network against Child Pornography (RCPI). This platform serves as a mechanism to report illicit and inappropriate content for minors on the Internet.

Key Actions of Each Stakeholder Group

The role of the political sphere extends beyond merely developing and implementing policies and regulations to promote a safe and healthy online environment for adolescents. It also involves allocating resources for research and closely collaborating with civil organizations and other stakeholders to implement initiatives and campaigns on the subject (Keen et al., 2020). However, collaborative efforts should focus on conducting research and developing regulations, policies, and educational programs that are sensitive to adolescents' experiences and specific needs regarding this critical issue. There should be a specific emphasis on emotional awareness and gender perspective (Idoiaga-Mondragon et al., 2024). This implies not only addressing the technical and legal aspects of online safety but also promoting a deeper understanding of the dynamics influencing online interactions and minors' consumption of sexual content. Yar (2020), for instance, urges the media to promote the production and distribution of educational and cultural content that fosters positive and healthy values concerning sexuality and emotional relationships. According to Rothman et al. (2017), the key lies in parents maintaining open and honest communication with their children, seeking resources and support to address questions and concerns related to sexual education and managing online pornography, with the assistance of professionals.

Regarding civil associations, Hyden (2023) argues that their activism is essential for raising awareness and mobilizing the political sphere regarding online pornography and its societal repercussions. Additionally, they play a crucial role in providing emotional support and guidance to minors who may be affected by exposure to such content. On the other hand, healthcare professionals can contribute through research and the development of prevention programs, as reflected in the *Guía para familias: adolescentes y uso de pornografía* (*Guide for families: adolescents and pornography use*), elaborated by experts in psychology and psychiatry (Testa et al., 2023b).

Stakeholders Establishing a Support Network Comprising Trained Professionals and Well-Informed Parents

It is advisable to provide continuous training for education and health professionals to keep them abreast of the online challenges confronting adolescents, enhancing their understanding of sexual misinformation and the associated risks linked to pornography consumption in this demographic. Furthermore, the implementation of parental guidance programs is suggested, emphasizing the significance of open communication regarding sexuality and secure utilization of the Internet (Davis et al., 2019). The active engagement of these stakeholder groups will not only complement governmental initiatives, but also contribute to the establishment of a supportive and nurturing environment.

In the realm of teacher training aimed at addressing students' access to and consumption of pornography, it is essential to highlight notable global initiatives. For instance, the Government of the Basque Country (Euskadi, 2024) has taken the lead in implementing a comprehensive initiative. This initiative aimed to equip educators with strategies and resources in this area. Similarly, civil organizations such as *Personal, social, health and economic* in the United Kingdom (PSHE, 2024) offer tailored educational programs to guide teachers on the effects and risks of accessing online pornography. According to Planting-Bergloo and Arvola-Orlander (2022), such training not only cultivates safer and healthier school environments, but also fosters open and constructive dialogue between teachers and students. This dialogue can help alleviate the stigma and shame typically associated with this topic.

FUTURE RESEARCH DIRECTIONS

Regarding future research directions, Davis et al. (2019) underscored the importance of exploring the influence of parenting styles, parents' experiences with pornography, and intrafamily dynamics on how parents address the topic of pornography with their children. Meanwhile, Testa et al. (2023a) advocate evidence-based research on adolescents to develop, adapt, and evaluate interventions specifically designed to address Problematic Pornography Use (PPU). They also emphasized the need to advance preventive research to mitigate the potential negative consequences stemming from pornography consumption among the adolescent population. In this context, Maheux et al. (2021) proposed establishing a unified definition and standard measure of pornography for adolescent participants, distinguishing between intentional and unintentional consumption of pornography in the digital environment, and understanding the mechanisms linking pornography consumption to concerns related to body and intimacy.

Thurman and Obster (2021), while not explicitly proposing future research directions in their work, suggest potential areas of focus based on the findings and gaps identified in the literature. They consider that potential research could revolve around: (a) Longitudinal studies to monitor changes in pornography consumption; (b) Investigations into the effectiveness of different regulatory approaches and technologies to limit minors' access to online pornography; and (c) Analyses of the role of peer influence and social networks in the exposure and consumption of pornography by adolescents. Additionally, Pau and Kirtava (2023) argued that this effort should continually address the constantly evolving nature of Internet addiction and problematic Internet use. They also emphasize the need for nationwide and international awareness campaigns, supported by comprehensive research to assess the impact of various approaches, considering different political and moral stances.

Ultimately, it would be pertinent to continue exploring the intersection between sexual education and MIL while also evaluating the effectiveness of programs or projects implemented within this framework. Additionally, researching the level of Media Literacy among adolescents in relation to pornography consumption and investigating how it can be enhanced to promote safer and more conscious navigation could be valuable areas of study. Finally, delving into the inclusion and effectiveness of sexual education and digital well-being in the school curriculum, identifying best practices, and identifying areas for improvement to comprehensively address the topic would be worthwhile.

REFERENCES

Advocates for Youth. (2024). *Rights, Respect, Responsibility: A K-12 curriculum*. 3Rs. https://bitly.ws/3eIfA

Alario-Gavilán, M. (2021). ¿Por qué tantos hombres se excitan sexualmente ejerciendo violencia? La invisibilización y la erotización de la violencia sexual contra las mujeres en la pornografía [Why do so many men become sexually aroused by violence? The invisibilisation and eroticisation of sexual violence against women in pornography]. *Atlánticas. Revista Internacional de Estudios Feministas*, 6(1), 190–218. doi:10.17979/arief.2021.6.1.7164

Alexandraki, K., Stavropoulos, V., Burleigh, T. L., King, D. L., & Griffiths, M. D. (2018). Internet pornography viewing preference as a risk factor for adolescent Internet addiction: The moderating role of classroom personality factors. *Journal of Behavioral Addictions*, *7*(2), 423–432. doi:10.1556/2006.7.2018.34 PMID:29788747

Alilunas, P., Khan, U., Marks, L. H., Waugh, T., & Chittick, K. (2021). Porn and/as pedagogy, sexual representation in the classroom: A curated roundtable discussion. *Synoptique*, *9*(2), 269–294. https://bitly.ws/3aqwa

Attwood, F., Smith, C., & Barker, M. (2018). 'I'm just curious and still exploring myself': Young people and pornography. *New Media & Society*, *20*(10), 3738–3759. doi:10.1177/1461444818759271

Barbero-Reyes, M. (2023). *Ni zorras, ni héroes. Guía para trabajar el consumo de pornografía en menores* [*Neither bitches nor heroes. A guide to working on the consumption of pornography by minors*]. Diputación de Granada. https://bitly.ws/3eIf9

Bernstein, S., Warburton, W., Bussey, K., & Sweller, N. (2022). Mind the gap: Internet pornography exposure, influence and problematic viewing amongst emerging adults. *Sexuality Research & Social Policy*, *20*(2), 599–613. doi:10.1007/s13178-022-00698-8

Beyens, I., Vandenbosch, L., & Eggermont, S. (2015). Early adolescent boys' exposure to Internet pornography: Relationships to pubertal timing, sensation seeking, and academic performance. *The Journal of Early Adolescence*, *35*(8), 1045–1068. doi:10.1177/0272431614548069

Byron, P., McKee, A., Watson, A., Litsou, K., & Ingham, R. (2021). Reading for realness: Porn literacies, digital media, and young people. *Sexuality & Culture*, *25*(3), 786–805. doi:10.1007/s12119-020-09794-6

Calvo-González, S. (2014). *Unidad didáctica de apoyo al programa de educación afectivo-sexual en la ESO. Ni ogros ni princesas. Identidades digitales* [*Didactic unit to support the affective-sexual education programme in ESO. Neither ogres nor princesses. Digital identities*]. Consejería de la Presidencia/Instituto Asturiano de la Mujer y Políticas de Juventud. https://bitly.ws/3eIcQ

Calvo-González, S. (2015). "Educación sexual mediática". Incorporando la alfabetización mediática crítica en un programa de educación sexual para educación secundaria obligatoria ["Media Sexuality Education. Incorporating critical media literacy in a sexuality education programme for compulsory secondary education]. *Revista de Estudios para el Desarrollo Social de la Comunicación*, *12*, 194–221. doi:10.15213/redes.n12.p194

Canh, L., M. Lucas., Cortelletti, F., & Valeriano, C. (2020). *Educación sexual integral. Guía básica para trabajar en la escuela y en la familia* [*Comprehensive sexual education: A basic guide for working in schools and families*]. Siglo XXI Editores.

Cerbara, L., Ciancimino, G., Corsetti, G., & Tintori, A. (2023). The (Un)equal effect of binary socialisation on adolescents' exposure to pornography: Girls' empowerment and boys' sexism from a new Representative National Survey. *Societies (Basel, Switzerland)*, *13*(6), 146. doi:10.3390/soc13060146

Charig, R., Moghaddam, N. G., Dawson, D. L., Merdian, H. L., & das Nair, R. (2020). A lack of association between online pornography exposure, sexual functioning, and mental well-being. *Sexual and Relationship Therapy*, *35*(2), 258–281. doi:10.1080/14681994.2020.1727874

Childnet International. (2018). *Myth vs Reality. A practical PSHE toolkit for educators to explore online pressures and perceived "norms"*. Childnet International/UK Safer Internet Centre. https://bitly.ws/3eIdz

Cowan, G., & Campbell, R. R. (1994). Racism and sexism in interracial pornography: A content analysis. *Psychology of Women Quarterly, 18*(3), 323–338. doi:10.1111/j.1471-6402.1994.tb00459.x

Cui, Z., Mo, M., Chen, Q., Wang, X., Yang, H., Zhou, N., Sun, L., Liu, J., Ao, L., & Cao, J. (2021). Pornography use could lead to addiction and was associated with reproductive hormone levels and semen quality: A report from the MARHCS study in China. *Frontiers in Endocrinology, 12*, 736384. doi:10.3389/fendo.2021.736384 PMID:34566897

Davis, A. C., Wright, C., Curtis, M., Hellard, M. E., Lim, M. S. C., & Temple-Smith, M. J. (2019). 'Not my child': Parenting, pornography, and views on education. *Journal of Family Studies, 27*(4), 573–588. doi:10.1080/13229400.2019.1657929

Davis, A. C., Wright, C. J., Murphy, S., Dietze, P., Temple-Smith, M. J., Hellard, M. E., & Lim, M. S. (2020). A digital pornography literacy resource co-designed with vulnerable young people: Development of "The Gist". *Journal of Medical Internet Research, 22*(6), e15964. doi:10.2196/15964 PMID:32348268

de-Miguel-Álvarez, A. (2020). On pornography and sexual education: Can "sex" legitimate humiliation and violence? *Gaceta Sanitaria, 35*(4), 379–382. doi:10.1016/j.gaceta.2020.01.001 PMID:32173052

Dudek, D., Woodley, G., & Green, L. (2022). 'Own your narrative': Teenagers as producers and consumers of porn in Netflix's Sex Education. *Information Communication and Society, 25*(4), 502–515. doi:10.1080/1369118X.2021.1988130

Emakunde. (2023). *El porno es una escuela de violencia contra las mujeres - tema* [*The porn industry as a achool of violence against women - topic*]. Emakunde. https://bitly.ws/3aqCU

Euskadi. (2024). *Educación apoya a docentes para erradicar las consecuencias del consumo de la pornografía entre jóvenes* [*Education supports teachers to eradicate the consequences of pornography consumption among youth*]. Euskadi.eus. https://bitly.ws/3eIkK

Fasih-Ramandi, M. (2019). Ethical and legal considerations in dealing with adolescents' exposure to cyber pornography. *Bioethics Journal, 9*(34), 81–93. https://acortar.link/yti835

Frangos, C. C., Frangos, C. C., & Sotiropoulos, I. (2011). Problematic Internet use among Greek university students: An ordinal logistic regression with risk factors of negative psychological beliefs, pornographic sites, and online games. *Cyberpsychology, Behavior, and Social Networking, 14*(1-2), 51–58. doi:10.1089/cyber.2009.0306 PMID:21329443

Fritz, N., Malic, V., Paul, B., & Zhou, Y. (2021). Worse than objects: The depiction of black women and men and their sexual relationship in pornography. *Gender Issues, 38*(1), 100–120. doi:10.1007/s12147-020-09255-2

Gámez-Guadix, M., Mateos-Pérez, E., Wachs, S., Wright, M., Martínez, J., & Íncera, D. (2022). Assessing image-based sexual abuse: Measurement, prevalence, and temporal stability of sextortion and nonconsensual sexting ("revenge porn") among adolescents. *Journal of Adolescence, 94*(5), 789–799. doi:10.1002/jad.12064 PMID:35719041

García-Rojas, A., & Salcines-Talledo, I. (2023). Pornografía y sexualidad [Pornography and sexuality]. In A. D. García-Rojas, I. Salcines-Talledo, N. González-Fernández, A. Ramírez-García & M. P. Gutiérrez-Arenas (Coords.), *Guías educomunicativas para familias. Educación afectiva y sexual en familia* [*Educational-communicative guides for families. Affective and sexual education in the family*] (pp. 30–31). Grupo Comunicar Ediciones. https://bitly.ws/3eBaV

Gesser-Edelsburg, A., & Elhadi-Arabia, M. A. (2018). Discourse on exposure to pornography content online between Arab adolescents and parents: Qualitative study on its impact on sexual education and behavior. *Journal of Medical Internet Research*, *20*(10), e11667. doi:10.2196/11667 PMID:30305264

Goh, P. H., Phuah, L. A., & Low, Y. H. (2023). Pornography consumption and sexual health among emerging adults from Malaysia: An observational study. *Sexual Health*, *20*(2), 134–147. doi:10.1071/SH22181 PMID:36848630

Goldsmith, K., Dunkley, C. R., Dang, S. S., & Gorzalka, B. B. (2017). Pornography consumption and its association with sexual concerns and expectations among young men and women. *The Canadian Journal of Human Sexuality*, *26*(2), 1–12. doi:10.3138/cjhs.262-a2

Herbitter, C., Norris, A. L., Nelson, K. M., & Orchowski, L. M. (2022). Understanding associations between exposure to violent pornography and teen dating violence among female sexual minority High School students. *Journal of Interpersonal Violence*, *37*(17-18), NP17023–NP17035. doi:10.1177/08862605211028314 PMID:34215165

Hyden, H. (2023). Pornography. The politics of legal changes. An opinion article. *Frontiers in Sociology*, *8*, 1250012. doi:10.3389/fsoc.2023.1250012 PMID:38089013

Idoiaga-Mondragon, N., Eiguren-Munitis, A., Ozamiz-Etxebarria, N., & Alonso-Saez, I. (2024). Let us educate on pornography: Young education students' representations of pornography. *Sexuality Research & Social Policy*. doi:10.1007/s13178-023-00930-z

Jhe, G. B., Addison, J., Lin, J., & Pluhar, E. (2023). Pornography use among adolescents and the role of primary care. *Family Medicine and Community Health*, *11*(1), e001776. doi:10.1136/fmch-2022-001776 PMID:36650009

Keen, C., Kramer, R., & France, A. (2020). The pornographic state: The changing nature of state regulation in addressing illegal and harmful online content. *Media Culture & Society*, *42*(7), 1175–1192. doi:10.1177/0163443720904631

Levin, D. S., & Hammock, A. C. (2020). School context and content in Canadian sex education. *The Canadian Journal of Human Sexuality*, *29*(3), 323–338. doi:10.3138/cjhs.2019-0046

Li, L., Wang, X., Tang, S., & Wang, J. (2023). Family functioning and problematic internet pornography use among adolescents: A moderated mediation model. *Frontiers in Public Health*, *11*, 1199835. doi:10.3389/fpubh.2023.1199835 PMID:37397734

Liang, B., & Lu, H. (2012). Fighting the obscene, pornographic, and unhealthy – an analysis of the nature, extent, and regulation of China's online pornography within a global context. *Crime, Law, and Social Change*, *58*(2), 111–130. doi:10.1007/s10611-012-9380-3

Löfgren-Mårtenson, L., & Månsson, S. A. (2010). Lust, love, and life: A qualitative study of Swedish adolescents' perceptions and experiences with pornography. *Journal of Sex Research*, *47*(6), 568–579. doi:10.1080/00224490903151374 PMID:19731132

López-Pacheco, J. A. (2021). The (re)emergence of the discourse of 'gender ideology' in Latin America: Protests, public attention, and government responses. *Estudios Politicos*, *60*, 145–177. doi:10.17533/udea.espo.n60a07

Macilotti, G. (2020). Online child pornography: Conceptual issues and law enforcement challenges. In A. Balloni & R. Sette (Eds.), *Handbook of research on trends and issues in crime prevention, rehabilitation, and victim support* (pp. 226–247). IGI Global. doi:10.4018/978-1-7998-1286-9.ch013

Maddocks, S. (2022). Feminism, activism and non-consensual pornography: Analyzing efforts to end "revenge porn" in the United States. *Feminist Media Studies*, *22*(7), 1641–1656. doi:10.1080/14680777.2021.1913434

Maheux, A. J., Roberts, S. R., Evans, R., Widman, L., & Choukas-Bradley, S. (2021). Associations between adolescents' pornography consumption and self-objectification, body consumption, and body shame. *Body Image*, *37*, 89–93. doi:10.1016/j.bodyim.2021.01.014 PMID:33582530

Martellozzo, E., Monaghan, A., & Adler, J. (2020). Researching the affects that online pornography has on UK adolescents aged 11 to 16. *SAGE Open*, *10*(1), 1–11. doi:10.1177/2158244019899462

Martin-Hald, G., & Malamuth, N. M. (2008). Self-perceived effects of pornography consumption. *Archives of Sexual Behavior*, *37*(4), 614–625. doi:10.1007/s10508-007-9212-1 PMID:17851749

McCormack, M., & Wignall, L. (2024). Pornography, social media, and sexuality. In *Handbook of social media use online. Relationships, security, privacy, and society* (pp. 309–329). Academic Press., doi:10.1016/B978-0-443-28804-3.00011-9

MediaSmarts. (2024). *Use, understand & engage: A digital media literacy framework for Canadian schools*. MediaSmarts. https://bitly.ws/3eBiN

Meilani, N., Hariadi, S. S., & Haryadi, F. T. (2023). Social media and pornography access behavior among adolescents. *International Journal of Public Health Science*, *12*(2), 536–544. doi:10.11591/ijphs.v12i2.22513

Meilani, N., Setiyawati, N., & Onyapidi-Barasa, S. (2020). Factors related pornographic access behaviour among high school students in Yogyakarta, Indonesia. *Malaysian Journal of Public Health Medicine*, *20*(2), 123–130. doi:10.37268/mjphm/vol.20/no.2/art.801

Ministerio de Educación. (2021). *Oportunidades curriculares de educación integral en sexualidad [Curricular opportunities for comprehensive sexuality education]*. Minedu/UNFPA. https://bitly.ws/3a8nJ

Navas-Garcés, A. E., & Nuñez-Ruiz, J. (2021). La violencia digital en México - Ley Olimpia [Digital violence in Mexico - Olympia law]. *Criminalia*, *87*, 709–724. https://bitly.ws/3a8gX

Pappas, S. (2021). Teaching porn literacy. *American Psychological Association*, *52*(2), 54. https://acortar.link/KcA0xI

Pau, L. F., & Kirtava, Z. (2023). International survey & analysis of laws and regulations addressing internet addiction and/or problematic usage of the internet. *World Journal of Public Health, 8*(1), 8–14. doi:10.11648/j.wjph.20230801.12

Pawlikowska, A., Szuster, E., Kostrzewska, P., Mandera, A., Biernikiewicz, M., Sobieszczanska, M., Rozek-Piechura, K., Markiewicz, M., Rusiecka, A., & Kalka, D. (2022). Internet addiction and Polish women's sexual functioning: The role of social media, online pornography, and game use during the COVID-19 pandemic - Online surveys based on FSFI and BSMAS questionnaires. *International Journal of Environmental Research and Public Health, 13*(13), 8193. doi:10.3390/ijerph19138193 PMID:35805852

Pekal, J., Laier, C., Snagowski, J., Stark, R., & Brand, M. (2018). Tendencies toward Internet-pornography-use disorder: Differences in men and women regarding attentional biases to pornographic stimuli. *Journal of Behavioral Addictions, 7*(3), 574–583. doi:10.1556/2006.7.2018.70 PMID:30203692

Planting-Bergloo, S., & Arvola Orlander, A. (2022). Challenging 'the elephant in the room': The becomings of pornography education in Swedish secondary school. *Sex Education, 24*(1), 16–30. doi:10.1080/14681811.2022.2137487

Prichard, J., Spiranovic, C., Watters, P., & Lueg, C. (2013). Young people, child pornography, and subcultural norms on the Internet. *Journal of the American Society for Information Science and Technology, 64*(5), 992–1000. doi:10.1002/asi.22816

Principi, N., Magnoni, P., Grimoldi, L., Carnevali, D., Cavazzana, L., & Pellai, A. (2022). Consumption of sexually explicit internet material and its effects on minors' health: Latest evidence from the literature. *Minerva Pediatrics, 74*(3), 332–339. doi:10.23736/S2724-5276.19.05367-2 PMID:30761817

PSHE. (2024). *Addressing pornography through PSHE*. PSHE Association. https://bitly.ws/3eIkU

Raine, G., Khouja, C., Scott, R., Wright, K., & Sowden, A. J. (2020). Pornography use and sexting amongst children and young people: A systematic overview of reviewers. *Systematic Reviews, 9*(283), 283. Advance online publication. doi:10.1186/s13643-020-01541-0 PMID:33280603

Revelo-Morejón, M. A. (2016). *Efecto del uso frecuente de pornografía en la expectativa del acto sexual de usuarios masculinos* [Effect of frequent use of pornography on the sexual act expectancy of male users] [PhD thesis, Universidad San Francisco de Quito]. https://bit.ly/3uYscMh

Rivera, R., Santos-Velasco, D., Cabrera-García, V., & Docal-Millán, M.-C. (2016). Online and offline pornography consumption in Colombian adolescents. *Comunicar, 24*(46), 37–45. doi:10.3916/C46-2016-04

Rodríguez-Castro, Y., Martínez-Román, R., Alonso-Ruido, P., Adá-Lameiras, A., & Carrera-Fernández, M. V. (2021). Intimate partner cyberstalking, sexism, pornography, and sexting in adolescents: New challenges for sex education. *International Journal of Environmental Research and Public Health, 18*(4), 2181. doi:10.3390/ijerph18042181 PMID:33672240

Román-García, O., Bacigalupe, A., & Vaamonde Garcia, C. (2022). Relación de la pornografía mainstream con la salud sexual y reproductiva de los/las adolescentes. Una revisión de alcance [Relationship of mainstream pornography to adolescent sexual and reproductive health. A scoping review]. *Revista Española de Salud Pública, 95*, e202108102. https://bit.ly/48GZeOP PMID:34267175

Rothman, E., Daley, N., & Alder, J. (2020). A pornography literacy program for adolescents. *American Journal of Public Health, 110*(2), 154–156. doi:10.2105/AJPH.2019.305468 PMID:31855489

Rothman, E. F., Paruk, J., Espensen, A., Temple, J. R., & Adams, K. (2017). A qualitative study of what us parents say and do when their young children see pornography. *Academic Pediatrics, 17*(8), 844–849. doi:10.1016/j.acap.2017.04.014 PMID:28450081

Sanders, T., Trueman, G., & Keighley, R. (2023). Non-consensual sharing of images: Commercial content creators, sexual content creation platforms and the lack of protection. *New Media & Society*. doi:10.1177/14614448231172711

Scull, T., Malik, C., Morrison, A., & Keefe, E. (2021). Promoting sexual health in high school: A feasibility study of a web-based media literacy education program. *Journal of Health Communication, 26*(3), 147–160. doi:10.1080/10810730.2021.1893868 PMID:33779520

Segato, R. (2003). Las estructura de género y el mandato de violación. [The gender structure and the mandate of rape] In R. Segato (Ed.), *Las estructuras elementales de la violencia. Ensayos sobre género entre la antropología, el psicoanálisis y los derechos humanos* [*The elementary structures of violence. Essays on gender between anthropology, psychoanalysis, and human rights*]. (pp. 21–55). Universidad Nacional de Quilmes.

SFUSD. (2017). *Be real. Be ready.* SFUSD. https://bitly.ws/3eC25

Sharma, N., & Bleich, E. (2019). Freedom of expression, public morals, and sexually explicit speech in the European court of human rights. *Constitutional Studies, 5*, 55. https://acortar.link/DFOfzn

Sharpe, M., & Mead, D. (2021). Problematic pornography use: Legal and health policy considerations. *Current Addiction Reports, 8*(4), 556–567. doi:10.1007/s40429-021-00390-8 PMID:34518793

Shek, D. T., & Ma, C. M. (2012). Consumption of pornographic materials among Hong Kong early adolescents: A replication. *TheScientificWorldJournal, 406063*, 1–8. doi:10.1100/2012/406063 PMID:22778698

Shor, E., & Golriz, G. (2019). Gender, race, and aggression in mainstream pornography. *Archives of Sexual Behavior, 48*(3), 739–751. doi:10.1007/s10508-018-1304-6 PMID:30187150

Sommet, N., & Berent, J. (2022). Porn use and men's and women's sexual performance: Evidence from a large longitudinal sample. *Psychological Medicine, 53*(7), 3105–3114. doi:10.1017/S003329172100516X PMID:35135634

Svedin, C. G., Donevan, M., Bladh, M., Priebe, G., Fredlund, C., & Jonsson, L. S. (2023). Associations between adolescents watching pornography and poor mental health in three Swedish surveys. *European Child & Adolescent Psychiatry, 32*(9), 1765–1780. doi:10.1007/s00787-022-01992-x PMID:35524827

Testa, G., Mestre-Bach, G., Chiclana-Actis, C., & Potenza, M. N. (2023a). Problematic pornography use in adolescents: From prevention to intervention. *Current Addiction Reports, 10*(2), 210–218. doi:10.1007/s40429-023-00469-4

Testa, G., Villena, A., Mestre, G., & Chiclana, C. (2023b). *Guía para familias. Adolescentes y uso de pornografía* [*A guide for families. Adolescents and pornography use*]. UNIR/Dale la Vuelta/ Colegio Oficial de la Psicología de Madrid. https://bitly.ws/3eIka

Thurman, N., Nalmpatian, A., & Obster, F. (2022). Lessons from France on the regulation of Internet pornography: How displacement effects, circumvention, and legislative scope may limit the efficacy of Article 23. *Policy and Internet, 14*(3), 690–710. doi:10.1002/poi3.293

Thurman, N., & Obster, F. (2021). The regulation of internet pornography: What a survey of under-18s tells us about the necessity for and potential efficacy of emerging legislative approaches. *Policy and Internet, 13*(3), 415–432. doi:10.1002/poi3.250

Vahedi, Z., Sibalis, A., & Sutherland, J. E. (2018). Are media literacy interventions effective at changing attitudes and intentions towards risky health behaviors in adolescents? A meta-analytic review. *Journal of Adolescence, 67*(1), 140–152. doi:10.1016/j.adolescence.2018.06.007 PMID:29957493

Vangeel, L., Eggermont, S., & Vandenbosch, L. (2020). Does adolescent media use predict sexual stereotypes in adolescence and emerging adulthood? Associations with music television and online pornography exposure. *Archives of Sexual Behavior, 49*(4), 1147–1161. doi:10.1007/s10508-020-01677-z PMID:32180100

Vertongen, R., van Ommen, C., & Chamberlain, K. (2022). Adolescent dilemmas about viewing pornography and their efforts to resolve them. *Journal of Adolescent Research*. Advance online publication. doi:10.1177/07435584221133307

Voicu, S. N., & Crăciun, I. (2023). Preventive online safety education for teenagers. *International Journal of Legal and Social Order, 3*(1). doi:10.55516/ijlso.v3i1.165

Willis, M., Bridges, A. J., & Sun, C. (2022). Pornography use, gender, and sexual objectification: A multinational study. *Sexuality & Culture, 26*(4), 1298–1313. doi:10.1007/s12119-022-09943-z

Wright, P. J., & Herbenick, D. (2022). Pornography and relational satisfaction: Exploring potential boundary conditions. *Archives of Sexual Behavior, 51*(8), 3839–3846. doi:10.1007/s10508-022-02406-4 PMID:36042069

Yar, M. (2020). Protecting children from internet pornography? A critical assessment of statutory age verification and its enforcement in the UK. *Policing, 43*(1), 183–197. doi:10.1108/PIJPSM-07-2019-0108

Yunengsih, W., & Setiawan, A. (2021). Contribution of pornographic exposure and addiction to risky sexual behavior in adolescents. *Journal of public health research, 10*(s1), jphr.2021.2333. doi:10.4081/jphr.2021.2333

ADDITIONAL READING

Ballester-Arnal, R., García-Barba, M., Castro-Calvo, J., Giménez-García, C., & Gil-Llario, M. D. (2022). Pornography consumption in people of different age groups: An analysis based on gender, contents, and consequences. *Sexuality Research & Social Policy, 20*(2), 766–779. doi:10.1007/s13178-022-00720-z

Behun, R., & Owens, E. W. (2019). *Youth and internet pornography: The impact and influence on adolescent development (Adolescence and society)*. Routledge. doi:10.4324/9780429423147

Butler, J. (2000). The force of fantasy: Feminism, mapplethorpe, and discursive excess. In D. Cornell (Ed.), *Feminism and Pornography* (pp. 487–508). Academic. doi:10.1093/oso/9780198782506.003.0027

Pathmendra, P., Raggatt, M., Lim, M. S., Marino, J. L., & Skinner, S. R. (2023). Exposure to pornography and adolescent sexual behavior: Systematic review. *Journal of Medical Internet Research*, 25, e43116. doi:10.2196/43116 PMID:36853749

Save the Children. (2020). *(Des)información sexual: Pornografía y adolescencia* [*Sexual (mis)information: Pornography and adolescence*]. Save the Children España.

Waltman, M. (2021). *Pornography: The politics of legal challenges*. Oxford University Press. doi:10.1093/oso/9780197598535.001.0001

KEY TERMS AND DEFINITIONS

Age Verification: Mechanism to confirm that a person attempting to access certain online content, such as pornography, meets the required minimum age.

Comprehensive Sexual Education: Educational approach that addresses various aspects of human sexuality, promoting knowledge and skills for making informed and healthy decisions throughout life.

Explicit Content: Visual, auditory, or textual material that clearly and directly presents content of a sexual or graphic nature.

Freedom of Expression: The fundamental right allowing individuals to articulate their thoughts, ideas, and opinions without censorship or restraint, fostering open communication and the exchange of diverse perspectives in democratic societies.

Gender Stereotypes: Preconceived and simplified beliefs or ideas attributing specific roles, behaviors, and characteristics to individuals based on their gender.

Individual Variability: Recognition of individual differences among adolescents as key factors in the relationship between pornography and sexual attitudes.

Media and Information Literacy (MIL): Skill to analyze, interpret, and produce media messages, empowering individuals to effectively and critically navigate the diverse media landscape.

Mental Health: The overall well-being of an individual's cognitive and emotional state, encompassing factors such as psychological resilience, emotional balance, and the ability to cope with life's challenges.

Normalization Effect: Process by which repeated exposure to certain stimuli, such as explicit content, leads individuals to perceive and accept those stimuli as typical or socially acceptable.

Sexual Misinformation: Circulation of inaccurate, misleading, or false information related to sexual topics. This may include misunderstandings regarding anatomy, reproduction, and safe sexual practices, among other aspects.

Compilation of References

Achiebe, C. (1999). *Things fall apart*. AWS.

Acosta Buralli, K., & Cevasco, J. (2022a,19-21 July). *The role of causal connectivity and note-taking condition in the comprehension of spoken and written discourse about the importance of comprehensive Sex Education by Argentine college students*. [Conference]. 32nd Annual Meeting of the Society for Text and Discourse. Society for text and discourse.

Acosta Buralli, K., Pispira, J., Cevasco, J., & Silva, M. L. (2023). Development of psychoeducational materials on integral sexual education and prevention of gender violence based on evidence. *Salud, Ciencia y Tecnología - Serie de Conferencias, 2*, 124. https://doi.org/ doi:10.56294/sctconf2023124

Acosta Buralli, K., & Cevasco, J. (2022b). Educación sexual integral en la formación de docentes de educación física en Argentina y México [Comprehensive Sexual Education in the training of Physical Education teachers in Argentina and Mexico]. *Lecturas Educación Física y Deportes, 27*(288), 2–15. doi:10.46642/efd.v27i288.3386

Adams, A., Lea, S. G., & D'Silva, E. M. (2021). Digital technologies and interventions against gender-based violence in rural areas. *International Criminal Justice Review, 31*(4), 438–455. doi:10.1177/10575677211040413

Advocates for Youth. (2024). *Rights, Respect, Responsibility: A K-12 curriculum*. 3Rs. https://bitly.ws/3eIfA

Agnew, E. (2021). Sexting among young people: Towards a gender sensitive approach. *International Journal of Children's Rights, 29*(1), 3–30. doi:10.1163/15718182-28040010

Aguzie, D. O., & Umunakwe, B. O. (2019). The contributions of philosophy in sustaining education in Nigeria. *Multidisciplinary Journal of Social Science Education*, 114–124. (Maiden edition).

Aguzie, D. O., Umunakwe, O. B., & Akaire, C. B. (2019). Aristotle's philosophy of gender inequality: Its implications for transformative leadership practices in the Nigerian politics. *Interdisciplinary Journal of Gender and Women Development Studies, 3*(1), 138–153.

Ahmed, N., Flisher, A., Mathews, C., Jansen, S., Mukoma, W., & Schaalma, H. P. (2006). Process evaluation of the teacher training for an AIDS prevention programme. *Health Education Research, 21*(5), 621–632. doi:10.1093/her/cyl031 PMID:16740671

Aizcorbe, G. M., & Gallo, M. N. (2023). La psicoeducación como una tecnología educativa [Psychoeducation as an educational technology]. *Innova Educa, 3*(3), 79–92.

Ajzen, I., & Fishbein, M. (2005). The Influence of Attitudes on Behavior. In D. Albarracín, B. T. Johnson, & M. P. Zanna (Eds.), *The Handbook of Attitudes* (pp. 173–222). Lawrence Erlbaum Associates, Inc.

Akers, R. (2017). *Social Learning and Social Structure: A general theory of crime and deviance*. Tranaction Publishers. doi:10.4324/9781315129587

Al Areqi, R. (2016). Hybridity/hybridization from postcolonial and Islamic perspectives. *Research Journal of English Language and Literature, 5*(1), 53–61. https://bit.ly/3BQdY10

Alario-Gavilán, M. (2021). ¿Por qué tantos hombres se excitan sexualmente ejerciendo violencia? La invisibilización y la erotización de la violencia sexual contra las mujeres en la pornografía [Why do so many men become sexually aroused by violence? The invisibilisation and eroticisation of sexual violence against women in pornography]. *Atlánticas. Revista Internacional de Estudios Feministas, 6*(1), 190–218. doi:10.17979/arief.2021.6.1.7164

Albulescu, I. (2018). The historical method in educational research. [AJHSSR]. *American Journal of Humanities and Social Sciences Research, 2*(8), 185–190.

Alessi, D., Barrena, M. A., & Ronconi, M. F. (2023). Desafíos políticos y pedagógicos en torno a la ESI [Political and pedagogical challenges around CSE]. In A. Peláez, M. Incháurregui, & M. Severino (Eds.), Escribir la ESI: saberes, debates y desafíos desde experiencias docentes [Writing the ESI: knowledge, debates and challenges from teaching experiences]. Editorial de la Universidad Nacional de La Plata (EDULP).

Alexander, R. (2020). *A dialogic teaching companion*. Routledge. doi:10.4324/9781351040143

Alexandraki, K., Stavropoulos, V., Burleigh, T. L., King, D. L., & Griffiths, M. D. (2018). Internet pornography viewing preference as a risk factor for adolescent Internet addiction: The moderating role of classroom personality factors. *Journal of Behavioral Addictions, 7*(2), 423–432. doi:10.1556/2006.7.2018.34 PMID:29788747

Alexopoulos, C., Stamou, A. G., & Papadopoulou, P. (2022). Gender representations in the Greek primary school language textbooks: Synthesizing content with critical discourse analysis. [IJonSES]. *International Journal on Social and Education Sciences, 4*(2), 257–274. doi:10.46328/ijonses.317

Al-Faham, H., Davis, A. M., & Ernst, R. (2019). Intersectionality: From Theory to Practice. *Annual Review of Law and Social Science, 15*(1), 247–265. doi:10.1146/annurev-lawsocsci-101518-042942

Alilunas, P., Khan, U., Marks, L. H., Waugh, T., & Chittick, K. (2021). Porn and/as pedagogy, sexual representation in the classroom: A curated roundtable discussion. *Synoptique, 9*(2), 269–294. https://bitly.ws/3aqwa

Almeida, L. (2003). As Meninas Más na Literatura de Margaret Atwood e Lucía Etxebarría. *Espéculo: Revista de Estudios Literarios, 25*.

Alnajjar, E. A. M. (2021). The impact of a proposed science informal curriculum on students' achievement and attitudes during the Covid-19. *International Journal of Early Childhood Special Education (INT-JECSE), 13*(2), 882–896. doi:10.9756/INT-JECSE/V13I2.211131

Alsawalqa, R. O., & Alrawashdeh, M. N. (2022). The role of patriarchal structure and gender stereotypes in cyber dating abuse: A qualitative examination of male perpetrators experiences. *The British Journal of Sociology, 73*(3), 587–606. doi:10.1111/1468-4446.12946 PMID:35644007

Álvarez, E. (2019). ¿Qué saben los maestros de primaria sobre educación sexual? Procesos de formación docente en torno a la educación sexual y la sexualidad: Estudio de casos. Área Temática 08. Procesos de Formación, COMIE. 1–10. https://www.comie.org.mx/congreso/memoriaelectronica/v15/doc/0661.pdf

Álvarez, J. L., & Jurgenson, G. (2011). Travestismo, transexualidad y transgénero. *Revista De Estudios De Antropología Sexual, 1*(3), 55–67. https://revistas.inah.gob.mx/index.php/antropologiasexual/article/view/573

Álvarez-Suárez, L. (2020). Patologización e invisibilización de la identidad de género en España: ¿Qué debemos aprender de la legislación argentina? [Pathologization and invisibilization of gender identity in Spain: What should we learn from the Argentinean legislation?]. *Opinión Jurídica [Legal Opinion], 19*(39), 85–109. https://bit.ly/3tGDKTG

Compilation of References

Ameigeiras, A. R. (2006). El abordaje etnográfico en la investigación social [The ethnographic approach in social research]. In I. Vasilachis de Gialdino (coord.), Estrategias de investigación cualitativa [Qualitative research strategies] (pp. 107-151). Gedisa.

Ammaturo, A., & Cevasco, J. (2023). The Role of the Establishment of Causal Connections and Elaboration Question Answering Tasks in the Comprehension of Spontaneous Narrative Discourse by Argentine College Students. *Reading Psychology*, *45*(2), 1–22. doi:10.1080/02702711.2023.2276453

Amnesty International. (2017). *What is online violence and abuse against women?* Amnesty International. https://www.amnesty.org/en/latest/campaigns/2017/11/what-is-online-violence-and-abuse-against-women/

Andujar, N. (January, 2024). *Los musulmanes conversos blancos como puente hacia el asimilacionismo* [White convert Muslims as a bridge to assimilation]. https://bit.ly/42LriPN

Angrosino, M. V. (2015). Recontextualización de la observación. [Recontextualisation of the observation] In *N.K. Denzin & Y.S. Lincoln (coords.) Manual de investigación cualitativa. Volumen IV Métodos de recolección y análisis de datos [Handbook of qualitative research. Volume IV Methods of data collection and analysis]*. (pp. 203–234). Gedisa.

Arbeláez, M., & Onrubia, J. (2014). Análisis bibliométrico y de contenido. Dos metodologías complementarias para el análisis de la revista colombiana [Bibliometric and content analyses. Two complementary methodologies for the analysis of the Colombian journal Educación y Cultura] *Revista de Investigaciones UCM*, *14*(23), 14–31. doi:10.22383/ri.v14i1.5

Arcila-Calderón, C., Blanco-Herrero, D., & Valdez-Apolo, M. B. (2020). Rechazo y discurso de odio en Twitter: Análisis de contenido de los tuits sobre migrantes y refugiados en español [Rejection and hate speech on Twitter: Content analysis of tweets about migrants and refugees in Spanish]. *Revista Española de Investigaciones Sociológicas*, *172*(172), 21–40. doi:10.5477/cis/reis.172.21

Arday, J., & Mirza, H. S. (2018). *Dismantling race in higher education: racism, whiteness and decolonising the academy*. Palgrave Macmillan. doi:10.1007/978-3-319-60261-5

Arnau-Sabatés, L., & Montané-Capdevilla, J. (2010). Aportaciones sobre la relación conceptual entre actitud y competencia, desde la teoría del cambio de actitudes. *Electronic Journal of Research in Educational Psychology*, *8*(3), 1283–1302. doi:10.25115/ejrep.v8i22.1416

Arslan, H. (Ed.). (2018). *An introduction to education*. Cambridge Scholars Publishing.

Ascraft, A., & Murray, P. (2017). Talking to parents about adolescent sexuality. *National Centre for Biotechnology Information*, *64*(2), 305–320. PMID:28292447

Asher, K. (2017). Spivak and Rivera Cusicanqui on the Dilemmas of Representation in Postcolonial and Decolonial Feminisms. *Feminist Studies*, *43*(3), 512–524. doi:10.1353/fem.2017.0041

Asociación Marroquí. (2022). *Mujeres tras el velo* [Women behind the veil]. Asociación Marroquí. https://bit.ly/48v4B3o

Astle, S., Toews, G. L., Topham, L., & Vennum, A. (2022). To talk or not to talk: An analysis of parents' intentions to talk with children about different sexual topics using the theory of planned behaviour. *Sexuality Research & Social Policy*, *19*(2), 705–721. doi:10.1007/s13178-021-00587-6

Attwood, F., Smith, C., & Barker, M. (2018). 'I'm just curious and still exploring myself': Young people and pornography. *New Media & Society*, *20*(10), 3738–3759. doi:10.1177/1461444818759271

Awan, I. (2016). Islamophobia on social media: A qualitative analysis of Facebook's walls of hate. *International Journal of Cyber Criminology*, *10*(1), 1–20. doi:10.5281/zenodo.58517

Azhar, S. (2023). "Too weak to fight, too scared to scream": Understanding experiences of sexual coercion of Black female adolescents through digital storytelling. *Sexualities, 13634607231212841*, 13634607231212841. doi:10.1177/13634607231212841

Badriah, S., Tambuala, F., Herlinah, L., Mariani, D., Nurcahyani, L., & Setiawan, H. (2023). The effect of comprehensive sexual education on improving knowledge, attitudes, and skills in preventing premarital sexual behavior in adolescents. *KONTAKT-Journal of Nursing & Social Sciences related to Health & Illness, 25*(1), 50-56. doi:10.32725/kont.2023.004

Baiocco, R., Pistella, J., & Morelli, M. (2020). Coming Out to Parents in Lesbian and Bisexual Women: The Role of Internalized Sexual Stigma and Positive LB Identity. *Frontiers in Psychology, 11*, 1–11. doi:10.3389/fpsyg.2020.609885 PMID:33363501

Bajo-Pérez, I. (2022). Gender violence through Instagram: Descriptive study of women residing in Spain between 18 and 35 years old. *Sociología Y Tecnociencia, 12*(2), 271–283. doi:10.24197/st.2.2022.271-283

Bambú, T. (2019, March 27). El feminismo radical, un gran incomprendido. *Pikara Magazine*. https://www.pikaramagazine.com/2019/03/feminismo-radical-incomprendido/

Bamkin, S. (2020). The taught curriculum of moral education at Japanese elementary school: The role of classtime in the broad curriculum. *Contemporary Japan, 32*(2), 218–239. doi:10.1080/18692729.2020.1747780

Banz Liendo, C., & Valenzuela Schmidt, M. (2004). *La intervención psicoeducativa en la escuela y el rol del psicólogo educacional* [Psychoeducational intervention in school and the role of the educational psychologist]. Ediciones Universidad Diego Portales.

Barabás, A. & Bartolomé, M. (1999). Configuraciones Étnicas en Oaxaca. [Ethnic Configurations in Oaxaca]. Ethnographic Perspectives for Autonomies [Perspectivas Etnográficas para las Autonomías]. INAH, INI.

Barbero-Reyes, M. (2023). *Ni zorras, ni héroes. Guía para trabajar el consumo de pornografía en menores* [Neither bitches nor heroes. A guide to working on the consumption of pornography by minors]. Diputación de Granada. https://bitly.ws/3eIf9

Bárcenas Bautista, C. (2008). La mujer española y la deconstrucción del discurso misógino en Crónica del desamor, La función delta, y Te trataré como una reina de Rosa Montero. [Tesis Doctoral, University of Houston].

Barozzi, S., & Ruiz-Cecilia, R. (2020). Training in gender and sexual identities in EFL teaching. Participants' contributions. *Onomázein. Revista de Lingüística. Filología y Educación, 6*(6), 84–103. doi:10.7764/onomazein.ne6.05

Barragán, F., & Pérez-Jorge, D. (2020). Combating homophobia, lesbophobia, biphobia and transphobia: A liberating and subversive educational alternative for desires. *Heliyon, 6*(10), 1–14. doi:10.1016/j.heliyon.2020.e05225

Barrientos-Delgado, P., Montenegro, C., & Andrade, D. (2022). Perspectiva de Género en Prácticas Educativas del Profesorado en Formación: Una Aproximación Etnográfica. *Revista Internacional de Educación para la Justicia Social, 11*(1). doi:10.15366/riejs2022.11.1.013

Barriuso-Ortega, S., Heras-Sevilla, D., & Fernández-Hawrylak, M. (2022). Análisis de programas de educación sexual para adolescentes en España y otros países / Analysis of sex-education programs for teenagers in Spain and other countries. *Educare (San José), 26*(2), 329–349. doi:10.15359/ree.26-2.18

Barthes, R. (1957). *Mythologies*. Editions du Seuil.

Bartholomaeus, C., Riggs, D. W., & Andrew, Y. (2017). The capacity of South Australian primary school teachers and pre-service teachers to work with trans and gender diverse students. *Teaching and Teacher Education, 65*, 127–135. doi:10.1016/j.tate.2017.03.006

Compilation of References

Bauman, S., Toomey, R. B., & Walker, J. L. (2013). Associations among bullying, cyberbullying, and suicide in high school students. *Journal of Adolescence*, *36*(2), 341–350. doi:10.1016/j.adolescence.2012.12.001 PMID:23332116

Baym, N. K. (2006). The Emergence of On-line Community. In S. Jones (Ed.), *Cybersociety: communication and community* (pp. 35–68). Sage.

Bayrakdar, S., & King, A. (2021). LGBT discrimination, harassment and violence in Germany, Portugal and the UK: A quantitative comparative approach. *Current Sociology*, 1–21. doi:10.1177/00113921211039271

Bégin, J. Y., Bluteau, J., Arseneault, C., & Pronovost, J. (2012). Psychoeducation in Quebec: Past to Present. *Ricerche Di Pedagogia E Didattica. Journal of Theories and Research in Education*, *7*(1). doi:10.6092/issn.1970-2221/2681

Begum, N., & Saini, R. (2019). Decolonising the Curriculum. *Political Studies Review*, *17*(2), 196–201. doi:10.1177/1478929918808459

Belli, L. (2013). La violencia obstétrica: otra forma de violación a los derechos humanos [Obstetric violence: another form of human rights violation]. *Revista Redbioética* [*Redbioethics Journal*], *1*(7), 25-34. https://redbioetica.com.ar/wp-content/uploads/2018/11/Art2-BelliR7.pdf

Berglas, N., Constantine, N., & Ozwe, E. (2014). A rights-based Approach to Sexuality Education: Conceptualization, Clarification and Challenges. *Perspectives on Sexual and Reproductive Health*, *46*(2), 63–72. doi:10.1363/46e1114 PMID:24785652

Bernstein, S., Warburton, W., Bussey, K., & Sweller, N. (2022). Mind the gap: Internet pornography exposure, influence and problematic viewing amongst emerging adults. *Sexuality Research & Social Policy*, *20*(2), 599–613. doi:10.1007/s13178-022-00698-8

Beyens, I., Vandenbosch, L., & Eggermont, S. (2015). Early adolescent boys' exposure to Internet pornography: Relationships to pubertal timing, sensation seeking, and academic performance. *The Journal of Early Adolescence*, *35*(8), 1045–1068. doi:10.1177/0272431614548069

Bezhanova, O. (2017). Rosa Montero's La carne: Questioning the Culture of the Transition. *Cincinnati Romance Review*, *43*, 134–149.

Bhabha, H. K. (1994). *The location of culture*. Routledge.

Bhambra, G. K., Gebrial, D., & Nisancioglu, K. (2018). *Decolonising the university*. Pluto Press. doi:10.2307/j.ctv4ncntg

Bhardwaj, S., & Hooda, K. (2022). Impact of innovative process in teaching –learning. [AJCS]. *Amity Journal of Computational Sciences*, *3*(2), 19–23.

Boccardi, F. (2023). La diversidad sexual en el discurso estatal de la Educación Sexual Integral en Argentina. Un análisis sociosemiótico de los materiales didácticos oficiales. [Sexual diversity in the state discourse of Comprehensive Sexual Education in Argentina. A socio-semiotic analysis of official teaching materials]. *Espacios en Blanco. Serie Indagaciones*, *33*(2), 31–31. doi:10.37177/UNICEN/EB33-375

Bogner, J., Hadley, W., Franz, D., Barker, D. H., & Houck, C. D. (2023). Sexting as a Predictor of First-Time Sexual Behavior among At-Risk Early Adolescents. *The Journal of Early Adolescence*, *43*(4), 516–538. doi:10.1177/02724316221113351

Bondestam, F., & Lundqvist, M. (2020). Sexual harassment in higher education–a systematic review. *European Journal of Higher Education*, *10*(4), 397–419. doi:10.1080/21568235.2020.1729833

Bonfil, P. (2014). Introducción [Introduction]. En P.Bonfil (coord.), Derechos y salud sexual y reproductiva entre jóvenes indígenas: hacia la construcción de una agenda necesaria [Sexual and reproductive health and rights among indigenous young people: towards the construction of a necessary agenda] (pp. 13-42). GIMTRAP.

Borruso, M. M. (2002). *Hombre, mujer y muxe'en el Istmo de Tehuantepec*. Plaza y Valdés.

Bosse, C. (2007). Becoming and Consumption: The Contemporary Spanish Novel. Lexington

Bourgois, P. (2001). The Power of Violence in War and Peace. Post-Cold War Lessons from El Salvador. *Ethnography*, *2*(1), 5–34. https://escholarship.org/uc/item/8w69708b. doi:10.1177/14661380122230803

Brah, A. (1991). Difference, diversity, differentiation. *International Review of Sociology*, *2*(2), 53–71. doi:10.1080/03906701.1991.9971087

Breuner, C. C., Mattson, G., Breuner, C. C., Adelman, W. P., Alderman, E. M., Garofalo, R., Marcell, A. V., Powers, M. E., Mph, M., Upadhya, K. K., Yogman, M. W., Bauer, N. S., Gambon, T. B., Lavin, A., Lemmon, K. M., Mattson, G., Rafferty, J. R., & Wissow, L. S. (2016). Sexuality Education for Children and Adolescents. *Pediatrics*, *138*(2), e20161348. doi:10.1542/peds.2016-1348 PMID:27432844

Briseño-Maas. M. L.; & Bautista-Martínez, E. (2016). La violencia hacia las mujeres en Oaxaca. En los caminos de la desigualdad y la pobreza [Violence against women in Oaxaca. On the roads of inequality and poverty]. *Revista LiminaR. Estudios Sociales y Humanísticos* [*Journal LiminaR. Social and Humanistic Studies*], *XIV* (2), 15-27.

Brookfield, S. D. (2012). Critical theory and transformative learning. In E. W. Taylor & P. Cranton (Eds.), *The handbook of transformative learning: Theory, research, and practice* (pp. 131–146). Jossey-Bass.

Brown, A. (2015). *Hate speech law: A philosophical examination*. Routledge. doi:10.4324/9781315714899

Brown, A., & Ishmail, K. J. (2019). Feminist theorizing of men and masculinity: Applying Feminist Perspective to Advance College Men Maculinity Praxis. *Threshold*, *42*(1), 17–35.

Bucheli, M., & Rossi, M. (2019). Attitudes toward intimate partner violence against women in Latin America and the Caribbean. *SAGE Open*, *9*(3). doi:10.1177/2158244019871061

Budapest Convention. (2001). *Convention on CyberCrime*. Budapest Convention. https://bit.ly/3IaGaO2

Bunjevac, N. (2018). *Bezimena*. Fantagraphics.

BusseR.LischewskiJ.SeeberS. (2019). Do non-formal and informal adult education affect citizens' political participation during adulthood? *JSSE - Journal of Social Science Education, 18*(4), 5–24. doi:10.4119/jsse-1443

Butler, J. (1990). *Gender trouble: Feminism and the subversion of identity*. Routledge.

Butler, J. (2017). *Cuerpos aliados y lucha política: hacia una teoría performativa de la asamblea / Allied bodies and political struggle: towards a performative theory of the assembly*. Paidós.

Butler, J. (2020). *Sin miedo. Formas de resistencia a la violencia de hoy / Without fear. Forms of resistance towards today's violence*. Taurus.

Butler, L. C., Fissel, E. R., Gildea, B., & Fisher, B. S. (2023). Understanding intimate partner cyber abuse across partnership categories based on gender identity and sexual orientation. *Victims & Offenders*, *18*(1), 77–100. doi:10.1080/15564886.2022.2139032

Byron, P., McKee, A., Watson, A., Litsou, K., & Ingham, R. (2021). Reading for realness: Porn literacies, digital media, and young people. *Sexuality & Culture*, *25*(3), 786–805. doi:10.1007/s12119-020-09794-6

Compilation of References

Cáceres-Reche, M. P., Hinojo-Lucena, F. J., Navas-Parejo, M. R., & Romero-Rodríguez, J. M. (2019). The phenomenon of cyberbullying in the children and adolescents' population: a scientometric analysis. *Research in social sciences and technology, 4*(2), 115-128.

Callender, K. A. (2015). Understanding antigay bias from a cognitive-affective-behavioral perspective. *Journal of Homosexuality, 62*(6), 782–803. doi:10.1080/00918369.2014.998965 PMID:25530128

Calsamiglia, H., & Tusón, A. (1997). *Las cosas del decir. Manual de análisis del discurso* [The things of saying. Discourse analysis manual]. Editorial Ariel.

Calvo-González, S. (2014). *Unidad didáctica de apoyo al programa de educación afectivo-sexual en la ESO. Ni ogros ni princesas. Identidades digitales* [Didactic unit to support the affective-sexual education programme in ESO. Neither ogres nor princesses. Digital identities]. Consejería de la Presidencia/ Instituto Asturiano de la Mujer y Políticas de Juventud. https://bitly.ws/3eIcQ

Calvo-González, S. (2015). "Educación sexual mediática". Incorporando la alfabetización mediática crítica en un programa de educación sexual para educación secundaria obligatoria ["Media Sexuality Education. Incorporating critical media literacy in a sexuality education programme for compulsory secondary education]. *Revista de Estudios para el Desarrollo Social de la Comunicación, 12*, 194–221. doi:10.15213/redes.n12.p194

Camero Callo, P. A. (2023). *Diseño de material psicoeducativo para contribuir en el bienestar psicológico afectado por la infodemia por Covid-19 en jóvenes cusqueños. [Design of psychoeducational material to contribute to the psychological well-being affected by the Covid-19 infodemic in young people from Cusco]* [Undergraduate Thesis, Universidad San Ignacio Loyola]. USIL Repositorio Institucional. https://hdl.handle.net/20.500.14005/13045

Camps, V. (2021). *Tiempo de cuidados: otra forma de estar en el mundo / Care time: another way of being in the world.* Arpa.

Canh, L., M. Lucas., Cortelletti, F., & Valeriano, C. (2020). *Educación sexual integral. Guía básica para trabajar en la escuela y en la familia* [Comprehensive sexual education: A basic guide for working in schools and families]. Siglo XXI Editores.

Cannon, C., Lauve-Moon, K., & Buttell, F. (2015). Intimate partner Violence through Poststructural feminism, Queer Theory and the Sociology of Gender. *Social Sciences (Basel, Switzerland), 4*(3), 668–687. doi:10.3390/socsci4030668

Cannon, C., Lauve-Moon, K., & Buttell, F. (2015). Re-Theorizing Intimate Partner Violence through Post-Structural Feminism, Queer Theory, and the Sociology of Gender. *Journal of Social Sciences, 4*, 668–687.

Cano Abadía, M. (2021). *Judith Butler. Performatividad y vulnerabilidad / Judith Butler. Performativity and vulnerability.* Shackleton.

Carman, M., Mitchell, A., Schlichthorst, M., & Smith, A. (2011). Teacher training in sexuality education in Australia: How well are teachers prepared for the job? *Sexual Health, 8*(3), 269–271. doi:10.1071/SH10126 PMID:21851765

Carosio, A. (2023). Embarazo adolescente, desigualdad y violencia en América Latina y el Caribe. [Teenage pregnancy, inequality and violence in Latin America and the Caribbean] In K. Batthyány (Ed.), *Desigualdades y violencias de género en América Latina y el Caribe [Inequalities and gender-based violence in Latin America and the Caribbean].* (pp. 117–212). CLACSO.

Carrera-Fernández, M. V., Almeida, A., Cid-Fernández, X. M., Vallejo-Medina, P., & Rodríguez-Castro, Y. (2019). Patrolling the boundaries of gender: Beliefs, attitudes and behaviors toward trans and gender diverse people in Portuguese adolescents. *International Journal of Sexual Health, 32*(1), 40–56. doi:10.1080/19317611.2019.1701170

Carrera-Fernández, M. V., Cid-Fernández, X. M., Almeida, A., González-Fernández, A., & Lameiras-Fernández, M. (2018). Attitudes Toward Cultural Diversity in Spanish and Portuguese Adolescents of Secondary Education: The Influence of Heteronormativity and Moral Disengagement in School Bullying. *Revista de Psicodidáctica*, *23*(1), 17–25. doi:10.1016/j.psicod.2017.07.004

Carrera-Fernández, M. V., Lameiras-Fernández, M., Blanco-Pardo, N., & Rodríguez-Castro, Y. (2021). Preventing violence toward sexual and cultural diversity: The role of a queering sex education. *International Journal of Environmental Research and Public Health*, *18*(4), 1–15. doi:10.3390/ijerph18042199 PMID:33672323

Carrera-Fernández, M. V., Lameiras-Fernández, M., Rodríguez-Castro, Y., & Vallejo-Medina, P. (2014). Spanish adolescents' attitudes toward trans people: Proposal and validation of a short form of the Genderism and Transphobia Scale. *Journal of Sex Research*, *51*(6), 654–666. doi:10.1080/00224499.2013.773577 PMID:23767992

Carrillo Zeiter, K. (2005). ...El amor y otras mentiras": Mujeres, sexo y amor en las novelas de Lucía Etxebarría. In A.-S. Buck & I. Gastón Sierra (Eds.), *El amor, esa palabra...": El amor en la novela española contemporánea de fin de milenio* (pp. 41–53). Iberoamericana Editorial Vervuert.

Casey, E., Carlson, J., Two Bulls, S., & Yager, A. (2018). Gender Transformative approaches to engaging men in gender-based violence prevention: A review and conceptual model. *Trauma, Violence & Abuse*, *19*(2), 231–246. doi:10.1177/1524838016650191 PMID:27197533

Castañeda, A. J. (n.d.). La enseñanza de la iglesia católica sobre la educación sexual según familiaris consortio, 37. *Aciprensa* https://www.aciprensa.com/Familia/edusex1.htm

Castelo-Rivas, W. P., Posligua-Castillo, M. J., Ruiz-Cordova, V. L., Apolo-Apolo, C. I., & Carpio-Chamba, J. L. (2023). Influencia de la Autoestima y el Apoyo Familiar en la Prevención del Sexting Adolescente. *Ciencia Latina Revista Científica Multidisciplinar*, *7*(4), 9995–10018. doi:10.37811/cl_rcm.v7i4.7684

Cava, J., & Musitu, G. (2002). *La convivencia en la escuela*. Paidós.

Cava, M. J., Castillo, I., Tomás, I., & Buelga, S. (2023). Romantic myths and cyber dating violence victimization in Spanish adolescents: A moderated mediation model. *Cyberpsychology (Brno)*, *17*(2). doi:10.5817/CP2023-2-4

Centre for the Study of Violence and Reconciliation. (2016). *Gender Based Violence in South Africa: A brief Review*. Centre for the Study of Violence and Reconciliation.

Cerbara, L., Ciancimino, G., Corsetti, G., & Tintori, A. (2023). The (Un)equal effect of binary socialisation on adolescents' exposure to pornography: Girls' empowerment and boys' sexism from a new Representative National Survey. *Societies (Basel, Switzerland)*, *13*(6), 146. doi:10.3390/soc13060146

Cevasco, J., & Acosta, K. (2023). Construction of coherence in the comprehension of narratives: Studies on the importance of the establishment of causal connections, gaps in current research and future directions. *Papeles del Psicólogo*, *44*(1), 45–54. doi:10.23923/pap.psicol.3010

Cevasco, J., Muller, F., & Bermejo, F. (2020). The role of discourse marker presence, causal connectivity and prior knowledge in the comprehension of topic shifts. *Current Psychology (New Brunswick, N.J.)*, *39*, 1072–1085. doi:10.1007/s12144-018-9828-4

Cevasco, J., & van den Broek, P. (2017). The importance of causality processing in the comprehension of spontaneous spoken discourse. *Ciencia Cognitiva*, *11*(2), 43–45.

Cevasco, J., & van den Broek, P. (2019). Contributions of causality processing models to the study of discourse comprehension and the facilitation of student learning. *Psicologia Educativa*, *25*(2), 159–167. doi:10.5093/psed2019a8

Chalaune, B. S. (2021). Paulo Freire's critical pedagogy in educational transformation. *International Journal of Research-GRANTHAALAYAH, 9*(4), 185–194. doi:10.29121/granthaalayah.v9.i4.2021.3813

Chan, A. S. W. (2023). Letter to the editor: Advocating worldwide social inclusion and anti-discrimination among LGBT community. Journal of Homosexuality, 70(5), 779–781. https://doi.org/ doi:10.1080/00918369.2021.2004869

Chandra-Mouli, V., Gómez, L., Plesons, M., Lang, I., & Corona, E. (2018). Evolution and Resistance to Sexuality Education in Mexico. *Global Health, Science and Practice, 6*(1), 137–149. doi:10.9745/GHSP-D-17-00284 PMID:29602869

Chan, E. (2023). Technology-facilitated gender-based violence, hate speech, and terrorism: A risk assessment on the rise of the incel rebellion in Canada. *Violence Against Women, 29*(9), 1687–1718. doi:10.1177/10778012221125495 PMID:36226437

Charig, R., Moghaddam, N. G., Dawson, D. L., Merdian, H. L., & das Nair, R. (2020). A lack of association between online pornography exposure, sexual functioning, and mental well-being. *Sexual and Relationship Therapy, 35*(2), 258–281. doi:10.1080/14681994.2020.1727874

Chazan, B. (2022). *What is 'education'? Principles and pedagogies in Jewish education.* Palgrave Macmillan., doi:10.1007/978-3-030-83925-3

Chiang, J. T., Chang, F. C., & Lee, K. W. (2021). Transitions in aggression among children: Effects of gender and exposure to online violence. *Aggressive Behavior, 47*(3), 310–319. doi:10.1002/ab.21944 PMID:33570759

Childnet International. (2018). *Myth vs Reality. A practical PSHE toolkit for educators to explore online pressures and perceived "norms".* Childnet International/UK Safer Internet Centre. https://bitly.ws/3eIdz

Cicogna, M., & Rossellini, F. (Producers), & Pasolini, P. P. (Director). (1969). *Medea* [Film]. Euro International Film.

Cifuentes-Zunino, F., Pascual, J., & Carrer-Russell, C. (2020). Acoso escolar por orientación sexual, identidad y expresión de género en institutos de educación secundaria catalanes. *Revista de Educación Inclusiva, 13*(2), 153-174. https://revistaeducacioninclusiva.es/index.php/REI/article/download/604/584

Civila, S., De-Casas-Moreno, P., García-Rojas, A. D., & Hernando-Gómez, A. (2023). TikTok and the caricaturing of violence in adolescent romantic relationships. *Anàlisi: Quaderns de Comunicació i Cultura, 69,* 75–91. doi:10.5565/rev/analisi.3632

Civila, S., & Jaramillo-Dent, D. (2022). #Mixedcouples on TikTok: Performative hybridization and identity in the face of discrimination. *Social Media + Society, 8*(3). doi:10.1177/20563051221122464

Cogan, C. M., Scholl, J. A., Lee, J. Y., Cole, H. E., & Davis, J. L. (2021). Sexual violence and suicide risk in the transgender population: The mediating role of proximal stressors. *Psychology & Sexuality, 12*(1-2), 129–140. doi:10.1080/19419899.2020.1729847

Cole, T., Policastro, C., Crittenden, C., & McGuffee, K. (2020). Freedom to post or invasion of privacy? Analysis of US revenge porn state statutes. *Victims & Offenders, 15*(4), 483–498. doi:10.1080/15564886.2020.1712567

Coll, C., Palacios, J., & Marchesi, A. (1992). *Desarrollo Psicológico y Educación II.* Psicología de la educación escolar [Psychological Development and Education II: Scholar education psychology]. Alianza.

Collier-Harris, C. A., & Goldman, J. D. G. (2017). What educational contexts should teachers consider for their puberty education programmes? *Educational Review, 69*(1), 118–133. doi:10.1080/00131911.2016.1183592

Colmeiro, J. (2011). Nation of Ghosts? Hunting, Historical Memory and Forgetting in Post-Franco Spain, *452F. Electronic journey of theory of literature and comparative literature, 4,* 17-31

Comisión Interamericana de Derechos Humanos (CIDH). (2014). *150 Período de Sesiones: Salud materna y denuncias de violencia obstétrica en México*. https://tinyurl.com/wjyfkwn

CONAPO. (2021a). Segunda fase de la Estrategia Nacional para la Prevención del Embarazo Adolescente 2021-2024 [*Second phase of the National Strategy for the Prevention of Adolescent Pregnancy 2021-2024*]. CONAPO. https://www.gob.mx/cms/uploads/attachment/file/703251/Segunda_fase_de_la_ENAPEA_2021-2024_ajuste_forros_030222_small.pdf

CONAPO. (2021b). La situación Demográfica de México [*Mexico's Demographic Situation*]. CONAPO. https://www.gob.mx/conapo/documentos/la-situacion-demografica-de-mexico-2021

CONEVAL. (2019). La pobreza en la población indígena de México, 2008-2018 [*Poverty among Mexico's indigenous population, 2008-2018*]. CONEVAL. https://www.coneval.org.mx/Medicion/MP/Documents/Pobreza_Poblacion_indigena_2008-2018.pdf

Conradie, P. J. (1977). The literary nature of Greek myths: A critical discussion of G. S. Kirk's views. *Acta Classica, 20*, 49–58.

Corcoran, E., Doty, J., Wisniewski, P., & Gabrielli, J. (2022). Youth sexting and associations with parental media mediation. *Computers in Human Behavior, 132*, 107263. doi:10.1016/j.chb.2022.107263

Correa, A. (Director). (2017). *Medea* [Film]. YouTube. https://goo.su/fKsUgy

Correia, R. (2006) Encouraging critical reading in the EFL classroom. *English Teaching Forum, 1*, 16–27.

Cosme, G. (2021). A Social Learning Understanding of Violence. *Academia Letters, Articles 1019*. doi:10.20935/AL1019

Costa, P. A., Carneiro, F. A., Esposito, F., D'Amore, S., & Green, R. J. (2018). Sexual Prejudice in Portugal: Results from the First Wave European Study on Heterosexual's Attitudes Toward Same-Gender Marriage and Parenting. *Sexuality Research & Social Policy, 15*(1), 99–110. doi:10.1007/s13178-017-0292-y

Cotton, A. (2021). *The importance of educating girls and women – the fight against poverty in African rural communities*. United Nations. https://n9.cl/ebm89

Coulter, R. W. S., Colvin, S., Onufer, L. R., Arnold, G., Akiva, T., D'Ambrogi, E., & Davis, V. (2021). Training preservice teachers to better serve LGBTQ high school students. *Journal of Education for Teaching, 47*(2), 234–254. doi:10.1080/02607476.2020.1851137 PMID:33986557

Council of Europe. (2001). *Common European Framework of Reference for Languages: Learning, teaching, assessment*. Council of Europe. https://rm.coe.int/1680459f97

Council of Europe. (2004). Introduction. Questions about the question. Chap. 1. In *Islamophobia and its consequences on young people*. European Youth Center. http://bit.ly/397kb6x

Council of Europe. (2014). *The Council of Europe Convention on preventing and combating violence against women and domestic violence*. Council of Europe. https://bit.ly/4246DpQ

Council of Europe. (2015). *Gender Equality Strategy 2014 – 2017*. Council of Europe. https://rm.coe.int/1680590174

Council of Europe. (2018). *Gender equality strategy 2018-2023*. Documents and Publications Production Department, Council of Europe. https://goo.su/JyW5E

Council of Europe. (2020). *Common European Framework of Reference for Languages: Learning, teaching, assessment. Companion volume*. Council of Europe. https://bit.ly/3PSYsaa

Council of the European Union. (2023). *Violence against women* (infographic). https://bit.ly/3SypFkJ

Compilation of References

Cowan, G., & Campbell, R. R. (1994). Racism and sexism in interracial pornography: A content analysis. *Psychology of Women Quarterly*, *18*(3), 323–338. doi:10.1111/j.1471-6402.1994.tb00459.x

Cowan, R. (2010). A stranger in a strange land: Medea in Roman republican tragedy. In H. Bartel (Ed.), *Unbinding Medea: Interdisciplinary approaches to a classical myth from antiquity to the 21st century* (pp. 39–52). Legenda.

Coyle, D., & Meyer, O. (2021). *Beyond CLIL: Pluriliteracies teaching for deeper learning*. Cambridge University Press. doi:10.1017/9781108914505

Crenshaw, K. (1989). Demarginalizing the Intersection of Race and Sex: A Black Feminist Critique of Antidiscrimination Doctrine, Feminist Theory and Antiracist Politics. *University of Chicago Legal Forum*, *1989*, 1. https://chicagounbound.uchicago.edu/uclf/vol1989/iss1/8

Creswell, J. W. (1998). *Qualitative inquiry and research design: Choosing among five traditions*. Sage Publications, Inc.

Criado Pérez, C. (2020). *La mujer invisible. Descubre cómo los datos configuran un mundo hecho por y para los hombres / The invisible woman. Discover how data shapes a world made by and for men*. Editorial Seix Barral.

Cripps, J., & Stermac, L. (2018). Cyber-sexual violence and negative emotional states among women in a Canadian university. *International Journal of Cyber Criminology*, *12*(1), 171–186.

Cui, Z., Mo, M., Chen, Q., Wang, X., Yang, H., Zhou, N., Sun, L., Liu, J., Ao, L., & Cao, J. (2021). Pornography use could lead to addiction and was associated with reproductive hormone levels and semen quality: A report from the MARHCS study in China. *Frontiers in Endocrinology*, *12*, 736384. doi:10.3389/fendo.2021.736384 PMID:34566897

Cumes, A. (2009). Multiculturalismo, género y feminismos: mujeres diversas, luchas complejas. *Participación y políticas de mujeres indígenas en contextos latinoamericanos recientes*, 29-52.

D'Ambrosi, L., Papakristo, P., & Polci, V. (2018). Social media and gender violence: Communication strategies for a "new education". *Italian Journal of Sociology of Education*, *10*, 76–89. doi:10.14658/PUPJ-IJSE-2018-2-6

D'Amore, S., Wollast, R., Green, R. J., Bouchat, P., Costa, P. A., Katuzny, K., Scali, T., Baiocco, R., Vecho, O., Mijas, M. E., Aparicio, M. E., Geroulanou, K., & Klein, O. (2022). Heterosexual University Students' Attitudes Toward Same-Sex Couples and Parents Across Seven European Countries. *Sexuality Research & Social Policy*, *19*(2), 791–804. doi:10.1007/s13178-020-00511-4

Dalton, M. (2010). *Mujeres: Género e Identidad en el Istmo de Tehuantepec, Oaxaca* [Women: Gender and Identity in the Isthmus of Tehuantepec, Oaxaca]. CIESAS.

Daudi, I. (2022). *Islamophobia and the West: The making of a violent civilization*. Taylor and Francis., doi:10.4324/9781003323105

Dávalos Vázquez, N. Q. (2017). Alguien ya robó mujer: virginidad y rito de paso en un barrio binnizá de Juchitán, Oaxaca [Someone has already stolen a woman: virginity and rite of passage in a Binnizá neighborhood in Juchitán, Oaxaca]. Master's thesis in Social Anthropology, El Colegio de San Luis.

Davies, C. (1994). *Contemporary Feminist Fiction in Spain. The Work of Montserrat Roig and Rosa Montero*. Berg.

Davis, A. C., Wright, C. J., Murphy, S., Dietze, P., Temple-Smith, M. J., Hellard, M. E., & Lim, M. S. (2020). A digital pornography literacy resource co-designed with vulnerable young people: Development of "The Gist". *Journal of Medical Internet Research*, *22*(6), e15964. doi:10.2196/15964 PMID:32348268

Davis, A. C., Wright, C., Curtis, M., Hellard, M. E., Lim, M. S. C., & Temple-Smith, M. J. (2019). 'Not my child': Parenting, pornography, and views on education. *Journal of Family Studies*, *27*(4), 573–588. doi:10.1080/13229400.2019.1657929

DBE. (2017). *DBE national policy on HIV, STIs and for learners educators, school support and officials.* Pretoria: Government Printers.

De Beauvoir, S. (1949). *El segundo sexo.* Éditions Gallimard.

de la Cadena, M. (1991). Las mujeres son más indias": Etnicidad y género en una comunidad del Cusco. [Women are more Indian: Ethnicity and gender in a Cuzco community]. Isis International Journal [Isis International Journal], 16.

de la Noy, K., Fay, W., Harris, L., Iwanyk, B., Jashni, J., McMillan, K., & Tull, T. (Producers), & Leterrier, L. (Director). (2010). *Clash of the titans* [Film]. Warner Bros. Pictures.

De Stéfano, M., Puche, L., & Pichardo, J. I. (2015). El compromiso de la investigación social en la construcción de otra escuela posible. *Revista Interuniversitaria de Formación del Profesorado*, *82*(29), 50-54. https://www.redalyc.org/pdf/274/27439665004.pdf

Degenaar, J. (2007). Discourses on myth. *Myth and Symbol*, *4*(1), 1–14. doi:10.1080/10223820701673973

Del Prete, A., & Pantoja, S. R. (2022). The Invisibility of Gender-Based Violence in the Social Network. *Gender Studies*, *11*(2), 124–143. doi:10.17583/generos.9045

del Río Ferres, E., Megías, J. L., & Expósito, F. (2013). Gender-based violence against women with visual and physical disabilities. *Psicothema*, *25*(1), 67–72. PMID:23336546

de-Miguel-Álvarez, A. (2020). On pornography and sexual education: Can "sex" legitimate humiliation and violence? *Gaceta Sanitaria*, *35*(4), 379–382. doi:10.1016/j.gaceta.2020.01.001 PMID:32173052

Denno, D. M., Hoopes, A. J., & Chandra-Mouli, V. (2015). Effective strategies to provide adolescent sexual and reproductive health services and to increase demand and community support. *The Journal of Adolescent Health*, *56*(1), S22–S41. doi:10.1016/j.jadohealth.2014.09.012 PMID:25528977

Denno, D., Hoopes, A., & Chandra-Mouli, V. (2015). Effective strategies to provide adolescent sexual and reproductive health services and to increase demand and community support. *Journal of Adolescence*, *56*(1), 1–14. PMID:25528977

Department of Education . (2019). *Relationships Education, Relationships and Sex Education (RSE) and Health and Education: Statutory Guidance for Governing Bodies, Properietors, Head Teachers, Principals, Senior Teachers Teams.* London: Dff.

Deping, L. (2009). A semiotic perspective of mythical discourse. *Chinese Semiotic Studies*, *2*(1), 1–19. doi:10.1515/css-2009-0103

Dey, A. (2020). Sites of exception: Gender violence, digital activism, and Nirbhaya's zone of anomie in India. *Violence Against Women*, *26*(11), 1423–1444. doi:10.1177/1077801219862633 PMID:31379258

Dhirani, L. L., Mukhtiar, N., Chowdhry, B. S., & Newe, T. (2023). Ethical dilemmas and privacy issues in emerging technologies: A review. *Sensors (Basel)*, *23*(3), 1151. doi:10.3390/s23031151 PMID:36772190

Dhrodia, A. (2018). Unsocial media: A toxic place for women. *IPPR Progressive Review*, *24*(4), 380–387. doi:10.1111/newe.12078

Di Marco, D., Hoel, H., & Lewis, D. (2021). Discrimination and exclusion on grounds of sexual and gender identity: Are LGBT people's voices heard at the workplace? *The Spanish Journal of Psychology*, *24*(e18), 1–6. doi:10.1017/SJP.2021.16 PMID:33745498

Díaz de Greñu, S., & Parejo, J. (2013). La promoción de la igualdad y el respeto de la diversidad afectivo sexual: Bases de un programa de orientación y tutoría para educación secundaria. *Revista Española de Orientación y Psicopedagogía*, *24*(3), 63–79. doi:10.5944/reop.vol.24.num.3.2013.11245

DIGEPO. (2019). *Síntesis del embarazo adolescente en el municipio de Juchitán de Zaragoza [Synthesis of adolescent pregnancy in the municipality of Juchitán de Zaragoza]*. DIGEPO.

Dionne, J. (2008). Los orígenes de la psicoeducación [The origins of psychoeducation]. In M. B. Vizcarra, & J. Dionne (Eds.), El desafío de la intervención psicosocial en Chile: aportes desde la psicoeducación [The challenge of psychosocial intervention in Chile: contributions from psychoeducation] (pp. 25-34). RIL editores.

Dodaj, A., Sesar, K., & Jerinić, S. (2020). A prospective study of high-school adolescent sexting behavior and psychological distress. *The Journal of Psychology*, *154*(2), 111–128. doi:10.1080/00223980.2019.1666788 PMID:31566509

Dodaj, A., Sesar, K., Pérez, M. O., Del Rey, R., Howard, D., & Gerding Speno, A. (2023). Using vignettes in qualitative research to assess young adults' perspectives of sexting behaviours. *Human Technology*, *19*(1), 103–120. doi:10.14254/1795-6889.2023.19-1.7

Dolev-Cohen, M., & Ricon, T. (2020). Demystifying sexting: Adolescent sexting and its associations with parenting styles and sense of parental social control in Israel. *Cyberpsychology (Brno)*, *14*(1), 6. doi:10.5817/CP2020-1-6

Domínguez, J., & Vázquez, E. (2015). Medidas de atención a la diversidad: Perspectiva del equipo de orientación específico. *Revista de Estudios e Investigación en Psicología y Educación*, *11*, 1–4. doi:10.17979/reipe.2015.0.11.87

Doniger, W. (2016). Invisibility and sexual violence in Indo-European mythology. *Social Research*, *83*(4), 847–877. doi:10.1353/sor.2016.0058

Donoso, T., & Velasco, A. (2013). ¿Por qué una propuesta de formación en perspectiva de género en el ámbito universitario? *Profesorado, Revista de Currículum y Formación del Profesorado*, *17*(1), 71-88. https://www.ugr.es/~recfpro/rev171ART5.pdf

Donoso-Vázquez, T., Hurtado, M. J. R., & Baños, R. V. (2017). Las ciberagresiones en función del género. *Revista de Investigación Educacional*, *35*(1), 197–214. doi:10.6018/rie.35.1.249771

Doyle, A. (2013, November 1). *Soft Skills List and Examples*. The Balance Careers; The Balance. https://www.thebalancecareers.com/list-of-soft-skills-2063770

Dudek, D., Woodley, G., & Green, L. (2022). 'Own your narrative': Teenagers as producers and consumers of porn in Netflix's Sex Education. *Information Communication and Society*, *25*(4), 502–515. doi:10.1080/1369118X.2021.1988130

Dueñas, J. M., Morales-Vives, F., Castarlenas, E., & Ferre-Rey, G. (2022). Trans students. Difficulties, needs and educational actions in Spain. *Gender and Education*, *34*(5), 529–544. doi:10.1080/09540253.2021.1971160

Dully, J., Walsh, K., Doyle, C., & O'Reilly, G. (2023). Adolescent experiences of sexting: A systematic review of the qualitative literature, and recommendations for practice. *Journal of Adolescence*, *95*(6), 1077–1105. doi:10.1002/jad.12181 PMID:37157169

Dunn, S. (2020). *Technology-facilitated gender-based violence: An overview*. Centre for International Governance Innovation. http://bit.ly/3HbrZb0

Duruoma, N. B., & Derefaka, A. A. (2019). Indigenous training and learning among the Agbaelu people of central Igboland, Nigeria. *Port Harcourt Journal of History & Diplomatic Studies, 6*(3), 1–16.

Dyasi, M. (2024, 1 20). *UNFPA Namibia*. Retrieved from Comprehensive Sexuality Education https://namibia.unfpa.org/en/news/importance-comprehensive-sexuality-education-africas-young-people-0

Eckert, S., O'Shay Wallace, S., Metzger-Riftkin, J., & Kolhoff, S. (2020). The best damn representation of Islam: Muslims, gender, social media and Islamophobia. *CyberOrient, 12*(1), 4–30. doi:10.1002/j.cyo2.20181201.0001

Eddo-Lodge. (2018). *Why I'm No Longer Talking to White People About Race*. Bloomsbury.

Educational News. (2019). *Types of education: Formal, informal & non-formal*. Educational News. https://n9.cl/m6kdi

ElSherief, M., Belding, E., & Nguyen, D. (2017). #NotOkay: Understanding gender-based violence in social media. *Proceedings of the International AAAI Conference on Web and Social Media, 11*(1), 52–61. 10.1609/icwsm.v11i1.14877

Emakunde. (2023). *El porno es una escuela de violencia contra las mujeres - tema* [*The porn industry as a achool of violence against women - topic*]. Emakunde. https://bitly.ws/3aqCU

Emeagwali, G. T. (2006). Africa and the textbooks. In G. T. Emeagwali (Ed.), *Africa and the academy* (pp. 1–30). Africa World Press, Inc.

Erken, A. (2021). United Nations Population Fund-The UNFPA strategic plan, 2022-2025 Annex 1. https://www.unfpa.org/unfpa-strategic-plan-2022-2025-dpfpa20218

Escamilla Gutiérrez, M., & Guzmán Saldaña, R. (2017). Educación Sexual en México ¿Misión de la casa o de la escuela? *Educación y Salud Boletín Científico de Ciencias de La Salud Universidad Autónoma Del Estado De Hidalgo, 5*(10). Advance online publication. doi:10.29057/icsa.v5i10.2478

Esu, A. E. O. (2011). The concept of curriculum. In A. F. Uduigwomen & K. Ogbinaka (Eds.), *Philosophy of education: An analytical approach* (pp. 122–134). Joja Educational Research and Publishers Limited.

Etxebarria, L. (1996). *Amor, curiosidad, prozac y dudas*. Debolsillo.

Etxebarría, L. (2000). *La letra futura*. Destino.

European Commission. (2023). *Issue paper on gender equality in and through education* (edited by B. van Driel, V. Donlevy & M. M. Roseme). Working Group on Equality and Values in Education and Training. European Education Area Strategic Framework. https://bit.ly/3HzxQXT

European Commission. (2023). *Issue paper on gender equality in and through education* (edited by B. van Driel, V. Donlevy & M. M. Roseme). Working Group on Equality and Values in Education and Training. European Education Area Strategic Framework. Publications Office of the European Union. https://bit.ly/3HzxQXT

European Commission. (n. d.). *Gender-based violence (GBV) by definition* [Webpage]. https://goo.su/ukD8cb

European Commission. (n. d.). *Gender-based violence (GBV) by definition*. European Commission. https://bit.ly/3U2jUNr

European Expert Group on Sexuality Education. (2016). Sexuality education – what is it? *Sex Education, 16*(4), 427–431. doi:10.1080/14681811.2015.1100599

European Institute for Gender Equality. (2018). *Gender equality and youth: the opportunities and risks of digitalization*. EIGE. doi:10.2839/09510

European Institute for Gender Equality. (2023). *Forms of gender-based violence*. European Institute for Gender Equality. https://bit.ly/47Tr4Hh

European Union Agency for Fundamental Rights. (2014). *Violence against women: An EU-wide survey.* Publications Office of the European Union. https://goo.su/BqG3Yi

European Union Agency for Fundamental Rights. (2019). *Report on minorities and discrimination.* EU. https://bit.ly/3Tcd4UO

European Union. (2019). *Key competences for lifelong learning.* Publications Office of the European Union. https://bit.ly/3SkQWHx

Eurydice. (2017). *Eurydice brief: Key data on teaching languages at school in Europe.* Eurydice European Unit. doi:10.2797/828497

Euskadi. (2024). *Educación apoya a docentes para erradicar las consecuencias del consumo de la pornografía entre jóvenes* [Education supports teachers to eradicate the consequences of pornography consumption among youth]. Euskadi.eus. https://bitly.ws/3eIkK

Evans, B. (2020). Myths of violence. *Journal of Humanitarian Affairs, 2*(1), 62–68. doi:10.7227/JHA.035

Ezeudu, F. O., Nkokelonye, C. U., & Ezeudu, S. A. (2013). Science education and the challenges facing its integration into the 21st century school system in a globalized world: A case of Igbo nation. *US-China Education Review B, 3*(3), 172–182.

Faith, B. (2022). Tackling online gender-based violence; understanding gender, development, and the power relations of digital spaces. *Gender, Technology and Development, 26*(3), 325–340. doi:10.1080/09718524.2022.2124600

Fajardo, D. P. C. (2022). Educación sexual integral en la escuela [Comprehensive sexual education at school]. *Revista Unimar, 40*(1), 136–151. doi:10.31948/Rev.unimar/unimar40-1-art7

Fang, J., Tang, S., Tan, X., & Tolhurst, R. (2020). Achieving SDG related sexual and reproductive health targets in China: What are appropriate indicators and how we interpret them? *Reproductive Health, 17*(84), 1–11. doi:10.1186/s12978-020-00924-9 PMID:32487257

Farsi, D. (2021). Social media and health care, part I: Literature review of social media use by health care providers. *Journal of Medical Internet Research, 23*(4), 1–21. doi:10.2196/23205 PMID:33664014

Fasih-Ramandi, M. (2019). Ethical and legal considerations in dealing with adolescents' exposure to cyber pornography. *Bioethics Journal, 9*(34), 81–93. https://acortar.link/yti835

Faur, E. (2019). La Catedral, el Palacio, las aulas, la calle. Disputas en torno a la Educación Sexual Integral [The Cathedral, the Palace, the classrooms, the street. Disputes around Comprehensive Sexual Education]. *Mora (Buenos Aires), 25*(1), 227–234.

Faur, E., & Gogna, M. (2016). La Educación Sexual Integral en la Argentina. Una apuesta por la ampliación de derechos. [Comprehensive Sexual Education in Argentina. A commitment to the expansion of rights] In I. E. Ramírez Hernández (Ed.), *Voces de la inclusión interpelaciones y críticas a la idea de "Inclusión" escolar* [Voices of inclusion, questions, and criticisms of the idea of School "inclusion"]. (pp. 195–227). Praxis Editorial.

Felipe, M. (2014). Reading habits of pre-service teachers / Trayectorias de lectura del profesorado en formación. *Culture and Education / Cultura y Educación, 26*(3), 448–475.

Ferguson, R. M., Vanwesenbeeck, I., & Knijn, T. (2008). A matter of facts… and more: An exploratory analysis of the content of sexuality education in The Netherlands. *Sex Education, 8*(1), 93–106. doi:10.1080/14681810701811878

Fernandez-Hawrylak, M., Alonso-Martínez, L., Sevilla-Ortega, E., & Ruiz-Ruiz, M. E. (2022). Inclusión de la Diversidad Sexual en los Centros Educativos desde la Perspectiva del Profesorado: Un Estudio Cualitativo. *Revista Internacional de Educación para la Justicia Social, 11*(2), 81–97. doi:10.15366/riejs2022.11.2.005

Fernández-Llebrez González, F. (2012). Malestares de género: identidad e inclusión democrática. *Foro interno: anuario de teoría política, 12*, 29-59.

Fernández-Tapia, J. (2021). Abuso sexual a niñas en Oaxaca:¿ problema legal o cultural? *Revista Innova Educación, 3*(3), 7–32. doi:10.35622/j.rie.2021.03.001

Figueroa Romero, D., & Sierra Camacho, M. T. (2020). Alertas de género y mujeres indígenas: interpelando las políticas públicas desde los contextos comunitarios en Guerrero, México. *Canadian Journal of Latin American and Caribbean Studies/Revue canadienne des études latino-américaines et caraïbes, 45*(1), 26-44.

Flores, Y. Y. R., Pérez, O. L., & Moreno, M. J. (2022). Resistencias y sincretismo indígena de mujeres tének y nahuas de San Luis Potosí, México, en la experiencia del autocuidado durante el embarazo y parto. *Revista de el Colegio de San Luis, 12*(23), 1–31. doi:10.21696/rcsl122320221409

Flynn, L. L. (1989). Developing critical reading skills through cooperative problem solving. *The Reading Teacher, 42*(9), 664–668.

FMI, ECMIA, y CHIRAPAQ. (2020). *Mujeres indígenas de las Américas a 25 años de Beijing. Avances, brechas y desafíos* [*Indigenous women of the Americas 25 years after Beijing. Progress, gaps and challenges*]. FMI, ECMIA, CHIRAPAQ.

Fondo de Población de las Naciones Unidas. UNFPA (2020). *Orientaciones técnicas y programáticas internacionales sobre educación integral en sexualidad fuera de la escuela*. https://www.unfpa.org/es/publications/orientaciones-tecnicas-y-programaticas-internacionales-sobre-educacion-integral-en

Fonllem, M. E. T. Género y sexualidad. Políticas públicas sobre los derechos sexuales y reproductivos en méxico (2000-2015). *Salud reproductiva, medio ambiente y género, 19*.

Fonner, V. A., Armstrong, K. S., Kennedy, C. E., O'Reilly, K. R., & Sweat, M. D. (2014). School based sex education and HIV prevention in low- and middle-income countries: A systematic review and meta-analysis. *PLoS One, 9*(3), e89692. doi:10.1371/journal.pone.0089692 PMID:24594648

Foradada, M., & López, S. (2023). El relato autobiográfico como método docente feminista / The autobiographical story as a feminist teaching method. *Educar, 59*(1), 83–97. doi:10.5565/rev/educar.1581

Foy, J. K., & Hodge, S. (2016). Preparing Educators for a Diverse World: Understanding Sexual Prejudice among Pre-Service Teachers. *Prairie Journal of Educational Research, 1*(1). doi:10.4148/2373-0994.1005

Frangos, C. C., Frangos, C. C., & Sotiropoulos, I. (2011). Problematic Internet use among Greek university students: An ordinal logistic regression with risk factors of negative psychological beliefs, pornographic sites, and online games. *Cyberpsychology, Behavior, and Social Networking, 14*(1-2), 51–58. doi:10.1089/cyber.2009.0306 PMID:21329443

Frankema, H. P. E. (2021). The origins of formal education in sub-Saharan Africa: Was British rule more benign? *European Review of Economic History, 16*(4), 335–355. doi:10.1093/ereh/hes009

Franks, M. A. (2022). Speaking of Women: Feminism and Free Speech. *Feminist Frictins: Key Concepts and Controversies*. Signs. http://signsjournal.org/franks/

Freyermuth-Enciso, M. G. (2014). La mortalidad materna y los nudos en la prestación de los servicios de salud en Chiapas: Un análisis desde la interculturalidad. *LiminaR, 12*(2), 30–45. doi:10.29043/liminar.v12i2.340

Compilation of References

Frías-Navarro, D., Monterde-i-Bort, H., Pascual-Soler, M., & Badenes-Ribera, L. (2015). Etiology of Homosexuality and Attitudes Toward Same-Sex Parenting: A Randomized Study. *Journal of Sex Research*, *52*(2), 151–161. doi:10.1080/00224499.2013.802757 PMID:24024528

Fritz, N., Malic, V., Paul, B., & Zhou, Y. (2021). Worse than objects: The depiction of black women and men and their sexual relationship in pornography. *Gender Issues*, *38*(1), 100–120. doi:10.1007/s12147-020-09255-2

Fuentes-Lara, C., & Arcila-Calderón, C. (2023). El discurso de odio islamófobo en las redes sociales. Un análisis de las actitudes ante la islamofobia en Twitter [Islamophobic hate speech on social networks. An analysis of attitudes to Islamophobia on Twitter]. *Revista Mediterránea de Comunicación*, *14*(1), 225–240. doi:10.14198/MEDCOM.23044

Future of Sex Education. (2020). *National Sex Education Standars, Core content and skills, K-12*. The Future of Sex Education.

Gamba, C. (2018). *La reflexión sobre nosotros/as mismos/as: los procesos de subjetivación docente y la educación sexual integral como tecnología de gobierno [Reflection on ourselves: the processes of teacher subjectivation and comprehensive sexual education as a technology of government]* [Master's thesis, FLACSO]. Repository FLACSO Andes.

Gámez-Guadix, M., Mateos-Pérez, E., Wachs, S., Wright, M., Martínez, J., & Íncera, D. (2022). Assessing image-based sexual abuse: Measurement, prevalence, and temporal stability of sextortion and nonconsensual sexting ("revenge porn") among adolescents. *Journal of Adolescence*, *94*(5), 789–799. doi:10.1002/jad.12064 PMID:35719041

Gamlin, J., & Berrio, L. (2020). Critical anthropologies of maternal health: Theorising from the field with Mexican indigenous communities. *Critical medical anthropology: Perspectives in and from Latin America*, 42-68.

Garaigordobil, M., & Oñederra, J. (2010). *La violencia entre iguales*. Pirámide.

García-Cano, M., & Hinojosa-Pareja, E. F. (2016). Coeducación en la formación inicial del profesorado: de la transversalidad a la vivencia a través de la ética del cuidado / Coeducation in initial teacher training: from transversality to experience through the ethics of care. Multiárea. *Revista de didáctica*, *8*, 61-86. doi:10.18239/mard.v0i8.1122

García-Cano, M., Buenestado-Fernández, M., Hinojosa-Pareja, E. F., & Jiménez-Millán, A. (2022). Innovación docente para la igualdad y para la diversidad en las políticas universitarias de España / Teaching innovation for equality and diversity in university policies in Spain. *Aula Abierta*, *51*(1), 75–84. doi:10.17811/rifie.51.1.2022.75-84

García-Cano, M., Hinojosa-Pareja, E. F., Buenestado-Fernández, M., & Jiménez-Millán, A. (2023). A statutory requirement: Teaching innovation for gender equality at university. *Women's Studies International Forum*, *96*, 102673. doi:10.1016/j.wsif.2022.102673

García-Rojas, A., & Salcines-Talledo, I. (2023). Pornografía y sexualidad [Pornography and sexuality]. In A. D. García-Rojas, I. Salcines-Talledo, N. González-Fernández, A. Ramírez-García & M. P. Gutiérrez-Arenas (Coords.), *Guías educomunicativas para familias. Educación afectiva y sexual en familia [Educational-communicative guides for families. Affective and sexual education in the family]* (pp. 30–31). Grupo Comunicar Ediciones. https://bitly.ws/3eBaV

Garduño, G. V. (2018). Educación Sexual: una polémica persistente. *Instituto Nacional para la Evaluación de la Educación*, *11*. https://www.inee.edu.mx/educacion-sexual-una-polemica-persistente/

Garrido, M. R., & Morales, Z. (2014). Una aproximación a la homofobia desde la psicología. Propuestas de intervención. *Psicología, Conocimiento y Sociedad*, *4*(1), 100–109. https://www.redalyc.org/pdf/4758/475847268005.pdf

Garriga i Setó, C. (2015). Una revisión crítica de los conocimientos actuales sobre la sexualidad y el género (II). *Aperturas Psicoanalíticas: Revista Internacional de psicoanálisis*, *51*. https://aperturas.org/articulo.php?articulo=0000918&a=Una-revision-critica-de-los-conocimientos-actuales-sobre-la-sexualidad-y-el-genero-II

Garzón Fernández, A. (2016). La educación sexual, una asignatura pendiente en España / Sexual education, a pending subject in Spain. *Biografía*, *9*(16), 195–203. doi:10.17227/20271034.vol.9num.16bio-grafia195.203

Gavey, N., Wech, A., Hindley, P., Thorburn, B., Single, G., Calder-Dawe, O., & Benton-Greig, P. (2023). Preventing image-based sexual coercion, harassment and abuse among teenagers: Girls deconstruct sexting-related harm prevention messages. *Sex Education*, 1–16. doi:10.1080/14681811.2023.2198205

Gay, R. (2014). *Bad Feminist: Essays*. Harper Perennial.

Gen H. Q. (2018). *How Obsessed Is Gen Z with Mobile Technology?* GenHQ. https://genhq.com/how-obsessed-is-gen-z-with-mobile-technology/

Gendreau, G. (1983). L'intervention, la formation et la recherche en psycho-éducation: Un bref retour sur le passé [Intervention, training and research in psycho-education: A brief look back at the past]. *Revue Canadienne de Psycho-Éducation*, *12*(2), 75–82.

Gentlewarrior, S., Martin-Jearld, A., Skok, A., & Sweetser, K. (2008). Culturally Competent Feminist Social Work. *Affilia*, *24*(3), 210–222. doi:10.1177/0886109908319117

Gesser-Edelsburg, A., & Elhadi-Arabia, M. A. (2018). Discourse on exposure to pornography content online between Arab adolescents and parents: Qualitative study on its impact on sexual education and behavior. *Journal of Medical Internet Research*, *20*(10), e11667. doi:10.2196/11667 PMID:30305264

Gilliam, M., Jagoda, P., Jaworski, E., Hebert, L. E., Lyman, P., & Wilson, M. C. (2016). "Because if we don't talk about it, how are we going to prevent it?": Lucidity, a narrative-based digital game about sexual violence. *Sex Education*, *16*(4), 391–404. doi:10.1080/14681811.2015.1123147

Gilroy, P. (2004). *Postcolonial melancholia*. Columbia University Press.

Giménez-Gualdo, A. M., Sánchez-Romero, E. I., & Torregrosa, M. S. (2022). El lado oscuro de internet. ¿Predice el cyberbullying la participación en sexting? *Revista Latinoamericana de Psicología*, *54*, 112–119. doi:10.14349/rlp.2022.v54.13

Girón Alconchel, J. L. (2023). Construcciones causales, consecutivas e ilativas. [Causal, consecutive and illative constructions] In G. Rojo, V. Vázquez Rozas, & R. Torres Cacoullos (Eds.), *Sintaxis del español* [*Spanish Syntax*]. (pp. 229–244). Routledge.

Goh, P. H., Phuah, L. A., & Low, Y. H. (2023). Pornography consumption and sexual health among emerging adults from Malaysia: An observational study. *Sexual Health*, *20*(2), 134–147. doi:10.1071/SH22181 PMID:36848630

Goikolea-Amiano, I. (2012). *Feminismo y piedad: un análisis de género en torno a las conversas al Islam* [Feminism and Piety: A gender analysis around women converts to Islam]. Universidad del País Vasco.

Goldfarb, E. S., & Constantine, N. A. (2011). Sexuality education. In B. Brown & M. J. Prinstein (Eds.), *Encyclopedia of Adolescence* (pp. 322–331). Elsevier Academic Press. doi:10.1016/B978-0-12-373951-3.00086-7

Goldfarb, E. S., & Lieberman, L. D. (2021). Three Decades of Research: The Case for Comprehensive Sex Education. *The Journal of Adolescent Health: official publication of the Society for adolescent. Medicine*, *68*(1), 13–27. doi:10.1016/j.jadohealth.2020.07.036 PMID:33468103

Goldsmith, K., Dunkley, C. R., Dang, S. S., & Gorzalka, B. B. (2017). Pornography consumption and its association with sexual concerns and expectations among young men and women. *The Canadian Journal of Human Sexuality*, *26*(2), 1–12. doi:10.3138/cjhs.262-a2

Compilation of References

Goldstein, A. (2020). Beyond porn literacy: Drawing on young people's pornography narratives to expand sex education pedagogies. *Sex Education, 20*(1), 59–74. doi:10.1080/14681811.2019.1621826 PMID:35814266

Gómez-García, S., Paz-Rebollo, M., & Cabeza-San-Deogracias, J. (2021). Newsgames frente a los discursos del odio en la crisis de los refugiados [News games against hate speech in the refugee crisis]. *Comunicar, 29*(63), 123–133. doi:10.3916/C67-2021-10

González-Falcón, I. (2019). *Variables didácticas y organizativas para la innovación y el liderazgo educativo. Guía docente*. Servicio de Publicaciones de la Universidad de Huelva.

Graaff, K. (2021). The implications of a narrow understanding of gender-based violence. *Feminist Encounters: A Journal of Critical Studies in Culture and Politics, 5*(1), 12. https://doi.org/ doi:10.20897/femenc/9749

Granero-Andújar, A. (2023). *Educación afectivo-sexual y colectivo LGTBIQ. Una relación de encuentros y desencuentros*. Octaedro. doi:10.36006/09142-1

Granero-Andújar, A., & Márquez-Díaz, J. R. (2022). Análisis de la normativa estatal española y autonómica andaluza en lo referido al colectivo LGTBI en el marco educativo. *Educare (San José), 26*(3), 1–24. doi:10.15359/ree.26-3.29

Graves, R. (2011). *The Greek myths: The complete and definitive edition*. Penguin.

Gray, H. (2013). Subject(ed) recognition. American Quarterly, 65(4), 771–798. https://doi.org/ doi:10.1353/aq.2013.0058

Gregorio, X. E., Silva, M. L., Pispira, J., & Rubbo, Y. (2023). The ideological discursive framework in femicide journalistic chronicles: María Soledad Morales' crime as a leading case. *Comunicación y Sociedad (Guadalajara), 8607*(0), 1–28. doi:10.32870/cys.v2023.8607

Grimal, P. (1992). *Dictionary of classical mythology*. Penguin.

Guerrero, D. G. (2017). Capítulo 10. Prevención del embarazo adolescente en el estado de Oaxaca mediante armonización de marco legal. *Índice*, 135.

Guindon, J. (1995). Les étapes de rééducation des jeunes délinquants...et des autres [*The stages of rehabilitation of young delinquents... and others*]. Sciences et Culture.

Gutiérrez España, J. A. (2021). *El intrépido vuelo de las mariposas istmeñas a la Ciudad de México. Muxeidad, identidad de género y corporalidad en contexto migratorio* [The intrepid flight of the Isthmian butterflies to Mexico City. Muxeidad, gender identity and corporeality in a migratory context].

Gutiérrez, N. (2017). Violencias en Oaxaca: pueblos indígenas, conflictos post electorales y violencia obstétrica. *Violencia y paz. Diagnósticos y propuestas para México*, 315-349.

Haberland, N. (2015). The case for addressing gender and power in sexuality and HIV education: A comprehensive review of evaluation studies. *International Perspectives on Sexual and Reproductive Health, 41*(1), 31–42. doi:10.1363/4103115 PMID:25856235

Hall, W. J., & Rodgers, G. K. (2019). Teachers' attitudes toward homosexuality and the lesbian, gay, bisexual, and queer community in the United States. *Social Psychology of Education, 22*(1), 23–41. doi:10.1007/s11218-018-9463-9

Hamilton, L., & Corbett-Whittier, C. (2012). Using case study in education research. *Sage (Atlanta, Ga.)*.

Hankivsky, O. (2020). Women's Health, Men's Health, and Gender and Health: Implications of Intersectionality. *Social Science & Medicine, 258*, 113136. PMID:22361090

Haralambos, M., & Holborn, M. (2004). *Sociology themes and prospective*. Harper Collins Publishers.

Harari, G. M., Müller, S. R., Stachl, C., Wang, R., Wang, W., Bühner, M., Rentfrow, P. J., Campbell, A. T., & Gosling, S. D. (2020). Sensing sociability: Individual differences in young adults' conversation, calling, texting, and app use behaviors in daily life. *Journal of Personality and Social Psychology*, *119*(1), 204–228. doi:10.1037/pspp0000245 PMID:31107054

Haraway, D. (1994). A manifesto for cyborgs: Science, technology, and socialist feminism in the 1980s. In S. Seidman (Ed.), *The Postmodern Turn New Perspectives on Social Theory* (pp. 82–116). Cambridge University Press. doi:10.1017/CBO9780511570940.007

Hard, R. (1997). *Apollodorus. The library of Greek mythology*. Oxford University Press. [trans.]

Harryhausen, R., & Schneer, C. H. (Producers), & Davis, D. (Director). (1981). *Clash of the titans* [Film]. Metro-Goldwyn-Mayer.

Hasinoff, A. A. (2015). *Sexting panic: rethinking criminalization, privacy, and consent*. University of Illinois Press. doi:10.5406/illinois/9780252038983.001.0001

Henry, N., & Powell, A. (2018). Technology-facilitated sexual violence: A literature review of empirical research. *Trauma, Violence & Abuse*, *19*(2), 195–208. doi:10.1177/1524838016650189 PMID:27311818

Henseler, C. (2003). *En sus propias palabras: escritoras españolas ante el mercado literario*. Torremozas.

Henseler, C. (2004). Pop, Punk, and Rock & Roll Writers: José Ángel MañAs, Ray Loriga, and Lucía Etxebarria Redefine the Literary Canon. *Hispania*, *87*(4), 692–702. doi:10.2307/20140874

Hequembourg, A. L., Livingston, J. A., & Wang, W. (2020). Prospective associations among relationship abuse, sexual harassment and bullying in a community sample of sexual minority and exclusively heterosexual youth. *Journal of Adolescence*, *83*(1), 52–61. doi:10.1016/j.adolescence.2020.06.010 PMID:32736276

Heras-Sevilla, D., & Ortega-Sánchez, D. (2020). Evaluation of sexist and prejudiced attitudes toward homosexuality in Spanish future teachers: Analysis of related variables. *Frontiers in Psychology*, *11*, 572553. doi:10.3389/fpsyg.2020.572553 PMID:33013607

Herbitter, C., Norris, A. L., Nelson, K. M., & Orchowski, L. M. (2022). Understanding associations between exposure to violent pornography and teen dating violence among female sexual minority High School students. *Journal of Interpersonal Violence*, *37*(17-18), NP17023–NP17035. doi:10.1177/08862605211028314 PMID:34215165

Heredia Espinosa, A. L., & Rodríguez Barraza, A. (2021). Antecedentes de la educación sexual en México a un siglo de su creación: eugenesia y moral. *Elementos 121*, 45–51. https://elementos.buap.mx/directus/storage/uploads/00000005801.pdf

Herek, G. M. (2004). Beyond "Homophobia": Thinking About Sexual Prejudice and Stigma in the Twenty-First Century. *Sexuality Research & Social Policy*, *1*(2), 6–24. doi:10.1525/srsp.2004.1.2.6

Hernáinz, E., & Márquez, D. (2011). *Manual Educativo para la Diversidad*. Fundación Reflejos de Venezuela, Unión Afirmativa de Venezuela y Amnistía Internacional Venezuela.

Hernández Castillo, R. A. (2010). Violencia de Estado y violencia de género: Las paradojas en torno a los derechos humanos de las Mujeres en México [State violence and gender-based violence: the paradoxes surrounding women's human rights in Mexico]. *Trace (México, DF)*, *57*, 86–98.

Hernandez, R. A. (Ed.). (2008). *Etnografías e historias de resistencia: mujeres indígenas, procesos organizativos y nuevas identidades políticas* (pp. 15–40). Centro de Investigaciones y Estudios Superiores en Antropología Social.

Herțanu, M., Soponaru, C., & Păduraru, E. A. (2023). Formal education vs. informal education in the Roma community - A silent confrontation where nobody wins. *Frontiers in Education*, *8*, 1–8. doi:10.3389/feduc.2023.1225113

Compilation of References

Hicks, S., & Jeyasingham, D. (2016). Social Work, Queer Theory and After: A Genealogy of Sexuality Theory in Neo-Liberal Times. *British Journal of Social Work, 46*(8), 2357–2373. doi:10.1093/bjsw/bcw103

Hill Collins, P. (1998). La política del pensamiento feminista negro. *Qué son los estudios de mujeres*, 253-312.

Hill, D. B. (2003). Genderism, transphobia, and gender bashing: A framework for interpreting anti-transgender violence. In B. Wallace & R. Carter (Eds.), *Understanding and dealing with violence: A multicultural approach* (pp. 113–136). SAGE., doi:10.4135/9781452231723.n4

Hill, D. B., & Willoughby, L. B. (2005). The Development and Validation of the Genderism and Transphobia Scale. *Sex Roles, 53*(7-8), 531–544. doi:10.1007/s11199-005-7140-x

Hinduja, S., & Patchin, J. W. (2014). *Cyberbullying: identification. Prevention and Response.* Cyberbullying Research Center. https://cyberbullying.org/Cyberbullying-Identification-Prevention-Response.pdf

Hooks, B. (2004). Mujeres negras. Dar forma a la teoría feminista. *Otras inapropiables. Feminismos desde las fronteras*, 33-50. ILSB (n/d). *Juventudes evalúan servicios de salud sexual y reproductiva a través de mecanismos de transparencia y rendición de cuentas en Oaxaca* [Youth evaluate sexual and reproductive health services through transparency and accountability mechanisms in Oaxaca]. ILSB. https://ilsb.org.mx/embarazoenadolescentes/assets/files/Oaxaca.pdf

Horsti, K. (2017). Digital Islamophobia: The Swedish woman as a figure of pure and dangerous whiteness. *New Media & Society, 19*(9), 1440–1457. doi:10.1177/1461444816642169

Huang, X., Zou, D., Cheng, G., Chen, X., & Xie, H. (2023). Trends, research issues and applications of artificial intelligence in language education. *Journal of Educational Technology & Society, 26*(1), 112–131. doi:10.30191/ETS.202301_26(1).0009

Huertas-Abril, C. A. (2018a). Inglés para fines sociales y de cooperación (IFSyC): Contextualización y justificación. [English for Social Purposes and Cooperation (ESoPC): Contextualisation and rationale]. In C. A. Huertas-Abril & M. E. Gómez-Parra (Eds.), *Inglés para fines sociales y de cooperación. Guía para la elaboración de materiales* [*English for Social Purposes and Cooperation: Guidance for materials design*]. (pp. 9–24). Graó.

Huertas-AbrilC. A. (2018b). Oral presentation rubric (EFL teaching and learning). doi:10.13140/RG.2.2.17163.36649

Huertas-AbrilC. A. (2018c). Rubric for written assignments. doi:10.13140/RG.2.2.30585.13920

Huertas-Abril, C. A. (2021). *Tecnologías para la educación bilingüe* [Technologies for bilingual education]. Peter Lang., doi:10.3726/b17576

Huertas-Abril, C. A., & Palacios-Hidalgo, F. J. (2023). New possibilities of Artificial Intelligence-Assisted Language Learning (AIALL): Comparing visions from the East and the West. *Education Sciences, 13*(12), 1234. doi:10.3390/educsci13121234

Human Rights Foundation. (2021). *Dismantling a culture of violence. Understanding violence against transgender and non-binary people and ending the crisis.* Human Rights Foundation. https://bit.ly/3Q1WZQ4

Hyden, H. (2023). Pornography. The politics of legal changes. An opinion article. *Frontiers in Sociology, 8*, 1250012. doi:10.3389/fsoc.2023.1250012 PMID:38089013

Ibrahim, R., Boerhannoeddin, A., & Bakare, K. K. (2017). The effect of soft skills and training methodology on employee performance. *European Journal of Training and Development, 41*(4), 388–406. doi:10.1108/EJTD-08-2016-0066

Ibrohimova, M., & Ziyaboyeva, S. (2022). English as a global language in XXI century. *The American Journal of Social Science and Education Innovations, 04*(1), 5–8. doi:10.37547/tajssei/Volume04Issue01-02

Icaza, R., & De Jong, S. (2018). Introduction: decolonization and feminisms in global teaching and learning: a radical space of possibility. In Decolonization and Feminisms in Global Teaching and Learning (pp. xv-xxxiv). (Teaching with Gender book series). Routledge.

Idoiaga-Mondragon, N., Eiguren-Munitis, A., Ozamiz-Etxebarria, N., & Alonso-Saez, I. (2024). Let us educate on pornography: Young education students' representations of pornography. *Sexuality Research & Social Policy*. doi:10.1007/s13178-023-00930-z

ILGA-Europe. (2023). *Annual Review of the Human Rights Situation of Lesbian, Gay, Bisexual, Trans and Intersex people in Europe and central Asia*. ILGA. https://www.ilga-europe.org/report/annual-review-2023/

ILSB. (2021). *Recomendaciones para prevenir el embarazo en adolescentes por medio de los servicios de salud sexual y reproductiva en Oaxaca [Recommendations for preventing adolescent pregnancy through sexual and reproductive health services in Oaxaca]*. ILSB. https://ilsb.org.mx/wp-content/uploads/2021/12/LPN_Incidencia_Oaxaca-H-web_VF.pdf

INEGI. (2018). *Encuesta Nacional de la Dinámica Demográfica (ENADID) 2018 [National Survey of Demographic Dynamics (ENADID) 2018]*. INEGI.

INEGI. (2020). *Censo de Población y Vivienda, 2020 [Census of Population and Housing, 2020]*. INEGI.

INEGI. (2021). *Encuesta Nacional sobre Diversidad Sexual y de Género*. INEGI.

INEGI. (2021). *INEGI- Censos de población y vivienda 2010-2020*. INEGI. https://cuentame.inegi.org.mx/monografias/informacion/mex/poblacion/diversidad.aspx?tema=me&e=15#:~:text=78%20%25%20de%20la%20poblaci%C3%B3n%20es%20cat%C3%B3lica

Iner, D., Mason, G., & Asquith, N. L. (2022). Expected but not accepted: Victimisation, gender, and Islamophobia in Australia. *International Review of Victimology*, *28*(3), 286–304. doi:10.1177/02697580221084115

INPI. (2017). *Etnografía del pueblo zapoteco del Istmo de Tehuantepec (Binnizá) [Ethnography of the Zapotec People of the Isthmus of Tehuantepec (Binnizá)]*. INPI. https://www.gob.mx/inpi/articulos/etnografia-del-pueblo-zapoteco-del-istmo-de-tehuantepec-binniza

Ioannis, PP. II. (1981). *Familiaris Consortio*. Libreria Editrice Vaticana.

IPPF European Network. (2012). *Sexuality Education in Europe and Central Asia*. IPPF European Network.

Iwunna, P., Ndukwu, E. C., Dioka, B. O., Alaribe, O. C., & Alison, O. J. (2021). History of Igbo people and education: A psychological implication. *Historical Research Letter*, *53*, 51–61.

Iyekekpolor, S. A. O., & Uveruveh, F. (2023). Curriculum development and evaluation: New dimensions to enriching Mathematics Education in Nigeria. *African Journal of Mathematics and Computer Science Research*, *16*(1), 8–13. doi:10.5897/AJMCSR2022.0913

Iyer, P., & Aggleton, P. (2012). *Sex education should be taught, fine…but we make sure they control themselves': teachers' beliefs and attitudes towards young people's sexual and reproductive health in a Ugandan secondary school*. University of Sussex. https://hdl.handle.net/10779/uos.23419181.v1

Jaffe, K. D., Dessel, A. B., & Woodford, M. R. (2016). The nature of incoming graduate social work students' attitudes toward sexual minorities. *Journal of Gay & Lesbian Social Services*, *28*(4), 255–276. doi:10.1080/10538720.2016.1224210

Jang, Y., & Ko, B. (2023). Online Safety for Children and Youth under the 4Cs Framework—A Focus on Digital Policies in Australia, Canada, and the UK. *Children (Basel, Switzerland)*, *10*(8), 1415. doi:10.3390/children10081415 PMID:37628414

Jhe, G. B., Addison, J., Lin, J., & Pluhar, E. (2023). Pornography use among adolescents and the role of primary care. *Family Medicine and Community Health*, *11*(1), e001776. doi:10.1136/fmch-2022-001776 PMID:36650009

Jiménez, R. (2019). Multiple victimization (bullying and cyberbullying) in primary education in Spain from a gender perspective. *Multidisciplinary Journal of Educational Research*, *9*(2), 169–193. doi:10.17583/remie.2019.4272

John, N., Casey, S. E., Carino, G., & McGovern, T. (2020). Lessons never learned: Crisis and gender-based violence. *Developing World Bioethics*, *20*(2), 65–68. doi:10.1111/dewb.12261 PMID:32267607

Johnson, M., & Majewska, D. (2022). Formal, non-formal, and informal learning: What are they, what are they, and how can we research them? Research report. Cambridge University Press & Assessment.

Juárez-Moreno, M., López-Pérez, O., Josefa Raesfelda, L., & Durán-González, R. E. (2021). Sexualidad, género y percepción del riesgo a la infección por VIH en mujeres indígenas de México [Sexuality, gender and HIV risk perception among indigenous women in Mexico]. *Saúde Soc. São Paulo, 30*(2), 1-12. https://doi.org/ doi:10.1590/S0104-12902021200399

Jung, H., & Choi, E. (2016). The importance of indirect teaching behaviour and its educational effects in physical education. *Physical Education and Sport Pedagogy*, *21*(2), 121–136. doi:10.1080/17408989.2014.923990

Kalimaposo, K., Mukando, M., Milupi, I., Mubita, K., & Hambulo, F. (2022). Men's Expeience of gender based violence in selected Compunds of Lusaka Urban. *International Journal of Social Science and Education Research Studies*, 717-733.

Kannan, J., & Munday, P. (2018). New trends in second language learning and teaching through the lens of ICT, networked learning, and artificial intelligence. *Círculo de Lingüística Aplicada a la Comunicación*, *76*, 13–30. doi:10.5209/CLAC.62495

Karaian, L., & Van Meyl, K. (2015). Reframing risqué/risky: Queer temporalities, teenage sexting, and freedom of expression. *Laws*, *4*(1), 18–36. doi:10.3390/laws4010018

Karakuş, G. (2021). A literary review on curriculum implementation problems. *Shanlax International Journal of Education*, *9*(3), 201–220. doi:10.34293/education.v9i3.3983

Karjo, C. H., & Ng, A. (2020). Hate speech propaganda from and against Muslims in Facebook posts. *International Journal of Cyber Criminology*, *14*(2), 400–416. doi:10.5281/zenodo.4766989

Karlsson, J., Jolles, D., Koornneef, A., van den Broek, P., & Van Leijenhorst, L. (2019). Individual differences in children's comprehension of temporal relations: Dissociable contributions of working memory capacity and working memory updating. *Journal of Experimental Child Psychology*, *185*, 1–18. doi:10.1016/j.jecp.2019.04.007 PMID:31077975

Karram, A. (2023). *Education as the pathway towards gender equality*. N9. https://n9.cl/miwacx

Karver, T. S., Sorhaindo, A., Wilson, K. S., & Contreras, X. (2016). Exploring intergenerational changes in perceptions of gender roles and sexuality among Indigenous women in Oaxaca. *Culture, Health & Sexuality*, *18*(8), 845–859. doi:10.1080/13691058.2016.1144790 PMID:26928352

Kattari, S. K., & Begun, S. (2017). On the margins of marginalized: Transgender homelessness and survival sex. *Affilia*, *32*(1), 92–103. doi:10.1177/0886109916651904

Keen, C., Kramer, R., & France, A. (2020). The pornographic state: The changing nature of state regulation in addressing illegal and harmful online content. *Media Culture & Society*, *42*(7), 1175–1192. doi:10.1177/0163443720904631

Kehily, M. J. (2002). Sexing the Subject: Teachers, pedagogies and sex education. *Sex Education*, *2*(3), 215–231. doi:10.1080/1468181022000025785

Kerbavaz, K. (2015). La lengua de Margarita: El silencio impuesto y la escritura activista en Crónica del desamor. *Revista de Filología y Lingüística de La Universidad de Costa Rica*, *41*(2), 55–65.

Keulder, C., & Amakoh, K. (2022). Amid progress on Women's Rights Namibians see gender based violence as a priority issue to adress. *Afrobarometer Dispatch*, (513), 1–19.

Kiekens, W. J., Baams, L., Fish, J. N., & Watson, R. J. (2022). Associations of relationship experiences, dating violence, sexual harassment, and assault with alcohol use among sexual and gender minority adolescents. *Journal of Interpersonal Violence*, *37*(17-18), NP15176–NP15204. doi:10.1177/08862605211001469 PMID:33719695

Kiss, L., Schraiber, L. B., Heise, L., Zimmerman, C., Gouveia, N., & Watts, C. (2012). Gender-based violence and socioeconomic inequalities: Does living in more deprived neighbourhoods increase women's risk of intimate partner violence? *Social Science & Medicine*, *74*(8), 1172–1179. doi:10.1016/j.socscimed.2011.11.033 PMID:22361088

Kluzer, S., & Pujol Priego, L. (2018). DigCompinto Action - Get inspired, make it happen. S. Carretero, Y. Punie, R. Vuorikari, M. Cabrera, & O'Keefe, W. (Eds.). JRC Science for Policy Report, EUR 29115 EN. Publications Office of the European Union. doi:10.2760/112945

Kluzer, S., Centeno, C., & O'Keeffe, W. (2020). *DigComp at work: the EU's digital competence framework in action on the labour market: a selection of case studies*. Publications Office. https://data.europa.eu/doi/10.2760/17763

Knights, V. (1999). *The Search for Identity in the Narrative of Rosa Montero*. Edwin Mellen Press.

Kolb, D. (2015). *Experiential learning: Experience as the source of learning and development*. Pearson.

Laje, A. (2019, december 2). *¿De dónde viene la ideología de género?* [Video]. Youtube. https://www.youtube.com/watch?v=dAaUhVTYfo0

Lakhotiya, A. (2023). *The role of education in promoting gender equality*. N9. https://n9.cl/7r3lqq

Lamas, M. (2018). ¿Activismo académico? El caso de algunas etnógrafas feministas. *Cuicuilco. Revista de ciencias antropológicas*, *25*(72), 9-30.

Lara-Garrido, A. S., Álvarez-Bernardo, G., & García-Berbén, A. B. (2023). Conocimientos hacia la Homosexualidad y Homonegatividad Moderna en Estudiantes de Educación Universitarios. *Revista Internacional de Educación para la Justicia Social*, *12*(2), 213–229. doi:10.15366/riejs2023.12.2.012

Latzman, N. E., D'Inverno, A. S., Niolon, P. H., & Reidy, D. E. (2018). Gender inequality and gender-based violence: Extensions to adolescent dating violence. In D. A. Wolfe & J. R. Temple (Eds.), *Adolescent Dating Violence. Theory, research, and prevention* (pp. 283–314). Academic Press. doi:10.1016/B978-0-12-811797-2.00012-8

Laursen, S., & Austin, A. E. (2020). *Building gender equity in the academy: Institutional strategies for change*. Johns Hopkins University Press. doi:10.1353/book.78724

Le Blanc, M. (2004). Qu'est-ce que la psychoéducation? Que devrait-elle devenir? Réflexion à la lumière de l'expérience montréalaise [What is Psychoeducation? What should it become? Reflection in light of the Montreal experience]. *Revue de psychoédcuation*, *33*(2), 289-304.

Le, H. V., Chong, S. L., & Wan, R. (2022). Critical reading in higher education: A systematic review. *Thinking Skills and Creativity*, *44*, 101028. doi:10.1016/j.tsc.2022.101028

Le, K., & Nguyen, M. (2020). How education empowers women in developing countries. *The B.E. Journal of Economic Analysis & Policy*, *21*(2), 511–536. doi:10.1515/bejeap-2020-0046

Lems, J. (2024). *Tomar la palabra. Islamofobia y participación política después del 15-M* [Taking the Floor: Islamophobia and Political Participation After the 15-M Movement]. Vernon Press.

Levin, D. S., & Hammock, A. C. (2020). School context and content in Canadian sex education. *The Canadian Journal of Human Sexuality*, 29(3), 323–338. doi:10.3138/cjhs.2019-0046

Levtov, G. R. (2013). *Promoting gender equity through schools: Three papers on schooling, gender attitudes, and interventions to promote gender equity in Egypt and India* [PhD thesis, University of Michigan]. https://n9.cl/pcatr

Ley Orgánica 1/2015, de 30 de marzo, por la que se modifica la Ley Orgánica 10/1995, de 23 de noviembre, del Código Penal. *Boletín oficial del Estado 77* de 31 de marzo de 2015, páginas 27061 a 27176. https://www.boe.es/eli/es/lo/2015/03/30/1

Ley Orgánica 11/1999, de 30 de abril, de modificación del Título VIII del Libro II del Código Penal, aprobado por Ley Orgánica 10/1995, de 23 de noviembre. *Boletín Oficial del Estado 104*, de 1 de mayo de 1999, páginas 16099 a 16102. https://www.boe.es/eli/es/lo/1999/04/30/11

Liang, B., & Lu, H. (2012). Fighting the obscene, pornographic, and unhealthy – an analysis of the nature, extent, and regulation of China's online pornography within a global context. *Crime, Law, and Social Change*, 58(2), 111–130. doi:10.1007/s10611-012-9380-3

Liebenberg, L. (2018). Thinking critically about photovoice: Achieving empowerment and social change. *International Journal of Qualitative Methods*, 17(1), 1609406918757631. doi:10.1177/1609406918757631

Li, L., Wang, X., Tang, S., & Wang, J. (2023). Family functioning and problematic internet pornography use among adolescents: A moderated mediation model. *Frontiers in Public Health*, 11, 1199835. doi:10.3389/fpubh.2023.1199835 PMID:37397734

Lismini, R., Narti, S., & Octaviani, V. (2023). Netnographic study of online gender-based violence (KBGO) on Twitter. *Journal of Science*, 12(2), 1645–1661. doi:10.58471/scientia.v12i02.1430

List, A., Brante, E. W., & Klee, H. L. (2020). A framework of pre-service teachers' conceptions about digital literacy: Comparing the United States and Sweden. *Computers & Education*, 148, 103788. doi:10.1016/j.compedu.2019.103788

Löfgren-Mårtenson, L., & Månsson, S. A. (2010). Lust, love, and life: A qualitative study of Swedish adolescents' perceptions and experiences with pornography. *Journal of Sex Research*, 47(6), 568–579. doi:10.1080/00224490903151374 PMID:19731132

López, F. (2008). Female Subjects in Late Modernity: Lucía Etxebarría's *Amor, Curiosidad, Prozac y Dudas. Dissidences*, 2(4)

López-Diosdado, M. (2016). Aprender a vivir juntos: una asignatura pendiente en la formación docente. *Revista Nacional e Internacional de Educación Inclusiva*, 9(2), 215-224. https://revistaeducacioninclusiva.es/index.php/REI/article/download/61/56

López-Pacheco, J. A. (2021). The (re)emergence of the discourse of 'gender ideology' in Latin America: Protests, public attention, and government responses. *Estudios Politicos*, 60, 145–177. doi:10.17533/udea.espo.n60a07

López, R., Hernández, D., & Martínez, K. P. (2023). Violencia Digital en las y los estudiantes de la Universidad Veracruzana. *Transdigital*, 4(8), 1–17. doi:10.56162/transdigital221

López-Sáez, M. Á., García-Dauder, D., & Montero, I. (2020). Correlate Attitudes Toward LGBT and Sexism in Spanish Psychology Students. *Frontiers in Psychology*, 11, e2063. doi:10.3389/fpsyg.2020.02063 PMID:32973622

Lugones, M. (2008). Colonialidad y género. *Tabula rasa*, (9), 73-102.

Lukolo, L., & van Dhyke, A. (2015). Parents' Participation in the Sexuality Education of Their Children in Rural Namibia: A Situational Analysis. *Global Journal of Health Science*, 7(1), 35–45. PMID:25560329

Lynch, K. R., & Logan, T. K. (2023). Rural and urban/suburban victim professionals' perceptions of gender-based violence, victim challenges, and safety advice during the COVID-19 pandemic. *Violence Against Women*, 29(5), 1060–1084. doi:10.1177/10778012221099987 PMID:35938486

Macilotti, G. (2020). Online child pornography: Conceptual issues and law enforcement challenges. In A. Balloni & R. Sette (Eds.), *Handbook of research on trends and issues in crime prevention, rehabilitation, and victim support* (pp. 226–247). IGI Global. doi:10.4018/978-1-7998-1286-9.ch013

Mackie, J. L. (1980). *The Cement of the Universe*. Clarendon Press. doi:10.1093/0198246420.001.0001

Maddocks, S. (2022). Feminism, activism and non-consensual pornography: Analyzing efforts to end "revenge porn" in the United States. *Feminist Media Studies*, 22(7), 1641–1656. doi:10.1080/14680777.2021.1913434

Madigan, S., Ly, A., Rash, C. L., Van Ouytsel, J., & Temple, J. R. (2018). Prevalence of multiple forms of sexting behavior among youth: A systematic review and meta-analysis. *JAMA Pediatrics*, 172(4), 327–335. doi:10.1001/jamapediatrics.2017.5314 PMID:29482215

Magezi, V., & Manzanga, P. (2019). Gender-based violence and efforts to address the phenomenon: Towards a church public pastoral care intervention proposition for community care intervention proposition for community development in Zimbabwe. *Hervormde Teologiese Studies*, •••, 1–9. doi:10.4102/hts.v75i4.5532

Maheux, A. J., Evans, R., Widman, L., Nesi, J., Prinstein, M. J., & Choukas-Bradley, S. (2020). Popular peer norms and adolescent sexting behavior. *Journal of Adolescence*, 78(1), 62–66. doi:10.1016/j.adolescence.2019.12.002 PMID:31841872

Maheux, A. J., Roberts, S. R., Evans, R., Widman, L., & Choukas-Bradley, S. (2021). Associations between adolescents' pornography consumption and self-objectification, body consumption, and body shame. *Body Image*, 37, 89–93. doi:10.1016/j.bodyim.2021.01.014 PMID:33582530

Mahmoudi, A., Khoshnood, A., & Babaei, A. (2014). Paulo Freire critical pedagogy and its implications in curriculum planning. *Journal of Education and Practice*, 5(14), 86–92.

Mahoso, T., Venketsamy, R., & Finestone, M. (2023). Cultural Factors Affecting the Teaching of Comprehensive Sexuality Education in Early Grades in Zimbabwe. *Global Journal of Human Social -Social Science: C Sociology and Culture*, 23(5), 1-13.

Mahtani, N. (2023, May 21). *La violencia digital en tiempos de la IA, ¿otra amenaza más para las mujeres?* [Digital violence in times of AI, another threat for women?] El País. https://bit.ly/48EhvNW

Maia, A. C. B., & Vilaça, T. (2017). Concepções de professores sobre a sexualidade de alunos e a sua formação em educação inclusiva. *Revista Educação Especial*, 30(59), 669. doi:10.5902/1984686X28087

Maio, G. R., Haddock, G., & Verplanken, B. (2019). *The psychology of attitudes and attitudes change* (3rd ed.). SAGE.

Makleff, S., Garduño, J., Zavala, R. I., Barindelli, F., Valades, J., Billowitz, M., Silva Márquez, V. I., & Marston, C. (2020). Preventing intimate partner violence among young people—A qualitative study examining the role of comprehensive sexuality education. *Sexuality Research & Social Policy*, 17(2), 314–325. doi:10.1007/s13178-019-00389-x

Makovhololo, P. (2017). Diffusion of Innovation theory for Infomation technology decision making in organisational strategy. *Journal of innovation theory for Information technology decision making in organisational strategy*, 461-481.

Maldonado, H. (2017). *La psicoeducación: Neo ideas para abordar problemáticas psicoeducativas* [Psychoeducation: Neo ideas to address psychoeducational problems]. Editorial Brujas.

Manrique, M. S. (2020). Tipología de procesos cognitivos. Uma ferramenta para análise educacional [Typology of cognitive processes. A tool for educational analysis]. *Educación (Lima)*, *29*(57), 163–185. doi:10.18800/educacion.202002.008

Manteiga, R. (1988). The Dilemma of the Modern Woman: A Study of the Female Characters in Rosa Montero's Novels. In R. C. Manteiga, C. Garlerstein, & K. McNerney (Eds.), *Feminine Concerns in Contemporary Spanish Fiction by Women* (pp. 113–123). Scripta Humanistica.

Maras, K., Sweiry, A., Villadsen, A., & Fitzsimons, E. (2024). Cyber offending predictors and pathways in middle adolescence: Evidence from the UK Millennium Cohort Study. *Computers in Human Behavior*, *151*, 108011. doi:10.1016/j.chb.2023.108011

Marcote, R. M. (1998). Voices of Protest in Rosa Montero's *Crónica del desamor*. *Neophilologus*, *82*(1), 63–70. doi:10.1023/A:1004237420813

Maria Michael, J., & Reyes, M. E. (2021). Cyberbullying victimization as a predictor of depressive symptoms among selected adolescents amidst the COVID-19 pandemic. *Makara Human Behavior Studies in Asia*, *25*(2), 145–152. doi:10.7454/hubs.asia.2161121

Marino, J. L., Lin, A., Davies, C., Kang, M., Bista, S., & Skinner, S. R. (2023). Childhood and Adolescence Gender Role Nonconformity and Gender and Sexuality Diversity in Young Adulthood. *JAMA Pediatrics*, *177*(11), 1176. doi:10.1001/jamapediatrics.2023.3873 PMID:37747725

Martellozzo, E., Monaghan, A., & Adler, J. (2020). Researching the affects that online pornography has on UK adolescents aged 11 to 16. *SAGE Open*, *10*(1), 1–11. doi:10.1177/2158244019899462

Martínez, C., Van Prooijen, J. W., & Van Lange, P. (2022). A threat-based hate model: How symbolic and realistic threats underlie hate and aggression. *Journal of Experimental Social Psychology*, *103*, 1044393. doi:10.1016/j.jesp.2022.104393

Martínez, J. L., González, E., Vicario-Molina, I., Fernández-Fuertes, A. A., Carcedo, R. J., Fuertes, A., & Orgaz, B. (2013). Formación del profesorado en educación sexual: Pasado, presente y futuro. *Magister*, *25*(1), 35–42. doi:10.1016/S0212-6796(13)70005-7

Martínez-Quiroga, P. (2015). Humor, feminismo y crítica social en la novela española contemporánea. *Bulletin of Spanish Studies: Hispanic Studies and Researches on Spain, Portugal, and Latin America*, *92*(6), 931–949. doi:10.1080/14753820.2014.947854

Martin-Hald, G., & Malamuth, N. M. (2008). Self-perceived effects of pornography consumption. *Archives of Sexual Behavior*, *37*(4), 614–625. doi:10.1007/s10508-007-9212-1 PMID:17851749

Martins, M. V., Formiga, A., Santos, C., Sousa, D., Resende, C., Campos, R., Nogueira, N., Carvalho, P., & Ferreira, S. (2020). Adolescent internet addiction – role of parental control and adolescent behaviours. *International Journal of Pediatrics & Adolescent Medicine*, *7*(3), 116–120. doi:10.1016/j.ijpam.2019.12.003 PMID:33094139

Masters, W. H., & Johnson, V. E. (2012). *El vínculo del placer*. Colección Relaciones Humanas Y Sexología, 1. GRIJALBO.

Masters, W. H., Levin, R. J., & Johnson, V. E. (1983). *El vínculo del placer: un nuevo enfoque del compromiso sexual*. Grijalbo.

Matambo, E. (2018). Formal against indigenous and informal education in sub-Saharan Africa: The battle without winners. *Indilinga*, *17*(1), 1–13.

Mateeva, E. (2022). Hate speech in election campaigns. *Media and Language*, *1*(11), 67–83. doi:10.58894/WTWA9930

Maxwell, J., & Chmiel, M. (2014). Notes toward a theory of qualitative data analysis. In U. Flick (Ed.), *The SAGE handbook of qualitative data analysis* (pp. 21–34). SAGE Publications. doi:10.4135/9781446282243.n2

Mazhambe, R., & Mushunje, M. (2023). Evidence generation for sustained impact in the response to from the SRHR Africa Trust Zimbabwe. *Frontiers in Global Women's Health*, 1–7. doi:10.3389/fgwh.2023.1135393 PMID:37746322

Mazzacani, D. (2019). Foreign languages for the labor market: An analysis of the role of compulsory education in Europe. *Revista Internacional de Organizaciones*, *23*(23), 39–58. doi:10.17345/rio23.39-58

Mbizvo, M., Kasonda, K., Muntalima, N.-C., Joseph, G., Inambwe, S., Namukonda, E., & Kangale, C. (2023). Comprehensive Sexuality Education Linked to sexual reproductive health services reduces early and unitended pregnancies among in-school adolescent girls in Zambia. *BMC Public Health*, *23*(348), 1–13. PMID:36797703

McCormack, M., & Wignall, L. (2024). Pornography, social media, and sexuality. In *Handbook of social media use online. Relationships, security, privacy, and society* (pp. 309–329). Academic Press., doi:10.1016/B978-0-443-28804-3.00011-9

McMaster, K. L., van den Broek, P., Espin, C. A., White, M. J., Rapp, D. N., Kendeou, P., Bohn-Gettler, C., & Carlson, S. (2012). Making the right connections: Differential effects of reading intervention for subgroups of comprehenders. *Learning and Individual Differences*, *22*(1), 100–111. doi:10.1016/j.lindif.2011.11.017

MediaSmarts. (2024). *Use, understand & engage: A digital media literacy framework for Canadian schools*. MediaSmarts. https://bitly.ws/3eBiN

Meilani, N., Hariadi, S. S., & Haryadi, F. T. (2023). Social media and pornography access behavior among adolescents. *International Journal of Public Health Science*, *12*(2), 536–544. doi:10.11591/ijphs.v12i2.22513

Meilani, N., Setiyawati, N., & Onyapidi-Barasa, S. (2020). Factors related pornographic access behaviour among high school students in Yogyakarta, Indonesia. *Malaysian Journal of Public Health Medicine*, *20*(2), 123–130. doi:10.37268/mjphm/vol.20/no.2/art.801

Mena, M. (2022). *Uso de redes sociales. Los jóvenes de 16 a 24 años, los más activos en redes sociales en España [Use of social media. Young people aged 16 to 24, the most active on social media in Spain]*. Statista. https://es.statista.com/grafico/28879/porcentaje-de-poblacion-que-ha-participado-en-redes-sociales-en-espana/#:~:text=Aunque%20las%20redes%20sociales%20han,alg%C3%BAn%20tipo%20de%20red%20social

Menabò, L., Skrzypiec, G., Slee, P., & Guarini, A. (2023). What roles matter? An explorative study on bullying and cyberbullying by using the eye-tracker. *The British Journal of Educational Psychology*, e12604. doi:10.1111/bjep.12604 PMID:37186299

Mena-López, M., & Ramírez Aristizábal, F. M. (2018). Las falacias discursivas en torno a la ideología de género. *Ex Aequo - Revista Da Associação Portuguesa de Estudos Sobre as Mulheres*, 37. doi:10.22355/exaequo.2018.37.02

Mendoza, A. (2018). X-ilah k'oha'an (parteras) y personal médico alópata en la atención del embarazo y el parto de mujeres mayas de Yucatán y Quintana Roo. *Salud reproductiva, medio ambiente y género, 55*.

Mendoza, B. (2010). La epistemología del sur, la colonialidad del género y el feminismo latinoamericano. *Aproximaciones críticas a las prácticas teórico-políticas del feminismo latinoamericano*, *1*, 19-36.

Menéndez, E. (1992). Modelo hegemónico, modelo alternativo subordinado, modelo de autoatención. Caracteres estructurales. *La antropología médica en México*, *1*, 97-111.

Compilation of References

Merrill, B. (2005). Dialogical feminism: Other women and the challenge of adult education. *International Journal of Lifelong Education*, 24(1), 41–52. doi:10.1080/026037042000317338

Meyer, E. J., Taylor, C., & Peter, T. (2015). Perspectives on gender and sexual diversity (GSD)-inclusive education: Comparisons between gay/lesbian/bisexual and straight educators. *Sex Education*, 15(3), 221–234. doi:10.1080/14681811.2014.979341

Michielsen, K., & Ivanova, O. (2022). *Comprehensive sexuality education: Why is it important? Study requested by the FEMM committee*. Policy Department for Citizens' Rights and Constitutional Affairs. European Parliament. https://bit.ly/48NaoSN

Millán, M. (2014). Alcances político-ontológicos de los feminismos indígenas. *Más allá del feminismo: caminos para andar*, 119-144.

Ministerio de Educación de la Nación Argentina. (2022). *Referentes Escolares de ESI. Educación Secundaria: parte 1* [*CSE School References. Secondary Education: Part 1*]. Ministerio de Educación de la Nación. Dirección de Educación para los Derechos Humanos, Género y ESI. http://www.bnm.me.gov.ar/giga1/documentos/EL007797.pdf

Ministerio de Educación. (2021). *Oportunidades curriculares de educación integral en sexualidad* [*Curricular opportunities for comprehensive sexuality education*]. Minedu/UNFPA. https://bitly.ws/3a8nJ

Ministerio de industria, energía y turismo. (2018). *Capacitación en materia de seguridad TIC para padres, madres, tutores y educadores de menores de edad*. Ministerio de industria, energía y turismo. https://alumnosayudantes.files.wordpress.com/2018/03/unidades-didacticas-sexting_secundaria_red-es.pdf

Ministerio de la Presidencia. (1977). *Los pactos de la Moncloa*. Secretaría General Técnica.

Ministry of Gender and Child Welfare. (2010). *National Gender Policy (2010-2020)*. Ministry of Gender and Child Welfare.

Mizan, R. M. (2022). What is curriculum? Definition and importance of curriculum. N9 https://n9.cl/7tnwn

Moallem, M. (2021). Race, Gender, and Religion: Islamophobia and Beyond. *Meridians (Middletown, Conn.)*, 20(2), 271–290. https://www.muse.jhu.edu/article/856874. doi:10.1215/15366936-9547874

Modecki, K. L., Minchin, J., Harbaugh, A. G., Guerra, N. G., & Runions, K. C. (2014). Bullying prevalence across contexts: A meta-analysis measuring cyber and traditional bullying. *The Journal of Adolescent Health*, 55(5), 602–611. doi:10.1016/j.jadohealth.2014.06.007 PMID:25168105

Mohanty, C. (2008). Bajo los ojos de occidente. Academia Feminista y discurso colonial. *Descolonizando el feminismo: teorías y prácticas desde los márgenes*, 1, 1-23.

Mohd Zin, Z., Wong, B. E., & Rafik-Galea, S. (2014). Critical reading ability and its relation to L2 proficiency of Malaysian ESL learners. *3L. The Southeast Asian Journal of English Language Studies.*, 20(2), 43–54. doi:10.17576/3L-2014-2002-04

Moldovan, O., & Bocoş-Binţinţan, V. (2015). The necessity of reconsidering the concept of non-formal education. *Procedia: Social and Behavioral Sciences*, 209, 337–343. doi:10.1016/j.sbspro.2015.11.245

Molero, F., Silván-Ferrero, P., Fuster-Ruiz de Apodaca, M. J., Nouvilas-Pallejá, E., & Pérez-Garín, D. (2017). Subtle and blatant perceived discrimination and wellbeing in lesbians and gay men in Spain: The role of social support. *Psicothema*, 29(4), 475–481. doi:10.7334/psicothema2016.296 PMID:29048306

Molla, C. (2021). *Sexting en adolescentes perfiles, prevalencias y desarrollo de la nueva escala de medida a-sexts* [Tesis doctoral, Universidad de Valencia].

Molla-Esparza, C., López-González, E., & Losilla, J. M. (2021). Sexting prevalence and socio-demographic correlates in Spanish secondary school students. *Sexuality Research & Social Policy, 18*(1), 97–111. doi:10.1007/s13178-020-00434-0

Monteiro, A. P., Guedes, S., & Correia, E. (2023). Cyber Dating Abuse in Higher Education Students: Self-Esteem, Sex, Age and Recreational Time Online. *Social Sciences (Basel, Switzerland), 12*(3), 139. doi:10.3390/socsci12030139

Montero Rodríguez, S. (2006). La autoría femenina y la construcción de la identidad en Crónica del desamor de Rosa Montero. *Revista de Filología y Lingüística de La Universidad de Costa Rica, 32*(2), 41–54. doi:10.15517/rfl.v32i2.4289

Montero-Fernández, D., García-Rojas, A. D., Hernando-Gómez, A., & Del-Río, F. J. (2022). Digital violence questionnaire. *Revista Electrónica de Investigación y Evaluación Educativa, 28*(2), 1–21.

Montero, R. (2009). *Crónica del desamor*. Alfaguara.

Moog-Grünewald, M. (Ed.). (2008). *Mythenrezeption. Die antike mythologie in literatur, musik und kunst von den anfängen bis zur gegenwart*. J. B. Metzler.

Mora-Cantallops, M., Inamorato-Dos Santos, A., Villalonga-Gómez, C., Lacalle-Remigio, J. R., Camarillo-Casado, J., & Sota-Eguizábal, J. M. (2022). *Competencias digitales del profesorado universitario en España: Un estudio basado en los marcos europeos DigCompEdu y OpenEdu* [The Digital Competence of Academics in Spain: A study based on the European frameworks DigCompEdu and OpenEdu]. Publications Office European Communities.

Morawska, A., Grabski, M., & Fletcher, R. (2015). Parental confidence and preferences for communication with their child about sexuality. *Sex Education, 15*(3), 235–248. doi:10.1080/14681811.2014.996213

Morelli, M., Urbini, F., Bianchi, D., Baiocco, R., Cattelino, E., Laghi, F., Sorokowski, P., Misiak, M., Dziekan, M., Hudson, H., Marshall, A., Nguyen, T. T. T., Mark, L., Kopecky, K., Szotkowski, R., Toplu Demirtaş, E., Van Ouytsel, J., Ponnet, K., Walrave, M, & Chirumbolo, A. (2021). The Relationship between Dark Triad Personality Traits and Sexting Behaviors among Adolescents and Young Adults across 11 Countries. *International Journal of Environmental Research and Public Health, 18*(5), 5102. doi:10.3390/ijerph18052526 PMID:33806314

Morell-Mengual, V., Gil-Llario, M. D., & Gil-Juliá, B. (2020). Prevalencia e influencia de la violencia homofóbica sobre la sintomatología depresiva y el nivel de autoestima. *Informació Psicològica, 120*, 80–92. doi:10.14635/IPSIC.2020.120.6

Moreno, F. (2015). Función pedagógica de los recursos materiales en Educación Infantil. *Revista de Comunicación Vivat Academia, 133*, 12–25. doi:10.15178/va.2015.133.12-25

Moreno-Sánchez, E. (2021). Violencia de género en la escuela: hay una oportunidad para la prevención. The Conversation.

Moreno-Sánchez, E. (Coord.). (2013). *La urdimbre sexista: violencia de género en la escuela primaria*. Aljibe.

Mori, C., Temple, J. R., Browne, D., & Madigan, S. (2019). Association of sexting with sexual behaviors and mental health among adolescents: A systematic review and meta-analysis. *JAMA Pediatrics, 173*(8), 770–779. doi:10.1001/jamapediatrics.2019.1658 PMID:31206151

Morrison, M. A., Kiss, M. J., Parker, K., Hamp, T., & Morrison, T. G. (2019). A systematic review of the psychometric properties of binegativity scales. *Journal of Bisexuality, 19*(1), 23–50. doi:10.1080/15299716.2019.1576153

Morrison, M. A., & Morrison, T. G. (2002). Development and validation of a scale measuring modern prejudice toward gay men and lesbian women. *Journal of Homosexuality, 43*(2), 15–37. doi:10.1300/J082v43n02_02 PMID:12739696

Morrison, M. A., & Morrison, T. G. (2011). Sexual Orientation Bias Toward Gay Men and Lesbian Women: Modern Homonegative Attitudes and Their Association With Discriminatory Behavioral Intentions. *Journal of Applied Social Psychology, 41*(11), 2573–2599. doi:10.1111/j.1559-1816.2011.00838.x

Morrison, M. A., Morrison, T. G., & Franklin, R. (2009). Modern and Old-fashioned Homonegativity Among Samples of Canadian and American University Students. *Journal of Cross-Cultural Psychology*, *40*(4), 523–542. doi:10.1177/0022022109335053

Morrison, T. G., Bishop, C. J., Morrison, M. A., & Parker-Taneo, K. (2016). A Psychometric Review of Measures Assessing Discrimination Against Sexual Minorities. *Journal of Homosexuality*, *63*(8), 1086–1126. doi:10.1080/00918369.2015.1117903 PMID:26566991

Mpofu, J. (2013). Relevance of formal education to third world countries national development. *Journal of Research & Method in Education (IOSR-JRME)*, *1*(5), 64–70.

Mullis, M., Kastrinos, E., Taylor, W. G., & Bylund, C. (2021). International Barriers to Parents-Child Communication about Sexual and Reproductive Health Topics: A Qualitative Systematic Review 21 (4). *Sex Education*, *21*(4), 387–403. doi:10.1080/14681811.2020.1807316

Muluneh, M. D., Stulz, V., Francis, L., & Agho, K. (2020). Gender based violence against women in sub-Saharan Africa: A systematic review and meta-analysis of cross-sectional studies. *International Journal of Environmental Research and Public Health*, *17*(3), 903. doi:10.3390/ijerph17030903 PMID:32024080

Muñoz-Fernández, N., Sánchez-Jiménez, V., Rodríguez-deArriba, M. L., Nacimiento-Rodríguez, L., Elipe, P., & Del Rey, R. (2023). Traditional and cyber dating violence among adolescents: Profiles, prevalence, and short-term associations with peer violence. *Aggressive Behavior*, *49*(3), 261–273. doi:10.1002/ab.22069 PMID:36585958

Myers, E. D. (1988). The Feminist Message: Propaganda and/or Art? A Study of Two Novels by Rosa Montero. In R. C. Manteiga, C. Garlerstein, & K. McNerney (Eds.), *Feminine Concerns in Contemporary Spanish Fiction by Women* (pp. 99–12). Scripta Humanistica.

Naciones Unidas. (2011). *Salud de la población joven indígena en América Latina. Un panorama general* [*Health of the young indigenous population in Latin America. An overview*]. Naciones Unidas.

Naeem, T. (2022). Muslims as terrorists: Hate speech against Muslims. *International Journal of Islamic Thought*, *22*(1), 114–124. doi:10.24035/ijit.22.2022.245

Nambambi, N., & Mufune, P. (2011). What is talked about when parents discuss Sex with Children: Family Based Education in Windhoek, Namibia. *African Journal of Reproductive Health*, *15*(4), 120–129. PMID:22571114

Namibia Statistical Agency. (2021). *Namibia National Gender Statistics Assessment*. Namibia Statistical Agency.

Navas-Garcés, A. E., & Nuñez-Ruiz, J. (2021). La violencia digital en México - Ley Olimpia [Digital violence in Mexico - Olympia law]. *Criminalia*, *87*, 709–724. https://bitly.ws/3a8gX

Navas-Luque, M. y Cuadrado-Guirado, I. (Coords.). (2020). *El estudio del prejuicio en Psicología Social*. Editorial Sanz y Torres.

Nematy, A., Namer, Y., & Razum, O. (2023). LGBTQI+ refugees' and asylum seekers' mental health: A qualitative systematic review. *Sexuality Research & Social Policy*, *20*(2), 636–663. doi:10.1007/s13178-022-00705-y

Nemoto, K. (2009). *Racing romance*. Rutger University Press.

Nepal, S., & Nepal, B. (2023). Adoption of digital banking: Insights from UTAUT Model. *Journal of Business and Social Sciences*, *VIII*(1), 17–34.

Neuschäfer, H.-J. (2011). Habíamos ganado la guerra: Sobre la obra de la autora catalana Esther Tusquets. In J. Reinstädler & D. Ingenschay (Eds.), *Escribir después de la dictadura. La producción literaria y cultural en las posdictaduras de Europa e Hispanoamérica* (pp. 137–142). Vervuert Verlag. doi:10.31819/9783954871094-007

Ng, H. H. (2020). Towards a synthesis of formal, non-formal and informal pedagogies in popular music learning. *Research Studies in Music Education, 42*(1), 56–76. doi:10.1177/1321103X18774345

Ngidi, L. Z., & Kaye, S. B. (2022). Reducing school violence: A peace education project in KwaZulu-Natal, South Africa. *South African Journal of Education, 42*(2), 1989. doi:10.15700/saje.v42n2a1989

Nielsen, L. B. (2002). Subtle, pervasive, harmful: Racist and sexist remarks in public as hate speech. *The Journal of Social Issues, 58*(2), 265–280. doi:10.1111/1540-4560.00260

Nieva de la Paz, P. (2004). *Narradoras españolas de la transición política: textos y contextos*. Fundamentos.

Norris, K., Lucas, L., & Prudhoe, C. (2012). Examining critical literacy: Preparing preservice teachers to use critical literacy in the early childhood classroom. *Multicultural Education, 19*(2), 59–62.

Norton, A. T., & Herek, G. M. (2012). Heterosexuals' attitudes toward transgender people: Findings from a national probability sample of US adults. *Sex Roles, 68*(11-12), 738–753. doi:10.1007/s11199-011-0110-6

Noveduc. (2024). *Comprehensive sexual education catalog*. Noveduc. https://www.noveduc.com/catalogo/educacion-sexual-integral/?mpage=2

Nwabude, A. A. R. (2022). Traditional African (the Igbo) marriage customs & the influence of the western culture: Marxist approach. *Open Journal of Social Sciences, 10*, 224–239. doi:10.4236/jss.2022.102016

Nyarko, K. (2014). Parental Attitude towards Sex Education at Lower Primary in Ghana. *International Journal of Elementary Education, 3*(2), 21–29. doi:10.11648/j.ijeedu.20140302.11

Nyirenda, J. E. (2018). The relevance of Paulo Freire's contributions to education and development in present day Africa. https://n9.cl/b1pv4

Obermaier, M., Schmuck, D., & Saleem, M. (2023). I'll be there for you? Effects of Islamophobic online hate speech and counter speech on Muslim in-group bystanders' intention to intervene. *New Media & Society, 25*(9), 2339–2358. doi:10.1177/14614448211017527

Observatorio Nacional de Tecnología y Sociedad. (2022). *Violencia digital de género: Una realidad invisible [Digital gender-based violence: An invisible reality]*. Observatorio Nacional de Tecnología y Sociedad. https://bit.ly/46SMO5H

Ofozoba, C. A. (2020). A philosophical reflection on gender inequality and the status of women in the 21st century Nigeria social environment. *The International Journal of Humanities & Social Studies, 8*(10), 123–129. doi:10.24940/theijhss/2020/v8/i10/HS2010-036

Ojeda, M., & Del Rey, R. (2022). Lines of action for sexting prevention and intervention: A systematic review. *Archives of Sexual Behavior, 51*(3), 1–29. doi:10.1007/s10508-021-02089-3 PMID:34791584

Ojeda, M., Del-Rey, R., Walrave, M., & Vandebosch, H. (2020). Sexting in adolescents: Prevalence and behaviours. *Comunicar, 28*(64), 9–19. doi:10.3916/C64-2020-01

Ojukwu, E. V., & Ibekwe, U. E. (2020). Cultural suppression of female gender in Nigeria: Implications of Igbo females' songs. *Journal of Music and Dance, 10*(1), 1–13.

Okoro, S. I. (2018). The Igbo and educational development in Nigeria, 1846-2015. [IJHCS]. *International Journal of History and Cultural Studies, 4*(1), 65–80. doi:10.20431/2454-7654.0401005

Compilation of References

Ollis, D. (2016). 'I felt like I was watching porn': The reality of preparing pre-service teachers to teach about sexual pleasure. *Sex Education, 16*(3), 308–323. doi:10.1080/14681811.2015.1075382

Onuora, N. T., Obiakor, E. E., Obayi, J. I., & Chinagorom, L. C. (2019). Igbo traditional education: A panacea to the nation's unemployment debacle. *International Network Organization for Scientific Research (INOSR). Arts and Management, 5*(1), 42–55.

OPS. (2008). *La Salud Sexual y Reproductiva de los Adolescentes y los Jóvenes: Oportunidades, Enfoques y Opiniones [Adolescent and Youth Sexual and Reproductive Health: Opportunities, Approaches and Views]*. OPS.

Orcasita, L. T., Cuenca, J., Montenegro, J. L., Garrido, D., & Haderlein, A. (2018). Diálogos y Saberes sobre Sexualidad de Padres con Hijos e Hijas Adolescentes Escolarizados. *Revista Colombiana de Psicología, 27*(1), 41–53. doi:10.15446/rcp.v27n1.62148

Ortega, R., Elipe, P., Mora-Merchán, J. A., Genta, M. L., Brighi, A., Guarini, A., Smith, P. K., Thompson, F., & Tippett, N. (2012). The emotional impact of bullying and cyberbullying on victims: A European cross-national study. *Aggressive Behavior, 38*(5), 342–356. doi:10.1002/ab.21440 PMID:22782434

Öz, R., & Kayalar, T. M. (2021). A comparative analysis on the effects of formal and distance education students' course attendance upon exam success. *Journal of Education and Learning, 10*(3), 122–131. doi:10.5539/jel.v10n3p122

Palacios-Hidalgo, F. J., & Huertas-Abril, C. A. (2024, in press). Socially and Culturally Responsive Language Teaching: Queering the EFL classroom. In E. F. López-Medina, G. Beacon, M. Quinterno & X. Sotelo (Eds.), Queer studies in ELT. Brill.

Palacios-Hidalgo, F. J. (2023). Introducing the Socially and Culturally Responsive Language Teaching approach. In B. Pizà-Mir, J. G. Fernández-Fernández, M. M. Cortès-Ferrer, O. García-Taibo, & S. Baena-Morales (Eds.), *Currículum, didáctica y los Objetivos de Desarrollo Sostenible (ODS): Reflexiones, experiencias y miradas [Curriculum, didactics and the Sustainable Development Goals (SDGs): Reflections, experiences and perspectives]*. (pp. 950–966). Dykinson., https://bit.ly/3NqnddF

Palacios-Hidalgo, F. J. (2024 in press). The role of technology in Socially and Culturally Responsive Language Teaching: Exploring its potential in the language classroom. In *IA aplicada a la enseñanza y el aprendizaje [AI applied to teaching and learning]*. Dykinson.

Palacios-Hidalgo, F. J., Cosin-Belda, C., & Huertas-Abril, C. A. (2023). Queering EFL teaching through English for Social Purposes and Cooperation: A teaching proposal for Primary Education. In F. J. Palacios-Hidalgo & C. A. Huertas-Abril (Eds.), *Promoting inclusive education through the integration of LGBTIQ+ issues in the classroom* (pp. 139–160). IGI Global., doi:10.4018/978-1-6684-8243-8.ch008

Palacios-Hidalgo, F. J., & Huertas-Abril, C. A. (2023b). The potential of English for Social Purposes and Cooperation for the development of digital literacy. In P. Escudeiro, N. Escudeiro, & O. Bernardes (Eds.), *Handbook of research on implementing inclusive educational models and technologies for equity and diversity* (pp. 37–68). IGI Global., doi:10.4018/979-8-3693-0453-2.ch003

Palacios-Hidalgo, F. J., & Huertas-Abril, C. A. (Eds.). (2023a). *Promoting inclusive education through the integration of LGBTIQ+ issues in the classroom*. IGI Global., doi:10.4018/978-1-6684-8243-8

Panchaud, C., Keogh, S., Stillman, M., Awusabo-Asare, K., Motta, A., Sidze, E., & Monzon, A. (2019). Towards Comprehensive Sexuality Education: A comparative Analysis of the Policy environment surrounding school-based sexuality education in Ghana, Peru, Kenya, and Guatemala. *Sex Education, 19*(3), 277–296. doi:10.1080/14681811.2018.1533460

Pappas, S. (2021). Teaching porn literacy. *American Psychological Association, 52*(2), 54. https://acortar.link/KcA0xI

Pashang, S., Khanlou, N., & Clarke, J. (2019). The mental health impact of cyber sexual violence on youth identity. *International Journal of Mental Health and Addiction, 17*(5), 1119–1131. doi:10.1007/s11469-018-0032-4

Pau, L. F., & Kirtava, Z. (2023). International survey & analysis of laws and regulations addressing internet addiction and/or problematic usage of the internet. *World Journal of Public Health, 8*(1), 8–14. doi:10.11648/j.wjph.20230801.12

Pawlikowska, A., Szuster, E., Kostrzewska, P., Mandera, A., Biernikiewicz, M., Sobieszczanska, M., Rozek-Piechura, K., Markiewicz, M., Rusiecka, A., & Kalka, D. (2022). Internet addiction and Polish women's sexual functioning: The role of social media, online pornography, and game use during the COVID-19 pandemic - Online surveys based on FSFI and BSMAS questionnaires. *International Journal of Environmental Research and Public Health, 13*(13), 8193. doi:10.3390/ijerph19138193 PMID:35805852

Pekal, J., Laier, C., Snagowski, J., Stark, R., & Brand, M. (2018). Tendencies toward Internet-pornography-use disorder: Differences in men and women regarding attentional biases to pornographic stimuli. *Journal of Behavioral Addictions, 7*(3), 574–583. doi:10.1556/2006.7.2018.70 PMID:30203692

Penna, M. (2015). Homofobia en las aulas universitarias: Un meta-análisis. *Revista de Docencia Universitaria, 13*(1), 197–200. doi:10.4995/redu.2015.6445

Pérez, V. M.-O. (2021). Pedagogía social y educación social. *Revista Educação Em Questão, 59*(59). Advance online publication. doi:10.21680/1981-1802.2021v59n59ID24018

Peterson, J., & Densley, J. (2017). Cyber violence: What do we know and where do we go from here? *Aggression and Violent Behavior, 34*, 193–200. doi:10.1016/j.avb.2017.01.012

Pichardo, J. I., & de Stefano, M. (2020). *Somos Diversidad. Actividades para la formación de profesionales de la educación formal y no formal en diversidad sexual, familiar, corporal y de expresión e identidad de género.* Ministerio de Derechos Sociales y Agenda 2030, y Ministerio de Igualdad. https://www.igualdad.gob.es/ministerio/dglgtbi/Documents/SomosDiversidad_DIGITAL_0707.pdf

Pichardo, J. I., & Puche, L. (2019). Universidad y diversidad sexo-genérica: Barreras, innovaciones y retos de futuro. *Methaodos. Revista de Ciencias Sociales, 7*(1), 10–26. doi:10.17502/m.rcs.v7i1.287

Pick De Weiss, S., Diaz R., Andrade Palos, P., & Gribble, J.N. (1993). Teenage sexual and contraceptive behavior: the case of Mexico. *Advances in Population: psychosocial perspectives*, 1:229-49.

Pick, S., Givaudan, M., & Poortinga, Y. H. (2003). Sexuality and life skills education: A multistrategy intervention in Mexico. *The American Psychologist, 58*(3), 230–234. doi:10.1037/0003-066X.58.3.230 PMID:12772430

Piedalue, A., Gilbertson, A., Alexeyeff, K., & Klein, E. (2020). Is gender-based violence a social norm? Rethinking power in a popular development intervention. *Feminist Review, 126*(1), 89–105. doi:10.1177/0141778920944463

PiJoos. I. (2017). *Sexual assault claims at primary school: Lesufi slams principal.* News24. https://www.news24.com/news24/sexual-assault-claims-at-primary-school-lesufi-slams-principal-20171123

Pispira, J., Cevasco, J., & Silva, M. L. (2022). Gender-based violence in Latin America (Ecuador and Argentina): Current state and challenges in the development of psychoeducational materials. *Discover Psychology, 2*(1), 48. doi:10.1007/s44202-022-00060-4

Planting-Bergloo, S., & Arvola Orlander, A. (2022). Challenging 'the elephant in the room': The becomings of pornography education in Swedish secondary school. *Sex Education, 24*(1), 16–30. doi:10.1080/14681811.2022.2137487

Plato, N. (2022). Advantages and disadvantages of education and its implementation. *Global Science Research Journals, 3*(3), 1–2. doi:10.15651/2437-1882.22.3.038

Compilation of References

Pon, P. (2009). Cultural Competency as New Racism: An Ontology of Forgetting. *Journal of Progressive Human Services*, *20*(1), 59–71. doi:10.1080/10428230902871173

Potvin, P. (2003). Pour une alliance réussie entre la pratique et la recherche en psychoéducation [For a successful alliance between practice and research in psychoeducation]. *Revue de Psycho-Éducation*, *32*(2), 211–224.

Pourkazemi, R., Janighorban, M., Boroumandfar, Z., & Mostafavi, F. (2020). A comprehensive reproductive health program for vulnerable adolescent girls. Pourkazemi et al. *Reproductive Health 17* (3), 1-6. PMID:31915022

Powers, R., Cochran, J., Maskaly, J., & Sellers, C. (2017). Social Learning Theory, Gender and Intimate Partner Violencnt Victimisation: A strucrural Equation Approach. *Journal of Interpersonal Violence*, 1–27. PMID:29294768

Praeg, L., & Baillie, M. (2011). Sexual violence: Mythology, infant rape and the limits of the political. *Politikon: South African Journal of Political Studies*, *38*(2), 257–274. doi:10.1080/02589346.2011.580126

Pratama, M. P., Sampelolo, R., & Lura, H. (2023). Revolutionizing education: Harnessing the power of artificial intelligence for personalized learning. *Klasikal: Journal of Education. Language Teaching and Science*, *5*(1), 350–357. doi:10.52208/klasikal.v5i2.877

Prichard, J., Spiranovic, C., Watters, P., & Lueg, C. (2013). Young people, child pornography, and subcultural norms on the Internet. *Journal of the American Society for Information Science and Technology*, *64*(5), 992–1000. doi:10.1002/asi.22816

Principi, N., Magnoni, P., Grimoldi, L., Carnevali, D., Cavazzana, L., & Pellai, A. (2022). Consumption of sexually explicit internet material and its effects on minors' health: Latest evidence from the literatura. *Minerva Pediatrics*, *74*(3), 332–339. doi:10.23736/S2724-5276.19.05367-2 PMID:30761817

Priyatni, E. T., & Martutik. (2020). The development of a critical–creative reading assessment based on problem solving. *SAGE Open*, *10*(2), 2158244020923350. doi:10.1177/2158244020923350

PSHE. (2024). *Addressing pornography through PSHE*. PSHE Association. https://bitly.ws/3eIkU

Puchner, L., Markowitz, L., & Hedley, M. (2015). Critical media literacy and gender: Teaching middle school students about gender stereotypes and occupations. *The Journal of Media Literacy Education*, *7*(2), 23–34. doi:10.23860/jmle-7-2-3

Quezada, F. (2016). Una medida de la homonegatividad breve, unidimensional e independiente de los efectos positivos y negativos: Evidencia de validez de la escala de Wrench en Chile. *Salud y Sociedad*, *7*(1), 10–28. doi:10.22199/S07187475.2016.0001.00001

Quijano, A. (2002). Colonialidad del poder, globalización y democracia [Coloniality of power, globalisation and democracy]. Revista de Ciencias Sociales [Social Science Journal], 4 (7-8), 1-23.

Raeburn, D. (2004). *Ovid. Metamorphoses. A new verse translation*. Penguin Books. [trans.]

Raine, G., Khouja, C., Scott, R., Wright, K., & Sowden, A. J. (2020). Pornography use and sexting amongst children and young people: A systematic overview of reviewers. *Systematic Reviews*, *9*(283), 283. Advance online publication. doi:10.1186/s13643-020-01541-0 PMID:33280603

Rajan, V. G. J. (2011). *Myth and violence in the contemporary female text*. Routledge.

Ramírez Aranda, J. M. González. González. J. M., Cavazos. Ríos. J. J., & Ríos. Garza. T. (2006). Actitudes de los padres sobre sexualidad en sus hijos, valores y medidas preventivas de SIDA. *RESPYN, Revista Salud Pública y Nutrición*, *7*(1). https://respyn.uanl.mx/index.php/respyn/article/view/159

Ramírez Botero, A. (2017). La intervención psicoeducativa y la psicología educativa: Una diferencia necesaria. [Psychoeducational intervention and educational psychology: A necessary difference] In M. Riaño Garzón, S. Carrillo Sierra, J. Torrado Rodriguez, & J. Espinosa Castro (Eds.), *Contexto educativo: convergencias y retos desde la perspectiva psicológica* [*Educational context: convergences and challenges from the psychological perspective*]. (pp. 35–57). Ediciones Universidad Simón Bolivar., doi:10.17081/bonga/1158.c3

Ramírez Izúcar, C. (2022). Retos para la Prevención del Embarazo en Adolescentes en Oaxaca [Challenges for the Prevention of Adolescent Pregnancy in Oaxaca]. *Oaxaca Población siglo XXI* [*Oaxaca Population 21st century*], 47, 31-40. https://productosdigepo.oaxaca.gob.mx/recursos/revistas/revista47.pdf

Ramos, A. M. G. (2020). Cyber-activism Against Sexual Violence: # BringBackOurGirls. *Debats: Revista de cultura, poder i societat*, (5), 233-244. doi:10.28939/iam.debats-en.2020-13

Rata, E. (2019). Knowledge-rich teaching: A model of curriculum design coherence. *British Educational Research Journal*, 45(4), 681–697. doi:10.1002/berj.3520

Raza, S. A., Qazi, W., Umer, B., & Khan, K. A. (2020). Influence of social networking sites on life satisfaction among university students: A mediating role of social benefit and social overload. *Health Education*, 120(2), 141–164. doi:10.1108/HE-07-2019-0034

Rebolledo, R., & González-Araya, F. (2023). Exploring the benefits and challenges of AI-language learning tools. *International Journal of Social Sciences and Humanities Invention*, 10(01), 7569–7576. doi:10.18535/ijsshi/v10i01.02

Rebollo-Catalan, A., & Mayor-Buzon, V. (2020). Adolescent bystanders witnessing cyber violence against women and girls: What they observe and how they respond. *Violence Against Women*, 26(15-16), 2024–2040. doi:10.1177/1077801219888025 PMID:31779537

Reed, L. A., Tolman, R. M., & Ward, L. M. (2017). Gender matters: Experiences and consequences of digital dating abuse victimization in adolescent dating relationships. *Journal of Adolescence*, 59(1), 79–89. doi:10.1016/j.adolescence.2017.05.015 PMID:28582653

Reis, J., & Seidl, A. (1989). School Administrators, Parents, and Sex Education: A Resolvable Paradox?. *Adolescence*, 24(95)-639–645.

Resett, S. (2019). Sexting en adolescentes: Su predicción a partir de los problemas emocionales y la personalidad oscura. *Escritos de Psicologia*, 12(2), 93–102. doi:10.24310/espsiescpsi.v12i2.10060

Revelo-Morejón, M. A. (2016). *Efecto del uso frecuente de pornografía en la expectativa del acto sexual de usuarios masculinos* [*Effect of frequent use of pornography on the sexual act expectancy of male users*] [PhD thesis, Universidad San Francisco de Quito]. https://bit.ly/3uYscMh

Reyes Alavez, DRamírez Vargas, R. (2022). Preventing Adolescent Pregnancy in Oaxaca [Prevención del Embarazo en Adolescentes en Adolescentes en Oaxaca [Preventing Adolescent Pregnancy in Oaxaca]. Oaxaca Población siglo XXI [Oaxaca Population 21st century], 47, 41-45.

Riggs, D. W., & Treharne, G. J. (2017). Queer Theory. In B. Gough (Ed.), *The Palgrave Handbook of Critical Social Psychology* (pp. 101–121). Springer Link. doi:10.1057/978-1-137-51018-1_6

Rivera Cusicanqui, S. (2010). Ch'ixinakax utxiwa: una reflexión sobre prácticas y discursos descolonizadores [Ch'ixinakax utxiwa: a reflection on decolonising practices and discourses]. Tinta Limón.

Rivera, R., Santos-Velasco, D., Cabrera-García, V., & Docal-Millán, M.-C. (2016). Online and offline pornography consumption in Colombian adolescents. *Comunicar*, 24(46), 37–45. doi:10.3916/C46-2016-04

Rodríguez-Castro, Y., & Alonso-Ruido, P. (2015). Analysis of the speeches of the young people on violence in intimate relationships. *Revista de Estudios e Investigación en Psicología y Educación, 2*, 015–018. doi:10.17979/reipe.2015.0.02.235

Rodríguez-Castro, Y., Lameiras-Fernández, M., Carrera-Fernández, V., & Vallejo-Medina, P. (2013). Validación de la Escala de Homofobia Moderna en una muestra de adolescentes. *Anales de Psicología, 29*(2), 523–533. doi:10.6018/analesps.29.2.137931

Rodríguez-Castro, Y., Martínez-Román, R., Alonso-Ruido, P., Adá-Lameiras, A., & Carrera-Fernández, M. V. (2021). Intimate partner cyberstalking, sexism, pornography, and sexting in adolescents: New challenges for sex education. *International Journal of Environmental Research and Public Health, 18*(4), 2181. doi:10.3390/ijerph18042181 PMID:33672240

Rodríguez-Darias, A. J., & Aguilera-Ávila, L. (2018). Gender-based harassment in cyberspace. The case of Pikara magazine. *Women's Studies International Forum, 66*, 63–69. doi:10.1016/j.wsif.2017.10.004

Rogers, E. (1962). *Diffusion of Innovations*. Free Press.

Román-García, O., Bacigalupe, A., & Vaamonde Garcia, C. (2022). Relación de la pornografía mainstream con la salud sexual y reproductiva de los/las adolescentes. Una revisión de alcance [Relationship of mainstream pornography to adolescent sexual and reproductive health. A scoping review]. *Revista Española de Salud Pública, 95*, e202108102. https://bit.ly/48GZeOP PMID:34267175

Romero, G. (2023). Los regímenes de género escolares como geopolíticas educativas estratégicas. Aportes para pensar la transversalidad de la Educación Sexual Integral [School gender regimes as strategic educational geopolitics. Contributions to think about the transversality of Comprehensive Sexual Education]. *La ventana. Revista de estudios de género, 7*(57), 41-74.

Romero, G. (2021). Sentidos en disputa en torno a la "transversalización" de la educación sexual integral en Argentina [Disputed meanings around the 'mainstreaming' of comprehensive sexual education in Argentina]. *Revista Mexicana de Investigación Educativa, 26*(88), 47–68.

Ronconi, L., Espiñeira, B., & Guzmán, S. (2023). Educación sexual integral en América Latina y el caribe: Dónde estamos y hacia dónde deberíamos ir [Comprehensive sexual education in Latin America and the Caribbean: Where we are and where we should go]. *Latin american legal studies, 11*(1), 246-296. doi:10.15691/0719-9112Vol11n1a7

Rood, B. A., Reisner, S. L., Puckett, J. A., Surace, F. I., Berman, A. K., & Pantalone, D. W. (2017). Internalized transphobia: Exploring perceptions of social messages in transgender and gender-nonconforming adults. *International Journal of Transgenderism, 18*(4), 411–426. doi:10.1080/15532739.2017.1329048

Rosa, R., Drew, E., & Canavan, S. (2020). An overview of gender inequality in EU universities. *The Gender-Sensitive University*, 1-15.

Rosenfelt, K., Columbus, C., Barnathan, M., & Radcliffe, M. (Producers), & Columbus, C. (Director). (2010). *Percy Jackson & the Olympians: The lightning thief* [Film]. 20th Century Fox.

Ross, C. B. (2006). Sex, Drugs and Violence in Lucía Etxebarria's Amor, curiosidad, Prozac y dudas. In A.-P. Durand & N. Mandel (Eds.), *Novels of the Contemporary Extreme* (pp. 153–162). Continuum International Publishing Group.

Rothman, E. F., Paruk, J., Espensen, A., Temple, J. R., & Adams, K. (2017). A qualitative study of what us parents say and do when their young children see pornography. *Academic Pediatrics, 17*(8), 844–849. doi:10.1016/j.acap.2017.04.014 PMID:28450081

Rothman, E., Daley, N., & Alder, J. (2020). A pornography literacy program for adolescents. *American Journal of Public Health, 110*(2), 154–156. doi:10.2105/AJPH.2019.305468 PMID:31855489

Rudoe, N., & Ponford, R. (2023). Parental attitudes to school- and home-based, sex and health education:Evidence from a crosssectional study in England and Wales, Sex Education. *Sex Education*. doi:10.1080/14681811.2023.2257602

Rugut, E. J., & Osman, A. A. (2013). Reflection on Paulo Freire and classroom relevance. *American International Journal of Social Science*, *2*(2), 23–28.

Ruíz Medrano, E. (2011). Un breve recorrido bibliográfico por la historia de los pueblos zapotecos de Oaxaca [A brief bibliographic tour through the history of the Zapotec peoples of Oaxaca] [*Anthropological Dimension*]. *Dimensión Antropológica*, *18*(52), 57–80.

Russell, S. T. (2011). Challenging homophobia in schools: Policies and programs for safe school climates. *Educar em Revista*, *39*(39), 123–138. doi:10.1590/S0104-40602011000100009

Russell, S. T., Bishop, M. D., Saba, V. C., James, I., & Ioverno, S. (2021). Promoting School Safety for LGBTQ and All Students. *Policy Insights from the Behavioral and Brain Sciences*, *8*(2), 160–166. doi:10.1177/23727322211031938 PMID:34557581

Saad, L. (2020). *Me and White Supremacy. How to Recognise your Privilege, Combat Racism and Change the Word*. Quercus Books.

Sacán, J. G., & Villafuerte, F. U. (2023). Resultados de conocimientos, actitudes y prácticas (CAPS) de la primera cohorte del curso Reconoce, Oportunidades Curriculares en ESI [Knowledge, attitudes and practices (KAP) results of the first cohort of the Recoce, Curricular Opportunities in CSE course]. In M. Samudio Granados, & C. Terán Fierro (Eds.), Educación integral de la sexualidad: reflexiones críticas desde distintas miradas [Comprehensive sexuality education: critical reflections from different perspectives] (pp. 169-190). Universidad Nacional de educación del Ecuador.

Sachse, M., Azalia Pintado, P. S., & Lastra, Z. (2012). Calidad de la atención obstétrica, desde la perspectiva de derechos, equidad e interculturalidad en centros de salud en Oaxaca [Quality of obstetric care from the perspective of rights, equity and interculturality in health centres in Oaxaca] [*CONAMED Journal*]. *Revista CONAMED*, *17*(1), s4–s15.

Sadana, R. (2002). Definition and measurement of reproductive health. *Bull Wold Health Organ*, 407-9.

Sáez Delgado, F., López Angulo, Y., Mella Norambuena, J., Sáez, Y., & Lozano Peña, G. (2023). Programa psicoeducativo aplicado en el profesorado como mecanismo de retribución a las escuelas participantes de una investigación [Psychoeducational program applied to teachers as a remuneration mechanism for schools participating in research]. *LATAM Revista Latinoamericana de Ciencias Sociales y Humanidades*, *4*(1), 3728–3741. doi:10.56712/latam.v4i1.522

Safitri, P. (2021). Peer Education sebagai Upaya pencegahan HIV/AIDS. [JAK]. *Jurnal Abdimas Kesehatan*, *3*(1), 87–92. doi:10.36565/jak.v3i1.161

Saleiro, S. P., Ramalho, N., de Menezes, M. S. y Gato, J. (2022). *Estudo Nacional sobre as necessidades das pessoas LGBTI e sobre a discriminação em razão da orientação sexual, identidade e expressão de género e características sexuais*. Comissão para a Cidadania e Igualdade de Género.

Samara, M., Burbidge, V., El Asam, A., Foody, M., Smith, P. K., & Morsi, H. (2017). Bullying and cyberbullying: Their legal status and use in psychological assessment. *International Journal of Environmental Research and Public Health*, *14*(12), 1449. doi:10.3390/ijerph14121449 PMID:29186780

Sánchez Sáinz, M. (2019). *Pedagogías Queer. ¿Nos arriesgamos a hacer otra educación? / Queer Pedagogies. Do we risk doing other education?* Catarata.

Sánchez-Sainz, M., Penna-Tosso, M., & Rosa-Rodríguez, B. (2016). *Somos como somos: Deconstruyendo y transformando la escuela*. Los Libros de la Catarata.

Compilation of References

Sanders, T., Trueman, G., & Keighley, R. (2023). Non-consensual sharing of images: Commercial content creators, sexual content creation platforms and the lack of protection. *New Media & Society*. doi:10.1177/14614448231172711

Sardinha, L., Maheu-Giroux, M., Stöckl, H., Meyer, S. R., & García-Moreno, C. (2022). Global, regional, and national prevalence estimates of physical or sexual, or both, intimate partner violence against women in 2018. *Lancet*, *399*(10327), 803–813. doi:10.1016/S0140-6736(21)02664-7 PMID:35182472

Scandurra, C., Picariello, S., Valerio, P., & Amodeo, A. L. (2017). Sexism, homophobia and transphobia in a sample of Italian pre-service teachers: The role of socio-demographic features. *Journal of Education for Teaching*, *43*(2), 245–261. doi:10.1080/02607476.2017.1286794

Schalet, A. (2000). Raging hormones, regulated love: Adolescent sexuality and the constitution of the modern individual in the United States and The Netherlands. *Body & Society*, *6*(1), 75–105. doi:10.1177/1357034X00006001006

Scheim, A. I., Baker, K. E., Restar, A. J., & Sell, R. L. (2022). Health and health care among transgender adults in the United States. *Annual Review of Public Health*, *43*(1), 503–523. doi:10.1146/annurev-publhealth-052620-100313 PMID:34882432

Schneider, M., & Hirsch, J. S. (2020). Comprehensive sexuality education as a primary prevention strategy for sexual violence perpetration. *Trauma, Violence & Abuse*, *21*(3), 439–455. doi:10.1177/1524838018772855 PMID:29720047

Schreier, M. (2014). Ways of doing qualitative content analysis: Disentangling terms and terminologies. *Forum Qualitative Sozialforschung / Forum: Qualitative. Social Research*, *15*(1). doi:10.17169/fqs-15.1.2043

Scull, T., Malik, C., Morrison, A., & Keefe, E. (2021). Promoting sexual health in high school: A feasibility study of a web-based media literacy education program. *Journal of Health Communication*, *26*(3), 147–160. doi:10.1080/10810730.2021.1893868 PMID:33779520

Segal, R. (2021). *Myth analyzed*. Routledge.

Segato, R. L. (2015). The Critique of Coloniality in Eight Essays. And an anthropology on demand [The Critique of Coloniality in Eight Essays. And an anthropology on demand]. Prometheus.

Segato, R. (2003). Las estructura de género y el mandato de violación. [The gender structure and the mandate of rape] In R. Segato (Ed.), *Las estructuras elementales de la violencia. Ensayos sobre género entre la antropología, el psicoanálisis y los derechos humanos* [The elementary structures of violence. Essays on gender between anthropology, psychoanalysis, and human rights]. (pp. 21–55). Universidad Nacional de Quilmes.

Senís Fernández, J. (2001). Compromiso feminista en la obra de Lucía Etxebarría. *Espéculo. Revista de Estudios Literarios*, *18*.

Setty, E. (2020). *Risk and harm in youth sexting: Young people's perspectives*. Routledge. doi:10.4324/9780429277344

SFUSD. (2017). *Be real. Be ready*. SFUSD. https://bitly.ws/3eC25

Share, J. (2009). *Media literacy is elementary: Teaching youth to critically read and create media*. Peter Lang. doi:10.3726/978-1-4539-1485-4

Sharma, N., & Bleich, E. (2019). Freedom of expression, public morals, and sexually explicit speech in the European court of human rights. *Constitutional Studies*, *5*, 55. https://acortar.link/DFOfzn

Sharpe, M., & Mead, D. (2021). Problematic pornography use: Legal and health policy considerations. *Current Addiction Reports*, *8*(4), 556–567. doi:10.1007/s40429-021-00390-8 PMID:34518793

Shay, S. (2016, June 13). *Decolonising the curriculum: it's time for a strategy*. The Conversation. https://theconversation.com/decolonising-the-curriculum-its-time-for-a-strategy-60598

Shek, D. T., & Ma, C. M. (2012). Consumption of pornographic materials among Hong Kong early adolescents: A replication. *TheScientificWorldJournal, 406063*, 1–8. doi:10.1100/2012/406063 PMID:22778698

Shih, Y. H. (2018). Some critical thinking on Paulo Freire's critical pedagogy and its educational implications. *International Education Studies, 11*(9), 64–70. doi:10.5539/ies.v11n9p64

Shor, E., & Golriz, G. (2019). Gender, race, and aggression in mainstream pornography. *Archives of Sexual Behavior, 48*(3), 739–751. doi:10.1007/s10508-018-1304-6 PMID:30187150

Shor, I. (1999). What is critical literacy? *The Journal of Pedagogy, Pluralism and Practice, 1*(4), 2. https://bit.ly/4a0xl5j

Sidze, E., Keogh, M., Mulupi, S., Egesa, C., Mutua, M., Muga, W., & Chimaraoke, I. (2017). *From Paper to Practice: Sexuality Education Polcies and their implication in Kenya*. Guttmacher Institute and African Population and Health Research Centre.

Sieder, R. (2017). Introduction. Indigenous women and legal pluralities in Latin America: rethinking justice and security [Introduction. Indigenous women and legal pluralities in Latin America: rethinking justice and security]. In Rachel Sieder (Ed.), Exigiendo justicia y seguridad: Mujeres indígenas y pluralidades legales en América Latina [Demanding Justice and Security: Indigenous Women and Legal Pluralities in Latin America] (pp.13-50). CIESAS.

Simmonds, S., Roux, C., & Avest, I. T. (2015). Blurring the boundaries between photovoice and narrative inquiry: A narrative-photovoice methodology for gender-based research. *International Journal of Qualitative Methods, 14*(3), 33–49. doi:10.1177/160940691501400303

Simpson, E. K., & Helfrich, C. A. (2014). Oppression and Barriers to Service for Black, Lesbian Survivors of Intimate Partner Violence. *Journal of Gay & Lesbian Social Services, 26*(4), 441–465. doi:10.1080/10538720.2014.951816

Siziba, E. (2020). (Submitted in). Gemder-Based Violence in Zimbabwe: Acritical analysis of Institutional Response. *Partial Fulfilment of the Requirement of the Doctorof Philosophy in Sociology: University of Pretoria*.

SmahelD.MachackovaH.MascheroniG.DedkovaL.StaksrudE.ÓlafssonK.LivingstoneS.HasebrinkU. (2020). *EU Kids Online 2020: Survey results from 19 countries*. EU Kids Online. doi:10.21953/lse.47fdeqj01ofo

Smith, P. K., & Steffgen, G. (Eds.). (2013). *Cyberbullying through the new media: Findings from an international network*. Psychology Press. doi:10.4324/9780203799079

Soleimani, V. (2023). Sexist hate speech against women. In O. Pérez de la Fuente, A. Tsesis, & J. Skrzypczak (Eds.), *Minorities, free speech and the internet* (pp. 137–152). Routledge. doi:10.4324/9781003274476-11

Solsten, E., & Meditz, S. W. (1990). Spain, a Country study. Department of the Army.

Sommet, N., & Berent, J. (2022). Porn use and men's and women's sexual performance: Evidence from a large longitudinal sample. *Psychological Medicine, 53*(7), 3105–3114. doi:10.1017/S003329172100516X PMID:35135634

South Africa Country. (2018). *Prevention of Violence against women and girls Stakeholder Network Analysis*. South Africa: South Africa Country Report.

Souto-Otero, M. (2022). Validation of non-formal and informal learning in formal education: Covert and overt. *European Journal of Education Research, Development and Policy*, 365–379. doi:10.1111/ejed.12464

Spanish Constitution. (1978). *The Spanish Constitution, passed by the Cortes Generales in Plenary Meetings of the Congress of Deputies and the Senate held on October 31, 1978. Ratified by the Spanish people in the referendum of December 6, 1978. Sanctioned by His Majesty the King before the Cortes on December 27, 1978.* https://bit.ly/437rpVT

Sperling, J. (2021). Comprehensive sexual health education and intersex (in)visibility: An ethnographic exploration inside a California high school classroom. *Sex Education*, *21*(5), 584–599. doi:10.1080/14681811.2021.1931834

Spires, R. C. (1996). *Post-Totalitarian Spanish Fiction*. University of Missouri Press.

Spivak, G. C. (1988). Can the subaltern speak? In C. Nelson & L. Grossberg (Eds.), Marxism and the interpretation of culture (pp. 271–313). Macmillan.

Spivak, G. C. (2011) *Can the Subaltern Speak?* Editorial El cuenco de plata. [1988]

Stahl, G., Keddie, A., & Adams, B. (2023). The manosphere goes to school: Problematizing incel surveillance through affective boyhood. *Educational Philosophy and Theory*, *55*(3), 366–378. doi:10.1080/00131857.2022.2097068

Staley, S., & Leonardi, B. (2016). Leaning In to Discomfort: Preparing Literacy Teachers for Gender and Sexual Diversity. *Research in the Teaching of English*, *51*(2), 209–229. doi:10.58680/rte201628875

Staley, S., & Leonardi, B. (2019). Complicating What We Know: Focusing on Educators' Processes of Becoming Gender and Sexual Diversity Inclusive. *Theory into Practice*, *58*(1), 29–38. doi:10.1080/00405841.2018.1536916

Statista Research Department. (2023a, November 3). *Number of women that were killed in gender violence assaults in Spain from 2003 to 2022*. Statista Research Department. https://bit.ly/3RxlXpX

Ștefăniță, O., & Buf, D. M. (2021). Hate speech in social media and its effects on the LGBT community: A review of the current research. *Romanian Journal of Communication and Public Relations*, *23*(1), 47–55. doi:10.21018/rjcpr.2021.1.322

Stoilova, M., Livingstone, S., & Khazbak, R. (2021). *Investigating Risks and Opportunities for Children in a Digital World: A rapid review of the evidence on children's internet use and outcomes. Innocenti Discussion Paper 2020-03*. UNICEF Office of Research – Innocenti. https://lc.cx/oZifpZ

Stoilova, M., Livingstone, S., & Khazbak, R. (2021, february). *Investigating Risks and Opportunities for Children in a Digital World: A rapid review of the evidence on children's internet use and outcomes*. UNICEF, 1–82.

Strauss, A., & Corbin, J. (2016). *Bases de la investigación cualitativa: técnicas y procedimientos para desarrollar la teoría fundamentada / Bases of qualitative research: techniques and procedures to develop grounded theory*. Universidad de Antioquia.

Subirats, M. (n. d.). *La evolución de las políticas públicas de igualdad [The evolution of public policies on equality]*. https://bit.ly/3uXfj50

Svedin, C. G., Donevan, M., Bladh, M., Priebe, G., Fredlund, C., & Jonsson, L. S. (2023). Associations between adolescents watching pornography and poor mental health in three Swedish surveys. *European Child & Adolescent Psychiatry*, *32*(9), 1765–1780. doi:10.1007/s00787-022-01992-x PMID:35524827

Szasz, I., & Lerner, S. (1998). *Sexualidades en México: algunas aproximaciones desde la perspectiva de las ciencias sociales*. El Colegio de México. doi:10.2307/j.ctvhn0bgv

Tabassum, F. R. (2003). Women who choose Islam. *International Journal of Mental Health*, *32*(3), 31–49. doi:10.1080/00207411.2003.11449590

Taylor, S., Calkins, C. A., Xia, Y., & Dalla, R. L. (2021). Adolescent perceptions of dating violence: A qualitative study. *Journal of Interpersonal Violence*, *36*(1-2), 448–468. doi:10.1177/0886260517726969 PMID:29294897

Temple, J. R., Le, V. D., van den Berg, P., Ling, Y., Paul, J. A., & Temple, B. W. (2014). Brief report: Teen sexting and psychosocial health. *Journal of Adolescence*, *37*(1), 33–36. doi:10.1016/j.adolescence.2013.10.008 PMID:24331302

Testa, G., Villena, A., Mestre, G., & Chiclana, C. (2023b). *Guía para familias. Adolescentes y uso de pornografía [A guide for families. Adolescents and pornography use]*. UNIR/Dale la Vuelta/ Colegio Oficial de la Psicología de Madrid. https://bitly.ws/3eIka

Testa, G., Mestre-Bach, G., Chiclana-Actis, C., & Potenza, M. N. (2023a). Problematic pornography use in adolescents: From prevention to intervention. *Current Addiction Reports*, *10*(2), 210–218. doi:10.1007/s40429-023-00469-4

That, V. V., Vinh, P. P., & Dung, Q. M. (2021). Methods of historical data analysis and criticism in historical research. *Baltic Journal of Law & Politics*, *14*(2), 244–256. doi:10.2478/bjlp-2021-00019

The Met (uploader). (2020-present). *The Gorgon's head, 1925. From the vaults* [Film]. YouTube. https://goo.su/RRWwrT

Thurman, N., Nalmpatian, A., & Obster, F. (2022). Lessons from France on the regulation of Internet pornography: How displacement effects, circumvention, and legislative scope may limit the efficacy of Article 23. *Policy and Internet*, *14*(3), 690–710. doi:10.1002/poi3.293

Thurman, N., & Obster, F. (2021). The regulation of internet pornography: What a survey of under-18s tells us about the necessity for and potential efficacy of emerging legislative approaches. *Policy and Internet*, *13*(3), 415–432. doi:10.1002/poi3.250

Thusi, X., & Mlambo, V. (2023). South Africa Gender Based Violence: An Exploration of a single sided Account. *EUREKA Social and Humanities*, (2), 73–80. doi:10.21303/2504-5571.2023.002734

Tomczyk, Ł. (2020). Skills in the area of digital safety as a key component of digital literacy among teachers. *Education and Information Technologies*, *25*(1), 471–486. doi:10.1007/s10639-019-09980-6

Tovmasyan, G. (2022). The Nuanced Forms of Sexual Violence in the Online Environment. In S. Bedi (Ed.), *Cyber crime, regulations and security contemporary issues and challenges* (pp. 254–263). The Law Brigade Publisher., doi:10.55662/book.2022CCRS.015

Trabasso, T., & Sperry, L. L. (1985). Causal relatedness and importance of story events. *Journal of Memory and Language*, *24*(5), 595–611. doi:10.1016/0749-596X(85)90048-8

Tran, T., Ho, M. T., Pham, T. H., Nguyen, M. H., Nguyen, K. L. P., Vuong, T. T., Nguyen, T. H., Nguyen, T. D., Nguyen, T. L., Khuc, Q. L. V., & Vuong, Q. H. (2020). How digital natives learn and thrive in the digital age: Evidence from an emerging economy. *Sustainability (Basel)*, *12*(9), 1–21. doi:10.3390/su12093819

Truszczynski, N., Singh, A. A., & Hansen, N. (2022). The discrimination experiences and coping responses of non-binary and trans people. *Journal of Homosexuality*, *69*(4), 741–755. https://dooi.org/10.1080/00918369.2020.1855028. doi:10.1080/00918369.2020.1855028 PMID:33331799

Tsuchiya, A. (2002). The "New" Female Subject and the Commodification of Gender in the Works of Lucía Etxebarria. *Romance Studies*, *20*(1), 77–87. doi:10.1179/ros.2002.20.1.77

Turban, J. L., & Ehrensaft, D. (2018). Gender identity in youth: Treatment paradigms and controversies. *Journal of Child Psychology and Psychiatry, and Allied Disciplines*, *59*(12), 1228–1243. doi:10.1111/jcpp.12833 PMID:29071722

Ukaegbu, P., & Oguejiofor, J. O. (2022). Marginalization of women in Igbo tradition: Myth or reality? *Nnamdi Azikiwe Journal of Philosophy*, *13*(2), 271–283.

Compilation of References

Umunakwe, B. O. (2023). Philosophical mediation between patriarchal theory and feminism: A reflection on Igbo society. In D. Okocha, M. Yousaf, & M. Onobe (Eds.), *Handbook of research on deconstructing culture and communication in the global south* (pp. 283–295). IGI Global. doi:10.4018/978-1-6684-8093-9.ch018

UNAIDS. (2013). *Gender-Based Violence (GBV) in Namibia: An exploratory assessment and Mapping of GBV Response services in Namibia*. UNAIDS.

UNAM. (2019, July 26). *La UNAM te explica: Transexualidad*. Fundación UNAM. https://www.fundacionunam.org.mx/unam-al-dia/la-unam-te-explica-transexualidad/

UNAM. (2021, September 3). Mexico, first place in teenage pregnancies among OECD countries. *Boletín UNAM*. UNAM. https://www.dgcs.unam.mx/boletin/bdboletin/2021_729.html

UNESCO (2021). *The journey towards comprehensive sexuality education: global status report*. UNESCO. doi:10.54675/NFEK1277

UNESCO. (2018). *El rol del sector de educación en la EIS*. UNESCO. https://csetoolkit.unesco.org/es/toolkit/el-caso/el-rol-del-sector-de-educacion-en-la-eis

UNESCO. (2018). *International technical guidance on sexuality education. An evidence-informed approach*. UNESCO. https://bit.ly/2NX4KG4

UNESCO. (2018). *International technical guidance on sexuality education: an evidence-informed approach*. UNESCO. doi:10.54675/UQRM6395

UNESCO. (2018). *International technical guidance on sexuality education: An evidence-informed approach; overview*. UNESCO. https://bit.ly/44JqCcN

UNESCO. (2018). *Orientaciones técnicas internacionales sobre educación en sexualidad Un enfoque basado en la evidencia*. UNESCO. https://unesdoc.unesco.org/ark:/48223/pf0000265335

UNESCO. (2019). *From ideas to action: addressing barriers to comprehensive sexuality in the classroom*. UNESCO. https://unesdoc.unesco.org/ark:/48223/pf0000371091

UNESCO. (2019). *Gender, media & ICTs: new approaches for research, education & training*. UNESCO. https://unesdoc.unesco.org/ark:/48223/pf0000368963

UNESCO. (2021). *The journey towards comprehensive sexuality education: Global Status Report*. UNESCO.

UNESCO. (2024, 01 20). *UNESCO Namibia*. Namibia Comprehensive Sexuality Education. https://education-profiles.org/sub-saharan-africa/namibia/~comprehensive-sexuality-education

UNESCO. UNAIDS, UNFPA, UNICEF, UN Women, & WHO. (2018). *International technical guidance on sexuality education. An evidence-informed approach*. https://bit.ly/42gvHKn

UNFPA. (2014). *Operational guidance for comprehensive sexuality education. A Focus on Human Rights and Gender*. UNESCO. https://www.unfpa.org/sites/default/files/pub-pdf/UNFPA_OperationalGuidance_WEB3_0.pdf

UNFPA. (2014). UNFPA Operational Guidelines for Comprehensive Sexuality Education: A Human Rights and Gender-Based Approach [UNFPA Operational Guidelines for Comprehensive Sexuality Education: A Human Rights and Gender-Based Approach]. UNFPA.

United Nation Women. (2023). *How Technology-Facilitated Gender-Based Violence Impacts Women and Girls*. UN Women. https://bit.ly/42SFiqO

United Nations & European Union. (2017). *Spotlight Initiative to end violence against women and girls*. UN. https://www.spotlightinitiative.org/

United Nations Development Programme. (2023, May 30). *Sara: La nueva herramienta de inteligencia artificial para combatir la violencia de género en Centroamérica* [Sara: The new artificial inteligence tool to fight gender-based violence in Center America]. United Nations Development Programme. https://bit.ly/3MbWZL9

United Nations Fund for Population Activity . (2015). *Incorporating comprehensive sexuality education within Basic and Higher education of Learning in KwaZulu- Natal* . KwaZulu Natal: UNFPA.

United Nations. (2015). *The sustainable development goals*. UN. https://sdgs.un.org/es/goals#history

United Nations. (2015). *Transforming our world: the 2030 Agenda for Sustainable Development*. UN. https://sdgs.un.org/2030agenda

United States Agency International Development. (USAID). (2008). *Education from a gender equality perspective*. USAID. https://n9.cl/4fu4h

Ur, P. (2012). *A course in English language teaching* (2nd ed.). Cambridge University Press. doi:10.1017/9781009024518

Uwak, S. O. (2018). Curriculum definition: A misleading philosophy. *International Journal of Advancement in Development Studies*, *13*(2), 27–34.

Vahedi, Z., Sibalis, A., & Sutherland, J. E. (2018). Are media literacy interventions effective at changing attitudes and intentions towards risky health behaviors in adolescents? A meta-analytic review. *Journal of Adolescence*, *67*(1), 140–152. doi:10.1016/j.adolescence.2018.06.007 PMID:29957493

Valdés, S., Ulm Yarad, D., & Moreno, C. (2021). ¿Qué obstáculos perciben los docentes respecto a la implementación de la educación sexual integral en las escuelas secundarias? [What obstacles do teachers perceive regarding the implementation of comprehensive sexuality education in secondary schools?]. *Revista de Educación en Biología, 3*(Número Especial), 249-251. https://congresos.adbia.org.ar/index.php/congresos/article/view/704

Valeggia, C. R., & Snodgrass, J. J. (2015). Health of Indigenous Peoples. *Annual Review of Anthropology*, *44*(1), 117–135. doi:10.1146/annurev-anthro-102214-013831

Van der Wilk, A. (2021). *Protecting women and girls from violence in the digital age: the relevance of the Istanbul convention and the Budapest convention on cybercrime in addressing online and technology-facilitated violence against women*. Council of Europe.

Van Ouytsel, J., Ponnet, K., & Walrave, M. (2020). Cyber dating abuse: Investigating digital monitoring behaviors among adolescents from a social learning perspective. *Journal of Interpersonal Violence*, *35*(23-24), 5157–5178. doi:10.1177/0886260517719538 PMID:29294845

Van Ouytsel, J., Van Gool, E., Walrave, M., Ponnet, K., & Peeters, E. (2017). Sexting: Adolescents' perceptions of the applications used for, motives for, and consequences of sexting. *Journal of Youth Studies*, *20*(4), 446–470. doi:10.1080/13676261.2016.1241865

Van Ouytsel, J., Walrave, M., De Marez, L., Vanhaelewyn, B., & Ponnet, K. (2021). Sexting, pressured sexting and image-based sexual abuse among a weighted-sample of heterosexual and LGB-youth. *Computers in Human Behavior*, *117*, 106630. doi:10.1016/j.chb.2020.106630

Van Ouytsel, J., Walrave, M., Lu, Y., Temple, J. R., & Ponnet, K. (2018). The associations between substance use, sexual behavior, deviant behaviors and adolescents' engagement in sexting: Does relationship context matter? *Journal of Youth and Adolescence*, *47*(11), 2353–2370. doi:10.1007/s10964-018-0903-9 PMID:30073509 van Wijlen, J., & Aston, M. (2019). Applying post-structuralism as framework for exploring infant feeding interactions in the neonatal intensive care unit. *The CanadiAN Journal of Critical NursinDiscourse*, *1*, 59–72.

Vangeel, L., Eggermont, S., & Vandenbosch, L. (2020). Does adolescent media use predict sexual stereotypes in adolescence and emerging adulthood? Associations with music television and online pornography exposure. *Archives of Sexual Behavior*, *49*(4), 1147–1161. doi:10.1007/s10508-020-01677-z PMID:32180100

Vannucci, A., Ohannessian, C. M., & Gagnon, S. (2019). Use of multiple social media platforms in relation to psychological functioning in emerging adults. *Emerging Adulthood*, *7*(6), 501–506. doi:10.1177/2167696818782309

Vanwesenbeeck, I., Westeneng, J., De Boer, T., Reinders, J., & Van Zorge, R. (2016). Lessons learned from a decade implementing Comprehensive Sexuality Education in resource poor settings: The World Starts With Me. *Sex Education*, *16*(5), 471–486. doi:10.1080/14681811.2015.1111203

Varela, J. J., Savahl, S., Adams, S., & Reyes, F. (2020). Examining the relationship among bullying, school climate and adolescent well-being in Chile and South Africa: A cross cultural comparison. *Child Indicators Research*, *13*(3), 819–838. doi:10.1007/s12187-019-09648-0

Vargas, M. A. F., Aguilar, C. A., & Jiménez, A. G. (2012). Educación sexual: Orientadores y orientadoras desde el modelo biográfico y profesional [Sexual education: Counselors from the biographical and professional model]. *Educare (San José)*, *16*, 53–71. doi:10.15359/ree.16-Esp.7

Vater, K. J. (2020). *Between Market and Myth: The Spanish Artist Novel in the Post-Transition, 1992-2014*. Bucknell University Press.

Vázquez, N. Q. D. (2017). *Alguien ya robó mujer: virginidad y rito de paso en un barrio Binnizá de Juchitán.*

Venketsamy, R. (2020). A comprehensive reproductive health program for vulnerable adolescent girls. *Reproductive Health*, *13*(13), 1–6.

Venketsamy, T., & Kinear, J. (2020). Strengthening comprehensive sexuality education in the curriculum for the early grades. *South African Journal of Childhood Education*, *10*(1), 1–9. doi:10.4102/sajce.v10i1.820

Veronica, L. (2022). Formal education: Understanding its meaning and importance. *International Journal of Education Research and Review*, *10*(2), 1–2.

Vertongen, R., van Ommen, C., & Chamberlain, K. (2022). Adolescent dilemmas about viewing pornography and their efforts to resolve them. *Journal of Adolescent Research*. Advance online publication. doi:10.1177/07435584221133307

Vickery, J. R. (2017). *Worried about the wrong things: Youth, risk, and opportunity in the digital world*. MIT Press. doi:10.7551/mitpress/10653.001.0001

Vidal-Moscoso, D., & Manríquez-López, L. (2016). El docente como mediador de la comprensión lectora en universitarios [The teacher as a mediator of reading comprehension for university students]. *Revista de la Educación Superior* [Journal of Higher Education]. *XLV*, *177*(1), 95–118.

Villora, B., Yubero, S., & Navarro, R. (2019). Cyber dating abuse and masculine gender norms in a sample of male adults. *Future Internet*, *11*(4), 84. doi:10.3390/fi11040084

Virgara, J. L., & Whitten, T. (2023). A systematic literature review of the longitudinal risk factors associated with juvenile cyber-deviance. *Computers in Human Behavior*, *141*, 107613. doi:10.1016/j.chb.2022.107613

Vizcaíno-Cuenca, R., Romero-Sánchez, M., & Carretero-Dios, H. (2024). Making visible the myths about cybersexual violence against women: An analysis of social reactions toward victims on Twitter. *Journal of Interpersonal Violence, 08862605231222876*, 08862605231222876. Advance online publication. doi:10.1177/08862605231222876 PMID:38243759

Voicu, S. N., & Crăciun, I. (2023). Preventive online safety education for teenagers. *International Journal of Legal and Social Order, 3*(1). doi:10.55516/ijlso.v3i1.165

Wachs, S., Gámez-Guadix, M., & Wright, M. (2022). Online hate speech victimization and depressive symptoms among adolescents: The protective role of resilience. *Cyberpsychology, Behavior, and Social Networking, 25*(7), 416–423. doi:10.1089/cyber.2022.0009 PMID:35639126

Wade, P. (2000). Raza y etnicidad en Latinoamérica [Race and ethnicity in Latin America]. Abya-Yala. doi:10.26530/OAPEN_625258

Warrier, S. (2021). Inclusion and Exclusion: Intersectionality and Gender-Based Violence. In R. Geffner, J.W. White, L. K. Hamberger, A. Rosenbaum, V. Vaughan-Eden, V.I. Vieth, Handbook of Interpersonal Violence and Abuse Across the Lifespan: A project of the National Partnership to End Interpersonal Violence Across the Lifespan (NPEIV) (pp. 2539-2552). Springer International Publishing.

Warwick, I., Chase, E., Aggleton, P. y Sanders, S. (2004). *Homophobia, sexual orientation and schools: A review and implications for action.* DfES.

Wekesah, F. M., Nyakangi, V., Onguss, M., Njagi, J., & Bangha, M. (2019). *Comprehensive Sexuality Education in Sub-Sahara Africa.* Forum for African Women Educationalist.

WHO, & BZgA (World Health Organization Regional Office for Europe, & German Federal Centre for Health Promotion). (2010). *Standards for Sexuality Education in Europe: A Framework for Policy Makers, Education and Health Authorities and Specialists.* WHO. https://bit.ly/3TnWxx2

WHO. (2006). *Defining sexual health: Report of a technical consultation on sexual health.* World Health Organization.

Willet, A., & Etowa, J. (2023). A Critical Examination of epistemologival congruence between intersectionality and feminist post structuralism: Towards an intergrated frameworkfor health related research. *Nursing Inquiry, 30*, 1–12.

Williams, C. (2023). Education and awareness raising to encourage formalisation. In C. Williams (Ed.), *A modern guide to the informal economy* (pp. 240–260). Elgar Publishing., doi:10.4337/9781788975612.00019

Willis, M., Bridges, A. J., & Sun, C. (2022). Pornography use, gender, and sexual objectification: A multinational study. *Sexuality & Culture, 26*(4), 1298–1313. doi:10.1007/s12119-022-09943-z

Wilson, K. (2016). Critical reading, critical thinking: Delicate scaffolding in English for Academic Purposes (EAP). *Thinking Skills and Creativity, 22*, 256–265. doi:10.1016/j.tsc.2016.10.002

Wirtz, A. L., Poteat, T. C., Malik, M., & Glass, N. (2020). Gender-based violence against transgender people in the United States: A call for research and programming. *Trauma, Violence & Abuse, 21*(2), 227–241. doi:10.1177/1524838018757749 PMID:29439615

Wolak, J., Finkelhor, D., Walsh, W., & Treitman, L. (2018). Sextortion of minors: Characteristics and dynamics. *The Journal of Adolescent Health, 62*(1), 72–79. doi:10.1016/j.jadohealth.2017.08.014 PMID:29055647

Wolford-Clevenger, C., Zapor, H., Brasfield, H., Febres, J., Elmquist, J., Brem, M., Shorey, R. C., & Stuart, G. L. (2016). An examination of the Partner Cyber Abuse Questionnaire in a college student sample. *Psychology of Violence, 6*(1), 156–162. doi:10.1037/a0039442 PMID:27014498

Compilation of References

Women, U. N. (2023, September 21). *Facts and figures: Ending violence against women*. UN Women. https://bit.ly/3PDc49g

Wood, G. (2013). The Naturalist Inheritance in *Amor, curiosidad, prozac y dudas* by Lucía Etxebarria. *Hispanic Research Journal*, *14*(3), 273–290. doi:10.1179/1468273713Z.00000000049

World Economic Forum. (2023). *Global gender gap report 2023*. World Economic Forum. https://bit.ly/499gQ6B

World Health Organization. (2015). *Sexual health, human rights and the law*. World Health Organization. https://apps.who.int/iris/bitstream/handle/10665/175556/9789241564984_ eng.pdf

World Health Organization. (2021). *Violence against women*. World Health Organization. https://www.who.int/es/news-room/fact-sheets/detail/violence-against-women

World Health Organization. (2021a). *Violence against women prevalence estimates*. World Health Organization. https://bit.ly/3IbPGQX

World Health Organization. (2021b). *Violence against women*. World Health Organization. https://bit.ly/40xAdBu

World Wide Web Foundation. (2020). *Survey - Young people's experience of online harassment*. Web Foundation. https://webfoundation.org/docs/2020/03/WF_WAGGGS-Survey-1-pager-1.pdf

Wright, P. J., & Herbenick, D. (2022). Pornography and relational satisfaction: Exploring potential boundary conditions. *Archives of Sexual Behavior*, *51*(8), 3839–3846. doi:10.1007/s10508-022-02406-4 PMID:36042069

Yadav, P., & Horn, D. M. (2021). Continuums of violence: Feminist peace research and gender-based violence. In T. Väyrynen, S. Parashar, É. Féron, & C. C. Confortini (Eds.), *Routledge handbook of feminist peace research* (pp. 105–114). Routledge. doi:10.4324/9780429024160-12

Yahner, J., Dank, M., Zweig, J. M., & Lachman, P. (2015). The co-occurrence of physical and cyber dating violence and bullying among teens. *Journal of Interpersonal Violence*, *30*(7), 1079–1089. doi:10.1177/0886260514540324 PMID:25038223

Yañez, A. G. B., Alonso-Fernández, C., & Fernández-Manjón, B. (2023). Systematic literature review of digital resources to educate on gender equality. *Education and Information Technologies*, *28*(8), 1–26. doi:10.1007/s10639-022-11574-8 PMID:36747612

Yang, S. O., Baik, S. H., & Jeong, G. H. (1999). Analysis of materials for sexual education in Korea. *Journal of Korean Academy of Community Health Nursing*, *10*(2), 508–524.

Yar, M. (2020). Protecting children from internet pornography? A critical assessment of statutory age verification and its enforcement in the UK. *Policing*, *43*(1), 183–197. doi:10.1108/PIJPSM-07-2019-0108

Yehya, F. M. (2021). Promising Digital Schools: An Essential Need for an Educational Revolution. *Pedagogical Research*, *6*(3), 1–10. doi:10.29333/pr/11061

Yunengsih, W., & Setiawan, A. (2021). Contribution of pornographic exposure and addiction to risky sexual behavior in adolescents. *Journal of public health research*, *10*(s1), jphr.2021.2333. doi:10.4081/jphr.2021.2333

Yustika, G. P., & Iswati, S. (2020). Digital literacy in formal online education: A short review. *Dinamika Pendidikan*, *15*(1), 66–76. doi:10.15294/dp.v15i1.23779

Yuvi. (2020). *Disadvantages of formal, informal and non-formal education*. Yogiraj Notes. https://n9.cl/gk3is

Zachari, A., Sabri Nawar, Y., & Javaherizadeh, E. (2018). The impact of sexuality in advertisements on consumers purchase behaviour: A social media perspective. *The Business and Management Review*, *9*(4), 1–18.

Zine, J. (2016). *Between orientalism and fundamentalism: Muslim women and feminist engagement*. In K. Hunt K. & Rygiel (Eds.), *Gendering the war on terror* (pp. 34-40). Routledge. https://bit.ly/47Eeb4C

Zulli, D., & Zulli, D. J. (2020). Extending the Internet meme: Conceptualizing technological mimesis and imitation publics on the TikTok platform. *New Media & Society*, *24*(8), 1872–1890. doi:10.1177/1461444820983603

About the Contributors

Mariana Buenestado Fernández, PhD in Educational Sciences from the University of Córdoba (Spain), works as a professor and researcher in the Department of Education at the University of Cantabria (Spain). Her career includes outstanding collaboration in research projects focused on diversity, inclusive education and digital competence. She highlights her priority interest in the transversal integration of gender in these fields. In addition, she has actively participated in teaching innovation projects, contributing to the implementation of avant-garde methodologies that promote inclusion and equity in the educational field. Dr. Mariana Buenestado-Fernández, Universidad de Cantabria, Spain (buenestadom@unican.es) Av. de los Castros, s/n,Santander, Spain 39005, ES

Azahara Jiménez-Millán (ella/she/her) works at the Department of Education, University of Cordoba (Spain). She has a degree in Education and Nursing, a Master's degree in Inclusive Education and a PhD in Social Sciences from the University of Cordoba. She is a member of Research Group SEJ-477 'Education, Diversity & Society'. Her main research focuses on the diversity and inclusion, leadership for social justice, and education policies.

Francisco Javier Palacios-Hidalgo (él/he/him) belongs to the Department of English and German Philologies of the University of Córdoba (Spain). He is a member of the Ibero-American Network of Bilingual and Intercultural Education (IBIE) and the Research Group HUM-1006 'Research in Bilingual and Intercultural Education' (EBeI). His research focuses on the teaching of English as a foreign language, language and bilingual education teacher training, educational technologies, teacher digital literacy and queer pedagogy.

***

Karen Acosta Buralli is a Psychologist and Professor of Psychology, graduated from the University of Buenos Aires, Argentina. She obtained a diploma in Comprehensive Sexual Education from the National University of San Martín, Argentina. She has worked as a teacher at the University of Buenos Aires and at the National University of Córdoba, Argentina. She received a doctoral scholarship from the National Research Council Scientific and Technical (CONICET), Argentina. His main area of interest related to comprehension of materials of Comprehensive Sexual Education.

Berenice Alfaro Ponce has a degree in Social Sciences from the Autonomous University of the State of Hidalgo (UAEH). During her doctorate she did a research stay as an ERASMUS scholar at the University of Łódź in the MISEAL project, her master's degree in Human Rights and Democracy by FLACSO. She is a member of the National System of Researchers level 1. Her research experience has focused on the topic of Education and Interculturality, Technology, Transnationalism and Public Policy and with this last topic she was awarded for her co-authorship with the International Award for Excellence in interdisciplinary Social Sciences 2022 granted by The Interdisciplinary Social Sciences Journal Collection. She currently holds a postdoctoral position at the Institute for Research on Obesity at the Tecnológico de Monterrey where she collaborates on several projects: Food Policies with UNICEF (which was awarded and assigned in September 2023), Digital Health with Elcano Foundation and works on food systems issues where she is interested in using the citizen science and community science approach as a participatory methodology for the analysis of the different actors. She is also a founding member of the Network for Research and Cooperation in Intercultural Studies (RICEI) and collaborates as a member of the Mexican Network for the Development and Incorporation of Educational Technologies in Latin America (RED LATe).

Blanca Berral-Ortiz graduated in Early Childhood Education at the University of Granada with Extraordinary End of Degree Award; Master in Research and Innovation in Curriculum and Training. Predoctoral Research Staff in Training attached to the Department of Didactics and School Organization of the University of Granada (Spain) in the Faculty of Education Sciences. Member of the AREA Research Group (Analysis of Educational Reality) (HUM-672), where he develops as lines of research the educational inclusion and digital competence from the development of literacy. She participates in teaching innovation projects focused on teaching through technology with mobile learning resources to improve learning; Inverted classroom and immersive technological resources (xr) for the development of digital competence in future education professionals (Inmer), among others. ORCID ID: email: blancaberral@ugr.es

Mónica Bonilla-del-Río is Assistant Professor in the Journalism, Audio-visual Communication, Advertising, and Public Relations programs at the European University of the Atlantic (Spain). She earned her Ph.D. from the Interuniversity Communication Program, specializing in Educommunication and Media Literacy at the University of Huelva. Additionally, she holds an Official Master's Degree in Communication and Audiovisual Education from the University of Huelva, a Master's Degree in Emotional, Social, and Creative Education from the University of Cantabria (Self-titled); and a Bachelor's Degree in Early Childhood Education from the University of Cantabria. Active member of the Ágora Research Group (Andalusian Research Plan: HUM-648) and Alfamed Joven, affiliated with the Euro-American Interuniversity Network Alfamed, she is dedicated to the exploration of media competence for citizenship. Her research focus encompasses educommunication, disability, and digital and social inclusion.

Chakabwata William holds a PhD in Curriculum and Instruction obtained from University of South Africa on 27 September 2023.He also holds a master degree in Curriculum and arts education which he earned from University of Zimbabwe. He has taught at Midlands State University in Namibia and also at Namibia University of Science and Technology(NUST).

About the Contributors

Sabina Civila FPI Predoctoral Researcher . PhD candidate in the Interuniversity Communication program (Málaga, Huelva, Sevilla y Cádiz) in the Educommunication line. Master in strategic communication and communication innovation (Malaga, Huelva, Seville and Cádiz), and Graduated in Advertising and Public Relations from the University of Cádiz. Researcher at the 'Ágora' Research Group (HUM-648). Currently he focuses his research on social networks, educommunication, media literacy and Islamophobia.

Rosa Elena Durán González completed her Bachelor's Degree in Education with emphasis in school management at the Universidad Pedagógica Nacional, her Specialization in Teaching and her Master's Degree in Educational Sciences at the Universidad Autónoma del Estado de Hidalgo, being a CONACyT scholarship holder. In June 2009, she concluded her Doctorate studies in Educational Sciences at the Universidad Autónoma de Estado de Hidalgo. She has teaching and management experience in basic education. She has participated in refresher courses for elementary school teachers in School Supervision 161 and Sector 13 of Pachuca Hgo. She has been a reader of Master's thesis at UPN and has presented papers in national and international congresses with the theme of Curriculum and Gender. Since her master's studies, she collaborated in the SEP SEByN CONACyT project "Equitable classrooms, a social and cultural construction", as well as in the project "Evaluation of the socioeconomic and cultural situation of indigenous migrant children in the city of Pachuca, Hidalgo". She contributed in the elaboration of the Methodological Guide of the Integral Curricular Redesign and has advised educational programs of redesign and new offerings in the Educational Reform of the UAEH. She collaborated with a team of UAEH researchers in the external evaluation of PRONIM (Migrant Children's Program) at the national level. She has participated in several research projects, in courses of improvement and has several publications.

Tú Anh Hà is currently a Research fellow at Rovira i Virgili University, Spain. Her research interests include education for sustainability, critical literacy, multilingualism, methods of integrating equality and equity in the class, education for peace, intercultural education, and early childhood education. She can be contacted at: tuanh.ling@gmail.com ORCID: 0000-0002-6450-3390

Cristina A. Huertas-Abril, Associate Professor, belongs to the Department of English and German Philologies of the University of Córdoba (Spain), where she teaches at the Faculty of Education Sciences and Psychology. She is a member of the Research Group HUM-1006 'Research in Bilingual and Intercultural Education' (EBeI). Her research mainly focuses on Computer-Assisted Language Learning (CALL), teaching English as a Foreign Language, bilingual education and teacher training.

Adrián Salvador Lara Garrido is a temporary substitute lecturer at the University of Almeria and PhD in Educational Sciences from the University of Granada (Spain). His main line of research focuses on sexual orientation, gender diversity and expression in education. He collaborates in projects on the knowledge and attitudes of professionals in the educational field towards LGTB people, being principal investigator on one occasion.

José Ramón Márquez Díaz is a Professor in the Department of Pedagogy. PhD in Social and Educational Sciences from the University of Huelva (Spain). His current lines of research are educational innovation, teacher training, attention to diversity, affective-sexual diversity, gender violence and bullying. He has published several communications at national and international conferences, books and book chapters in prestigious publishers, and articles in indexed and non-indexed journals. Finally, he completed a research stay at the University of Eastern Finland (Finland).

José Antonio Martínez Domingo Predoctoral contract at the University of Granada, he is Predoctoral Research Staff in Training. Graduated in Primary Education with specialization in Physical Education and Master in Research and Innovation in Curriculum and Training, he is currently doing his PhD in Educational Sciences. Member of the research group RITE (SEJ-607) and Analysis of Educational Reality (AREA, HUM-672). Her lines of research focus on digital competence, social networks, new teaching-learning methodologies, teaching innovation and technological resources.

Adriana Medina-Vidal is a specialist in human behaviour and education with a gender perspective. PhD in Anthropology since 2018 at the Centro de Investigaciones y Estudios Superiores en Antropología Social (CIESAS). She carried out her post-doctoral research at the Institute for the Future of Education of the Tecnológico de Monterrey (2022-2023), where she collaborated in the research, publication and generation of projects that promote the development of the competence of reasoning for complexity in university students. She has carried out several research stays in national and international universities. At present, her work as an independent consultant focuses on gender, entrepreneurship and education.

Ronika Mumbire works for the civil society in Zimbabwe where she is a leading figure on improving the welfare of women in that country. She has is a passionate about improving the welfare of women particularly those who live in rural areas. She may be contacted at ronikamumbire@gmail.com

Mazal Oaknín (FHEA) is Associate Professor (Teaching) and Spanish Language Coordinator at University College London, where she teaches Spanish language, literature and translation at UG and PG levels. She is the Project Lead of the "Tackling the BAME-BIPOC Awarding Gap" project and the "Fighting the BIPOC Awarding Gap Project Through Reverse Mentoring" project, as well as the co-director of the e-Expert Seminar Series in Translation and Modern Language Education" (UCL and University of Córdoba). Mazal is the co-editor of Literatura política y política literaria en España: Del Desastre del 98 a Felipe VI (Peter Lang, 2015) and author of Writing, Feminism and the Media in Spain (Peter Lang, 2019). Her co-edited volume Innovation in Translation Education: A New Focus on EDI will appear in UCL Press in 2024.

Adrian Palma-Patricio is a Professor and Researcher at the Universidad Autónoma de la Ciudad de México. Professor Palma Patricio has obtained his PHD in Anthropology at Centro de Investigaciones y Estudios Superiores en Antropología Social in 2018. His research interests include gender and sexuality, masculinities, indigenous people and health promotion. He has presented his work at a number of conferences in México. He is the author e.g. of "Masculinidades indígenas migrantes" wich appers in the book "Aportaciones al estudio e intervención de las masculinidades" published by Juan Pablos editor (2021), or "México y la sexualidad entre varones" compilated in the book "Y si hablas de…de tu ser hombre?: Violencia, paternidad, homoerotismo y envejecimiento en la experiencia de algunos varones" published by El Colegio de México (2014).

About the Contributors

Elisa Pérez Gracia Graduated in Primary Education with a specialty in foreign language (English). She holds two PhD, the first one in Languages and Cultures, and the second one in Education, both from the University of Córdoba, Spain, and obtaining CUM LAUDEM. She is a professor and researcher in the area of Didactics and School Organization of the Department of Education of the University of Córdoba, and she is a member of the Research Group of the Andalusian Research and Innovation Plan "Education, Diversity and Society" (EDISO; SEJ-477). Her main lines of research have to do with educational inclusion and equity and teacher training. She has published diverse research articles in international high impact journals, and she has presented in diverse national and international conferences the main results of her research projects and studies. Currently, her research work focuses mainly on the field of inclusion policies in higher education from the perspective of inequality. She is part of the research group of the I Inclusion Diagnosis Project at the University of Córdoba and the European UNITE Project to improve learning using inclusive digital resources.

Elizabeth-Guadalupe Rojas-Estrada is a scholarship recipient from the National Council of Humanities, Science, and Technology (Conacyt-Mexico). Currently, she is pursuing a Ph.D. in the Inter-University Doctoral Communication Program at the University of Huelva (UHU). She holds a Master's Degree in Communication from the Pontifical Catholic University of Valparaíso (Chile) and a Bachelor's in Communication from the Meritorious Autonomous University of Puebla (Mexico). She is a member of the Ágora research group (UHU) and serves as the President of the Alfamed Young Network, an organization dedicated to promoting media and information literacy. Her research interests include the analysis of media competence presence in the curriculum and public policies associated with fostering digital citizenship.

José-María Romero-Rodríguez has a D. in Educational Sciences from the University of Granada (Extraordinary Doctoral Thesis Award). Regarding his academic training, he has a degree in Pedagogy from the same University, having obtained the National Prize for End of Degree in University Education (Third Prize) and Extraordinary Prize End of Degree; Master's Degree in Research and Innovation in Curriculum and Training, at the same University and; University Master's Degree in Innovation and Knowledge Management from the University of Malaga. He is currently Assistant Professor at the Department of Didactics and School Organization of the Faculty of Education Sciences of the University of Granada (Spain) and coordinator of the Bibliomaker Educación UGR. Author of more than 100 scientific articles of impact (JCR and Scopus) on the use of Information and Communication Technologies (ICT) for the improvement of teaching and learning and on the risks associated with the problematic use of the Internet. He has made academic and research stays in different institutions such as Tecnológico de Monterrey (Mexico), Palacký University Olomouc (Czech Republic), University of Aveiro (Portugal), Polytechnic Institute of Coimbra (Portugal), Universidad Distrital Francisco José de Caldas (Colombia), Universidad Estatal a Distancia-UNED (Costa Rica), University of Camagüey (Cuba) and University of Padua (Italy).

Francisco Sánchez is Assistant Professor in the University of Córdoba. He graduated from the University of Cádiz in Classical Philology and English Studies. He completed successfully a Master's Degree in Teacher Training and a Master's Degree in International Communication. Francisco Sánchez also finished a PhD dissertation in Arts and Humanities with merits. His research focuses on Latin political treatises during the Spanish and Portugueses Renaissance, on Classical Receptions and on the application of critical approaches to Classics, both in research and teaching.

Bruno Onyinye Umunakwe is currently a Ph.D. student with University of Nigeria, Nsukka in the department of Philosophy. He is also, a remote degree applied health student with Brigham Young University, Idaho. Bruno has published and contributed in several reputable journals and books. His area of academic interests include, African studies, human rights philosophy, philosophy of education, bioethical issues, public health especially mental issues. Bruno is diligent, innovative and responsive. He has engaged in different community health outreach.

Juan-José Victoria-Maldonado is a research teaching staff attached to the group SEJ-655: Laboratory for Innovation in Education (LabinED) and Analysis of Educational Reality (AREA, HUM-672) of the University of Granada. Graduated in Early Childhood Education and subsequently the Master in Research and Innovation in Curriculum and Training at the University of Granada. His curriculum vitae includes a large number of publications of book chapters in high impact publishers such as Dykinson or Octaedro and articles for different journals (Frontiers in Education, Education Sciences, Journal of Technology and Science Education...). The main line of research is digital competence in the training of future teachers in order to improve the curricula within the initial teacher training.

Arantxa Vizcaíno-Verdú is Associate Professor at the Business and Communication School of UNIR (Universidad Internacional de la Rioja, Spain), working within the Department of Marketing and Communication. Academically, she holds a PhD in Communication (University of Huelva), an MA in Communication and Audiovisual Education (UHU), a BA in Advertising and Public Relations (University of Alicante), and a Certificate of Higher Education in Plastic Arts and Design – Illustration (Massana School of Barcelona). Professionally, she is Key Regional Leader of the 'TikTok Cultures Research Network', and Section Editor & Social Media Manager for the Revista Mediterránea de Comunicación (Scopus Q1/Q2). She is also researcher in the COYSODI group at UNIR, external research collaborator in the COMPUBES group at the University of Alicante, and alumnus of the Influencer Ethnography Research Lab (IERLab). Her research focuses on the analysis of transmedia storytelling, fandom, and popular culture on social media and the Internet.

Index

A

Abuse 14, 23-24, 26-27, 29-30, 36, 46, 58, 64-65, 71-73, 75, 83, 90-91, 93-94, 97, 99-101, 113, 124, 142, 148, 186, 188, 192, 194-195, 202, 204, 208, 212, 214, 222-227, 249, 259, 262, 271, 278
Active Listening 83, 160, 169, 215
Adopted 25, 36, 126, 143, 232, 266
Africa 22-29, 32-33, 38-39, 41, 62, 99, 127, 130-131, 133, 213, 224-225
Age Verification 269, 283-284
AIALL 189-190, 193-197, 202-204, 206, 209-210
Artificial Intelligence 81-82, 145, 189-190, 193, 206, 208-210, 220, 232, 237, 239
Asexual 25, 114
Assault 27-28, 40, 83, 91, 99, 101, 191, 193, 226, 229
Assisted Language Learning 189-190
Attitudes 2, 23, 26-27, 30-31, 37, 41-42, 58, 65, 83-85, 100, 103, 107, 109-110, 112, 114, 117, 121, 129, 131, 152-167, 169-170, 176, 182-183, 186, 190, 204, 209, 212-217, 220, 222, 229, 232-233, 242, 244, 248, 254, 266, 268, 270, 283-284
Awareness 12-14, 46, 56-59, 63-66, 74-76, 81, 84-85, 92-98, 100, 104, 106-108, 117, 120, 126-127, 136, 145, 147, 151, 160, 194-195, 202, 204, 210, 212-222, 233, 237, 239-240, 243, 246, 248, 251-252, 254-255, 257-258, 263, 271-272, 275-276

B

Binnizá 1-2, 6, 9-10, 14, 16, 18-20
Bisexual 25, 114, 153, 155-156, 163, 165-166

C

Causal Connection 178, 188
Causal Network Model 174, 188
Child Protection 252
Classical Reception 149-150
Classical Tradition 136, 141, 150
Classics 135, 142, 144, 147, 149-150
Clause 178-179, 181, 188
Collaborative Sexuality Teaching Models 102
Community 1-2, 5-12, 14, 16, 20-23, 25, 29, 31-32, 35-39, 85, 89, 95-99, 101, 106-108, 110, 114, 125, 128-130, 155, 160-161, 165, 173, 175, 180, 187, 205, 219, 230, 233, 235-236, 239, 243, 259, 265, 279
Comprehensive Sex Education 22, 102, 106, 108, 111-112, 114, 182, 206, 265
Content Analysis 44, 54-55, 60, 241, 278
Cooperative Learning 135, 146, 150, 161, 195
Critical Approaches to Classics 150
Critical Classics 135
Critical Literacy 44-45, 49-52, 55-62
Critical Pedagogy 126, 130-132
Critical Reading 44-45, 50, 52, 54, 59-61
Critical Thinking 44-45, 49, 52-54, 56-57, 61-62, 66, 81, 97, 101, 126, 132, 136, 142, 145, 175, 195, 204
CSE 6, 23-38, 63, 67, 70, 79, 153, 158-160, 162, 171-182, 185-186
Curriculum 6, 22-26, 28-32, 35, 37-38, 41-42, 45-46, 51, 62, 76, 78, 82, 85, 102-103, 114, 116-125, 127, 129-132, 153, 155, 161, 172, 174, 193, 207, 220, 254, 256, 273, 276

D

Decoloniality 3, 20
Dialogic Talk 87, 101
Diffusion 22-23, 33-40, 42
Digital Behavior 263
Digital Sphere 211-212, 216-217
Discourse 4, 33, 43, 59, 110, 135-137, 139, 141-142, 145-148, 150-151, 174, 176-177, 180-183, 230, 234, 244, 269, 279-280
Discourse Analysis 59, 135, 137-138, 177, 180, 183
Discrimination 1, 5, 11-13, 20, 24, 30, 37, 42, 47-

48, 58, 66-67, 79, 88-91, 108-109, 116, 124, 133, 152-153, 155-162, 166-167, 169, 190-194, 204-205, 208, 210, 214-215, 229-230, 232-235, 238-241, 244-245

E

Early Childhood Sexuality Curriculum 102
EDI 64, 73-75, 79
Education 1-2, 5-8, 10, 13-14, 19, 22-32, 34-35, 38-42, 45-46, 48-51, 54, 58-64, 66, 69, 71-77, 79, 81-88, 91-107, 109-119, 121-133, 136, 151-153, 159-166, 168-177, 182-195, 197, 202, 204-209, 211-214, 216-217, 219-227, 233-234, 237, 239-240, 243, 246, 248, 250-255, 257-263, 266-268, 271-273, 275-284
English for Social Purposes and Cooperation (ESoPC) 206
Experiential Learning 135, 142, 146-147, 149-150, 219
Explicit Content 228, 247-249, 252, 263-265, 268, 270, 272-273, 284

F

Feminised Genders 143, 150
Feminism 4, 33-34, 38, 42-43, 74, 79, 98-99, 109, 132, 149-150, 163, 168, 235, 242, 244, 280, 284
Feminist Pedagogy 81-82
Formal Education 14, 116-119, 122-124, 127, 129-133, 173
Franco Regime 63, 65, 67, 69, 79-80
Freedom of Expression 104, 212, 234, 259, 269, 282, 284

G

Gender 2-6, 8, 10-14, 16-18, 20, 23-25, 27-42, 44-62, 64-66, 69, 72, 74-97, 99-102, 108-110, 112, 114-118, 122, 124, 126-129, 131-133, 142-143, 148-150, 153-157, 160-163, 165-166, 168-175, 177-178, 180, 182, 186-192, 195-197, 201, 204-205, 207-213, 215-216, 219, 222-227, 229-236, 238-242, 244-245, 251, 258, 265, 270, 272, 275, 278, 280, 282-284
Gender Based Violence (GBV) 23, 27, 30
Gender Bias 47, 58, 62
Gender Equality 26-27, 44-59, 62, 64, 69, 72, 76, 79, 81-82, 84-85, 95-97, 99, 116, 118, 131-133, 143, 148, 173, 175, 190-192, 195, 205, 211-213, 223, 226, 232, 239
Gender Islamophobia 229-230, 244

Gender Perspective 12-14, 20, 81-82, 115, 173, 211, 224, 233, 275
Gender Roles 6, 11, 18, 26, 58, 83-84, 97, 124, 142, 157, 191, 230, 265, 270
Gender Stereotypes 48, 50, 58, 60, 64-65, 75, 86, 94-95, 189, 191, 196, 204, 212, 214, 216, 222, 232, 244, 265, 270, 284
Gender Violence 11, 48, 58-59, 81-84, 86-97, 100, 102, 109, 171-174, 177-178, 180, 182, 188, 208, 211, 222-223, 227, 229-231
Gender-Based Violence 1-2, 4-6, 8, 11-12, 15, 17, 23, 25, 30, 39, 41, 44, 58, 63-67, 69, 72-76, 80, 83-85, 89, 97-98, 100, 114, 135, 141-142, 148-150, 162, 180, 185, 188-190, 205-214, 216, 222-223, 226, 229-233, 236-237, 239-241, 243-244
Gender-Based Violence Prevention 148
Girl-Child 116-118, 124, 126, 128-129, 133

H

Harassment 8, 29, 69, 82-83, 89, 91, 98-99, 101, 190-192, 204, 212-215, 217, 226-228, 232, 237, 239-240, 243, 259
Hate Speech 192, 223, 229-230, 233-234, 236-243, 245
Healthy Relationship 63-64, 72, 75, 80
Hegemonic Medical Model 9, 14, 20
Heteronormativity 155, 157, 163, 169
Higher Education 41, 60-61, 76, 85, 87, 92, 94-98, 100, 119, 151, 169, 195, 224
Homophobia 46, 155-156, 163, 165, 167-169
Homosexual 33, 115, 155-158, 169

I

Image Cyberbullying 227
Implementation 2, 22, 24-25, 28, 30-31, 35, 37, 42, 82, 85, 93, 120, 131-132, 154-155, 162, 171-177, 181-182, 187-188, 213, 217, 220, 237, 247-248, 252, 257, 274-275
Inclusive Language 49, 58, 108, 115, 161, 169, 203
Inclusiveness 127, 134
Indigenous Traditional Medical System 1, 9
Indigenous Women 1-2, 4-9, 11-14, 17-19
Individual Variability 270, 284
Initial Training 152
Innovation 22-24, 28, 30-31, 33-39, 43, 62, 73, 82, 99, 106, 127, 209, 240-241
Intercultural Approach 12, 20
Interpersonal Relationships 80, 142, 215, 248-249, 251, 257, 263, 266
Intersectionality 1-4, 15, 20, 42, 74, 84-85, 98-99,

Index

226, 233, 238
Intersex 25, 115, 143, 165, 168
Intervention 28, 32, 39, 45, 50, 52-57, 85, 98, 113, 152-153, 159, 161, 169, 173, 183-186, 208, 220, 222, 251, 256-257, 261, 272, 282
Intervention Strategy 169
Islam 231, 233-245
Islamophobia 229-230, 233-234, 238, 241-242, 244-245

L

Language Teaching and Learning 189, 193, 195
Lesbian 78, 115, 153, 156-157, 163, 165-167
Lucía Etxebarria 64-65, 75, 77-79

M

Meaningful Learning 160, 169
Media and Information Literacy (MIL) 273, 284
Media Literacy 49, 51-52, 60, 211, 238, 240, 265, 269, 271, 273, 276-277, 280, 282-283
Mental Health 27, 73, 75, 193, 207, 219, 224, 243, 249, 251, 261, 264, 268, 282, 284
Metanarrative 43
Minors 102-104, 246-255, 257-258, 262-264, 269, 271-277, 281
Modern Homonegativity 152-153, 157-159, 162, 169
Multicompetent Model 154, 156-157, 159, 170
Multicompetent Model of Attitude 154, 159, 170
Muxes 10, 20
Mythical Discourse 138, 148, 150
Mythology 135-137, 139, 141-145, 147-149, 151

N

New Masculinities 101
Nonbinary 115
Non-Consensual Sexting 217, 221, 227-228
Normalization Effect 270, 284

O

Obstetric Violence 1, 8, 12-13, 15
Online Education 252, 262-263
Online Grooming 227-228
Online Harassment 190, 192, 213-214, 217, 226-227
Online Pornography 265-266, 271, 273, 275-277, 279-281, 283
Online Protection Measures 246-248, 252, 257, 263
Online Safety Education 283
Online Security 220, 263-264

P

Pansexual 115
Parents and Caregivers 22, 31, 35
Paternalism 134
Patriarchy 3-4, 10, 90, 116
Photographic Narration 81, 85
Photovoice 86, 95, 99-101
Post-Colonialism 75, 235, 245
Poststructural 22, 33-34, 38, 42-43
Poststructural Feminism 22, 33-34, 38, 42
Pre-Service Teacher 58, 62, 188, 209
Prevention 6, 16, 19, 26, 29, 41, 48, 82-83, 86, 89, 92-93, 95-98, 100-101, 104, 106, 113-114, 135, 148, 152-153, 159-160, 162, 170-174, 177-178, 180, 182, 184, 186, 188, 195, 202, 207-208, 211-212, 215-216, 219-220, 224, 246, 253-257, 259, 261, 263, 275, 280, 282
Prevention Strategy 100-101, 113, 170, 186, 188, 208
Psychoeducation 171-173, 176-177, 180, 182-185, 188

Q

Qualitative Approach 1
Qualitative Research 15, 100, 127, 259
Queer 25, 38, 74, 83, 100, 115, 137, 143, 150, 154-155, 160, 165, 167, 169, 190, 204, 207, 259
Queer Pedagogy 160

R

Racism 76, 78, 151, 156, 167, 245, 278
Recommendations 13, 18, 23, 37, 46, 49, 55, 72, 105, 159, 172, 180, 237, 239, 246, 252, 259, 266, 272-273
Reflexivity 37, 43
Research 5, 8, 14-16, 25-26, 33, 35-36, 38-39, 41-42, 49, 54, 58-61, 73-74, 79, 82, 86-87, 94, 98-101, 103, 107-108, 112, 117-118, 122, 126-132, 143, 145-149, 154, 160-161, 163-165, 168, 176, 180-186, 192-193, 195, 204, 206-208, 213-214, 219-221, 223-226, 229-231, 234-235, 238-241, 243-244, 246-247, 249-251, 257, 259, 261-263, 266, 268-270, 275-281, 283-284
Revenge Porn 227, 232, 249, 258, 271, 278, 280
Reverted 229-232, 234-237, 239-240, 245
Risks 8, 23, 25, 113, 159, 194, 202, 204, 215-217, 219, 223, 233, 246-254, 257-258, 261, 263, 265-266, 268, 271-272, 275
Rogers Diffusion of Innovation Theory 22
Rosa Montero 64, 75-78

S

Sexting 213-214, 217, 221, 224-225, 227-228, 246-250, 252-264, 278, 281
Sextortion 227-228, 249, 251, 262, 264, 278
Sexual Cyberbullying 213-214, 216, 218-220, 228
Sexual Education 2, 6-7, 13, 22-23, 26, 31, 42, 99, 103-108, 110, 171-173, 175, 182-188, 268, 272-273, 275-279, 284
Sexual Identity Impersonation 228
Sexual Misinformation 266, 268, 271-273, 275, 284
Sexuality 2-8, 10-11, 13-14, 18-19, 22-23, 25-27, 29-32, 35-36, 38-42, 45-46, 60-61, 63-64, 66, 69, 71-77, 79, 82, 84, 91, 100-108, 110-115, 152-153, 155, 158-160, 164-165, 174-176, 183-188, 190, 195, 205, 207-208, 211-212, 216, 225, 247, 254, 261, 266-270, 272-273, 275, 277, 279-280, 283-284
Shared Responsibility 110-111, 222, 252, 264
Social Categories 2, 20
Social Media 45, 48, 52, 114, 205, 216, 223, 227, 229-230, 232-241, 243-244, 247, 254-255, 259-260, 262, 268, 270, 272, 280-281
Socially and Culturally Responsive Language Teaching 189-190, 194, 207, 209-210
Socio-Emotional Skills 73, 76, 80, 220
Solutions 13, 45, 53, 65, 105, 220, 237, 239, 246, 252, 269
Spanish Contemporary Literature 64, 75
Spanish Transition 64, 75, 80
Strategies 9, 13-15, 39, 51, 81, 83-84, 86-89, 92, 94-99, 110, 127, 152-153, 159-162, 171, 173, 175-176, 178, 181, 192, 213-214, 216-223, 237-238, 251-252, 254-256, 258-259, 263, 266, 271-273, 275

T

Teacher Training 37, 58, 61-62, 93, 99, 153, 159-160, 162, 171-172, 175-176, 180, 182-183, 187-188, 272, 275
Teaching Proposal 189-190, 195, 204, 207
Text 3, 5, 44-45, 48, 50-57, 62, 66, 82, 87, 104, 112, 141, 143, 145-146, 149-150, 177-182, 187-188, 201, 209, 227, 239, 250-252, 257, 260
Textual Analysis 63, 69, 72-73, 80
Textual Comprehension 51, 56-57, 62
TGNC 190-193, 210
Traditional Igbo Society 116, 118, 124-128, 134
Training 9, 12, 32, 37, 58-59, 61-62, 77, 85, 92-93, 95, 99, 106-107, 119, 122, 130, 152-153, 159-164, 171-172, 175-176, 179-180, 182-184, 187-188, 195, 202, 204-205, 211, 217-218, 225, 238, 246, 252-253, 255, 257-258, 272, 275
Trans and Gender Non-Conforming People 189, 210
Transphobia 156, 163, 165, 168, 170, 192, 208

U

University Teaching 81-82
University-Level Teaching 135-136, 144

V

Velas 11-12, 20

W

Women 1-11, 13-19, 23-25, 27-30, 33-34, 36-37, 39, 41, 43, 46-49, 53-54, 56-57, 60-61, 63-67, 69-78, 81, 84-86, 88-94, 96, 98-101, 103, 105-106, 109-110, 115, 118, 124-125, 128-133, 142-144, 148-151, 156-157, 162-163, 166-167, 170, 173, 177, 180, 183, 187, 189-192, 197, 201-203, 205-208, 210-214, 216-217, 222-223, 225-226, 229-244, 271-272, 276, 278-279, 281-282

Y

Young People 6, 12-13, 15, 22-27, 29, 35, 104, 106-107, 112, 176, 183, 185, 217-223, 226, 241, 243, 247-252, 257-258, 260-261, 263, 266, 272, 277-278, 281

Z

Zapotec 6-7, 10, 12, 18-20

Publishing Tomorrow's Research Today

Uncover Current Insights and Future Trends in Education
with IGI Global's Cutting-Edge Recommended Books

Print Only, E-Book Only, or Print + E-Book.
Order direct through IGI Global's Online Bookstore at www.igi-global.com or through your preferred provider.

ISBN: 9781668493007
© 2023; 234 pp.
List Price: US$ 215

ISBN: 9798369300749
© 2024; 383 pp.
List Price: US$ 230

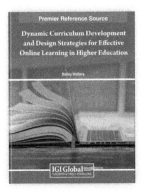

ISBN: 9781668486467
© 2023; 471 pp.
List Price: US$ 215

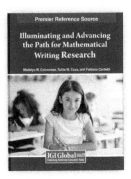

ISBN: 9781668465387
© 2024; 389 pp.
List Price: US$ 215

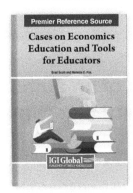

ISBN: 9781668475836
© 2024; 359 pp.
List Price: US$ 215

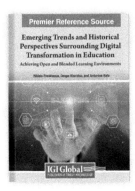

ISBN: 9781668444238
© 2023; 334 pp.
List Price: US$ 240

Do you want to stay current on the latest research trends, product announcements, news, and special offers?
Join IGI Global's mailing list to receive customized recommendations, exclusive discounts, and more.
Sign up at: www.igi-global.com/newsletters.

Scan the QR Code here to view more related titles in Education.

www.igi-global.com   Sign up at www.igi-global.com/newsletters   facebook.com/igiglobal   twitter.com/igiglobal   linkedin.com/igiglobal

Ensure Quality Research is Introduced to the Academic Community

Become a Reviewer for IGI Global Authored Book Projects

 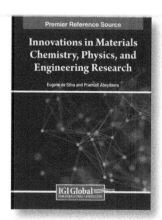 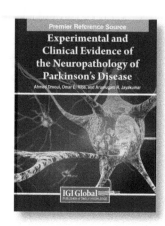 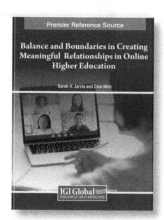

The overall success of an authored book project is dependent on quality and timely manuscript evaluations.

Applications and Inquiries may be sent to:
development@igi-global.com

Applicants must have a doctorate (or equivalent degree) as well as publishing, research, and reviewing experience. Authored Book Evaluators are appointed for one-year terms and are expected to complete at least three evaluations per term. Upon successful completion of this term, evaluators can be considered for an additional term.

If you have a colleague that may be interested in this opportunity, we encourage you to share this information with them.

Recommended Titles from our e-Book Collection

Innovation Capabilities and Entrepreneurial Opportunities of Smart Working
ISBN: 9781799887973

Advanced Applications of Generative AI and Natural Language Processing Models
ISBN: 9798369305027

Using Influencer Marketing as a Digital Business Strategy
ISBN: 9798369305515

Human-Centered Approaches in Industry 5.0
ISBN: 9798369326473

Modeling and Monitoring Extreme Hydrometeorological Events
ISBN: 9781668487716

Data-Driven Intelligent Business Sustainability
ISBN: 9798369300497

Information Logistics for Organizational Empowerment and Effective Supply Chain Management
ISBN: 9798369301593

Data Envelopment Analysis (DEA) Methods for Maximizing Efficiency
ISBN: 9798369302552

Request More Information, or Recommend the IGI Global e-Book Collection to Your Institution's Librarian

For More Information or to Request a Free Trial, Contact IGI Global's e-Collections Team: eresources@igi-global.com | 1-866-342-6657 ext. 100 | 717-533-8845 ext. 100

Are You Ready to Publish Your Research?

IGI Global
Publishing Tomorrow's Research Today

IGI Global offers book authorship and editorship opportunities across three major subject areas, including Business, STM, and Education.

Benefits of Publishing with IGI Global:

- Free one-on-one editorial and promotional support.
- Expedited publishing timelines that can take your book from start to finish in less than one (1) year.
- Choose from a variety of formats, including Edited and Authored References, Handbooks of Research, Encyclopedias, and Research Insights.
- Utilize IGI Global's eEditorial Discovery® submission system in support of conducting the submission and double-blind peer review process.
- IGI Global maintains a strict adherence to ethical practices due in part to our full membership with the Committee on Publication Ethics (COPE).
- Indexing potential in prestigious indices such as Scopus®, Web of Science™, PsycINFO®, and ERIC – Education Resources Information Center.
- Ability to connect your ORCID iD to your IGI Global publications.
- Earn honorariums and royalties on your full book publications as well as complimentary content and exclusive discounts.

Join Your Colleagues from Prestigious Institutions, Including:

Australian National University
MIT Massachusetts Institute of Technology
Johns Hopkins University
Tsinghua University
Harvard University
Columbia University in the City of New York

Learn More at: www.igi-global.com/publish
or Contact IGI Global's Aquisitions Team at: acquisition@igi-global.com

Individual Article & Chapter Downloads
US$ 37.50/each

Easily Identify, Acquire, and Utilize Published Peer-Reviewed Findings in Support of Your Current Research

- Browse Over **170,000+ Articles & Chapters**
- **Accurate & Advanced** Search
- Affordably Acquire **International Research**
- **Instantly Access** Your Content
- Benefit from the *InfoSci® Platform Features*

" *It really provides* an excellent entry into the research literature of the field. *It presents a manageable number of* highly relevant sources *on topics of interest to a wide range of researchers. The sources are* scholarly, but also accessible *to 'practitioners'.* "

- Ms. Lisa Stimatz, MLS, University of North Carolina at Chapel Hill, USA

Milton Keynes UK
Ingram Content Group UK Ltd.
UKHW051601021224
3319UKWH00046B/1467